Sor Juana

FIEL

Copia de otra que de si hizo, y de su mano pinto la R. M. Juana Ynés de la Cruz. Fenix de la America, Gloriosо de su tiempo de su Sexo. Honrra de la Nacion de este Nuevo Mundo, y arguمento de las admiraciones, y elogios del Antiguo. Nacio el dia 12. de Nov: del año de 1651. a las onze de la noche. Recivio el Sagrado Habito de el Maximo D. S. S. Geronimo en su Convento de esta Ciudad de Mexico. de edad de 17. años. Ymurio Domingo 17. de Abril de el de 1695. de edad 4 o . y 4. años, cinco meses, cinco dias, y cinco horas. Requiescat in pace. Amen.

Portrait of Juana Inés de la Cruz

Sor Juana

OR, THE TRAPS OF FAITH

OCTAVIO PAZ

Translated by Margaret Sayers Peden

THE BELKNAP PRESS OF
HARVARD UNIVERSITY PRESS
CAMBRIDGE, MASSACHUSETTS
1988

Library of Congress Cataloging-in-Publication Data
Paz, Octavio, 1914–
  [Sor Juana Inés de la Cruz, o, Las trampas de la fe. English]
  Sor Juana / Octavio Paz ; translated by Margaret Sayers Peden.
    p. cm.
  Translation of: Sor Juana Inés de la Cruz, o, Las trampas
  de la fe.
  Bibliography: p.
  Includes index.
  ISBN 0-674-82105-X (alk. paper)
    1. Juana Inés de la Cruz, Sister, 1651?–1695. 2. Authors,
Mexican—17th century—Biography. 3. Nuns—Mexico—Biography.
I. Title.
PQ7296.J6Z72513 1988   88-3002
861—dc19   CIP
[B]

Preface

O N HER LIFETIME, Sor Juana Inés de la Cruz was read and admired not only in Mexico but in Spain and all the countries where Spanish and Portuguese were spoken. Then for nearly two hundred years she
and her works were forgotten. After the turn of this century taste
changed again, and she began to be seen for what she really is: a universal poet. When I started writing, around 1930, her poetry was no longer
a mere historical relic but had once again become a living text. What
sparked the revival, in Mexico, was a small book by a poet, Amado
Nervo; his *Juana de Asbaje*, 1910, dedicated "to all the women of my
country and my race," can still be read with pleasure. Between 1910 and
1930 numerous scholarly works appeared, devoted primarily to un-
earthing and establishing the texts. The labors of Manuel Toussaint were
followed by those of Ermilo Abreu Gómez, who gave us the first modern
editions of *First Dream*, the *Carta atenagórica*, and the *Response to Sor
Filotea*.

Sor Juana's writings appealed greatly to the Mexican poets of the
time, above all Xavier Villaurrutia, who edited her sonnets and *endechas*, and Jorge Cuesta. In those years, spurred by Cuesta's enthusiasm,
I read Sor Juana's poems for the first time; I was especially taken by the
sonnets. It was not until 1950, in Paris, that I began to read her again.
The magazine *Sur* was planning to commemorate the tercentenary of
her birth and asked me for an article. I accepted the assignment, went to
the Bibliothèque Nationale, dug into the old editions, and wrote a little
essay, the distant ancestor of this book.

Like an almost cyclically recurring presence, Sor Juana reappeared twenty years later. In 1971–72 I was to be the Charles Eliot Norton Professor of Poetry at Harvard University, and was invited to give a course or two in addition to the Norton Lectures. When asked what the subject of one of the courses would be, without giving it much thought I replied, "Sor Juana Inés de la Cruz." By then Alfonso Méndez Plancarte had published his exemplary edition of her complete works. I went back and read her again, and read what had been written about her, much of which I had forgotten or had not known. The Harvard libraries provoked and satisfied my curiosity. In the stacks I used to encounter Raimundo Lida; we would talk of Sor Juana, of music, of hermetic numerology. I gave the course again at Harvard in 1973, and in 1974, at the Colegio Nacional, delivered a series of lectures on Sor Juana, her life and her work. Afterward it occurred to me, in reviewing the notes and materials I had accumulated, that I might draw upon them for a book that would be simultaneously a study of the age in which she lived and a consideration of her life and her works, a blend of history, biography, and literary criticism. I began to write intermittently, with many interruptions, and by 1976 had completed the first three parts; then nothing, for several years. Finally, feeling a twinge of remorse, I returned to the unfinished manuscript and, in the first half of 1981, wrote the last three parts.

My book is not the first on Sor Juana, nor will it be the last. The bibliography of writings, in many languages, on her person and her work is large and constantly growing. I owe much to my predecessors, and have tried to give them due credit in the course of the book. I am also indebted to a number of friends for their help and encouragement, especially Jose Luis Martínez, who gave me full access to his library, provided photocopies of several books, and gave me the benefit, as always, of his friendship and his advice; and Antonio Alatorre, who generously and rigorously reviewed the pages of the Spanish text.

For the English-language edition, I have made a few changes with the book's new audience in mind. I have deleted occasional observations addressed to my fellow countrymen, and have pruned certain passages—for example, analyses of intricate Spanish verse forms—unlikely to be of interest to those who do not read Spanish. In addition, I have compressed the discussion of Sor Juana's principal biographers and the overview of the publication history of her works and have shifted them from the opening pages of Parts Two and Five, respectively, to a section of Notes on Sources at the back of the book.

I have used the text of the Méndez Plancarte edition, the *Obras completas* published in four volumes by the Fondo de Cultura Económica in Mexico City, and have referred to the poems by their numbers in that edition.

O.P.

Translator's Acknowledgments

This translation could not have been completed without the assistance of the Center for Inter-American Relations and the generous support of the National Endowment for the Humanities and the Witter Bynner Foundation for Poetry. My personal gratitude goes to Rosario Santos, Susan Mango, and Steven Schwartz.

I am indebted to more people than can be listed here for the help and information I received from them; it is my hope that they will recognize themselves and accept my appreciation. Among that large number, I am especially grateful to Luis Harss, who read this translation for Harvard University Press with informed care, and whose suggestions, along with those of other editors, improved it. Last, but always first, my enduring thanks to William Peden.

M.S.P.

Contents

Illustrations

. . . al ánimo arrogante
que, el vivir despreciando, determina
su nombre eternizar en su rüina.

. . . *to the undaunted spirit*
that, disdaining life, determines
to immortalize itself in ruin.

—*First Dream*

Prologue

History, Life, Work

*O*F THE MAJOR POETS of our hemisphere, a number are women, among them Juana Inés de la Cruz, Emily Dickinson, Gabriela Mistral, Marianne Moore, and Elizabeth Bishop. It is not hard to see that these five have several things in common, apart from their sex. All, for example, were unmarried and all lived somewhat at the fringes of their time and their world, vitally conscious of their singularity both as women and as poets. Nevertheless the distinctiveness of Sor Juana, of her personality as well as her work, is the most pronounced. Indeed, her case is unique. The others are modern figures—Emily Dickinson belongs to the late nineteenth century and the other three to the twentieth—whereas Juana Ramírez (her original name) lived in the twilight era of the Hispanic seventeenth century, the period of the Spanish empire's decline, and in a faraway place, the city of Mexico. There are additional factors that set her apart: she was a nun, and she was an illegitimate child.

There was nothing ordinary about her person or her life. She was exceptionally beautiful, and poor. She was the favorite of a Vicereine and lived at court, courted by many; she was loved and perchance she loved. Abruptly she gives up worldly life and enters a convent—yet, far from renouncing the world entirely, she converts her cell into a study filled with books, works of art, and scientific instruments and transforms the convent locutory into a literary and intellectual salon. She writes love poems, verses for songs and dance tunes, profane comedies, sacred poems, an essay in theology, and an autobiographical defense of the right of women to study and to cultivate their minds. She becomes famous, sees her plays performed, her poems published, and her genius applauded in all the Spanish dominions, half the Western world. Then suddenly she gives up everything, surrenders her library and collections, renounces literature, and finally, during an epidemic, after ministering to stricken sisters in the convent, dies at the age of forty-six.

No less than her life, her literary work sets her apart from most of our great writers. What is surprising above all is its extent and variety: she cultivated almost all verse forms, from the popular ballad to the love sonnet and the burlesque epigram. She wrote a long philosophical poem that reminds one not of her contemporaries but of such modern poets as Valéry and Eliot. She was the author of religious plays in which theology occupies the place that philosophical and political theories have in serious drama today. Finally, she was a remarkable essayist. It is not easy to find in the history of Pan-American literature a body of work offering such a variety of themes and subjects, united almost always to perfection of form.

The word "seduction," with its varied resonances, intellectual and sensual, conveys the nature of the attraction the figure of Sor Juana exerts. When she entered the convent, her confessor, the Jesuit Antonio Núñez de Miranda, is said to have rejoiced, for (according to his contemporary biographer) "having recognized . . . the uniqueness of her erudition coupled with her beauty, which attracted the attention of many who would like to know her and would happily court her, he was wont to say that God could not do greater harm to this realm than by allowing Juana Inés to remain in the public eye." Father Núñez' fears were realized, although in a way he could not have foreseen. Neither the scarcity of information about the crucial episodes in her life nor the dispersal of most of her personal papers and her voluminous correspondence has shielded Juana Inés from the public eye. For more than half a century her life and work have intrigued and fascinated scholars and critics. Why, when so young and beautiful, did she choose to become a nun? What was the true nature of her emotional and erotic inclinations? What is the significance and the place of her *First Dream* in the history of poetry? What were her relations with the ecclesiastical hierarchy? Why did she renounce her lifelong passion for writing and learning? Was that renunciation the result of a conversion or an abdication? This book is an attempt to answer such questions as these.

The enigma of Sor Juana is many enigmas, those of her life and those of her work. It is clear that an author's life and work are related, but the relation is never simple: the life does not entirely explain the work, nor does the work explain the life. There is something in the work that is not to be found in the author's life, something we call creativity or artistic and literary invention. Among the studies of Sor Juana are two that illustrate the limitations of the approach that attempts to find in the life an explanation of the work. The first is the biography written by the Jesuit Diego Calleja, her contemporary. He was her first biographer. Calleja depicts Sor Juana's life as a gradual ascent toward saintliness; when he notes some contradiction between this idealized life and the import of her work, he either minimizes or glosses over the contradiction. The work becomes an illustration of the nun's life, that is, an edifying tract. At the opposite pole we find a German professor, Ludwig Pfandl. Influenced by psychoanalysis, he diagnoses Sor Juana as the victim of a father fixation that leads to narcissism, a neurotic personality in whom strongly masculine tendencies predominate. For Father Calleja, Sor Juana's work is an allegory of her spiritual life; for Pfandl it is a mask for her neurosis. In either case Sor Juana's writing ceases to be a literary work; both critics read her work as a projection of her life—a saintly life for Calleja and a neurotic conflict for Pfandl. The work becomes a hieroglyph of the life; as work of art, it vanishes.

I do not deny that biographical interpretation is one way to approach a work. It is, however, a path that goes only to the threshold; to comprehend truly, we must cross it and step inside. At that moment, the work is detached from its author and becomes autonomous. Immersed in reading, we are no longer interested in the subconscious motives that may have led Cervantes to write *Don Quixote*. Nor are we interested in his intentions; that is a matter of interpretation and we—tacitly, by the mere act of reading his book—superimpose our interpretations upon his. The work shuts out the author and opens to the reader. The author writes impelled by conscious and unconscious forces and objectives, but the sense of the work—and the pleasures and surprises we derive from the reading—never coincides exactly with those impulses and objectives. A work responds to the reader's, not the author's, questions. The reader stands between the work and the author. Once written, the work has a life of its own distinct from that of its author, a life granted by its successive readers.

In contrast to the biographically oriented critics, others approach the text as an independent and autonomous entity. They begin with the justified assumption that the work has characteristics that cannot be explained by the author's life. It is valid to see in Sor Juana's poems certain traits that, even if psychological in origin, are departures from the styles prevailing in her time. These distinctive traits make her work unique and self-sufficient. Nevertheless, even though it seems to us—and indeed is—unique, it is clear that Sor Juana's poetry is related to other past and contemporary works, from the Bible and the Church Fathers to Góngora and Calderón. Those works form a tradition, and thus present themselves to the writer as models to be imitated or rivals to be equaled. The study of Sor Juana's work takes us immediately to other works, and these works, to the intellectual and artistic climate of their time, to everything that constitutes "the spirit of an age." Spirit and, something even more powerful, *taste*. To a writer's life and work we must add a third term: society, history. Sor Juana is strongly individual and her work is undeniably unique; at the same time, the woman and her poems, the nun and the intellectual, exist within the context of a society, New Spain at the end of the seventeenth century.

My intention is not to explain literature through history. The value of sociological and historical interpretations of works of art is all too limited. Yet it would be absurd to close our eyes to this elementary truth: poetry is a social, a historical, product. To ignore the relation between society and poetry would be as grave an error as to ignore the relation between a writer's life and his work. Freud warned us that psychoanalysis cannot entirely explain artistic creation; and in the same way that there are elements in art and poetry that cannot be reduced to psychological and biographical explanations, there are elements that cannot be reduced to historical and sociological explanation. In what sense, then, is it valid to attempt to place the things that are unique to Sor Juana—her life and work—within the context of the history of her world, the aristocratic society of the city of Mexico in the second half of the seventeenth century? We are facing complementary realities. Both life and work unfold within a given society and thus are intelligible only within the history of that society; at the same time, its history would not be what it is without the life and works of Sor Juana. It is not enough to say that Sor Juana's work is a product of history; we must add that history is also a product of her work.

I have stated that a work exists not in isolation but in relation to other works, past and present, that are its models and its rivals. I must add that there is another, no less determinant, relationship: that of work to reader. Much is written today about the reader's influence on the work, and on the author himself. In every society there is a system of prohibitions and sanctions: the domains of what can and cannot be done. There is another area, usually broader, that is also divided into do's and don'ts: what can and cannot be said. Authorizations and prohibitions encompass a range of nuances that vary from society to society. Even so, they can be divided into two broad categories, the expressed and the implicit. The implicit prohibition is the more powerful; it is what is never voiced because it is taken for granted and therefore automatically and unthinkingly obeyed. The ruling system of repressions in each society is based upon this group of inhibitions that do not need to be monitored by consciousness.

In the modern world, the system of implicit authorizations and prohibitions exerts its influence on writers through their readers. An unread author is an author who is a victim of the worst kind of censorship, indifference—a censorship more effective than the Ecclesiastical Index. It is possible that the unpopularity of certain genres—poetry, for example, following Baudelaire and the Symbolists—is a result of the implicit censorship of a democratic and progressivist society. Bourgeois rationalism is, in a manner of speaking, constitutionally averse to poetry. Hence poetry, from the beginnings of the modern era—that is, since the last years of the eighteenth century—has been a form of rebellion. Poetry is not a genre in harmony with the modern world; its innermost nature is hostile or indifferent to the dogmas of modern times, progress and the cult of the future. Of course some poets have sincerely and passionately believed in progressive ideals, but their works say something quite different. Poetry, whatever the manifest content of the poem, is always a violation of the rationalism and morality of bourgeois society. Our society believes in history: newspapers, radio, television, the *now;* poetry, by its very nature, is atemporal.

In other societies, in addition to the anonymous community of ordinary readers, there is a group of privileged readers called the Archbishop, the Inquisitor, the Secretary General of the Party, the Politburo. These are fearsome readers, and they had as much influence on Sor Juana Inés de la Cruz as her admirers. In her *Response to Sor Filotea de la Cruz* she left us a confession: "I want no quarrel with the Holy Office." Her dread readers are a part—and a significant part—of her work. Her work tells us something, but to understand that something we must realize that it is utterance surrounded by silence: the silence of the *things that cannot be said.* The things she cannot say are determined by the invisible presence of her dread readers. When we read Sor Juana, we must recognize the silence surrounding her words. That silence is not absence of meaning; on the contrary, what cannot be said is anything that touches not only on the orthodoxy of the Catholic Church but also on the ideas, interests, and passions of its princes and its Orders. Sor Juana's words are written in the presence of a prohibition; that prohibition is embodied in an orthodoxy supported by a bureaucracy of prelates and judges. An understanding of Sor Juana's work must include an understanding of the prohibitions her work confronts. Her speech leads us to what cannot be said, what cannot be said to an orthodoxy, the orthodoxy to a tribunal, and the tribunal to a sentence.

This brief description of the relation between author and readers, between what can and cannot be said, omits an essential fact: usually the author is a part of the system of tacit but imperative prohibitions that forms the code of the *utterable* in every age and society. Nevertheless, not infrequently, and almost always in spite of themselves, writers violate that code and say what cannot be said, what they and they alone *must* say. Through their voices speaks that *other* voice: the condemned voice, the true voice. Sor Juana's contemporaries soon perceived in her voice the outburst of the other voice. That was the cause of the misfortunes she suffered in the last years of her life, for such transgressions were, and are, punished with severity. Furthermore, it is not unusual that in some societies, as in seventeenth-century New Spain, the writer himself becomes an ally, even an accomplice, of his censors. In the twentieth century, by a kind of historical regression, there are abundant examples of writers and ideologues who have become their own accusers. The similarity between Sor Juana's final years and these contemporary examples led me to choose as subtitle of my book "The Traps of Faith." The phrase is not applicable to all of Sor Juana's life, nor does it define her work; but I believe that it does describe an evil common to her time and our own. The recurrence of the evil is worth emphasizing, and that is why I have used the phrase: as a warning and example.

A work survives its readers; after a hundred or two hundred years it is read by new readers who impose on it new modes of reading and interpretation. The work survives because of these interpretations, which are, in fact, resurrections: without them there would be no work. The text transcends its own history only by being assessed within the context of a different history. I believe I can say in conclusion: understanding the work of Sor Juana demands an understanding of her life and her world. In this sense my book is an attempt at restitution; I hope to restore to their world, to seventeenth-century New Spain, Sor Juana's life and work. In turn, Sor Juana's life and writings can restore her distant world to us, her twentieth-century readers. This restitution is historical, relative, and partial, a twentieth-century Mexican's reading of the work of a nun of seventeenth-century New Spain. We can begin.

Part One

The Kingdom of New Spain

I

A Unique Society

SOCIETY IS DEFINED as much by how it comes to terms with its past as by its attitude toward the future: its memories are no less revealing than its aims. Although we Mexicans are preoccupied—or, more accurately, obsessed—with our past, we lack a clear idea of who we have been. What is more serious, we have no desire to know. We live between myth and negation; we enshrine certain periods, we forget others. These exclusions are significant; just as there is psychic censorship, there is historical censorship. Our history is a text in which some passages are written in black ink and others in invisible ink. One of the periods that have been scribbled over and revised with greatest zeal is that of the viceroyalty of New Spain. There are two popular versions of Mexican history, and in each the image of New Spain is distorted and diminished.

The first version can be summarized as follows: Mexico was born with the Aztec state, or even earlier; it lost its independence in the sixteenth century and recovered it in 1821. According to this idea, between Aztec and modern Mexico there is not only continuity but identity; both are the same nation, which is why we say that Mexico *recovered* her independence in 1821. New Spain was an interregnum, a historical parenthesis, a vacuum in which nothing of importance occurred. It was the period of the Mexican nation's bondage. The rule of Montezuma, although it may have oppressed all other Indian nations, was indigenous, but the viceroyalty was a rule by foreigners—hence Independence as restoration. This version is colored by myth. The second version draws on biological metaphor: Mexico's roots are sunk in the pre-Hispanic world; the three centuries of New Spain, especially the seventeenth and eighteenth, were a period of gestation; Independence signaled the nation's maturity, its coming of age. The second is the more rational version, but in overemphasizing evolution it overlooks interruptions and differences.

The truth is that the history of Mexico is a history in the image of its geography: abrupt and tortuous. Each historical period is like a plateau surrounded by tall mountains and separated from the other plateaus by precipices and divides. The Conquest was the great chasm, the dividing line that split our history in half: on the far side lies the pre-Columbian world; on the near side, the Catholic viceroyalty of New Spain and the secular and independent Republic of Mexico. The second period embraces two opposite but equally peripheral offshoots of Western civilization. The first, New Spain, was a historical reality that ran counter to the current of Western civilization, that is, against the flow of emerging modernity. The second, the Republic of Mexico, was a hasty adaptation of that modernity, which has distorted our traditions without making us a truly modern nation.

The slash line of the Conquest was so clean and deep that most of us are tempted to view the pre-Columbian world as a seamless whole. It was not so. It, too, was marked by divisions and interruptions. First of all, we note a spatial division that characterized the history of Mesoamerica from the neolithic age: nomadic versus sedentary peoples. This division was both geographical and cultural: north and south, the barbaric and the civilized—or, as the Aztecs saw it, Toltecs and Chichimecs. In the area inhabited by the sedentary peoples, the seat of Mesoamerican civilization, we find a great diversity of cultures, languages, and states, from the Olmecs to the Toltecs, Zapotecs, Mixtecs, and the many-branched Maya family, itself divided into many city-states. Historically this diverse world can be divided into two main periods. The first was the so-called classical period, Teotihuacán, Monte Albán, and the Maya city-states, which lasted until the ninth century. It was followed by two more strictly historical epochs, Tula and Mexico-Tenochtitlán. But however radical these distinctions, they define phases of a single civilization. The great break, I must repeat, was the Conquest, which was a watershed between civilizations.

We twentieth-century Mexicans, even those of pure Indian descent, look on the pre-Columbian world as a world on the *other side,* not only distant in time but across the cultural divide. Clearly—although official opinion does not accept it—there are greater affinities between independent Mexico and New Spain than between them and pre-Hispanic societies. The proof is that our attitude toward the Indian world is not very different from what it was in colonial days. New Spain, especially during the seventeenth and eighteenth centuries, was committed to a recovery of the pre-Columbian past, after first subjecting it to a curious idealization; at the same time, it continued in the north the Christianizing of the Indians begun by the first Franciscans and Dominicans. Independent Mexico, particularly the twentieth-century Mexico spawned in the Mexican Revolution, has persisted in both enterprises: recovery of the Indian past—for purposes of self-justification and idealization—and the integration of indigenous groups into Mexican society. Our anthropologists and rural schoolteachers are the heirs of the sixteenth- and seventeenth-century missionaries. The ideas and the rhetoric have changed, but not the general movement of history. This movement unfolds in contradictory and complementary directions: while racially we are becoming more and more a mestizo nation, socially and culturally we are becoming more and more Western.

Far from revealing a linear continuity, this brief overview of Mexican history has shown the existence of three distinct societies. I am not alone in this perception; Edmundo O'Gorman maintains that "our past is made up of three closely related historical entities: first, the Aztec empire; second, the viceroyalty of New Spain; and third, the nation of Mexico."[1] I must add that each of these societies is separated from the other by a negation. The Indian world was negated by New Spain; New Spain, nonetheless, cannot be understood without the Indian world, both as an antecedent and as a secret presence that pervades practices, customs, family and political structures, economic systems, crafts, legends, myths, and beliefs. In turn, New Spain was negated and at the same time prolonged by the Republic of Mexico. Each negation contains within it the negated society—usually as a masked, a veiled, presence. Many of the constituent elements of the pre-Hispanic world reappear in New Spain and are part of modern Mexico. The influence of New Spain was the more decisive: it gave us our language, religion, and culture. In sum, there is continuity, yes, but one that was interrupted time and time again.

These breaks and interruptions do not exclude a secret and persistent continuity. Teotihuacán was the religious, political, military, and economic center of ancient Mexico from the second millennium before

Christ to the time of its downfall in the seventh century. The collapse of this great city did not mark the end of its influence in history. In myth and legend it became the archetype for all the societies that followed. First it inspired Tula, the militarist state that replaced the Toltecs in the valleys of Mexico and Puebla. Tula, in turn, served as a model for Mexico-Tenochtitlán. The image of Mexico-Tenochtitlán—significantly equated with that of Rome—reappears in the seventeenth and eighteenth centuries in the imperial city of Mexico. Although the defeats and setbacks since Independence have dissipated the chimera of empire—the legacy of Mexico-Tenochtitlán and New Spain—the modern republic has maintained Aztec and Spanish centralism even while imitating North American federalism. Continuity, then, but also superimposition: upon the ruins of a pre-Columbian world, conquered but not dead, arose a different society, New Spain, which reached its peak in the eighteenth century and in turn disintegrated during the civil wars of the first half of the nineteenth century. Upon the remains of New Spain was erected a smaller Mexico, the republican Mexico of Juarez and his successors. This third Mexican society, our own, is still evolving.

NEW SPAIN RESEMBLES neither pre-Columbian nor modern Mexico. Nor was it a replica of Spain, even though it was a territory under the rule of the Spanish crown. What were its relations with the mother country? Was it truly a colony? That depends on what is meant by "colony." Originally the word referred to the settling, peaceful or violent, in a foreign country of a group from a different country. The newly arrived eject—at times, exterminate—the natives; they do not form an independent entity but maintain their political and religious ties with the home country. The movement for independence comes later, when the descendants of the first colonists begin to feel they are different from the mother country. Greek colonies in the ancient world and English colonies in New England are examples of what originally was understood by "colony." In this sense New Spain was never a colony, although probably the *criollos,* the locally born citizens of Spanish descent, had a "colonial" consciousness in the seventeenth and eighteenth centuries. And in the modern sense of the word? We have only to consider for a moment the colonies held until recently by Great Britain, France, Holland, and Belgium to recognize their enormous differences from New Spain and the other possessions of the Spanish crown.

The English colonies in America were settled by groups with religious, political, and economic motives. Like the Greeks, the English hoped to found communities in the image of those in the homeland. Unlike the Greeks, however, many of those colonists were religious dissenters. Hence the dual influence of religion and utopianism in the formation of the political democracy of the United States. The social contract was, in its beginnings, religious. Religious motives also inspired the Spanish, but whereas the English founded their communities to escape an orthodoxy, the Spanish established theirs to expand one. For one group the founding principle was religious freedom; for the other, the conversion of the natives to an orthodoxy and a Church. The conquistadors undertook the Conquest at their own risk; in a way, it was a private undertaking. But it was also an imperial enterprise. Cross, sword, and crown—a fusion of the military, the religious, and the political. Two words define Spanish expansion: conquest and conversion. These are imperial words, and medieval words as well. The conquest of America by the Spanish and the Portuguese resembles neither Greek nor English colonization but, rather, the Christian crusades or a Muslim holy war. Even the conquistadors' "thirst for gold" corresponds to the Muslim and Christian warriors' looting and pillage.

Another distinguishing feature of New Spain should be noted: it was one of several kingdoms subject to the crown, in theory equal to the kingdoms of Castile, Aragon, Navarre, and Leon. In the eighteenth century the reforms of Charles III modified the arrangement, but even then New Spain did not become a true colony. The wars of independence of the possessions of the Spanish crown in America belong more to the tradition of the struggles of Catalonia and Portugal against the hegemony of Castile than to the history of modern revolutions. The liberal ideology of the Spanish American movement for independence obscured and distorted the true nature of the separation from Spain: the republican and democratic ideals of the groups that directed the struggle for independence did not correspond to the historical reality of Spanish America. There was no bourgeoisie or intellectual class to criticize the absolute monarchy or the Church. The classes that effected independence were unable to implant democratic and liberal ideas because there was no organic bond between them and those ideas.

Why did Spanish American revolutionaries appropriate the ideas of the Enlightenment and the American Revolution? Because they felt that there was no political model in their own tradition that could provide the intellectual and moral justification for their rebellion. To all appearances, they were correct. I say "to all appearances" because there *was* a Spanish tradition of struggle for autonomy and independence: Catalonia, Aragon, the autonomous cities of Castile, the Basques. It was a buried tradition, however, and though still alive, it was not widely known. It was, in fact, a mere embryo of a true political model. Instead of rethinking and revising that tradition, instead of bringing it up to date and applying it to new circumstances, Spanish Americans (and also liberal Spaniards) preferred to appropriate the political philosophies of the French, English, and North Americans. It was understandable that Spanish Americans would want to claim those ideas and would hope to implant them in their own countries, for those were the ideas of emerging modernity.

The contradiction between the ideals of independence and Spanish American reality was particularly visible in Mexico. Although the movement toward autonomy originated among criollo groups during the eighteenth century, if not earlier, at the time of independence Spanish Americans appropriated the revolutionary ideas of the *Encyclopédie* and of the Founding Fathers of North American democracy as if they were a ready-made philosophy. Something similar happened later with positivism and is happening now with Marxism. I will reiterate a point I have often made: our history, from the perspective of modern Western history, has been ex-centric. We have had no age of critical philosophy, no bourgeois revolution, no political democracy: no Kant, no Robespierre, no Hume, no Jefferson.

The *other* tradition, our tradition, surfaces from time to time. For example, when in 1813 Fray Servando Teresa de Mier proposed to establish Mexico's historical and legal right to independence, he did not refer to French or North American examples but wrote: "We Americans [Mexicans], being equal in rights to the Spanish, endeavored to establish tribunals and congresses from the moment the monarchs of Spain and the Indies submitted to Napoleon . . . You, the Spanish, have stripped your King of his sovereignty, and thus the tie that bound the Americas to him has been broken, and a sovereign people has been formed."[2]

This is impeccable reasoning, and it proves that New Spain was considered not a colony but a kingdom, with the same rights and obligations as those of other kingdoms in the empire. The overthrow of the Spanish monarch had broken the pact that through him united the Spanish and American nations. Fray Servando underscores the fact that the King was the King of Spain and the Indies, and that New Spain owed loyalty to the Spanish monarch, not to Spain. Therefore, once the King had been deposed by Napoleon, the Mexican people regained their sovereignty. At the same time, Fray Servando's reasoning expresses with great clarity the essential contradiction of New Spain. This contradiction was not based on the antagonisms between rich and poor or between subjected natives and European oppressors, as is so often claimed in pseudo-Marxist arguments. The contradiction that produced the explosion of revolutionary insurgence originated not from the base of society but from its summit: the schism between criollos and Spaniards. The inferior status of the criollos—in politics, the administration, and the military, not in the sphere of wealth—did not conform to the status of the kingdom of New Spain within the empire. New Spain was a kingdom like other kingdoms, but the criollos were not treated as equal to their kinsmen born in Spain. This, allied to the revolt of landless peasants, was the cause of the wars of independence.

NEW SPAIN WAS UNIQUE not only for its situation within the empire but also for its internal structure. In the following pages I will sketch the nature of that historical and social reality. But we should keep in mind that it was an immense and rapidly changing reality, which was at the peak of its expansion during the seventeenth and eighteenth centuries. As proof, we have only to remember that the Spaniards and criollos pushed as far north as San Francisco and beyond. New Spain was an enormous land, prosperous and peaceful. In spite of occasional uprisings, hunger, epidemics, and riots, it was public order, not turmoil, that prevailed during these three centuries.

When we speak of the differences between New Spain and Spain, we immediately think of the differences that distinguish a dependent entity from its mother country. Spain ruled Mexico, and it was the peninsular Spanish who occupied the apex of the social structure. In the economic sphere, Spain removed from Mexico more riches than she returned. There is another disparity, one that not everyone has noted: Catholicism was a new religion in America and an old one in Spain, a creative force in New Spain and one on the defensive in the Old World. I refer, of course, to the second half of the seventeenth century and most of the eighteenth. While Mexico, however falteringly, was developing, Spain was declining as rapidly as she had expanded a century before.

As for the political realm: the stability and relative calm of the viceroyalty contrast markedly with the turmoil and intrigues of the court in

Madrid—especially from the end of the reign of Philip IV through the long rule of Charles II. First under the regency of the Queen Mother and her inept ministers, then under the disastrous governments of John of Austria and the indecisive Medinaceli and Oropesa, Spain suffered both unrest and indignities: internally, general economic and cultural decline; externally, reverses, defeats, and humiliations. The Spanish empire was of sound body but its central nervous sytem was severely damaged.

THE MODERN AGE IS DISTINGUISHED by two features that are *not* found in New Spain. The first is the expansion of the central government at the expense of local autonomy. The second, related to the first, is equality before the law: a single law for all, and all equal before that law. The disappearance of the medieval system of special jurisdictions corresponds to the growth of the centralized state with its national bureaucracy. But in New Spain the state, although strongly centralized and with a powerful bureaucracy, protected local interests and special jurisdictions. Native communities were ruled by the laws of the Indies, and there were different statutes for the various other ethnic groups: blacks, mulattos, mestizos, criollos, and Spaniards. Specific laws governed religious orders and the secular church, while others applied to the landholders, merchants, miners, artisans, brotherhoods, and guilds. This is why the historian Richard M. Morse defines New Spain as a pluralistic society ruled by a markedly hierarchical and paternalistic system of special jurisdictions for a large number of divergent groups.[3]

The groups that composed this society had no political representation; as a result, Mexicans were poorly prepared for democracy. At the same time, it would be inaccurate to say that New Spain was feudal in the strict sense of the word. The latifundium, the property system based on large estates, prevailed, but the landholders were strongly dependent on central authority. One of the characteristic features of Spanish history is that feudalism, because it was relatively weak in Spain, strengthened rather than weakened the monarchy. In New Spain, likewise, centralism triumphed over the aspirations of an embryonic feudal class.

Alongside the system of large estates there was collective ownership of land. A system of communal landholding known as the *calpulli* dated from the pre-Hispanic period and was based on blood and religious ties. Barrios were laid out spatially according to the four cardinal points, or four points of the cosmos, and the land was not divisible or transferable.

The crown had an interest in protecting such communal property because it limited the economic and political power of the aristocratic criollo landowning class, the only group with potential separatist leanings. One of the causes of the break with Spain was the failure of this policy: the criollo landowners grew too powerful while simultaneously an enormous class of landless peons was created.

The clergy composed the second group of collective landowners. I should clarify that we are not dealing here with a single proprietor but with many: the religious orders and the secular clergy. The aggregate of their possessions was enormous; by the end of the seventeenth century more than half of the land was in the hands of the Church. The power of the Church can be compared to that of two modern institutions: large capitalist corporations and political bureaucracies, especially those that rule communist countries. Such organizations exert their power in overlapping areas of public activity: economic, administrative, political, and, in the case of the Church and contemporary political bureaucracies, ideological. A triple monopoly, over the means of production, the products, and the conscience of the producers. These similarities should not obscure significant differences: large capitalist companies exercise an economic, not a political or ideological, monopoly; and although the Church, like a communist bureaucracy, had jurisdiction over morality, it did not, like such bureaucracies, have a monopoly of political power.

The intricate network of associations, brotherhoods, and artisans' guilds also deserves mention here. The state had the right to demand services or contributions from the private sector, but in contrast to the situation in a capitalist society, the responsible entity was the guild or corporate group, not the individual. Such rendering of services might be in money or in labor. Taxes, state monopolies, prohibitions against manufacturing certain goods: this is what Max Weber, speaking of Egypt and the Hellenistic world, called the "mercantilism" of the patrimonial system.[4]

In a patrimonial system as defined by Weber, the professional army excludes natives of the country from positions of high command. This restriction was one of the criollos' principal complaints against the Spanish. Another distinguishing characteristic of such a society is its concept of guilt and innocence before the law. In New Spain the two poles of justice were not, as in modern society, the legality or illegality of the sentence but rather its severity or mildness. The determining principle was *grace*. When Sor Juana asked the Viceroy to spare the life of a man condemned to death, she did it in the following terms (in poem 25):[5]

> Any man can take a life
> but only God can breathe life in;
> thus only through the gift of life
> may you hope to resemble Him.

The Christian ruler was not, like our presidents, the embodiment of the law but, rather, of divine design.

The attitude toward education is also significant. Weber notes two typical forms of education in the patrimonial system, both of which existed in New Spain. The first is education as a special province of the clergy and members of the dominant church; the second is university education. In the sixteenth and seventeenth centuries, European university education began to enlighten the social group that later, toward the end of the eighteenth century, was to form the bureaucracy of modern societies. In Mexico, however, the war for independence and the civil disputes of the nineteenth century interrupted the modernization of the national bureaucracy. In the first third of the twentieth century this process was again interrupted by the Mexican Revolution. The result was that as recently as the middle of this century Mexico did not have a modern bureaucracy.

AFTER THIS OUTLINE it is not difficult to accept Richard M. Morse's definition of the mode of governance of New Spain. With certain reservations and provisos that I shall enumerate later, it is clear to me that this regime corresponds to one of the two forms of traditional rule defined by Max Weber: patrimonialism. The other is feudalism. Patrimonialism can be defined as the rule of one, aided by trusted advisers; that is, government as an extension of the royal house. Feudalism consists of rule by a privileged few. In a patrimonial regime the central authority must strive to prevent the excessive growth of an independent aristocracy of landowners who enjoy hereditary privileges. In New Spain, a distrustful central authority assiduously monitored the activities of the criollos.

The Viceroy of New Spain was also the governor and captain general, as well as the presiding officer of the Real Audiencia. His four titles designated four distinct functions and jurisdictions. First, as Viceroy, he was the alter ego of the monarch; as governor general, he was a kind of first minister or chief of state charged with the administration and operation of the kingdom; as captain general he directed the administration of military affairs (the captaincy general was not strictly a military assignment and did not involve command of troops, just as a modern president does not conduct military operations although he is, ex officio, chief of the armed forces); as presiding officer of the Real Audiencia he administered justice and directed the general policies of the nation (here we note an overlap between the political and judicial). The historian Ignacio Rubio Mañé, who has studied the subject in depth, points out the vagueness of these functions and jurisdictions. He also observes that in addition to the lack of clear demarcation among the four offices, the authority of the offices was at times in contradiction. For example, the territorial limits within which the Viceroy exercised his authority did not coincide with the boundaries of his power as presiding officer of the Audiencia, or as governor, or captain general.[6] This ambiguity in functions, jurisdictions, and duties was not accidental: it was intended to increase the viceroys' dependency.

Because of the vastness of his domains, the Spanish monarch had to ensure the loyalty of those who governed distant lands in his name. Thus no Viceroy was granted a long tenure, undoubtedly in order to deny him the opportunity to further his own ambitions. The first viceroys, says Rubio Mañé, "were not assigned specific terms, and the Emperor, Charles V, made sure that they governed *for whatever period was the will of the King.*" Even so, by the end of Charles V's reign it was the custom to limit the post of Viceroy of Peru to a period of six years. In 1629, over the opposition of the majority of the members of the Council of the Indies, the Count-Duke de Olivares succeeded in changing the phrase "the will of the King" to a specific appointment of three years. Obviously the term could be extended if the monarch so desired. Of the four viceroys who were patrons of Sor Juana, the Marquis de Mancera served nine years, Fray Payo de Rivera six years, the Marquis de la Laguna six years, and the Count de Galve seven.

Another safeguard: viceroys could not bring sons, daughters, sons-in-law, or daughters-in-law to New Spain. According to a royal decree of 1660 this arrangement was inviolable. It was a custom, as reported in the same decree, that had endured from "time immemorial." Indeed, it appears in every patrimonial regime from ancient times through the Renaissance—and is still practiced by totalitarian communist governments today. This ban made virtual hostages of the Viceroy's family. Another form of control was the institution of the *visitador,* or royal inspector. The precedent for this office similarly is found in antiquity and in the Middle Ages, for example, in the *missi dominici* (personal representatives) of Charlemagne. Rubio Mañé tells us that "because of the rigor of his procedures, the Viceroy as well as the Audiencia always dreaded the arrival of a *visitador.*" Many of these inspectors were famous for their severity. But "the King's principal instrument for controlling the Viceroy was a judgment of his performance, the *juicio de residencia.*" This judgment was begun at the end of the Viceroy's term; the investigation lasted six months. The judge was guided in his inquiry by "the sealed letter of instructions the Viceroy had received at the time of his appointment." Rubio Mañé summarizes: "When the Viceroy showed unusual enterprise, he invited the crown's jealousy and thus assured that obstacles would be placed in the way of all his projects."

The Viceroy was the presiding officer of the Real Audiencia, but his relation to this body, which was a sort of government council, was determined by a subtle interplay of checks and balances. The Real Audiencia of Mexico was composed of a presiding officer (the Viceroy), eight judges, four criminal magistrates, two prosecutors (one for criminal and the other for civil affairs), a chief constable, and a number of lesser functionaries. The Viceroy did not participate in the judicial functions of the Audiencia; in this area his presidency was purely honorific. By contrast, he had full jurisdiction and far-reaching powers in the political arena: "The right conceded to the Audiencia by the crown to limit the broad powers of the Viceroy was not granted in such a way as to diminish the authority of the monarch's alter ego." The Audiencia's independence of the Viceroy was guaranteed specifically by the judges' right to communicate directly with the King without intervention of any kind by the Viceroy. On the other hand, the Viceroy, by virtue of a royal decree of 1602, had the right to "take testimony and to initiate investigations against the judges." The Audiencia, thanks to a royal decree of 1610, could convene without the Viceroy, "to consider matters relating to him or his family." The Viceroy, of course, "was guaranteed freedom to express his opinions to the King, to recommend certain procedures, and at times to countermand orders sent to him. The ritual phrase 'Obey, but do not fulfill' was widely known."[7]

How to sum up relations between the Viceroy and the Audiencia? As a system of checks and balances, but also as a play of mirrors. The Real

Audiencia represented not power but the restraint of power; it was both the limit of the Viceroy's will and the eyes and ears of the absent monarch. No Viceroy could govern without its cooperation, support, and approval. The Audiencia represented the continuity of the Spanish state during the absence of the Viceroy or at his death, until such time as the *pliego de mortaja*, the sealed "death letter," could be opened, revealing the name of the Viceroy's successor. If it was neither the voice that issued orders nor the arm that executed them, the Audiencia was the ear that listened and the mind that deliberated, without whose counsel no decision could be made. The Audiencia was an example of the deliberate ambiguity in the division of functions that typified the Spanish overseas system: if it was not the court of first instance, it was the *other* court. New Spain was an intricate web of influences, powers, and jurisdictions. A counterbalance to the political and judiciary power of the Viceroy and the Audiencia was the moral and religious power of the Archbishop of Mexico. He, in turn, found a rival in the Bishop of Puebla, the other great city. And both of them were confronted by powerful religious orders. The quarrels among the Princes of the Church could be terrible, as Sor Juana Inés de la Cruz could testify with bitterness in the last years of her life.

2

The Dais and the Pulpit

MY SKETCH OF NEW SPAIN is by no means a complete description. But my purpose is more modest: to draw a general picture of the world into which Sor Juana Inés de la Cruz was born and in which she lived and wrote. I have commented on New Spain's dependence on the mother country, on how mercantilism and the latifundium system defined its economy and patrimonialism its politics. Historians who have studied this period tend to omit or barely mention another aspect that was equally important, especially in the case of Sor Juana: the viceregal court. New Spain was a typical court society. Many recent observations about the institution of the court are directly applicable to the two American courts of the time, that of Mexico City and that of Lima. In passing, I should note that the only two Spanish American nations with a court were also the only two that had centralized political systems prior to the arrival of the Europeans. It was the court, the center and summit of society, that made the whole system comprehensible. In addition to exerting a decisive influence on political and administrative life, the court served as a model for social life. Without the court we cannot understand Sor Juana; not only did she live in it as a young woman, but her life itself can be seen as the history of her relationship—intimate but also fragile and unstable—with the viceregal palace.

A theater of social and cultural activities no less than of intrigues and political decisions, the viceregal court was a radial center of morality, literature, and aesthetics; it profoundly influenced both social life and individual destinies. The court set an example for courtesy, mores, and styles; it governed the manner of loving and eating, of burying the dead and courting the living, of celebrating birthdays and mourning the departed. "The criterion that determines what events we must remember," says Valéry in the prologue to *Regards sur le monde actuel*, "is the one that measures changes in social codes." These codes are none other than those of courtesy and urbanity. The viceregal court performed a dual civilizing role: it transmitted the models of aristocratic European culture, and it offered for emulation a way of life different from those of the Church and the university, the two other great institutions of the time. Compared to them, the court represented a more aesthetic and vital mode of life. The court was the secular world—a ballet, not always vain and often dramatic, in which the true characters were human passions, ranging from sensuality to ambition, moving within a strict and elegant geometry.

The transition from medieval to modern society was achieved through the absolutist state. The primary political and cultural instrument of the absolute monarchy was the court, which transformed quarreling feudal barons into the ruler's servants, that is, into courtiers and bureaucrats. The court of France was the supreme model for all the Western world, especially in Sor Juana's time. The historian Irving A. Leonard remarks, with a touch of puritanical reproof, that Sor Juana's patron the twenty-eighth Viceroy, the Marquis de la Laguna and Count de Paredes, held sway "amidst a viceregal court perhaps consciously imitating the profligacy, luxury, and immorality of the contemporary Versailles of Louis XIV." [1]

Norbert Elias reproaches historians and sociologists for their lack of attention to the phenomenon of the court. He observes that scholars concerned with economic structure call this period "mercantilist"; those who study it from the perspective of the state call it "absolutist"; those who examine the mode of government and administration tend to use Weber's term "patrimonialism." How, Elias asks, can they close their eyes to the fact that for three hundred years the court was the model for what today we call "civilization" and the Middle Ages called "curteisie"? He adds that the aristocratic society of the court—the last great nonbourgeois institution of the West—survived in two forms: as a legacy, and as an inverted image of courtly civilization. [2] In effect, the bourgeoisie imitated—and still imitates—certain forms of courtly life, while simultaneously and from the beginning moving, in terms of basic attitudes, in a direction exactly opposite to the ideals of the court. Imitation by adoption and, one might say, by contradiction. Bourgeois morality—

ascetic, prudent, sober, scornful of luxury—is anticourtly; bourgeois mores, in aesthetic and erotic ideals and fantasies, pay homage to courtly culture. The bourgeois counts pennies but wishes he were an aristocrat. Here, too, the lack of continuity between modern Mexico and New Spain is apparent: Mexico, when it became independent, broke with the tradition of the viceregal court but did not adopt the attitudes or morality of the Western bourgeoisie.

Another distinctive nonmodern trait of New Spain is orthodoxy. Here the contrast with later colonial societies is fundamental. As we know, indifference toward religious matters has characterized imperialist expansion during the modern era. Colonial powers of the nineteenth and twentieth centuries have had no interest in converting the inhabitants of conquered territories. The example of India clearly illustrates the difference between premodern and modern dominion. Islamic rule converted more than a third of the population, and today, excluding Pakistan and Bangladesh, some fifty million Indians are Muslims; after more than two centuries of British rule, the Christians in India number scarcely ten million. For the Muslim conqueror, the Indian convert was a "brother"; for the British administrator, the Christian Indian was still a "native." The same indifference toward religious orthodoxy distinguishes the policy of the other great colonial powers of the nineteenth century. The reason is to be found in the origins of the modern state and its ideology, bourgeois liberalism in its several shadings. Here a brief digression is in order.

Evolution toward modernity divides into two parallel paths: that of countries in which modernity followed the triumph of the Reformation, and that of countries such as France, which entered modernity *without* Protestantism. In France, modernity was expressed as a criticism of absolute monarchy, of the court, and of the ancien régime, but also as an attack against the Catholic Church. From its beginnings French democracy was colored by anti-Catholicism and anticlericalism; it was a secular movement, in spite of the nebulous deism of some of its supporters. There was, however, a religious element—anti-Rome and anti-Jesuit in sentiment—which in France fulfilled a function similar to the role of Protestantism in Nordic countries: Jansenism. Jansen's theology was decisive in the formation of a modern moral conscience in France. The absence of this element in Spain and in her American possessions may explain, in part, why we do not have an authentic modernity. In Protestant countries—especially England and Holland—as in France, modernity was an inner attitude, a matter of conscience, before it was politics and action. In contrast, Spanish American rationalism was not free inquiry but an acquired ideology, which is precisely why our anticlericalism was highly rhetorical. The origins of English and of North American democracy, deeply influenced by Dutch example, were religious: Anglo-Saxon democracies were born of a religious movement, the Reformation. This is the decisive but never-mentioned difference between Anglo-Saxon and Latin democracies; they spring from diametrically opposed attitudes toward the traditional religion of the West.

The indifference toward religious orthodoxy of a colonial power such as France is explained by the secular nature of the bourgeois state during the time of imperialist expansion. How does one explain the same indifference among the English Protestant colonists who reached America shortly after the Spanish? Richard M. Morse recalls a passage from Martin Luther's "Open Letter to the Christian Nobility" that clearly illustrates the spirit of Protestant colonization. For Luther, an unoccupied land or a land populated by pagans was a savage land; thus he equated the natural world with paganism. If Christians found themselves in a savage land, their duty was not to convert the pagans but to elect their own religious leaders. The American Indians were a part of nature and so, like all things of the earth, were contaminated by sin and death; they were something to be tamed or exterminated. Moreover, the idea of the salvation of one's neighbor never enters the Calvinist ethic because only divine grace, not human action, can save man. Predestination is the cornerstone of Calvinism. The drama of religion is reduced to a dialectic between the creator and the created. As the intermediaries between the individual conscience and God are suppressed, the evangelizing mission of Christianity disappears. In turn, and by virtue of a similar logic, religion offered a foundation for democracy. The text that Morse quotes from Luther is explicit: "If a little group of pious Christian laymen were taken captive and set down in a wilderness, and had among them no priest consecrated by a bishop, and if there in the wilderness they were to agree in choosing one of themselves, married or unmarried, and were to charge him with the office of baptizing, saying mass, absolving and preaching, such a man would be as truly a priest as though all bishops and popes had consecrated him."[3] Election by the people not only legitimizes authority, it *consecrates* it. Nothing similar exists in all of Catholic tradition.

The contrast with New Spain could not be greater. Evangelization was the justification for the Conquest and, later, for Spanish and Portuguese domination. The conversion of infidels is not exclusively a Christian concept; it is also—and perhaps to an even greater degree—Islamic. From its beginnings Islam resorted to conversion by conquest. Sixteenth-century Spain and Portugal were emerging from centuries of Islamic influence; thus it is not an exaggeration to see in the conquest and the evangelization of America a process in which the Muslim precedent was no less a determining factor than the Catholic faith. Anyone who lives in India can see the differences between Islamic and Portuguese rule on one hand and English rule on the other. The Muslims and Portuguese destroyed Hindu temples with the same zeal that Cortés devoted to tearing down the idols of the great pyramid of Cholula; upon those ruins, sometimes with the very stones, they erected superb mosques and cathedrals. The English respected native cults and temples; they were interested first and foremost in administering the empire. The results were the churches of Goa, the mosques of Delhi, and in Bombay the railway station.

As it defines itself, every society defines other societies. That definition almost always takes the form of a condemnation: the *other* is the barbarian. The duality of ancient times, Greeks vs. barbarians, is repeated in the Middle Ages, although the terms have been inverted: pagans vs. Christians. Beginning with the eighteenth century, medieval dichotomy becomes modern duality: civilization vs. barbarism. The word "civilization" was anticipated early in the sixteenth century by another term first defined by Erasmus of Rotterdam in a brief tract, *De civilitate morum puerilium*. Soon, says Norbert Elias, there was a French *civilité*, an Italian *civiltà*, and even a German *Zivilität*.[4] Elias does not report a Spanish *civilidad*, although the word had already been recorded by the grammarian Nebrija. The reason seems obvious to me: the word was not in common use. The *Diccionario de autoridades* of the Spanish Royal Academy lists two meanings for *civilidad:* urbanity and politeness, but also lowness and baseness. The second usage was the more common. In regard to the word *civil*, the *Diccionario* explains that although in the strict sense "it was equivalent to urbane, courteous, and polite . . . , the word is not used in this way but is applied only to one who is despicable, mean, base, or of low condition." The Corominas dictionary indicates that in Spanish the word was used to mean the opposite of knightly, reflecting the original opposition between *militaris* and *civilis*.[5] So in Spain and its territories until the eighteenth century, *civilidad* was pejorative in connotation, unlike its cognates in the rest of Europe.

The unusual development of *civilidad* in Spanish is another example of the persistence of premodern traits in our culture. *Civilidad*, civility, is a word that related to the aristocratic circle of the court, while *civilizado*, civilized, is a bourgeois word indicating the educated and progressive man. In Spain, although there was a court society, a different set of key words was used, all permeated with the martial and the religious. Social hierarchies could be translated into religious values: *honra*, honor, was synonymous with purity of lineage, and purity of lineage had religious connotations. Ideas of purity and impurity are essentially religious, as seen in the example of the Indian caste system. In Spain, undoubtedly because of centuries of coexistence and struggle with Islam, these concepts refer to martial and seignorial functions as well as to lineage. The key word that defined and justified the historical actions of Spain and the existence of her empire was *evangelization*—evangelization understood as conversion, even if by holy war. The medieval dichotomy of pagan vs. Christian assumed greater force and immediacy in New Spain than in the mother country: Catholicism vs. all *others* (Indian idolaters, Protestant sects, Moors, Jews, and Judaizers). Orthodoxy created a dualism, a definitive line of demarcation. Its authority relied on both the law and the sword, the Church and the state. Spain was, at the dawn of the modern age, again different from other European states. In them central power was strengthened, and in them, in one way or another, state and nation—two separate entities until then—became one. But no other nation-state identified as totally as Spain with a single religion.

Spanish orthodoxy fed on the Neoscholasticism of Francisco Suárez[6] and his disciples. There is a clear connection, Morse states, between Neothomism and the patrimonial society of New Spain. Although this doctrine was devised for thirteenth-century Europe, in its new Spanish version it adapted marvelously to New Spain, perhaps even better than to Europe. Neothomism considers society to be "a hierarchical system in which each person and each group serves the purpose of a general and universal order that transcends them," according to Morse. Society is not a composite of individual atoms, as in modern political philosophy, but an association of subsocieties and subgroups. The system is hierarchical, but the hierarchy is not a product of a social contract; it belongs to the universal and natural orders. Hierarchy provides a governing principle capable of righting wrongs, abuses, and injustices through the person of a universally accepted sovereign. The ruler's authority originates in the people; nevertheless, the ruler is responsible not to society but to God. Neothomism was a philosophy destined to offer a logical and rational justification of the Christian revelation. In turn, the teaching and defense of the Christian revelation formed the basis of the Spanish empire. Religious orthodoxy was the foundation of the political system.

This marriage of idea with political power is profoundly antimodern: nineteenth- and twentieth-century democracies are systems that do not postulate any ideology that lies beyond the boundaries of discussion and criticism. More precisely, the only ideology of the modern state, at least theoretically, is one that guarantees the coexistence, and the free discussion and criticism, of all ideas. The orthodoxy of the bourgeois state is the absence of orthodoxy. Thus the modern state is based on a principle completely opposed to the one that ruled New Spain and similarly today inspires communist societies. The total fusion of idea and power was at the root of the historical "mission" of the Spanish empire, as today it is at that of the communist state. The justification of Spanish expansionism was evangelization; for communism, it is revolutionary proselytizing. The contradiction that corrodes universalist ideologies and inevitably ends by destroying them is that they do not, in fact, transcend the specific social entities we call nations, classes, peoples, and ethnic and cultural groups. New Spain is a good example of this commonplace: from within the bosom of a vast philosophical, political, and religious universalism—imperial Spain—emerged the criollo sense of a distinct identity that evolved into Mexican nationalism.

IF FROM SOCIAL and political structures and forms we turn to the composition of New Spain's population, we find a similarly motley and complex reality. At the base were the Indians; at the apex, the Spaniards and criollos. Even the Indians, divided—by Jacques Lafaye's classification—into nomadic and sedentary peoples, were not a monolithic group.[7] In contrast to the sedentary peoples, the nomads did not experience the abrupt obliteration of their cultures and for a long while preserved their religious beliefs and their shamans. The sedentary populations, bound to the land and to mining, were those who suffered most deeply the severe disruption of the Conquest. At the time of the Spaniards' arrival, Mesoamerican society was enmeshed in a period of continuous wars, probably begun several centuries earlier with the fall of Teotihuacán. Military defeat and the ensuing servitude were no novelty for the Indians; the true and terrible novelty was the destruction of their civilization. The change in social, political, and religious systems was total. That change began with the demolition of their temples and religious monuments and the physical annihilation of the two ruling groups, the aristocracy and the caste of priests and shamans. The destruction of the temples, statues, and paintings was tantamount to the abolition of their symbols; the extermination of the priestly caste, to the extirpation of their memory and consciousness.

The military triumph of the Spanish was seen as a change in religion: the Indian gods disappeared over the mythical horizon. But a society that believes in cyclic time sees the end of one cycle as the beginning of another. The door through which the old gods exit is the door through which new gods enter. New gods? The flight of the Indians' gods was but their return under other names. The Conquest left great masses of Indians in spiritual orphanhood. This situation of total psychic dispossession made possible their conversion to Christianity: baptism was the path by which they could become part of the religious, juridical, and political order of New Spain. Baptism opened the doors to the new society and at the same time was the return passage to the ancient sacred world. Indians became Christians; the Christians' God, virgins, and saints were Indianized. From the beginning Indian Christianity was an instinctive and popular form of syncretism. This syncretism profoundly influenced the beliefs of criollos and mestizos.

The sixteenth century was one of evangelization and of building, a century of architects and masons and their works: convents, churches, hospitals, cities. The art and science of constructing cities is a political art. Civilization is primarily urbanism; by that I mean, more than a vision of world and men, a civilization is a vision of men in the world and men as a world: an order, a social architecture. The seventeenth and eighteenth centuries continued the era of construction: plazas, churches, government buildings, aqueducts, hospitals, convents, palaces, schools. The cities of New Spain are the image of an order that embraced an entire society, this world and the afterworld. Even today, disfigured and affronted by the tastelessness of our plutocracy, the megalomania of our politicians, and the obtuseness of our technocrats, Mexican cities restore our faith in the genius of our people. The seventeenth century witnessed the expansion of territory; a peace only occasionally interrupted by the uprisings of nomadic tribes and incursions of pirates; the growth of cities and, along with them, the twin sisters of luxury and culture. A society rich and sensuous, but devout and superstitious; obedient to royal power and submissive to the mandates of the Church, but shaken by strange deliriums that were both funereal and licentious.

In the seventeenth century the split at the peak of society became more clearly defined. Political and military power was Spanish; economic power was criollo; religious power tended to be shared between them—a delicate balance not broken until Independence. The criollo's resentment of the Spaniard, already perceptible in the sixteenth century, was accentuated in the seventeenth. The criollo considered himself a loyal subject of the crown, but could not help being conscious of his inferior status. The Spanish bureaucracy disdained him: the criollo was and was not Spanish. He felt the same ambiguity toward the land where he had been born and would be buried: it was and was not his. Constant vacillation: like the Indians, the criollos were born here, but like the Spanish, they were from there. Criollo patriotism was ambivalent: love for the ancestral land beyond the sea and love for the native land. In the seventeenth century these conflicting sentiments were expressed not in political terms but in subtly shaded emotions, religion, and art.

If the criollo, born of Spanish blood, was the victim of ambiguity, the mestizo, born of mixed blood, was doubly so: he was neither criollo nor Indian. Rejected by both groups, the mestizo had no place either in the social structure or in the moral order. In the light of traditional moral systems—the Spanish, based on honor, and the Indian, based on the sacredness of family—the mestizo was the living image of illegitimacy. From this feeling of illegitimacy grew his insecurity, his perpetual instability, his tendency to swing between extremes: from courage to panic, from exaltation to apathy, from loyalty to treachery. Cain and Abel in a single soul, the mestizo vacillated between moral nihilism and abnegation, derision and fatalism, jest and melancholy, lyricism and stoicism.

In a society in which the division of labor conformed more rigidly than in others to social hierarchies, the mestizo was literally a man without resource or recourse. A true pariah, he was destined to the most dubious livelihoods: from beggary to banditry, from vagrancy to soldiering. In the seventeenth and eighteenth centuries, the underworld was recruited from among the mestizos; in the nineteenth, mestizos gravitated to the police and the army. A spectacular career: bandit to policeman to soldier to guerrilla to local boss to political leader or university professor to chief of state. The ascent of the mestizo was a result not solely of demographic trends—today mestizos make up the majority of the Mexican population—but equally of his capacity to live and survive under the most adverse conditions, of his daring, strength, skill, fortitude, ingenuity, adaptability, industry, and resourcefulness. And of a basic fact of life: among the groups that composed the population of New Spain, it was the mestizos who authentically embodied that society, they were its true children. They were not, like the criollos, Europeans who had decided to put down roots in a new land; neither, like the Indians, were they a given reality, blending into the landscape and the pre-Hispanic past. They were New Spain's true novelty. More important, they made New Spain not only new but *other*. In the seventeenth century, however, the mestizo influence was barely appreciable. The mestizos and mulattos of Sor Juana's *villancicos* are primarily picturesque and semicomic characters.

3

Syncretism and Empire

$\mathscr{S}$IXTEENTH-CENTURY RELIGIOUS POLICY with regard to the Indian civilization was a tabula rasa. The early missionaries wanted to save the Indians, not their idols or beliefs. The interest of a Sahagún[1] in ancient Indian religions implied neither acceptance nor tolerance of their myths. When Sahagún noted a similarity between Indian and Christian rites—for example, communion with hallucinogenic mushrooms, confession, and ritual cannibalism—he hastened to denounce that similarity as deceit, a trick of the devil. The missionaries' attitude toward Indian religions and beliefs can be summed up in Robert Ricard's expression "a break with the past." But it was difficult to ignore the Indian religion and the analogy between many of its rituals and those of Christianity. It was also difficult to forget that, by virtue of grace, humankind had an innate knowledge of the divinity.

Another often-debated theme was that of the preaching of the Gospel in the New World. Jacques Lafaye quotes the opinion of Solórzano Pereira, stated in his *Política indiana,* that the conversion of the Indians had been reserved by God to the Spanish monarchs and their ministers and vassals, since "before our arrival the Gospel was unknown in· the New World."[2]

A different view was expressed by Antonio de la Calancha (1584–1654), an Augustinian friar who believed that shortly before the destruction of the temple of Jerusalem—that is, some seventy-two years after the birth of Christ—the Gospel had been taught in the West Indies, probably by St. Thomas. This explained the similarities between Christianity and certain beliefs held by American Indians. It is not possible here to recapitulate the many phases of that polemic. I shall merely state that by the seventeenth century a radical change had taken effect. The tabula rasa policy had been supplanted by what one might call a policy of linkage, which endeavored to establish a bridge of communication, more supernatural than natural, between the native and Christian worlds. This new syncretism, in contrast to the popular syncretism of the Indians, proposed not to Indianize Christianity but, rather, to seek prefigurations and signs of Christianity in paganism.

Seventeenth-century syncretism was the work of Jesuit theologians and historians and of sympathetic intellectuals such as Carlos de Sigüenza y Góngora.[3] The policy of the Jesuits in New Spain was no different from their general strategy for other regions of the world, especially China. The spiritual and intellectual nucleus of the strategy was a vision of world history as the gradual unfolding of a universal and supernatural truth. The sum of that truth was Christianity and the passion of Jesus; in other parts of the world and in other ages, the same mystery had been manifest, not fully, but in symbols and signs and coincident marvels. Seventeenth-century Jesuit syncretism could be compared to the policy of St. Paul: the apostle universalized the doctrine of Jesus by cutting the umbilical cord that joined the Church of Jerusalem—dominated by James, the brother of Jesus—with Judaism. St. Paul's knife was Hellenism. The Jesuits' intent, also, was universalization, but in a much broader sphere than the Mediterranean. The road to that universalization led through the ancient beliefs and practices of India, China, and Mexico. A striking example was the famous controversy over Confucian ritual. To strengthen their position in the court of the Son of Heaven, the Jesuits maintained that the rites performed during ancestor worship—which was central to the Confucian system—were not incompatible with Christian beliefs. The syncretism of the Society of Jesus met the opposition of the Dominicans and Franciscans, who obtained a papal denunciation of the Society's thesis.

The other risk run by the Jesuits was that of provoking the suspicion, even the enmity, of national states—as indeed occurred a century later in their confrontation with the Bourbons. If the universalism of the Society of Jesus brought them into conflict with the politics of absolutist states, their syncretism was similarly capable of feeding or inspiring national and separatist tendencies in the bosom of those states. This is precisely what happened in New Spain in the seventeenth century, the century of the awakening of criollo spirit. I have pointed out the limitations of criollo patriotism, as well as the criollo's ambivalence toward his two worlds, Indian and Spanish. In the seventeenth century criollo identity—to avoid the equivocal word "nationalism"—was expressed in artistic creation and philosophical and religious speculations in which the image of *New* Spain appears, more or less veiled, as the *Other* Spain. With some confusion, the criollo felt he was heir to *two* empires, Spanish and Indian. With the same contradictory fervor with which he exalted the Hispanic empire and detested the Spanish, he glorified the Indian past and disdained the Indians. Criollos themselves did not clearly perceive this contradiction. Aristocratic prejudice prevented them from seeing in living Indians the descendants of Mexico-Tenochtitlán; in their eyes, the Aztec empire had been a society of warriors governed by wise and prudent rulers. The mere fact that the Aztec city-state was called an empire reveals the degree to which the indigenous world was misunderstood by the seventeenth century. The image of Rome had blended with that of Mexico-Tenochtitlán.

The dreams and aspirations of the criollos—their need to sink their roots in Mexican soil and still maintain loyalty to the Spanish crown, their Catholic faith and their eagerness to legitimize their presence in a world only recently baptized—would never have been formulated or expressed without the Society of Jesus. The awakening of criollo spirit coincided with the rise of the Jesuits, who displaced the Franciscans and Dominicans to become the most powerful and influential order in New Spain. The Jesuits were more than teachers to the criollos; they were their spokesmen and their conscience. The union between criollo aspirations and the great Jesuit plan for world unification produced extraordinary works in the sphere of religious beliefs, as well as in art and history. Jesuit syncretism, joined to emerging criollo patriotism, not only modified traditional attitudes about Indian civilization but motivated a kind of resurrection of that past. The influence of classical humanism was also crucial in that resurrection: through historical analogy, the erudition and imagination of the seventeenth century Romanized Mexico-Tenochtitlán. The Aztec world was transformed in the imperial mirror of humanism. Mexico-Tenochtitlán was an American Rome and, like the Latin capital, was the seat of first a pagan, then a Christian, empire. In the image of the imperial city of Mexico one could recognize both criollo patriotism and the Jesuit dream of Christian universalism embracing all societies and all cultures.

The Jesuits' enterprise must be viewed within the perspective of the

Counter-Reformation and also as a facet of European expansion in Asia and America. The discovery of America, the unknown continent, and of China, the unknown civilization, precipitated a crisis in Catholic theology and in the conscience of its missionaries. For fifteen hundred years millions of souls in America had been deprived of the grace of baptism. The new lands and their new inhabitants seemed to contradict the verse of the Gospel in which the resurrected Christ appeared unto the apostles and bade them to go into *all* the world and preach the Gospel to *every* creature (Mark 16:15). The solutions to this enigma were many and ingenious. The Franciscans adopted Joaquim of Floris' doctrine of a spiritual and allegorical interpretation of the Gospel.[4] Other theologians, among them a majority of the Jesuits, maintained that the Indians' ancient beliefs—either by virtue of natural grace or because the Gospel had been preached in America prior to the arrival of the Spaniards— contained a glimmering of the true faith, even though only confused memories of the doctrine survived. In the seventeenth century this belief was extended and affirmed. It was a viewpoint—as developed later in a tract written by Fray Servando Teresa de Mier in justification of the movement for independence—that implicitly undermined the basic principle of Spanish domination in America, evangelization.

The discovery of Chinese civilization had confronted the missionaries with a different enigma: a society in many ways superior to the Christian, but governed by a bureaucracy of intellectual "atheists," the mandarins. The Jesuits were particularly impressed by an empire that was hierarchical and at the same time peaceful. They saw in that society, despite its vastness and the complexity of its institutions, an example of social harmony founded less on force of authority than on judicious political and moral organization. The Confucian ethic was a chain of loyalties and mutual responsibilities descending from superior to inferior. Ancestor worship, respect for the head of the family, and devotion to the Emperor were the triadic manifestation of a single principle, and that principle was none other than natural religion. The Jesuits believed that if they could succeed in converting the Emperor, it would then not be difficult—because of the very dynamic of the system—to convert the mandarins and, finally, all of the people. Everything in their policy toward Emperor K'ang Hsi was directed to that proposition: to find a point of contact between Christianity and Confucianism. To "adapt and absorb" the Chinese culture into Christianity, says D. P. Walker, "it was necessary to establish . . . that the writings ascribed to Confucius, and other ancient Chinese classics, were compatible with Christian ethics and monotheism, and with good, 'natural' religion."[5]

Although it may seem strange, the source of Jesuit syncretism is to be found in the Neoplatonic hermeticism of the Renaissance. This movement was impregnated with ancient philosophy and rationalism, with science and magic. The doctrines of the *Corpus Hermeticum* were one of its intellectual and emotional components. The *Corpus* was a body of texts comprising the revelations and teachings of Hermes Trismegistus, a legendary figure believed to have lived before Plato, possibly a contemporary of Moses. In 1460 a Byzantine sold Cosimo de' Medici a manuscript containing most of the treatises that make up the *Corpus Hermeticum*. Although Cosimo had already entrusted Marsilio Ficino with the translation of Plato, he ordered him to put aside the work of the Greek philosopher and immediately to undertake the translation of the revelations of Hermes Trismegistus. Cosimo's attitude and Ficino's obedience are not surprising; they were following a tradition that went back as far as Lactantius and Clement of Alexandria. According to this tradition, Plato had been inspired by the doctrine of Hermes; to translate him was to go directly to the source. (In my discussion of Sor Juana's *Allegorical Neptune* and *First Dream,* chapters 11 and 24, I will return to this subject.)

From Renaissance hermetic philosophy were born two opposing currents. One flows from Ficino and Pico della Mirandola to Cornelius Agrippa, Giordano Bruno, and Tommaso Campanella, then spreads throughout Europe, inspiring the French Academies, the Elizabethan occultist John Dee, and the German Rosicrucian movement.[6] Through various libertine and occultist sects of the seventeenth and eighteenth centuries, one branch of this current merged into the socialist movement, especially as defined by Fourier, while the other fed modern poetic theory, from the romantics to our contemporaries. The astral religion of Bruno and Campanella is the source both of socialism and of the theory of universal correspondences held by the early German and English romantics, by Nerval and Baudelaire, by the symbolists, by Yeats, and by the surrealists. The society of the stars was the dual archetype for the political society and for the society of words. In the former, liberty and necessity resolve into a harmonious accord called justice; in the second, that same accord becomes a poetic analogy, the system of universal correspondences.[7] The second current, represented primarily by the Jesuits, attempted to reconcile non-Christian religions with Roman Catholicism.

Although the direct source of Jesuit syncretism was Renaissance hermeticism, I have also noted an antecedent in certain Church Fathers' interpretation of pagan philosophers. In his correspondence with Father Joachim Bouvet, Leibniz, who followed with interest the work of the Jesuits in China, praised the famous missionary Matteo Ricci (Li Matou) "for having followed the example of the Fathers of the Church who interpreted Plato and other philosophers in a Christian sense."

Had the grand plan of the Society of Jesus been realized, a unification of diverse civilizations and cultures would have been achieved under the sign of Rome. What is extraordinary in this enterprise, especially from a religious point of view, is its disconcerting combination of piety and calculation, faith and Machiavellianism. The Jesuits intended to convert the Chinese not through the evangelization of peasants, craftsmen, and merchants but by proselytizing the Emperor and his court. The idea behind this plan for world conversion led not to the kingdom of God, that is to say, to the end of this world, as in the Franciscan millenarianism of the sixteenth century, but to the ascendant movement of universal history. It is not surprising that in the seventeenth century the chosen site for attempting such an enterprise was precisely that of a great universal empire: China under the Ch'ing dynasty. Nor is it surprising that the other theater of experimentation was the land of the ancient Mexican empire.

I have noted how by analogy the attributes of imperial Rome were projected into the Aztec state. This image, first conceived by historians influenced by classical humanism, became in the seventeenth century the model of the most daring speculations. It was a rare conjunction, a kind of triadic historical consonance: humanism, Jesuit theology, and the aspirations of the criollo aristocracy of New Spain. In the shadow of Jesuit syncretism was born a project that was not entirely dissipated until the second half of the nineteenth century: the founding of a Mexican empire that was to be heir to both Spanish and Aztec worlds.

IN THE ALTERED CIRCUMSTANCES of the second half of the seventeenth century, the apparition of the Virgin of Guadalupe, in the sanctuary of an Indian goddess, confirmed the uniqueness of New Spain. It was a true *sign,* in the seventeenth-century religious sense of the word, that suggested a mysterious connection between the pre-Columbian world and Christianity. The apparition of the Virgin was a mark of divine favor conferred on this northernmost Spanish American nation and of its capital, imperial Mexico City. Although devotion to the Virgin was common before the seventeenth century, it was in the century of the criollo that this devotion became a national cult. The second half of the century, in fact, erupted into a kind of Guadalupe frenzy. Like a pious variation of baroque style, Guadalupe paintings and sculptures and poems multiplied, to say nothing of churches and sanctuaries built in her name. Sigüenza y Góngora wrote in her honor his *Primavera indiana* (*Indian Spring*) and the *Glorias de Querétaro* (*Glories of Querétaro*); Sandoval y Zapata dedicated to her a memorable sonnet in which he compared the metamorphosis of the roses in the icon of the Virgin to that of the Phoenix:

> More blessed than the Phoenix, roses, you die;
> from ashes will arise its feathered form,
> but from your death is holy Mary born.

The citizens of New Spain literally were in love with the Virgin. In 1648, in a work that profoundly affected all of New Spain, Miguel Sánchez proclaimed the Virgin of Guadalupe "the first criollo woman." But she was and is still more than that "first woman." The Virgin of Guadalupe was a point of union among criollos, Indians, and mestizos, the answer to their triple orphanhood: Indians, because Guadalupe-Tonantzin was the transfiguration of their ancient female deities; criollos, because the Virgin's apparition made the land of New Spain more of a real mother than Spain had been; mestizos, because the Virgin did and does represent reconciliation with their origins and the end to their illegitimacy.

The cult of the Virgin of Guadalupe was but one of the manifestations of seventeenth-century syncretism. Another was the argument that the Gospel had been taught prior to the arrival of the Spanish by none other than the apostle St. Thomas, known among the Indians as Quetzalcoatl. The learned Carlos de Sigüenza y Góngora, an ex-Jesuit who throughout his life unsuccessfully sought to be reinstated into the Society, was one of those whose attempt to understand and exalt the Indian past was characterized by erudition and intellectual audacity. Among the many lost works of Sigüenza y Góngora—and we can only lament the missing manuscripts and the dispersion of his library and his collection of Mexican antiquities—is one we know only by its title: *The Phoenix of the West, the Apostle St. Thomas, Found under the Name of Quetzalcoatl among the Ashes of the Ancient Traditions Preserved on the Stones, on*

Toltec and Teochichimec Teoamoxtles and in Mexican Songs. Fortunately we do have the notes of a friend of his, a Portuguese Jesuit named Manuel Duarte. Apparently Sigüenza y Góngora's treatise was based on notes left him by Duarte.[8]

In 1680, on the occasion of welcoming a new Viceroy, Don Tomás Antonio de la Cerda, Marquis de la Laguna and Count de Paredes, Mexico City erected two triumphal arches, one conceived by Sor Juana and the other by Sigüenza y Góngora. Sigüenza's arch broke with all precedent. The figures that adorned these baroque monuments had invariably been taken from Greco-Roman mythology or ancient history; Sigüenza's arch featured the effigies of Aztec emperors. The title of the pamphlet describing the arch was explicit: *Theater of Political Virtues That Constitute a Ruler, Observed in the Ancient Monarchs of the Mexican Empire.* The Aztec rulers Itzcóatl, Ilhuicamina, Axayácatl, Montezuma, Cuauhtémoc, and even the god Huitzilopochtli, whom Sigüenza y Góngora also classified as an emperor—these were the models of governance the criollo proposed to a Spanish Viceroy.

Sigüenza y Góngora was a close friend of a descendant of the kings of Texcoco, Don Juan de Alva Ixtlilxóchitl. This noble Indian owned a collection of antiquities that he bequeathed to Sigüenza on his death. Despite his fondness for Indian antiquities and his friendship with Alva Ixtlilxóchitl, the scholar looked with suspicion on Indians in general. His attitude expresses very clearly the ambiguity of his era, divided between admiration for the Indian empire and fear of its descendants. Once, to protect the city from the danger of major flooding, Sigüenza, acting in his capacity as engineer in charge of public works, directed the cleaning of a clogged canal in the area of the Puente de Alvarado, the site of the defeat suffered by the conquistadors on July 10, 1520 (the episode known as the Noche Triste, Night of Sorrow). Amid the debris removed by the workers were hundreds of clay figurines, all representing Spaniards and all either decapitated or with blood-red paint around the throat or over the heart. Sigüenza immediately communicated news of his find to the Viceroy and the Archbishop—the dreaded Aguiar y Seijas—and warned them that such objects of superstition were more than sufficient proof that the Indians detested the Spanish and that they were planning for them the fate that had befallen Cortés and his men on the Noche Triste.[9] Years later, during the tumult of June 8, 1692, Sigüenza y Góngora risked his life to save the archives of the municipal building from the fire. This was clearly an act of heroism and of love for the history of his people. At the same time, however, he wrote an account of the disturbance in which he blamed the Indians and the *castas* (people of all combinations of races) for what had occurred. Sigüenza attributed the cause of the rebellion not to oppression by the Spanish or the incompetence of the authorities or to the scarcity of maize, but to the malevolence and drunkenness of the Indians. The figure of Sigüenza y Góngora, admirable and contradictory, is an image of the New Spain of the latter half of the seventeenth century. This is the world in which Sor Juana Inés de la Cruz was born and lived.

IF ARCHITECTURE IS THE ART that best embodies the characteristics and ideas of a society, New Spain can be pictured as one vast plaza on which, fronting and confronting one another, stand the palace, the city hall, and the cathedral: the ruler and his court; the people, within their various hierarchies and jurisdictions; and religious authority. Outside the plaza stand three additional buildings: the convent, the university, and the fortress. The convent and the university were centers of learning; the fortress defended the nation from external forces. The convent and the university were also fortresses defending New Spain, not against pirates and nomadic tribes but against time. Neoscholasticism had a stronghold in every cell and every hall. The enemy was history, that is, the form assumed by historical time in the modern age—criticism. New Spain was made not to change but to endure. A construct that aspired to an existence outside time, New Spain had as its ideal neither change nor the modern consequence of change, the cult of progress. Rather, its ideal was stability and permanence; its vision of perfection was to imitate, on earth, the eternal order. In a society of this nature, criticism meant a return to the original principle; it must, in other words, be directed toward the infractions of and deviations from the principles on which the society was founded, not toward the principles themselves.

The modern age has been the negation of the ideas and beliefs that inspired New Spain. It was born as a movement of radical criticism— criticism of the principles themselves, not of the imperfections of man and his institutions; thus criticism has been viewed as the mother of change, the principle that sets history in motion. But before becoming the religion of criticism and change, modernity was first the criticism of religion: the Reformation. Except that the criticism of the Reformation, unlike the criticism of eighteenth-century philosophers, was deeply religious, not antireligious. Here, then, is where New Spain differs not only from the modern world but particularly from New England. In their beginnings the English colonies, like the Spanish, were societies with a religious foundation. But the Protestant ethic was based in criticism of papist and Roman religion, while the Spanish Catholic ethic was a defense of that religion. New Spain was no less religious than New England but from its inception was designed to oppose criticism, that is, history and change. The philosophy that justified its existence was defensive: guardian of the faith of Rome, Neoscholasticism was also the defender of monarchy and empire.

In the seventeenth century New Spain was a more vigorous, prosperous, and civilized society than New England, but it was a society closed to the world outside and, even more important, to the future. While toward the end of the eighteenth century the religious democracy of New England was transformed into the political democracy of the United States, New Spain, incapable of resolving her internal contradictions, exploded and, in the nineteenth century, collapsed. For the United States, passage from a traditional to a modern society was a natural step; the bridge was Protestantism. The dilemma facing Mexican criollos on the day following Independence may have been insoluble: continuity condemned the nation to immobility, and change demanded a violent break, a rending and tearing. Continuity and change were not complementary as in the United States but, rather, antagonistic and irreconcilable. Mexico changed, but that change tore her apart. The wound remains unhealed to this day.

4

A Transplanted Literature

ON THE BROAD MEANING of the word "culture," New Spain was a cultured society: not only was Spanish culture—language, religion, art, morality, customs, myths, and rituals—fully incorporated, it was substantially modified, and adapted with great originality to conditions in America. In the more limited sense of the word, however—that having to do with education, with the production and communication of intellectual, artistic, and philosophical innovations—only a small portion of the population could be considered cultured. By that I mean that only a small minority had access to the Church and the university, the two great educational institutions of the age. It followed that, confined to the academies, universities, and religious seminaries, the culture of New Spain was an erudite culture for the erudite. I have mentioned the markedly religious flavor of that society; theology was the queen of sciences and all learning was centered about her. Similarly distinctive was the blending of the Christian tradition with classical humanism: the Bible with Ovid, St. Augustine with Cicero, and St. Catherine with the Erythraean sibyl.

A rival to the Church and the university, the court was also a great center of aesthetic and cultural propagation. The aristocracy was fond of literature and art; the taste of the patrons and nobles of the seventeenth and eighteenth centuries was better and more refined than that of our politicians and bankers. As today we find diversion in crossword puzzles and intellectuals compose political manifestos, the courtiers and clerics of the seventeenth century solved poetic riddles and wrote *décimas* and sonnets. Courtly language belongs to a chosen group and tends to become a veiled and coded speech understood only by initiates. Courtly literature inexorably moves toward hermeticism, although its mysteries are aesthetic rather than religious or philosophical. Courtly hermeticism veils no transcendental truths; it protects the privileged from the intrusions of the common people. Gongorism was not the same as Symbolism; it was an aristocratic aesthetic, while French Symbolism was, or attempted to be, a poetics of initiation, a secret knowledge that verged on religious revelation.

A literature for the few, erudite, academic, profoundly religious (in a dogmatic rather than a creative sense), hermetic, and aristocratic, the literature of New Spain was written by men to be read by men. There were exceptions; we can point, for example, in the first half of the seventeenth century, to the mediocre poems of María Estrada de Medinilla. It is nonetheless truly extraordinary that the most important writer of New Spain was a woman, Sor Juana Inés de la Cruz. The markedly masculine character of culture in New Spain is a fact whose true significance has not been grasped by the majority of Sor Juana's biographers. Neither the university nor any other school of higher learning was open to women. The only means by which women might penetrate the closed world of masculine culture was to slip through the half-open doors of the court and the Church. Although it may seem strange, the two places where men and women could congregate for the purpose of intellectual and aesthetic communication were the convent locutory and the palace drawing room. Sor Juana made use of both.

Another distinctive feature of the period: the culture was, above all else, oral—the pulpit, the university chair, and the salon. Few books were published, most of them religious; the works of Sor Juana, for example, were printed in Spain. The intellectual animation, the passion and cleverness with which subtle points of erudition and philosophy were debated, must not obscure the essentially dogmatic nature of the culture. The university and the Church were the depositories of the codified learning of the age, the licit learning uncontaminated by heresy. The function of the university, as a guardian of orthodoxy, was to defend the principles on which the society was based, not to question or debate them. In some ways orthodoxy was more stringent in New Spain than in the mother country, as is seen in the prohibition against printing novels and other works of fiction. The theater, too, on occasion was the victim of the zeal of certain intolerant archbishops and prelates. In spite of all this, New Spain was not entirely unreceptive to new ideas. A modern historian has shown that many books forbidden by the Inquisition were widely read.[1] In his writings, Sigüenza y Góngora shows evidence of some familiarity with Gassendi, Kepler, Copernicus, and Descartes. It was about this time as well that the influence of the renowned German Jesuit Athanasius Kircher was at its peak.

LITERATURES, LIKE TREES AND PLANTS, are born of a land and in it flourish and die. But literatures, also like plants, may be carried abroad to take root in a foreign soil. Spanish literature traveled during the sixteenth century; transplanted to America, it was slow to take root. In Mexico and Peru the process of adapting Spanish literature was different from that in other parts of America. I am referring not only to how rapidly the viceroyalties of New Spain and Peru became rich and complex societies with great urban centers like Mexico City and Lima, but also to the prior existence, in both countries, of advanced civilizations. Argentines, for example, do not suffer the presence of the impalpable shadow of the *other* language between themselves and their land. The language disappeared along with the bones of those who spoke it, the Indians exterminated in the nineteenth century. In contrast, in Mexico and Peru everything alludes to pre-Hispanic civilizations, from the names of objects, plants, and animals to the sites where our cities now stand.

More than a vision of a world, a civilization *is* a world—a world of objects and especially a world of names. In Spanish poetry, heir to both Greco-Roman and Judeo-Christian traditions, grapes, as well as being the fruit that gives us wine, allude to two divinities: Christ and Bacchus. In turn, wine is central to two convivial occasions that are the highest expression of Western-Mediterranean culture: the banquet and the holy mass, philosophical dialogue and the sacrifice of the Son of Man. The ancient Mexicans had plants that fulfilled the dual functions of the grape, but merely in naming them the differences become apparent: the maguey cactus, the peyote cactus, and hallucinogenic mushrooms. Although the maguey yields pulque, a liquor that could be considered the homologue of wine in its function as an intoxicant, the transfiguring and symbolic features of wine are more closely approximated in peyote and hallucinogenic mushrooms. Wheat replicates the dualism of wine: Ceres and Demeter, Christ and holy communion. In Mexico, maize assumes the place of wheat. Universal nourishment analogous to bread, maize, like the Christian host, was also a material metaphor for the divine mysteries. Among the rituals associated with maize, one, recorded by Tor-quemada,[2] particularly impressed Sor Juana: during a ceremony cele-brated in the Great Temple of Mexico-Tenochtitlán, the devout ate pieces of the god Huitzilopochtli, an idol made of maize and drenched in blood. The resemblance to the Eucharist must have been at once stun-ning and scandalous.

From its inception, New Spanish literature was aware of its duality. The shadow of the *other,* a ghostly language, composed not of words but of murmurs and silences, was already evident in the poetry of the sixteenth century. In the following century, as seen in the *loas* preceding Sor Juana's plays *El divino Narciso* (*The Divine Narcissus*) and *El cetro de José* (*Joseph's Staff*), that *other* is confronted and questioned, but only for the purpose of integration and absorption. In the nineteenth century the ghost becomes an idea, and only in the twentieth century is it made flesh to speak with its own voice. Indigenous literature could not be fully understood and evaluated in the sixteenth, seventeenth, and eighteenth centuries. When he translated Nezahualcóyotl, Fernando de Alva Ixtlilxóchitl[3]—doubly unfaithful, since Nezahualcóyotl was nei-ther Christian nor Roman—transformed him into a Christian Horace. The discovery and the assimilation of non-Western arts and literatures began in Europe during the eighteenth century, gained impetus with ro-manticism, and culminated in the first half of the twentieth century. Changes in European aesthetic sensibilities opened to modern Mexicans the way to understanding pre-Hispanic arts and poetry. That discovery came relatively late: even in 1920, a poet as attuned to Mexican identity as Ramón López Velarde was insensitive to pre-Columbian art. In fact, only in my generation did Aztec poetry influence the poets of Mexico.

From the beginning, the poetry of New Spain branched into two cur-rents: cultivated verse, and the popular or traditional poetry derived from Spain. A third branch was the didactic literature whose purpose was the evangelization of the natives. Traditional poetry arrived in Mex-ico with the conquistadors; cosmopolitan poetry appeared with their sons. In our sixteenth century, popular *romances* coexisted alongside Renaissance sonnets, religious songs with Neoplatonic tercets, and bawdy rondels with pastoral poems that transplanted Tasso's *Aminta* to the volcanos of Anáhuac and the lakes of Michoacán. At one extreme were poems closely related to song and dance, with abbreviated and assonant lines, a poetry with its roots in the Middle Ages, in which the erotic song served as model for the religious *villancico.* At the other extreme was an Italianate and Latinate poetry nourished in the aesthetic of the late Renaissance and in the mannerism of Sannazaro and Bembo. The two currents were mutually fertilizing. In the sixteenth century Francisco de Terrazas (1525?–1600?), a descendant of a conquistador, represents the sententious and cosmopolitan poetry derived from Garcilaso and Herrera. He wrote a rather tedious epic poem about Cortés, left unfinished, and a few exquisite sonnets, one of them, quite memorable, on the subject of two feminine legs. In contrast to this aristocratic poet we find the transparent songs of Hernán González de Eslava (1534–1601?). He, too, in a few sonnets and in certain love poems in *lira* form, shows signs of the Italianate and cultivated tendency; the remainder of his work consists of *villancicos* and traditional religious songs that assure him a privileged position in the history of our lyric.

In the prologue to the first volume of his anthology *Poetas novohispanos*,[4] Alfonso Méndez Plancarte quotes the noted Spanish critic Menéndez Pelayo's opinion of Bernardo de Balbuena (1561?–1627): "one of the great poets of the Spanish language." This may be exaggeration; it is not exaggeration to say that Balbuena is one of the most opulent and colorful. Spanish critics attributed certain baroque traces in his work to the exuberance of Mexican nature. Apart from the fact that the landscape around Mexico City cannot be called exuberant, it is more appropriate to seek the origins of Balbuena's verbal richness in the history of styles than in styleless nature. One of Balbuena's works is a long poem in praise of Mexico City (*Grandeza mexicana* [*Mexican Majesty*], 1604); he was also author of a pastoral novel in verse (*Siglo de Oro en las selvas de Erífile* [*Golden Age in the Forest of Eriphyle*], 1608) and of a verse epic fantasy (*El Bernardo, o victoria de Roncesvalles* [*Bernardo, or Victory at Roncesvalles*], 1624). Everything else he wrote was lost, in manuscript, during the Dutch burning and sacking of Puerto Rico in 1625. Balbuena, who was Bishop of Puerto Rico, died two years after this disaster. At a time when Spanish poets were singing the shepherd's solitude, praising simple village life, and inveighing against life in the city as the origin of envy, ambition, greed, and licentiousness—a theme that Góngora turned to again and again in his *Solitudes*—Balbuena's poem is a paean to the city, commerce, and urban life. The passion, writes Balbuena, that constructed in the center of a lake the wonder of Mexico City, was self-interest, "a sun that sheds its light on all the world ... the hidden strength and source of political life," the foundation of all cities and all civilized life. Self-interest is the source of culture, the creator of social hierarchies and of the inevitable inequality among men. A return to nature would be a return to barbarism, where "in confusion we should all be equal."

The Augustinian Miguel de Guevara is an enigma. Some years ago a Guevara manuscript dated 1638 was found containing several admirable sonnets in *conceptista* style, among them the famous "I am not moved, my God, to love you by promises of Heaven . . ." Was Guevara the author, or was he merely the copyist? Scholars tend to agree that the latter is more probable.

The last poet in Méndez Plancarte's first volume is Juan Ruíz de Alarcón (1580?–1639). He is surely one of the great dramatic poets of our language, but can he be called Mexican? He was born in Mexico of a criollo family and studied here, but his work was written in Spain for the Spanish stage. The case of Alarcón is extreme but not exceptional; the same question can be asked of the other poets I have named. The history of New Spain's poetry reflects that of the mother country.

Renaissance forms and modes predominated in the sixteenth century; they were adapted to Spanish by Garcilaso and reached a slightly artificial and overly elaborate perfection with Fernando de Herrera. Garcilaso's poetry and, still more, Herrera's are expressions of mannerism more than of high classicism. Thus the roots of Mexican poetry are to be found not in the Middle Ages, or in an unlikely "classicism," but, rather, in the period of the sixteenth century that witnessed the transition from Renaissance to baroque: mannerism. The passage toward the baroque leads through mannerists like Terrazas and Balbuena. Two characteristics mark the New World baroque: it was the richest of our literary periods, and it was the longest, lasting well into the middle of the eighteenth century. Long-lived and rich, this period was also strikingly original. It is often said that the Mexican baroque is a chapter in the Spanish baroque, which is, in turn, a chapter in the European baroque. This summary definition overlooks the great originality of the Spanish baroque—in Góngora, Quevedo, Lope de Vega, and Calderón—and within that originality, the not easily dismissed figure of Sor Juana Inés de la Cruz. The theme of the baroque in the literature of New Spain leads to a moment's reflection.

MODERN CRITICISM HAS STRUGGLED to define the difference between the baroque style proper and mannerism. That difference escaped Heinrich Wölfflin and his followers: they did not perceive that mannerism, a style that began in Italy around 1520 and ended about 1570, intervened between the Renaissance and the Baroque period. Ernst Robert Curtius goes further and suggests that the more general term "mannerism" be substituted for the word "baroque," which is in his opinion too closely linked to a specific historical period.[5] According to Curtius, mannerism is a tendency that surfaces throughout the history of styles: there is a Greek and a Roman mannerism, a medieval and a modern mannerism. This German critic believes that the baroque prevalent in sixteenth- and seventeenth-century Europe and America is but one of the cyclical expressions of mannerism. Quite possibly Curtius is correct, but few have followed his proposal for changing the nomenclature of literary periods.

Other authors consider that far from being an intermediate style between Renaissance and baroque, mannerism is a form of the latter. According to one of these critics, mannerism would be the "ingenious, intellectual, and paradoxical component of the baroque," as represented by Donne, Herbert, Sponde, and Quevedo. The other component, which this critic calls high baroque, is simply the Gongorism described in our old manuals: a "decorative, exclamatory, extravagant form typified by Crashaw, Marino, D'Aubigné, and Góngora."[6] There is nothing new in this opinion. The differences between the two styles are well known and can be summarized as follows: the first mode is *conceptista*, paradoxical, philosophizing, and markedly intellectual; the second is metaphorical, pictorial, and conspicuously aesthetic. In the first, the conceit triumphs; in the second, the image. One is directed toward the intellect; the other, toward sight and the other senses.

It is not necessary to accept these criteria to perceive the difficulty in making a clear division between baroque and mannerist styles. One of the critics who has written most perceptively on the subject—one of the earliest as well, Erwin Panofsky—points out that "it is admittedly difficult to isolate the distinctly new characteristics from the sum total of this literature, and almost impossible to subsume them under a single concept."[7] The transition from the Renaissance to mannerism was imperceptible, as was the passage from mannerism to the baroque. Mannerist elements exist within the baroque—one might even say the baroque is a new and different combination of mannerist elements—and baroque characteristics are found in mannerism. Nevertheless, to introduce a little order, even if the somewhat illusory order of taxonomy, it is convenient to separate mannerism from the baroque. The former is the

ultimate consequence of the Renaissance, its negation as well as its exaggeration. It is at the same time the necessary antecedent of the baroque. But we must treat all such designations with caution and irony.
We can strangle in them, as if in jungle lianas. Deluded by the demon of
classification, Professor Helmut Hatzfeld labeled Cervantes and Racine
as baroque and Góngora as mannerist.[8] We may best simplify by saying
that in a general history of the Greco-Roman tradition and Western literature as outlined by Curtius, the "early baroque" of the sixteenth century and the "high baroque" of the seventeenth would each be a cyclic
manifestation of mannerism; in a specific history of sixteenth- and
seventeenth-century European and Spanish American literature it is
preferable to identify two distinct periods: mannerism and the baroque.

In New Spain, as I have pointed out, mannerism would be represented
in its incipient phase by Terrazas, and in its more essential and developed
form by Bernardo de Balbuena. Or should we call Balbuena baroque
because of his verbal lavishness, his abundant use of color, and his love
of brilliant metaphor? Be that as it may, it is clear that there is a basic
difference between the work of these two poets and that of the seventeenth-century poets Luis de Sandoval y Zapata and Sor Juana Inés de
la Cruz. The latter is more complex and appears as closed forms ruled
by the laws of contrasts, while in the former one finds "a multiplicity of
floating elements," the key characteristic, according to Harold B. Segel,
of mannerism.[9] Having said this, I repeat: the differences between mannerist and baroque styles must not be exaggerated; they have common
boundaries and at times merge together. It is revealing that several of the
poets, such as Tasso and Guarini, whom modern critics consider most
representative of Italian mannerism, are precisely those the ultrabaroque
Gracián quotes with appreciation in his *Agudeza y arte de ingenio* (*Wit
and Art of Cleverness*).

With some frequency, the baroque has been explained as a consequence of historical, psychological, and religious factors: the crisis of
Catholicism, the struggles of the Reformation and the Counter-
Reformation, the defeat of the Spanish armada, inflation and economic
crisis in Spain, the discoveries in astronomy and physics that sent Thomism and Neo-scholasticism reeling. All this produced, or coincided
with, a spiritual crisis characterized by continuous tension between body
and soul, faith and doubt, sensuality and awareness of death, the instant
and eternity. This psychic and moral discord was resolved in a violent,
dynamic art permeated with the dual awareness of the world's fragmen-

tation and its unity, a chiaroscuro of contrasts, paradoxes, twisted inversions, and scintillating affirmations. For other critics, the baroque is not art's response to history but a moment in the history of art; to them the baroque is the highest point in a process of aesthetic refinement begun during the Renaissance. Others believe that mannerism and the baroque are not so much the expressions of the great disturbances and revolutions in seventeenth-century society, ideas, and beliefs as the result of changes in the artist's position in regard to society and his work: as soon as collectors and cognoscenti appreciated the artist's personality more than the subject of his works, *manner* predominated.[10] Mannerism and the baroque represent the triumph of the creator's subjectivity over the dual tyranny of aesthetic canon and natural model.

None of these ideas excludes the others. Nor is any of them excluded by Curtius' thesis that the periodic appearance of mannerist and classic tendencies in the West, from Lycophron to Mallarmé and Pound, reveals a kind of rhythm in the history of styles. That that rhythm exists is evident to me. Its relation to historical and social change is less clear: I do not see how the use of hyperbaton and periphrasis can be the consequence of the victory of the Battle of Lepanto or the revocation of the Edict of Nantes. Nor do I see the relation between Apollinaire's *calligrammes* and unemployment in the vineyards. No one, however, would deny the correspondence between the history of a society and the history of its arts. Somehow, mannerist periods correspond to epochs of crisis. Similarly, there is an obvious, if not clearly understood, relation between the emergence of subjectivism and the several expressions of mannerism: baroque, romantic, symbolist, modernist. In the course of this book I will have occasion to explore more concretely and in more detail the relations between Sor Juana's writing and crisis in the viceregal world.

THE REDISCOVERY OF BAROQUE POETRY is relatively recent. Wölfflin considered baroque art decadent, and it was not until the avant-garde movements of our century that the great baroque writers were again held in esteem. It is anything but coincidence that Eliot's influence should have stimulated a reevaluation of Donne; neither was it by chance that the Spanish poets of the Generation of 1927, especially Gerardo Diego and Dámaso Alonso, inspired the revival of Góngora. What has been overlooked—or at least not sufficiently emphasized—is the analogy the Spanish poets of that period, specifically Gerardo Diego, discovered between Góngora's poetry and the avant-garde aesthetic.

Vicente Huidobro, the initiator of modern poetry in our language, preached an art of invention in which the image created a reality independent of and even contrary to natural reality. Not unrealism or surrealism but antirealism, or, better, metarealism. His was a poetics that sought to turn its back on nature and reality. Góngora, Dámaso Alonso has said, created metaphors that were equations raised to the third degree: his raw material was neither spoken nor literary language but, rather, the metaphor of the metaphors of those languages. This describes exactly the images of Huidobro and the Hispanic avant-garde.

The similarities between the aesthetic doctrine of the baroque, as expressed in the seventeenth century by a Gracián or a Pellegrini, and the ideas of the avant-garde are striking. For Gracián, "a conceit is an act of comprehension that ex-presses the correspondences that exist among objects." The cleverness will be all the greater the less visible the correspondence. Pierre Reverdy's well-known definition of the poetic image is nothing more than a variation of Gracián's formula: "The image is born not of comparison but of the bringing together of two realities. . . . The greater the distance between the objects and the greater the necessity to establish relations among them, the stronger and more effective the image will be." It is difficult to believe that Reverdy had read Gracián. This coincidence between baroque and avant-garde poetics is not a question of influences but rather a question of an affinity operating as much in the sphere of the intellect as in sensibilities. The baroque poet hoped to astonish and astound; Apollinaire proposed exactly the same thing when he extolled surprise as one of the basic elements of poetry. The baroque poet attempts to discover the secret relationships among things, exactly as affirmed and practiced by Eliot and Wallace Stevens. These similarities are all the more remarkable when one considers that the baroque and the avant-garde spring from totally different origins, one from mannerism, the other from romanticism. The solution to this small mystery is perhaps to be found in the role played by form in both baroque and avant-garde aesthetics. Baroque and avant-garde are both formalisms.

Although the baroque and romanticism are mannerist, the similarities between them cloak very profound differences. Each, reacting against classicism, proclaimed an aesthetic of the abnormal and the unique; each presented itself as a transgression of norms. But while the romantic transgression centers on the subject, the baroque transgression focuses on the object. Romanticism liberates the subject; the baroque is the art of the metamorphosis of the object. Romanticism is passionate and passive; the baroque is intellectual and active. Romantic transgression culminates in the apotheosis of the subject or in its fall; baroque transgressions lead to the appearance of an unheard-of object. Romantic poetics is the negation of the object through passion or irony; the subject disappears in the baroque object. Romanticism is explosion; the baroque is implosion. The romantic poem is spilled time; the baroque is congealed time.

The words "wit" (cleverness, ingenuity) and "conceit" define baroque poetry; "sensibility" and "inspiration," the romantic. Wit *invents;* inspiration *reveals.* The inventions of wit are conceits—metaphors and paradoxes—that discover the secret correspondences that unite beings and things among and with themselves; inspiration is condemned to dissipate its revelations—unless a form can be found to contain them. That is, romanticism is condemned to rediscover the baroque. This is precisely what Baudelaire, before anyone, did in modern times. Passionate, romantic mannerism evolved into formalism: first symbolism and then the avant-garde. Like classic art, the baroque aspires to dominate the object—not by balance, however, but by the irritation of contradictions. Thus, like the avant-garde, it is at once romantic and classic. It is vertigo and stasis; congealed movement. In a memorable phrase, Gracián expresses the dual tension of all mannerism, its romantic origins and its classic ambition: "Wit attempts excesses and achieves marvels."

NEW SPAIN'S BAROQUE POETRY was a transplanted poetry. Her poets had their eyes fixed on Spanish models, especially Góngora. Although Góngora's influence was substantial, it was not unique; Lope de Vega, Quevedo, and others, especially Calderón, are not to be overlooked. The very number of colonial poets is surprising.[11] The majority were clerics and rather mediocre, but they wrote in one of the great periods of our language, and in general their works are superior to those of our barren neoclassical and clamorous romantic periods. Some, like Juan de Palafox, Bishop of Puebla, wrote poems more typical of the preceding century, in which echoes—pleasing echoes—of St. John of the Cross can be heard. Most of these poets abandoned themselves with frenetic delight to the complexities and artifices of *culteranismo*. In the mid-seventeenth century we find two authentic poets, Agustín de Salazar y Torres and Luis de Sandoval y Zapata, who wrote a number of amazing sonnets. Sandoval y Zapata recalls Quevedo, but a Quevedo in whom violent chiaroscuro was transformed into a kind of visual harmony. In a sonnet dedicated to a beautiful woman seen on a balcony at sunset, he writes:

> The dying Sun gives birth to blazing pyres,
> but you, as evening falls, more brightly shine,
> your incandescence shedding love, and life.

An impoverished descendant of a conquistador, Sandoval y Zapata also wrote an interesting historical *romance* praising the Ávila brothers—friends and followers of Martín Cortés—who were beheaded in Mexico City for plotting the independence of Mexico. The *romance* is not patriotic in tone; it expresses the grievances of a particular group of people.

After several centuries of oblivion, Sandoval y Zapata's work has finally been collected and published.[12] Much is lost—plays, poems, prose. Only thirty-four sonnets, several *romances* and *décimas,* and an essay have been discovered: bits and pieces, but magnificent bits and pieces. Agustín de Salazar y Torres fared better; two volumes of his writings were published in Madrid under the title *Cítara de Apolo (Apollo's Lyre,* 1681 and 1689). Salazar y Torres was born in Spain, came to Mexico at the age of three, left New Spain when he was not yet twenty, and died in Spain at the age of thirty-three. Spanish or Mexican? More accurately, Spanish *and* Mexican. He was a lyric poet and dramatist noted for his metrical inventions. Calderón praised him, and Sor Juana imitated him more than once. His work reveals a spectrum of influences, moving principally between Góngora and Calderón, but he is not overwhelmed by these powerful personalities. He is an exquisite poet in whom musicality of verse is allied to sensuality of description, as seen in this fragment from *El baño de Procris (Procris Bathing):*

> As if a needle to the magnet drawn,
> I gazed, bedazzled,
> while to the flowing crystal where I'd knelt
> moments before,
> she gave herself—a glowing ship of ice;
> then artful Love,
> by beauty blinded,
> did, even so, conspire
> to heat the waters with his lustful fire.

In the second half of the century there was an even greater number of poets, none of whom is notable with the exception of Sor Juana. She stood alone, surrounded by a chorus of undistinctive, although, it is true, well-tempered, voices. The most famous of that group was Carlos de Sigüenza y Góngora (1645–1700). He is one of the great figures of the seventeenth century, great not for his poems—well constructed, dignified, and boring—but for his scientific and historical works. Additional names could be listed of decorous mediocrities who wrote ornate, oratorical poems to be declaimed in contests and ceremonies. Such poetry was characteristic of the age, encouraged by the university and the Church. As today we have literary prizes, the seventeenth century had its competitions, called "jousts" and "palestras" in the manner of feudal tourneys. Sor Juana praised the author of one such poem:

> Enigma to your art is naught,
> like Oedipus, you penetrate:
> physically, if final cause be known,
> logically, should there be debate.

Irving A. Leonard dedicates two entertaining chapters of his book about New Spain to poetry competitions and to some of the peculiarities of baroque verse: *ecos* (echoes); acrostics; alliteration; poems with two or three possible readings; *retrógradas,* reversible poems that could be read from first to last line and from last to first; centos, poems made from the verses of other poems, almost always those of Góngora; *paranomasías,* words identical in spelling except for one vowel; word play in which the letters of a word are reversed; and other clever games.[13] Under the double contamination of neoclassical and romantic aesthetics, the one enamored of decorum and the other of spontaneity, it is the custom among modern critics to disdain such games. An injustice; these are legitimate resources of poetry.

Wit and conceit also characterize baroque prose, particularly sacred writings. The sermon was the seventeenth-century equivalent of the essay. As a woman, Sor Juana could not preach sermons, but she could write criticism of them. This is precisely what she did in her celebrated *Carta atenagórica (Athenagoric Letter)*. A perfect example of how the poet appropriated the predominantly masculine forms of the culture of her century, the *Carta* reveals another characteristic of that society: theology as a mask for politics. Often the only purpose of theological debate using Scholastic conceits of extraordinary abstraction and subtlety was to mask controversy among individuals and groups. Theology in the seventeenth century fulfilled the same polemical function as do social ideologies and politics in the twentieth: dispute over the interpretation of a passage from the Scriptures was a way in which power struggles and personal squabbles were expressed.

In contemporary times the intellectual polemic unfolds on the pages of newspapers and magazines; in the seventeenth century differences were aired from the pulpit and only occasionally appeared in print. We know that the *Carta atenagórica* provoked many debates and more than one heated attack, as reported by Sor Juana herself, in a tone somewhere between fear and pleasure. In spite of the uproar caused by this polemic, the only extant condemnation of the nun's position is a pamphlet containing a sermon refuting her arguments, written by a Valencian priest, Francisco Xavier Palavicino.[14] The lack of written testimony, however, does not mean that the debate did not (it did, for many years) stir the opinions of cultivated persons. Previously, in describing seventeenth-century literature, I stated that it was a literature for the few, masculine, erudite, *conceptista,* sententious, ingenious, clerical, and courtly. I also pointed out that another distinguishing feature was the importance of the spoken word: a culture of the pulpit and the university chair, but also of the salon. The tripartite division of society was reflected in the forms of intellectual exchange: the sermon in the church; the lesson in the lecture hall; the salon at court and in the homes of the wealthy. The cloister occupied an intermediate position between court and church. It is no secret that monasteries and convents, especially the latter, although essentially religious, were centers of intense worldly life in addition to being hubs of economic and commercial activities. The ambiguous correspondence between the celestial and the earthly "courts" was duplicated in the religious communities of Mexico City.

Certain authors, deceived or bedazzled by the originality of Mexican colonial baroque creations—palaces, churches, poems—have interpreted them as the first fruit of an emerging national spirit. Although specifically Mexican themes—the Conquest, native legends, the "majesty" of Mexico City, the landscape of Anáhuac—appear in the poems of this period, it would be questionable to claim that they are expressions of "literary nationalism." It was natural—the very aesthetic of the baroque demanded it—that cultivated poetry should assimilate native elements. Not for the sake of nationalism, however, but out of fidelity to the aesthetic of the strange, the unique, the exotic. In her songs and *villancicos* Sor Juana made clever use of the popular speech of mulattos and criollos, and even of the Indian language Nahuatl. She was motivated not by nationalism but by its exact opposite, a universalist aesthetic that delighted in recording picturesque details and in highlighting specificities. The Catholic politics of the Spanish empire corresponded to the catholic aesthetic of baroque art.

I do not deny the obvious: that there is a convergence between criollo sensibility and baroque style in the field of architecture and in letters (and in more mundane areas such as cuisine). This accounts for the frequent felicity of the artistic expressions of the time. The explanation for this phenomenon is not, however, to be found in criollo nationalism. I have described the limitations and ambiguities of the criollo's patriotism, divided as he was between fidelity to the empire and his vital need to differentiate himself from the Spanish world, torn between his loyalty as a subject of the crown and his feeling that in matters of justice and personal dignity he was mistreated by the bureaucracy in Madrid. Nonetheless, evidence of criollo separatist tendencies does not appear until well into the eighteenth century. Baroque criollismo, with its unique flavor, was involuntary. Indeed, the existence of that uniqueness was a consequence of baroque universality.

Styles in art always spread beyond national boundaries; this was particularly true of the baroque. It extended from Vienna to Goa, from Prague to Quito. The baroque welcomed all specificities and all exceptions—among them Góngora's "Mexican feathered mantle"—precisely for being the aesthetic of the strange. The goal of the baroque was to astonish and astound; that is why it sought out and collected all extremes, especially hybrids and monsters. Conceit and cleverness are the sirens and hippogriffs of language, the verbal equivalents of nature's fantasies. In such love for the strange we find both the secret of baroque art's affinity with criollo sensibility and the source of its fruitfulness. To the baroque sensibility the American world was marvelous, not only for the vastness of its geography, the fantasy of its fauna, the delirium of its flora, but for the bizarre customs and institutions of its ancient civilizations. Among all these American marvels there is one that from the beginning, from the writings of Terrazas and Balbuena, was glorified by the criollo: his own being. In the seventeenth century the aesthetic of the strange expressed with rapture the strangeness of the criollo. In such enthusiasm it is not difficult to find an act of compensation; psychic insecurity lies at the root of this attitude. Ambiguous fascination: the exact opposite of the Frenchman of the same century, the criollo saw himself not as a confirmation of the universality represented in every human being but as the exception each of us is.

It has often been said—both in praise and deprecation—that the Mexican baroque was an exaggeration of its Spanish models. Indeed, like all imitative art, the poetry of New Spain attempted to surpass its models: it was the extreme of baroqueness, the apogee of strangeness. This excess is proof of its authenticity, something that cannot be said of either our neoclassical or romantic poetry. Each of them, too, was an imitation, but a pallid and faded imitation reflecting the lack of affinity between those poets and the models they proposed to imitate. In contrast, the unique aesthetic of the Mexican baroque corresponded to the historical and existential uniqueness of the criollo. Their relationship was not one of cause and effect, but of affinity and coincidence. The criollo breathed naturally in a world of strangeness because he was, and knew himself to be, a strange being.

Part Two

Juana Ramírez
1648–1668

5

The Ramírez Family

$\mathcal{F}$ROM THE MIDDLE of the eighteenth to the end of the nineteenth century Sor Juana Inés de la Cruz suffered the same neglect and indifference that obscured almost all the great poets of the baroque period, even Góngora himself. The last reprinting of the three volumes of her work appeared in 1725, and it was not until 1940 that the first modern edition was published.[1] Even more destructive than the indifference of two centuries was the dispersal of the archives and libraries of the convents as a result of the laws promulgated under Juarez:[2] what survived the carelessness and venality of men fell victim to the mice. Among the irreparable losses were Carlos de Sigüenza y Góngora's "Oración fúnebre" ("Funeral Oration") and various manuscripts of Sor Juana's—a play, a treatise on morality, and other papers. Especially regrettable is the loss of her correspondence. She is known to have exchanged letters with a great many people in Spain.

Castorena y Ursúa, the editor of the third volume of her writings, reported that some of her papers were in Andalusia, in the hands of Don Juan de Orve y Arbieto, who had edited the second volume of her works. According to Castorena, the manuscripts of the first volume were in the Hieronymite archives of the Escorial; they had been deposited there by the Countess de Paredes, who was responsible for their publication. In 1950, in the preface to the first volume of his edition of the *Complete Works,* Alfonso Méndez Plancarte lamented, "To this day, as far as we know, no one has searched in Madrid for this correspondence or for the manuscripts of the first two volumes; nor has anyone looked for Orve y Arbieto's papers in Seville or its environs."

For the study of Sor Juana's life we must rely on two basic texts: her letter to the Bishop of Puebla, Manuel Fernández de Santa Cruz (*Respuesta a Sor Filotea de la Cruz* [*Response to Sor Filotea de la Cruz*]), and the brief biography written by the Jesuit priest Diego Calleja. We can also turn to a few mentions of her by her contemporaries and to a handful of legal and religious documents, such as her certificate of baptism, her will and those of her mother and sisters, some contracts of purchase and sale, and her profession of faith.[3]

Although the two biographical texts contain a great deal of information, they suffer from lacunae and other defects. The *Response* to the Bishop of Puebla was written in a spirit of defensiveness and in the throes of a bitter polemic. It contains fascinating revelations but fails to mention a crucial period—the years at court—and is similarly silent on other aspects of her life. It is not an autobiography but a self-defense. When the third and last volume of her works was published in Madrid in 1700, *Fama y obras póstumas del Fenix de México, Décima Musa, poetisa americana* . . . (*Fame and Posthumous Works of the Phoenix of Mexico, Tenth Muse, Poetess of America* . . .), the *nihil obstat* for the book was issued by Diego Calleja. More than an imprimatur, it is a biography. Calleja had never met Sor Juana but he knew several persons, like the Marquis de Mancera, who had been her friends. He also maintained a lengthy correspondence with Sor Juana. His account is not a true biography in the modern sense of the word, but an edifying narrative in which the smallest incidents in her life were seen as supernatural signs and signals of an ascent toward virtue and saintliness. Calleja avoids anything that might cloud her reputation and says nothing that sheds any light on the two great enigmas that have so intrigued her modern admirers: why she embraced the religious life and why she later renounced literature. One example of Calleja's method: he sees a portent of Sor Juana's religious vocation in the fact that she was born in a room called "the cell." This is legend contaminating history, Christian marvel dissolving prosaic reality.

Juana Ramírez de Asbaje was born in San Miguel Nepantla, a village in the foothills of Popocatépetl. She says in a poem,

> I was born where solar rays
> stared down at me from overhead,
> not squint-eyed, as in other climes.

According to Calleja, she came into the world on November 12, 1651. There is good reason to believe he was mistaken. No baptismal entry has been found recording her name and that of her parents. It is not likely it will be found; in those days the names of the parents of illegitimate children were not entered in the church registry. But scholars have found a certificate of baptism in the parish of Chimalhuacán, the jurisdiction to which Nepantla belonged. It records the baptism on December 2, 1648, of a girl child: "Inés, daughter of the Church; the godparents were Miguel Ramírez and Beatriz Ramírez." Miguel and Beatriz Ramírez were the brother and sister of Juana Inés' mother, Isabel. It is almost certain that the Inés of the entry of 1648 is our Juana Inés. Thus she was three years older than her biographer reported and she was illegitimate, for that was the meaning of "daughter of the Church." Her mother's will confirms the baptismal entry in Chimalhuacán. In that document the criolla Doña Isabel Ramírez de Santillana declares that she is mother of six children, five female and one male, all illegitimate, the first three conceived with Pedro Manuel de Asbaje and the other three with Captain Diego Ruiz Lozano.

Juana Inés' father, Pedro Manuel de Asbaje y Vargas Machuca, was a Basque, according to Sor Juana. Nothing else is known about him. Calleja portrays him as an impoverished nobleman who had sought fortune in the New World. Even the spelling of his name is uncertain: Asbaje or Asvaje or Azuaje? A curious fact: two baptismal records of 1666 in the parish of Chimalhuacán were signed by a friar F. (or H.) de Asvaje.[4] Who is F. de Asvaje? A relative of Pedro Manuel de Asbaje? Could that friar be the real father of Juana Inés and her two older sisters? Admittedly, this supposition cannot be proved and may seem unfounded, but it is not totally preposterous. In that century—the trials of the Inquisition so attest—relations between priests and single or married women were far from rare.

The enigma of Juana Inés' father, aside from being baffling, is one of the real obstacles confronting her biographers. Who was he? What were his origins? What became of his family? There is no doubt that the Ramírez family, and Sor Juana herself, did everything possible to keep Pedro Manuel de Asbaje in the shadows. They succeeded. He is a disembodied man, a ghost.

Juana Inés scarcely mentions her father's name. She did not see him from the time she was a small child, if she knew him at all. She had no connection with her father's relatives and never speaks of them. Although she called herself a "legitimate daughter," she must have been aware of the gossip surrounding her origins. A savage epigram (95), in which she replies to an "insolent" critic, reveals that Juana Inés was sensitive to rumors:

> Not to be born of an honorable father
> would be a blemish, I must own,
> if receiving my being from no other
> I had not known it was his alone.
>   Far more generous was your mother
> when she arranged your ancestry,
> offering many a likely father
> among whom to choose your pedigree.[5]

Those who have commented on this epigram have not noticed that it refers not so much to her bastardy as to her father's origins. Was Asbaje not "honorable" because he was a plebeian or because he had committed some crime or misdeed?

Before entering the convent, Juana Inés used her mother's name. In the portrait painted by Andrés Islas (1772) there is an inscription that reads clearly: "In the lay world she was known as Doña Juana Ramírez, for so she signed her name." Her will confirms the inscription: "In the lay world my name was Doña Juana Ramírez de Asbaje." One exception: to celebrate the completion of the metropolitan cathedral (1667), several "poetic descriptions" of the building, called "dedications," were published; in one of them appears a sonnet in homage to the book's author, the priest Diego de Ribera, written by "Doña Juana Inés de Asbaje." This is one of her earliest poems; she was twenty years old and still living in the viceregal palace as a lady-in-waiting to the Marquise de Mancera. It is possible that at court she was known as Juana Ramírez de Asbaje or Asvaje. Until she took the veil she had remained in the circle of her mother's family. The convent in which she took her vows, San Jerónimo, was reserved exclusively for criollo women, and several other women of her family were nuns in San Jerónimo. Thus, both family and social considerations explain the use of her maternal name, although the satisfaction with which she alludes to her Basque ancestry is patent.

Juana Inés' maternal family was criollo on both sides, and her step-father, her sisters' husbands, and her half brother's wife as well were criollo. Pedro Ramírez de Santillana and Beatriz Rendón, her maternal grandparents, were of Andalusian origin and came from Sanlúcar de Barrameda. A landholder of moderate means, Pedro Ramírez had leased two haciendas, both the property of the Church: first in Nepantla, where Juana Inés was born, and then in Panoayán, where she grew up. In that region the land is fertile; the two haciendas, particularly the one in Panoayán, which exists today, were productive and yielded a good profit. Pedro Ramírez was granted the lease to the hacienda of Panoayán for "three lifetimes," that is, through his lifetime and those of his daughter Isabel and his granddaughter María. Later, again "for three lifetimes," the hacienda passed to Juana Inés' half brother, Diego Ruiz Lozano, and to his descendants. Thus Panoayán was in the hands of the Ramírez family for five generations.

There were many military men and clerics in the family, as was usual in that time and at that social level. The senior Diego Ruiz Lozano was a lance captain, and his son also took up arms as a career and was captain of the same corps. One of Isabel Ramírez' sisters, María, married the wealthy Juan de Mata, a man of influence and good standing in the viceregal palace. One of Sor Juana's half sisters, Inés Ruiz Lozano, was married to José Miguel de Torres, secretary of the university and poet of some renown. Their son José Diego de Torres also became secretary of the university and a poet like his father and aunt. Another of the Torres family—the Mercedarian Fray Miguel de Torres—was a friend and biographer of Manuel Fernández de Santa Cruz, the Bishop of Puebla and friend and protector of Sor Juana.

A notable characteristic of Sor Juana's family is the independence, fortitude, and energy of the women. Sor Juana's mother, Isabel Ramírez, managed the hacienda of Panoayán from her father's death in 1656 until her own in 1688—more than thirty years. Her daughter María succeeded her and administered the hacienda until the time of her death. Another daughter, Josefa, was no less enterprising; when abandoned by her husband she sought the help of Sor Juana, who secured a loan on some jewels, and bought a hacienda in the Chalco region. It is impossible not to admire these spirited women, considering the age in which they lived. (And my admiration for Isabel Ramírez grows when I remember that she never learned to read.) Managing a hacienda was not, and is not, an easy task; it requires considerable physical vigor, skill, tenacity, and authority. The proprietor not only has responsibility for the land, the stock, and the equipment but is the head of a community.

Landholders, clerics, captains, nuns: how did these people reconcile their strong beliefs with Isabel Ramírez' love affairs? How were the sisters of Juana Inés able to marry and how did she herself succeed in being accepted into the palace to become a lady-in-waiting to the Vicereine? How can the harmony among sisters and mother be explained? We must modify our ideas about seventeenth-century morality. Sexual orthodoxy was much less rigorous than religious orthodoxy. The Ramírezes were a typical criollo family, as were their relatives, the Matas, the Ruiz Lozanos, the Torreses. Contemporary documents reveal that the behavior of Isabel Ramírez was far from being a scandalous exception. Everyone accepted without reserve the existence of natural children, and José Miguel de Torres, secretary of the university and father of several clerics and nuns, found nothing particularly censurable in the bastardy of his wife or that of many of his nieces and nephews.

As for Sor Juana's sisters, María Ramírez, a full sister, had three children: Isabel María de San José (who became a nun in the convent of San Jerónimo), Lope, and Ignacio. María is said to have been married to Lope de Ulloque, but the only evidence for this is her death certificate. Neither of her two sons took their father's surname; their uncle by marriage, Dr. José Miguel de Torres, gives only their mother's name when he mentions them in his will. Isabel Ramírez' will, executed a year before her death in 1687—when her daughter María's three children had all been born—is explicit: "I direct that three hundred gold pesos be given to the said María de Asbaje, my daughter, of maiden state . . ." In the record of Isabel María de San José's profession of faith in 1688, written in the hand of Sor Juana Inés de la Cruz, who was the archivist and secretary of San Jerónimo at the time, one reads that the novice was the daughter of María Ramírez and Captain Fernando Martínez de Santolaya.[6] Furthermore, in that same year, Isabel María de San José made her own will, according to the custom of novices when they took the veil, and in it she declared herself to be "a natural daughter of Captain Fernando Martínez de Santolaya, who delivered me as such to Mother Juana Inés de la Cruz, and she in her charity raised me."[7] In the light of these facts, the feminism widely attributed to Sor Juana takes on a new coloration. Her satire of men and her defense of women cease to be opinion; they are a moral, even visceral, reaction to lived experiences.

Two documents confirm the solicitude with which Juana Inés sheltered her abandoned niece. In a deposition made in 1683, she contests a claim by her nephew Francisco de Villena, son of her sister Josefa, to some jewelry and silverware actually belonging to "a girl whom this deposer has in her charge."[8] This girl must have been Isabel María de San José. Years later, in 1691, Juana Inés sought to invest fourteen hundred gold pesos—some months later she added another six hundred pesos—in lands belonging to the convent of San Jerónimo, "so that for my lifetime the administrator of said convent will deliver to me the corresponding income, and afterward to Sister Isabel María de San José, my niece."[9]

The case of Sor Juana's other full sister, Josefa, is not much different from that of María. She, too, had children out of wedlock. She married José de Paredes in 1664, but two years later he abandoned her. Yet she had four children. The mystery clears as soon as it is learned that Josefa subsequently lived in Mexico City with Francisco de Villena. The four children inherited Don Francisco's property and his name. There is a deposition by her cousin, the poet José Diego de Torres, in which it is confirmed that all four—José Felipe, Francisco, Rosa Teresa, and María—were children of Josefa Ramírez de Asbaje and Francisco de Villena. In his deposition, José Diego de Torres affirmed that he knew them "as if he had educated them." Which was true: his father, José Miguel de Torres, had been the children's tutor and, after Francisco de Villena's death, Josefa's legal representative. One of the sons, José Felipe, became a cleric and probably is the author of an elegy written at Sor Juana's death, "América, no llores" ("Weep Not, America").

The younger Diego Ruiz Lozano, Juana Inés' half brother, was also, as he attested in his will, the father of an illegitimate son. An interesting footnote: Pedro Ramírez, Sor Juana's grandfather, says in his will that he owed Diego Ruiz Lozano, "a neighbor of this province, one hundred pesos or slightly less." There is little doubt that by that date—1655—the Diego Ruiz Lozano mentioned in the will was Isabel's lover (his son and namesake Diego was born about 1656),[10] and it is unlikely that Pedro Ramírez was unaware of his daughter's liaison with his creditor.

The behavior of the Ramírez women—that of the men must have been even more free—does not seem to have had any great effect on their reputation. Ruiz Lozano's two daughters married well-known and respectable men; the natural daughters of Josefa Ramírez also married, and all the grandsons found positions in the Church, the university, and the military. Political and religious orthodoxies are implacable in regard to heretical ideas, but not to the passions of the senses. There is abundant testimony regarding the libertine manners of New Spain. The traveler Thomas Gage gathered anecdotes about the lechery, avarice, and licentiousness of the clergy with rancorous glee. Other travelers were astounded by the looseness of women and by the ease with which the Spanish and their descendants, criollos and mestizos, satisfied their appetites. It was reported that at the end of the seventeenth century two thousand *arrobas* of pulque entered Mexico City every day, and much more on Tuesdays and Saturdays. The *pulquerías* and taverns were serviced by girls, but male prostitution was not unknown: "[It was] held for certain that to attract customers these publicans have a provision of persons of both sexes for evil commerce."[11] The police could not enter taverns or brothels. Nevertheless, this century was also the century of missionaries like Father Kino, mystics like Catalina Suárez, and austere ascetics like the Archbishop of Mexico, Francisco Aguiar y Seijas, and Father Antonio Núñez de Miranda, Sor Juana's confessor.

Again and again the extreme religiosity of the era has been emphasized, as well as its extreme sensuality. The violent contrast between asceticism and dissoluteness appears throughout the Baroque Age, in all countries and classes. Often austerity and laxity come together in a single person: John Donne is the author of libertine poems like the elegy "Going to Bed" as well as devout sermons. In Quevedo's poems there is an unending dialogue between soul and arse, bones and excrement. The outcry, composed of shock and admiration, produced by the icy eroticism of Marino's *Adonis* can be compared to the passions later awakened by the novels of Lawrence, Joyce, and Proust. The great literary invention of the Baroque Age—the conceit or union of opposites—expresses with extraordinary precision the character of the era. But the case of seventeenth-century baroque society is not unique: rigor and debauchery, radical pessimism and exalted sensuality, asceticism and eroticism, often go together. In another book I have tried to show how the dialogue between *body* and *nonbody* unfolded in India.[12] There is a kind of correspondence between artistic mannerism and the conjunction of body and nonbody. In antibaroque eras there is a rigid separation between body and nonbody, matter and spirit. This separation, in the sphere of art, is expressed as a clear distinction between drawing and color. Mannerist periods, on the other hand, in the domains of art and thought as well as in morality and eroticism, are ruled by the principle of *coincidentia oppositorum*.

The social and physical conditions of New Spain favored the manifestation of all these contrasts. From the beginning, the attraction of America was contradictory: for the Franciscan missionaries it was the continent where the millennium prophesied by Joaquim of Floris would be fulfilled. For the majority of lay persons and for many of the clergy, America represented the hope of instant riches. The open spaces gave some a sensation of recapturing their personal freedom, while others felt they had gained a new spiritual kingdom. The strange food, the colors, the landscapes, the women with different skin and eyes (Indian, mestizo, mulatto), the complicity of the sun and the vegetation, the voluptuousness of the climate—all this stirred the imagination, and, with the imagination, the senses. Contemporary demographic studies have shown that the birthrate of the Spanish increased in New Spain. The explanation lies not in an impossible biological mutation but in the changes of geographic and social milieu: the new conditions were more favorable to the pleasures of the senses and less favorable to the morality of repression. A modern scholar, scandalized by the sexual mores of New Spain in the seventeenth century, cites the case of a clergyman considered unusual because, in spite of his wealth and good looks, he was believed to have died a virgin.[13] Countless clerics were charged and sentenced for having seduced their parishioners. The lax sexual morality of the Mexican people is surely a legacy of New Spain. It is unwise to condemn it: if machismo is a tyranny that darkens relations between man and woman, erotic freedom illumines them.

6

May Syllables Be Composed
by the Stars

*T*OLERANCE FOR THE ABERRATIONS of appetite but intransigence in matters of opinion and belief; allowance for the straying body but not the wayward soul: such was the way of the world in which Juana Inés was born and lived. But what was she like, what were her home and her people like? We know very little about her childhood, and that little is the glimmer she herself, always reticent, allows us in the *Response* to the Bishop of Puebla and in other passages of her writing. Several times she alludes to her sunny, lively, and playful spirit. We know of her cleverness in conversation, her skill in argument, and the felicity and grace of her improvisations. The wit and charm that distinguished her in her maturity must have been present in her childhood as imagination and mischievousness. The adult Juana Inés, devoted to her intellectual labors, gives us a glimpse of another Juana Inés: the little girl engrossed in her childish games, at once serious and impassioned, fond of skipping and singing but also of listening to the stories of the maids and the legends of her elders. Unlike St. Teresa, she must have been given more to dreaming than to adventure, and more to reflection than to dreaming.

A solitary child, a child who plays by herself, a child absorbed in herself. Above all, a curious child. That was her sign and her destiny: curiosity. Curious about the world and about herself, about what happened in the world and what happened inside herself. Her curiosity quickly became intellectual passion: *What is it?* and *What is it like?* were questions repeated throughout her life. In the *Response* she tells us: "Once in my presence two young girls were spinning a top, and scarcely had I seen the motion and the figure described when I began, out of this madness of mine, to meditate on the effortless *motus* of the spherical form, and how the impulse persisted even when free and independent of its cause." [1] From the beginning, intellectual curiosity was her great passion, or, rather, the sublimation of great passion. In the same *Response* she tells that when she was three she succeeded, not without deception and pleading, in persuading the teacher of one of her older sisters to give her lessons. She also tells us that she did not eat cheese because she had been told it made one slow-witted, and her "desire for learning was stronger than the desire for eating." By the time she was six or seven she knew how to read and write. Then she asked her mother to send her to the university dressed as a man. Following the predictable refusal, she consoled herself by studying and reading in her grandfather's library. Determined to learn grammar, she cut off several inches of her hair, and when, after a period of time she had set herself, she still had not mastered the lessons, she cropped it again: it did not seem to her that a head should be "adorned with hair and naked of learning."

It is not surprising that Sor Juana's fragmentary recollections of her childhood have been one of the sources of the hypothesis of her "masculinity." But in order to understand these episodes fully, we must place them within the context of her early life. We must visualize the little girl in her home, her elders and their conflicts, her sisters and their games, the nursemaids and their tales, illnesses and chores, pleasures and holidays, the ups and downs of family life on a hacienda clinging to a mountainside on the boundary between cold and warm zones, between the snows of Popocatépetl and the tropical cane fields of the plain. Unfortunately, Sor Juana scarcely mentions her family in her autobiographical account and tells us nothing at all of what was doubtless a key to her mental world: the nature of her ties with her mother and her mother's two consorts.

Her parents' separation and the appearance of the new lover, Diego Ruiz Lozano, must have affected her deeply. Thus the first question we must ask is, what was the nature of her relationship with Pedro Manuel de Asbaje? If it is impossible to answer this question entirely, it is not impossible to give an answer that seems at least plausible. Did she know her father? I have already said it is improbable that she did. It does not seem likely that Asbaje lived with Isabel in her parents' house. In any case Juana Inés would not have seen him—if she ever knew him—after the separation; it is an established fact that Asbaje disappeared entirely from Isabel's life. The separation must have occurred by the time Juana Inés was five or six years old, if not before.[2] The fact that Sor Juana almost never mentions her father is further proof of Pedro Manuel de Asbaje's desertion.

All these circumstances lead me to believe that Sor Juana had no relationship with her father, only with his absent figure. Relations with the absent are entirely subjective; the absent one is a projection of our desires, hatreds, and fears. We experience absence as a vacuum, but it is a vacuum we fill with our imagination. What was Juana Inés' image of her father? Every child's projection of the paternal image is complex and contradictory; hers must have been singularly so. Undoubtedly, three figures blended together in her image of paternity: that of her biological father, Pedro Manuel de Asbaje; that of his substitute and rival, Diego Ruiz Lozano; and that of the grandfather with whom she lived and who, almost surely, was a strong father figure. But her grandfather died in 1656, when she was about eight. In the meantime, the silence surrounding her father's absence must have given her and her sisters a rather fanciful idea of him. As a grown woman Juana Inés never spoke of him except indirectly and in order to refer to her Basque ancestry. At any rate, it is impossible to believe that her father's image would not have been tinged with the rancor she must have felt over his desertion. Rancor and, perhaps, secret and grudging admiration.

Juana Inés must have known that Pedro Manuel de Asbaje's absence was permanent. And permanent, irrevocable absence is the absence of the dead. Perhaps before Asbaje's physical death—sometime before 1669, that is, prior to her entering the convent[3]—she killed and buried him symbolically. A frequent compensation of children and lovers is to kill in dreams the loved one who has deserted them. By this I mean that for Juana Inés not only was the father absent, he was a ghost. Her love poems revolve around an image, an imaginary form held by memory or desire, not a physical lover. The beloved appears as a creature of smoke, a shadow sculpted by the mind. Sometimes that shadow is of a dead man. A notable example is the justly famous poem in *liras* (213) in which a woman weeps over the absence of her deceased husband. In that poem Sor Juana plays the role of the widow with a conviction that goes beyond baroque rhetoric. The theme fascinated her: there is another poem (78), in *endechas* no less impassioned than the *liras,* in which, as stated in the heading, "she expresses even more vividly the feelings suffered by a woman who had greatly loved her dead husband."

The ambiguity of her feelings toward the image of her father is unquestionable. The absent father, if not dead, had disappeared. His absence provoked nostalgia and idealization: in our fantasy the absent loom large as either heroes or monsters. Maybe her feelings were not those of pride but those of grief and shame: how could she have known whether he was adventurer or wretch, dissolute hidalgo or unworthy priest? In any case, the image she had of her father, as I have said, was a mixture of resentment, nostalgia, and—why not?—secret admiration. If, as her attitude suggests, she killed him in her imagination and buried him in silence, her poetry exhumed him, transfiguring them both: she was his widow and he her dead husband. On first consideration, this fantasy seems to invert a Freudian archetype: boys symbolically kill their fathers and girls their mothers. In the case of Juana Inés, if my supposition is true, the girl child kills her father, not her mother, indicating an inversion of sex and of values. A double transgression: killing the image of her father and thus assuming the masculine, not the maternal, image. But this "masculinization" is in turn negated by a second psychological shift: Juana Inés converts the paternal fantasy into a phantom of her husband and transforms herself into his widow. Thus she achieves identification with the mother—Asbaje's real, if not legal, widow—and the "masculinization" is changed into "feminization": in her mind Juana Inés takes her mother's place. A further ambiguity: the substitution is completed when she becomes a nun. The convent is not a renunciation, it is the path toward transmutation: the nun is a poet. Through poetry she revives the dead and marries them. As will be seen, one of her poetic archetypes was Isis, the Egyptian goddess who is not only the universal mother of seeds, plants, and animals but, as the inventor of writing, a symbol of intellect. There is still another secret and striking analogy between the "widow" Juana Inés and the goddess: Isis revives her brother-husband Osiris and marries him. The figure of Isis embodies a double maternity, one natural and the other symbolic. The second transcends the first, and Sor Juana recognized herself in it. She also identified herself with maidens of antiquity who similarly transform natural into symbolic or spiritual maternity, poetically or divinely inspired to produce poems and prophecies. This is the secret theme of her life, as I hope to show in this book—though I can seek only to glimpse, not to *know,* who Juana Inés was.

It is not easy to imagine what her feelings were for Diego Ruiz Lozano. They surely were no less complex than her feelings for the ghostly

Asbaje. Except that if the distinguishing mark of her relationship with the latter was absence, what joined her to Ruiz Lozano was the exact opposite: he was a creature of flesh and blood. Her mother's new lover must have been seen by Juana Inés as an interloper and usurper. In her childhood mythology the two antagonistic, but complementary, figures in which virility crystallized were her father and stepfather, the ghost and the intruder. The first was a disembodied reality, smoke that slipped through her fingers. The second was an all too physical presence, an alien body that occupied and profaned the places reserved for the head of the house. Those places are simultaneously sacred and intimate: the armchair in the living room, the head of the table, the conjugal bed. The alien presence is the palpable expression of power in its most naked and unlawful form: usurpation.

Here I must risk a hypothesis that seems extremely likely to me, although it cannot be verified. Ruiz Lozano fulfilled a compensatory function in the dialectic of guilt and punishment. The tyranny of the stepfather was punishment for the symbolic death of the father. The virility of the ghost was incarnate in Ruiz Lozano but its corporeal form was aggression. Fantasy was at work again: the aggressor was not the real Diego Ruiz Lozano but a figure created by Juana Inés' guilt feelings.

The actual relationship between her and her stepfather must not have been too bad. I have pointed out that in 1672 Diego Ruiz Lozano placed his two daughters—Antonia, fourteen, and Inés, thirteen—in the convent of San Jerónimo, to "remove them from worldly perils" and so that "they may be in the company of Mother Juana Inés de la Cruz, cousin [half sister] of the aforementioned girls." In his deposition, Diego Ruiz Lozano pledged payment for their food and lodging and, "should the case arise," three thousand pesos for each girl's dowry. Neither of the two made her profession. But Juana Inés' real relationship as a grown woman with Diego Ruiz Lozano is not necessarily consistent with the ambiguous feelings and images he must have inspired during her childhood.

The contrast between the two images of virility, father and stepfather, can be expressed as passivity versus activity. The passivity of the ghost excites the activity of the imagination; the aggressive presence of the intruder, on the other hand, provokes a defensive withdrawal. Before her stepfather, Juana Inés reins herself in, retreats into herself. The instinctive movement inward prefigures the convent cell and her solitude among books. Before her father's ghost, Juana Inés gives rein to her fantasy. The movement outward foreshadows the gesture with which, as a writer, she will spell out the figures of her desires and speculations. In the combination of the two motions is the germ of her inordinate capacity to develop mind over body.

The ghost that haunts her thoughts and the intruder who dominates the home are figures inextricably bound to her mother and, therefore, to her. Her relationship with her mother—the most complex and most difficult to penetrate—must have been determined by the opposition of the two masculine images, the ghost and the intruder. The mother compensates for absence not with her imagination but with another presence. That presence is not one of usurpation or instability; it is permanence and stability. The mother embodies a kind of legitimacy, not legal but earthly, carnal. She is the home, the earth. Her powers are exercised in a kingdom opposite to the one in which Juana Inés gives rein to her own: not the world of dream and its phantoms but that of real reality. Maybe Juana Inés felt a kind of affectionate repulsion toward her, the fascination that introverted, intellectual temperaments sometimes feel toward powerfully animal natures. A fascination that does not exclude rejection. Although her life was the negation of her mother's life, how can we fail to see it also as an oblique homage? In order to understand the contradictory relationship that almost surely united Juana Inés with her mother—admiration, jealousy, pity, resentment—the mother must be seen as the young Juana Inés saw her: at the center of the home, at the same time queen and scandal of the family. In a world of strong passions and weak individuals, ruled by contradictory winds, the mother is the lodestar that attracts all wills, either energizing or neutralizing them: the lady of lightning and of calm.

Juana Inés stands among the ghost of her father, the presence of her stepfather, and the enormous earthly reality of her mother. The mother represents the fusion of opposites in Juana Inés—not spiritually but physically, carnally. Juana Inés' life and work will be an attempt to spiritualize this carnal fusion, to transmute it: in this alchemy, art will replace the alchemist's fire. In her poems, when she refers to her writing, she frequently speaks of giving birth or aborting; in "El epinicio al conde de Galve" ("Epinicion to the Count de Galve") the pythoness of Delphi is described in truly extraordinary terms, "although virgin, pregnant with divine concepts." The image is a portrait of the Sor Juana who in turn presents herself as a sublimation of the maternal figure. *Conceptismo* serves her admirably for this kind of paradox; through paradox is achieved the marvel of "frenzy that is sanity." The transgression of the logical order produces a new spiritual reality, the conceit. An intellectual transgression that is no less marvelous than her mother's carnal transgression. Sor Juana is unwed but fecund, like her mother: one engenders mortal creatures, the other, mental ones.

The grandfather is her other link to masculine power. Sor Juana says in the *Response* that as a child she lived with her mother and her grandfather. Her grandfather spent the last years of his life on the hacienda of Panoayán; he was devoted to books and culture. In 1930 a learned bookseller, Demetrio García, found a copy of Octaviano della Mirandola's anthology of Latin poets, *Illustrium poetarum flores,* published in Lyon in 1590. The copy first belonged to Pedro Ramírez and then to Juana Inés. The scholar Ermilo Abreu Gómez examined the volume and reported that her signature appears on the first page: "[property] of Juana Inés de la Cruz, the worst," a form of self-humiliation she repeated on a page of the convent of San Jerónimo's Book of Professions: "I, the worst woman in the world, Juana Inés de la Cruz." Ramírez' name appears on the title page. There are numerous marginal notes, not all in the same hand. According to Abreu Gómez, "At least two persons have written them . . . The main ones record very curious bits of information, some erudite and some personal; we may conclude that their author was knowledgeable about classic literatures . . . We also learn that this Ramírez was married and of some social standing . . . Other notes record the years when the volume was in use (1646–1652), which supports the idea that in fact it could have belonged to the nun's grandfather."[4]

The anthology contains fragments from Virgil, Ovid, Horace, Juvenal, Persius, Lucan, Seneca, Boethius, Plautus, Catullus, Martial, Lucretius, Propertius, Tibullus, and others. This Latin anthology of della Mirandola's (a relative of Pico?) confirms what Sor Juana herself tells: her grandfather had "many and varied" books and she read them all, and "there were not enough punishments, or reprimands, to prevent me from reading." This little confession is precious: the filial relationship between the child and the old man assumed the form of an intellectual initiation.

The figure of the grandfather is ambiguous: he takes the place of the father, but he is also beyond masculinity. Whereas the alien presence of Ruiz Lozano accentuates the aggressiveness of virility, the grandfather's old age transcends it. Not only is the grandfather compensation for the father's absence, he also represents the sublimation of masculine sexuality. The ambiguity operates in both directions, positive and negative: if old age diminishes virility, it also transmutes it. The negative sign becomes positive because the grandfather owns a treasure no less esteemed than virility, a library. Virility is life that engenders life, but life subject to time and death. In contrast, books, also a masculine sign, do not age; they are congealed time, sexuality purified of any accidents of event, procreation, or death. Books are the answer to the carnality of the mother and the aggressive sexuality of men.

Her grandfather's books opened the doors to a world which neither her mother nor her sisters could enter: a man's world. A world, paradoxically, closed to most men, even to Diego Ruiz Lozano and her father. A world of clerics, scholars, and elderly men where the aggressiveness of masculine sexuality disappeared or was transformed. The function of books was manifold: compensation for the original double flaw, her illegitimate birth and her father's absence; substitution for the dominating presence of the intruder Diego Ruiz, through books that are gentled and purified sexuality; and sublimation of sexuality by asexual, nonfleshly, ideal virility. Sublimation through culture resolved her conflict for a time. The cost was great: letters—the signs of things—took the place of things. From then on Juana Inés lived in a world of signs, and she herself, as seen in her portraits, became more and more a sign What did that sign say? This is the question she asked herself until she died, and the question this book attempts to answer.

The world of books is a world of the elect, where material obstacles and everyday risks diminish until they evaporate almost completely. The true reality, books say, is ideas and the words that signify them; reality is language. Juana Inés inhabits the house of language. That house is peopled not by men and women but by beings more real, more enduring, and more consistent than those of flesh and blood: ideas. The house of ideas is stable, secure, solid. In this fierce and changing world one place is unassailable: the library. There Juana Inés finds not only refuge but a space that replaces the home, with its conflicts and its ghosts. The decision years later to enter the convent is easier to understand in the light of that childhood discovery. The convent is the equivalent of the library, as she herself indicates in her *Response* to the Bishop of Puebla. In turn, convent and library are compensation for the stepfather and substitute for the father. And they fill the same emotional need, since cell and library are rooted in the same soil of infantile desire.

It is no accident that the Spanish language calls the womb the "maternal cloister." In cloistering herself, Juana Inés completes her withdrawal. It is a return to the infantile state. The cell-library is the maternal cave, and to enclose oneself in it is to return to the world of our origin. Childhood autoerotism is an attempt to restore the prenatal paradise in which there is no distinction between subject and object. Reading eventually replaces autoerotism: in the passivity of reading, subject and object fuse again, on a higher level. In reading, the self can finally expand and sway like an object; the subject alternately contemplates and forgets itself, sees itself in what it reads and is seen by it. The cell and the library are rhythmic time: a return to the cradle gently rocking on the tide of being.

The analogy between reading and the original situation can be extended. To begin to live, to grow, is a painful process: our life begins as a separation and ends in an uprooting. In the prenatal world desire and satisfaction are one and the same; birth means disjunction, and therein lies the punishment of having been born. That punishment is also the source of self-awareness: we sense our ego as distinct from the *other*. But there is a marvelous substance that suspends the conflict between desire and satisfaction: maternal milk. In it pleasure and necessity are joined. Nursing narrows the gap between subject and object. Unity is reestablished and for a moment one and *other* are indistinguishable. In an image that is doubly admirable—for its visual precision and its spiritual insight—Hölderlin says that the child hangs from its mother's breast like fruit from the branch. So it does: the child again becomes part of the body from which it was born. The substance that heals the wound is milk, maternal sap.

Popular metaphors are unfailingly precise: if we love a person we say that we drink her in with our eyes. Substituting the eye for the mouth as the organ of desire is part of the vital process; the expression "drink in with our eyes," by its plasticity and energy, is a metaphor that not only evokes but convokes the primal state. In turn, reading is a metaphor of that metaphor: with his eyes the reader drinks in the milk of wisdom and, precariously, reestablishes in the sphere of imagination and thought the broken unity between subject and object. The reader places his consciousness in abeyance and delves deeply into an unknown world. Does he go in search of himself? He goes, rather, in search of the place from which he was torn. All reading, even when it ends in disagreement or a yawn, begins as an attempt to regain wholeness. However avid for novelty the reader may be, what he vaguely seeks is recognition, the place of his origin.

Reading is a double metaphor. On the one hand it reproduces the original infantile state: writing is the magic milk with which we try to dispel the separation between subject and object. On the other hand, it reminds us of an ancient and complex analogy. Since the beginning of time man has seen in the starry sky a living body bathed in rivers of shining, fiery milk; this vision of an immense female body in the cosmos is closely allied to another: stars and constellations combine in celestial space to trace figures, signs, and forms. Primordial milk is transformed into a vocabulary, the starry sky is a language. Stellar milk is destiny, and the figures traced by the stars are those of our history. Milk is life and knowledge. As old as astrology, this metaphor has marked our civilization; it has been sign and design. Sign is design, and the sentences written by the stars are man's history: the signs of the stars are the milk we suck as children, and that milk contains everything we are and everything we will be.

Reading the sky or its double, the page, drinking the stellar milk, will not undo the knot of fate, but can at least help us understand our condition: it can give us knowledge, if not freedom. In a hierarchical society like Sor Juana's, in which birth determined name and rank and was also the basis of social order, learning—the milk of wisdom—was one of the surest recourses against the misfortune of a plebeian or illegitimate birth. For Juana Inés reading undoubtedly served that healing function: learning cleansed her of her bastardy. More than once she must have remembered the infant Hercules and Jupiter's strategy in bestowing divinity on him. In a book that was widely read in her time, which she, an enthusiast of treatises on mythology, must have read and reread—I am referring to *Teatro de los dioses de la gentilidad* (*Theater of the Pagan Gods*) by the Franciscan Baltasar de Vitoria—the origin of the Milky Way is explained:

> As Hercules was illegitimate, and a bastard, being the son of the god Jupiter and of Alcmene, wife of Amphitryon, and was of a diminished and only partial divinity . . . it was his father's wish to make him legitimate and wholly a god, to confer the divinity lacking to him . . . and so that Jupiter might count him as one among the gods, and that he not lack for anything, he waited until one day he found his wife Juno sleeping, and charged the goddess Pallas to bring the sleeping child to be suckled by the

sleeping goddess, but as the child [took] the breast greedily, the goddess
awakened, and when she saw the theft that was being made of her milk
she drew back angry and offended; as she pulled her breast from the child's
mouth, milk spilled across the sky and, curdling and clotting, formed the
Milky Way.[5]

Hercules' legitimation through the theft of divine milk is replicated in
Juana Inés' reading her grandfather's books without her family's knowledge.

The drops of stellar milk are the syllables that write our destiny. In
the syllables of those constellations, St. Augustine and Freud read the
signs of the life urge and the death wish: the deification of the ego and
the fascination for nothingness, damnation, and death. But if reading
those signs does not produce happiness—we cannot return to the paradise of the prenatal state, nor ascend, like Hercules, to immortality—it
does offer the only freedom within our reach: that of self-knowledge.
Sor Juana reads in her cell-womb-library, and that reading is a liberation. Enclosure is transformed into a universe of signs, and the cloister
opens toward a limitless space: the sky. It is a pulsing space filled with
signs: the constellations are letters, and the letters form an intricate network of roads and paths, labyrinths and spirals. Reading is a pilgrimage,
a "going toward." The reader not only deciphers the letters but walks
along the paths traced by the writing. Following them, he leaves the
cloister that enclosed him and wanders through the open spaces. Reading is freedom, and as the reader reads, he reinvents the very things he
reads, and so participates in universal creation. Or, as Sor Juana says in
a glowing line, "May syllables be composed by the stars." The stars
compose sentences but it is she who writes them. The return to infancy
is resolved in transcending the infantile state, and through knowledge
narcissism is dissolved in self-criticism. The cell-library completes infancy and at the same time exorcises it.

The image of the library as the refuge where Juana Inés' emotions are
enfolded and where her mental activity unfolds must be completed by
another image that bears on will and character: library as treasure
house. Every treasure has its guardians, its dragons; every treasure is
barred in a castle or buried in a cave. The image of the treasure calls up
the figure of the hero and his exploits. These exploits are epic violations,
heroic profanations. Juana Inés must storm the fortress and take possession of knowledge, as the pirates of her time sacked captured galleons.
Knowledge is transgression. She herself says so: she reads all books and

there are "not enough punishments, or reprimands, to prevent me." The transgression is a movement toward maleness. As a girl, she cuts her hair and wants to wear men's clothing; as a young woman, she neutralizes her sex beneath the habits of the nun; as an adult, in her great poem *Primero sueño* (*First Dream*) she identifies with the hero Phaethon. Such is the eminently social and not psychosomatic origin of masculinity: books are forbidden wealth and possessing such treasure denotes a transgression; these circumstances are imposed on Juana Inés not so much by biology as by the nature of the society she lives in. The library is a treasure consisting of books made by men, collected by men, and distributed among men. To possess that collected learning, she must do what all thieves do, not excluding the heroes of myth: disguise herself. Masculinity is a disguise imposed on Juana Inés by society, as is her profession as a nun. Her bastard origins and her father's absence lead her to the library, and the library, to the convent. In this way social and personal psychological circumstances fuse. Her life is a series of choices, imposed by necessity, that she adopts with open eyes.

The choice of Phaethon as a model parallels the impossibility of distinguishing between the personal and the social, freedom and fate. Like her, Phaethon is a bastard, son of Apollo and the nymph Clymene. But the theme of honor and of Phaethon's attempt to prove his honor through rash action is not Sor Juana's theme, although it must have influenced her choice of the young hero as an archetype. She is excited by Phaethon because he is the transposition, in the mythic world, of her childhood state, even of her entire life. To learn is audacity, violence: the library is transformed into open space, like the mental sky of *First Dream,* from whose height plummets the overreaching youth, struck down by Zeus. The sky and its analogue—the page on which the letters of the poem are constellations—become battlefields. The figure of Phaethon falling from the heights, one of the most intense and least abstract images of *First Dream,* is a metaphor of her transgression: the audacity that prompts the admonitions of her elders. At the end of her life the situation repeats itself: the same audacity is cause for punishment by her superiors. Learning as transgression implies punishment of learning. For most of the Spanish poets of her era, Phaethon is an example of imprudence and its punishment. For Sor Juana that punishment is a consecration.

The sky Phaethon falls from is a verbal sky, the strophes of *First Dream.* A space filled with verbs, nouns, and adjectives, space traversed by the circular movement of tropes and metaphors: the imaginary space of solitude. A double solitude: the reader's and the self-taught writer's. In the *Response* Sor Juana complains again and again that she studied alone, she had no teachers, her only confidants were mute books. And mirrors, she could have added. Her poetry is filled with mirrors and the companions to mirrors, portraits. True, mirrors and portraits are baroque commonplaces and appear in all the poets of the period; even Góngora's monstrous Polyphemus sees himself portrayed in the "neutralities" of the mirror of the sea and is amazed: that single eye in his clouded forehead is the sun itself in the center of the sky. In Juana Inés the function of mirrors and portraits is both rhetorical and symbolic. For her the aesthetic of mirrors is also a philosophy and a morality. The mirror is the agent for the transmutation of infantile narcissism into self-contemplation; through a process analogous to reading, which converts reality into signs, the mirror turns the body into an image made of reflections. In the mirror, the body becomes simultaneously visible and untouchable. It is the triumph of eyes over touch. Subsequently, the image of the mirror is transformed into an object of knowledge. From eroticism to contemplation and from contemplation to criticism: the mirror and its double, the portrait, are a theater where seeing is metamorphosed into learning. A learning that to the baroque sensibility is disillusioned learning.

In many poems Juana Inés takes delight in the dialectic between the portrait and the model, the image in the mirror and the original, appearance and reality. The true reality is that of appearance. Both are copies of essence, but appearance is more real than reality because it is more pure; I mean, less subject to accident and contingency. Nevertheless, there is an interlocutor, invisible but eloquent, that criticizes appearance: time. The sonnet to her portrait, a portrait painted with "false syllogisms of colors," is a variation of a courtly and funereal theme: the coquette and the skull. At the crux of the baroque opposition between flesh and skeleton, Sor Juana places thought: the mirror's reflections are also mental reflections. Portraits and mirrors are emblems of speculation. The transmutation is radical: the appearances that have become reflections are resolved into a cluster of conceits. Although the essence of the world is ideal and intellectual, appearances are borne and flow away on the current of time. The conceit is nothing but the ultimate reflection on the vanity of things and the world. The conceit shines for a moment in the page-mirror and vanishes; like everything and everyone, it is time being dissipated.

Implicit in Juana Inés' childhood situation were the events of her adult life: renunciation of marriage; the cell-library of the convent; rebellion against authority; and even the argument of *First Dream*. I am not suggesting a rigid psychological determinism but pointing out the conjunction between character and social circumstances. This conjunction does not exclude freedom, although within fairly narrow limits; we are the critics as well as the accomplices of our fate. The life and work of Juana Inés can be summed up in a single sentence: knowledge is a transgression committed by a solitary hero who then is punished. Not the glory of knowledge—denied to mortals—but the glory of the act of knowing. Transgression demands masculinization; in turn, masculinization resolves itself into neutralization, and neutralization, as we have seen, into a return to femininity. Sor Juana's ultimate victory is to adopt the Neoplatonic maxim: souls have no sex. She arrives at this victory by the same process that leads her from self-contemplation to self-knowledge, from the mirror to the book, and from the book to writing. Twists and turns of fate: the dialectic of infantile desire in its crystallizations, repressions, and sublimations, opens out into the image of the library and the cell. Opens out and, as in the figure of the seashell, closes in: Juana Inés constructs her spiral house—her work—with the very substance of her life. Every turn is an ascent toward knowledge, and every turn encloses her further in herself. The image of the shell finally evaporates: Sor Juana is alone in the vast expanse of her lucid dream. The library vanishes like the obelisks and pyramids of the chimerical Egyptian landscape evoked in *First Dream*.

7

The Trials of Juana Inés

ON THE RESPONSE TO SOR FILOTEA DE LA CRUZ there is a gap: Juana Inés passes abruptly from her childhood to her entrance into the convent of San Jerónimo. She thus skips over a decisive period of her early life, including her years in the viceregal court. According to Father Calleja, she was sent to Mexico City when she was eight "to live with her grandfather, where she fed her hunger for learning with a number of books she found in his home, books that had no other use than to encumber a writing desk." Sor Juana places the episode of her grandfather's books prior to her departure for Mexico City and underlines that fact by saying that as a consequence of her reading, when she reached the capital "many marveled not so much at my natural wit as at my memory, and at the amount of learning I had mastered at an age when many have scarcely learned to speak well." But in one detail Sor Juana and Calleja agree: she went to Mexico City when she was still a child of about eight or ten. Pedro Ramírez, her grandfather, died in January of 1656, and Juana Inés undoubtedly left the hacienda of Panoayán shortly thereafter. Early in 1669, when she was twenty, she entered the convent of San Jerónimo; so she had lived some twelve years on her own, first with relatives and then at court. The relatives who received Juana Inés in Mexico City were her maternal aunt Doña María Ramírez and her husband, the wealthy Juan de Mata.

Why was she sent to Mexico City, far from her mother and sisters? Was she unwanted at home? About the time of Pedro Ramírez' death a new man had entered his daughter Isabel's life: Captain Diego Ruiz Lozano. As I have said, the first child of Isabel Ramírez and Diego Ruiz

Lozano was born in those years. That may be the reason why Isabel decided to send Juana Inés to live with the Matas. If my hypothesis is correct, 1656 was a pivotal year in her fate: her departure for Mexico City coincided with the disappearance of her grandfather and the appearance of her half brother, Diego. These two events must have marked her deeply. It is not impossible, furthermore, that Juana Inés' presence on the hacienda of Panoayán was not entirely to Diego Ruiz Lozano's liking, if, in fact, he did live there once Pedro Ramírez died. We do not know whether her older sisters, María and Josefa, also Asbaje's children, were sent away to live with other relatives. In any case, only the death of her grandfather and the presence of her mother's new lover can explain why, when still a child, Juana Inés lived away from home with wealthy relatives.

What kind of life did she lead in the Mata home? What were her duties? We do not know. However affectionate her aunt and uncle and cousins may have been, she must often have felt lonely. Solitude again presents itself as her natural element, her native state: Juana Inés is a plant that grows in arid land. Her way through the world is a separation from that world and a delving into herself. During the years spent in the Mata home she must have completed the psychological process of withdrawing into herself. Added to the feeling of being unwanted in her own home, almost surely, was the pain of being a ward. Even if she did not suffer humiliation—how can we ever know?—it is certain that she soon realized she had no place in the world. Study, more than her relations with her family, was again her shield against others and against herself. Through Calleja we know that she learned Latin in twenty lessons and that her teacher was Martín de Olivas, to whom she later dedicated an elaborate acrostic sonnet comparing him to a no lesser figure than Archimedes.

I have spoken of solitude, not isolation. Juana Inés' life in the Mata home was far from that of an anchorite; one can be lonely amid the hubbub of the world, and that was probably true in her case. The testimony of Calleja is conclusive: "Rumors flew of an ability never yet seen in one of so few years; and keeping pace with her years, so grew her cleverness, thanks to her care for her studies, and likewise her comely appearance, thanks to the care of nature alone, which in this case did not wish to confine such subtlety of spirit in a body that would greatly envy it, or like a miser conceal such treasure by hiding it in rocky soil." Her portraits and her repute confirm Calleja's words: Juana Inés was not only clever but pretty. Somewhat coquettishly, she paints herself in the beautiful and cultured Doña Leonor, the heroine of her secular play *Los empeños de una casa* (*The Trials of a Noble House*), 388:

> To tell you I was born with beauty
> will be forgiven, I presume,
> this truth is witnessed by your eyes
> and proved as well by misfortune.

Leonor is beautiful, clever, and poor, exactly like Juana Inés. But there is a difference: Leonor lives with her father, Juana Inés has no one. Her popularity was a two-edged sword since, as Calleja says colorfully, Juana Inés ran the risk that "her cleverness would subject her to unhappiness and, no less unhappily, her beauty to pursuit." Whether because her relatives thought that she would find her place at court or because they did not want the responsibility of having in their home a prodigy as fragile as Juana Inés—beautiful, virginal, and unprotected—they took her to the viceregal palace and presented her to the newly arrived Vicereine, Doña Leonor Carreto, Marquise de Mancera. Juana Inés had spent eight years with the Matas and was fifteen when the new Viceroy and his wife arrived in Mexico (1664). The intelligence, the charm, and possibly the helplessness of the girl immediately impressed the Marquise. Juana Inés was at once admitted into her service, "which she entered," says Calleja, "as the lady Vicereine's favorite."

DON ANTONIO SEBASTIÁN DE TOLEDO, Marquis de Mancera, was an ambitious and astute politician. He was very close to Queen Mariana of Austria and owed to her in great part his long and ultimately brilliant career. His wife was lady-in-waiting to Queen Mariana from the time of Mariana's arrival in Madrid and her marriage to Philip IV (1649). Undoubtedly his wife's origins won him the post: like so many of the Madrid aristocracy of the time, Leonor Carreto's family was German. Her father had served the Emperor of Austria as an ambassador and died in Madrid in 1651 while carrying out his duty. In 1680 her brother, Otón Enrique Carreto, Marquis de Grana, once more represented his country, serving as Emperor Leopold's ambassador at the court of Charles II. The Marquis de Mancera and the Marquis de Grana were friends and allies in the political intrigues of that era: beyond their kinship, they were united by common interests, since both belonged to the Austrian faction and had suffered the hostility of John of Austria, bastard brother of

Charles II.[1] Don Antonio Sebastián de Toledo aspired to be chancellor of state, and the viceroyalty of New Spain was a steppingstone to that position. So in 1664, already fifty-three years old, he obtained the post, undoubtedly aided by his well-connected wife. The next year Philip IV died and his widow became regent. Mancera was an able administrator and a prudent Viceroy, but contemporary chronicles remember him less for his political abilities—all the more notable as those were the years of great misgovernment in Madrid—than for an obsequious indiscretion: in 1666 he gave the Queen a filigree box containing a thousand duros of four pesos each, and Mariana promptly passed on the gift to her favorite and first minister, the German Jesuit Juan Evardo Nithard.[2] The incident confirms that the absolute monarchy conceived of the state as a personal patrimony.

If Mancera was an astute courtier and skillful politician, Leonor Carreto was clever, vivacious, haughty, and perhaps a bit saucy. Her brother, the Marquis de Grana, had the reputation of being both intelligent and obese; she was known only for the former. She was blonde, beautiful, and, like her husband, fond of luxury. The couple were famous for their extravagance, more with state money than with their own fortune: the Marquis de Mancera left a deficit in the public treasury of over a hundred thousand pesos. They were also criticized for always arriving late at religious services. In spite of all this, the Marquis demonstrated throughout his political career—in Mexico and during his long years at the Madrid court—subtlety, caution, and an uncommon capacity to survive political changes and upheavals.

Also notable was the couple's fondness for literature. Leonor Carreto was not an ordinary person; if she had been, she would not have taken such an interest in Juana Inés, nor would she have protected her so unhesitatingly. Her husband felt the same fascination, and many years later, back in Madrid, as Calleja reports, he still remembered his wife's young protégée. Juana Inés rapidly conquered Doña Leonor Carreto's affection. "The lady Vicereine," says Calleja, "could not live an instant without her Juana Inés." It has been said that Vicereine's affection for her was maternal. This is not probable: the Vicereine had a daughter of her own, who was married in Mexico in 1673.[3]

Leonor was slightly more than thirty years old when she came to New Spain, some fifteen years older than Juana Inés. But it was not so much the difference in age as the young criollo girl's defenselessness that must have influenced the Marquise's feelings. In spite of the fact that, strictly speaking, Juana Inés was not an orphan, her situation was not very different from an orphan's: she was illegitimate, away from home, lacking her father's protection. Perhaps the Vicereine's affection was a composite of selfishness and admiration, sympathy and pity. Juana Inés was an agreeable companion, obliging and discreet; to these utilitarian and mundane considerations was added amazement at a marvel of intelligence and learning; and to amazement, the pity a forsaken young girl inspires.

It was a relationship of superior to inferior, of protectress to protégée, but one in which there was also recognition of an exceptional young woman's worth. Obviously Juana Inés' intellectual gifts impressed the Vicereine no less vividly than her beauty. Calleja says that her attendance on the Vicereine did not take time from her studies because "talking to the lady Vicereine was a continuation of them." This confirms that Leonor Carreto loved literature and that she must have been a person of sensitivity and refinement. There have been celebrated masculine friendships based on the shared passion for ideas, the arts, or the sciences. But this experience, one of the highest we can aspire to, is not exclusively male: the relationship, tinged with mutual admiration, that joined these two women was such a friendship of the spirit. A friendship imbued—at least in its written expressions—with an exalted Platonism and sprinkled with homages of devoted obeisance. These sentiments of loving friendship were legitimized, in a manner of speaking, by the philosophical and literary conventions inherited from Renaissance Neoplatonism.

Did Leonor Carreto influence her young friend? In one of the three funerary sonnets she wrote on the death of her patroness—"Unhappy lyre whereon your music played . . ." (189)—Juana Inés hints that the Vicereine's advice and friendship had been helpful in her first attempts at poetry. Like her other poems dedicated to female friends, these poems are marked by a tone of passion both devoted and restrained. The passion in these sonnets to Laura—the poetic name Juana Inés gave to Leonor Carreto in an allusion to Petrarch and to their own Platonic sentiments—is less intense and more reserved than in the poems dedicated to María Luisa Manrique de Lara y Gonzaga, Countess de Paredes.

Juana Inés lived in the company of the Viceroy and Vicereine from the time she was sixteen until she was twenty—decisive years in a woman's life, especially at that time, when women were more precocious. The Manceras' court was brilliant, and numerous soirées, entertainments, and ceremonies were held in the palace. Although we do not know whether her duties in the service of the Vicereine provided an opportunity to meet young noblemen, Calleja tells us that she was surrounded by "the refined aura of flattery." He does not, of course, allude to any specific love affair, but it would be absurd to discount entirely flirtations and amorous play. Sor Juana's personality, her happy nature, her taste for the world, the pleasure she received and gave in social exchanges, her narcissism, and, finally, the flirtatiousness she never entirely lost, suggest this possibility. If the nun was worldly, why would she not have been so before she was bound by religious vows? In many poems she alludes to the parties and balls in the palace with a knowledge that is not secondhand. One example is the *romance* in which, as the subtitle says, "one of the ladies-in-waiting in the Viceroy's palace tells of drawing lots on New Year's" (36). In this courtly game the *caballeros* were distributed among the ladies by lot, an arrangement, says Sor Juana, in which pleasure and chance went hand in hand:

> [Then let the lots fall where they may,]
> for well we know, the Fairest here
> may draw the lot of anyone,
> but won will be by only one.

Juana Inés must have played this game while she lived in the palace. Other of her writings reveal a similar experience of flirtatious play: the *letras* to be sung and danced, the *redondillas, seguidillas, endechas, billetes, sainetes,* and secular plays.

In his introduction to volume 4 of Sor Juana's *Complete Works,* Alberto G. Salceda, in examining the poet's secular dramas, comments relevantly on one of the *sainetes,* skits, presented at the first performance of *The Trials of a Noble House.* The subtitle of the first *sainete* is "De palacio" ("At the Palace") and in it the characters, called "palace entities," compete for a rather strange prize: not the ladies' favor but their scorn.[4] Salceda thinks this is a kind of appendix to a hypothetical "treatise on love" scattered throughout Sor Juana's works. The *sainete,* this critic adds, is not "strictly about love, but about a simulacrum of love, curious and typical of its time, known by the designation *galanteo de palacio*" (palace flirtation). In truth, the *sainete* is not an exception; related themes and motifs appear in many other poems.

To give an idea of what the *galanteos de palacio* were, Salceda quotes a long description by the Duke de Maura.[5] Almost everything the Spanish historian says about the royal court in Madrid is applicable to the Mexican viceregal court, which closely imitated the former. From the time of Philip IV, when the royal seat was definitively established in Madrid, it was a common practice among the great families of the Spanish nobility to send their daughters to court as ladies-in-waiting to the Queen. The girls lived in the palace, participated actively in court life, and were present at all processions, receptions, balls, entertainments, and ceremonies. There is nothing more natural than that amatory relationships should have been formed between the Queen's ladies and the courtiers—except that, "as among the male assemblage there was a scarcity of young single men, as most were serving at some distance from the court, or had not yet acquired sufficient rank to frequent it, the stable or shifting couples that were constantly joining together, separating, changing, and interchanging, consisted usually of a married man and an unmarried woman." Those relationships "were entered upon by mutual consent" and were of course dissolved at the moment the status of the Queen's lady-in-waiting was changed by marriage.

The Duke de Maura's description merits some thought. The *galanteos de palacio* were an exception to the general rule. That rule prescribed that marriages were arranged by the families of the bridegroom and bride; social and economic considerations took precedence over the will or affections of the betrothed. Erotic relations—the domain of subjectivity and of powers indifferent, even contrary, to financial and social hierarchies—could not develop except outside matrimony and as a breach of the social order. Consent operated only in the liberated lives of the single men and, in the case of young noblewomen, in the *galanteos de palacio*. This custom is another example of the nature of love in the West, the extraordinary invention of our civilization.

From its inception, the idea of love in the West was linked to transgression; the institution described by the Duke de Maura is merely a variant of this general rule. In the seventeenth century transgression flowed within two strictly defined channels. One was social: amatory games that were the domain of members of the court. The second had to do with gender: there was a basic difference between what was permitted to men and what was permitted to women. That difference was determined by physiology: there was the danger that children would be born of those premarital unions. The freedom of the single man was almost unlimited, a fact that accounts for the large numbers of bastard children; on the other hand, the *galanteos* of the young noblewoman almost never resulted in procreation, whether because full sexual union was not consummated or because the lovers resorted to practices like coitus interruptus and, in secret, abortion. The *galanteos de palacio* were an institution that simultaneously and contradictorily stimulated erotic freedom and limited its realization. The contradiction cut deeper: on the one hand, infractions were encouraged and, tacitly, approved; on the other, an insurmountable obstacle was raised to their legitimation. The ladies' gallants were married and, should there be a child, the usual reparation of marriage could not be demanded. The dualism of this curious custom lay in the fact that the transgression was not legalized but was, nevertheless, approved.

The *galanteos de palacio* mark a moment in the erotic history of the West. The code of courtesy is intimately linked with the code of gallantry; both are attempts to regulate, within the enclosed space of the palace, the game of the passions, without drowning the passions but limiting as much as possible the havoc caused by their violence. The origin of courtesy and gallantry is found in Provence: the first courtly society of the West flowered there. Along with a philosophy and a physics of love, Provence, influenced by Arabic eroticism, elaborated an erotic code: courtly love.

The *galanteos de palacio* reproduce, although in a more frivolous way, the relationship between the ladies and troubadors of the twelfth and thirteenth centuries. But they invert the formula: in Provence it was the ladies who were married and their gallants unwed. This difference is revealing. Provence exalted woman, gave her a certain freedom, and placed her in a situation of relative autonomy in connection with men and male institutions. The defeat of Provence and of Catharist heresy was also the defeat of courtly love. In the fires ignited by Simon de Montfort and the Dominican inquisitors, the Catholic Church burned both Albigensian heretics and freedom for women. The difference between New Spain's *galanteos de palacio* and Provence's courtly love does not nullify their essential similarity. Both societies were characterized by two essential qualities that distinguish Western eroticisn from all other types, transgression and idealization. In New Spain we find extramarital relationships and a sexual union that was unconsummated or at least did not result in children; in the courtly love tradition, intense eroticization of social life—ceremonies and parties centering upon the illicit relations between ladies and gallants—and at the same time sublimation of erotic passion.

Platonism fits naturally within this social context: love ascends from body to soul—and souls, as Sor Juana never tired of repeating, have no sex. In its beginnings Western love was predominantly homosexual. I am thinking, of course, of Athens and of Plato, who was the first to confer philosophical and spiritual dignity on love, to convert it into a scale of knowledge and a form of contemplation. Among the Alexandrian and Roman poets, creators to no lesser degree than Plato and other philosophers of the myth and concept of love, erotic passion was fundamentally heterosexual—although bisexuality was not unknown—and was linked to jealousy, that is, to the will of the woman who was loved. The poets discovered something that Plato was unaware of: the freedom of the beloved. The reason is probably historical: in Alexandria and especially in Rome, women of the upper classes knew a freedom and autonomy—legal, economic, social, and erotic—that was unthinkable in Athens. For Plato the person who is loved, even in that person's most elevated form, is an object, whether of pleasure or of spiritual contemplation; for Catullus and Propertius, the beloved is a free entity, a human being with whom we undertake a difficult relationship in which our own freedom is exercised and compromised. For Plato love is knowledge; for the poets, acknowledgment.

Antiquity bequeathed to us the two central notes in our idea of love: we love a person's body but also, and above all, we love the soul; and that person, in possessing a unique soul, is a free being and not an object. The roots of unique love are found in this idea of the individual soul that dwells in every body. The history of love is indissolubly linked to the history of the soul. When they discovered the soul—"that drop of foreign blood in Greek culture," as Erwin Rohde says—philosophers discovered love: human beings are unique because their body is the house (or prison) of a soul, that immortal spark. To the ancient world woman was an object or a function: courtesan, mother, pythoness. Platonism, and, especially the love poetry of Catullus and Propertius, decisively transformed the amorous relationship by converting the beloved into a subject with a soul, that is, a person possessing a free will.

Poetic imagination formulated for the first time an enigma that has fascinated the West and served as the theme of our poems, novels, comedies, and tragedies: love is a strange combination of fate and freedom. Through the power of a philter or other magic that paralyzes or changes our will, we can fall in love with someone unworthy, even perverse, as Catullus tells us repeatedly. Thus the problem of the existence of evil and its terrible attraction also appears in love, however scandalous this may have been to Plato and his disciples. If love as fate brings us face to face with the mystery of evil and suffering—why do we love our damnation?—love as freedom confronts us with another, no less terrible, mystery: the transmutation of subject into object, and of object into subject. Again: in love we seek not so much knowledge, as Plato desired, as acknowledgment; when we choose the object of our love we want that person also to choose us. The dialectic of erotic choice makes a subject of the object and vice versa. Love proposes an impossibility, but that impossibility is the condition of love: making a me of you and a you of me.

The Arabs inherited Platonism, incorporated it into Sufi mysticism, and transmitted it to the Provençals. Through the heirs to Provence—Cavalcanti, Dante, Petrarch—this conception reached the Neoplatonic Florence of the Medici, where, reformulated, it would become the spiritual sustenance of the great modern poets and novelists. Love is a spiritual experience for us of the West; furthermore, it is a road that leads to the contemplation of essences or the union with true reality. That is why it is not synonymous with procreation: it is a transgression—also a sublimation—of the social order as represented by marriage and family. Although originating in the body and indissolubly bound to it, love in its essence is spiritual.

All these concepts, as they were reelaborated through Renaissance Neoplatonism and through sixteenth- and seventeenth-century Hispanic poetry and theater, reappear in the writing of Sor Juana. For example, the idea of love as a spiritual passion that transcends the sexes is found as early as Marsilio Ficino's letters to his friends. From this perspective Juana Inés' impassioned poems to María de Gonzaga, Countess de Paredes, will seem less strange to modern readers.

Although inspired in a philosophy of love that goes back to Provence, the *galanteos de palacio* were meant to introduce a little order into a closed society in which individuals of both sexes were forced to live in a certain intimacy, not to illustrate an idea about love. More than an ideology of love, they formed a code of erotic coexistence. The *galanteos de palacio* were part of what could be called society's "hygiene of the passions." In a certain way, institutions of that nature were (and are) the counterpart and complement to prostitution. All erotic rites are socialized sexuality; the *galanteos de palacio* were sexuality transformed into theater: a ballet of the passions, a sexual ceremony that evoked the strutting of peacocks in the same way that tourneys were a metaphor for combats between stags. Tourneys belong to the last stage of feudal society; the *galanteos de palacio* represent the world of seventeenth- and eighteenth-century court society. In one case, an allegory of erotic combat; in the other, a dance of male and female planets around a sun-king.

All the time she was lady-in-waiting to the Vicereine, Juana Inés participated in these worldly rites; before being converted into the conceits of her poems, they were experiences she had lived. Here it is appropriate to correct another of the errors many of her biographers have fallen into, the assumption that her rank as lady-in-waiting to the Vicereine offered her the possibility of marriage. The Matas placed her in the viceregal palace either because they wanted to rid themselves of the responsibility of having her in their home or so that Juana Inés would gain polish at court—not, in any case, for her to marry. Marriage was eliminated because the gallants were almost always married. Most important of all, marriages were arranged between heads of family, and central to the negotiations was something Juana Inés did not have—a dowry.

Juana Inés' status at court must have been brilliant. Her status, not her situation. The first was due to personal merits: beauty, discretion, elegance; the second is based in the social hierarchy: name, rank, fortune. The former is transitory; the latter is engraved in the unchanging order of court society. Juana Inés moved nimbly among the palace whirlwinds and soon became one of their centers. Her preeminence derived not only from her virtues but also, I venture to say, from one of her least admirable character traits: her taste for flattery and fondness for a none-too-subtle adulation of the powerful. This unfortunate inclination is, in addition, a further proof of her narcissism and coquetry, and also of her psychic insecurity. At the same time, that insecurity had its roots in her social circumstances: the irregularity of her birth, her lack of resources, and, most decisively, the absence of family. If it is true that adulation flowers in hierarchical societies, it is also true that adulators are recruited from among those who have no fixed place in society.

Her diplomatic arts, her beauty, her vivaciousness, and her sunny nature do not entirely explain the secret of her popularity. Intelligence and learning were the keys that opened the doors of viceregal society to her. From the time she was very young she revealed an extraordinary mastery in writing verse. Her first two datable poems (185 and 202), written during her years at court when she was about eighteen, before entering the convent, are surprising in their perfection of form and sureness of hand. I am referring to the funeral sonnet in honor of Philip IV (1666) and to the poem dedicated to the priest Diego de Ribera (1667). In *The Trials of a Noble House* (388) she portrays herself in the tale told by Doña Leonor:

> Such was my eagerness to learn,
> from my earliest inclination,
> that studying far into the night,
> and with most eager application,
> I accomplished in a briefer span
> the weary toil of long endeavor,
> with diligence, commuting time
> through the fervor of my labor;
> within a very little time
> I was the target of all eyes,
> admired, the center of attention,
> so immoderately eulogized
> that laurels won through industry
> were glorified as gifts of God.
> I was, through all my native land,
> recipient of praise and laud,
> the quality of veneration
> formed by communal acclaim;
> and as the things that all were saying,
> to good purpose, or in vain,
> by elegance of face and bearing
> were not in any way gainsaid,
> too soon, a general superstition
> was so insistent and widespread
> that the idol they'd created
> now the people deified.
> To foreign lands, to distant realms,
> Fame spread the tidings far and wide,
> and the persuasion distance lends
> gave credence to these false reports.
> Then Fervor, wearing spectacles
> whose lens reality distorts,
> saw talents of most modest worth
> disproportionately magnified.

What is notable, apart from the vanity these lines reveal, is the clarity of Sor Juana's vision of fame and its ambiguous enchantment: name and renown are both blessing and damnation. This is one of the fundamental themes of the *Response;* it also appears in some of her best sonnets and *romances.*

Calleja tells a curious anecdote that corroborates what Sor Juana says about herself. Although Calleja's account seems to be at least in part a pious invention—it suggests a transposition of the episode of the child Jesus before the learned sages of the temple—it is good evidence. The Marquis de Mancera never forgot Juana Inés, and many years after he left Mexico he told Calleja, in the Jesuit's words:

> The honorable Marquis de Mancera, who is living today—and may he live many more years [Calleja was writing this in 1700, five years after Sor Juana's death]—has twice told me that as he was uncommonly astonished on seeing such diversity of knowledge in Juana Inés . . . he wanted to ascertain the truth and to learn whether such amazing wisdom was innate or acquired . . . and so he gathered together one day in his palace all the men of letters in the university and the city of Mexico. They numbered some forty, of varied professions, such as theologians, scripturists, philosophers, mathematicians, historians, poets, humanists, and not a few of those we like facetiously to call "parlor wits," those who although not having as the purpose of their studies a university appointment, nevertheless, with their native wit and general erudition, are wont, and not in vain, to judge soundly on all things . . . So on the appointed day they gathered for this curious and remarkable competition, and the honorable Marquis testifies that the human mind cannot conceive what he witnessed, for he says that "in the manner that a royal galleon"—here I transcribe His Excellency's words—"might fend off the attacks of a few canoes, so did Juana extricate herself from the questions, arguments, and objections these many men, each in his specialty, directed to her." What study, what understanding, what mental prowess, and what memory must be necessary for this!

Calleja concludes by saying that Juana Inés had confirmed in one of her letters that what the Marquis de Mancera had told him was true.

At that moment, just when her learning and her wit had captured the admiration of the learned and of court society, adulated for her beauty and cleverness, at nineteen years of age, she entered the convent of San José de las Carmelitas Descalzas (the Discalced Carmelites) as a novice. The order was severe, and after a brief time a frightened Juana Inés returned to the world. Her Catholic biographers maintain that she left for reasons of health, but there is not a single text or document to prove this supposition, except for one rather vague allusion by Father Oviedo, Núñez de Miranda's biographer. Once more we are faced with a pious legend. The truth is that Juana Inés was unable or unwilling to bear the harshness of the order. Calleja omits this episode, and if it had not been for Luis González Obregón, a modern scholar, we would still not know that she spent three months with the Carmelites. If the rigor of the order discouraged her, it did not change her mind. A year and a half later, not without considerable doubt and thought, she took her vows—but this time in an order known for the mildness of its discipline. On the twenty-fourth of February of 1669 she took the veil in the convent of San Jerónimo. She was not yet twenty-one.

8

Taking the Vows

$\mathcal{E}$VERYONE WHO HAS APPROACHED the figure of Sor Juana has asked the same question: why, when nothing in her life indicated a religious vocation and she was widely admired, did she leave the court and seclude herself in a convent? The answers are as varied as the interpreters. One of the answers, the most popular one, attributes Juana Inés' decision to an unhappy love affair. The hypothesis of a disappointment in love includes a broad range of interpretations: the beloved died; the beloved was beyond reach, because of Juana Inés' poverty, her illegitimate birth, or whatever; the beloved was unworthy, undistinguished; the beloved forsook her. All these and other suppositions are variants of the old romantic theme of the Obstacle. It is one of the ingredients—more exactly, it is *the* ingredient—of the traditional image of love. The necessary complement to the idea of love as transgression is that of love as Obstacle. This interpretation of Sor Juana's decision stems from a critical error: reading a baroque text through romantic eyes.

It is not possible, many critics allege, that Juana Inés could have lived in the whirlwind of the court for five years—the most impressionable years in a woman's life, when her whole being opens to her senses and her senses open to the outer world—and have emerged unscathed. I have already said that it would be absurd to discount the possibility of some curvetting and amorous play. She may have fallen in love or believed, as happens at that age, that she was in love. But no loves, happy or unhappy, profound or frivolous, drove her to the convent. Marriages were arranged between families, and the determining factors were social and financial considerations, not the will of the betrothed. In love or not, Juana Inés had no dowry and scarcely any family. Who was her father, and where was he?

And the *galanteos de palacio?* Those games, as we have seen, not only did not have marriage as an end but specifically excluded it. Neither was the nature of those games—erotic *rites de passage*—particularly favorable to what today we call romantic love. The testimony of one of the autobiographical sections of *The Trials of a Noble House* (388) will perhaps save me the need for further evidence. Through Doña Leonor, Juana Inés indirectly describes her situation at court:

> Amid such unrestrained applause,
> with my attention claimed by all
> in all the throng I could not find
> for my regard a worthy mark;
> and so, belovèd of so many,
> I took not one into my heart.
> My own virtue I defended
> in assemblies, fearlessly,
> with danger I avoided danger,
> with injury countered injury.
> With modesty that all admired
> I praised those who lauded me,
> and thus I countered my censure
> of my affability.

Juana Inés' description could not be more frank and confirms what I have said about the mores of the viceregal palace. At no moment does she speak of marriage or even invoke the possibility; her game is reduced to "defending her virtue." A dangerous game because it consists of not refusing absolutely, but refusing while fueling the fire. The nature of the *galanteos de palacio* places in doubt the existence of a tragic love affair. Further, Sor Juana's psychology militates against this hypothesis. In addition to her extreme intellectualism—adverse to married life—her attitudes toward men and women must not be forgotten. In her poems the former are ghosts, disembodied shadows; the latter, real presences. In an essay of 1950 I wrote that "it would be excessive to speak of homosexuality; it is not excessive to observe that she herself does not hide the ambiguity of her feelings." It is extremely difficult to have a clear idea about these feelings. The situation of a woman of her century and her means must be taken into account. An unmarried girl, especially one in Juana Inés' peculiar circumstances, who displayed her love for a man in public would have lost her reputation immediately; on the other hand, a loving friendship between women was permissible if they were of elevated rank and their sentiments idealized.

The argument based on hidden character traits may seem gratuitous, even fanciful. It is scarcely necessary to explain that the existence of repressed or sublimated tendencies, whether or not they were known to her, does not exclude the possibility of love for or love affairs with one or many men. I repeat: I perceive an ambiguity in Sor Juana's relations with some women friends, but those inclinations, as expressed in her poems, are synonymous with more complex sentiments, not with lesbianism. Gide said, "Only a simple way of thinking about feelings makes us believe that there are simple feelings." The undeniable attraction she felt for a few women could have been a sublimation of an impossible passion for a man, forbidden to her as a nun. But during her years as lady-in-waiting to the Vicereine, might she not have suffered a passion for one of the lords who attended the entertainments at court? I have already said that although the existence of such a passion seems doubtful, I do not entirely discount it. It is not impossible that Juana Inés fell in love while she lived in the palace, but that love, whether unhappy or happy, would not have been the cause of her profession as a nun. She was not eligible to be married because she lacked a dowry, a father, and a name. But why not accept what she herself tells us: that she felt no inclination toward marriage? We must make a careful distinction, as was made in her time, between love and matrimony. We tend to confuse them, but for Juana Inés and her century, they were totally separate. In her situation a love affair could not lead to marriage. Besides the lack of a dowry and a father, there was a further impediment: the lack of a vocation for marriage. We must accept the confidences she offered us. Sor Juana belonged to a class of women who, when it can be avoided, flee the married state. Antiquity bequeathed us two female archetypes, Venus and Diana. It is clear that Juana Inés' personality was closer to the second than the first: Diana is the goddess not of marriage but of the chaste and solitary life of the huntress. All this confirms what I indicated earlier: the real or supposed existence of one love or several could not have been a determining cause for her decision.

There is another, no less decisive, argument against a love affair: what documents do we have? There is no letter or any other indication that could be valid proof of such a consuming love. None of Sor Juana's contemporaries even hinted at the existence of a clandestine love. On this subject, as is natural, Sor Juana's silence is absolute. So is Calleja's.

Of course, there are the love poems. There are many, and some are very profound. All of them reveal a perfect knowledge of what could be called the dialectic of love: jealousy, coolness, absence, loss, requited love. Two reasons keep me from accepting the testimony of the poems. First, we do not know the dates of those *romances, endechas,* and sonnets. Second, the poetry of that period is not confessional poetry. Sincerity was a value for the romantics, as it is for us moderns; it was not so for the poets of the seventeenth century. Baroque poetry presents the reader with archetypical schemes of love and of the passions, but the reader must not or cannot infer that those texts have any confessional value.

The erotic knowledge revealed in Sor Juana's poems and secular plays is learning codified through tradition rather than the result of experience: a rhetoric, a casuistry, and even a logic. It has been said that a treatise on love may be derived from Sor Juana's poems, and this is true because they are conceits and archetypes, not confessions. Granted, several poems strike a note that seems to verge on confession. In general these are poems about solitude, not love, and poems in which the theme of half-stoic, half-Christian disillusion predominates. The sensual, impassioned, direct tone is found not in the love poems but almost always in those of loving friendship dedicated to Lysis and to other woman friends, such as the enchanting Belilla of a few unforgettable *endechas* (71). Coincidence or veiled homage: Belilla is the pet name of her niece and protégée, the novice Isabel María de San José, illegitimate like herself, whom she sheltered as a young girl and to whom she left on her death the revenue from two thousand gold pesos deposited in the convent.

Among the poems on sacred themes there is a *romance* (56) that contains lines many critics consider to be a true confession:

> Now I recall (were it not so!)
> how I loved in other days,
> it was madness far exceeded,
> immoderation, far outpaced;
> But as it was a bastard love,
> and of antitheses composed,
> oh, how readily it vanished
> once its defects were exposed.

Sor Juana immediately compares this love composed of antitheses to divine love. These are impressive verses and I am tempted to see them as an authentic confession, but I have one doubt: is this not a variant of one of the archetypes of the religious poetry of the age? The theme is traditional and so is the manner of treating it. Thus as testimony of a love affair its value is doubtful. Still, I am of a divided mind; as one critic has noted, there is a kind of ambiguity between the profession of love for God, the theme of the poem, and the sudden irruption of a personal memory. Oscillation between the fiction demanded by the genre and the confession of a lived experience. I realize that this interpretation is frag-ile: it is based on an impression, not on any real fact. But is that not enough? I find the entire poem disconcerting: some fragments are mark-edly theological, others fit the pattern of sacred verses, and in others the tone and expression seem to be from a poem on secular love. It is a disquieting mixture. But not even in this poem—much less the love poems—can we be sure the poet is referring to her personal experience. Sor Juana's love poems are illustrations of a metaphysic, an aesthetic, and a rhetoric that came from Dante and Provençal poetry, were inher-ited by Petrarch, and inspired the poets of the Renaissance and the Ba-roque period.

THE MAJORITY OF CATHOLIC CRITICS think that Juana Inés chose the religious life because of an authentic vocation, that is, because she heard the call of God. It is evident that Juana Inés was a sincere Catho-lic; her orthodoxy is not in doubt. But in her time the convents were filled with women who donned their habits because of worldly consid-erations and needs, not as a response to a divine call. Sor Juana's case was no different from that of girls today who seek a career that will offer both economic security and social respectability. The religious life, in the seventeenth century, was a profession. This did not imply impiety or lack of faith: the majority of clerics and nuns were sincere Catholics and modest Church functionaries. Women donned the habit when, because of family arrangements, lack of fortune, or for some other reason, they could not marry, or if they were alone in the world without the support of a male.

The convent was a haven. But not every woman could enter; it was necessary to have a dowry and belong to a reputable family. The cere-mony of taking the vows was solemn, with godparents, guests, music, and flowers. Poor women—widows, orphans, abandoned women— found refuge in the hospices founded in principal cities by the Church and by a few benevolent and wealthy patrons. The Bishiop of Puebla,

Manuel Fernández de Santa Cruz, founded two homes for the "many poor women who wished to keep intact the flower of their purity—but in their meekness feared to lose it either because they were very poor or very beautiful."[1] The biography of another benefactor contains this panegyric: "One cannot deny the heroism, the magnificence, of the work of cloistering women who . . . being unable to enter convents, shed tears in manifest peril in the lay world."[2] Entering the convent was a common solution in that time. The case of Sor Juana was not exceptional: in her own family, besides her niece Isabel María de San José, two daughters of her half sister Inés also took their vows in San Jerónimo.

Nothing in Sor Juana's earlier life reveals a particular religious disposition. During the years when she was lady-in-waiting to the Vicereine she distinguished herself for her beauty, her wit, and her learning, not her devotion. Nor, it must be admitted, did she demonstrate excessive piety during the twenty-six years she lived in San Jerónimo. In this sense the reproaches of Fernández de Santa Cruz and the much more severe recriminations of Núñez de Miranda were justified. Calleja himself, though reluctantly, cannot but recognize that Sor Juana was lukewarm in her devotions: "Twenty-seven years she lived the life of a nun without the seclusion that earns ecstatics their glory and good name but substantially fulfilling her religious obligations." Father Oviedo goes further and relates that her confessor Núñez de Miranda constantly counseled her to dedicate less time "to her renown and to continuing correspondence by spoken and written word with those outside." The *Response* corroborates what Calleja and Oviedo said.

In spite of everything I have just stated, the majority of Catholic critics, for reasons easier to understand than to justify, consider Juana Inés' decision to become a nun the expression of a spiritual conflict that was resolved in a genuine renunciation of the world. This question is crucial because it is inextricably linked to the other enigma of her life: the crisis of her last years. Robert Ricard is the critic who has argued the religious-vocation hypothesis with greatest rigor and coherence. For the French historian, Sor Juana's case is similar to that of Pascal: just as Pascal, in his first conversion, abandoned a worldly career to ascend to the "order of the spirit," Sor Juana left the viceregal court because of her eagerness for knowledge; in his second conversion, Pascal renounced learning to enter the "order of charity," and Sor Juana renounced knowledge for the love of God. Ricard is guilty of the error in reasoning called *petitio principii:* in order to prove there was a first conversion, he takes for granted the existence of a second. The truth is that the renunciation of learning at the end of her life was not a voluntary act; it was, rather, as will be seen, a humiliation imposed by ecclesiastical authorities following a battle of more than two years. As for the "first conversion": Juana Inés, unlike Pascal, could not renounce a worldly career she never had. She was a helpless girl alone in the world.

It is impossible to know Juana Inés' state of mind during the years immediately prior to her becoming a nun. But it is not impossible to try to reconstruct that moment and to glimpse the causes that precipitated her decision. *The Trials of a Noble House* can again give us some clues. The situation of Doña Leonor in the first act is a transference of Juana Inés' situation at court: she is beautiful, clever, cultivated, and "admired, the target of all eyes." Both Juana Inés and Leonor are poor, and both are semi-orphaned. Here the symmetry ends: Leonor is without a mother, while Juana Inés has no father. This difference determines the divergent directions their lives will take. Juana Inés lives without male protection; Leonor's father protects her and when her honor is endangered does not hesitate to demand satisfaction by marriage or by blood. Faithful to their symmetrically opposed destinies, Leonor marries and Juana Inés goes to a convent. Was the absence of a father so decisive, or was Sor Juana's play more a projection of her wishes and obsessions than an adaptation of her life?

In Juana Inés' situation during these years I note three basic and enduring circumstances, along with others that, although temporary, are in the end no less decisive. These basic circumstances are her bastardy, her poverty, and the absence of her father. None of them could be the sole reason for her becoming a nun, but each contributes powerfully to that outcome. There is, furthermore, a certain hierarchy to the causes. The least important perhaps was the bastardy, which did not prevent either of her sisters from marrying. If poverty was in fact a major obstacle, it was not insuperable, as the example of her sisters again shows. Nevertheless, there is a clear contrast between the fortunes of the daughters of Diego Ruiz Lozano, who was well-to-do, and those of the ghostly Pedro Manuel de Asbaje: Inés Ruiz Lozano married a university professor, and her sister, Antonia, a landowner; María and Josefa de Asbaje, abandoned by their husbands, lived unconventional lives and had children by different fathers. Pedro Manuel de Asbaje was a name; Diego Ruiz Lozano, a real presence. His will reveals him as a paterfamilias who loved his children and carefully guarded his property. When his daughters approached puberty, he took them from their mother and placed them in the convent of San Jerónimo under the care of their half sister Juana Inés. Later, he arranged marriages with men of good social position. The difference between the situation of Ruiz Lozano's daughters and that of Asbaje's must have made its impression on Juana Inés. It is understandable that the examples of her mother and her two sisters may have frightened her: was that what awaited a woman alone in the world? With more realism than her modern biographers, Father Calleja succinctly explains her predicament: "The good countenance of a poor woman is a white wall every fool wants to foul."

Sor Juana's will (February 23, 1669) contains a moving passage. In such documents novices renounced their possessions, and Juana Inés says: "I declare that in the keeping of Doña Isabel Ramírez, my mother, I have two hundred forty pesos of gold coins, which quantity was given and granted to me by Captain Don Juan Sentís de Chavarría: I declare them to be my worldly goods." Those coins were all her fortune. Who was this captain who made her a gift of the pesos, and what connection did he have with Juana Inés or with the other women in her family? None. Like her patron Velázquez de la Cadena, he was a rich and charitable man: Knight of the Order of Santiago, generous benefactor of the Colegio de San Gregorio, established by the Jesuits for the education of Indian nobility.[3] Chavarría made other donations, for pious as well as educational projects, all of them through his and Sor Juana's spiritual adviser, Núñez de Miranda, among them the gift of his hacienda, San José de Oculman, to the same Colegio. The mention of Chavarría in Sor Juana's will confirms what Father Oviedo said about the decisive intervention of Núñez de Miranda. The Jesuit not only allayed Juana Inés' moral scruples but obtained the gifts of money needed for her to enter the convent.

While she lived in the palace, Juana Inés must often have had these thoughts: I have no fortune, I have no name, I have no father. She was lady-in-waiting to the Vicereine, but viceroys occupied their posts for only a few years and then left, never to return. After the Marquis and Marquise de Mancera, who? Return to the Matas and live as a ward of that wealthy family? But would they accept her again? Besides, how could she forget that Juan Mata had specifically placed her in the palace, if not to get rid of her, at least with the intention that she make her own way in the world? When after spending three months in the harsh order of the Carmelites Juana Inés changed her mind and left the convent, she did not go to her home, or the Matas', but to the palace, to the Marquise de Mancera. This indicates that her only home was the palace. A temporary home, one that she would have to leave the day the Manceras returned to Spain.

Again and again her reflections must have led her to the same place: the convent door. Her protectress, Leonor Carreto, must have urged her to accept that solution. The fact that the Marquise and her husband attended the ceremony of Sor Juana's taking the veil is an indication that they favored the project and probably facilitated it. Who in that milieu would find it illogical or cruel that a pretty and unprotected twenty-year-old girl should seclude herself in a convent? I do not know whether another factor has been considered: it was not easy to enter a convent, and if Juana Inés had not spent those years in the viceregal palace, she might not have found a sponsor to pay her dowry. It might even be argued, without great exaggeration, that the palace was her stepping-stone to the convent. Perhaps her family placed her with the Vicereine with the idea that through her protection and connections Juana Inés would find a sponsor and benefactor.

The person who encouraged her with the greatest energy, sagacity, and authority, calming her fears and dissipating her doubts, was Father Antonio Núñez de Miranda. Theologian, professor of philosophy, and censor for the tribunal of the Inquisition, Núñez de Miranda was the confessor of the Viceroy and Vicereine, and so, says Oviedo, "often being in the palace, . . . offered to assist her in any way he was able." Núñez de Miranda had been rector of the famous Colegio de San Pedro y San Pablo and had the reputation of being a great homilist. These talents, and his post as censor for the Holy Office, had earned him renown. His special purview was nuns. He visited the convents frequently, he was spiritual adviser to many nuns, and he had written a handbook for them. It was surely because of his influence that the wealthy Pedro Velázquez de la Cadena paid Juana Inés' dowry (three thousand pesos, a sizable sum and more than her half sisters took to their husbands when they were married). Father Oviedo praises this talent of Núñez de Miranda's: "He negotiated dowries without number, and many were those that were settled by his industry and diligence, thus protecting many needy maidens and consecrating them as brides of Christ in the sacred seclusion of the cloister."[4]

Oviedo himself reports that from the moment Father Núñez met Juana Inés he had been zealous in her behalf. That zeal was so extreme, and the relations between the Hieronymite nun and the Jesuit so prolonged and complex, that Oviedo devotes an entire chapter of his biography of Núñez to describing them. In those pages he attempts to cleanse Núñez of the faults that many attribute to him, including the excessive harshness that led him to forbid her writing poetry and pursuing her studies. Sor Juana, on the other hand, he accuses of being ungrateful, conceited, and ungovernable. The polemical tone of those passages is revealing, and demonstrates that even then there was talk of the persecutions that clouded Sor Juana's last years. The theme of Sor Juana's unhappy relations with the Church hierarchy is not an invention of modern anticlericalism, as some have said; it comes to us from Sor Juana's own time. The break between the nun and her spiritual adviser was cruel, and even more cruel the reconciliation, which she achieved only with submission. But in the period before she became a nun, while Juana Inés vacillated, asking herself whether her intellectual passions were compatible with religious obligations, Núñez laid her scruples to rest and comforted her; he was not harsh but fatherly, obliging, not inflexible. Fishers of souls are awesome because they are also seducers. Oviedo records that when Juana Inés decided finally to take her vows, Núñez' joy was so great that he paid for the festivities and invited "the most notable and illustrious members of the ecclesiastical chapters and secular councils, sacred orders, and nobility of Mexico City, and on the eve of the profession arranged the altar lights with his own hands."[5]

The passages of the *Response* relating to her becoming a nun are memorable for their elusiveness and reticence. Sor Juana says something without saying it; with a gesture she erases what she has said, and as she is erasing it, says it again. It is worthwhile to reproduce this long and sinuous paragraph, in spite of the fact that it has been quoted many times:

> And so I entered the religious order, knowing that life there entailed certain conditions (I refer to superficial, and not fundamental, circumstances) most repugnant to my nature; but given the total antipathy I felt toward marriage, I deemed convent life the least unsuitable and the most honorable I could elect if I were to ensure my salvation. To that end, first (as, finally, the most important) was the matter of all the trivial aspects of my nature . . . , such as wishing to live alone, and wishing to have no obligatory occupation to inhibit the freedom of my studies, nor the sounds of a community to intrude upon the peaceful silence of my books.

For a complete understanding of this declaration two circumstances must be kept in mind: the person writing it is a nun, and she is writing to a Bishop, her superior, to defend herself from certain attacks and to justify her passion for profane literature. The passages must be placed within the general context of the *Response,* considering her innate passion for learning. Sor Juana's declaration has two parts: in the first she refers to the principal reason that led her to take the veil; in the second, she alludes to the incompatibilities between her intellectual vocation and life in a religious community. I shall address the latter in another part of this book. In regard to the former, Sor Juana states that with respect to the most important end—that is, her salvation—the religious state was "the least unsuitable and the most honorable" she could elect. Thus she proclaims the perfectly orthodox primacy of spiritual over temporal ends: we are in this world to save ourselves and win everlasting glory. But her decision to choose the convent is subordinate to a clause that determines the whole paragraph: "but given the total antipathy I felt toward marriage." This declaration is the heart of the *Response,* and not only of that document but of her entire life. Sor Juana was not oblivious of the fact that there are other roads to salvation and that among them, for women, the most normal and most often followed is marriage. Not for her. Thus the decision to become a nun is subordinate, and is a consequence of another, earlier, decision: antipathy to the married state. There is not a hint of an allusion to the call of God or to a spiritual vocation; with extraordinary frankness, Sor Juana expounds a rational decision: since she does not want to marry, the convent is the least unsuitable and most honorable way to ensure her salvation. The suitable way would have been marriage; the dishonorable, to live unmarried in the world, which, as Calleja says, would have exposed her to being the white wall fouled by men. Juana Inés' choice was not the result of a spiritual crisis or a disappointment in love. It was a prudent decision consistent with the morality of the age and the habits and convictions of her class. The convent was not a ladder toward God but a refuge for a woman who found herself alone in the world.

Up to this point I have examined the negative responses, so to speak, that may have motivated Juana Inés to become a nun. Those considerations were, as has been seen, strictly worldly, based on concerns that were as much financial as social and moral. The word that defines those concerns is not "saintliness" but "propriety." But her decision cannot be reduced to those reasons. We know that she was extremely hesitant and that, even once she had decided, the harshness of the Carmelite order frightened her and she left the convent. Núñez' arguments and counsel, as well as the moderation of the Hieronymite order, finally persuaded her. But that edifice of reasonable reasons was raised on something more fundamental: her antipathy to marriage. That was the vital foundation of her attitude. Was she sincere when she wrote this sentence? Or did she merely want to disguise the fact that for a girl in her situation the prospects for a good marriage were rather doubtful and that the cloister was preferable to the course her two sisters had followed? Sor Juana was not always truthful—again and again, for example, she stated that she was legitimate—but in this case we have no reason to doubt her sincerity. Her interests and passions coincided. Everything we know about her, and everything her work tells us, corroborates her disinclination toward marriage. It is easy to imagine her at court and in the cloister, dancing in a ballroom or singing in a choir, chatting in a garden or in a locutory; we know she experienced, enjoyed, and suffered the powerful emotions of literary glory, of loving friendship, and perhaps of love itself—but can we imagine her in a home with husband and children?

Why this antipathy to marriage? To think that she felt a clear aversion to men and an equally clear attraction to women is absurd. In the first place, because even if that supposition were true, it is not likely that while she was still so young she knew her true inclinations; in the second, because only by attributing to her an intellectual and sexual license more appropriate to a Diderot heroine than to a girl of Juana Inés' age and social class in New Spain could she cold-bloodedly have chosen as refuge an institution inhabited exclusively by persons of the sex that supposedly attracted her. No, her words, as I have stressed repeatedly, indicate little or no aptitude for domestic life. In our century more and more women, without renouncing love, have preferred not to marry. That was unimaginable in the seventeenth century; outside marriage there were but two roads: a life, at best, like that of Juana Inés' sisters, or the convent. I underscore once again that in the seventeenth century the word "marriage," except in plays, did not mean *love* but a married woman's life as it is described ideally by Fray Luis de León and satirically by Quevedo. Apart from this distaste for a life of hearth and home—because of what she saw as a child and an adolescent?—it is futile to try to learn what her true sexual feelings were. She herself did not know.

Antipathy to marriage is linked to another cause, which I find conclusive. From the beginning, from the years when she read her grandfather's books behind her family's back, the transposition and transmutation of her inclinations was at work: learning is the other, the positive, face of her antipathy to marriage. She does not want to marry because she wants to learn. She loves learning. She is sparing in details of the reasons for her repugnance for married life; on the other hand, with an effusiveness not totally free of coquettishness, she speaks at length of her eagerness for knowledge. The movement toward the masculine is mingled with the process of apprenticeship: in order to learn, one must be a man, or be like a man. Disguising herself as a man, cutting her hair, and, finally, neutralizing her sexuality beneath a nun's habits are sublimations or, better, translations of her wish: she wants to possess masculine values because she wants to be *like* a man. That "like" is a bridge and, simultaneously, the sign of distance that cannot be bridged. That is why in the second stage of the process, she burns the bridge, turns against men, defends women, and anticipates modern feminism.

Antipathy to marriage, love of learning, masculinization, neutralization: all these resolve into a no less powerful word, solitude. When it was imposed on her, she transformed it into an accepted, even chosen, destiny. First, a solitary child lost among her elders; later, a solitary girl in the bustle of the social world. She secluded herself in a convent not in order to pray and sing with her sisters but in order to live alone with herself. She was mistaken: she had exchanged the hubbub of the world for that of the cloister. But in 1669 the convent seemed to be the solution; if her destiny was learning, she could not be learned in the lay world either married or single. She could, on the other hand, be learned as a nun. The contradictions between her intellectual vocation and life in the midst of a religious community, although foreseen—as she recalls with a touch of bitterness in the *Response*—emerged later. I must add that even if she wished to live alone, she did not wish to live in isolation. She always loved intellectual communication, and this very communication—her living in continuing correspondence with the world outside—was what Núñez de Miranda most often censured her for. Alone but not isolated, Sor Juana lived in her world and with her world. The same is true of what I have called, somewhat inexactly, her "masculinity": it exists alongside the most intense femininity. If there is such a thing as a feminine temperament, in the most arresting sense of the word, it is that of Sor Juana. She fascinates us because the most extreme oppositions come together in her without ever completely blending. Perhaps this is the secret of her compelling vitality: few beings are as alive as she—after being buried for centuries.

As we have seen, in 1667 she entered the convent of the Carmelites as a novice, and a few months later, repentant, left the convent. Did she repent of her second and definitive choice? We will never know. Some of her poems reveal bitterness, anguish, discouragement, but do we not find the same emotions in the work of poets who lived in the world? She complained of the intrusions of her companions in the cloister; had she remained at court, would she not have been exposed to even more intolerable interference? The decision to become a nun was, in her circumstances, the best one, perhaps the only one, she could make. Nevertheless, she must have had moments of doubt and weakness. More than once she must have lamented being bound to an irrevocable solution. We moderns, accustomed to changing our occupation and way of life, cannot fully realize the meaning of a decision that binds us for a lifetime. This is the subject of a revealing sonnet (149). The title describes very well the terrible decisions that like hers cannot be appealed: "Spiritedly, She Considers the Choice of a State Enduring unto Death." The theme of glory in defeat—symbolized, as in *First Dream,* by the figure of Phaethon, her protector and hero—blends with her ungovernable longing for what her life might have been, but was not. With lucidity and melancholy Sor Juana considers the spirit that led her to choose a state that ends only with death. And it seems to her that, even at the risk of being struck down, it would have been loftier and more heroic to seize the reins of the chariot of the Sun and live a life exposed to danger:

> Were the perils of the ocean fully weighed,
> no man would voyage, or, could he but read
> the hidden dangers, knowingly proceed,
> or dare to bait the bull to frenzied rage.
> Were prudent rider overly dismayed,
> should he contemplate the fury of his steed
> or ponder where its headlong course might lead,
> there'd be no reining hand to be obeyed.
> But were there one so daring, one so bold
> that heedless of the danger he might place,
> upon Apollo's reins, emboldened hand
>   to guide the fleeting chariot bathed in gold,
> the diversity of life he would embrace
> and never choose a state to last his span.

Part Three

Sor Juana Inés de la Cruz
1669–1679

9

Life in the Convent

At THE END OF THE SEVENTEENTH CENTURY in Mexico City, according to Gemelli Carreri, who was there in 1698, there were twenty-nine religious communities of monks and twenty-two of nuns.[1] The population of the city numbered some twenty thousand Spanish and criollos and some eighty thousand Indians, mestizos, and mulattos. We should not be surprised by the numbers of people in religious communities; I have already noted that for the majority of monks and nuns the cloister was a career, a profession. This does not mean, of course, that there were but few with authentic callings; the temper of the century was religious, as ours is scientific and technical. The function of the cloisters was threefold: religious, in the narrow sense of the word, as exemplified in the austerities of the Carmelites; worldly, in providing an occupation to thousands of men and women who otherwise would have found themselves without a livelihood; and societal: in welfare, charity, and teaching.

The work of religious communities in the area of education was massive. It scarcely bears mentioning that from the seventeenth century the Society of Jesus had been the educator of criollo society; in the seventeenth and eighteenth centuries, artistic and intellectual culture in New Spain was stamped with the methods and aims of the Jesuits. The intellectual achievement in the nunneries was inferior to that in the male Jesuit institutions; with the acknowledged exception of Sor Juana Inés, artistic, philosophical, and scientific contributions were insignificant. On the other hand, the nuns distinguished themselves in teaching at the elementary and intermediate levels. Because of the nuns, there was a female culture in Mexico, however poor that culture may seem to us. The nuns also instructed young and adolescent girls in music, theater, dance, and art, as well as skills such as sewing, embroidery, and cooking. The testimony of Thomas Gage is meticulous:

> Gentlemen and citizens give their daughters to be brought up in these nun-neries, where they are taught to make all sorts of conserves and preserves, all sorts of needlework, all sorts of music, which is so exquisite in that City, that I dare be bold to say, that the people are drawn to their churches more for the delight of their music than for any delight in the service of God. More, they teach these young children to act like players; and to entice the people to their churches, they make these children act short dialogues in their choirs, richly attiring them with men's and women's apparel . . . These are so gallantly performed that there have been many factious strifes and single combats . . . for defending which of these nun-neries most excelled in music and in the training up of children.[2]

Gage perhaps exaggerates. But not much. The convents were not only centers of learning; they maintained hospitals, poorhouses, and homes for orphans and the elderly, and they offered asylum to the forsaken. Religious orders fulfilled two functions today discharged by the state—education and charity.

The convent population reflected the complexity of Mexican colonial society, with its vertical and horizontal divisions. There were convents for Spanish women and for criollo women, a convent exclusively for the descendants of the conquistadors, and another, Corpus Christi, for In-dian noblewomen. This diversity corresponded to the multiplicity of hierarchies and jurisdictions representing the different communities in New Spain. It was not easy to enter a convent: purity of lineage was as strict a requirement as the dowry and the ability to incur the major expense of the ceremony of profession. That is why—for appearance' sake—Juana Inés declared at the time she took her vows that she was the legitimate daughter of Pedro de Asbaje and Isabel Ramírez. It was for the same reason that in 1672 Diego Ruiz Lozano placed his two daughters in San Jerónimo in the custody of their "cousin," Sor Juana Inés de la Cruz. These irregularities reveal that although the rules were severe, enforcement was lax.

Dowries ranged between three and four thousand pesos. This was a sizable sum, but on a number of occasions devout potentates like Juana Inés' sponsor Pedro Velázquez de la Cadena paid the dowries of novices with limited means. Isabel María de San José, Sor Juana's niece, was similarly favored by a protector who contributed her dowry and assumed responsibility for the expenses of the ceremony of profession.

New Spain was dotted with huge, solid, and often beautiful convents and monasteries. Besides serving as religious and cultural centers, they were economically very productive. The orders sold the products resulting from the labor and industry of the nuns and their assistants, and were also engaged, as major landholders, in the agricultural market and other lucrative operations. It is known, for example, that investments in the business affairs of the convent of San Jerónimo yielded an interest of five percent annually. Earnings from the sale of the convent's orchard and garden produce were significant. Another source of income was the leasing of haciendas and farms to individual agriculturists like Pedro Ramírez, Juana Inés' grandfather. In the cities, the orders owned plots of land, buildings, houses, and at times entire neighborhoods; they were not strangers to urban speculation. Gemelli Carreri sums up the situation of the convents in this phrase: "Stanno tutti sopprabondantemente richi." In a way the religious orders—male as well as female—resembled modern corporations, although with an important qualification: the orders were rich but their shareholders (monks and nuns) were not. Instead, their economic activities were directed toward a purpose that transcended the personal (their community, their Church), which in turn was governed by values not of this world. But their religious focus did not, of course, prevent the wealth of the convents from being reflected in the beauty and magnificence of the buildings and in the breaking and relaxing of rules.

The immensity of the buildings was due not only to the wealth of the orders and the magnitude of their cultural and economic undertakings but also to the number of people living within their walls. I have referred to how the convents differed according to the nuns' origins and the amount of their dowries. The convent population was composed of nuns, servants (maids and slaves), "girls," and lay sisters. The "girls" were children whose families had placed them in the convent's keeping, sometimes for life; the lay sisters were women who had resolved to withdraw into the sanctuary of convent walls, although without taking vows. Nuns brought their own maids and slaves to the convent. The ratio of servants to nuns is revealing: there were three maids for each nun. In some convents the ratio was even higher: five maids per nun. How were such large numbers of women housed? In a book containing invaluable information, Josefina Muriel reports that "each nun had her own cell; on occasion they were large enough to house an entire family comfortably."[3] Cells were sold and rented. The recent work of reconstruction at the convent of San Jerónimo has revealed that the majority of the cells had two stories. Thus, when a cell was sold to Sor Juana in 1691, the record of sale indicates that it was sold with "upper and lower floors." Each cell had a bathroom, a kitchen, and a sitting room, in addition to sleeping quarters. Some were larger still. In truth, the convents were small cities and the cells were apartments or even, at times, small houses constructed around enormous patios. "Each of the large cells houses a nun, a 'girl' or 'girls' entrusted to her care, her personal maids, and her favorites." This last category *me laisse rêveur.*

Although the rules mandated communal life, "each nun lived privately . . . As common rooms there were only a sewing room and those necessary for the exercise of prayers, discipline, and questions of governance." Usually the cells were supplied with at least a small kitchen, so that in most convents the rule of communal meals was never, or almost never, enforced. Neither was the rule of sewing together in a communal sewing room. This situation lasted until the end of the eighteenth century, and many nuns protested when there was an attempt to change the rule. The nuns of the order of the Immaculate Conception alleged that "their constitutions did not oblige them to eat in the same hall . . . and there was no recourse but to grant them dispensation from communal life."[4] Despite the general vow of poverty, in many convents the nuns could receive incomes, have personal possessions and jewels, and, through intermediaries, engage in various financial activities. Laxity in regard to the vow of poverty extended to clothing and personal adornment. At the end of the seventeenth century, in the convent of Jesús María (Immaculate Conception) the nuns wore jet bracelets, rings, and pleated scapulars and coifs. The Hieronymites dressed like the nuns of the Immaculate Conception. The portraits of Sor Juana do not evoke the rigors and austerities of ascetic life but, rather, the elegance of aristocratic society—good taste as a style of religious life.

The convents were small republics, although subject to external authority. The Hieronymites were responsible to the Archbishop, and the prioress had to request permission for such transactions as the sale of a cell to Sor Juana. Similarly, before the poet could invest two thousand gold pesos in the convent's farms, she was obliged to obtain the Archbishop's permission. Both cases were mere formalities; in general, the required authorizations were automatically granted. In essence, the convents ruled themselves, and higher authorities intervened only in extreme situations. The autonomy of the convents—never absolute, of course—was increased by virtue of the plurality of jurisdictions and powers. If one authority denied a request, the favor of a different authority could be sought. More than once, conflicts arose between convents and the authorities to whom they were responsible; to settle these disputes—interminable, costly, and tangled—it was necessary to appeal to Madrid and Rome. The relationship between the convents and the responsible authorities did not often degenerate into conflict, but in the case of disagreement the convents invariably sought the support of a third party: the Viceroy, a different Prince of the Church, or patrons in the Spanish court or the Vatican. As will be seen, the convent of San Jerónimo was not exempt from these tensions during the tenure of Archbishop Aguiar y Seijas.

Every three years, by secret vote, the nuns elected their superiors and dignitaries. The hierarchy consisted of the prioress or abbess, assisted by a vicaress, one or several instructors of novices, a gatekeeper, two or more disciplinarians, a manager (finances), some arbitrators who resolved debated cases, a bookkeeper (treasurer), an archivist, and in some convents a librarian. These were rotating offices, but a nun could be reelected to a post. Sor Juana was archivist and bookkeeper. She seems to have distinguished herself in the second duty. Twice reelected, she held that post for nine years. As is to be expected, the election of the abbesses awakened strong passions among supporters of various candidates. The convents experienced the rebellions, quarrels, intrigues, coalitions, and reprisals of political life. Frequently nuns complained to the Archbishop and other church authorities about the tyrannies of one of the abbesses. In 1701, Josefina Muriel reports, "there was a mutiny of nuns in the convent of the Immaculate Conception against the abbess, whom they wanted to kill." Physical violence was not unknown; besides corporal punishment and physical assaults, there was one case of a nun who was murdered by the sisters.

Another rule only partially observed was that of confinement within the cloister. The nuns did not go out, it is true, but they received visitors. It is known that in addition to the Vicereine and her ladies, the Viceroy and his retinue often came to the convent. The convents were also frequently visited by homilists, theologians, and other distinguished personages, both clerical and secular. There were numerous religious functions, after which those attending visited the nuns in their locutories;

thus true salons were formed. Nonreligious entertainments—singing, dancing, and brief theatrical performances—were performed in the patios of the convents, usually by the girls who were studying with the nuns. The audiences for these spectacles were composed not only of clerics but also of the lords and ladies of the court. Opportunities to see and mingle with outsiders was not limited to festivals and ceremonies. Again, Gage: "It is ordinary for the Fryers to visit their devoted nuns, and to spend whole days with them, hearing their music, feeding on their sweet-meats. And for this purpose they have many chambers which they call Loquitorios, to talk in, with wooden bars between the nuns and them, and in these chambers are tables for the Fryers to dine at; and while they dine the nuns recreate them with their voices." Gage's descriptions may seem fantastic, but it is attested that Fray García Guerra, Archbishop of Mexico, was an assiduous visitor to the Royal Convent of Jesús María. The objects of the visits of His Excellency the Archbishop were two nuns, instructors in music and culinary arts. Fray García took pleasure in listening to their worldly songs and savoring their tidbits.[5]

The nuns received their visitors unveiled, despite the fact that they were expressly forbidden to uncover their faces in the presence of outsiders. Neither was separation by the wooden bars strictly observed, and at times the nuns sat in the same room with their visitors. Curiously, just as actresses have devotees today, in New Spain there were those who paid court to nuns. The custom dated from the Middle Ages, as evidenced by many songs, licentious poems, and reports. It throve in New Spain and reached such proportions that when the austere Aguiar y Seijas was named Archbishop, one of his first measures was to combat it. Antonio de Robles notes impassively in his *Diario de sucesos notables* (*Record of Notable Events*): "5 January 1682. Notification to the nuns of La Concepción and San Jerónimo not to receive or allow male devotees at the iron grilles and porter's gate."

The other face of license is asceticism. New Spain in the seventeenth century was a battleground for sexuality and death. Their combat was an embrace, frequently mortal. The dialogue between the two signs that define us and (in)determine us (that is, make us human: creatures of uncertainty), the sign *body* and the sign *nonbody*, assumed in the Baroque Age a sumptuous and bloody form, voluptuous and cruel. The ascetic ranted like a lover, the lover mortified himself like an ascetic. If the convents of New Spain did not produce either great mystics or great theologians, they were prodigal in the number of penitents and flagellants. These nuns excelled in exquisite confectionary arts, and in the no less exquisite arts of martyring themselves and their sisters. In his chronicle of the convent of the Immaculate Conception, Sigüenza y Góngora relates many cases in which ascetic practices were literally stained with blood. The events he describes at times resemble undiscovered chapters of *Justine ou les malheurs de la vertu*. One such story can be read as an anticipatory confirmation of Wilde's paradox on art. Sigüenza reports that the nun Antonia de Santa Clara asked the abbess and the sisters to brand on her face the words *Esclava del Santísimo Sacramento* (Slave of the Most Holy Sacrament). How can one fail to recall that on her forehead, branded by the red-hot iron, Lisarda, the heroine of Mira de Amescua's play, bears the words "slave of the devil"?[6] Life imitates art but elects symmetrical opposition. The German scholar Ludwig Pfandl collects these examples with gratification and uses them to stress his image of a Juana Inés in the grasp of a dark sexual delirium and tortured by obsessive visions of self-castration.[7]

Sigüenza y Góngora also relates many miracles and marvels. For example, a nun falls from a second floor, where she is caring for a sick woman; as she falls, she commends herself to the protection of St. Joseph, and in that instant, before touching the ground, she soars upward, back to the place from which she had fallen. Sigüenza y Góngora—cosmographer, mathematician, reader of Descartes and Gassendi—gives no sign of doubting such miracles or deploring the mortifications and penances to which the nuns subjected themselves. To fault him for that is to forget the Holy Office, and that is to forget a lot; Sigüenza could not, without grave danger, condemn the nuns' flagellations or question their miracles. He later adopted a similar attitude toward the marvels and mortifications of Aguiar y Seijas. As for Sor Juana, what is amazing is the fact that although she lived in that ambiance she did not lose her reason but was always able to preserve a distance between her intellect and the dark seductions of asceticism, miracles, and false mysticism. Sor Juana was "human, all too human," not in the tragic sense of Nietzsche but in the absence of a wish to be either saint or devil. She never renounced reason, although at the end of her life she was forced to renounce literature. If she was not seduced by saintliness, neither was she tempted by the vertigo of damnation. More accurately, like other great spirits, she suffered—but resisted—two temptations, ecstasy and debasement. She wanted only to be what she was: a lucid mind.

THE CONVENT OF SANTA PAULA of the Order of San Jerónimo was founded in 1586.[8] It began as an extension of the order of its founder, the nun Isabel de Guevara, who was from the Royal Convent of the Immaculate Conception. From its inception, the new convent was intended for criollo women. The building was large, solid, austere, and without much architectural distinction. It was, on the other hand, one of the most spacious in the city, covering almost fourteen thousand square yards. The historian Francisco de la Maza, author of a number of perceptive studies on Sor Juana and her time, says:

> The nuns of San Jerónimo followed the conventual rule of St. Augustine, although they cannot properly be called Augustinian. They wore habits resembling those of their founders, the sisters of the Immaculate Conception. The tunic was white, with very full tapered sleeves; the coif was also white, and the veil and scapular were black . . . Over the scapular, at their breast, they wore a metal or parchment escutcheon painted with some religous scene. The black thong of the order of St. Augustine girded the waist, and an enormous rosary floated from the neck to the knees.[9]

The scenes depicted on the escutcheons, as Sor Juana's portraits attest, are decidedly mannerist, with a stylization that verges on affectation and an indefinable sensuality that is at once saccharine and morbid. In Juan de Miranda's portrait of Sor Juana, the oldest we have, she is caressing with her left hand, in a gesture more feminine than devout, the beads of an enormous rosary, as if it were a necklace. In that portrait, as in the poetic conceit and in the morality of the period, the mannerist principle of the conjunction of opposites triumphs.

The nuns of San Jerónimo, as in the majority of the convents of New Spain, lived "private lives," that is, they did not observe the rule of communal life; each lived in her own cell and there cooked, ate, sewed, prayed, and received visits from the other nuns. Connected with the convent was a school for girls. Many girls lived in the convent as boarders from the age of seven until their education was complete. The school was celebrated for its classes in music, dance, and theater. From the time she took the veil, Sor Juana participated in the theatrical and musical activities of the convent. Besides her *villancicos,* she composed many songs for *loas,* and the lyrics for several "dances and provincial airs" written for an entertainment held in San Jerónimo in honor of the Marquis and Marquise de la Laguna. She also began—it was left unfinished—a treatise on music, *El caracol* (*The Conch Shell*), which has been lost. By all indications, including what she herself relates in an epistolary poem to the Countess de Paredes, *The Conch Shell* was an adaptation, intended for use in her school, of Pietro Cerone's musical treatise *El melopeo y maestro* (*Music and Master*). And the rule of cloister? The regulations of San Jerónimo were as relaxed as those of the Immaculate Conception; the viceroys and their companions frequently visited the convent, and the nuns received these visitors in the locutory and even the sacristy, without a veil. They conversed, they debated, they composed and recited poems, they solved riddles and puzzles, and they sang and played worldly music.

Unlike the convent of the Immaculate Conception, which had its chronicler in Sigüenza y Góngora, San Jerónimo had no historian, nor is it likely ever to have one. Like the other convents of New Spain, the convent of the Hieronymites kept very complete records; for generations the nuns gathered documentation so that someday the history of their house could be written. They also had a library that probably contained rare and valuable books. The civil wars of the nineteenth century, and the laws Juarez enacted in 1859 against the religious orders, dispersed the archives and libraries of Mexican convents. To measure the significance of that dispersal and that loss, we have only to remember that those libraries and archives were the richest in all of New Spain. Juarez' reforms destroyed a precious part of Mexico's history and thus contributed substantially to the process of self-mutilation that has made us a people without a memory. What was not lost forever was removed from the country and now is found in American libraries and archives. The records of San Jerónimo did not escape this general fate. Many disappeared; others were acquired by libraries and scholars abroad; only a few remained in Mexico. Among the latter is the *Rules and Constitutions Which by Apostolic Authority Must Be Observed by the Nuns of the Supreme Doctor St. Jerome, in This City of Mexico* (1702). By reading those rules we can imagine what daily life must have been in Sor Juana's convent, although bearing in mind that many of the regulations, especially those relating to communal life and isolation from the outside world, were not observed.

Activities began at six in the morning with the prayers of the first of the canonical hours, the "prime." Immediately following, the mass, which was required and was heard in the choir. At eight, breakfast: bread, eggs, milk, butter. At nine, the prayers of the "tierce." Later, communal work in the "sewing room," from which no nun could be excused without the permission of the Mother Superior. This is one of the unobserved regulations. The nuns sewed in their cells, singly or in small groups. In no passage in her letter to the Bishop of Puebla does Sor Juana hint that she ever participated in the communal sewing sessions required by the rules. At twelve there were the prayers of the "sext" and, following that, the noon meal. Again, contrary to the mandate of the rule, meals were prepared in the cells. Meat was eaten except on Wednesday. At three, the "nones," and following the prayers, says Francisco de la Maza, "almost certainly there was a siesta."[10] At dusk there was a collation of preserved or fresh fruit. At seven, in the choir, "vespers," followed by dinner, recreation, the prayers of the "complin," and bed. "Matins" and "lauds" brought the night's sleep to a close. Rules specified that beds should have mattresses and pillows "but no sheets," and that the nuns should sleep in "*sayuela* and little scapular, girded and veiled." The *sayuela* was a coarse woolen gown. It is impossible to know whether these regulations were adhered to; I am inclined to believe not. The fasts of the Church were observed, and on Friday there was a "chapter meeting" at which routine matters were discussed, offenses considered, and penances imposed. De la Maza indicates that punishments ranged from reciting the Lord's Prayer to perpetual incarceration within the convent. I hasten to add that the penalties were generally light. Fridays were also dedicated to confession. Communion was not required except on major feast days.

One is struck by the monotony of this regimen. What is extraordinary is not that some nuns abandoned themselves to pious or cruel eccentricities but that they did not all go mad. For certain less-than-stable personalities, the tedium and the long hours of idleness encouraged delirious fantasies and, not infrequently, disgust and horror toward their sisters and themselves.

For the majority, convent life was a hotbed of gossip, intrigue, and conspiracy: all the variations of the passion for cabal, as Fourier called the love of power that leads us to form political cliques and coteries. This passion, says the great utopian, "is a calculating enthusiasm." The union of calculation and ambition is a secret poison that both stimulates and corrupts the life of closed associations: the court, the Church, the military, the university, the party, the academy. To achieve its aims, the passion for conspiracy—especially in its vulgar form, politicking—must seek the complicity of others. The price is high: in order to use others, the ambitious must in turn serve others. Sor Juana often complained of the intrigues and envy of her sisters; it is almost certain, furthermore, that her renunciation of literature was the result of a clerical cabal against her. But as will be seen, she, too, mastered this art composed of cunning, dissimulation, patience, and cold blood. She survived more than twenty years of convent life and ecclesiastic and palace intrigue by virtue of her skill as much as her moral and intellectual gifts. The way she used her relations with the viceregal palace reveals rare political acumen. Like the other women of her family, Juana Inés was strong and flexible, stubborn and sinuous, deferential but obstinate.

Although the nuns of San Jerónimo led "private lives," they saw each other continually in their cells, not just during the assemblies required for the daily liturgy—mass and the prayers corresponding to the seven canonical hours. Sor Juana alludes to these visits and social conversations; she calls them "obstructions" and offers several examples as proof: ". . . how I might be reading, and those in the adjoining cell would wish to play their instruments, and sing; how I might be studying, and two servants who had quarreled would select me to judge their dispute; or how I might be writing, and a friend would come to visit me, doing me no favor but with the best of will, at which time one must not only accept the inconvenience, but be grateful for it. And such occurrences are the normal state of affairs." The vow of poverty was similarly ignored. I have pointed out that nuns owned jewels and other property, invested money for interest, and profited from various lucrative financial dealings. There was an explicit prohibition against giving and receiving gifts, but Sor Juana received many presents, some very valuable, and also gave gifts to friends, especially the vicereines. It is not inconceivable that the convent itself, interested as it was in maintaining good relations with the viceregal palace, paid for those presents.

In the light of this brief description, the question of whether Juana Inés carried out her religious duties loses significance. The rule was relaxed, and infractions were numerous and widespread. She did not distinguish herself by either her fervor or her rigor. Neither, however, did she transgress seriously against the rule, nor was she negligent. Juana Inés almost always maintained her lucidity and emotional balance; she kept herself at an equal distance from the deplorable license and idleness of the majority of her sisters and the no less deplorable mortifications, eccentricities, and cruelties of the others. By this I do not mean that she was "normal"; no one is. She was a woman who moved with ease, at times with elegance, through a dangerous and mined terrain. It should be added that almost never, as she skirted precipices and pitfalls, did her smile abandon her.

LIKE ALL THE CONVENTS of New Spain, the convent of San Jerónimo was a two-story, rectangular building constructed around a vast patio. But the combined action of the years, necessity, and the nuns' fantasies transformed its geometrical simplicity into a true labyrinth. Open spaces became occupied by small, capricious constructions: galleries, interior balconied rooms, passageways, cubicles built on the flat roof, small fountains. The restoration currently in progress has revealed that the two floors that usually made up one cell—a singularly inappropriate word to describe such lodgings—were joined by an interior stairway. A curious detail: the majority of the cells contained a tub and braziers for heating bath water, evidence that the nuns washed their bodies with the same zeal their servants devoted to scrubbing floors and polishing ritual objects. Some fifty nuns lived in the convent in addition to the "girls," the women given asylum, and the servants and slaves—more than two hundred women in all. Each nun arranged her cell according to her tastes and in keeping with her means. Sor Juana's cell, to judge by what can be seen of it in her portraits, was elegant, even slightly theatrical. According to a tradition handed down by the nuns of San Jerónimo, one we have no reason to question, her cell was on the southeast corner of the cloister, at the corner of Monserrate and Verde streets.[11] There is a large window in the room on the second floor, so that on clear days, which most were, Sor Juana could see the Valley of Mexico and the two volcanos of her childhood.

The cells housed not only the nuns but the maids and the girls entrusted to the nuns' care. During her first years in the convent Sor Juana was attended by her slave, Juana de San José, a mulatto girl four years younger than she, whom Sor Juana's mother had given her when she became a nun. The slave lived with her some ten years; in 1683 she and her infant son were sold by Sor Juana to her sister Josefa for two hundred fifty gold pesos. Probably Sor Juana's two half sisters, Antonia and Inés, also lived with her for a brief time in 1673, and later her niece and protégée Isabel María de San José, until she became a nun. It is not known whether Sor Juana had other maids or slaves. I am inclined to believe she did; with the passing years, her financial situation became more and more comfortable, in spite of the fact that on one occasion she declared herself to be "a poor nun." For reasons I shall explain later, she must have wanted to provide against future contingencies.

It is impossible to reconstruct the details of Sor Juana's life during her first years as an ordinary nun. But one can draw a general picture of this life. I have mentioned the rules of the order and the daily routine imposed by them, primarily the communal prayers at canonical hours. Aside from this obligation, the nuns were free to devote themselves to their chores, their private devotions, or conversation with their sisters. They had many free hours, and Sor Juana dedicated a major part of hers to reading, studying, and writing. By her own testimony as well as general information we have about her, we know that she was an omnivorous reader. In another part of this book I shall go more deeply into the subject of her reading and the much-disputed topic of her library. For now I shall point out only that her readings were more broad and varied than profound. To "keep abreast" and fill in gaps in her learning—as is always the case with the self-taught—she read a great many encyclopedias and other compilations of what we would today classify as general information, such as manuals and treatises on mythology, philosophy, jurisprudence, and history. She also wrote profusely. Her literary works are as notable for quantity as for diversity of subject; she was also an indefatigable letter writer. She had correspondents both in America and in Spain. One of them was Father Diego Calleja. In a beautiful elegy dedicated to her memory—it appears without the author's name in *Fame and Posthumous Works* (1700), but it is undoubtedly his—he tells how Sor Juana became his correspondent. A true fisher was she, not of souls but of partners in dialogue:

> by chance she read one of my poems,
> a work of years more slight than subtle:
> one tearfully I laugh to limn;
> then wrote me, praising my poor verse
> as if its rantings were sublime.
> We judge wise who sings our praises,
> especially in the absence of the wit
> that sinks what seemingly it raises.
> I answered, awaiting every day
> her news, maddened by the fleet,
> assured the seas held it at bay.
> And each epistle brought to me,
> in phrases wrought in finest tones,
> the gold of generosity . . .

The correspondence with Calleja, as he reports, had begun some twenty years earlier, that is, about 1680. During those years Juana Inés wrote so much and with such brilliance and vigor that the Jesuit admitted he was outdone:

> to follow her was all in vain,
> as if across a stony ground
> a footsore ox chased bounding fawn.

Sor Juana's eagerness for written communication betrays a certain opportunism, an immoderate anxiety to know and be known. Vanity, yes, but also solitude; smothering, asphyxia. It was not only the convent; the entire country—her whole world—was too small for her. Her true contemporaries were to be found not in Madrid or Lima or Mexico but in a Europe that in the latter half of the seventeenth century was opening to the modern era on which Spain had turned its back. Have those papers, written with such passion and motivated by the need to hear and be heard, been lost forever? When we confront the loss of Sor Juana's correspondence, the melancholy invariably awakened by the study of our past turns to desperation. It is said that the passion that corrodes the Spanish peoples is envy; worse and more destructive is neglect, creator of our deserts.

To read and to write is to converse with others and with oneself. In both cases, our respondent is an absence-presence that speaks to us without a tongue and hears us without ears. Sor Juana says it in one of the convoluted figures so beloved of her era: "Hear me with your eyes . . . hear me, deaf, for my plaint is mute." She conversed not only with the ghosts that spring from books or the imagination but with flesh-and-blood people. A scandalized Father Oviedo reports that she stopped writing letters only when she was in the locutory chatting with visitors. Her friendship with Leonor Carreto was not interrupted when she became a nun; on the contrary, it is well known that the Vicereine and her husband, the Marquis de Mancera, "had the custom of attending chapel for vesper prayers, and then chatting in the locutory with Sor Juana."[12] They were accompanied by close friends and members of the court who had known the young nun during her years in the palace. Especially frequent among the visitors were clerics and laypersons devoted to letters, one of whom, Juan Ignacio de Castorena y Ursúa, left us an account of those visits. Of course, Castorena was but a boy in those years, and his commentary refers to a later period. But the gatherings in 1680 must not have been very different from those in 1670.

Castorena was rector of the University of Mexico, professor of scripture, Bishop of Yucatan, author of sermons, and editor of the first newspaper in Mexico, *La Gazeta de México*. He was a great friend of Sor Juana's, her defender in a bitter hour, and it is to him that we owe the edition of the third volume of her writings, *Fame and Posthumous Works*. This is Castorena's description of those gatherings in the locutory: "Happier [than her readers] were those of us who had the privilege of being her listeners; whether arguing the most difficult questions with Scholastic rigor, advancing with greatest delicacy her comments on various sermons, or spontaneously composing verses in divers languages and meters, she astounded us all, and won the acclamation of the most severe critic among the assembled courtiers." The locutory had become a salon, and there, as in all salons, the participants set off verbal fireworks, improvised poems and games, and gossiped. "In various Talk th' instructive hours they past, . . . At every Word a Reputation dies."[13]

Manuel Fernández de Santa Cruz, the man who later would play such a decisive role in the life and destiny of Sor Juana, must occasionally have been among those attending these gatherings. Fernández de Santa Cruz was a native of Palencia and had been a canon in Segovia. He was an erudite theologian, skillful administrator, and cautious politician. He was named Bishop of Chiapas and came to New Spain in 1673; as soon as he arrived, however, he was ordered to serve as Bishop of Guadalajara. He was a friend and protégé of Fray Payo Enríquez de Rivera, in those years Archbishop of Mexico and later Viceroy. There is no doubt that Juana Inés and Fernández de Santa Cruz were good friends. In the prologue to his edition of Sor Juana's criticism of Father Vieyra, the *Carta atenagórica*, 1690, the Bishop, speaking of himself in third person, recalls that it was "many years ago he kissed her hand," and that from that time he "remained enamored of her soul, and that affection has not been cooled by distance or time." While Bishop of Guadalajara, Fernández de Santa Cruz was in Mexico City several times; in 1675 he was consecrated by Fray Payo and in 1676 promoted to the position of Bishop of Puebla. The bishopric of Puebla was second in importance in all of New Spain, and more than once its Bishop was a rival to the Archbishop of Mexico City.

The relationship between Sor Juana and Fernández de Santa Cruz must have been quite close, as we shall see in the final section of this book, although they never violated hierarchical order. He was a man and she a woman, he a Prince of the Church and she a simple nun. The Bishop counsels her and she declares her obedience. At the same time, the superior is fascinated by the wit of the subordinate, and recognizes in her a tacit and invisible superiority. Sor Juana must have enjoyed a privileged relationship with the prelate, for one of her nephews, Fray Miguel de Torres, was his intimate and later would be his biographer. Fray Miguel was the son of Sor Juana's half sister Inés and José Miguel de Torres, secretary of the university. It is not inconceivable that Sor Juana's friendship with Fernández de Santa Cruz contributed to Fray Miguel's obtaining the position. We know that on various occasions Sor Juana used her influence and connections to favor her relatives. And it is not illogical to suppose that she and Santa Cruz belonged to a circle centering upon Fray Payo. Thus little by little a web of relationships is drawn in which personal and group interests are no less decisive than intellectual and aesthetic affinities.

SOR JUANA SEVERAL TIMES ALLUDES to her frail health. We know that on at least one occasion she was seriously ill. That was during her first years in the convent, around 1671 or 1672. The disease was typhoid fever. Two poems resulted from her illness: a sonnet dedicated to Laura (Leonor Carreto) and an epistle in the form of a *romance* addressed to Fray Payo Enríquez de Rivera. The subject of the sonnet is the same as that of the *romance:* the experience of death. Sor Juana uses the same metaphor in both: the Fates appear, and with them the deadly scissors. The sonnet (186) reads:

> To cut the spindled thread she had not spun,
> I saw her gaping scissors' stroke begun.

And the *romance* (11):

> From that fatal implement,
> a sound that echoed in my ears:
> like brothers, bound yet enemies,
> the blades of those relentless shears.

If the poems share the same theme, they are very different in treatment. The sonnet is an exercise in *metaphysical* amatory poetry, while the *romance* is an example of seventeenth-century epistolary poetry in which burlesque is blended with the serious, and erudition with fantasy. Both are models of the styles of the era. In the sonnet Sor Juana uses the real experience of death to build through clever antitheses and parallelisms to the inevitable final "surprise." Her mastery of the medium is only that; there is no passion, only, as the title promises, ingenuity. As Fate is about to snatch away Sor Juana's life, she realizes it is not hers to claim, but Laura's. She closes her scissors and retreats:

> Defeated, at that instant she withdrew,
> and left me there to die only for you.

The sonnet is notable for the perfection of its composition. But it is a shame that two such deeply felt experiences—loving friendship for Laura and fear of death—were turned into a verbal construct driven by the mechanics of rhetoric rather than true poetic spirit.

The *romance* is a request to Fray Payo to administer the sacrament of confirmation. Her plea is the excuse for telling him, in seriocomic terms, of her illness and fever-induced delirium. An experience that a modern imagination would have explored psychologically and described in realistic terms is Sor Juana's pretext for citing Ovid and Virgil, Clotho and Atropos, Sisyphus and Tantalus, the Lethe and the Styx. Her hell is a literary hell, but one, fortunately, with comic relief. In the second, less entertaining part of the poem Sor Juana remembers that she is a nun and a Christian; she shudders at the danger now behind her and, although she does not consider herself deserving of hell, gazes with apprehension "from Purgatory / upon the harsh, allotted place." Following these lines the poem becomes an exposition of Christian doctrine and ends, predictably, in praise of Fray Payo, "Preeminent Prince," whom she sees in her fantasy in the heights of glory, a Pope, pontifical staff in hand. Courtly adulation is a note that appears again and again in her poems.

Both poems are impersonal—impersonal in a paradoxical way. The biographical element, the "experience," is the nucleus of both; but it has been neutralized by being expressed in archetypal forms: concepts, antitheses, Latin erudition, Christian theology, courtly formulas. In the autobiographical eclogue *Amarilis,* Lope de Vega recounts his fanciful love affair with Marta de Nevares, but all his confessions are transfigured—frequently stereotyped—in the mold of pastoral poetry. In the baroque century, in order to be recognizable, individual experience had to accommodate itself to archetypes conceived in philosophy and rhetoric. The personal and unique tones of each experience evaporated in favor of the generic, abstract, and universal. A lived experience was transformed from something entirely personal into yet another variation—a specimen—of a vital and moral typology. In Sor Juana's sonnet, real and actual death is changed into a rhetorical figure, converted into a phrase in an amatory conceit; in the *romance,* the same experience is transformed into erudition and burlesque poetry.

Sonnet and *romance* are two exercises by an extremely intelligent disciple, one who is capable of rivaling her masters but who does not exceed them. The sonnet is reminiscent of the conceptual games of Lope de Vega; the *romance,* although less daring, of the violent chiaroscuro of Quevedo. More than a precise influence, the names of these two poets suggest two extremes: they are the boundaries within which she moves. She does not follow either; at times she approaches Góngora; at times, Calderón or Polo de Medina, or even poets we no longer remember, like Anastasio Pantaleón de Ribera. With exquisite taste and a sure sense of proportion, she embraces the style—the styles—of her era. I stress the words "taste" and "proportion," because from the beginning these two qualities are present in her work. Her sensitivity was acute and balanced, intelligent and lucid: a finely calibrated scale that weighed words, their meanings, their shades of meaning.

In 1673 a new Viceroy—a descendant of Columbus—was named, Don Pedro Nuño Colón de Portugal, Duke de Veragua. Although the Marquis and Marquise de Mancera left the viceregal palace, they did not immediately return to Spain; as Antonio de Robles records, they remained six months longer in the city, living in the home of the Count de Santiago. The change surely was not a surprise to Sor Juana; viceroys held their posts for relatively brief periods, and the Marquis de Mancera had already served longer than the traditional term. In her heart of hearts, she must have been happy that she had decided in time to become a nun: where would she have gone if she had had to leave the palace at the departure of her protectors? The possibility of returning to the Matas might not have been open to her, even had they been disposed to receive her again in their home, because about that same time Don Juan de Mata died, and his widow, Sor Juana's aunt María Ramírez, died shortly after, in 1680.

The Duke de Veragua had obtained the viceregency in a way that even in that era, accustomed as it was to the sale of positions and sinecures, was somewhat scandalous. Traditionally, to fill important appointments like that of Viceroy, the Council of State and the Council of Castile presented three names to the King. Prime Minister Valenzuela, a resourceful man, had conceived of a remedy for the ailing public treasury: to award the posts to the highest bidder among the nominees. But before carrying out his plan, to assuage Queen Mariana's scruples and his own, he consulted theologians about the legitimacy of this solution. The theologians approved the idea, and so Don Pedro Nuño de Portugal, his purse lighter by fifty thousand ducats, was named Viceroy of New Spain. He arrived in Mexico City on November 16, 1673, and made his ceremonial entry on December 8. Four days later, unexpectedly, he died. Consternation was all the greater when it was learned that he had died without taking the sacraments. Thus the poor Duke derived no benefit from the enormous sum he had laid out. Sor Juana wrote three sonorous and sculpted sonnets in his memory, a true baroque mausoleum (190, 191, 192). Perfect sonnets, but as courtly ceremony, not religious ritual. Empty sonnets. Nonetheless, each contains felicitous verses that demonstrate the power and resources of baroque rhetoric—as in this line from the second sonnet: "applause you came, as paradigm you died," and, in the third, "*Here lies* are letters that are writ on stone: / but in our hearts are scribed the words *Here lives.*"

The Marquis and Marquise de Mancera left Mexico City on April 2, 1674; en route to Veracruz, on April 21, in the town of Tepeaca, Leonor Carreto died suddenly. Robles records that when she was exasperated by insistent favor-seekers, Leonor had always said, "Go to the column at Tepeaca."[14] The Archbishop officiated at the pontifical funeral ceremonies in the cathedral, and there were also prayers offered in San Jerónimo to the salvation of her soul. What must Sor Juana have felt on the death of her friend and protectress? She wrote three sonnets (187, 188, 189), but the emotions she must have felt—dispossession, grief, even, perhaps, despair—were purified in passing through the at once ethical and aesthetic sieve of poetic form. If only we had her correspondence we might be able to glimpse her true feelings. Surely she exchanged letters with the widower, the Marquis de Mancera—who, as I have said, always remembered her with admiration and affection—and in those letters the two must have referred to the years when Juana Inés had been so close to the Vicereine.

The three sonnets to Laura (Leonor Carreto) are of the same perfection of composition as those dedicated to the Duke de Veragua, but they are more translucent. Their language is not sculpture but aerial architecture. Body, in these poems, is the shadow of soul; rhyme is the echo of an idea. Personal feelings, subjected to the dual tyranny of the baroque aesthetic and decorum, are decanted, sublimated, and congealed. The first sonnet exalts her friend's physical beauty: "the heavens, by her beauty held in thrall / stole Laura off, and bore her to their heights." The second is strongly Platonic: the immortal soul, "from the embrace of beauteous prison [the body] now released / . . . ascends to don its crown of morning stars." Sor Juana could not resist the temptation of the witticism, and she ends this sonnet with a slightly blasphemous hyperbole: to compensate for the body in which it had lived, the soul requires the expanse of "all the heavens." The third sonnet contains a quatrain I find enchanting. It begins with a confidence—that Leonor influenced her poetry—and ends with the very modern image of the writer who sees herself writing:

> Unhappy lyre whereon your music played,
> be still, its echoes call to you in pain,
> misshapen are the letters that here fall,
> black teardrops from my melancholy pen.

Fray Payo Enríquez de Rivera was named Viceroy, and thereby two powers were joined: the scepter and the staff. His administration was uneventful and mediocre, as, by Chuang-tsu's definition, all good governments must be: no internal rebellions or oppressions, and no external victories or disasters. His relations within the Audiencia, as well as with the ecclesiastic hierarchy, were peaceful. Manuel Fernández de Santa Cruz, his protégé and friend, was Bishop of Puebla. Unlike Aguiar y Seijas, Fernández de Santa Cruz had no quarrels with the religious orders, and none of his measures evoked controversies or resentment. Fray Payo realized that some satisfaction had to be given to the aspirations of the criollos—a policy followed by Fernández de Santa Cruz—and during his administration it was decreed by royal edict that authority in the monasteries and convents should alternate between Mexicans and Spaniards. Thus it is not surprising that, judging by all indications, relations between the Viceroy-Archbishop and the convent of San Jerónimo were extremely cordial and fluid. Fray Payo was sympathetic, even protective, toward Sor Juana. One anecdote serves to illustrate the Archbishop-Viceroy's benevolent feelings for her and how he protected her from jealousy and envy. Once a Mother Superior complained of Sor Juana's haughtiness—an imputation that was perhaps not entirely false, since in a veiled way Oviedo makes the same charge—and accused Sor Juana of having rudely said, "Quiet, Mother, you are a silly woman." The Archbishop wrote in the margin of the complaint, "Prove the contrary, and I shall pass judgment."

A lack of documentation prevents us from detailing the life and writing of Sor Juana during the period of Fray Payo's viceregency. Sor Juana was twenty-six years old when Leonor Carreto died; by the end of the Archbishop's term she was thirty-one. What did she do during that time? What were her ideas, her preoccupations? What were her discoveries and disappointments? Her conflicts? What did she read, and with whom did she talk? Most important: what did she write? In spite of the paucity of information, we know some things: Juana Inés devoured books during those years, as can be seen in the erudition so ostentatiously displayed a little later in 1680 when writing her *Allegorical Neptune*. Through this text we can, to a certain point, reconstruct her readings, as will be seen. But we are in the dark about what she wrote. Between 1676 and 1679 we can date, with some certainty, only five *villancicos;* a *loa* to the Immaculate Conception ("Loa de la Concepción"); another *loa*, "A los años del rey" ("On the Birthday of King Charles II"); and a little poem praising a work (which one?) by Fray Payo. To this meager list we might add four *villancicos* attributed to her and, possibly, the epistolary *romance* offering her best wishes on the occasion of the birthday of her sponsor, Captain Don Pedro Velázquez de la Cadena. It is likely that other compositions—religious, amatory, and philosophical—as well as satires and courtly homages, also belong to this period.

It is impossible to date Sor Juana's poems. In addition to the faulty documentation—originals as well as manuscript copies of her works have been lost—it would be pointless to seek internal evidence: there is no perceivable evolution in her style. Like Minerva from Jupiter's brow, Sor Juana's poetry was born fully formed. With the exception of two or three poems that reveal the hesitancy of a talented apprentice—for example, the sonnet on the death of Philip IV, the earliest poem to which we can give a date (1666?)—her mastery is constant. Some poems are better than others; some are weakened by a certain haste and other defects, but all have been written by a poet in full control of her style. More accurately, styles. She had several—all those typical of her age—and all, as I have said, were distinguished by her handling of chiaroscuro and her sense of form and proportion. Sor Juana's poetic personality is to be found not in the biographical content of her poems or in her style but in her aesthetic. What is personal and unmistakable is not what she tells us but the way in which she tells it. The originality of her work must be sought not in impossible confessions or even in veiled confidences but in the perfection of form. Within a given form, what distinguishes it is the accent, the *tone*.

Fray Payo retired from the government of New Spain on October 7, 1680. He had been Viceroy for seven years and Archbishop of Mexico for thirteen. Before that he had been Bishop of Guatemala, so the most significant parts of his career belong to America. One scholar has underscored Fray Payo's humility, his return to the Convento del Risco in Spain after having declined the bishopric of Cuenca and the presidency of the Council of the Indies. To balance the portrait a little, I must add that Fray Payo accepted the royal favor of an annual income of four thousand ducats, one-fifth a Viceroy's salary in the seventeenth century (twenty thousand ducats). The treasury of Mexico paid this pension. The royal pension was but a drop in the ocean: Fray Payo was a member of the highest nobility (the house of the Dukes de Alcalá) and his family was one of the richest in Spain. His aunt, the Duchess de Alcalá, was the mother of the Duke de Medinaceli, appointed just about that time (1680) to be prime minister to Charles II.

Since he was a brother of the Duke de Medinaceli, the new Viceroy, Don Tomás Antonio de la Cerda, the Marquis de la Laguna, was also Fray Payo's cousin. Don Tomás de la Cerda was forty-two years old when he arrived in Mexico. His powerful and influential family was one of the oldest of the Spanish nobility. Among his ancestors were Alfonso el Sabio and St. Louis of France. His wife, María Luisa Manrique de Lara y Gonzaga, Countess de Paredes de Nava, was from a no less illustrious family. She was related to the Gonzaga family, the Dukes of Mantua, through her father, while through her mother she descended from the Manriques, who had given Spain a succession of statesmen and famous writers: Chancellor López de Ayala, Fernán Pérez de Guzmán, the poet Jorge Manrique, Admiral Hurtado de Mendoza, the Marquis de Santillana, Gómez Manrique, and others. The Countess de Paredes was thirty-one when she came to Mexico, almost exactly Sor Juana's age. The Marquis and Marquise de la Laguna lived in Mexico about eight years, from November 1680 to April 1688. This would be the richest and fullest period in Sor Juana's life.

10

Political Rites

$\mathcal{T}$HE SPANISH EMPIRE, whatever our judgment in regard to its historical significance, was an imposing political edifice. If the discovery and conquest of America was astounding, no less so was the construction of a complex social and administrative architecture that held together until the beginning of the nineteenth century. The empire had to confront two obstacles that were on first view insuperable: the heterogeneity of the peoples who composed it, and the vast expanse of its territory. In regard to the second, in order to appreciate what was accomplished, we must keep in mind the limited means of communication the central power had at its command prior to the invention of the steamship. Travelers embarked in Cadiz and some three months later, after stopovers in the Canaries and the Antilles, arrived in the insalubrious port of Veracruz. Not a destination but a pause: there began the slow ascent to the cities of the high plateau. From the time they disembarked, voyagers confronted the other reality that along with the vastness characterized the empire: the diversity of the nations under its domain.

The road each new Viceroy traveled from Veracruz to Mexico City was a true ritual pilgrimage that can be seen as political allegory. The historian Ignacio Rubio Mañé records that "once the fleet was within the Gulf of Mexico, from the sounding at Campeche a messenger ship went on ahead to carry the news of the Viceroy's imminent arrival in Veracruz. A gentleman carrying the letters of appointment went with the ship."[1] In Veracruz the civil and military authorities, the governor, and the clergy received the new Viceroy; following the symbolic presentation of the keys of the city, a Te Deum was celebrated. The Viceroy remained a few days in the port city, visited the castle of San Juan de Ulúa, and reviewed the state of the fortifications. Then, escorted by a company with bugles and standards, he started on the road to Jalapa. "All along the way Indian officials and governors came out to receive him, having ordered the road to be swept and decorated, presenting strands of flowers along with courteous speeches in their tongues."[2] The next stage ended in Tlaxcala, a traditional ally of the Spanish, whose friendship had been decisive during Cortes' struggle against the Aztec state. Here the ceremony was a rich web of historical and political allusions:

> The Viceroy made his public entrance on horseback . . . Before him came his scouts and a viceregal page carrying a standard which on one side was embroidered with the royal arms, and on the reverse, the arms of the Viceroy. There followed a large number of Indians with drums, small flutes, and other musical instruments, and carrying on tall poles the banners or emblems of their peoples; the Corps of Tlaxcala, composed entirely of Indian nobility, preceded the Viceroy, holding long ribbons attached to the bridle of the horse he was riding: the councilmen wore over their clothing mantles of fine cotton on which were embroidered the crests of their families and peoples; the Viceroy was followed by his grooms, his retinue, and his escort, all amidst a great throng; and arriving at the end of the High Street, he found before him a façade ornamented with hieroglyphs referring to his person, and at that place was also performed a *loa* befitting the occasion. Later, he proceeded to the parish church to hear the Te Deum, and then to royal houses where lodging had been arranged for him. He remained in Tlaxcala three days, during which time there were bullfights and other diversions. Then he continued on his road to Puebla, where he was received with the greatest solemnity, again entering on horseback, and there he usually remained a week amid festivities and honors.[3]

Thus, before reaching the capital, the new Viceroy made "public entrances" into three cities: the port of Veracruz, associated with the landing of Cortés and the initiation of the Conquest; Tlaxcala, the capital of the Indian republic allied with the conquistadors; and Puebla, founded by the Spanish, a rival to the capital of the viceroyalty, a city that in the symbolic geography of New Spain represented the criollo pole, while Tlaxcala represented the Indian.

The outgoing and the incoming viceroys met in Otumba. There they celebrated the ceremony of the exchange of the scepter of command, the symbol of authority. The site could not have been more appropriate:

Otumba had been the theater of the first great Spanish victory following the defeat of the Noche Triste. But Otumba had not always been the place where the change of command was effected: "The exchange of the scepter first took place in Cholula; that was in the sixteenth century, but in 1580 Otumba began to be used for this ceremony."[4] Cholula is the other city associated with the history of the Conquest of Mexico. In the pre-Hispanic era it had been the religious capital of the high plateau, so that within the religious symbolic system it stood in complementary opposition to Villa de Guadalupe, as Tlaxcala stood against Puebla on the plane of secular history. In short, each of these ceremonies had a specific historical significance; at the same time, each was related to the others. The whole formed a system of symbolic relationships; religious meanings were interwoven with the historical to form, in a manner of speaking, a legal and political allegory. That allegory was the ideal portrait of a society: New Spain.

These festivities constituted a political liturgy. Their function was twofold. In the first place, they were a ritual restatement of the bonds that united the King with his subjects in New Spain; second, they served to join the two nations that, at least juridically, composed the kingdom—the Spanish and Indian nations. In the rite a dual relationship was realized symbolically: that of the lord with his vassals, and that of the people with themselves. In this second sense the celebrations performed a vital function: the fusion of classes, groups, and hierarchies. The political ceremony was a true fiesta, by which I mean a collective act wherein symbols were embodied and made palpable. It was the return of the society to its origins, to the pact that had founded it; a pact expressed vertically in the bond that joined the lord with his vassals, and horizontally in the original wholeness to which the parts of the social body were being restored. Return was both restatement of the past and a new beginning.

The last stage in the entrance of the viceroys was governed by an elaborate and complex ritual in which every element of society participated: the Audiencia, the Metropolitan Church, the university, the military, the religious orders, and the guilds and brotherhoods—not excluding those of Indians, mulattos, and *castas*. The viceroys were received in Villa de Guadalupe; following that, they visited Chapultepec, where they spent a night or even, as in the case of the Marquis de la Laguna, several days. The meaning and the symbolism of these stops leaps to the eye. Villa de Guadalupe, where the Virgin associated with Mexican Catholicism and pre-Hispanic religions had appeared; Chapultepec, another site impregnated with history, but secular rather than religious: the Aztec empire and its descendant, the kingdom of New Spain.

The Viceroy made his entrance into the city under a canopy. The ceremony of this canopy had specific political connotations: "to receive with canopy," says the *Diccionario de autoridades* (1726–1739), "is a public demonstration made only for Pope, Emperor, or Kings on entering a city or village of their domain." The privilege of the baldachin was, in the case of the viceroys, limited to the day of their grand entrance; it was an attribute of sovereignty. In the plaza of Santo Domingo, the site of the Holy Office, the municipality erected a triumphal arch, and it was there the ceremony of the presentation of the keys to the city was enacted. Afterward the Viceroy and his retinue proceeded to the doors of the cathedral, where the cathedral chapter had erected another arch, less imposing than the one at Santo Domingo. A Te Deum was sung in the cathedral, and the Viceroy swore before the Archbishop and the chapter to defend the Catholic faith and the Church and its privileges. From the cathedral the Viceroy marched to the palace. There, in the audience chamber, the last ritual act was performed: the Viceroy assumed his post by taking an oath in which he swore vows of loyalty to his monarch, solemnly promising to fulfill his duties as a Christian Prince.

Two traditions, both European, were joined in the rite of the Viceroy's assumption of power: the *triumph* and the *entrée*. The origins of the triumph go back to Rome. It was the highest honor that could be accorded a victorious general. The conquering troops paraded through triumphal arches erected by the city; the general, dressed in the purple tunic and gold-embroidered toga of a Capitoline Jupiter, held a laurel branch in his right hand and in his left the eagle-topped scepter. The Renaissance revived the Roman triumph but transformed it from a military ceremony to a civic rite celebrating the entrance of a sovereign into a city of his rule. The characteristic feature of the Roman festival, the triumphal arch, survived, but the military parade of conquering soldiers and captives became a cortège, half religious procession, half popular fiesta.

The Renaissance triumph overlaid a more ancient tradition that had survived until the century of the Baroque: the entrée. The Spanish word *entrada* has gradually lost the meaning it held prior to the eighteenth century, one that survives in the French. According to the *Petit Littré*, the *entrée* is a *ceremonie solennelle avec laquelle un personnage consi-*

dérable entre ou est reçu dans une ville. Our *Diccionario de autoridades* says almost the same thing: "Public function in which a King, an ambassador, or a major personage makes a solemn entrance, presenting himself to the public with great ostentation." Both these definitions, however, omit one essential element: the *entrance,* as described in chronicles from the end of the Middle Ages, was not only a solemn ceremony but a public festival.

The Renaissance transformed the medieval entrance into a Roman-style triumph. The entrée was essentially spectacle, the manifestations of the relationships of vassalage: the people proffering themselves in the spectacle of receiving and honoring their lord. The Renaissance introduced the triumphal arches and other elements that evoked the Roman past and at the same time announced the new absolutist state. In turn, the baroque profoundly altered the Renaissance triumph. The addition of masks, dancers, and disguises, as well as the erection of triumphal arches that were real enigmas requiring explanations, changed the entire nature of the festival. The entrance, without ceasing to be a political rite, became an allegory, and the ceremony moved toward theater. Richard Alewyn recounts that in 1550 Henry II entered the city of Rouen, famous for its maritime commerce, along an avenue of trees whose trunks had been painted "in imitation of those in Brazil." Hundreds of parrots and monkeys leaped and screeched in the leafy branches. In the treetops, huts had been constructed to shelter three hundred clay-bedaubed men and women, "bare, in accordance with the custom of the savages of America, of any coverings on parts that nature demands should be hidden."[5] Almost imperceptibly the military parade turned into pantomime and the religious procession into theatrical allegory.

By the end of the seventeenth century the triumph declined because of the increasing indifference of one of its constituencies: the bourgeoisie. The last great example of the triumph, says Alewyn, was the entrance in 1635 of the Cardinal-Infante Ferdinand II into Antwerp. The spectacle was organized by Rubens. Until the eighteenth century the common people of the cities and villages continued to take part in the festivities of receiving their sovereign and other important personages, but by now the bourgeoisie was no longer actively involved. In short, the baroque theatricalized politics and converted a rite like the entrée of a prince into a popular pantomime and allegory. Thus began the reign of illusion and that of its contradictory complement, criticism. The festival left the city plaza and took refuge in the hamlet and the baroque palace. It would not be until the French Revolution that the public celebration would be revived. A bloody resurrection.

In Spain and its domains the evolution was different. Rather, there was no real evolution. First, the Spanish bourgeoisie—or, more accurately, bourgeoisies—did not perform the critical and dissident functions that characterized the middle classes of Nordic Europe and France. Second, the public festival, secular or religious, has always occupied a prominent place in the calendars of our Hispanic nations and in the sensibility and fantasy of our peoples. This is not the place to examine the reasons for the persistence of our public festivals. It is almost certainly a matter of still another premodern trait, one allied to the relative weakness of our bourgeoisies: we have fiestas for the same reasons we did not have an Enlightenment. But while this explanation is not inaccurate, it omits other, no less important factors that relate to what can only be called the singular history of Spain. A unique history that never entirely adapted itself to the European model.

The historian Pierre Chaunu points out that the Spanish concept of urban space corresponds to the symbolism of the fiesta. Every one of our towns, from hamlet to city, has a point of convergence, a gathering place—the plaza. The fiesta takes place in the plaza, and in its course it fulfills the dual function I referred to above: the fusion of the different elements composing the society, and the affirmation of the bonds between the lord and his vassals. Pierre Chaunu says: "The fiesta expressed the monarch's privileged connection with the public. Thus it played a primary role in building the state. The fiesta has a special place in world history."[6] This function, I shall add in passing, still exists in Mexico: the celebration of September 15 (the Cry of Independence) has been and still is a true public fiesta, an annual affirmation of the legitimacy of the Mexican state and the unity of the nation.

Two different currents are united in the Hispanic entrée. The first has popular and traditional origins: the festival in which, since the time of the pagans, the people have celebrated the rotation of the days, months, and years. This popular and religious festival found in New Spain a corresponding form in indigenous celebrations and rituals. Spain imported the entrée proper—incorporating the triumph—from Burgundy. In the fifteenth century the dukedom of Burgundy, a civilization as aborted as that of Provence, was a preview of what courtly society and the European absolutist state would later be. When Charles V imported into Spain the political and administrative methods of the court of Burgundy, he concurrently imported the *joyeuse entrée*. Burgundian influence in Spain began in 1518 with a festival that scandalized austere Castilians: the ostentatious entrance into the cities and villages of Spain of the young monarch and his retinue. The *joyeuse entrée* was the expression of a state that was much stronger and more centralized than the state of Castile. Compared with the complex and refined political structures in France and Flanders, the Spanish monarchy was still an unsophisticated and embryonic institution. In societal symbolism, the entrée represented the dawn of the absolutist state.

The fortunes of history dictated that the legacy of the Catholic kings should fall upon a prince who though descended from a German dynasty was Burgundian by culture and education. Charles V was German only through his grandfather, the Emperor Maximilian, himself the son of a Portuguese mother. Charles was born in Ghent and spent his childhood in Burgundy under the tutelage of his aunt, Margaret of Austria, and everything in his education prepared him for "a Burgundian destiny."[7] His language was French; all his life he spoke German and Spanish badly. Even his name was chosen in memory of the unfortunate Charles the Bold. The influence of Burgundian civilization in the sphere of public administration, in governmental and economic systems, as well as in art and festival, marked Spain forever. In the area that interests me here, that of sensibility, it is enough to recall two inseparable and hostile urges that dwell in our souls: the fiesta and our obsession with death. Two tragic forms of excess and dissipation that are the legacy of Burgundy.

The legacy took root in the sixteenth century in the valley of Anáhuac, similarly a land of dance and sacrifice, laughter and penance. The persistence of the Burgundian heritage in the art and sensibility of our peoples sheds light on certain affinities and similarities that I have often wondered about. Is there a more Spanish painter than Ensor, especially in a composition like *The Entrance of Christ into Brussels,* a canvas from which a good part of Diego Rivera's painting derives? The Valle-Inclán who dreamed up the grotesqueries of *Tirano Banderas,* is he not a great Flemish writer, one who might have been the master of Michel de Ghelderode? What has rather superficially been called the baroque nature of the Spanish peoples—our propensity for antithesis, chiaroscuro, the mask and the conceit—may be nothing other than the expression of a steadily flowing Burgundian undercurrent.

How to explain the continued presence of Burgundy in our art and sensibility? Two answers occur to me, not mutually exclusive but complementary. The first is noted by Chaunu: Burgundian civilization not only marked the end of the Middle Ages—its waning, as Huizinga has called it—but was also a kind of prophecy of the Baroque. This would explain the survival of the Burgundian strain that, fused with our baroque heritage, is still prevalent among us. The second is the anomaly of our historical evolution: the superimposition of various historical times and types of civilization. Our history has followed no single unbroken pattern—the straight line of the evolutionists, the zigzag of the dialecticians, or the circle of the neoplatonists. Our history has been a discontinuous process of fits and starts: at times a dance, at others a lethargy interrupted by a sudden violent awakening. Again and again we Spanish and Spanish Americans rub our eyes and ask: what time is it in world history? Our time never coincides with other times. We are always either ahead or behind. In the case of Mexico, pre-Columbian multiplicity must be added to Spanish: like the Spain of Charles V, the Mexico of Montezuma was a mixture of many societies, tongues, and nations. For all these reasons, eras and styles do not pass in Hispanic countries; they exist side by side, nourishing and devouring one another. Many currents converge and explode in the Mexican fiesta, an eruption not only of forms but of historical spaces and times. The history of the Mexican fiesta is still to be written.

Triumphal arches suffered the same evolution as the other arts during the baroque period. As if they were materialized conceits, not physical objects, they were steadily transformed into monumental enigmas. Canvases and all available surfaces of walls and columns were covered with reliefs, medallions, emblems, and inscriptions. The monument became a text, and the text an erudite charade. To decipher the meaning of the monument, learned explications and expositions were required. Like Marchel Duchamp's *Large Glass*, unintelligible without the notes of his *Green Box,* baroque triumphal arches had as obligatory complement a book that with the most extravagant erudition ingeniously explicated the paintings, emblems, and inscriptions.

The Baroque Age, simultaneously fascinated with and rent by the coexistence of opposites—sensuality and death, faith and doubt, the soirée and the cell—was irresistibly drawn toward the dissolution of the very forms of which it was enamored. The arches were destined for a brief life. Two faces of the same coin: the Baroque created many marvels but constructed them hurriedly and of perishable materials. The seduction of death does not entirely explain the phenomenon; the baroque festival was a holocaust demanding sacrifice, destruction. An aesthetic of excess becomes the art of dissipation. The Baroque invented plethoric and inflated forms that faded at their frenetic peak, attracted by the void. The baroque festival is an *ars moriendi*. The greatest artists of the age did not hesitate to devote their time and talent to creating ephemera: Velázquez and Calderón, Inigo Jones and Ben Jonson, Rubens, Bernini, Le Brun, Racine, Molière, all created triumphant forms destined for immolation at the precise instant of their triumph. Apotheosis and sacrifice of form.

Many aspects of the baroque festival are mysterious to us. Perhaps by comparing it to the "happening," a festival in vogue two decades ago, we may understand it better. What the baroque festival and the "happening" have in common is their fascination with death, although their responses to this fascination differ. The "happening" is intended as a transgression of the social—moral, aesthetic, even rational—order; the baroque festival, in contrast, is a celebration. In the one case, order is disrupted; in the other it is fulfilled, in a spectacle that literally consumes as it is consummated. The baroque festival is a representation in which even death is extravagantly attired and masked; the dynamism, sensuality, and movement of the festival culminate in a mausoleum, that is, in a monument—whether of stone or of words. The "happening" is the precise opposite of the monument: destruction, even self-destruction. Unlike the baroque festival, the "happening" lacks an explanatory text; if it had one it would be unintelligible: pure negation of text. The baroque festival is the exaltation of culture in its supreme form; it is the illusion of form and, at the same time, the dissipation of that form. Ruled by an aesthetic that alternately demonstrates the illusion and disillusion of form, the baroque festival exalts culture. The "happening" is a rebellion against culture, and therefore is the destruction not only of form but of meaning. The destruction of meaning mandates the destruction of language: between speech and silence, the "happening" elects the scream. The negation of language carries within it the negation of representation; the "happening" is a spectacle whose true theme is the destruction of representation. The "happening" is the nihilism of violence, the spasm of a West in the grip of self-loathing.

ON MAY 8, 1680, the Marquis de la Laguna was named Viceroy of New Spain. Although viceroys were named for a term of three years, on the next day, by secret royal decree, the Marquis was granted, in advance, an extension of three years.[8] The influence of his brother, the Duke de Medinaceli, was then at its zenith. By October of that same year, the Marquis and his wife were in New Spain. The Viceroy-Archbishop, Fray Payo de Rivera, received them in Otumba on October 17, and there, following established tradition, the transfer of the scepter of command was carried out. Afterward the new Viceroy and his wife visited Villa de Guadalupe and spent several days in Chapultepec. The solemn entrance was made on November 30.

The new Viceroy and Vicereine, as I have said, were members of the highest nobility. Don Tomás Antonio de la Cerda, third Marquis de la Laguna, was the younger brother of the eighth Duke de Medinaceli, then prime minister to Charles II. He had been captain general of the Andalusian coast and counselor of the Indies. He had been named to serve in the government of Galicia, but the King changed his mind—probably owing to the influence of the Marquis' brother—and named him Viceroy of New Spain. Unlike the subtle Marquis de Mancera and the prudent Fray Payo, both skillful governors, Don Tomás de la Cerda was a mediocre politician and an incompetent statesman. He was not even greatly gifted as a courtier, as would be seen when the Duke de Medinaceli fell from royal favor. Upon his return from New Spain in 1689, the Marquis de la Laguna was named majordomo to the new Queen, Maria Anna of Neuburg; with the post he obtained an appointment as lifetime grandee, a major concession achieved through the major investment of two hundred thousand gold crowns (the Marquis was extremely wealthy). He had little success in his appointment as majordomo: he was sent to a designated port to welcome the new wife of Charles II, but because of a storm the convoy had to alter its course and put ashore elsewhere. The new Queen felt slighted by her reception, and to add to the difficulty the Marquis de la Laguna arrived several days late. These lapses in protocol provoked royal disfavor, but it was not of long duration. Neither was the Marquis; he died on April 22, 1692, three years after returning from New Spain.

The wife of the Marquis de la Laguna, María Luisa Manrique de Lara y Gonzaga, was of an equally illustrious and affluent family. She was the eldest daughter of a prince of the Holy Roman Empire, Vespasiano de Gonzaga, related by marriage to the reigning house of Mantua and captain general of Valencia; her mother, María Inés Manrique de Lara, was descended from a famous family in the history and literature of Spain.

María Luisa was, on her father's side, a princess of the house of Mantua, but she used the title she inherited from her mother, Countess de Paredes.[9] Her husband also used that title, along with his own, Marquis de la Laguna. The Countess had married Tomás de la Cerda in 1675, in the royal palace of Madrid, five years before their arrival in Mexico.

María Luisa, a woman of great energy and decisiveness, was said to be beautiful, and if we are to judge by Sor Juana's poems, she was extremely so. She must also have been discreet, sensitive, and intelligent, for otherwise it would be difficult to explain her admiration for Sor Juana and her passionate interest in her writings. In addition to being the inspiration for many of Sor Juana's poems, she urged her to write one of her best works, *El divino Narciso* (*The Divine Narcissus*). We also owe to the Countess the publication of Sor Juana's first collection, *Inundación castálida* (*Castalian Inundation*). We are unable to draw a portrait of this fascinating woman or of her husband; instead we are limited to occasional glimpses. Both, she especially, were sensitive and cultivated, and their passion for the arts, poetry, theater, and music was as great as their love for pomp and luxury. In that world good manners were an aesthetic initiation; at times love of social forms, the culture of the senses, was imperceptibly transformed into love of artistic form, the culture of the spirit. What a shame that lack of information prevents us from knowing them more intimately. One of the great flaws in Hispanic literature is the dearth of memoirs. We have no Saint-Simon, no Sévigné.

The custom of building triumphal arches to celebrate the entrée of viceroys goes back to the earliest years of New Spain. In his *Teatro de virtudes políticas* (*Theater of Political Virtues*), Sigüenza y Góngora says that Mexico City, "with inexpressible magnificence, has erected such triumphal arches or façades since December 22, 1528—the day the first Audiencia that came to govern these lands was welcomed—until the present time." Manuel Toussaint cites among the triumphal arches in Mexico City the one built in honor of Viceroy-Archbishop Fray García Guerra in 1611, painted "by no less than Luis Juárez, great artist of our Golden Age, and described by no less than Mateo Alemán." Following European example, the theme and the architecture of these monuments were entrusted to established poets and artists, as was the composition of the obligatory accompanying text. Sor Juana emphasizes this point in one of the first pages of her *Allegorical Neptune:* "To make resplendent the triumphal arches erected in honor of the viceroys come to govern this most noble kingdom has been the concern of many finely sharpened quills because, according to Plutarch, *preclara gesta praeclari indigent orationibus* [illustrious deeds demand illustrious rhetoric]."[10] Alberto G. Salceda mentions a number of arches in the seventeenth century.[11] Their titles—the titles of the accompanying texts—are revealing: *Astro mitológico político* (*Mythological-Political Star*); *Marte Católico* (*Catholic Mars*); *Ulises verdadero* (*The True Ulysses*); *Elogio panegírico y dibujo de ínclito Eneas* (*Eulogistic Panegyric and Portrait of an Illustrious Aeneas*); *Simulacro histórico y político de príncipe escondido bajo la alegoría de Cadmo* (*Historical and Political Simulacrum of Prince Cloaked in the Allegory of Cadmus*); *Zodíaco ilustre* (*Illustrious Zodiac*); *El nuevo Perseo* (*The New Perseus*).

Sigüenza was entrusted with the arch at Santo Domingo and Sor Juana with the cathedral arch. Aside from the obvious honor and benefits, the commission offered each of them the opportunity to seek the favor of the new Viceroy. As writers of indeterminate status, they both needed that favor: she was a learned nun whose father no one knew; he was a professor of mathematics and astrology noted for his irritability and unpunctuality. Although today they are the outstanding figures of their century, to their contemporaries they were suspect: Sor Juana because of her origins, and Sigüenza because he had been expelled from the Jesuit order (for nocturnal escapades while a student in the Colegio del Espíritu Santo in Puebla). But in a government like that of New Spain—the Viceroy at the center, like a sun, and around him the courtiers, planets with no light of their own—the light of power could dispel any shadow or strain. Until then Sor Juana had lived under the protection of the Marquis and Marquise de Mancera and, following their departure, that of Fray Payo. Now that the Viceroy-Archbishop had relinquished his dual responsibilities, she was without a patron. The commission from the ecclesiastic chapter could perhaps open the palace doors to her. It is not inconceivable that it was at Fray Payo's suggestion that Sor Juana had been made responsible for the cathedral arch. At any rate, the chapter would not have dared name her without his consent. This is additional proof, contrary to Francisco de la Maza's supposition, that Sor Juana did indeed enjoy Fray Payo's friendship. The position of Sigüenza y Góngora was even less secure; although, over opposition, he had obtained the professorship in mathematics and astrology at the university, his petition for reinstatement to the Jesuit order had twice been rejected.

Sigüenza y Góngora indicates that the plaza of Santo Domingo was the place where the city traditionally erected the arch to welcome its viceroys. He gives the names of the artists who executed his design and affirms that, "in the judgment of the well-informed in art, it was one of the most exquisite and unique creations of the age." The entire text of the *Theater of Political Virtues* is permeated with the exalted patriotism I alluded to in Part One of this book. Sigüenza was a champion of the cause of New over Old Spain. He begins his written text by proclaiming the superiority of the Mexican capital: "The imperial, most noble City of Mexico is the head of Occiseptentrional America." Later he expounds an idea that must have flattered criollos but which Spaniards must have thought extravagant, even dangerous: the arches that Mexicans build for their viceroys should not be called "triumphal," because the word is used "in memory of Roman triumphs and derived from battles of bloody invasions, for never was an arch erected for anyone who had not robbed at least five thousand enemies of their lives . . . Europe needs such bloodthirsty celebrations but we Americans exult in not feeling the need to achieve blessings of such nature . . . If we have always had the experience of princes who governed without bloodshed, how can the pageant with which Mexico welcomes those who come in love be called 'triumphal'?"

Sigüenza's attitude must not be confused with modern pacifism. The latter is a form of political, even revolutionary, action. It is a means to achieve political goals; for Sigüenza, however, pacifism was the result of a stage of civilization. His pacifism is a reproach to warlike, barbaric Europe; Europeans persisted in calling Americans savages, and Sigüenza replies by demonstrating that true civilization is incompatible with war. What is curious is that when he mentions the "bloody invasions" of the Europeans, he fails to note—or pretends not to note—the example right before his eyes: the Spanish conquest of Mexico. In Sigüenza's attitude we find again the contradiction that undermined the criollo dream and ended by tearing it apart.

Sigüenza did not hesitate to carry his reasoning to its logical conclusion. With full awareness of the political significance of the entrance, he criticizes the custom of "adorning it with mythological conceptions from mendacious fables." Thus, motivated by love for his country and faithful to the true spirit of the ceremony, he declares that he prefers to make the welcoming arch for the Count de Paredes a monument to truth and the art of governing. No better way than to turn his eyes not to pagan fables but to his own Mexico—specifically, to Mexico's ancient history. The examples of good government and political virtues that Sigüenza offers the Viceroy are "the Mexican emperors who actually resided in this most renowned empire of America." The title of the arch could not be clearer: *Theater of Political Virtues That Constitute a Ruler, Observed in the Ancient Monarchs of the Mexican Empire, Whose Effigies Adorn the Arch Erected by the Very Noble Imperial City of Mexico.* The models of political wisdom the learned criollo proposed to the Viceroy were Itzcóatl, Tizoc, Moctezuma Ilhuicamina, and other Aztec sovereigns. An unusual guest among these historical personages: the tribal god Huitzilopochtli. Sigüenza justifies his inclusion by arguing that Huitzilopochtli was not a divinity "but a chieftain and leader of Mexicans in the voyage that by his command was undertaken in search of the provinces of Anáhuac." In the Aztec god Sigüenza sees a figure who embodies the traits of Moses and Aeneas, that is, the two paradigms of his time: the Bible and classical antiquity.

Sigüenza's attitude conforms to the general tenor of criollo sentiment as it had been formulated and shaped by the Society of Jesus. This sentiment, as I have indicated, coincided in part with the designs and policies of the Jesuits in America and China. Jesuit universalism was founded on a peculiar syncretism that attempted to make the Catholic religion compatible with ancient Mesoamerican religions and, in the case of China, Confucianism. Such a procedure demanded a radical alteration of non-Christian and, at times, Christian beliefs. The transformation of a pre-Hispanic divinity such as Huitzilopochtli into a legendary leader can be explained within this policy of intellectual confiscation. For the Franciscans and the first missionaries, the Aztec gods were devils; for the Jesuits and ideologues like Sigüenza y Góngora, they were historical figures. The Franciscans wanted to put an end to the ancient religions, while the Jesuits wanted to utilize them. And in order to utilize these religions, they had to be stripped of the supernatural.

It was difficult to incorporate the figure of the devil Huitzilopochtli into an arch intended to honor a Spanish Viceroy, but less so when the Aztec god was converted into a flesh-and-blood leader who had founded a city and a state. The story of Huitzilopochtli's feats was modeled on those of the heroes of Greco-Roman antiquity and biblical patriarchs. Sigüenza closed his eyes to the Conquest; that is, he ignored the fact that between the Aztec empire and the kingdom of New Spain a bloody event had intervened. That deliberate oversight had an ideological purpose: to ensure the continuity between Mexico-Tenochtitlán and imperial Mexico City. The analogy with Rome, seat of a pagan empire and later the center of Christianity, was understood by all. In the maneuver of appropriation and transfiguration of the Indian past, humanism played a decisive role: Mexico saw itself in the mirror of Rome.

The *Theater of Political Virtues* is not an isolated example of Sigüenza's political and historical philosophy. I have already mentioned his vision of Quetzalcoatl—for him, not a pre-Hispanic god but none other than the apostle St. Thomas. What was the learned criollo's reaction to the arch conceived by Sor Juana, who had specifically chosen a pagan fable as theme? Sigüenza explains that the object of his criticism of the triumphal arch is not "to discredit what Sister Juana Inés de la Cruz devised for the arch erected by the Holy Metropolitan Church of Mexico City." He knows "that there is no pen that can rise to the towering eminence where hers excels," and that "in her, Mexico enjoys what in previous centuries the Graces apportioned among those learned women who in history books were objects of veneration and amazement." As for Sor Juana's unusual theme, Sigüenza triumphantly pulls another prodigious interpretation from his sleeve: "Neptune is not a chimerical King or a fabled deity, but an individual who actually existed, and one of whose glories was to have been the progenitor of the American Indians." This interpretation of pagan mythology was but an extreme application of the method whereby Huitzilopochtli was converted into an Emperor and Quetzalcoatl into a Christian apostle.

If Sigüenza's interpretations are surprising, even more surprising is the fact that they were tolerated by the Spanish authorities. Indifference? Ignorance? Inattention? Lafaye thinks that "it was acceptable to paint effigies of the emperors of Anahuac on the occasion of a Viceroy's reception because the Indian past had lost its power of subversion."[12] The Marquis de la Laguna could not suspect that a century later the criollos would use Sigüenza's historical metaphors as ideological ammunition against Spanish domination. Nevertheless, Lafaye's opinion needs to be slightly modified. Sigüenza's attitude, it is true, was an expression of criollo society's "self-affirmation," long before there was any discernible movement toward separatism. Nevertheless, it is difficult to ignore the political nature of his statements on American pacifism and on the teaching of Christianity in Mexico prior to the arrival of the Spanish. And it is similarly difficult to overlook his obsessive reiteration of the analogy between the Roman and Mexican empires, and the markedly polemical and anti-European tone of his reasoning. Similar ideas appear in the Jesuits' interpretations of the Chinese empire and Confucian religion. Sigüenza y Góngora was not unique; his ideas were variations on a prevalent doctrine held, more or less consciously, by other writers of the time, members of the Society of Jesus and those close to it. It would be an error to read a defense of political independence into Sigüenza's ideas; it is not an error to see in them the unexpected conclusions a still-nebulous criollo patriotism had drawn almost unintentionally from the syncretist universalism of the Jesuits. Two currents combined in Sigüenza's attitude. The ideas came from the syncretism propagated by the Jesuits; the sentiments, from the confused aspirations of criollo society.

11

The World as Hieroglyph

*N*OTHING COULD BE FURTHER from the patriotic and historical interpretations of Sigüenza than the arch devised by Sor Juana: *Allegorical Neptune, Ocean of Colors, Political Simulacrum, Erected by the Noble, Holy, and August Metropolitan Church of Mexico City, in the Magnificent Allegorical Concepts of a Triumphal Arch Solicitously Consecrated and Lovingly Dedicated to the Joyful Entrance of the Most Excellent Don Tomás Antonio de la Cerda, Count de Paredes, Marquis de la Laguna, Viceroy, Governor, and Captain General of Our New Spain.* It is worth our while to consider this title—the title of the booklet accompanying the arch—for a moment. Why "Allegorical Neptune"? Because the pagan god serves as a symbol of the Spanish Viceroy to New Spain. Sor Juana's aquatic allegory undoubtedly flows from the verbal similarity between one of Tomás de la Cerda's titles—Marquis de la Laguna (Marquis of the Lake) —and the fact that Mexico City had been founded on a lake. "Ocean," not only because it is Neptune's dwelling place but because Sor Juana says, "as Vincenzo Cartari notes, [Neptune and Oceanus] were very similar in their portrayal; and with good reason, for they indicated one and the same thing." "Ocean of Colors"—first, because the colors and the lines are allegories of the virtues and attributes of Neptune, and second, because these virtues and attributes are so numerous as to form a true ocean. Thus "the mythological colors and symbolic lines" of the arch, being allegories of Neptune's qualities, were also those of the Marquis de la Laguna. The arch, "in voices of colors, publishes the triumphs" of the Viceroy. "Political Simulacrum," because the arch was the model of the virtues of kings and princes such as Neptune and the Viceroy.

The arch was built in front of the west door of the cathedral. It had a single façade some thirty yards high and sixteen wide and was made of wood, cloth, and plaster. The structure cannot have been very solid, for it was scarcely a month in construction. Sor Juana describes its three basic parts and their architectural styles—Corinthian, composite, and Doric; the simulated jaspers and bronzes; the columns, bases, and panels or canvases with their paintings, effigies, and Spanish and Latin inscriptions. She does not mention the artists who executed her design, but praises their work. Rather convenient praise, since it affords her the opportunity, with no false modesty, to praise her own inscriptions as well: if the lines, figures, and colors of the arch attract the "eyes of the common people," the inscriptions capture the "attention of the well-informed." Among the principal attractions of the arch was the representation of Neptune and his wife, Amphitrite, on the first and central canvas, naked and standing on a seashell pulled by two "swimming monsters." A revealing detail about Sor Juana, who was a master of the art of courtly praise; her idea of representing the Viceroy and Vicereine as Neptune and Amphitrite allowed her to say, as she notes in the "Razón de la fábrica alegórica" ("Rationale of the Allegorical Invention"): "For the faces of the two sea gods, the brush stole the perfections of their Excellencies, although falling short (especially in the case of the Most Excellent Lady Marquise) of the original, however beautiful the results." The Marquise must have been enchanted by such adulation.

The image of Neptune and Amphitrite was taken from Vincenzo Cartari's famous treatise on mythology, *Le imagini de i dei de gli antichi*. In the "Argumento del primer lienzo" ("Theme of the First Canvas"), Sor Juana points out that the engraving in Cartari's book was inspired by a description from Pausanias. What is Sor Juana's source for this information? In Part One of this book I referred to Baltasar de Vitoria's *Theater of the Pagan Gods*. In the chapter devoted to Neptune, Vitoria, too, refers to Pausanias when he speaks of Cartari's engraving, and adds, "How they painted Neptune Cicero reports and Cartari presents to us." Although Sor Juana the bibliophile delighted in citing her sources, she never mentioned Vitoria. When the *Allegorical Neptune* is compared to the *Theater of the Pagan Gods,* however, it becomes obvious that Sor Juana's information and her quotations—both in reference to the gods of antiquity and authorities in mythology—are frequently the same as those in Vitoria's work. The number of duplicated passages precludes any possibility of coincidence. It is not unreasonable to presume that instead of obtaining the original sources, Sor Juana consulted compilations and available treatises like Vitoria's, and Juan Pérez de Moya's *Filosofía secreta* (*Secret Philosophy*), another very popular contemporary treatise on mythology. Like so many self-taught scholars, she concealed the fact that her information was secondhand. In her favor, I can say that she utilized the collective learning transmitted through mythological works with few appreciable variations.

It is not likely that Sor Juana personally supervised the construction of the arch: she was forbidden by the rule of cloister to leave the convent. She undoubtedly directed the work from her cell. She also wrote a small volume in explication of her allegory. It is divided into two parts. The first, in prose, contains the dedication, the rationale of the allegorical invention, and detailed descriptions of the motifs and subjects of the eight canvases, four bases, and two intercolumniations. Each of these descriptions ends with a brief poem—a *décima,* an octet, a quatrain, a Latin epigram—except the central canvas, which concludes with a sonnet. The second part is in verse, the "Explicación sucinta del arco" ("Succinct Explication of the Arch"). In fact, it is a recapitulation and metrification of the descriptions of the first part. Manuel Toussaint believes that it dates from 1680 and that the complete edition, consisting of the two parts, is of a slightly later date, perhaps 1681. If that were so, the "Succinct Explication" (in verse) would be Sor Juana's second publication. Her first is the *Villancicos a San Pedro* (*Villancicos for St. Peter*), which appeared in 1677.

Various episodes in the story of Neptune, transposed into allegories of the deeds—real or imagined—of the Marquis de la Laguna and all related to the imperial city of Mexico, were represented on the canvases, bases, and intercolumniations. For example, the third canvas depicted the story of Delos—also in Vitoria's book—which Neptune changed from a floating to a stable island—an allusion to Mexico-Tenochtitlán, originally built "on isles of floating grasses / by blind and ignorant heathen." On the fourth canvas Aeneas was saved from Achilles' persecution by the god, an archetype of the Marquis, "like the Father of the Winds, all-powerful, / who when offended waxed more merciful." On the fifth canvas Neptune defended the learned centaurs from the mace of Hercules, and the Marquis, like the sea god, was "for letters, the greatest refuge known."[1] The sixth canvas showed the Dolphin, Neptune's ambassador, "a scaled Cicero," before an aloof Amphitrite and transformed into a constellation: "O Mexico, applaud your Neptune

. . . The Dolphin blazes in the sky, announcing with his augury that all is well." On the seventh, the god allows himself to be bested by Minerva in their competition to be patron of Athens, a defeat that is a victory, for, contrary to what is generally believed, Minerva is not the daughter of Jupiter but of Neptune, that is, of wisdom itself, "as Natalis Comes records, following Pausanias." And so on.

The arch and its two explications, in prose and verse, contained two petitions. The first, symbolized on the second canvas by the painting of "a city invaded by the salty ocean's wrath," asked the Viceroy to complete the project of draining the basin of Mexico City, as Neptune had contained in a lake the waters of the Peneus River. Sor Juana sums up her request in an *octava real* with the motto *Opportuna interventio:* "quede ya la cabeza de Occidente / segura de inundantes invasiones" (now may the center of the West / be safe from inundating floods). On the eighth canvas was a painting of the cathedral of Mexico City as it was then, still uncompleted; opposite was the Wall of Troy, whose construction was attributed to Neptune. Sor Juana again closely followed Vitoria; like the Spanish mythologist she counterposes the view of Ovid, who ascribes the wall to Apollo, to that of Virgil, who says it is the work of Neptune. Sor Juana quotes the same lines from Ovid and Virgil that Vitoria quotes. Finally, she asks the Viceroy to complete the temple and concludes the allegory with another *octava real*.

The *Allegorical Neptune* is a perfect example of what is admirable and execrable in baroque prose: interlaced with prosopopeias, echoes, labyrinths, emblems, paradoxes, wit, and antitheses, sparkling with Latin quotations and Greek and Egyptian names, in interminable, sinuous phrases, slowed but not overburdened by its trappings, it advances across the page with a certain elephantine majesty. No matter: the abundance of quotations, references, and literary allusions—four or five to a page—gives us a rather complete picture of Sor Juana's readings and of her intellectual and literary preferences.

Although it is less interesting, the section in verse, "Succinct Explication," has greater aesthetic value. In spite of being a commissioned work, it contains, as always, felicitous lines and passages. The dedication, in octosyllabic lines of assonant rhyme, fulfills a threefold purpose: to praise the new Viceroy, the outgoing Viceroy (Fray Payo), and the chapter. Expert in courtly matters, Sor Juana excels in the art of ingenious flattery. The remaining parts—eight, one for each canvas—are written in the traditional form for this kind of composition, the *silva*. Once again, we wonder at her mastery of versification. Every line is a living, flexible whole: syllables propelled by accent and caesura combine and separate, rise and fall, with an undulation that evokes the sea or a field of wheat.

Sor Juana's versification is one of the most elegant and refined in Spanish. Few poets in our language equal her, and those who surpass her can be counted on the fingers of one hand. The *silva* was written in the light (and shadow) of Góngora. Light and shadow controlled by a less rich and powerful, but more reflective, temperament. Splendors moderated to a restrained radiance: "a radiant constellation / on a transparent throne." The "Succinct Explication" ends with a sonnet in which, among convolutions and reverberations, appear two tercets with Neoplatonic resonances. Sor Juana invites the Viceroy to pass beneath the arch and enter the cathedral:

> Then, enter, and if for such stateliness
> the temple be too small, love will create
> another in our souls, of greater strength,
>   that ideal porphyries will consecrate:
> so formal is your sovereign majesty,
> we immaterial temples dedicate.

The arch was an allegorical portrait of Tomás de la Cerda. The section in prose justifies this allegory and develops it. It begins by explaining that in order to represent their gods—immaterial beings that "lacked all visible form"—the ancient Egyptians resorted to hieroglyphs, "and this they did not only with deities, but with all invisible things, such as days, months, and weeks." For the same reasons and also "out of reverence and respect," it was not illogical "to seek ideas and hieroglyphs that represent symbolically some of the countless prerogatives that illumine the Count de Paredes." Farther on, Sor Juana explains why she chose a fable from antiquity as an allegory of the Viceroy and why that does not invalidate her comparisons: because "fables have their basis in true events; and those the heathens called gods were really excellent princes . . . or the inventors of things." Neptune seemed to her to be a "drawing of His Excellency as accurate as the concordance of their deeds will prove." She then sets forth the genealogy and deeds of Neptune, with quantities of quotations from mythologists then in favor (Cartari, Pierio Valeriano, Comes, Textor) and of classical poets and authorities (Macrobius, Cicero, Pliny, Ovid, Homer), not excluding the Church Fathers and the Bible.

The genealogy of Neptune that Sor Juana presents is not uncommon for her time, but it is tendentious. Later I shall try to demonstrate the rationale for this curious genealogy. According to Juana Inés, Neptune's mother was "the goddess Opis or Cybele, who is the same as Isis, as both names represent the Earth, which they called *Magna Mater* . . . Isis signifies the same in Comes: *Io modo Luna dicta est, modo credita est Terra*" (Io is now called Moon, now thought to be Earth). The transformation of Opis into Isis, Isis into Io, and Io into a cow allows her, following the mythological treatises of the time, to accentuate the Egyptian nature of the goddess and, by derivation, that of her son, who thereby is no longer Neptune, the Greek and Roman god of the sea; rather, without ceasing to be Neptune, he is also Harpocrates (Horus), divinity of silence, son of Isis, worshiped by the Egyptians in the form of a boy-god. Sor Juana was fascinated by the figure of Harpocrates (she refers to him again in *First Dream*) and recalls that St. Augustine called him "the great god of silence." This allusion also appears in the *Theater of the Pagan Gods* (chapter 13: "On Harpocrates, God of Silence"). Sor Juana follows Vitoria very closely—again, without mentioning him—in her remaining references to this Egyptian divinity, as when she explains that Harpocrates is the god the Greeks called Sygalion.

At some point the weaving of analogies that is the substance of all syncretism unravels. Neptune is Harpocrates and Harpocrates is silence and silence is Sygalion, but is Neptune silence? The relationship between Neptune and silence stretches so thin that it threatens to break. With feigned ingenuousness Sor Juana confesses that she "had never seen in any author" (although she adds immediately, with a certain coyness, "of the few I have mastered") "the reason why the ancients venerated Neptune as the god of silence." The truth is that Neptune, god of the sea, violent and awesome, was associated with the taming of horses and with navigation, not with silence. Nevertheless, twisting still more the thread of analogy, Sor Juana ventures an explanation: "Because he is the god of the waters, whose children, fish, are mute, as Horace said: *O mutis quoque piscibus / donatura cygni, si libeat, sonum* (Oh, to mute fish, if you so wished, you could give the song of swans)." The explanation is not an explanation, and the quote from Horace is not relevant, except to change the stormy and unpredictable Neptune into a hermetic and silent god.

The same quotation from Horace appears in Vitoria, in connection not with Neptune, however, but with silence and its deities, Harpocrates, Sygalion, Angirona or Angerona.[2] And there are other examples:

all of Sor Juana's citations and associations during this period came from Vitoria (who, for his part, had taken them from Valeriano, Cartari, and others). In order to appreciate our poet's methods, it is enlightening to compare texts from Sor Juana and Vitoria.

Sor Juana:

> For which reason, his being master of silence, they depicted Pythagoras as a fish, for among all the animals only the fish is mute; and so went the ancient proverb: *pisce taciturnior* [more silent than a fish]; and the Egyptians, according to Pierius, chose it as a symbol of silence; and Claudian says that Rhadamanthus turned the loquacious into fish, so that with eternal silence they make amends for their garrulity: *Qui iusto plus esse loquax, arcanaque suevit / prodere, piscosas fertur victurus in undas: / ut nimiam pensent aeterna silentia vocem* [He who was more than ordinarily talkative, a betrayer of secrets, was carried off, a fish, to live in the waters amid his kind, to atone in eternal silence for his garrulity].

Vitoria:

> Pythagoras was the great master of teaching silence, and thus his disciples depicted him as a fish: because among all the animals only the fish is mute, and it was an ancient proverb: *pisce taciturnior,* more silent and more mute than the fish: and so the Egyptians chose the fish, according to Pierius, as a symbol of silence . . . and Claudian attributes mute silence to fish when he presents Rhadamanthus, judge of hell, condemning to hell loquacious and talkative men who have made so bold as to discover and make known hidden secrets, and in punishment he transformed and converted them into fish, and these are the verses of Claudian: *Qui iusto plus esse . . .*

Syncretist genealogy: the archetype of the Marquis de la Laguna was not truly the Greco-Roman Neptune, but a composite divinity in whom were allied different attributes and deities, among them, and principally, an Egyptian boy-god (Horus) in the Hellenized form of Harpocrates. Sor Juana's process of transformation tended to intellectualize and internalize Neptune in order to convert him, the stormy god who was the progenitor of terrifying monsters like Polyphemus and the giant Antaeus, into a civilizing deity whose attributes were sapience, culture, and art. As for Isis:

> This greatly celebrated Isis was that queen of Egypt whom Diodorus Siculus so justly praises from the first lines of his *History* . . . ; Plutarch

wrote an entire book on the subject; Valerianus Pierius, many chapters; Plato, many praises, and in Book II of *Legib.* [*Laws*], in treating Egyptian music, said: *Ferunt antiquissimos illos apud eos concentus Isidis esse poemata* [They claim that the songs that have been preserved for such a long time were the compositions of Isis].

Thus Isis was a poet in addition to being the goddess of wisdom.

After she portrays Neptune, Sor Juana compares him with Tomás de la Cerda. Although preposterous, the comparison is not without ingenuity: Neptune is the son of Saturn and Tomás de la Cerda is of royal blood; Neptune is the son of Isis (Wisdom) and Tomás de la Cerda is a descendant of Alfonso el Sabio (Alfonso the Wise); Neptune is the brother of Jupiter, the sky god, and Tomás de la Cerda is the brother of the Duke de Medinaceli (*coeli,* of the sky); Neptune is the god of water and Tomás de la Cerda is the Marquis de la Laguna (of the Lake); Neptune, god of buildings, built the wall of Troy and Tomás de la Cerda is the Count de Paredes (of walls); Neptune invented the art of horseback riding and Tomás de la Cerda is a *marqués,* a Celtic word that means prefect of knights; the sign of Neptune is the trident and in Tomás de la Cerda's viceregal scepter are represented three powers: martial, civil, and criminal.

The Countess de Paredes also figured in the arch. In addition to the first canvas, on which she appeared as Amphitrite, naked and standing on a seashell, she was represented on the two intercolumniations. On one, the sea itself was the hieroglyph of the beauty of María Luisa Manrique de Lara: "The beauty of María is the sea (*Mar*) in her eyes." The Countess was of the house of Mantua, so that the other intercolumniation depicted "a ship on the high seas and overhead the Morning Star" (Venus), with the rhymed explanation: "From Mantua, her fairest light / sailed 'cross the ocean from afar: / in such a star upon the sea, / the sea beheld its lucky star."

THE *ALLEGORICAL NEPTUNE* begins with a comparison between Egyptian hieroglyphs and the arch erected in honor of the Viceroy. For Sor Juana the arch was but another hieroglyph among the vast allegorical representations composing the universe. The seventeenth century was the century of emblems, and only from and within that emblematic conception of the universe can we understand Sor Juana's attitude. The interest in hieroglyphic writing in the fifteenth century stimulated the birth of the art of emblems that two centuries later, in the hands of the Jesuits, was converted into a system of interpreting the world and into a peda- gogical and didactic tool.[3] But hieroglyphs and emblems were more than representations of the world; the world itself was hieroglyph and em- blem. Not only writing was seen in them—that is, a means of represent- ing reality—but reality itself. Among the attributes of reality was sym- bolic being: rivers, rocks, animals, stars, human beings—everything was a hieroglyph at the same time it was itself. Signs acquired the dignity of being; they were not a representation of reality, they were reality itself, or, more exactly, one of its versions. If the reality of the world was em- blematic, everything and every being was a symbol of another. The world was a fabric of reflections, echoes, and correspondences.

The conjunction between the emblematic vision of the universe and Neoplatonism was fateful. The encounter took place in the Florence of Cosimo de' Medici, and its first protagonists were Marsilio Ficino, Pico della Mirandola, and their disciples and friends. The fact that Egyptian hieroglyphs were indecipherable gave them an ontological status distinct from that of mere linguistic sign. (Only with Champollion did Egyptian writing lose this dignity.) Furthermore, precisely because they were Egyptian, the hieroglyphs were a kind of mysterious materialization of original wisdom, as it had been revealed to man by the authors of the ancient theology, the teachers of Plato and Plotinus. Among these first philosophers, the first and wisest had been Hermes Trismegistus. From its beginnings, Renaissance Neoplatonism was a hermeticism, and that hermeticism was an "Egyptianism." In his preface to the *Pimander,* one of the treatises in the *Corpus Hermeticum,* Ficino says: "In that time in which Moses was born flourished Atlas the astrologer, brother of Pro- metheus the physicist and maternal grandfather of the elder Mercury, whose grandson was Mercurius Trismegistus . . . , who has been called the founder of theology." Ficino attributed the invention of hieroglyphs to Hermes. He saw in them—and not only in them but in the pyramids, obelisks, and other monuments of Egypt—symbolic expressions, mate- rial forms in which that original wisdom, or "first theology," had been revealed.

The "Egyptian" interpretation of Platonism was not a novelty. The philosopher Iamblichus (250?–330?) had already attempted a fusion be- tween Near Eastern rituals, especially Egyptian, and Platonic philoso- phy. Greco-Roman antiquity from the time of Herodotus was fascinated with Egypt. Egyptian religion, especially the cult of Isis, had a profound impact in Syria, Asia Minor, Greece, Rome, and, later, Gaul and Germany. To the religion of Isis we owe one of the most beautiful novels of our civilization—Apuleius' *Golden Ass*—as well as Plutarch's essay on Isis and Osiris. Greek syncretism turned the god Thoth, author of the arts and sciences, into Hermes "Thrice-great" (Trismegistus) of hermetic tradition. There has been a great deal of discussion about the importance and degree of truly Egyptian elements contained in hermetic gnosticism. For Festugière the ideas are essentially Greek, although the varnish is Egyptian.[4] Bloomfield thinks that "these writings are chiefly the product of Egyptian Neoplatonists who were greatly influenced by Stoicism, Judaism, Persian theology and possibly native Egyptian beliefs, as well as, of course, by Plato, especially the *Timaeus*."[5] Thus was born a chimerical Egypt whose fantastic characteristics would be accentuated by the Renaissance and the Baroque.

In the sixteenth century Neoplatonic hermeticism spread through Europe. Its influence permeated literature and poetry, as well as philosophy and theology. In the Valois court, protected alternately by Diane de Poitiers and Catherine de' Medici, poets professed a Neoplatonism impregnated with hermeticism. One of the central figures of that great poetic moment was Pontus de Tyard (1521?–1605), the Bishop of Châlons. A poet admired by Ronsard, a friend of Maurice Scève, and bard of Louise Labé, Tyard did not fear to affirm that the mystery of the Christian Trinity was prefigured in "Egyptian" tradition: "From the holy school of Egypt . . . has come down to us the secret doctrine and the wisdom of the ternary number." In England, Neoplatonic hermeticism influenced Sir Philip Sidney and from the influence of his circle was prolonged until the seventeenth century and the Cambridge Neoplatonists. Two of the books Giordano Bruno published during his stay in England—*Spaccio della bestia trionfante* (*The Expulsion of the Triumphant Beast*) and *De gli eroici furiori* (*The Heroic Frenzies*)—are dedicated to Sidney. Recently Frances A. Yates has speculated that Shakespeare may have found in Bruno a model for Berowne, the courtly poet in *Love's Labor's Lost*.

Three elements must be identified in Renaissance Neoplatonic hermeticism: the authentically philosophical, a mixture of genuine Platonism and of ideas taken from the *Corpus Hermeticum*, the Cabala, and other sources; the new science, especially astronomy and physics; and a magic vision of the universe derived from alchemy, astrology, and other occult sciences. About the latter it must be said that the "magi" of the sixteenth century, such as John Dee, through their constant manipulation of and experimentation with the natural elements, opened the way to the empiricism of modern science. Scientific and magic preoccupations were so tightly imbricated that it is impossible to separate them. This is true not only for such minor figures as Cornelius Agrippa and John Dee but also for Giordano Bruno and Tommaso Campanella. Bruno appropriates the ideas of Copernicus and for the first time gives them a philosophical formulation; at the same time, he uses the new physics and astronomy to justify magic. With the intention of returning to this subject in the chapter on *First Dream,* I shall merely mention now the fusion between hermeticism and Egyptianism. In his *Expulsion of the Triumphant Beast,* Bruno says: "Egypt, the great monarchy of letters and nobility, is the father of our fables, metaphors, and doctrines." When he refers to Egyptian writing, following the belief of his time, he confuses hieroglyphs with emblems—the Hellenistic period had already committed the same error—and says that "with those sacred letters . . . which were images—the Egyptians captured with marvellous skill the language of the gods."[6]

The seventeenth century is the dividing line between this kind of thinking and modernity. Hermeticism began to decline when in 1614 a Huguenot who had taken refuge in the court of James I, the Hellenist Isaac Casaubon, proved that the *Corpus Hermeticum* dates from the first centuries of the Christian Era. The triumph of Cartesian thought and the advances of physics and Newtonian astronomy precipitated the decline of hermeticism. Nevertheless, it survived throughout the seventeenth century not only in esoteric religious movements such as Rosicrucianism but also in figures who exercised a great intellectual influence on their age. Among these are the Englishman Robert Fludd and the German Jesuit Athanasius Kircher, of universal renown in their century. Fludd was celebrated for his polemic with Father Mersenne, a friend of Descartes, and with Kepler. Kircher still awaits a modern biography.[7] Fleeing the Swedish occupation of Germany, he first sought refuge in Avignon and later took up residence in Rome. He lived there some forty years, until his death. He accumulated a rich collection of Oriental antiquities, books, and scientific manuscripts and instruments. Kircher was a prolific author, and his words were widely read and esteemed in his century. Frances A. Yates describes him as a seventeenth-century Pico della Mirandola and points out that he aimed to make a synthesis of the great religious traditions that included areas unknown to Pico, such as

Mexico and Japan, which had been covered by the Jesuit missions. Kircher's syncretism was broader than Sigüenza's, but it was subject to the same spiritual policy and was inspired in a similar proposal: a Christian synthesis of universal religions.

A man of great ingenuity and persuasiveness, a scholar possessed—as are many of our contemporaries—by a mania for exclusivist interpretation, Kircher believed that in the Egyptian civilization he had found the universal key for deciphering all the enigmas of history. Naturally, that was the Egypt of the hermetic tradition. In several books that were widely celebrated and commented on—*Prodromus Coptus* (1636) and *Oedipus Aegyptiacus* (1652)—he demonstrated with awesome erudition and eloquence that India, China, and ancient Mexico owed their arts, religions, sciences, and philosophies to the Egypt of the hermetic tradition. Four examples among thousands: Confucius is none other than the savant called Thoth by the Egyptians and Hermes by the Greeks; the Brahmans adore Isis in their pagodas and wear linen and carry staffs like Egyptian priests; the diviners and seers of Mexico followed the Egyptian hierophants and Indian gymnosophists in their rites; it was Egyptian example that inspired the builders of the Mexican pyramids. The *Oedipus Aegyptiacus* contains a chapter on the parallelism between Egyptian and American religions. Kircher's readers in New Spain must have seized upon these ideas with enthusiastic and understandable emotion.

In Kircher's work Jesuit syncretism reaches a totality that embraces all times and all places. Catholic Rome is the center upon which all religions converge, and the prefiguration of that center, a true bridge between Christianity and other religions, is ancient Egypt and her prophet Hermes Trismegistus. The *Oedipus Aegyptiacus* is studded with quotations from the *Corpus Hermeticum,* especially from the *Pimander* and the *Asclepius.* Kircher, like Pontus de Tyard, believed that Hermes had intuited the mystery of the Trinity. Kircher's great passion, says Yates, was hieroglyphs, and, like everyone of his time, he saw them as emblems, that is, not as writing but as symbolic pictures concealing divine truths: "Hermes Trismegistus, the Egyptian, who first instituted the hieroglyphs, thus becoming the prince and parent of all Egyptian theology and philosophy, . . . engraved his opinion for all eternity on lasting stones and huge rocks. Thence Orpheus, Musaeus, Linus, Pythagoras, Plato, Eudoxus, Parmenides, Melissus, Homerus, Euripides, and others learned rightly of God and of divine things."[8] The hieroglyphs thus became symbolic representations, emblems, of the ideas in the *Pimander* and other hermetic treatises.

Hermeticism also penetrated into Spain, but there its traces are less visible than in Italy, France, England, and Germany. The orthodoxy of the Spanish monarchy and its belligerent policy in religious matters explain the rather discreet, even underground, nature of Spanish hermeticism. But it was not as insignificant as the usual stereotyped vision of Spanish history supposes. Its influence has been discovered in no less a person than Juan de Herrera, Philip II's architect. An English scholar, René Taylor, has shown that both Herrera and Philip II collected hermetic works.[9] According to Taylor, there is considerable similarity between the magical-architectural preoccupations of Herrera and those of John Dee, Elizabeth's astrologer, who was Bruno's friend and guide during his stay in London. Taylor says: "Both were mathematicians . . . At the same time side by side with their interest in rational mathematics went a passion for *mathesis,* or 'mystical' mathematics . . . They were both . . . enthusiastic Lullists . . . interested in Hermetism, astrology . . . and Cabala." Taylor adds that Philip II not only had Dee's works in his library but had met him personally, for the English magus had cast his horoscope. The relationship between Dee and certain Spanish circles interested in these matters must have been rather intimate; among Dee's belongings recently acquired by the British Museum is an obsidian Aztec mirror. Dee was in the Low Countries and during his stay was visited by many nobles from the retinue of Charles V. One of them must have presented the Mexican mirror to him.[10]

The theme of hermeticism in Hispanic letters of the sixteenth and seventeenth centuries has not been studied, but even though our information is incomplete and fragmentary, it is not far-fetched to suggest that its influence was greater than has been reckoned. A rigorous study is needed on the subject, similar to those on the poets of the Pléiade in France or on Spenser and Sidney in England. One focus of such a study would have to be Lope de Vega's Platonism. Even a summary examination of *La Dorotea*—one of his most personal works, not only because it is semi-autobiographical, but also because it expresses his philosophy of love and is a repertory of his ideas and readings—instantly reveals his familiarity with Neoplatonism. Citations and allusions to Ficino, Pico della Mirandola, and Leo Hebraeus abound, as do references to Natalis Comes, Alciati, and Textor.

The "Aprobación" (imprimatur) of the *Theater of the Pagan Gods* was issued by Lope de Vega. In the chapter dedicated to Hermes ("On Mercurius Trismegistus, Grandson of the God Mercury"), Vitoria says: "Mercurius the philosopher [that is, Thoth] had the surname Trismegistus because he was great in three things: great in the Priesthood, great in the science of Philosophy, and very great in Theology . . . because he comprehended some of the mysteries of the Holy Trinity and professed them." This syncretist interpretation of some of the treatises of the *Corpus Hermeticum* was current, as has been seen, among Neoplatonists. Vitoria adds: "None of the ancient philosophers speaks words more faithful to, and more to the letter of, the Holy Scripture, than Mercurius Trismegistus: and in the book called *Asclepius,* in the fourth chapter, Trismegistus treats the matter of the creation almost exactly as Moses wrote it in Genesis." In his "Aprobación" Lope de Vega says that Father Vitoria's book contains "a most important lesson for the comprehension of many books whose moral the ancient philosophy clothes in many fables . . . and in whose ornaments the theologians of the heathen, from Mercurius Trismegistus to the divine Plato, found, through symbols and hieroglyphs, the explanation of the nature of things—as recorded in the *Pimander* and the *Timaeus*—which, as sacred matters, the Egyptians carefully hid from the common people."

12

Sister Juana and the Goddess Isis

$\mathcal{F}$OLLOWING THIS DIGRESSION it will be easier to understand Sor Juana's attitude as well as the true meaning of the *Allegorical Neptune*. I have pointed out that in the first pages of the prose explication Sor Juana says that Neptune descended from Isis. She thus converts him into an Egyptian deity. There were several arguments—some historical and mythological, some personal and self-serving—for such an identification. The syncretist cult of Osiris/Serapis was born during the reign of Ptolemy I. That cult was disseminated by Egyptian merchants and seamen through all the Mediterranean ports.[1] The popularity of the cult of Serapis in the seaports explains why he was sometimes identified with Poseidon and later with Neptune. But Sor Juana was most interested in reinforcing the ties between Neptune and wisdom. In order to make him the son of Isis, she avails herself of Sigüenza y Góngora's method, a method universally employed by Renaissance and baroque mythologists. Sor Juana points out that Cartari "mistakes" Minerva for Isis—that is, he confuses and fuses them. In truth, both goddesses are one, the one to whom "authors of old have given many names: Apuleius calls her Rhea, Venus, Diana, Bellona, Ceres, Juno, Proserpina, Hecate, and Rhamnusia. Diodorus Siculus says that Isis is the one who was called Moon, Juno, and Ceres; Macrobius is of the opinion that she is the Earth, or the nature of things." In spite of these many names and attributes, Sor Juana maintains that "it is not difficult to ascertain who this so oft mentioned Isis is": all her names are ways to label wisdom. For proof she cites the words of Jacques Bolduc, an author often quoted by Vitoria: "The ancients gave divers names to wisdom, all of them originating from someone's having feigned, in order to lend authority to their doctrine, some attending goddess to whose direction was owing, they said, all that the sciences had achieved, such as the Egeria of Numa, the Urania of Avitus, and the Ennoia of Simon Magus." Thus Isis is one of the names of wisdom, the most illustrious, since it is linked to the hermetic tradition of Egypt in which pagan wisdom and biblical revelation are joined.

It is truly amazing that among the ancient names of wisdom Sor Juana lists that of the consort of Simon Magus—a person described as a charlatan in the Acts of the Apostles—whom various Christian authors and Fathers of the Church, among them Justin Martyr, Hippolytus, Irenaeus, and Tertullian, vehemently denounced in blackest terms. Sor Juana must have been aware that the consort of the gnostic Simon was named Helena and that he had found her in a brothel in Tyre; Simon said that the fallen Ennoia (Epinoia), that is, the "Thought" of God, had taken refuge in the body of the prostitute. No less surprising is the fact that Sor Juana—here in agreement with the gnostics and heretics—attributes a gender to Mind, and the female gender at that. And, in fact, like *sophia* (wisdom), the words *ennoia* and *epinoia,* frequently used by gnostics and meaning "thought" or "idea," are feminine.[2] The idea of the Fall is common to gnosticism and to Christianity, but in the former there is an element essentially foreign to the Christian vision of the universe: belief that Mind is female. The gnostic sees the world in pairs, all of them derived from a dualist principle: *nous* (mind, spirit) and *epinoia* or *ennoia* (thought). That is why it has been said that gnosis can be seen as "a great sexual mystery." Sor Juana knew of these ideas indirectly, through syncretist treatises on mythology, Father Kircher's books, and other works influenced to a greater or lesser degree by the speculations of Neoplatonic hermeticism. Thus she affirms that wisdom is essentially female and, without saying so explicitly, insinuates that what we call mind or idea is also female.

These ideas were clearly heretical, and that is undoubtedly why Sor Juana relies on an astonishing etymology for Isis. Again she refers to Bolduc, who, "following well-reasoned arguments," says: "From Mizraim and Heber, the first teachers of the Egyptians and men renowned for their divine wisdom, and through their doctrine bearing on religion, we know that the name Isis derived from an iterated Hebrew name. That name is *Is,* which means Man."

This etymology protects her from any suspicion: the goddess Isis is the personification of wisdom, but her origin is doubly masculine: Is-

Is = twice male. Furthermore, the Hebrew origin of the name lends to the wisdom embodied in Isis a character different from and superior to that of the Greek *sophia,* the Latin *sapientia,* or the gnostic *ennoia.* The wisdom of Isis is directly linked with biblical revelation, although this supernatural origin was later obscured through centuries of paganism. In the same way that the mystery of the Holy Trinity is visible in the doctrines of Hermes Trismegistus, there is an intimation of biblical revelation in the Egyptian wisdom of Isis. As Sor Juana describes: "But this name of Isis [she is referring to the original Hebrew] is not that of any ordinary wisdom [that is, profane wisdom] but that of Heber and Mizraim, as Bolduc himself explained: 'So that the cow that means Isis, or divine Wisdom, according to the men who were the first leaders in Egypt following the flood, that is, Mizraim and Heber, was, by some indications, different from the one that existed later.'" And Sor Juana concludes triumphantly that there was a time, before there were pagans and idolators, when Isis "represented only wisdom"—the true wisdom that had its origins in the Bible.

This bizarre etymology of Isis is not merely a baroque oddity or a theological sophistry intended to protect Sor Juana against doctrinaire attacks, but reveals, once again, Sor Juana's contradictions: it is a deliberate exaltation of the female condition that, simultaneously, expresses a no less deliberate will to transcend that condition. Wisdom is female, but the goddess who personifies wisdom signifies doubly Man. (Is this not also the paradox of the modern feminist movement?) The mythological enigmas in which Sor Juana took such pleasure are masks that reveal as they conceal. But it is possible to discern still another element in her predilection for Isis. A goddess whose name is the symbolic doubling of Man and who is the female archetype of highest learning—both profane and divine—Isis is also the "universal mother," the Magna Mater: Earth, and nature itself. Since the Greeks, Isis had been identified with Demeter, Aphrodite, Hera, and Io. In the case of Io, the connection was more direct: the majority of mythologists relate that Io, turned into a cow and pursued by Juno's gadfly, takes refuge in Egypt, where a compassionate Jupiter restores her to human form. The Egyptians, says Vitoria, "adored her in the figure of a cow and called her the goddess Isis." Sor Juana repeats this version and quotes the same verses from Ovid that Vitoria uses to illustrate his account, although she omits the mythologist's beautiful translation: "From woman to cow, from cow into goddess, for her spirit and beauty, thus was she changed."

The identification between Isis and Cybele was a little more difficult, but not impossible: according to Cartari, Cybele was the "great mother," and Isis was also the universal mother. The same was true of the wife of the awesome Saturn and mother of Neptune, the goddess Opis, frequently confused with Rhea and Cybele. All these goddesses resolve into Isis, who in turn is transformed into a kind of secret—although loudly proclaimed—emblem for Sor Juana Inés de la Cruz. The nun, a "renowned and learned woman," projects her longings and desires onto the divinity venerated by Apuleius, one in whom motherhood and wisdom are combined. All the obsessions of Juana Inés are contained in the figure of the goddess: Isis is the image of motherhood and, at the same time, "the model of Egyptian wisdom." Juana Inés, through Isis, transposes the "masculinity" inherent in culture and the sexlessness afforded by her nun's habits into a kind of ideal femininity and symbolic universal motherhood. The French jurist André Tiraqueau "placed Isis in the catalog of learned women: and learned she was, in great measure, because she was the inventor of Egyptian letters." The goddess becomes confused with knowledge, that is, *she is knowledge:* "Finally, she had not only all the qualities of one who is wise, but those of wisdom itself, which was conceived in her." This idea is not in contradiction with what may be deduced from Sor Juana's interpretation in a different passage of the name of Isis: doubly Man. In the same way that the symbolic motherhood of the goddess, mother of signs, transcends natural motherhood, her being transcends mere human knowledge, which is masculine. Never ceasing to be Woman, Isis is doubly Man: in her, both sexes, without being annulled, are reconciled and transfigured. She is wisdom incarnate. An extraordinary ambition: Juana Inés, nun and virgin, is of the line of Isis, and her name will one day appear on that list of "learned women."

The identification with Isis, universal mother of seeds, living beings, and signs—that is, doubly mother—conceals a third element: one even more decisive, because it illuminates the true, if not entirely conscious, sense of the attraction Juana Inés feels for Isis and causes her to identify with her. In Part Two I alluded to the ease with which in some of her poems Sor Juana adopts the role of "widow." I pointed out that perhaps she killed her absent father in her imagination or, at least, experienced that absence as the equivalent of death. The second state of the process was when her poetic imagination transformed the ghost of her father into the image of a dead husband, and she became a widow. The analogy with the myth of Isis and Osiris is disturbing and significant. According to the traditional account, the god Set murders Osiris, cuts him into pieces, and scatters the pieces across the Earth. Isis weeps for him, one by one finds the fourteen pieces of the divine corpse, assembles them, and revives her dead husband. The story of the resurrection of Osiris completes the identification of the "widow" Juana Inés with the goddess: motherhood resolves into the symbolic resurrection of the past and its dead. The agents of the resurrection are signs: letters and poetry. Thus by means of a long and sinuous deviation—in every sense of the word—Juana Inés returns to femininity and motherhood. This detour is the equivalent of the pilgrimage of Isis and her hardships while searching for the remains of Osiris. But "masculinization" for the purpose of appropriating masculine learning (signs and letters) and the "neutralization" of her sex beneath her religious habits are not so much stages in a return to natural femininity and motherhood as they are the successive steps in a pilgrimage—which is itself a transfiguration—toward the *other* motherhood represented in Isis: Juana Inés is the mother of living poetic works.

The transformation of Io into Isis allows her to identify the cow with wisdom, and thus to explain with curious reasoning why "learned men imaged themselves [by this she means represented themselves] as a bull . . . [It was] as a symbol of wisdom that they sacrificed the bull to Neptune." The theme of the cow and Isis, in the hermetic tradition, is linked with that of the Egyptian cross. A notable example of this syncretist interpretation is found in the rooms of Pope Alexander Borgia in the Vatican. Frescoes by Pinturicchio representing the history of Io and her transformation into Isis decorate those halls. In one of the frescoes, in the so-called Room of the Saints, Isis is seen at the center, seated on a throne, with the emblems of her wisdom; Moses is on her right and Hermes Trismegistus on her left. In another of the frescoes, Apis—a symbol, in turn, of the bull of the Borgias—is shown worshiping the cross. Another and even stranger syncretist emblem: that cross, in the form of the letter *tau*, is none other than the so-called Egyptian cross that according to tradition was found in the temple of Serapis. An Egyptian emblem converted into a *sign* of the Christian prefigurations of hermeticism. Ficino recorded this tradition; Pico and others disseminated it; Bruno adopted it as additional proof that Christianity had appropriated and deformed the ancient rites and symbols of astral religion (a belief that cost him his life). Almost a century later, undoubtedly through Kircher, the tradition reached Sor Juana, who adopted it, as we shall see at the proper time, as the theme for a *villancico*.

The only quotation in Italian in all of Sor Juana's work is from Boccaccio, and it appears in the *Allegorical Neptune*. It does not seem likely that Sor Juana knew Italian; probably she used a secondary source. In the chapter he dedicates to Venus, Vitoria mentions the same lines ("It is right, Cytherea, that in my realms / you should feel at home, since you were born in them"). Two of Boccaccio's works correspond to the tastes and concerns of Sor Juana: *De genealogia deorum gentilium* (*On the Genealogy of the Pagan Gods*) and *De claris mulieribus* (*On Famous Women*). We do not know whether Sor Juana read those works, but through Vitoria, Cartari, and others she surely had knowledge of their contents. The most complete anthology of texts on Isis is found in those works by Boccaccio.[3] The transformation of Io into Isis appears in both. Boccaccio's sources were Ovid and Macrobius, two authors well known to Sor Juana; part of the theme of *First Dream,* as will be seen, is probably taken from Macrobius. Another of the authors cited in the *Allegorical Neptune* is the poet Pietro Crinito, a member of the Neoplatonic circle of Florence, a friend of Pico della Mirandola, and author of a collection of dialogues Sor Juana may have read: *De honesta disciplina.* Mirrorings of erudition: Sor Juana quotes an ancient Latin verse quoted by Crinito, although he does not mention his source: *Isis arte non minore protulit aegiptias* (With no less art, Isis conceived Egyptian letters).

The most frequently cited authors in the *Allegorical Neptune* are, naturally, mythologists. All are tied, directly or indirectly, to hermetic syncretism. Frances A. Yates reports that prominent among the books in John Dee's library were "the usual Renaissance reference books: the *Hieroglyphica* of Pierio Valeriano, the *Mythologia* of Natalis Comes, the *Emblems* of Alciati." These are the authors that appear again and again in the *Allegorical Neptune*. Pierius was the great authority on hieroglyphic and allegorical subjects but Vincenzo Cartari offered something of particular interest: *Le imagini de i dei de gli antichi* contains a systematic comparison between Greco-Roman and Egyptian divinities. The illustrations frequently display on facing pages the Greek and Egyptian forms of their divinities. It seems that Giordano Bruno found the inspiration for his *Expulsion of the Triumphant Beast* in Cartari's illustrations. As I have said, Sor Juana took from that volume the figures of Neptune and Amphitrite painted on the central canvas of her arch.

A CUBE FORMED OF MIRROR-CONCEITS, the *Allegorical Neptune* reproduces itself: each of its allusions is reflected in another—that is, in turn, projected onto another, and so on. In reading it, we glimpse a Sor Juana Inés de la Cruz very different from the one traditionally presented by her biographers and critics. I emphasize, first of all, the "Egyptian" coloration of her reading and her intellectual tastes. The importance of this preoccupation may even be measured quantitatively. As proof, a glance at the index of names appearing in volume 4 of her *Complete Works* will suffice. The word "Egypt" appears thirty-one times, and the names of Egyptian personages, cities, rivers, and places, another fifty-one times. This computation does not include synonyms and adjectives (Gypsy, Pharaonic, Egyptian, and others) or mentions of monuments, objects, and cultural themes (such as pyramids, oracles, and hieroglyphs). Sor Juana is yet another victim of one of the intellectual diseases of her age: Egyptomania. This obsession extended to the Enlightenment and nineteenth-century romanticism. To it we owe, among other works, Mozart's *Magic Flute*. Second, I would point out that Sor Juana's erudition was more general than profound. I have shown that frequently she used secondary sources derived from compendia, collections, and manuals. Finally, her knowledge was not very current; Neoplatonic hermeticism had flourished a century earlier. Was she unaware of the new ideas and discoveries? I do not think so. Vitoria, who cannot be suspected of heresy, quoted Copernicus, although later subscribing to the astronomy of Tycho Brahe. If Sigüenza y Góngora knew Descartes and Gassendi, how could she not know them? She did not quote them because it was not prudent: she wanted no quarrel with the Holy Office. Sor Juana's society, like modern totalitarian societies, suffered not only from the evil of censorship but from an even more painful evil, self-censorship.

Among Sor Juana's favorite readings were the works of Father Athanasius Kircher. Her very real admiration for him can be seen in the number of times she quotes him; his name, written in Latin, can be read on the spines of several of the books in the background of the portraits of Sor Juana painted by Miranda and Cabrera. The *Allegorical Neptune* is a work of Kircherian inspiration, although Sor Juana never quotes the German Jesuit in it. The syncretist vision of Isis comes from Kircher, as does her mania for Egypt. In *Oedipus Aegyptiacus*, a work Sor Juana undoubtedly knew and studied, Kircher expounds at length on the cult of Isis and Apis, linking it with the hermetic tradition and constantly seeking the hidden connection between Neoplatonic Egypt and Christianity. One of the book's illustrations depicts Isis—"Polymorphus daemon"—robed in all her attributes, following the well-known description of Apuleius. In the *Allegorical Neptune* there is more than one echo of all this: many of Sor Juana's ideas are taken from *Oedipus Aegyptiacus,* a work described by one critic as "a display of erudition composed of incontrovertible names and facts at the service of fiction."[4] But Kircher's books contain more than fantastic hypotheses based on literary erudition; they are encyclopedias of the learning of the age. Kircher was interested in physics (especially optics), astronomy, and the natural sciences. In spite of his inclination toward capricious hypotheses and interpretations, the Jesuit was a true savant and was in contact with the best minds in Europe. Leibniz was interested in Kircher's idea of attributing Egyptian origin to Chinese ideograms, although in the end he rejected it: "I know that some [he was referring to Kircher] have believed that the Chinese were once a colony of the Egyptians, based on a supposed resemblance between their graphic characters, but that resemblance is illusory . . . Egyptian characters are popular . . . while the Chinese probably are more intellectual."

Sor Juana was familiar with Kircher's historical and mythological speculations as well as his scientific works. In her letter to the Bishop of Puebla she refers to Kircher's book on magnetism: "The Reverend Father Athanasius Kircher, author of the learned study *De magnete . . .*" She had also read his famous treatise *Ars magna lucis et umbrae,* as is evident from the passage in *First Dream* on the magic lantern.

Three conflicting currents flow together in Kircher's work: Catholic syncretism, as represented in the seventeenth century by the Society of Jesus; the "Egyptian" Neoplatonic hermeticism inherited from the Renaissance; and new astronomical and physical concepts and discoveries. More than a synthesis of these contradictory elements, Kircher offered his readers a superimposition of facts, ideas, and fantasies. The seventeenth century was fascinated with this extraordinary amalgam of learning and rational delirium. In New Spain his influence was not limited to Sor Juana. Sigüenza y Góngora's will testifies to his popularity. In that moving document, after bequeathing to the Library of San Pedro y San Pablo his books on mathematics and astronomy, his Mexican antiquities, and his collection of manuscripts in Spanish and Nahuatl, Sigüenza says: "I also give to the [Most Reverend Fathers] M.R.PP. my set of the works of Father Athanasius Kircher, so that with the four I am lacking, to be found in the aforesaid Library of San Pedro y San Pablo, the said set will be complete." So not only were the works of Kircher read and commented on by intellectuals and scholars like Sigüenza and Sor Juana, they were found in the libraries of Jesuit schools. For Sor Juana, Kircher's work was a window through which she could view the most daring speculations and the discoveries of the new science without the danger of being accused of heresy. Through Kircher, an orthodox author, she glimpsed the vast territories that stretched beyond the boundaries drawn by the Church. Territories at once real and chimerical: an abstract Egypt dotted with obelisks incised with magic signs and mathematical formulas, pedantic enigmas, and scientific instruments.

The case of Kircher is extreme but not unique. The blending of the beliefs and ideas of hermetic Neoplatonism, alchemy, the Cabala, and notions from the new science was common in the seventeenth century. Few minds were immune to the fascination of Hermes Trismegistus and the Egyptian hieroglyphs. It must again be emphasized that without hermeticism, alchemy, and magic speculations, the empiricism of modern science would not have been possible. From the free and irreverent attitude of the "magi" toward nature, from their intense interest in natural phenomena, emerged the basic notion of *experimentation*. In this sense, Sor Juana's autobiographical *Response* is an impressive testimony, for in its pages, for the first time in the history of Hispanic thought, appears a truly modern attitude toward nature. Sor Juana's point of view was not that of traditional philosophy nor that of religion: she was not interested either in cosmic order or in supernatural miracles but, rather, in natural phenomena. This attitude, however, would have been unimaginable without the interpretations and speculations that minds like Kircher's had contributed during that time.

Finally, I want to emphasize another point about Kircher, perhaps the most significant: he was one of the links in the chain that runs from the Neoplatonic Florence of the end of the fifteenth century to the illuminist sects that during the final years of the eighteenth century opened the way to romanticism and to the visionary socialism of a Fourier. For example, in 1775, on the eve of the French Revolution, Kircher's name, along with Fludd's, appears frequently in the great controversies on magnetism. Once again, as in the sixteenth and seventeenth centuries, the amalgam of empirical science and esotericism is repeated: "At the moment when Montgolfier is mastering the atmosphere and Franklin is capturing lightning, Mesmer is attempting to subdue spirit energies."[5] Through Kircher, Sor Juana is tied to a universal and still-living tradition, a tradition that has inspired the poets of our civilization from the Renaissance to contemporary times. But this tradition, by its very nature, has always flowed underground. Only now have we begun to learn about its origins and perceive its ramifications. It is extraordinary that one of those ramifications is found in an end-of-the-seventeenth-century Mexico and that it can be traced in one of the most complex, rigorous, and intellectually rich texts of Spanish-language poetry, *First Dream*.

Although derived from the same sources, Sor Juana's syncretism develops in a direction opposite to Sigüenza's. Historical and political concerns are not central to her thought. On the other hand, she is obsessed by the place of women in the world of the mind; hence her pensive questioning of Isis. There is in her a philosophical tone not found in Sigüenza: she wants to know how the world is made. Each, the learned criollo and the poet, verges on heterodoxy, but for different reasons and in different areas. It has often been said that Sor Juana is greatly superior to Sigüenza as a writer. It must be stated that this superiority is not merely a matter of style. Sigüenza's mind was not inclined toward synthesis, while Sor Juana's was to a high degree. She also surpassed him in her capacity to connect facts, concepts, and situations. Both faculties, that of connecting and that of synthesizing, are philosophical in the sense of Baudelaire's definition: "Imagination is the philosophical faculty par excellence."

A commissioned work and an example of courtly adulation, the *Allegorical Neptune* is unique. Not a mere curiosity, as some scholars have said, but a document in the history of ideas in the Hispanic world. The opinion of an obscure contemporary, the scholar John van der Ketten, is worth noting. In his *Apelles symbolicus,*[6] a catalogue of symbols and allegories, he cites the *Allegorical Neptune* with this unusual praise: "Some of the symbols reveal an acuity greater than might be expected of a virgin." Sor Juana would have been pleased by such praise. In a poem written years later she compares herself to the

> [virgin, yet] pregnant
> with divine concepts,
> maiden Pythoness
> of Delphi . . .

The arch of the *Allegorical Neptune* was in fact a hieroglyph. More exactly, an emblem, an enigma. A riddle based on three terms that, like the illustrations in Cartari's book, were mirrored figures: Neptune and the Viceroy; Amphitrite and the Vicereine; Isis and, unseen, Sor Juana Inés de la Cruz. At the center of this enigma fashioned of conceits and interwoven with erudite allusions—invisible but present, like the mysterious spirits that animated Hermes' statues—was Sor Juana herself.

Part Four

Sor Juana Inés de la Cruz
1680–1690

13

Flattery and Favors

$\mathcal{T}$HE GOVERNMENT OF John of Austria, the illegitimate son of Philip IV who had presented himself as the "savior" of Spain, ended in fiasco. At his death, after interminable months of chaos, Juan Tomás de la Cerda, Duke de Medinaceli, was named first minister. He was married to the ambitious Catalina of Aragon, who was as wealthy as he. The Duke enjoyed the friendship of Charles II; he was not lacking in intelligence, but he had neither will nor imagination: "in external as in internal affairs, Medinaceli relied on the age-old axiom of mediocre statesmen, which says that to govern is to compromise, and to compromise is to yield." [1] The most memorable action of his government was the auto-da-fé of June 18, 1680, in which the King and Queen "participated"—such ceremonies were public spectacles—along with Spanish grandees, dignitaries of the Church, and one hundred eighteen accused, almost all of humble condition, vagrants, religious lunatics, peddlers, prostitutes, adulterers, and a handful of unfortunate Judaizers. Thirty-four were burned in effigy, because they had died or were fugitives; eighteen were turned over to the civil executioner, who burned most of them at the stake. The political objective of this auto-da-fé, according to the historian Modesto Lafuente, was to divert a public aroused by the government's economic blunders. Medinaceli was entangled in disputes with both queens and with the King's confessor. Weakened by a stroke, his power undermined by constant palace intrigues, in April 1685 he was forced to resign. From that time, he lived on his estates in Andalusia.

The government of the Marquis de la Laguna was no more auspicious than that of his brother. His arrival coincided with an insurrection of

Indians in what is now New Mexico. He never succeeded in subduing them throughout the six years of his viceregency. He was even less successful in regard to the pirates who constantly threatened and ravaged the coastal areas. The most famous of those incursions was the capture and sacking of Veracruz. In spite of the fact that for more than a year French, English, and Dutch ships had been plundering Mexican seas and threatening the ports, in May 1683 Veracruz was taken by surprise and almost without resistance by buccaneers under the command of the Frenchman Nicolas Agramont and the famous Lorencillo. The occupation and sacking of the city lasted two weeks, from the seventeenth to the thirtieth of May. The pirates withdrew when the Viceroy of Mexico paid the one hundred fifty thousand pesos demanded for the ransom of hostages. They took thirteen hundred slaves with them—"in full view of the Spanish fleet," which had been in the vicinity since the twenty-eighth. Meanwhile, the Vicereine was expecting a child—the child to whom Sor Juana would dedicate lavish eulogies in verse—and only after his wife recovered did the Marquis decide to undertake the journey to Veracruz, on July 17, two months after the sacking. Once he reached the port he had no course but to declare the governor guilty and sentence him to be beheaded. The governor appealed to the Council of the Indies; his sentence was stayed and he was deported to Spain.[2]

In spite of the Marquis de la Laguna's calamitous defense of the coasts and the sparse initiative and energy he displayed in governing, the situation of New Spain during those years compares favorably with that of the mother country. J. H. Elliott points out that "between the death of Don Juan José and the fall of his mediocre successor, the Duke of Medinaceli, in 1685, Castile's fortunes reached their nadir."[3] Because of the natural decentralization of the Spanish empire, which amounted to a sort of unplanned federalism—"federalism by default"—the provinces and colonies did not experience the exhaustion of Castile. While viceroys and vicereines came and went, "in America the colonial aristocracy was able to build up great estates unchecked by interference from a central government which had struggled so hard in the sixteenth century to retain control over its new domains."[4] Intellectual and cultural paralysis was added to economic and political. There is no doubt that this cultural inertia was the result of the closed, dogmatic, and formalistic nature of the education imparted by the Church, particularly the Jesuits, at the end of the seventeenth century, which contrasted strongly with the awakening of the modern age elsewhere in Europe. Another reason, Elliott notes, was "the moral and intellectual bankruptcy of the ruling class," a phenomenon that fifty years earlier had perturbed the Count-Duke de Olivares. The English historian asks, Was this the result of a biological flaw brought about by interbreeding among the members of the governing class, or the result of a flaw in the political, economic, and cultural systems?

The subject of historical decline is inexhaustible, and in any case goes beyond the limits of this book. Suffice it to say that the unmistakable sign of all such declines is the loss of a national plan. Members of the ruling class suddenly feel that the plan elaborated by their fathers and grandfathers is no longer viable, but are incapable of conceiving a different one. In the sixteenth century the Castilian nobility produced great statesmen and military men; by the end of the seventeenth century their descendants were notable for their laziness, greed, and ignorance. When the ambassador of Louis XIV in Madrid, the Marquis de Villars, described in his memoirs the situation in the Spanish court, he cited as an example the Duke de Medina de las Torres, a prominent member of the Consejo de Estado, the supreme council, a man who had "spent all his life in Madrid in total idleness, occupied only in eating and sleeping."[5] The contrast between Spain and New Spain is again evident. During those years, as seen in the preceding chapters, a national plan was being formed that, although it was to undergo radical changes, would separate us from Spain one hundred forty years later and continue to animate our national life today.

The vitality of New Spain was especially visible in the area of culture: the existence of a Sor Juana was but one of the signs of an emerging society. Neither Sor Juana nor Sigüenza was an isolated case: they were central but not unique figures in a human panorama that was much richer than was thought until recently, one that still awaits investigation by historians. The ideas of Sor Juana's generation, and the artistic and intellectual forms in which they were expressed, were not their own; indeed they were already old: European culture had abandoned those ideas, and inquiring minds were venturing into new terrain. Even so, that generation's ardor, curiosity, and desire for learning are impressive. Situated between two worlds and two eras, it represents on the one hand a kind of golden Hispanic sunset—contrasting to the crepuscular grayness of Spain—and on the other a dawn prefiguring, perhaps, a new society.

THE YEARS OF the viceregency of the Marquis de la Laguna were the richest of Sor Juana's life. The limited information at our command—

her correspondence lost, the archives of the convent of San Jerónimo scattered, no memoirs or testimony from those who knew her and were in contact with her—prevents a full reconstruction of the period. We do know, however, that two of her major works, *The Divine Narcissus* and *First Dream,* date from those years. In addition, there were numerous commissioned and occasional poems. Whatever else their value, these offer us a glimpse of what her life must have been and the nature of her relations with the viceregal palace. More than half of her literary output consists of poems for ceremonial occasions: homages, epistles, congratulations, poems to commemorate the death of an Archbishop or the birth of a magnate. The majority of these compositions were written during the viceregency of Tomás de la Cerda, and almost all were dedicated to him, to his wife, or to their son, José María, born in Mexico in 1683. According to the *Complete Works,* there are two hundred sixteen extant poems by Sor Juana; among them, fifty-two, one fourth, are dedicated to the Marquis and Marquise de la Laguna. To these must be added brief theatrical works—*loas, saraos, bailes,* and, of course, the *Allegorical Neptune.* In other *loas,* written to celebrate the birthdays of Charles II, his first wife, Marie Louise d'Orléans, and the Queen Mother, Mariana of Austria, Sor Juana invariably found the opportunity to praise her protectors.

The variety of poetic forms utilized by Sor Juana in these pieces is remarkable: *romances, décimas, seguidillas,* sonnets. Her mastery is no less cause for admiration. Alfonso Méndez Plancarte, a specialist in such matters, justly emphasizes and expertly analyzes their meter, complexity of rhythmic structure, and felicity of rhyme. It cannot be repeated too often: Sor Juana is one of the great versifiers of the Spanish language. If they were notable for no other reason, these poems would engage our attention purely for their metric artistry. But we are also captivated by the rich images and graceful turns of phrase. Ingenious inventions are frequent, such as a character in one of the *loas* (377) who appears "clad in sunrays" and declaims:

> I am a Reflection
> of that blazing Sun
> who, among shining rays,
> numbers brilliant sons:
> when his illustrious rays
> strike a speculum,

on it is portrayed
the likeness of his form.[6]

Modern critics have complained of the triviality of many of these compositions, and several have deplored their overly colloquial tone. Aside from the fact that Sor Juana is never, or almost never, vulgar or tasteless—just the opposite of Lope and Quevedo—this reproach is particularly inappropriate today, when conversational language is used by almost every contemporary poet. Furthermore, in these poems colloquial expressions are rare; exactly the opposite criticism can be made: Sor Juana overuses learned allusions, artifice, and convolutions. But within the rather strict limitations of the genre, they generally display the same equilibrium that distinguishes her other poems. In a literature as given to extremes as the Hispanic, bounded by the awe-inspiring and the bizarre, the crude and the artful, Sor Juana is a marvel of temperance. I do not pretend that the dactylic *romances* in swinglike rhythms or the echoing *ovillejos* and courtly sonnets can be taken as models of great poetry, but I do believe they are examples of verbal mastery. Some are sonorous and others amusing, some elegant and others frivolous; almost all are intelligent, and many are dazzling. In a century such as our own, which has degraded language through the banalities of commercial and ideological propaganda, it is a pleasant and bracing exercise to stroll through Sor Juana's labyrinths of echoes and conceits, or to pause for a moment over her diaphanous combinations of sound and idea (377):

> In soft echoes are heard,
>> the bird;
> in flowing waters that sing,
>> the spring;
> in phrases' sweet shower,
>> the flower;
> in green-throated salute,
>> the shoot . . .

Our interest in these texts is not exclusively aesthetic; it is also historical. The poems are documents of a society and must be studied within the system of symbols with which that society simultaneously veils and reveals itself. They are disguises, but transparent disguises. Occasioned by a funeral, a birth, or some other social ritual, these compositions fall within the realm of ceremony. They must be read for what they truly were: not signs of an aesthetic or a morality, but of an etiquette. More precisely, ceremony is itself an ethic, a policy, and an aesthetic. In every society, particularly a rigorously hierarchical society like that of Sor Juana, etiquette is a system for the symbolic representation of social relationships. In this etiquette is expressed, in figurative and allegorical form, the order of the society's values and the innermost structure of the system that alternately unites and divides the groups and individuals that compose it. Etiquette is never explicit or literal; it is an emblematic language that can be deciphered only by those who have the key. That is why I spoke of "transparent disguises." Etiquette draws a line between those who know and those who do not, the courtier and the commoner. To speak that language is to belong to a society within a society. But etiquette is not innate; it demands an apprenticeship. To be courtly it is not enough to be noble; etiquette, which is a code, is also a culture.

Because it is tacit rather than explicit, etiquette, in the symbolic mode, faithfully represents the social order. Unlike moral and political codes, it plays especially with the values of the unspoken, the implicit, and the understood. Like morality and law, etiquette draws strict boundaries and legislates what can and cannot be done. It never says *no,* however; rather, *only this far.* An *only this far* based on conditions that are implicit, not expressed. Etiquette, in essence, is a figurative language, and thus verbal artistry can be seen in turn as a superior and more complete form of the same symbolic system. This correspondence reveals the true nature of Sor Juana's poems. They are not palace diversions; or, rather, in being so, they perform a public function; they are verbal emblems of an understood relationship in the body politic. Although this relation assumes many forms, it can be reduced to its simplest: the bond that unites the lord and his vassals.

Ceremony appears as a choreography of attitudes, actions, and words. It is a geometry that expresses a world vision: an animated mirror reflecting with allegorical figures the natural order of things and beings. And that order is a projection of the supernatural order: the three kingdoms of nature are duplicates of the divine kingdom, in the same way that the royal court is a copy of the heavenly court. A ceremony is a ritual in which, as if in a game of mirrors, the three levels of reality are reflected: divine, natural, and political. Each of the participants, not excluding the spectator, has his place in the ceremony; that place is hierarchical and scrupulously adheres to rank. In turn, this hierarchical order in some sense reproduces the order of things and beings in the universe, from plants to stars and from animals to angels. So the order of things and the order of heaven are really only projections of the order of civilization: of social power and authority, classes and genders, generations and individuals.

Referring to Chinese civilization, Marcel Granet quotes a sentence from the *Li Chi* (*Book of Rites*) that is perfectly applicable to courtly society in New Spain at the end of the seventeenth century: "When Music is perfect, there is no rebellion; when Rites are fulfilled, there are no disputes."[7] Etiquette proposes to a royal society a political archetype: social order is a chain of powers, loyalties, and subordinations extending in two directions, one vertical, the other horizontal. The first links the prince to his subjects; the second, the vassals to each other. The vertical relationship is threatened by the rebellion of the people, from the Spanish grandee to the commoner, as well as by the tyranny of the lord; the second is threatened by rivalries between classes and among equals. Ceremony is regulated according to this twofold disposition—the high and the low, the center and the periphery—not abruptly but through countless gradations.

In almost all of Sor Juana's courtly poems, and very markedly in the *loas*, the order of the cosmos coincides with the social order. Poetry and the other arts—music and dance—represent an intermediate kingdom in which the reflections of the orders of the universe and society are interwoven. The system of metaphoric equivalences is at once simple and rich. The King is the sun and rules the four elements as if they were the various ranks of an Assembly. The elements argue among themselves, but music converts their discord into harmony, and all four render fealty to Charles II, "the sovereign pastor." In another *loa*, life, nature, majesty, and loyalty debate like academicians and theologians until their disharmony resolves into a chorus. In several of these plays the ranks double or triple: corresponding to the sun, the heavens, and time, which belong to the natural world, are the human attributes of prudence, youth, and happiness. In the *loa* for Marie Louise d'Orléans, the most intellectual of Sor Juana's *loas*, the characters are faculties of the soul—reason, will, and memory. Each exercises control over one aspect of time: memory, over the past, "the protocol of the world"; will, over the present, "the flexible instant" that "begins as present and ends as past"; reason over the future, the "sublime parapet, impregnable rampart" reserved for "the Creator alone."

A ballet of conceits and figures, a prodigious repertory of poetic rhythms and forms, characters, ideas, and deities pirouette through Sor Juana's courtly poetry, all moved by a single gravitational force: the loyalty of vassal to lord, the love of the prince for his subject. Courtly order is cosmic order, and poetry merely reproduces the dual hierarchy of the universe and society. On the one hand, triumph of form; on the other, substitution of ideology for reality. The sun of Sor Juana's *loas* was the feeble and obtuse Charles II; the planets and luminaries that surrounded him, inept courtiers, rapacious politicians, and stupid noblemen. In all closed and despotic societies, ideology finally supplants reality. At times the discrepancy between the ignoble real world and the exalted rhetoric that cloaks it becomes both enormous and grotesque. In *loa* V (378), written to mark the birthday of Charles II, Apollo appears on the stage and summons the planets to announce to them that the monarch, the Spanish sun, has just completed his twenty-third year, an occasion for them to reiterate, like the gods they are and in the best astrological tradition, "the benign influences" they had granted him at "his illustrious birth." Saturn steps forward and bestows authority; Jupiter follows with the gift of power, Mars with courage, Apollo with learning, Venus with beauty, Mercury with eloquence, and Juno with achievement (today, less genteelly, we would say "success"). Sor Juana could not have seen an Adonis or a Mercury or a Mars in the sickly and frightened Charles II, but she did not find it ridiculous to compare him to those ancient deities. Reality had vanished from that society, displaced by ideology and its conventions.

In addition to idealization, courtly poetry fulfilled a more humble, but more immediately practical, purpose. As she provided the viceregal court with an aesthetic ritual, Sor Juana was establishing a privileged relationship between the convent and the palace. The courtly poet attracts the prince's favor, in the primary sense of the word "attract." Political metaphor is essentially theological: the prince's favor is a replica of divine grace. There are also erotic resonances: the attraction the vassal feels for his lord, and the lord's fascination for his favorite, evoke the magnetism between the bodies and souls of lovers. This dual symbolism evolved in specific situations that justified and reinforced it. Reinforcement was particularly pertinent to the case of the nuns of the convent of San Jerónimo. It was essential for them, faced with a tyrannical and capricious Archbishop, to turn to the protection and friendship of a Viceroy whose brother was the King's prime minister. Later, in considering the crisis provoked by the *Carta atenagórica*, I shall examine in greater detail the relationship between Sor Juana and Archbishop Aguiar y Seijas. For now, I shall only note that in New Spain, a society of strict and immutable hierarchies but numerous jurisdictions, in order to offset the power of its customary superior, every entity sought the protection of a second power. If the Archbishop of Mexico was the immediate authority and if his authority, unlike Fray Payo's, was exercised imperiously and carelessly, it was natural and understandable that the convent should seek the friendship of the palace.

More than once I have referred to Sor Juana's tact and political skills. She and Sigüenza y Góngora had made the two triumphal arches with which Mexico City and the Church chapter welcomed the Marquis and Marquise de la Laguna. Sigüenza did not succeed in ingratiating himself with the Viceroy and instead sought the rather uneasy protection of the erratic Aguiar y Seijas. In contrast, Sor Juana soon enjoyed the favor of the palace and became the friend and confidante of the Countess de Paredes. Through the poems that celebrate the birthdays of her protectors and other such festivities, we can appreciate the alacrity with which the nun won their friendship. The Viceroy and his wife arrived in Mexico in November 1680, and in either that or the following year Sor Juana honored Tomás de la Cerda's birthday with a *romance* that also extolled the virtues of his wife. Other poems followed—*romances, décimas, glosas*, sonnets, *endechas, loas*—until the pair's departure from Mexico in 1688. The tone of those poems grew more and more intimate and the friendship expressed in them more intense. Extravagant eulogies were mixed with pleas, and picturesque adulation with declarations of exalted love. Was Sor Juana sincere? Yes and no: hyperbole was the norm in that day. Courtesy was second nature to the aristocracy and the upper ranks of the clergy. The model for that courtesy was the relationship between superior and inferior, symbolized by that between King and courtier, Heaven and planets, God and his creatures.

Many of these poems were written to accompany gifts or to acknowledge them. Sor Juana received many, frequently valuable, presents. She kept them in her study along with her books, where they were viewed by the sisters with amazement and curiosity. Among them were some that shed an oblique light on her life in the convent—for example, a plumed diadem like those worn by Aztec chieftains, probably of quetzal or hummingbird feathers, sent to her by the Countess de Paredes. Sor Juana reciprocated with the gift of a sweetmeat of nuts "concocted" by Apollo himself, and a *romance* (23). The naturalness with which she accepted the gift and the ease with which she expressed her thanks raised the eyebrows of her punctilious modern editor, Méndez Plancarte, although he ends by saying that the saucy proverb at the end of the poem was "innocently employed." Was the explanation necessary?

> I shall don it, ma'am,
> for thus crowned may my head
> more fittingly be used
> as a rug for you to tread.
> Many kisses, at your feet,
> I give you in return,
> for "kisses freely given
> will no reproval earn."

There was a constant flow of gifts, notes, flowers, sweets, and portraits between palace and convent. Juana was not a wealthy woman; what sources did she draw upon to reciprocate María Luisa's gifts? She sent more than poems and sweets and flowers. On one occasion she gave the Countess a stroller for her infant son; on another, a small ivory retable; on another, some rare fish. Among Sor Juana's talents was her shrewdness in financial matters. Although poets and intellectuals tend not to be good businessmen, there are exceptions: Pope earned a great deal of money with his poems and his translations of Homer. Sor Juana's skill in administering the convent's funds was acknowledged by the sisters, who several times elected her treasurer. The Church chapter paid her two hundred pesos for the *Allegorical Neptune,* and she lost no time in thanking them with adulatory *décimas* and a play on words: "For an unworthy Arch [*Arco*] you gave / a treasure chest [*arca*] of infinitely greater worth." Sor Juana's greatest gain, however, was having access to the Viceroy and Vicereine and winning their confidence. It is entirely possible that the convent paid for many of these gifts. It was to the nuns' advantage to be on good terms with the palace, especially since their relations with Archbishop Aguiar y Seijas were far from perfect. If all this is kept in account, Sor Juana's position is revealed clearly: on the one hand, she serves the convent and is its intermediary and spokeswoman with the Viceroy and Vicereine; on the other, the favor of the palace strengthens her position in the convent and gives her independence from and influence over the sisters.

Among the poems dedicated to the Viceroy and Vicereine are several containing petitions. In one she asks Tomás de la Cerda to spare the life of one Antonio de Benavides, who had impersonated a Field Marshal, the Marquis de San Vicente. In another poem (125) she asks the Countess de Paredes to free an Englishman named Samuel (who was he, and what was his offense?). There are also *décimas* accompanying a written request to a judge, and others in which she seeks justice for a widow. Why does she ask for Benavides' life and Samuel's freedom? Does she do it *motu proprio* or is she the spokeswoman for other interested parties? I am inclined to believe the latter: Sor Juana could not have had any personal interest in Benavides, the unknown Samuel, or the anonymous widow of the *décima*. I fear that these petitions, in addition to confirming her influence with the Viceroy and Vicereine, help explain how she moved away from poverty to enjoy not only comfort but remarkable affluence.

I attempted to explain in Part One of this book that New Spain was a society in which the ruler treated the government as his private patrimony and its functionaries as his servants and members of his family. The conditions that limited the power of the Viceroy—the Audiencia, the *visitador,* the *juicio de residencia*—constituted a political restraint but did not deny the patrimonial nature of the viceregal government. They did not deny it, because the viceroyalty reproduced the markedly patrimonial characteristics and political structures of the mother country. In a world of hierarchies that were fixed, but subject to changes dictated by the will or caprice of the ruler, favor translated not only into prestige, influence, and power but, inevitably, into material rewards. This is a situation, *mutatis mutandis,* that still prevails in Mexico. A ruler's benevolence toward his subjects took the form of gifts and favors ranging from appointment to a public post to granting pardon to a criminal. Appointments and favors could be bought, whether directly from the official or, more frequently, through intermediaries such as court favorites and protégés. The Duke de Veragua bought the viceregency of New Spain, and the Marquis de la Laguna himself, in 1689, bought his rank as Spanish grandee and the post of chief majordomo to Queen Maria Anna of Neuburg, second wife of Charles II. The practice was widespread in the courts of Europe and, of course, the viceroyalties.

Only with the birth of the modern state, toward the end of the eighteenth and the beginning of the nineteenth century, as Max Weber and Norbert Elias have shown, did the practice come to be considered bad. And it was more for utilitarian than for ethical reasons that it was judged so: because it was irrational and uneconomical.

Some of Sor Juana's biographers, with the best of faith, speak of the nun's "humanity." Human she was, and humane, but her excellent qualities should not blind us to the morality of her day. Here, as in the case of her having become a nun, we attribute modern sentiments, reactions, and attitudes to her. Her interventions on behalf of third parties were not limited to the occasions we are aware of through her poems. We know, for example, that she received a loan of two thousand gold pesos on the jewelry of one of her sisters, and that she herself, in a dispute with a nephew who had demanded the return of that collateral, declared with a certain pride that she had been granted the sum "as a favor . . . and not because the gems were valued at a thousand pesos." If she was motivated by humaneness in asking for Benavides' life and Samuel's liberation, why do we know nothing of other philanthropic acts? I understand the repugnance with which my opinion will be received, but everything we know about Sor Juana leads to the conclusion that she practiced what today we call influence peddling. To condemn her for that would have astounded her contemporaries. Patronage was one side of the coin. The other was charity: as we saw, the wealthy Juan de Chavarría bequeathed an estate for the support of the priests who taught Indian children their letters, and Sor Juana was able to take her vows thanks to the generosity of Pedro Velázquez de la Cadena and the same Chavarría.

Sor Juana's worldly poetry fulfilled a dual purpose: it was a courtly ritual impregnated with political symbolism, and it was a means of privileged communication between the convent and the palace. At the same time, her relationship with the Viceroy and Vicereine strengthened her position in the cloister, sheltering her—at least for a time—from envy and meddling. But practicality and self-interest were only one aspect of that relationship; the other, perhaps more important, was a mixture of generous sentiments: gratitude, friendship, and something beyond and distinct from those emotions. The affection Sor Juana felt for the Countess de Paredes, to judge by the tone of the poems she addressed to her, soon turned into a feeling so intense that it can only be called love. Through these poems we can see that her loving friendship was reciprocated with the same effusiveness. There are so many poems written to María Luisa Manrique de Lara, the emotions so intense, that they cannot be ignored. One thing is certain: from 1680, the relationship with the Countess de Paredes became the emotional center of Sor Juana's life. When Sor Juana met the Countess she was a mature woman. She was thirty-one; she had survived a difficult youth—abandonment by her family, the years with the Matas, straitened finances, doubts about becoming a nun, the illness of 1673—and she was at the height of her talent and in the best years of her life. The Countess was almost exactly her age. She had been born in October 1649, one year later than Sor Juana. She was childless when she arrived in Mexico; she had suffered several miscarriages. (Her only son, José María, who inherited his father's title and both their fortunes, was not born until 1683.) The friendship with María Luisa was beneficial for Sor Juana; it gave her independence and security in her relations with her sister nuns in San Jerónimo. And we owe to it several unforgettable poems. For these reasons, the relationship of the two women demands separate consideration.

14

Council of Stars

MOST OF SOR JUANA'S BIOGRAPHERS, while aware of her relationship with María Luisa Manrique de Lara, have preferred to skirt the issue, although one bookishly self-assured scholar, Ludwig Pfandl, armed only with a few texts on psychiatry, has attempted to uncover the secrets of her soul. In this matter, I believe exactly the opposite of what Sartre believed: no human being is entirely transparent to others—or even to himself. Thus I do not attempt to reveal the convolutions of Sor Juana's innermost being but, rather, approach her life and her work with a hope of understanding them in all their contradictory complexity. I add that this understanding can be no more than an approximation, a glimpse. No soul, no life, can be reduced to a biography, and even less to a psychiatric diagnosis. Freud said that the content of every dream is nearly infinite: what, then, can be said of a life, composed of thousands of dreams and thousands of acts, some realized and others frustrated? None of the historians of ancient times, including Plutarch, proposed in their biographies to reveal the entire life and character of their heroes: they wished only by using their most salient characteristics to show them as human beings. Sartre wrote three thick volumes on Flaubert, but Flaubert remained as elusive as before. A biography should not pretend to duplicate its subject or reveal that subject fully; both tasks are impossible. Nevertheless, although no one truly knows his lover or his friends, we all have some knowledge of them. This knowledge allows us to understand them, to sympathize with their feelings, and even at times to divine their reactions. The object of biography is to convert the remote person into a more or less intimate friend.

An understanding of the person Sor Juana may have been depends on our—also relative and approximate—understanding of history. Her world was very different from ours. The first and most notable difference—particularly true in her case: she was a creature of words who lived for and because of the word—relates to language. Sor Juana spoke and wrote Spanish, the language I write in today, but during the three centuries that have passed since her death linguistic forms have changed, as well as the import and even the meaning of words. The language of her courtly poems sounds exaggerated to us: to call the King a sun, to call his princes stars, to call the marquises and countesses goddesses, seems reprehensible adulation as well as unacceptable extravagance. But for Sor Juana and her world, these were implicit values. Her hyperboles and resounding adjectives were part of a system of metaphors, metonymies, and synecdoches founded on a triple equivalence: the order of the universe was that of society, and both were reflected in that of the familial House. No one believed that the pitiful Charles II was truly the sun; at the same time, in the code of political and aesthetic emblems, the King—whichever King—was a sun. Our equivalences are duller but no less popular: Commander-in-Chief for the President, First Lady for the President's wife.

Sor Juana's language reflects the absolutism and patrimonialism of her century. As it reflects them it transfigures them, but without altering their context. With no sense of embarrassment she calls herself the servant, even the slave, of the Viceroy and Vicereine. She knew perfectly well that she was neither; in identifying herself in this way she was merely following a social and political convention. The favorites and protégés of the grandees were members of their House: that is why they were called *familiares,* "of the family." The state was the House of all. This equivalence extended into a series of ideas and practices. On the one hand, it was bound to the concept of property: the King or the potentate used public wealth as if it were his own; this was why posts could be sold, and he could consider his functionaries, not excluding his ministers and counselors, as "members of his household," that is, as his domestic servants. The very titles of the highest palace positions allude to this situation: privy counselor, chamberlain,[1] and royal stewards (from *stig-wita,* house dweller) and stewardesses. On the other hand, as head of the House the lord was a father image; relations between him and his courtiers and protégés were similar to the father-son relationship in all its ramifications.

The two orders blended together in everyday language. The lord was considered, alternately or simultaneously, as father and as proprietor; the exercise of power was colored with expressions that pertained as much to the domain of the right of property as to the family. In turn, the interpenetration between erotic and familial language was close and constant. It still is: today in Mexico a wife refers to her husband as *hijo,* son, and a husband calls his wife *madre,* mother. In the seventeenth century it was common for a man to call his beloved *dueño mío* (my master, using the masculine gender), and also *mi bien, mi tesoro,* or *mi prenda* (my wealth, my treasure, my gem). The vocabularies of proprietary, familial, and amatory relations were commingled in everyday expression: they were interchangeable metaphors and metonymies used in designating relations between lords and vassals. The usage was so widespread that no one would have found it strange that, like all the courtly poets of her time, Sor Juana constantly employed in her poems to the Countess de Paredes expressions that combined the rhetoric of lovers with legal and familial language. The faithfulness of the lover, the loyalty of the servant, and the affection of the son were synonyms that designated an identical devotion. They were not transgressions of general usage: their sense as well as their syntax obeyed not only courtly rhetoric but the deeply rooted ideology of the era.

The explanation I have just outlined is useful in understanding the context of Sor Juana's poems of loving friendship. But the poems are more than their context. It is impossible to read them as mere examples of courtly style and not perceive what is unique and individual in them. Under cover of consecrated expressions, others are slipped in that by their fire and their daring say something very different from the commonplace declarations of loyalty and devotion to lord or lady. Sor Juana herself was aware of the daring of certain expressions; nevertheless, rather than moderate them, she defended them by referring to Neoplatonism, thus calling even more attention to them. There are moments when her language becomes defiant. It is understandable that when people again began to read Sor Juana at the end of the last century, her early critics preferred not to linger over those poems: the nineteenth, the bourgeois, century was prudish and sanctimonious. But the unusual fervor of those poems did not escape the notice of Sor Juana's contemporaries. Their perplexity is similar to our own; they asked the same questions we ask ourselves: how to interpret them? In the first edition of the first volume of her works (*Castalian Inundation,* Madrid, 1689), which appeared during her lifetime, we find several evidences of that bewilderment. The subject demands a brief commentary.

We do not know who composed the titles and the brief explanatory notes that precede many of the poems in the *Castalian Inundation,* which were reproduced in subsequent editions. The title page lists as editor a Don Juan Camacho Gayna, a knight of the Order of Santiago. He was of the house of Medinaceli. Master of the Horse and major-domo to the Marquis de la Laguna; he had been, during the Marquis' viceregency, the mayor of San Luis Potosí; when the book appeared he was governor of the port of Santa María. It is difficult to believe that he composed the titles and notes. Probably his participation in the edition was limited to the use of his name. The Countess de Paredes had carried Sor Juana's manuscripts with her to Spain, and it is almost certain that she assumed the costs of printing: the book was a homage to her and to the house of Laguna. It is more credible to attribute the editing of those texts to one of three people: Father Luis Tineo, author of the imprimatur; Father Diego Calleja, who wrote a second and briefer imprimatur; or the anonymous author of the "Prologue to the Reader." I incline toward Calleja—with scant reason, I confess, but guided by what he would later write about Sor Juana and by his long-continuing interest in her.

Whoever was responsible for the editing judged it necessary to insert an "Advertencia," an explanatory note, immediately preceding the first poem dedicated to the Countess de Paredes.[2] Its wording, in its very scrupulous distinctions—typical of someone expert in matters of conscience, like the Jesuit Calleja—is significant: "Either her appreciation for being favored and celebrated, or her acquaintance with the illustrious gifts bestowed by Heaven on the Lady Vicereine, or that secret influence (which until today no one has been able to verify) of the humors or the stars, known as sympathy, or all of these together, generated in the poet a love utterly pure and ardent for her Excellency, as the reader will see in the whole of this book." The author of the note does not hide his wonderment and ventures three explanations, although without settling on any. It will be helpful to examine them one by one.

The first refers to the gratitude Sor Juana must have felt for the favors granted her by the Countess de Paredes. This explanation is in tune with the social and linguistic reality of the era, that is, the rhetoric of courtly society. I have already referred to the interpenetrations, in courtly language, of expressions belonging to patrimonial law, the social system, and the order of the universe: "master," "lord," "sun," and others. The mingling of courtly and erotic languages, nevertheless, merits a more thorough consideration. We do not know whether love, as has some-times been said, is an invention of the West; on the other hand, we do know that erotic language, as it has appeared in our poetry since the twelfth century, was born in the seignorial courts of Provence. There have been many discussions on the origins of Provençal poetry, both of its metric and strophic forms—Arabic or Latin verse?—and of its central theme, courtly love. Today it seems irrefutable that the influence of Arabic eroticism was a determining factor in the ideology of courtly love. In turn, the former received and elaborated the interpretations of Platonism made by Hellenizing Arab philosophers and Sufis.

No less decisive than these ideological and aesthetic factors was the nature of the society in which courtly love was born. From the beginning, says René Nelli, a dual tendency was present in the erotica of the troubadours: the chivalric, and what is more correctly termed the courtly. The first designates love "as it was actually practiced by the princes and their ladies," while "courtly love was the loving friendship, Platonic or semi-Platonic, that the troubadours, almost always of humble origin, professed to ladies of high rank, according to a traditional poetic ritual."[3] The Italian poets of the *dolce stil nuovo* received and recreated the idealistic tradition of courtly love, and since that time these concepts have continued to nourish the language and imagination of Western peoples. The origin of Sor Juana's poetry of loving friendship is to be found in the poetic forms of courtly love that blend the troubadour's expression of love (real or feigned) for his lady with the feudal vocabulary of the vassal's homage to his lord.

Robert Briffault does not find any essential difference between the poetry of the lords and that of the troubadours in regard to the concept of love.[4] He rejects with numerous examples the presumed Platonism of the latter—both seem to him naturalistic and sensual—but he agrees that their language differs. That difference proceeds not only from the difference in social rank—the first knights, the second commoners—but also from the function of the poetry. Knights used this poetry to express a real affection; they wrote their *cansós* as homage to their ladies: the poetry was the equivalent of the bouquet of flowers that today accompanies the gifts a lover gives his beloved. In all aristocratic societies "Venus and Mars have at all epochs been intimately associated: 'gallantry' and 'courtly manners' had reference to . . . both . . . warriors and lovers." In contrast, the poetry of the troubadours was a poetic fiction: in the courtly ceremonies of the castle the poet represented the knight-poet. His poem had to be *convincing,* not sincere. "Bernard de Vantadour celebrates in lascivious terms the personal charms of Aliénor of Aquitaine at a time when the latter was well on in her fifties." Briffault's explanation helps us better understand Sor Juana's poems to María Luisa Manrique de Lara: they were the homage of a professional poet to the poet's lord.

One may wonder: why to the Vicereine and not the Viceroy? The first—perhaps the only—answer to this question is that it would have been scandalous, given the morality of her time (and even ours), had Sor Juana directed to the Marquis de la Laguna poems in which she exalted his physical charms as highly as his moral virtues. It will be said that it was equally scandalous for a woman to refer to another woman in the terms Sor Juana used. No, it was not. Even if, as has been seen, certain expressions are perplexing, it was more easily understandable that a woman address her lady in those terms than her lord. The sensual expressions and amatory images could be accepted and read as metaphors and rhetorical figures for two true sentiments: appreciation and an inferior's devotion to her superior. That is why the anonymous author of the "Advertencia" offers the poet's gratitude as his first explanation for the tone of the poems. That gratitude, through a convention of the era, could be expressed in images from the tradition of erotic poetry. The blending of eroticism and vassalage has already appeared, as I mentioned previously, in the first flowering of Provençal poetry and had been perpetuated by the poets of the Renaissance and the Baroque.

Nelli points out that one of the distinctive notes of courtly love is submission to the lady, and that this theme rules and determines all others. It is already present in the formative period of courtly love—that is, in chivalric erotica, with William IX, Duke of Aquitaine: "No man can triumph in love unless he submit all his being to the will of his lady." The word William uses is *obedienz:* the lover is the servant of the lady. This submission frequently assumes the form of feudal homage. It was inevitable that "the juridical vocabulary of the era should be used to express the new relations of loving fidelity. But homage to the lady was not an inherent rite of vassalage: feudal institutions in themselves cannot explain why about 1120 it occurred to the great barons to subject themselves to their beloved, like vassals to their lords. The starting point was devotion to the lady: that devotion adopted the social form of the relationship of vassalage."[5] Vassalage was symbolic and was inscribed not in the laws of reality but in those of ceremony. According to Nelli, the

Provençals took the idea of the submission of the lover from Arabic erotica. This is a convention that is not present either in Gallo-Roman or Germanic tradition or in the Christianity of the time. The great lords of Provence almost surely were inspired in the example of the Arabic courts of Andalusia: "Submission is beautiful for the free man who falls in love," said Al-Hakam, Caliph of Cordoba.

The theme of submission to the beloved woman is closely associated with another theme, also of Arabic origin: "William IX at times called his mistress *mi dons* [my lord], and the *senhal* [pseudonym or sign masking the identity of the lady] by which she was characterized was masculine: *Bon Vezi* [Fair Neighbor]. Thus the singular custom of masculinizing the beloved object dates from the eleventh century." This custom can be interpreted as a transposition of the bond of feudal vassalage, but it also indicates that the lady was being accorded the supreme distinction in the human relations of the ancient and medieval worlds: that of friendship between men. For all these reasons, "Spanish Arabs bestowed masculine titles on their beloved: *Sayyide,* my lord; *Mulaya,* my master." The two themes—submission to the lady, and her masculinization— reappear in later erotica, especially in the sixteenth and seventeenth centuries. So although in its origins erotic poetry appropriated the juridical and seignorial language of feudalism, converting the amorous relationship into a symbolic facsimile of the bond between lord and vassal, courtly poetry, reversing the trend, confiscated amorous rhetoric and employed it in palace etiquette: the bond between the courtier and his lord was analogous to that of love. In turn, the age-old friendship between free men appeared, transformed, in love. In the seventeenth century examples of this curious eroticization of etiquette abound, in poetry, in theater, and in the novel.

All human relationships, private as well as public, are symbolic, but this symbolism is clearest and most constant in political and religious ceremonies. Metaphors—double and triple in the Baroque period— turned around a few elements: sun, magnet, heart. All of them appeal to a kind of universal magnetism: centers of the world, givers of heat and light, were simultaneously incarnations of power and love. In Sor Juana's poems to the Countess de Paredes we find all the motifs of traditional amatory poetry transformed into metaphors of the relationship of gratitude and dependence that united the nun with her Vicereine. In appearance these poems merely reiterate the rhetoric of the era: the poetry of the seventeenth century is bursting with sonnets, *décimas, romances, octavas,* and *letrillas* in which appear—ad nauseam—expressions similar to those in Sor Juana's poems. Not even the greatest poets—Góngora, Quevedo, Lope, Calderón—are immune to the vice of courtly adulation, and in all of them the conversion of amatory into courtly language is constant. The difference is that in the case of Sor Juana that transposition is carried to the most daring and delirious extremes. Furthermore—and this is decisive—her exaltation, far from seeming artificial, as in the courtly poems of other poets, in certain poems achieves the intensity that distinguishes authentic passion from rhetorical affectation. Nor are the poems exempt from the blend of eroticism and religion that appears in the amorous poetry of all times. Again and again Sor Juana says that she is a servant, enamored, a slave, a lover; in the most fervent passages she also calls herself an idolator and a believer.

The poets of the Renaissance and the Baroque, following Greco-Roman antiquity, called their beloved "goddess" and made a cult of their love. Although Sor Juana uses and abuses such literary devices, there comes a moment when they are insufficient. Then she uses more passionate expressions closer to true religion than to mythological conventions. The mingling of eroticism and religion is universal and belongs to all epochs. Christian and Muslim mystics, believers in a single God, used expressions typical of erotic passion with the same ardor as, although with less crudeness than, the Indian mystics, whether polytheists or worshipers of Emptiness. The latter have converted the Buddhist concept of Emptiness (*Prajna Paramita,* the supreme wisdom) into a divinity with the semblance of a beautiful and bejeweled naked girl who, like Bernini's *St. Teresa,* offers herself with a gesture of abandon. In turn, the poets of all languages and civilizations have used in their poems the religious metaphors and symbolic expressions of the liturgy and theology. Sor Juana also carried this convention to extremes; hence it is not surprising that she has been criticized for those audacities that verge on heresy. One example, among others, is *romance* 27, which ends with this declaration:

> [Give my greetings to my masters,]
> And to God, Lady, that seeing
> the Heaven of your perfection,
> He rise again, on this our
> holy day of resurrection.[6]

Sor Juana's poems conform to, but at the same time exceed, the theme of gratitude to the protectress. Many of these poems break with models of mere praise. It is true that the expressions used by Sor Juana also appear in hundreds of courtly poets, but always with a cool and impersonal tone. Góngora's sonnets and *octavas* to the Marquise de Ayamonte or the Count de Niebla may surprise us with their wit or luminous images—never because they express a personal sentiment. The same is true of all the courtly poetry of that century. In contrast, in Sor Juana the stereotyped figures, the pompous commonplaces, and the ritual praise are immediately tinged with personal feeling: they are confidences, expressions, as she herself says, of an impassioned and frequently melancholy wit. These are personal poems addressed to a flesh-and-blood person. Although they are more or less official homages to a Vicereine, the most intense among them—and there are many—are declarations of amorous admiration. At the risk of seeming monotonous, I must repeat: Sor Juana's poems to María Luisa are often at variance with the courtly genre and constitute a world apart, of which they are the only examples in the poetry of the period.

At this point we must move to the second explanation given by the author of the "Advertencia": that "her acquaintance with the illustrious gifts bestowed by Heaven on the Vicereine" led Sor Juana to employ these singular expressions. We cannot know whether the real María Luisa corresponded to the picture Sor Juana paints of her. My impression—setting aside courtly adulation and the exaggerations motivated by Sor Juana's fervor—is that the Countess must have been an extraordinary being. Most of those who have studied this matter believe as I do. If she had not been intelligent and sensitive she would not have been Sor Juana's friend, nor would she have taken such a passionate interest in her poetry. What a shame that we know so little about her and that we must reconstruct her friendship with Sor Juana through the poems alone. The information we have of her physical charms is no less favorable than that of her moral virtues. It is true that through the eyes of palace adulation a deformed duke was an Adonis, an inept prime minister was a Lycurgus, and defeated generals were Alexanders and Caesars. But it is impossible that the woman described in the at once artful and sensual terms of the decasyllabic *romance* 61—one of the most exquisite, daring, and seductive amatory compositions of baroque poetry—could have been ugly. Sor Juana never tires of praising "the beautiful proportion" of María Luisa, and constantly links the physical to the moral: her love, although spiritual, is born of the sight of her friend's beauty. In this the Platonism is overt: corporeal beauty is the first step in the scale of love.

The sentiments expressed in the poems that Sor Juana dedicated to the Countess de Paredes spontaneously evoke, in a cultivated spirit like that of the author of the "Advertencia," the theory of sympathy ruled by the dual influence of the stars and the humors. These ideas had come down from antiquity, and by 1689, the year of the publication of the *Castalian Inundation,* were already being displaced by the new physics and the new psychology and physiology. But not in end-of-the-seventeenth-century Spain, a society still closed to the changes that in those years were transforming the sciences and philosophy. Furthermore, the reach of those changes and discoveries should not be exaggerated: for the majority of intellectuals and poets of the century the physics and psychology of the Renaissance still obtained. It must, in addition, be confessed that the astrological theory of love, however chimerical it may seem to us, held greater consistency for Sor Juana's contemporaries than the doctrines of psychoanalysts and psychiatrists hold for us. I am not, of course, speaking of *truth*—if, in fact, this word has any meaning in relation to men and their ever-changing natures—but of *consistency*. Shocking as this may sound, I believe that modern psychological theories have merely replaced a set of fantastic principles (humors, stars, spirits, affinities, and antipathies) with others no less fantastic (complexes, compulsions, the unconscious, archetypes). In a certain way, psychology today is nothing more than a translation of Renaissance psychology into modern scientific terms.

The division of human nature into four temperaments, each determined by a bodily humor, is ancient, appearing as early as Hippocrates. This theory, developed by Greco-Roman and medieval medicine, prevailed until the dawn of the modern age. As we all know, the four humors—blood, phlegm, choler or yellow bile, and black bile—were the cause of the four temperaments: sanguine, phlegmatic, choleric, and melancholic. The temperaments existed in relation to the four elements and were subject to the influence of the stars. The transformation of the theory of the four humors—purely physiological in origin—into a cosmological doctrine of passions and human types was the result of a long evolution that in ancient times extended from the Stoics to the Neoplatonists. Arab philosophers and physicians further developed the doctrine. Their versions were a major influence on the Christian West and prepared the way for the great flowering of Scholasticism in the thirteenth century. In turn, the poets of the *dolce stil nuovo* converted the doctrine into a poetics of love that continues to inspire us today. Finally, the Neoplatonic hermeticism of the Renaissance systematized it and gave it its final form. That was the fountain from which Sor Juana drank. The phrase—central to the "Advertencia"—referring to "that secret influence . . . of the humors or stars, known as sympathy," must be read in the light of this tradition.

FOR THE RENAISSANCE and the Baroque Age, man was a microcosm, a theater ruled by the same forces and powers that ruled the universe, although man was endowed with free will. Antiquity had deified the planets, and each of them was literally a god radiating powerful influences capable of altering the course of human lives. As C. S. Lewis observes, the word "influence" has lost much of its efficacy and has become vague and abstract; for the Renaissance and the Baroque Age—and, it goes without saying, for the Middle Ages—the influence of the stars was a kind of magnetism that combined material and spiritual forces. Sor Juana's editor Méndez Plancarte piously attempted to minimize her belief in astrology.[7] The truth is that most of her contemporaries, both in Europe and the New World, intellectuals included, continued to believe in astrology: "Orthodox theologians accepted the theory that the planets affect not only events and human psychology, but the life of plants and minerals as well."[8] The Church was not opposed to astrology but rather to an absolute astral determinism that denied free will; it also persecuted divination and adoration of the planets. Basically, the problem that confronted the Church was not very different from the one that has absorbed men since they began to reflect upon their strange earthly destiny: freedom versus predestination.

Sor Juana's ideas on this subject were those of her time. Like almost all her contemporaries, she believed in the powers of the stars. The entire argument of *loa* V (378), celebrating the birthday of Charles II, revolves around the effects of the planets on human destinies. Previously, in commenting on Sor Juana's courtly poetry, I referred to this composition and to the council of stars convoked by the Sun (Apollo) to corroborate the beneficent influences with which they had favored Charles II. This scene offers Sor Juana the opportunity to expound her ideas, the traditional ideas of her time, about astral influence. A good Catholic, she accepts free will, but as an exception and a privilege; in all else, the stars decree.

> Through a rare privilege
> and notable exception,
> God granted to the Will
> the right to take free action

(in acting for free choice,
which works to good or ill,
influence cannot force,
but predispose, the Will),
and the rest must fall to you,
whose influence conjoined
to some brings misery
and some exalts with joy.

The action of the stars, the elements, and the humors produced a universal *sympathy*. As in the case of *influence,* we run the risk of missing the sense of this word if we do not recall its history and its origins. For the Stoics, sympathy was universal *syn-pathos,* the force that bound the world together and prevented the dispersion of its elements. The philosopher Chrysippus says that "the world is in a state of union because of the *conspiring* and the accord of all things celestial and terrestrial."[9] The agent of that union was a life-giving and unifying breath that animated all things and all beings: the *pneuma.* The origin of the idea of love in the West is undoubtedly to be found in the *pneuma.* The Stoics probably took this concept from the physicians, who were in turn inspired by Aristotle. He had said that a breath, or astral *pneuma,* is found in semen and that the life of the embryo and the preservation of the species were owing to it. In the pneumatology of the physicians appear other breaths: the exhalations of the blood that were until the beginning of the modern age called "spirits." These spirits naturally must not be confused with angelic intelligences. According to Robert Burton, heir to ancient, medieval, and Renaissance medical sciences, "Of these spirits there be three kinds . . . *natural, vital, animal.*"[10] Other authors change the order, but in all of them the process is the same: the spirits are born of the blood as a tenuous faint ether or vapor; as they pass from the liver to the heart and from the heart to the head, they become increasingly purer. The spirit that dwells in the brain is the agent of fantasy. Fantasy was one of the internal senses, along with memory, common sense, judgment, and imagination. For the Scholastic (also for Sor Juana, as seen in *First Dream*) the functions of fantasy were higher than those of imagination.[11]

The Stoics inherited from the physicians the medical idea of the *pneuma* and turned it into the animating principle of the cosmos and of every human being. Originators of primordial fire, igneous breaths (*pneumata*) maintained the cohesion of the elements and united all things with themselves and with other things: through their work the world was a *system*. At the same time, the *pneuma* was the vital motor of every man, the soul of his soul, what gave him unity, and what caused him to relate to other men and to seek their friendship. Logic itself expressed this universal sympathy; it was an agreement between two more or less distant terms, reached by means of a third intermediary term. Giorgio Agamben, author of a fascinating book on the influence of the "pneumo-phantasmology" of antiquity and the Middle Ages on the art and thought of the West, says that for Zeno and Chrysippus "the *pneuma* was a corporeal principle, a subtle and luminous body . . . that entered into all beings and was the origin of growth and sentient life." [12] The *pneuma* was inborn, not a principle external to the body; it survived the death of the body and ascended to the sublunar region. The Neoplatonists' idea of the ethereal or astral body, still alive in the beliefs of many contemporary sects, is already present in embryonic form in these concepts of ancient Stoicism, also in the *spiriti* and *spiritelli* of Cavalcanti, Dante, and the poets of the *dolce stil nuovo*.

Galen called the Aristotelian *pneuma*, the transmitter of life located in the semen, "the vehicle of the soul." This was a felicitous expression and was later associated with the Platonic idea of the descent of the soul to the body. In a famous and obscure passage of the *Timaeus*, Plato says that the demiurge divided souls according to the stars; that is why souls have as their dwelling the stars corresponding to them. There they remain until the moment comes to descend and inhabit the body each has been assigned. At death, the soul of the just returns to his star; that of the evil and impious is condemned to being reincarnated, each time lower on the scale of being. Plato's myth and Galen's metaphor inspired Plotinus, Porphyry, and Proclus—also their heir Macrobius, a writer who undoubtedly influenced Sor Juana—in their concept of the astral body. The form of the astral body was spherical, but when it entered the physical body it assumed the body's shape; it was a kind of ethereal container for the soul. Its function was twofold: it served as the soul's vehicle in the descent from star to earthly body, and also as the bridge, the mediating term, between two opposing and irreducible realities— the body, mortal matter, and the incorporeal and immortal soul.

Without its ethereal body, the soul could not have communicated with its physical body or with the material world. Thus, with great subtlety, Neoplatonism tried to resolve a problem that still preoccupies contemporary philosophy and psychology: the relation between the immaterial mind and the material world of the senses. In its descent the soul moves through the different heavens and then the planets "inscribe their gifts on the container of subtle matter: the qualities and destiny of the future individual."[13] Thus the ethereal body is also the bearer of the inclinations of the soul, and of its passions and faculties. It is the agent, as are the humors at the other extreme, of sympathies and antipathies. The mental horizon on which Sor Juana's poems unfold, and the allusions of the "Advertencia" to stars and sympathy, begin to take on clearer form.

In the first pages of the *Vita Nuova,* Dante marvelingly and marvelously relates his first encounter with Beatrice, who was dressed in a pure color, blood red. In that instant "the vital spirit, the one that dwells in the most secret chamber of the heart, began to tremble violently . . . and trembling, it spoke these words: Here is a god stronger than I, who shall come to rule over me." At once the animal spirit awakened, which in turn alerted the spirits of the senses, especially those of sight. At the same time the natural spirit that resides in the liver, the one most inclined to bodily pleasures, wakened and began to weep. Dante was merely utilizing a commonplace; the theory of the vital spirits—vapors born of the blood—was current in his time. His immediate source, it appears, was Albertus Magnus, although the theme is also found in St. Thomas Aquinas.

In the course of the book there are other spirits, which enter and depart through the eyes of lovers and their ladies, do battle, penetrate the lover's heart, and there engrave the lady's image. These spirits are numinous like the *pneuma* and, as befits their nature, are transformed into sighs. They are the *spiritelli.* In the poems of Cavalcanti, they move ceaselessly through the bodily organs and shoot love's arrows through the eyes of the lady at her gallant. Servants of love, they "make men tremble and women humble." In one of his sonnets they appear fourteen times, once in each line. The physiology of love of the *dolce stil nuovo* poets has certain analogies with modern theories of communication and genetics. That physiology is a network of calls and replies: the sight of Beatrice wakes the vital spirits, which in turn alert the *spiritelli,* and this world of busy messengers is set in motion like our molecules and atoms or our telephone systems. Like genes and linguistic signs, the messenger spirits transmit information. They also resemble, not biologically or linguistically but in the epic-burlesque mode, the sylphs of *The Rape of the Lock.* Like Pope's creatures, they are breaths, sighs; like them, they are intelligent.

There is little similarity between the Neoplatonists' idea of the astral body, the transparent vehicle for the soul identified with the spirit of fantasy (*phantastikon pneuma*), and the *spiritelli* of Dante and Cavalcanti, although several authors of that era confused them. The vital spirits came from Arabic medical tradition. It is not necessary to elaborate on this; the Averroism of Cavalcanti is well known and has been widely studied. Dante's concepts were in many respects opposed to the naturalism of his friend, most markedly in his vision of love. For the somber Cavalcanti, love was an accident and was linked with death,[14] while for Dante it was the center that made the universe secure and allowed it to spin and to survive. Nevertheless, in the theory of the *spiriti* and *spiritelli*, the coincidence between the two friends was nearly absolute. They were even alike in the slightly sarcastic manner they adopted at times in speaking of the tiny and ethereal guests of the blood and the humors.

It is not difficult to understand why the ethereal vehicles of the soul do not appear in Dante's vision of love. This Neoplatonic concept contained two ideas incompatible with Christian dogma: the existence of the soul before birth and the disappearance of the body following death. (The resurrection of the dead is one of the principal mysteries of Christianity.) But astrology prevails in the thinking of the Florentine poet, almost always allied with numerology. Also central to Dante's poetry are distinctive traces of the Neoplatonic concept of the soul's destiny, its separation from the body and its ascent into the heavens, not only following death but also during exceptional moments such as ecstasy and certain kinds of dreams. Although the belief in the "voyage of the soul" through other worlds is ancient and appears both in central Asia and in pre-Columbian America, Dante inherited it from the Greco-Roman and Judeo-Christian traditions. In Sor Juana—although associated with knowledge, not with love—the theme of the voyage of the soul is similarly fundamental. Robert Klein points out that Dante transcended the opposition between Neoplatonism and naturalism, between the vehement Averroism of his friend Cavalcanti and the *gentilezza* of his admired Guinizelli, not by eliminating one of the two terms but by combining them. In the last sonnet of the *Vita Nuova*, anticipating the *Divine Comedy* and its voyage through the three realms, appear in succession "the medical mechanistic theories (*spirito* = *sospiro* [sigh]), a rational or allegorical explanation (*spirito* = *pensiero* [thought]) and 'shamanic' ecstasy (the ascent to heaven of the wandering spirit)."[15] The spirit is born as a sigh; it ascends and is transfigured in eyes that, as they see, *understand*:

When it has come to the desired place,
It sees a lady held in reverence,
And who shines so, that through her radiance
The pilgrim spirit gazes upon her.[16]

Marsilio Ficino believed in the ethereal body and in planetary influences. His affirmation of melancholy as a disposition that favored contemplation, love, and poetry was also a reaffirmation of the doctrines of astrology and the humors: black bile and the influence of Saturn were determinants in the melancholic temperament. This idea inspired and captivated many great artists and poets of the sixteenth and seventeenth centuries. No less decisive was his philosophy of love. Ficino was not an original philosopher, but his role is central in the history of affective emotions. Not only did he inherit and systematize the Western tradition of love poetry—Provençal poetry, the *dolce stil nuovo,* and Petrarch—but his reading of Plato was the first authentic interpretation of that Greek philosopher. Ficino invented the expression "Platonic love," and he was the first to formulate that kind of love in philosophical and psychological terms. Sor Juana probably did not read Ficino, although in the *Allegorical Neptune* she mentions one of his direct heirs, the Neoplatonic Florentine poet Pietro Crinito. No matter; the ideas expressed for the first time in Ficino's *De Amore* had, some two centuries later, already been converted into a commonplace of civilized peoples.

Along with the cosmological concept of love and the theory of the humors, the notion of universal sympathy also figures in Ficino's thinking. Not in the cosmo-mechanistic form of the Stoics, but as a kind of affinity among things and beings. The true name of that affinity is love, that is, the case of animate beings, attraction toward good. The good, which ranges from the useful to the perfect, resolves into goodness, and the supreme goodness is God.[17] Love is a desire to enjoy a special goodness, beauty. There are three kinds of beauty: beauty of bodies, beauty of sounds, and beauty of souls, corresponding to seeing, hearing, and intellect. For Ficino, love, even in its inferior form—attraction by the beauty of the body—is always contemplative and not sensual or sexual. Love describes a circle; it goes from God to his creature and from his creature, through love of the beautiful body and the noble soul, returns to God. Thus the highest form of human love—in truth, the only love that counts—is mutual love. This is an idea Sor Juana does not share: "love does not demand / a corresponding will." Ficino's concept of love, Kristeller points out, also encompasses two very different sentiments: friendship and charity. The latter is "the religious sentiment embracing all fellow men as brothers for the sake of God." The former is a concept that "originates in Greek philosophy and was first made the object of philosophical inquiry by Plato and even more by Aristotle." [18]

For all these reasons, love is not exclusively a union between a man and a woman. If true love—indistinguishable from charity and friendship—is mutual love and, essentially, love of God, "not only man and woman but also two men or two women may be united by a sentiment of love." Kristeller rejects the interpretation of some writers who have seen a veiled or sublimated homosexuality in Ficino's concept; no one in Ficino's day, he states, attributed these tendencies to Ficino or to his friends and disciples. Whether or not Kristeller's interpretation is well founded, and whatever the nature of Ficino's sexual inclinations may have been, a long tradition of love culminates in his ideas, in which distinct currents flow together, notably courtly love, the *dolce stil nuovo*, Dante's poetry, and Petrarch's *Canzoniere*. I emphasize that Ficino is not an end but a beginning; his ideas about love, surviving many vicissitudes and alterations, have nurtured the art, literature, and emotional lives of men and women for more than four centuries, until our own time. Today those concepts are disintegrating and there is nothing visible on the horizon to replace them. The most ominous of signs: the absence of signs.

The history of love in the West, from the chivalric poetry of William of Aquitaine on, can be seen as a dual process of liberation and sublimation. All peoples and civilizations have looked upon Eros with veneration and fear. His powers are particularly feared in hierarchical societies; love is a passion that levels classes, institutions, and precepts. Nevertheless, through a combination of internal and external circumstances, in the bosom of a feudal and chivalric society, love was integrated into the social order. And love at its most violent and subversive: as a violation of social hierarchies and a transgression of the institution of marriage. What was most notable was that this dual infraction—the troubadours were commoners while their ladies were both married and members of the highest nobility—assumed the form of a rite, outside the Church but no less venerated than the religious sacraments. The agents of the consecration were not oil, wine, and priest, but poetry, music, and troubadour. The poets of the *dolce stil nuovo* inherited this tradition, and Guinicelli, whom Dante considered to be the master of his generation, based his poetics on the identification between love and *gentilezza*. This latter was an aristocracy of the heart, in contrast to a nobility of the blood. Love made equals of lovers because it was founded on the nobility of souls. A dual subversion: poetry and love negated marriage, hierarchies, and lineage. Furthermore, they exalted woman and so restored her free will. Since the time of Alexandria and the Rome of Catullus and Propertius, all the great periods of erotic poetry have coincided with the freedom of women: they are the symptoms of a civilization's maturity.

The sublimation of sexuality was the price of the conversion of erotic violence into ritual. Eros is a destructive and creative god: what we call civilization—as taught by the most dissimilar masters, Plato, St. Augustine, and Freud—is simultaneously the repression and the sublimation of his powers. In all societies the two signs that define man, the sign *body* and the sign *nonbody,* set the stage for a bloody dialogue that is at times resolved in a momentary and unstable equilibrium.[19] In Provence the body was never totally denied, and sublimation assumed several equivocal forms. Among them, the most curious was the ceremony of the *asag,* a series of trials that culminated in the suitor's contemplation of his lady, naked; the suitor could lie beside her in bed, although without consummating sexual union. In Florence, sublimation took a stricter form and the relationship between lovers consisted of what another Platonist, Leo Hebraeus, would later call "visual copulation."

Repression is counterproductive and almost always ends in explosions or moral duplicity: Dante had several illicit extramarital affairs, and Petrarch had two illegitimate children by different women. In other cases, chastity ends by perverting the spirit, as seen in many ascetics. On the other hand, Platonic sublimation not only inspired great artists, it protected love both from the dissipation of libertinism and the frenzy of asceticism. Love is mortal and lethal, as a lucid and bitter Cavalcanti was the first to see. Love is gazing into another's eyes, but that game is soon transformed into fatal fascination: lovers lose their bodies and their souls. Or become bored. Love kills lovers or lovers kill love. To save it, and to be saved, their *united* gazes—following the battle of glances—must be directed upward. This was what Dante told us; in this lay the historical and psychological function of Platonism; and this is what today we can salvage from that tradition.

15

Religious Fires

$\mathscr{F}$ROM THE PERSPECTIVE of the tradition I have briefly reviewed, we can more easily understand the attitude of the readers of the poems Sor Juana addressed to María Luisa Manrique de Lara. Clearly they caused a certain amazement, for otherwise the "Advertencia" would not have been necessary. The tone of that note is also revealing, at once cautious and reassuring, as if to thwart any improper interpretation. But thus sanctioned, the poems conformed quite naturally to the context of a genre and a tradition. Those poems were simultaneously courtly poems and homages of gratitude, palatial adulation and declarations of a Platonic infatuation.[1] The process of sublimation initiated by courtly love and perfected by Renaissance Neoplatonism succeeded in legitimating passions and inclinations that were transgressions of sexual morality, such as relations outside marriage or between persons of the same sex. Thus, while such acts were almost always cruelly repressed, their sublimated expression was not. Contrast the severity with which the "abominable sin," homosexuality, was persecuted to the tolerance and even admiration with which Ficino's chaste but passionate friendships were viewed. Michelangelo and his exalted Platonism, as well as other artists and poets of the Renaissance, enjoyed the same tolerance. This attitude was not exclusive to the papal court and the Italian republics but extended to Elizabethan England and the France of the Valois. Almost always, these Platonic friendships were between men; I say almost always because there are also examples of sublimated Sapphism. One of the most notable is the "Élégie d'une dame enamourée d'une autre dame." Its author, Pontus de Tyard, was an intimate friend of Maurice

Scève and of Ronsard and the protégé of Diane de Poitiers; he was a devotee of Neoplatonic philosophy and the tradition of Hermes Trismegistus. A high dignitary of the Church, he was at the time of his death Bishop of Chalon.[2] In his opulent refuge, "dedicated to silent orgies of meditation," he wrote and later collected in his *Oeuvres poétiques* (1573), to no one's scandal, a curious poem exalting lesbian passion.

> Nostre Amour serviroit d'eternelle memoire
> Pour prouver que l'Amour de femme à femme épris
> Sur les masles Amours emporteroit le pris.[3]

Sor Juana's poems are not as direct as the "Élégie" of Pontus de Tyard. The sentiments they express—which were surely the sentiments she truly felt—are far more complex and ambiguous. Up to this point I have shown how and why it was possible, without provoking general reproach, to write in Mexico and publish in Madrid in the late seventeenth century poems with the theme of a loving friendship between two aristocratic women. But how did they themselves, Juana Inés and María Luisa, explain their affection? How did they justify it and not find it contrary to the reigning morality and to their situations—one a nun and the other married and a mother? The tradition that justified the poems also justified the authors of such poems. Their sentiments, as Sor Juana never tires of repeating and the titles of her poems emphasize, were honest, pure, and decent. Their affection, consecrated by poetry and philosophy, had been defined as the sublime combination of the three most elevated sentiments: love, friendship, and charity.

Sor Juana does not blush about feeling what she feels; she alludes again and again to the spiritual nature of her love. This is why she insists on the separation between soul and body. Every time this idea, more Platonic than Christian, appears, Father Méndez Plancarte frowns and calls it "poetic fantasy" or "philosophical nonsense." Unfortunately for all those who have wanted to ignore or diminish Sor Juana's Platonism, those "fantasies" not only figure constantly in her writings but are the axis on which *First Dream*, her greatest poem, turns. Sor Juana's Platonism, like that of so many in the Renaissance and the age of the Baroque, fitted within—or, more exactly, was grafted onto—the Scholastic tradition. The break with Scholasticism was not the result of Neoplatonic hermeticism, although that philosophy had prepared the way, but of Cartesianism and the scientific and philosophical revolution, two intellectual currents that touched Sor Juana only obliquely and from afar.

For her, Platonism was both a vital and an intellectual necessity. Without strict Platonic dualism, her sentiments and those of María Luisa would have become aberrations.

Because of her talent and her religious state, Sor Juana was not an ordinary woman. The same was true of the Countess: she was of the highest nobility, and in addition to being beautiful and clever, she was the Vicereine. Although it was for differing reasons, their positions placed both of them beyond ordinary norms and demands. That privileged situation, nevertheless, carried with it responsibilities and tedious obligations. In a certain way both women were prisoners of their rank. Sor Juana was not subject to a husband's authority, but she was subject to the Mother Superior of her convent and to the intrigues of the sisters. She was not of a religious temperament, as we have seen, and her true passion had always been learning. Solitary amid the flurry of San Jerónimo, willful and independent; one day inspired and the next spiritless; frequently afflicted by imaginary ills that were nonetheless as tormenting as physical illness—her true, her only, companions were the ghosts in her books. Although María Luisa's circumstances were different, her predicament was similar: affection that found no object. She was married to a mediocre man and, to judge by the portrait we have, one rather feeble and insignificant. Her life was a weary succession of ceremonies. We know that she was clever and vivacious and that she loved palace intrigue; while she was in Mexico she wrote constantly to Madrid asking for this and that, always seeking favors for her family and her protégés. The way she gathered together, transported, and succeeded in publishing the manuscripts of Sor Juana's first book, *Castalian Inundation,* is an indication of her energy and her independence. There is a parallel between María Luisa's courtly activities and Sor Juana's continuous literary correspondence. In both instances, busyness concealed an internal emptiness.

In terms of psychic economy—to use Freud's expression—Sor Juana's malady was not poverty but riches: a powerful but unused libido. That profusion, and its lack of object, are evident in the frequency with which images of female and male bodies appear in her poems, almost always converted into phantasmal apparitions. Sor Juana lived among erotic shadows. Her poems reveal, furthermore, that she was a true melancholic. I use this word in the sense given it by Ficino and Cornelius Agrippa, but also that of Freud; the two concepts are complementary. To the former, melancholy was a kind of internal emptiness (*vacantia*) that, in the best of humans, was channeled into aspiration toward higher ends. For Freud, melancholy is a state similar to grief; in both cases the subject confronts the loss of a desired object, whether because it is now lost or because it does not exist. The difference, of course, is that in the case of grief the loss is real, while with the melancholic it is imaginary. For Freud—the coincidence with Ficino is curious—in certain cases melancholy is associated with the opposite psychic disturbance: mania. That is, divine furor, the Platonist's *enthousiasmos,* or inspiration.

Neither religious nor conjugal life, neither conventual liturgy nor palace ceremony, could offer Juana Inés and María Luisa emotional or sentimental satisfaction. The nun was not St. Teresa, nor was the Countess Penelope. Further, both for nun and for Vicereine, an illicit relationship with men was excluded. According to the Duke de Maura, conjugal morality in the court of Charles II was strict, especially when compared with the courts of France and England. In New Spain the sanctions were no less strict; significantly, the chronicle of three centuries of viceregal history contains no scandalous story concerning a Vicereine. An excess of libido could not be directed toward an object of the opposite sex. A different object—a female friend—had to take its place. Transposition and sublimation: the loving friendship between Sor Juana and the Countess was the transposition; the sublimation was realized by means of the Neoplatonic concept of love—friendship between persons of the same sex. These relations, exalted and codified by poetry, corresponded perfectly both to the psychic needs of the women and to their social rank. If love was the *other* nobility, Platonic love-friendship was even more noble and heroic.

The hypothesis I have just outlined does not necessarily exclude the presence of Sapphic tendencies in the two friends. Neither does it include them. Any comment on this subject would be mere supposition; we lack facts and documents. The only thing that is sure is that their relationship, although impassioned, was chaste. As for the real person, the Countess de Paredes is not even a shadow for us, merely a name and its echo; although the figure of Sor Juana is slightly more real, just when we think we can grasp it, it eludes us, like the ghosts in her poems. I need not review what I have written about her childhood. For Sor Juana the pursuit of culture not only involved masculinization but carried with it the neutralization of sexuality. Neutrality is not synonymous with sterility; there is a moment when neutrality becomes symbolic fecundity: the nun Juana is Isis, lady of letters, and also the pythoness who makes predictions in her cave (her cell), pregnant not with child but with metaphors and tropes. Her mother had managed a large estate, mistress of herds and harvests; Sor Juana was mistress of a community of signs and concepts.

As we have seen, the examination of Sor Juana's erotic tendencies is inconclusive and ends with a question. In accord with the classic definition of the melancholic temperament, its two extremes were depression and mania. Between them lay the gamut of attitudes: masculinization and neutralization of the libido, identification with her grandfather and, contradictorily, with her mother. And always an exalted narcissism. But hers was a narcissism tempered by the lucidity of melancholy and the rapture of enthusiasm. The image in her mirror evoked the caress of her gaze and, an instant later, the severity of her criticism. So she sought another image that could free her from herself and captivate her; a ghostly shadow, a fleeting conceit, the face of a female friend. Was she aware of her complexity? Clearly she was: some of her best poems are an examination of that "amorous torment . . . that begins as desire / and ends in melancholy." She also realized that those conflicting impulses and sentiments, at once tyrannical and impalpable, resisted every attempt at a clear definition:

> I harbor a regard,
> so elusive in its tone that
> though I know how to feel,
> no feeling have I known.

These lines are from a poem on sacred love (56), but they could be about profane love. She took the opportunity, whatever the theme, to comment marginally on her thoughts about her state and the enigmas that dwelled within her. Of course no one has a perfect knowledge of his own being, and Sor Juana is no exception to this universal rule. But some, more lucid than others, know that they are a bundle of impulses and contradictory and secret passions. This knowledge Sor Juana did have; if anything distinguishes her, it is her lucidity. She did not deceive herself in the case of her relationship with the Countess de Paredes; on the contrary, as she expressed her sentiment, she justified it with the example of Platonic dualism. In one of the first poems she addresses to the Countess, she confesses that she lives bound "in the sweet chains / of your sacred lights." Soon the more familiar *tú* replaces *vos* and, in the way male poets address their ladies, she begins to call her by the Arcadian names of Lysis and Phyllis, as she had earlier called Leonor Carreto "Laura." In *romance* 19, one of the most impassioned, the anonymous author of the titles thought it necessary to insert this clarification: "Pure love, from afar and desiring nothing indecorous, can be as fervent as the most profane." From the first lines of this poem, her amorous cult verging on heresy—as Méndez Plancarte fully notes—she declares her Platonism in inflamed terms:

> originating in the heart,
> desire, in discord and dissension,
> kindles tainted holocausts,
> fires of bodily affection,
>   and only when born of the soul
> may the pure flame of consecration
> blaze brightly in religious fires
> of silence and of adoration.

Eight ingenious and impassioned verses in the Spanish original, with lines of audacious beauty: those "religious fires" are reminiscent of the greatest poets, a Donne or a Lope. Unevenly, and with a certain lassitude—prolixity is a defect that seventeenth-century poets were scarcely ever able to avoid—the poem continues, and in another intense passage Sor Juana says that she loves María Luisa like a moth, the "simple / lover that in blind circling / is prey to the flame," like the unwary hand of the child who cuts himself as he strokes the knife blade, as the sunflower loves the light, as air loves space, as fire loves matter, like "all natural things" that desire "lovingly unites / in bonds that bind them tight." She loves her, finally, for herself, for being who she is: Phyllis. When Sor Juana reaches this point, she explains the nature of her affection:

> There is no obstacle to love
> in gender or in absence,
> for souls, as you are well aware,
> transcend both sex and distance.

In the verses that follow, Sor Juana not only accepts but exalts the uniqueness of her affection: "ordinary beauty" follows a "natural course." María Luisa's does not. Hers is a "marvel, with royal privilege." The Provençal theme of the lady's sovereignty and its authority to break norms justifies her love-friendship. In *romance* 48 she returns to the theme of the separation of body and soul in no less unequivocal terms.

As its title explains, the poem is in reply to "a gentleman from Peru who sent her clay vessels while suggesting that she should become a man." Sor Juana replies with wit:

> As for the counsel that you offer,
> I promise you, I will attend
> with all my strength, although I judge
> no strength can make me a Tarquin;
>   for here we have no Salmacis
> whose crystal water, so they tell,
> to nurture masculinity
> possesses powers unexcelled.

Méndez Plancarte attributes Sor Juana's mention of the fountain of the nymph Salmacis (Ovid, *Metamorphoses,* 4.285–388) to inattention. This fountain did not transform maidens into youths, it changed Hermaphroditus into an androgyne. The transformation of woman into man, adds Méndez Plancarte, was the work of Isis, who changed Iphis into a man (Ovid, *Metamorphoses,* 9.666–797). A psychoanalyst would undoubtedly find this confusion significant. But maybe we do not need psychoanalysis to be able to explain this small error. To begin with, it is difficult to believe that Juana Inés, considering everything we know about her, would refer to the episode about Iphis: it was too similar to her own situation. Iphis, a Cretan girl who had been raised as a young man, in love with and betrothed to the maiden Ianthe, asks Isis to turn her into a man, and her request is granted. As a second point, it is likely that the origin of Sor Juana's confusion is to be found in Father Vitoria's treatise on mythology. Although Ovid states clearly that Hermaphroditus, on seeing himself changed and "his limbs become enfeebled," asked for, and obtained, from his parents Hermes and Aphrodite the concession that "whoever comes into this pool as man, shall go forth half-man, and be softened at the touch of the water," Vitoria's version says that "Hermaphroditus asked and was granted that all who bathed therein would have two sexual natures." In any case, Sor Juana later refers not to transformation into a male but to hermaphroditism:

> I have no knowledge of these things,
> except that I came to this place
> so that, if true that I am female,
> none substantiate that state.
>   I know, too, that *uxor,* woman,

> designated, in the Latin,
> only those who wed;
> and either gender may be virgin.

In the third verse she diminishes and almost places in doubt her female condition ("if true that I am female"), and in the final lines negates
it: being virgin, she is of both genders. These verses show not only that
she was aware of her conflict, but that, resolved by her religious vows
and her Platonism, it had ceased to be a conflict. She joined the order so
that no one should "substantiate" that she was a woman; because she
had not married and was virgin, her nature was still dual. She thus declares that spiritually she is an androgyne. That is why it is not proper
that she be looked upon as a woman:

> as I will never be a woman
> who as wife may serve a man.
> I know only that my body,
> not to either state inclined,
> is neuter, abstract, guardian
> of only what my soul consigns.

Her religious state has neutralized her sexuality, and her body is inclined
toward neither the masculine nor the feminine. But her soul responds to
other souls and may love them reciprocally, without differentiation in
gender. This theme is the motif of innumerable variations in *romances,
décimas, glosas,* and sonnets.

On the Platonic scale of love, the eyes and ears immediately precede
the supreme love, which is that of the mind. Seeing is an inferior form
of contemplation, and the true lover contemplates the beloved with
closed eyes. In a *glosa* addressed to Lysis, she asks:

> Though blinded by the sight of you,
> unseeing, must I feel resigned,
> if pleasures that are of the soul
> are also seen by one who's blind?

In a sonnet to Lysis (179) she carries to extremes "a lover's conceits":
her beloved's "beauty is unreachable," because merely the thought of
possessing it offends both her beloved's honor and her own love. This
gives rise to a paradox: "not to begin, simply, is what I begin." In the
same sonnet she affirms that supreme love does not seek to be requited.
This is an idea she repeats in many poems: the only "bliss" is that which

"neither can be deserved / nor dreamed of being achieved" ("To Lysis," 90). In the *sainete* "At the Palace," the prize to the winning gallant consists of loving without hope of reciprocation. Father Méndez Plancarte maintains that the Lysis of sonnet 179 is not the Countess de Paredes and that the person speaking is a man. Nevertheless, in the poems clearly addressed to María Luisa, Sor Juana repeats again and again her praise of unrequited love. The poems abound with allusions to those incidents and events that are generally associated with amorous relationships: jealousy, reproaches, absences, joy, gifts, meetings. In *romance* 18 she asks María Luisa's forgiveness for not having seen her or written to her for several days, and says that her religious duties had been the cause of the "intermission." Reproaches about absences come sometimes from her lips and other times from María Luisa's. *Romance* 27, written during the Lenten season, when visits to the convents were suspended, is one example:

> . . . I am downcast,
> too long from me are you absent,
> and my desires, thus disallowed,
> grow forty times more preva-Lent.
> My will is fasting, sorrowing,
> my intellect is held in pawn,
> my pleasures lie in idleness,
> my eyes have naught to gaze upon.
> If truth be told, beloved one,
> I know I do not overstate,
> when not with you, even my words,
> seem sounds that others fabricate.

Another poem (83), in *endechas reales,* states in still more tender terms her apologies for "not having waited to see you." She surely is alluding to visits the Countess made to the convent. These *endechas* are more notable for their direct and effusive tone than for poetic value. Sor Juana plays on the word *esperar,* which means both "to wait" and "to hope": to wait for a person and to hope for "what cannot be hoped or waited for," the blessing of love. At the end two verses stand out— "Enough of pain, / fair Master, enough"—that for the attentive reader immediately bring to mind a line from one of her best-known and most appreciated sonnets (164): "Enough of suffering, my love, enough." There are other poems of lesser quality that contain phrases as emphatic. For example (82):

> Thus, should I call you mine,
> I do not intend
> that mine you should be judged,
> merely that as yours I would be seen.

Reproaches motivated by a long silence reappear in a poem (91) in *redondillas*. On this occasion the one who complains is María Luisa, and it is Sor Juana who begs forgiveness for not having written. This occasion again opens the way to speaking in paradoxes. She praises silence, since her love, completely internal, suffices without need of externalization:

> In the passion of my love
> it was not heedless on my part
> to give powers to the heart
> once practiced only by the tongue.
> Herein my reasons I construe:
> because my passion was so full,
> I could see you in my soul,
> so in my soul I spoke with you.

In silence she loved her, and in silence she thought that the beloved also loved her, because "in imagining you / I found your favor." The inward happiness leads to rapture:

> To such madness I had come,
> in the blessing of your love,
> that, even imagined, your slightest boon
> could drive me to delirium.

But because the Countess orders her to speak, she speaks: "If to love your beauty is an unpardonable offense . . . so, too, it is one of which I never shall repent." And she concludes, not without audacity:

> This I find in my affection
> and more that I cannot convey;
> but you, from all I did not say,
> will sense the love beyond expression.

The boldness of the final lines appears in a different poem (90), also in *redondillas*. As if she had a presentiment of future interpretations of her poems, she states specifically that the reason she loves María Luisa is not that she was favored by her but that she is compelled by María Luisa's beauty. She does not want "gratitude to be confused with love."

Haughtily, she explains once again that the supreme love is love that does not expect reciprocation or reward:

> For when honorable regard
> equitably is returned,
> it is a prize for loyalty,
> and not for being loved, reward.

The *endechas* that describe "a feeling of distance and disdain" contain fewer conceits and affectations. This composition (77) is yet another of those exalting the superiority of absence over possession. The first four verses, in their ebb and flow, admirably express the vacillations, the approach and withdrawal of one disdained in love:

> I approach and I retire:
> who could find, were it not I,
> in what is absent to the eye
> a presence in what is afar?

Psychological accuracy is allied with precision of expression: to find "a presence in what is afar" goes right to the mark. The poem—and it is not unique—ends with expressions of amorous despair:

> I now must go, and not remain,
> To live far from your radiance
> where even my love-malady
> will serve to foster your disdain.

Among the great erotic pleasures are those of sight. Sor Juana did not deny herself those pleasures, and in her poems vision is as fundamental as the conceit. It can even be said that her conceits either begin in a visual image or lead to one. When she does not see, she evokes and fantasizes: she sees with her memory and with the eyes of that spirit of fantasy that sees when the artist closes his eyes. That spirit is the cherub hovering over Melancholy in Dürer's engraving and busily sketching figures in a notebook. Its agents are the *spiritelli* of Dante and Cavalcanti, who imprint in the heart of the enamored poet the phantasmal image of his lady. Sor Juana turns to those ghosts, at once funereal and passionate, elusive and obsessive, in many poems. The title of a poem I have already cited (142) fits perfectly within the tradition of the superiority of the ghost to the real person: "Because she holds her in her thoughts, she scorns as futile seeing her with her eyes." The pleasure of imagination is twofold, because it is seeing with the eyes and with the spirit.

Poetry has the gift of making the impalpable perceptible and the incorporeal visible. It is an art of embodiment, even though that embodiment is imaginary: words, rhythms, conceits. The best example is one of her most famous poems, a decasyllabic *romance* (61) entitled "She paints the harmonious proportions of the Countess de Paredes . . ." The poem was written after the Countess had returned to Madrid, since the title states that it was "remitted from Mexico." As the model was absent, it is a portrait drawn from memory and by fantasy.

Almost everyone who has commented on this poem "out of modesty has transferred his admiration from content to form, from *message* to *structure*."[4] It is true, the metric scheme is unusual and the interest it has roused is understandable, but no less noteworthy is the sequence of metaphors the poet unfolds before the reader, a series of variations on every part of the female body: hair, eyes, brow, lips, throat, breasts, waist, arms, legs, fingers, feet. There are few poems in the Spanish language that can equal the concentration and richness of this one, the eloquence of its images and the coordination of syntax with rhythmic movement. Even the artifice of the dactyls that begin each line, which sounds forced to the modern ear, conquers in the end. In its syntax, vocabulary, and erudite allusions, the aesthetic coordinates of the poem are Gongorist. The antecedent for this *romance* is one by Agustín de Salazar with the same meter and theme.[5] But the architecture of Sor Juana's poem is more solid, its inventiveness more stunning, and its lines more rigorous. It is not profuse, but rich, there is complexity, not confusion.

Almost all the great Spanish poets of the seventeenth century, including Góngora, were given to excess; at times, swept along by inspiration or enamored of their own gifts, they did not know how to stop. In spite of the aesthetic of the century and the example of her Spanish masters, by temperament and by intellectual and artistic inclination Sor Juana tended more toward economy and reserve. To know how far to go: this is the prelude to perfection. Sor Juana did not always achieve it, and she was often prolix. But some few poems reveal that she had learned the difficult art of knowing her limits. The decasyllabic *romance* is one of these. It combines opposing qualities that when joined together produce the rarest of effects, intensity and richness. Valéry, who loved Góngora, would have been enchanted with this poem. Its undeniable Gongorism is the robe of the period; beneath it throbs a naked woman. The images are verbal fans that simultaneously conceal and reveal eyes, breasts, brow, mouth.

There are other of Sor Juana's poems that celebrate the face and body of María Luisa, although none as brilliant and imaginative as this. Among the *billetes* and other occasional poems one *décima* (132), "She describes in detail . . . the portrait of a beauty," ends with a literary pun. The portrait is of Phyllis, and the reason for leaving it unfinished is that she has,

> . . . shod in gold,
> a foot so comely it takes only
> half a line.

In addition to the poems addressed to María Luisa, there are several in which Sor Juana describes other women. Most are amusing. Some are caricatures, like the one to "sour Gila" (72), which Sor Juana ends by saying that if the verses do not seem sufficiently sour, Gila can sprinkle "her bile" on them.

Comparing the poems that describe the female body with those mentioning the male body, one finds that there are more of the former and they are more explicit. We can see Sor Juana's women; her men are "ghostly shadows." Nevertheless, I reiterate that it is not possible to extract any conclusions about her personal erotic tendencies from an examination of the poems. In a masculine culture that idealized woman and instituted a poetic cult of the lady (even though the reality of the female condition did not correspond to the ideal image), description of the male body was unseemly—or scandalous, if the author of the description were a woman, and even more were she a nun. Poetic and rhetorical tradition included vocabulary and figures for naming parts of the female body, but very few of those phrases could be applied to the male body. This could explain why few descriptions of the male body appear in Sor Juana's poems and why those few are always vague and imprecise. As we consider this theme we confront once again what may be an insuperable historical limitation: on the one hand, the society in which Sor Juana lived—her culture, her ethic, her social hierarchies— help us to understand her; on the other, it conceals her from us. Her essential attitudes were responses, often unconscious, to the system of manners and prohibitions of the Catholic society of New Spain. Her most intimate and personal tendencies were indissolubly and secretly bound to the morality and customs of her era. There is a point at which the social is indistinguishable from the individual. Sor Juana, like each of us, is the expression and the negation of her time, its hero and its victim. That is why, like every human being, she is an enigma.

THE POEMS THAT HAVE as their theme the portraits of María Luisa and Juana Inés are of particular interest. There must have been several portraits, all lost. The title of *décima* 126 is revealing: "Accompanying a ring bearing the portrait of the Señora Countess de Paredes. She explains." The portrait was painted on a ring for the index finger so "that all may know / the ring indexes my devotion." But this miniature cannot be the same portrait referred to in *romance* 19 ("Phyllis, the daring of the brush / gave wings to my pen"), nor the one that inspired the *redondillas* "To the portrait of a proper beauty") (89). This poem consists of variations on the theme of an inanimate but cruel portrait and the lively distress of the enamored:

> O beautiful and cruel Copy,
> delighting in your tyranny,
> avow that you will pity me
> or yield your merciless beauty!

At the end of the poem appears an idea that must have been an obsession, given its prominence in other poems: the portrait is immune to time, but this victory reduces the subject to a rigid representation. The cruelty of the portrait reminds her of the cruelty of the original, which gives rise to dejection:

> O Lysis, of your comeliness
> contemplate the cruel copy
> which, more than in the same beauty,
> resembles you in heartlessness.
>   Enjoy, and live impartially
> —free of thankless time's deception—
> in the Original's perfection,
> and the Art's longevity.

The alliteration (comeliness, contemplate, cruel, copy) is felicitous.[6] Although beautiful, the last three lines elude the opposition between the original and the portrait. In the *décimas* of poem 103 Sor Juana hints at a solution: dejection before the impassive portrait is transformed into inward possession. Although this love monologue addressed to a portrait is somewhat theatrical, it does not derive from Calderón. A poetry of reflection and intimate self-analysis, it is heir to Petrarch:

> I reach to touch, to ascertain
> whether there is life in you:
> could life be lacking, is it true,
> in this which all my senses claimed?

> Can it be true that you disclaimed
> the living contact of this hand
> that provokes you to attend,
> to pay attention to my plight?
> Can those eyes be lacking light?
> Can utterance from those lips be banned?

The muteness and immobility of the portrait, having intensified the torment of absence, point the path to true love: inwardness. Again we see the theme of poem 91:

> Happy, I enjoy the blessing
> a cold enamel can consign:
> though my affection you decline,
> you may, when most intransigent,
> say you are indifferent,
> but not say that you are not mine.

This poem in *décimas* is complemented by another (102) in which the theme is a portrait of Sor Juana "sent to someone" (María Luisa). The two poems form a diptych and are like the obverse and reverse of the same reality. In the *Complete Works* both were included in a series that Méndez Plancarte entitled "De amor y de discreción" ("Of Love and Discretion"), surely to mitigate slightly the *in*discretion of the poems. The second poem is extraordinarily limpid. If the decasyllabic *romance* dazzles us, we are more profoundly moved by the transparency of the *décimas*. It is not an exaggeration to say that they are clear enough to see through. Sentiment is deep but controlled, and passion is lucid. In this poem Sor Juana again demonstrates her exquisite sense of moderation: in forty verses there is not one superfluous word. Midway between a play of conceits and sentimental confession, the poem is at once limpid and passionate:

> The one whose features here are drawn
> into your hands delivers me,
> for though a copy you will see,
> resemblance will not semblance spawn:
> in me you find her all transformed,
> and of her love she sends the palm;
> but do not marvel at the calm
> and silence that you find in me,
> yours is the liability,
> her soul she yielded without qualm.

Although María Luisa sees only Juana Inés' "copy" (her "resemblance") in the painting, she will find not a "semblance" of her affection but the real thing.[7] The last stanza of the poem is an example of the poetic conceit not in the tradition of a Quevedo or a Gracián but in that of Lope, "a terse, limpid form and extreme condensation of thoughts."[8] The portrait says that, more fortunate than the original, it will live with María Luisa. Being a painted figure will protect it from the torment of seeing itself unloved—and if María Luisa notices that the portrait lacks a soul, she can give it one, since María Luisa already has that of Juana Inés.

> And if it is that you should rue
> the absence of a soul in me,
> you can confer one, easily,
> from the many rendered you:
> and as my soul I tendered you,
> and though my being yours obeyed,
> and though you look on me amazed
> in this insentient apathy,
> you are the soul of this body,
> and are the body of this shade.

Of the many poems that the friendship with María Luisa Manrique de Lara left us, some are interesting as biographical and psychological documents, some few for their poetic value. The latter number fewer than ten, but among them are some of Sor Juana's most intense and beautiful poems. Two of them, which represent the two extremes of her poetic talent—the maximum in brilliance and the maximum in clarity—are minor masterpieces (a useful if worn expression): the decasyllabic *romance* (61) and the *décimas* (102) that accompany her portrait.

All these poems, in spite of the nonsequential order in which they were published, fit within the tradition of erotic poetry following Petrarch's *Canzoniere:* they are a series that tell and sing of the vicissitudes of passion. Sor Juana's poems allude to a personal story that, as we have seen, is impossible to clarify completely. Its mystery resembles that of Shakespeare's sonnets, although the poems are of less poetic value. What was the nature of her relationship with María Luisa Manrique de Lara? She, too, asked that question, and she responded with poems that say everything and nothing. Faithful to her poetic models, her poetry—of exaltation and praise, lament and reproach—always ends as questions and paradoxes. Since Petrarch erotic poetry has been, as much as or more than the expression of desire, a form of introspection, self-examination: as the poet sees his beloved, he also sees himself seeing her. Seeing himself, he sees in his innermost self, engraved on his heart, the image of his lady: love is phantasmal. This Juana Inés felt and expressed as few poets have felt and expressed it. Her poetry—alternatively exalted and reflective—revolves around endless metamorphosis: the desired body becomes a ghost, the ghost an unreachable presence.

16

The Reflection, the Echo

ALL EXTANT PORTRAITS of Sor Juana are copies of others, earlier lost or destroyed, that were painted during her lifetime. She mentions these portraits in her poems, as we have seen; further, the anonymous author of the elegiac tercets published in 1700 in *Fame and Posthumous Works* alludes to having once seen such a portrait.[1] But only toward the end of the nineteenth century was it suggested that Sor Juana herself might have painted at least one of those portraits, as well as a portrait of the Countess de Paredes. The first mention of her artistic abilities appeared in 1874 in *Hombres ilustres de México* (*Illustrious Figures of Mexico*), which contains a biography of Sor Juana by Gustavo Baz and a lithograph by Isiquio Iriarte with a caption reading, "After a self-portrait." This "self-portrait," then in Puebla, was bought by a North American collector in 1883 and now belongs to the Philadelphia Museum of Art; it appears as the frontispiece to this book. On the lower edge is an inscription that begins, "A faithful copy of another [portrait] of herself, painted by the hand of the R.M. [Reverend Mother, meaning Sister] Juana Inés de la Cruz." The caption gives rise to a minor enigma: was Sor Juana Inés de la Cruz a painter? Most of those who have studied Sor Juana have not questioned the authenticity of the inscription. A dissenting view is offered by Francisco de la Maza, who believes the portrait is a counterfeit. His arguments are not to be scorned and deserve further examination.[2]

It is very odd, argues de la Maza, that none of Sor Juana's contemporaries ever mentioned her painting skills, although her talents in other arts, from poetry to theology and from music to embroidery, were widely praised. Neither, he adds, did she allude to this gift in her poems, despite the fact that one of her favorite themes was the danger of illusion and disillusion as represented in portraits. In a *romance* (19) Sor Juana asks permission of María Luisa to paint her metaphorically, with words; she implies a preexisting portrait when she says, "Phyllis, the daring of the brush gave wings to my pen." Méndez Plancarte comments that "the Vicereine had allowed Sor Juana to paint her portrait, and thus she has the courage to express her affection in verse." Quite logically, de la Maza observes that although the poem mentions a brush, at no moment does it intimate that the brush was Sor Juana's. In the opinion of Méndez Plancarte, a poem (89) written in *redondillas*, "To the portrait of a proper beauty," follows the same theme: "How wise, Lysis, to permit / your likeness to be drawn . . ." Once again the poem does not state that Sor Juana painted the portrait. Each time that she uses "paint," "portray," "copy," or another similar word, it refers to the art of literature, that is, to a word picture of a person, place, or situation. Nevertheless, there is one poem that suggests that she painted, a *décima* (126) with the explanatory title "Accompanying a ring bearing the portrait of the Señora Countess de Paredes. She explains."

> This copy that is your semblance
> was by tenderness inspired,
> whereon a clumsy hand conspired
> to give emotion utterance . . .

Neither the title nor the poem itself persuades de la Maza: "We need only rephrase the title (knowing that the titles were almost always false, even distracting, in the early editions) to be accurate: 'Accompanying a ring bearing a portrait commissioned by her of the Señora Countess de Paredes,' for it is clear that Sor Juana says the copy 'was inspired,' that is, commissioned to be copied." I disagree. The titles in the first editions of Sor Juana's works are neither false nor distracting, but illuminating, which is why Méndez Plancarte retained them in his edition of the *Complete Works*. The phrasing of the poem, moreover, is ambiguous; was the "tenderness" that caused the portrait to be painted Sor Juana's, or that of an anonymous artist? This *décima* is followed by another (127) on the same theme. Here the miniature was "meant to limn your loveliness," but as it did not succeed, Sor Juana requests of Lysis that she overlook "the limitation / of a brush reft of finesse." It does not seem likely that Sor Juana would have criticized so severely a work by some-

Portrait of Sor Juana by Juan de Miranda

one other than herself. These two brief poems are the only evidence that might justify the belief that Sor Juana was a painter.

The Philadelphia portrait is undated; de la Maza believes that "if not from the nineteenth, it dates from the end of the eighteenth century." I am not at all sure. The painting—precisely because of the "preciosity" that so displeases de la Maza—must have been painted early in the eighteenth century. Of course this is a supposition; it is very difficult to determine the date of a painting without reference to other works by the same artist. De la Maza believes the painting to be a hoax, a copy of the portrait painted by Juan de Miranda. He bases his opinion on the similarity of their inscriptions. Indeed, the wording on both paintings does list the major events in Sor Juana's life—on the Miranda work, in greater detail—but from this we cannot conclude that one is a copy of the other. What is more likely is that both derived from a common source, Father Calleja's biography, whose errors are repeated in both. One finds a similarity—a correspondence, rather—in the phrasing of the two inscriptions: "Phoenix of America, Glorious Fulfillment of Her Sex, Honor of the Nation in This the New World, Subject of Admiration and Praise in the Old." But, once again, why conclude from this coincidence that the painting in Philadelphia is a copy of Miranda's? It could be the reverse. Nor is plagiarism an issue; rather, since the same language appears on all the oldest portraits of Sor Juana, is it not more likely that both painters used the same source? The only portrait with a different inscription is that by Miguel Cabrera (1750), although he, too, calls her the Phoenix of America.

If we compare the paintings themselves, in addition to the inscriptions, again the conclusion is contrary to de la Maza's. The two portraits are not alike either in the position of the figure or in composition or background or any other detail. We cannot conclude, strictly from a comparison of the paintings, that the Philadelphia painting is a copy of Miranda's or that the latter was inspired by the former; these are two distinct works whose only resemblance lies in their subject. Like de la Maza, however, I am struck by the fact that Sor Juana's contemporaries did not comment on her artistic abilities; but unlike de la Maza, I am not convinced that the attribution of the Philadelphia portrait is false. While the silence of her contemporaries is indeed odd, Sor Juana's fondness for painting is well known. Again and again in her poems she refers to this art, particularly the art of portraiture. Such an interest is not unusual; poets who have been painters abound, and painters who have been poets. Michelangelo excelled in both the plastic arts and poetry. Blake was a renowned engraver, and Victor Hugo's drawings have a charm of their own. Often painting is a complementary passion for a writer, his "innocent hobby"; witness Federico García Lorca, Jean Cocteau, and Xavier Villaurrutia. Perhaps for Sor Juana painting was merely a pastime, which would explain why her friends and her panegyrists never commented on it. Who ever mentions Quevedo's paintings? And yet Don Francisco did paint.

Juan de Miranda's portrait poses additional questions. The painting, which gained public attention in the nineteenth century, was first described by Luis González Obregón in an article published in *El Renacimiento* in 1894 and later collected in his popular book of chronicles and studies of the viceregal period, *Mexico viejo, 1521–1821*. González Obregón never saw the painting; at that time it was owned by the Hieronymite nuns, who were living in semi-hiding. But an acquaintance of González Obregón, a scholar named José María de Ágreda, who was related to the Bishop, not only saw the painting but copied from it the two inscriptions reported by González Obregón in his article. The first, as I have described, is a kind of dithyrambic and biographic compilation of the events in Juana Inés' life. The second reads as follows: "This copy of Sister Juana Inés de la Cruz was given to the Bursary of our Convent by Sister María Gertrudis de San Eustaquio, her spiritual daughter, being Bursar. In the year 1713. Miranda *fecit*." Nothing more natural than that Sister María Gertrudis should give to the bursary a portrait (a copy, as it was called at the time) of Sor Juana, who had three times been elected bursar of the community. It is important to note that in the other, longer inscription there was no mention, according to both González Obregón and Ágreda, either of a date or of Miranda's name. Until that day no one had seen the painting; then around 1940 it was learned that Señor Gustavo Espinosa Mireles had acquired it. In January 1944 the poet Jesús Flores Aguirre published a description of the painting accompanied by a photograph. In 1951 the painting was first publicly displayed during an exhibition of books and pictures relating to Sor Juana. A few years ago it was acquired by the National University, and today it hangs in the rectory building.

Now to turn to some mysteries about the painting. First, the painting in the rectory has one inscription, not two. The briefer inscription recording the gift of Sister María Gertrudis is missing. Were there two paintings, one of which has been lost? It seems strange that two such portraits should have been painted; it is also difficult to believe that Ágreda invented the second inscription. What, then, is the explanation? Jesús Flores Aguirre, who saw the condition of the painting when it came to light, reported that "the wrapped canvas had been standing on a wood support in some damp cellar, which had decayed the borders and damaged the part of the oil touching the ground." This might be the explanation; perhaps the second inscription was written along one of the borders and was effaced by dampness and exposure. Unfortunately, the hypothesis has one flaw. On the painting in the rectory, following the long inscription there is a blank space not large enough to allow room for the second and then, in black letters, "Miranda *fecit.*" There is no second legend and the portrait is not dated. Two possibilities, then: either the second inscription and the date were Ágreda's invention (but why? for what purpose?), or there were really two paintings and the one Ágreda mentions is a copy Miranda made in 1713 of a portrait he had painted earlier. If this is the case, then the painting in the rectory could be the original.

The second mystery is no less puzzling. The long inscription begins, "A Faithful Copy of the Celebrated Woman . . ." Among the accepted meanings of the word *copia,* copy, two are pertinent here. According to the *Diccionario de autoridades,* a copy is "a painting made in imitation of another in all the rigor of the art." The dictionary also offers this definition: "Copy. Often used to mean portrait." This second meaning was common in the seventeenth century, and Sor Juana used it again and again in her poems. The inscription says very clearly that the painting is a copy of Sor Juana, not of her portrait; that is, it is a painting from life. On the other hand, the inscription on the Philadelphia painting reads, "Faithful copy of another [painting] of herself, painted by the hand of the R.M. Juana Inés de la Cruz." In this case the word "copy" is used in both meanings, as an imitation of a painting and as a portrait. If Miranda's oil was also a copy, in the first sense of the word, why does the inscription not clarify this point? One may argue that because Sor Juana died in 1695 the date 1713 excludes the possibility that this was a portrait from life. But the inscription on the painting in the rectory has no date at all. The fact that critics insist on saying that it was painted in 1713 indicates that they are repeating secondhand information without having seen the painting. One further indication convinces me that this is an authentic portrait: it portrays an attractive woman with a full face, smooth skin, bright eyes, black eyebrows, a woman about thirty—the

Portrait of Sor Juana by Miguel Cabrera

age of Juana Inés during her friendship with the Countess de Paredes. We know that in 1713 Miranda was advanced in years; he wrote his will the following year. We also know that by 1694 he was a renowned painter with connections in high places. The rules of the convent of San Jerónimo were rather lax, and it is possible that Miranda, especially given the protection of the Countess de Paredes, was allowed to enter the cloister sometime between the years 1680 and 1688 in order to paint Sor Juana. The painting Ágreda saw, the one with two inscriptions, one of them bearing the phrase "In the year 1713. Miranda *fecit*," could be a copy of this earlier portrait. My supposition is plausible but, I must confess, highly speculative.

Either as a portrait from life or as a copy of another painting, our interest in the Juan de Miranda portrait is twofold. For one thing, it is the best we have of Sor Juana—along with the portrait by Miguel Cabrera, a copy of Miranda's painting. Second, the resemblance of the face to the one in the engraving by Lucas de Valdés and to that of the anonymous portrait in Philadelphia is remarkable. Whatever the artistic merits of these works, it is certain that they portray the same person. This is significant in itself, especially when we realize that these are the earliest surviving portraits of Sor Juana. Valdés' engraving was made during Sor Juana's lifetime; it appeared in the first edition of the second volume of her *Works,* published in Seville in 1692, and is surely a copy of the portrait the Countess de Paredes took with her to Spain. As a work of art it is inept, but the features are the same as those in the Philadelphia and Miranda paintings. No less remarkable is the fact that although our knowledge of Sor Juana's life is fragmentary, with many gaps and few facts, her face has survived through three centuries of neglect and civil disorders.

IN CONTRAST TO the silence concerning her ability to paint, her contemporaries praised her musical skills. Calleja mentions them, the anonymous elegy of 1700 alludes to them, and she herself displays them, with some satisfaction, in several of her writings. In a *romance* (21) addressed to the Countess de Paredes, she speaks of having begun the study of music as a "diversion from melancholy." The apprenticeship was arduous, and to lessen its rigors for future students, she conceived the idea of writing a treatise to simplify the rules. She called it *El caracol (The Conch Shell)* to signify that harmony is a spiral, not a circle. She did not send it to the Vicereine because it was "so unformed" that it was "unworthy" not only of her friend's hands but even of her own. Did she finish it? It has never been seen.

In 1930 the bookdealer Demetrio García discovered two books that had belonged to Sor Juana: Octaviano della Mirandola's anthology of Latin poets and a treatise on music by Pietro Cerone, *Music and Master.*[3] In his biography of Sor Juana, Ermilo Abreu Gómez published photocopies of two pages of that book on which Sor Juana had entered a handwritten note on semitones. The notation, unimportant in itself, is signed, "His disciple, Juana Inés de la Cruz." A surprising declaration; Cerone disapproved of women's involvement in music, which he said was a clear cause of their ruination and dishonor. Perhaps Sor Juana did not feel that his opinion included nuns: the habit had neutralized her womanliness. The note transcribed by Abreu Gómez led several critics to believe that there were other marginal notations by Sor Juana. Not so. I have examined the volume, which is today in the Mexican Library of Congress, and the only notation is the one published by Abreu Gómez. It is true that several folios are missing from the volume, among them the title page and index.

Whether Sor Juana ever composed music we do not know. Her interest in music, however, is clear. It was a threefold interest, practical, theoretical, and philosophical. In regard to the first, among the activities for which the convent of San Jerónimo was famous was the teaching of music, song, and dance. Father Calleja specifically refers to Sor Juana's activity as a teacher or instructor of solfeggio and music. Rather frequently there were programs in the convent patio in which girls sang, danced, and recited poems. Sor Juana participated in these performances; for example, she wrote six songs for an entertainment in honor of the Marquis and Marquise de la Laguna. In addition, she wrote, throughout her lifetime, *villancicos* that are among her best works and were sung in the cathedrals of Mexico City, Puebla, and Oaxaca and in other churches. If she did not write music, she was constantly in contact with those who did. And finally, lyrics for songs and dance tunes appear in her *loas,* plays, *autos sacramentales, sainetes,* and other theatrical works. In the seventeenth century the communication between poetry and music was constant. The great poets of Spain wrote melodies to be sung in their dramas and comedies; the first Spanish opera was written by Lope de Vega; and it was Calderón who created the *zarzuela. Loas* "were structured as musical prologues, . . . and *entremeses,* later called *sainetes,* were accompanied by pieces sung to the tune of popular airs."[4]

In addition to theatrical music, there was vocal music: *romances, letrillas,* and sonnets were also written to be sung. We do not know whether any of Sor Juana's poems were sung; it is not likely, although her *letrillas* and *bailes* undoubtedly had musical accompaniment, as did her *villancicos* and lyrics for sacred works. All this has been lost.

I have mentioned Sor Juana's interest in music theory. She was proud of her knowledge and took every opportunity to demonstrate it. One poem in *redondillas* (87) is captioned "She paints the symmetrical harmony that the eyes perceive in beauty, along with that of music." A triple play of reflections: her painting is verbal, and the terms in which the portrait is constructed are musical. The poem is inconsequential, but not the idea that inspired it: the theory of correspondences, which later would be rediscovered by the romantics and symbolists. Sor Juana inherited this idea from Neoplatonic hermeticism. The metaphors of these *redondillas* are rather labored, but in other poems she returns, with greater success, to correspondences and to the idea of the universe as a system of complementary unions and oppositions. In the *villancico* written for the Assumption (220), Mary is the "Divine Mistress of the Heavenly Chapel" who directs the universal choir. A cosmic solfeggio, from the lowest note, *ut* ("do"), up to and even beyond "sol" (the sun), to the "la" of *la Exaltata* (Mary). The procedure is the same as that in the previous poem: technical terms are used to contruct a poetic and theological allegory. Ternary measure is a metaphor for the Trinity, and Nature, being out of tune, has lost its cadence. That is, after the Fall it lost its original innocence. A beautiful image: sin as dissonance and wrong tempo.

Of all Sor Juana's "musical" poems, the most clever is the *loa* (384) celebrating the birthday of Elvira de Toledo, the wife of Gaspar de Sandoval, Viceroy of New Spain. The central personage is Music, accompanied by each of the six notes: *ut* (do), re, mi, fa, sol, and la (ti would be added later). Music directs the game, and the notes, carrying large placards or slates, form phrases praising the Countess and her husband. There are precedents for this game in the plays of Lope de Vega and Calderón. But the principal interest of this poem is found in the long speech by Music, expounding Sor Juana's musical philosophy. Traditionally, beauty was the concern of the eyes and harmony of the ears, although it had always been thought that there was a correspondence between them. Lope says in a well-known sonnet, "Marino, a great painter for the ears, / and Rubens, a great poet for the eyes." In Sor Juana's *loa*, Music begins by saying that it was not "folly" that she had been chosen as the patron of *all* beautiful things. There is a *conformity*—that is, a correspondence—between harmony and beauty:

> Although by different senses ruled,
> there is but a single measure
> that to the ear brings Harmony
> and Beauty to the eye admeasures.

Because of the limitations of our senses, we judge that there are many "different measures," each one corresponding to a different sense, and that this is the reason for the differences among what is seen, heard, tasted, or felt. But the soul, "there in the abstract," knows that an identical proportion rules taste and touch, hearing and sight. Beauty is nothing other than "a proportion that regulates perfectly / some parts with others." Beauty is not an absolute; it is a relationship. Beauty as structural balance is a doctrine that comes from Plato, passes through Scholasticism, and is bequeathed to the Renaissance; it is also a modern doctrine that both a Valéry and a Jakobson would approve. This is why, Sor Juana concludes, nothing can better represent beauty—that is, give an *idea* of it—than music.

Sor Juana's ideas derive from Cerone, an avowed Neoplatonist: "Music is none other than a consonant harmony of many and diverse things well proportioned and considered."[5] The doctrine that each of the arts is a "different musical meter" corresponding to a physical sense also appears in Cerone, although in a less succinct and elegant form. In both Cerone and Sor Juana can be seen a kind of compromise between Pythagorean tradition—the harmony of the spheres as a manifestation of divine order—and the more modern idea that aesthetic pleasure, as Descartes was writing at about that time, consists of "correspondence between the object and the senses." Cerone says, "A certainty: that one of the judges of harmony is the ear . . . that is, reason and hearing are two judges that always go together . . . Reason is guide and mistress of hearing." Reason is proportion, and its archetype is the unheard music of the spheres; the ear is the sensory organ of that universal correspondence.

Because it is harmony and accord, music is measure, and thus is manifest not only in sounds but in everything ruled by order and proportion.

Sor Juana's idea could be expanded slightly by saying that music is seen as well as heard. Platonism and Pythagoreanism had earlier inspired Fray Luis de Leon to say that, moved by music, the soul

> travels through the air
> until reaching the farthest of the spheres,
> and there, but differently, it hears
> the sounds of all eternity,
> the music that was the first to reach man's ear.

Music transports us to another realm, where a music plays that is inaudible to the senses but that reason perceives and translates for us. Sor Juana prefers to explore a different correspondence: Music, she says, is the most perfected idea of Time. She sets out to prove it in lines of eight syllables: What is the Sun (sol), fourth planet, "but a compass of gleaming gold / moved by an All-Powerful God"? Her *maxima* note, "composed of twelve parts," is Day—the hours are the single notes—while Night is the "*maxima* rest," similarly composed of twelve intervals. Also, in the "circular course" of the signs of the zodiac—"whose names harmonize with Music," the Sun, through the first six, rises higher in the heavens, and during the last, declines, until it has completed four "times," or seasons. And she concludes that Music is thus proved to be the hieroglyph of Time. To illustrate her concept of music as emblem of the universe, Sor Juana refers to an example well known in her time: geometrical lines can be "weighed" on scales. When volumes are converted into weights arranged proportionally and are struck, they

> will resound harmonically,
> as hammers have been known to do
> from earliest antiquity.

Sor Juana is alluding to the fable of the origin of music. It was believed that music derived from the invention of blacksmithing. Alberto G. Salceda, commenting on a passage of the *Response,* notes that Sor Juana took the example of the hammer from Cerone. The Neapolitan maestro, speaking of the "invention of the proportions," alludes to the chapter in Genesis (4:18–22) about the three sons of Lamech: Jabel, Tubalcain, and Jubal. In Cerone's version, one day "when Jubal entered the forge of Tubalcain his brother, he heard that the hammers were creating a harmony and pleasing sonority." As a lover of music and "in order to know what were the proportions that caused that sonority,"

Jubal weighed the hammers and then compared their weight with their sounds. So were born the notes and tones. But later Cerone gives a different version: in it he cites the authority of Boethius—the first student of music in the Christian West—in order to ascribe to Pythagoras the discovery "of musical proportions from the sound of hammers." Boethius had based his opinion on Macrobius, an author often consulted by Sor Juana.[6]

The story of Pythagoras and the hammers also appears in one of the works of Athanasius Kircher. Kircher published in two superbly illustrated volumes an encyclopedia of music he called (the prodigious title merits transcription) *Musurgia universalis, or the Great Art of Consonance and Dissonance, in Ten Books, in Which Is Treated All Doctrine and Philosophy of Sound, and in Which Are Expounded Both the Theory and Practice of Music in All Its Divers Forms, and Are Explained the Remarkable Powers and Effects of Consonance and Dissonance throughout the Universe, with Many New and Amazing Examples, Adapted for All Occasions, and Especially in Philology, Mathematics, Physics, Mechanics, Medicine, Politics, Metaphysics, and Theology* (Rome, 1650). Sor Juana undoubtedly knew those volumes. The *Musurgia universalis* was one of the most celebrated books of the celebrated Kircher, so famous that the Jesuit missionaries who journeyed to China in 1757 carried with them two dozen copies of it and two more of the three volumes of *Oedipus Aegyptiacus*. Samuel Pepys notes in his diary that in 1667 in London he purchased the two volumes by Kircher for thirty-eight shillings.[7]

The beautiful frontispiece of the *Musurgia* depicts a complex allegory composed of, in the upper center, the symbol of the Trinity and nine choirs of angels; in the center, the terrestrial globe; and on the lower left edge, the figure of the noble Pythagoras. He is resting on a block of stone on which is incised his famous theorem. In his right hand he holds a baton that points downward to a forge and anvil where four blacksmiths are at work. There are other correspondences between Kircher and Sor Juana. It is even possible that the title of her proposed musical treatise (*The Conch Shell*) was inspired by the German Jesuit. In a section of the *Musurgia* devoted to acoustics, he discusses trumpets and megaphones. There he explains that the helical form is the one best suited to this class of instrument, both because sound propagates within a spiral and because the spiral is the form of the inner and outer ears. Many of Kircher's inventions illustrated in the *Musurgia*—talking statues, megaphones, mechanical organs—borrow the form of the conch shell.[8] The idea of the resonances among music, the senses, and the affections and emotions—one of Sor Juana's favorite themes—also appears in Kircher. The work of the German Jesuit is said to be the first exposition of the baroque doctrine of correspondence between music and the passions and emotions.[9] Another idea shared by Sor Juana and Kircher—although it is as old as Pythagoreanism—is the correspondence between light and sound. The optical laws of reflection could be translated into those of acoustics: "sound is the ape of light." Reflection is a visual echo. Music as hieroglyph of the universe is also found in the *Musurgia*. Kircher cites Hermes Trismegistus: "Music is but the order governing things." That order is musical: beneath the rain of light from the Trinity, nine angelic choirs perform the music of the spheres in a concert of thirty-six parts, a number obtained by multiplying the two sacred numbers four and nine.

If music is geometry made sound, both are manifestations or translations of the divine word. In the *Response* Sor Juana says that the arts and sciences are connected because they are "steps for climbing . . . to the peak of Sacred Theology." Without geometry, "could one measure the Holy Ark of the Covenant and the Holy City of Jerusalem . . . and without being expert in music, how could one understand the exquisite precision of the musical proportions that grace so many Scriptures, particularly those in which Abraham beseeches God in defense of the Cities . . . ?" The cities are Sodom and Gomorrha (Genesis 18:20–32). When he learns that the Lord is going to destroy them, Abraham asks whether they will be spared if there are fifty just men in the city. Jehovah agrees, but then Abraham lowers the figure "to five less than fifty, which is a ninth, and is as mi to re; then to forty, which is a tone, and is as re to mi; from forty to thirty, which is a diatesseron, the interval of the perfect fourth; from thirty to twenty, which is the perfect fifth; and from twenty to ten, which is the octave, the diapason." Sor Juana concludes with an odd rationale: "And as there are no further harmonic proportions, [he] made no further reductions." Is that why Abraham ended his pious bargaining, because of musical misgivings?

The answer lies in the numerical-musical interpretation of the Scriptures. In a perceptive and erudite article on this passage of the *Response,* Raimundo Lida traces the antecedents of the arithmetical-musical reading of the Bible.[10] Through an obscure sixteenth-century author, Pietro de Bongo, he arrives at another no less abstruse, the Benedictine Ruperto de Deutz, who in the twelfth century composed an unfinished commentary on Genesis. When he turns his attention to the dialogue between God and Abraham, de Deutz explains the descending series (fifty, forty-five, thirty, twenty, ten) through Greek musical terminology, using a method that is essentially the same as Sor Juana's. The source of this mode of interpretation, of course, is to be found in the Pythagoreans. The arithmetical-musical explication of the Bible surely goes back to the Cabala, which was for its part influenced at a certain moment in its evolution by Neoplatonic numerical symbology. But there is no reason to look back to the twelfth century; we should not overestimate Sor Juana's erudition, or her knowledge of theology and patristics. She was familiar with the texts that were read in her time, and she was an avid reader of works that would correspond to the encyclopedias and reference books of our time. Often, as I have noted earlier, her quotations come not from a firsthand reading of her sources but from passages quoted and commented on in those encyclopedias. According to Lida, the immediate source of the passage in the *Response* referring to Abraham and his bargaining is found in Cerone. Cerone writes "not only in Heaven but in all things, Proportion is essential, and if it is absent, it is a sure indication that such things as are disproportionate have incurred the wrath of God."

In the light of these ideas, an aesthetic is transfigured into theology, and we can now understand why Sor Juana speaks of original sin as being discordant and having the wrong tempo. Cerone is more limited and prosaic—he was neither a poet nor a theologian—but no less categorical: "The harmony of the body in correspondence with virtues and good habits is consonance and musical harmony." The relation between virtue and music is frequently a theme in Greco-Roman antiquity, as well as in Confucianism and Indian treatises on music. These ideas also appear in Kircher's musical treatise: the movements of the soul, those of the body, and those of the stars obey the same principles and are manifestations of the same imperceptible harmony. The tenth book of the *Musurgia universalis* is concerned with universal harmony and is an ardent exposition, says Conor P. Reilly, of "the natural harmony of the vegetal, animal, and human worlds, the three in concordance with the music of the spheres, the angelic choirs, and the Great Divine Harmony."[11] From this perspective, the story of Creation itself can be seen as a musical invention. One of the most curious engravings in the *Musurgia universalis* represents the first chapter of Genesis, under the title

Harmonia nascentis mundi, as a baroque organ with forty-two pipes; from the pipes issue six circles, which are the six days of Creation: above, in the center, a dove traces a spiral that bears the words *Fiat lux;* at the left, a tier lower, are the waters and, at the right, the land; below them, from left to right, are the creation of the stars, of the plants and animals, and of Adam and Eve, standing beneath the tree. A triple reading of Genesis, visual, verbal, and musical.

Did Sor Juana play a musical instrument? Neither she nor any of her contemporaries says a word on this subject. In any case, she collected them: Father Calleja speaks of "her musical and mathematical instruments, of which she had many, precious and exquisite." It was natural for Father Calleja to refer to scientific and musical instruments in the same phrase; music and mathematics were sister arts, and the scientific apparatus of the time often included musical instruments. Joscelyn Godwin says that an example of Kircher's inventiveness, a kind of computer for composing music, survives in the Pepysian Library of Magdalene College in Cambridge. It is a contrivance—Kircher called it a "musarithmetic box"—with sliders on which are inscribed the rhythmic and melodic patterns which, in combination, produce melodies.[12] It is an invention that would have delighted Marcel Duchamp. I wonder whether that machine was also among the objects in Sor Juana's collection. What would her "precious and exquisite" instruments have been? Were they "speaking trumpets," music boxes, automatons that danced and sang, magnets, magnifying glasses, helioscopes, magic squares, astrolabes, mirrors, echo chests? One of the themes that consumed Sor Juana was the echo; another was the reflection. A major portion of her poetry revolves around these two motifs—or, more accurately, obsessions. Two magical objects, the mirror and the conch shell, that project two incorporeal progeny. In Sor Juana's symbolic system the echo, in the auditive mode, and the reflection, in the visual, are homologous; their values are interchangeable. Both are metaphors of the spirit: the echo is voice, word, music; the reflection is light, intelligence.

Sor Juana the collector—this is one of her characteristics that no one has noted, in spite of its obvious significance. We know that in her quarters she accumulated books, musical instruments, scientific apparatus, paintings, "gems, baubles, and other possessions that illustrious personages, even from afar, presented to her, drawn by her illustrious name" (in Calleja's words). Sor Juana's collection and her library confirm what we know about the sound state of her finances. Her collection was a mixture of objects of differing provenance, value, and merit; that is, it was an assemblage, born of accident and fancy more than of a plan. This kind of collection is more closely related to the magician's cave than to the museum gallery. Sor Juana, a child without a family or a permanent residence, found refuge in her cell and there built her house as the spider spins its web. Her house became as large as the world because it held a library and a collection of rare objects from the four corners of the earth. The collection and the library were her family: her parents, her brothers and sisters, her friends, her lovers, her children. They were also her realm. A realm at once spatial and temporal, concrete and imaginary; a realm in which the world, transformed into a collection, lost its hostility, reduced to a series of random and marvelous objects. The collection neutralized the world, turned it into a toy. She could admire each of those objects, venerate it as a center of magnetic radiation, caress it like a lover, rock it like a child, study it, take it apart, or throw it out the window.

The collection corroborates everything I said in Part Two about her childhood and about the significance of the cell: womb, library, conch shell. The outgoing and inward-turning sides of her nature that materialized, so to speak, in her cell are also represented in her collection. Her fondness for the spiral is not accidental: the shell is one of her psychic emblems. The other is the starry dome of the heavens. In the first, the world outside, the surf of the sea, spirals inward: the shell is the house of echoes. In the second, the interior life, the ideas and angelic intelligences, open out into the firmament in glowing and radiant configurations. The sky is not so much the opposite of the house as its luminous projection in open space. The sky, like the mirror, is a house of reflections.

Two emblems and a double movement that unfolds or draws back into itself. The echo spirals into the shell until it becomes silence; or, trumpeted forth, it becomes fame and the distortions of fame, gossip and slander. Or it ascends to become a hymn: music is a kind of starry sky that we hear but do not see. The reflection is immobilized in the portrait, dissipates in the image in the mirror, is refracted in the lens, slips through a crack, stretches along the ground, rises and reassembles in the mysterious order of the constellations, silent music we see but do not hear. The inward-outward motion—the twofold rhythm that rules her life and her work, her speech and her silence, her eminence and her final fall—is implied in her collection and in her library. In the first, the external becomes internal; in the second, intimacy opens outward. The library is her heaven, the collection her spiral shell.

17

Realm of Signs

IT IS SOR JUANA'S LIBRARY rather than her collection that has excited the curiosity of her biographers. Father Calleja says that "her solace was her library, where she went to console herself with four thousand friends, for that was the number of which it was composed, almost without cost; there was no one who printed a book who did not automatically contribute to it." Scholars have debated that figure, but it is clear that, whatever the number, Sor Juana had many books. While Calleja may have exaggerated, he did not invent. I would suggest fifteen hundred volumes at least. I base my supposition on the following: Irving A. Leonard cites the case of Melchor Pérez de Soto, a simple builder who owned seventeen hundred volumes. Leonard adds that the libraries of the well-to-do were more extensive.[1] In a cell the size of Sor Juana's, with its spacious rooms and high ceilings, two or three thousand volumes could be accommodated without difficulty.

By examining various libraries, the lists that booksellers remitted to the inquisitors for their examination, and other documents, Leonard reached the conclusion that the laws forbidding the circulation of certain books in New Spain were scarcely enforced at the end of the seventeenth century. Books came from places other than Spain, principally Lyon, Antwerp, and Brussels. The portraits by Miranda and Cabrera show shelf upon shelf of thick volumes. And if Sor Juana had only a few books, where did she read all the books she cites in her work? What probably *is* fantasy on Calleja's part is his statement that Sor Juana amassed those volumes "almost without cost." No doubt she was given many books, but however great her renown, it is hardly likely that publishers in Spain and elsewhere sent her every book they printed. A woman with an income of her own from money invested in the convent's business ventures, who owned jewelry, musical instruments, and scientific apparatus, surely had the wherewithal to buy books.

A library is the reflection of its owner. Sor Juana was a nun and a poet, devoted to theology and mythology, inquisitive about the sciences, a music lover, and a gatherer of unusual information. A nun by profession but a poet by birth; we must therefore begin with poetry and literature. In the forefront are the Spanish poets of the sixteenth and seventeenth centuries who formed her tastes, guided and inspired her. At times her *liras* and *silvas* recall Garcilaso, at other times St. John of the Cross; in her *romances* and *décimas* there are echoes of Lope de Vega, and also of Quevedo; in other poems the voice of Alarcón, blended with her own, is audible; the couplets in imitation of Jacinto Polo de Medina are famous; and some of her historical and mythological sonnets bear a family resemblance to those of Francisco de Rioja and Juan de Arguijo. But there were many other poets in her library: Fernando de Herrera, Fray Luis de León, Hurtado de Mendoza, Francisco de Figueroa, Esteban Manuel de Villegas, Bartolomé and Lupercio Leonardo Argensola, and the euphuists, such as Luis Carrillo y Sotomayor, the Count de Villamediana, Juan de Jáuregui, Pedro Soto de Rojas, and finally, to keep the list brief, Gabriel Bocángel and Anastasio Pantaleón de Ribera. Sor Juana suffered—more accurately, enjoyed—the influence of Góngora, and she must have read José de Pellicer and other commentators on the Cordovan poet. Góngora's light illuminates—or darkens—only one part of her poetry. Calderón's example was no less decisive; as a dramatic poet she is his disciple, and to his name should be added those of Agustín Moreto y Cabaña and Fernando de Rojas.

Besides the great *Romancero*,[2] a treasure shared by everyone in the sixteenth and seventeenth centuries, Sor Juana knew traditional poetry, both secular and religious (the distinction is nominal: their forms were the same and there was continuous interchange in vocabulary, images, and themes). Sor Juana's religious *villancicos* perhaps represent the best moments of that genre. In those wingèd songs she reveals a perfect assimilation of the anonymous tradition and of the poets who preceded her, José de Valdivielso, Lope de Vega, and Góngora. Several times I have referred to her mastery of meter; in addition to the constant reading of poets, anthologies, and collections of songs and poems, she must have studied the theorists of the period: Antonio de Nebrija, Fernando de Herrera, Juan Díaz de Rengifo, Gonzalo Correas—perhaps, too, Bishop Juan Caramuel, who according to experts was the most original although least read of those authors.[3] She must often have referred to Gracián's treatise *Agudeza y arte de ingenio* (*Wit and Art of Cleverness*), as well as his other works. There is a perceptible affinity between the Aragonese Jesuit and the Mexican nun. In addition to these serious readings, she would certainly have had lighter books, dramas and comedies, chivalric romances, and pastoral and picaresque novels. The list is plentiful: from the theater of Juan del Encina and Gil Vicente to the descendants of Calderón; from *Amadis of Gaul* and its progeny to Jorge de Montemayor's *Diana* and all the other Dianas, Amarylises and Galateas of Gil Polo, Cervantes, and Lope; from the *Quijote* to *Guzmán de Alfarache* and *El Buscón* (*The Rascal*). Epic poems—almost all on American themes—and religious epics would occupy one shelf, alongside imitations of Ariosto and Tasso. Nearby would be the works of Bernardo de Balbuena: *El Bernardo, Grandeza mexicana* and *Siglo de Oro*. Last, it would be unjust to overlook her contemporaries. Among Spaniards, Sor Juana esteemed José Pérez de Montoro. She also read León Marchante. In a letter, according to his own account, she praised the man who was to be her biographer, Father Diego Calleja. Among her contemporaries there is a forgotten poet, justly reinstated by Méndez Plancarte, the Hispano-Mexican Agustín de Salazar y Torres. In South America she had several admirers, such as the Count de la Granja and the Peruvian satirist Juan del Valle y Caviedes. In conclusion, two names, two extremes, defined the Spanish-language portion of the library, Góngora and Calderón.

Sor Juana read Latin and perhaps Portuguese. Because she quoted two verses from Virgil that had been translated into Italian by Boccaccio, some also believe that she knew Italian. This is not sufficient evidence; I have already shown that the verses are found in Vitoria and that Sor Juana merely transcribed them, repeating the accompanying commentary. But whether or not she read Italian, she undoubtedly knew Italian poetry. Its influence was predominant during the sixteenth and seventeenth centuries; Petrarch and Petrarchism had impregnated not only literature but the emotional life of Europe. In Spain, Boscán's translation of Castiglione's *Courtier* released a flood of imitations that lasted until the middle of the seventeenth century. Translations of Jacopo Sannazaro's *Arcadia*, Giambattista Guarini's *Pastor fido* (*The Faithful Shepherd*), Ariosto's *Orlando furioso,* and Tasso's *Gerusalemme liberata* were all circulated in Spanish. Ariosto and Tasso were imitated incessantly, as well as Pietro Bembo, Luigi Tansillo, and other poets infrequently read today. Sor Juana must have loved Jáuregui's charming if wordy version of Tasso's *Aminta*. She would also have read with pleasure the versions of Italian poets that Gracián included in his *Wit and Art of Cleverness,* among them the universally acclaimed Giambattista Marino. By contrast, the French poetry of her time, to say nothing of the English, was *terra incognita* for her. Did she read Quevedo's imitations of Joachim du Bellay's Roman sonnets? The question of Portuguese authors is not very clear; did she actually read Portuguese? In one of her *villancicos* to St. Peter (249), a Portuguese man speaks a mixture of Portuguese and Spanish in a comic passage. In her critique of Vieyra's sermon she praises "the noble Portuguese nation," but in all her work she quotes only two authors from that language, Vieyra himself and the Duchess de Aveyro. In any case, whether in Spanish or in the original, Sor Juana must have read Camoëns, Francisco Manuel de Melo, and others.

The mainstay of the library—alongside Spanish poetry and treatises on mythology—was Latin literature. Sor Juana's tastes were those of her era. Following a tradition that went back to the Middle Ages, the four great poets were Virgil, Horace, Ovid, and Lucan. The last was especially appreciated, since he was considered Spanish, like the two Senecas and Martial.[4] Besides these four poets, she quotes Statius, the forgotten Silius Italicus, and poets of the Late Empire seldom named today: Claudian and Ausonius. She also alludes to Juvenal, Persius, and, in spite of his sins against propriety, Martial. But not a word about Lucretius (with good reason) or, strangely, Tibullus. Changes of taste and of perspective: she mentions Propertius only once, buried in a list of names, and Catullus not at all. They are the two poets closest to modern sensibility.

Among prose writers she refers several times to Seneca the philosopher and to Cicero, less frequently to Quintilian, to Seneca the rhetorician, to Pliny the Younger and, of course, in reference to Isis, Apuleius. Pliny the Elder was one of her favorite authors, to judge by the frequency of citations. He was a writer very much to her taste because of the informational and encyclopedic nature of his works. Among historians she cites Tacitus and especially Julius Caesar. Two authors who were primary sources of information and who influenced the genesis of *First Dream* were Cicero and Macrobius. Her allusions to Greek literature are fewer. She knew it through Latin translations, a superficial knowledge derived from secondhand sources. Did she actually read the tragedians? Sophocles is quoted twice in the *Allegorical Neptune,* but those allusions—and the same happens with Euripides—are in my opinion not from the original but from the mythological studies she so often used. In one poem (38) she cites Aeschylus and Sophocles in a list of twenty poets from antiquity, from Homer to Propertius. Her Homer is not our Homer but the one from the hermetic tradition transmitted by Kircher and others.

The bookshelves in the Miranda and Cabrera paintings display very few works of literature; the overwhelming majority are theological treatises, volumes of ecclesiastical history, and mythology. This is a reflection of the period: what her contemporaries most admired in her was her theological learning and her erudition. Even discounting the painters' exaggeration, she must have had many books on religion. First of all, those she used every day: the *Brevario romano* (*Roman Breviary*), the lives of saints, the Holy Bible, and religious commentators such as Arias Montano. Also mystical and ascetic writings: St. Teresa, Fray Luis de Granada, St. John of the Cross, Sister Ágreda (María Coronel, the "St. Teresa of the baroque," as she has been called), and the Jesuit Luis de la Puente, very influential in his time although completely forgotten today. Sor Juana speaks with veneration—she calls him her father—of St. Jerome, the founder of her order and patron saint of translators. Among the books in Miranda's painting is an imposing volume on patristics. Indeed, she mentions several of the Church Fathers in her writings, among them Irenaeus, Eusebius of Caesarea, Lactantius, St. John Chrysostom, and Gregory Nazianzen. In the *Response* she alludes to the authors of the sacred hymns: St. Anthony, St. Bonaventure, St. Thomas. In the same passage she refers to Cassiodorus, one of the first to study musical theory. And since I have mentioned music, we must not overlook Cerone. Was he the only theorist she read?

Among the saints—doubly sainted—who loved learning, St. Isidore of Seville and his *Etymologiae* would have been essential. But the Church Father most often cited by Sor Juana, following St. Jerome, was St. Augustine. In the spiritual history of Christianity, St. Augustine is a touchstone; one is an Augustinian or a Thomist just as one is a Platonist or an Aristotelian. Augustianism—in one of its most extreme derivations, Jansenism—flourished during Sor Juana's century, although in a different intellectual and historical milieu: France. Unquestionably Sor Juana was aware of this current, but no allusion to it appears in her work. Jansenism had been condemned by the Vatican and was seen as an anti-Spanish as well as an anti-Jesuitical doctrine. Sor Juana's silence is indicative of the narrow limitations of Hispanic thought at the end of the seventeenth century. Besides, neither her character nor her mind was attuned to that tendency. There is nothing of Pascal in her, despite the fact that at the end of her life she, like the French philosopher, renounced secular learning.

Scholasticism was crucial in shaping her. What could be called the structure of her thought—that is, not only the ideas but the manner of ordering them—derives from that philosophy. It is nevertheless futile, as we have seen, to try to fit her thought into the Scholastic mold, as Father Méndez Plancarte and other Catholic critics have attempted to do. That Scholasticism played a decisive role in her intellectual development is not surprising. Neither is it by chance that on the bookshelves in Miranda's painting we see Peter Lombard (Magister Sententiarium), St. Thomas, and a disciple of Francisco Suárez, the Jesuit de la Puente. In Cabrera's portrait Peter Lombard's name recurs and those of Duns Scotus and Suárez appear. These names were more or less intellectual coordinates, and their inclusion in the library of a nun devoted to theology was obligatory. Did she read them or read about them in manuals?

The dominance of Scholasticism—a philosophy that elsewhere was dying out—is understandable in the New Spain of the end of the seventeenth century. The revival of Scholasticism in the second half of the sixteenth century was due above all to the Spanish theologians of the Society of Jesus and, foremost among them, to Francisco Suárez. At that time the Jesuits controlled the culture and higher education of both Spain and its overseas possessions. Suárez maintained the doctrine of St. Thomas and his version of Aristotelian tradition while incorporating Duns Scotus' criticism and attempting to adapt that philosophy to new historical conditions: the Catholic polemic against the Reformation and the emergence of national states in the form of absolute and imperial monarchies. Suárez' teaching, except in certain matters of political philosophy, became unofficially a kind of orthodox doctrine of the Spanish monarchy, and its most outstanding exponents and exegetes belonged to the Society of Jesus.

Sor Juana read Suárez and especially his followers and commentators. Among the authorities she mentions in the *Response* is Juan Díaz de Arce, a Mexican theologian who was an interpreter of Scripture. Her spiritual director for many years was another Jesuit theologian, Father

Núñez de Miranda. Her interest in theology and its subtleties explains her friendship with the Bishop of Puebla, Manuel Fernández de Santa Cruz, a renowned theologian. This same interest, an integral part of intellectual debates and logical argumentations, later led her to criticize Father Vieyra and thus to work her own ruin. Sor Juana seems to have been particularly receptive to Suárez' ideas on the thorny debate over divine grace and free will. Suárez upheld the position of another Jesuit, Luis de Molina, accused by the Dominicans (and later by the Jansenists and Pascal) of having extended too far the sphere of the human will and thus fallen into the heresy of Pelagius, who had affirmed that men could be saved without divine grace. In her critique of Vieyra—I shall examine the point in more detail in Chapter 25—Sor Juana appears to be not only in sympathy with Molina but bordering on Pelagianism.

Juridical and political reflection is important in Suárez' thought. He denied the divine right of kings: the authority of the monarch comes from the people, and the state is an expression of social consensus. He rejected Aristotle's idea that slavery was a part of natural law: there are no slaves by nature, all men are born free. He also opposed the right of conquest founded on conversion, the cornerstone of Spanish imperialism. There is not a trace of these admirable ideas in any of Sor Juana's writings, although their influence can be glimpsed in Sigüenza y Góngora. Sor Juana's silence on these topics confirms what I have said previously: all her life, perhaps because of her modest origins and her illegitimacy, she sought the protection of the powerful. She was extraordinarily prudent in matters of opinion: she respected authority and attempted to minimize any disagreement touching on religious or political orthodoxy. Her occasional difficulties with a Mother Superior were of a personal, not doctrinal, nature. Nevertheless, she lived in a stringently doctrinal society and at the end of her life found herself involved in a quarrel in which intellectual disagreement was no less decisive than personal rivalries.

The name of Aristotle appears on the spine of a volume in Miranda's painting. We do not know whether she read his works or merely the manuals and compendia that summarized and interpreted his philosophy. In her prose writings and in some poems she mentions Heraclitus and Democritus, Parmenides and Pythagoras. Since the early Renaissance, Heraclitus and Democritus had been paired in their contrasting reactions to melancholy: Heraclitus weeps, Democritus laughs. On the two occasions Sor Juana mentions them, she repeats that cliché.

As for Parmenides, she attributes to him a phrase that belongs to Epi-
menides, the legendary Cretan. The mention of Pythagoras in the *Allegorical Neptune* is copied from Vitoria. The name of Pythagoras comes
up again, predictably, in a poem about music. None of these allusions
indicates that Sor Juana had read those philosophers. And that is not
strange; because of her education, her religious vows, and the clerical
world in which she lived, she was more interested in theological subtleties than in philosophy. This does not mean that she was totally ignorant
of the ancients. Medieval and Renaissance theology was pervaded with
Aristotelianism, and with Platonism and Stoicism. Furthermore, the
reading of Plutarch, Cicero, Macrobius, and other writers had instructed
her in the doctrines of the ancient philosophers. Did she read Diogenes
Laertius? In the *Allegorical Neptune* she cites him, but in reference to
the Great Goddess. I suspect she is mistaking her sources.

Renaissance humanism did more than discover Plato, Plotinus, and
the *Corpus Hermeticum:* it disinterred other philosophers, offering to
the European consciousness a new and more truthful image of the
Stoics, the Epicureans, and the Skeptics. The resurrection of Lucretius
and the discovery of the atomism of Democritus were definitive in the
intellectual evolution of Galileo and of Giordano Bruno. No less decisive
for Descartes, not to mention Montaigne, was the reading of Sextus
Empiricus, the most complete version the West had (and has) of ancient
Skepticism. The Stoics, especially Seneca and Epictetus, exercised a profound influence in the sphere of morality. Perhaps out of prudence, Sor
Juana never mentions these themes, or Lucretius or Sextus Empiricus.
Or Montaigne, and—even more revealing—she mentions Erasmus only
once, in the *Allegorical Neptune*. Fifty years earlier Quevedo and Gracián had mentioned him openly. But she must have read parts of that
philosophical literature, in some cases directly and in others through the
interpretations and compendia that circulated in her time. Quevedo, besides translating some of Seneca's letters and offering a verse rendition
of Epictetus, wrote a curious treatise in which he defended Epicurus,
including him with the Stoics: *Nombre, origen, intento, recomendación
y descendencia de la doctrina estoica* (*Name, Origin, Design, Praise, and
Derivation of the Stoic Doctrine*). Quevedo cited Sextus Empiricus several times—showing that he knew him well—and wrote beautifully in
praise of "Señor de la Montaña" (Montaigne) and of the "book that
was written in French and is entitled *Essais*, a book so great that who-
soever in order to read it ceases to read Seneca and Plutarch, will read

Plutarch and Seneca." It is difficult to imagine that Sor Juana did not know and ponder this essay.

The system of ideas and convictions that Sor Juana inherited from the Neothomism of Suárez and his disciples was infiltrated by a new element, a "foreign body," in biochemical terms. It acted as an agent to relax rigid abstractions and was a stimulus to her thought as much as to her sensibility and imagination. I am referring to Neoplatonic hermeticism. I have already alluded to the doctrine of Platonic love in her poetic work and in her life. As in the rest of Europe, Platonic eroticism nourished Spanish literature following Garcilaso; the Spanish knew of the doctrine from its direct source, Marsilio Ficino, but principally from the work of his followers, Leo Hebraeus, Bembo, Sannazaro, and others. Hebraeus' *Dialoghi d'amore* (*Dialogues of Love*) were several times rendered into Spanish. A copy of that book surely sat on Sor Juana's bookshelves. The influence of Neoplatonism was equally profound in the sphere of thought and the sciences. Neoplatonism, as I have said, was at first indistinguishable from hermeticism. The various treatises that compose the *Corpus Hermeticum* are pervaded with Neoplatonism and with interpretations that Neoplatonists such as Iamblichus had made of Egyptian religions. This is why Renaissance Neoplatonism was also a hermeticism fascinated by "the Egyptian mysteries."

The religious and philosophical syncretism of the second and third centuries reflected in the *Corpus Hermeticum* gave rise to a new syncretism when those texts reappeared in the early Renaissance. It was not a movement of the common people, like the Reformation, but was limited to groups of intellectuals. There was a Catholic hermeticism, especially in France; a Protestant hermeticism in England and Germany; a clearly heretical hermeticism, that of Cornelius Agrippa; and even one that was anti-Christian: Bruno wanted to return to an astral religion. The influence of hermeticism and of Neoplatonism was greater in the sciences than in metaphysics. The Pythagorean and Neoplatonic vision of the universe as number and proportion stimulated Galileo, Copernicus, Kepler, and others. Galileo said that the book of nature was written with mathematical signs, an idea that would have seemed blasphemous to Dante. Opposing Scholasticism and its logical categories, hermeticism postulated an empiricism derived from magical principles that were inseparable from the manipulation and observation of matter. In this sense, its function in the birth of modern science was analogous to that of alchemy. Hermeticism declined when it was noted that, far from being the source of Platonism, Hermes Trismegistus was a figure of legend and his treatise a religious derivation of Neoplatonism. Nevertheless, as I have indicated, hermeticism, through figures like Fludd and Kircher, survived until the end of the seventeenth century. Kircher was a dominant influence on the intellectuals of New Spain, notably Sor Juana Inés de la Cruz and Carlos de Sigüenza y Góngora.

Although Kircher rejected the purported magic of Agrippa, Bruno, and other sixteenth-century hermeticists, in his work the boundaries between scientific empiricism and fantastic speculation are extremely tenuous. In many cases he sought an impossible accord between the new physics and the old. For example, in questions of astronomy he adopted the system of the Danish astronomer Tycho Brahe, which was a compromise between Copernicus and Ptolemy. Such a tendency perfectly suited the curiosity and hunger for knowledge of minds like Sor Juana's and Sigüenza's, doubly isolated from the world by their orthodoxy and by geographical distance.

The blend of erudition and fantasy in Kircher's writings is especially visible in his works in anthropology, history, and linguistics: his ideas on hieroglyphs, his "Egyptian" interpretation of the civilizations of China and Mexico, his book on Babel and the tongues, and so on. This aspect of his thought had a disastrous influence on Sigüenza y Góngora. It must have fascinated Sor Juana, for these were topics closely related to those in the sixteenth-century treatises on mythology that nourished her curiosity and her fantasy, treatises saturated with hermeticism and Neoplatonism. The titles of those books and the names of their authors appear again and again in Sor Juana's portraits and in her writings, especially the *Allegorical Neptune*.

The culture of the seventeenth century was symbolic and emblematic. It is the period, says Julián Gallego, of the triumph in painting of allegory over mythology.[5] In poetry, the fusion of the allegorical, the symbolic, and the mythological was constant: myths, and their heroes, were first of all examples, emblems. Hence the fundamental importance of books like Andrea Alciati's *Emblemata,* universally read and admired, and translated into Spanish by Bernardino Daza Pinciano (1549). This book surely was on Sor Juana's bookshelves, perhaps accompanied by the commentary of Sánchez de las Brozas and others whom Gallego mentions in his study of the culture of symbols in seventeenth-century Spain. Among the Spanish treatises on mythology, the most important and best known was Juan Pérez de Moya's *Filosofía secreta donde de-*

bajo de historias fabulosas se contiene mucha doctrina provechosa (Secret Philosophy in Which beneath Fabulous Stories Much Beneficial Doctrine Is Contained, 1611). Sor Juana does not mention this work, but neither does she mention Baltasar de Vitoria, in spite of the fact that she follows his *Theater of the Pagan Gods* extremely closely in her *Allegorical Neptune.* Among the non-Spanish writers, especially the Italians, I scarcely need repeat the names of Pierio Valeriano and his *Hieroglyphica;* Vincenzo Cartari, *Le imagini de i dei de gli antichi;* Natalis Comes, *Mythologiae;* Boccaccio's *De genealogia deorum,* and the famous encyclopedia of Ravisius Textor. In addition to Greco-Roman mythology, these books and Kircher's contained information about the gods of other civilizations, especially ancient Egypt. And through Juan de Torquemada and others, Sor Juana knew the mythology of ancient Mexico.

In the *Allegorical Neptune* she repeatedly mentions the philosophers, historians, naturalists, and poets of antiquity as her authority in mythological matters: Herodotus, a mine of information on Egypt; Homer, "the name in the mouth of all mythologists"; Pliny the Elder, a repertory of marvels and rarities; Plutarch, cited nine times, founder of the "school of mythology" and a great authority on Isis; Ovid, a fountain of fables and divinities. Sor Juana also takes pleasure in alluding to her learning in law, although again we must remember that it was principally canon law: papal bulls, ecumenical councils, and encyclicals. As for the historians, besides the Greeks and Latins I have mentioned, ecclesiastical history must be added, and the name of Father Mariana, the source for Sor Juana's *auto sacramental* on St. Hermenegild. And science? She cites Archimedes and Galen; in the portraits we see Hippocrates and various Latin tomes on anatomy, surgery, and pharmacy. Were they a fantasy of the artists? Fantasy and sad reality: nowhere do the names of the philosophers and scientists of her own time appear. The point deserves clarification.

It cannot be said that Sor Juana was totally ignorant of the philosophical and scientific thought of her time. I have pointed out that Irving A. Leonard demonstrates that proscribed books did, clandestinely, reach Mexico: astrology, magic, licentious novels, Bibles, Protestant commentary on the Scriptures, and even a few volumes of philosophy and science. Sigüenza y Góngora mentions Galileo, Kepler, Copernicus, Descartes, and Gassendi. It would be difficult to believe that Sor Juana could have kept those kinds of books in her cell and remained immune to scandal or danger; it is not difficult to believe that she read them in secret, or that during her conversations in the locutory she heard summaries and discussions of them. Not the slightest hint of any of this is evident in her writings, in contrast to those of Sigüenza y Góngora. In questions of orthodoxy, as we have seen, she was extremely prudent and reserved. Even so, fear and reticence do not totally explain her attitude. More venturesome, and with broader scientific knowledge than Sor Juana's, Sigüenza, too, did not cross the threshold into the modern age. Sor Juana's silence and Sigüenza's vacillation are only partially explained by fear of the Inquisition. An additional factor was ignorance: their information was imperfect and random. It was bound to be. Sigüenza y Góngora prided himself on being au courant about what was happening in European intellectual matters. A naive vanity; his writings reveal the contrary. It has been reported that he exchanged letters with Europeans eminent in astronomy and other sciences, but no one has seen any of those letters. I can understand that they might have been lost, like so many of his manuscripts, but what about the letters in the archives of the Europeans? Neither is there any proof that he was invited to the court of Louis XIV.

Sigüenza, Sor Juana, and the others lived in isolation, in a world closed to the future. Their intellectual culture was already, even for the time in which they lived, essentially an anachronism. The Sigüenza who mentions Descartes four times in his *Libra astronómica y filosófica* (*Astronomical and Philosophical Libra*) cites Kircher twenty-one times in the same work; the Sigüenza who can calculate an eclipse also maintains that Neptune was an Egyptian and "the progenitor of the American Indians." Sigüenza's modernity was ambiguous and contradictory; Sor Juana's was timid and imperfect. One of the reasons for the interest the two writers hold is their ex-centric situation: their lively intellect contrasts with the systems and ideas they worked with: defunct systems, trite ideas. Irving Leonard defined New Spain as a "neomedieval" society. The adjective is deserved, if not quite exact; New Spain was a society oriented toward opposing modernity, not achieving it. It is incontestable that proscribed books were read in New Spain; it is also clear that very few arrived and that those few had to be read in secret—and, first and foremost, that no mention could be made of them. A culture of silences, reticences, charades, and circumlocutions is not a modern culture. Sigüenza glimpsed the new intellectual landscape and immediately stepped back. Sor Juana closed her eyes.

The examination of Sor Juana's library reveals a world very distant from our own. The intellectual movement that began in the Renaissance with the new science and the new political philosophy is not represented in that collection of books. It will be said that the absence of Machiavelli, Hobbes, and Bodin is understandable. What about the absence of Montaigne, Bacon, and Descartes, or the silence in regard to Erasmus? Sor Juana's library is a mirror of the massive failure of the Counter-Reformation in the sphere of ideas. This movement presented itself as an answer to Protestantism and as a moral and intellectual renewal of the Catholic Church. Its not inconsiderable first fruits were sublime works of poetry, painting, music, sculpture, and architecture. Neither would it be fair to ignore the work of the Jesuits in humanistic studies or in the sciences. But based on its very suppositions, the movement was destined to ossify. If any society has merited the designation "closed society," in the sense given it by Karl Popper, that society was the Spanish empire. Defensive by nature, the monarchy and clergy constructed walls, sealed windows, and closed all doors with a double chain and padlock. The keeper of the keys was the Society of Jesus. The doors opened only from time to time, in order to expel some poor unfortunate. The alliance of political power and ideological orthodoxy invariably results in hierarchical societies that move toward immutability without ever entirely achieving it. The intellectual history of orthodoxies—whether of the Counter-Reformation in Spain or of Marxism-Leninism in Russia—is the history of the mummification of learning.

18

Different from Herself

And different from myself
I wander among your quills . . .

*E*XAMINING SOR JUANA'S LIBRARY allows us to understand better her sonnet "in praise of the astronomical science" of Father Eusebio Kino. In it she refers to the Jesuit's writings on the comet of 1680 that had excited Europe and America. A curious story. In Mexico the comet had caused widespread panic. Sigüenza y Góngora, who was an astronomer but also a stargazer (he had published almanacs containing predictions and horoscopes, although he later denounced astrology), fired off a *Manifesto filosófico contra los cometas despojados del imperio que tenían sobre los tímidos* (*Philosophical Manifesto against Comets, Now Divested of Their Dominion over the Fearful,* January 1681). The pamphlet was dedicated to the Countess de Paredes, one of the ladies frightened by the comet. Belief in the ominous influence of comets was very old. Since Aristotle it had been thought they were sublunary bodies formed by terrestrial vapors. It was also believed they were a portent and cause of disasters. But the old ideas were changing, if slowly. Galileo had maintained that comets came from outer space, beyond the moon, a hypothesis that was soon confirmed by other astronomers. This was the end of a medieval belief inherited from Aristotle, that the heavenly spheres—pure, incorruptible, immutable—could not be sullied by impure bodies such as comets. Sigüenza y Góngora expounded a moderate thesis in his essay: he denied that comets announced or were bearers of misfortune, but he "openly recognized that he was ignorant of the true significance of the phenomenon, and affirmed that, in any case, it should be venerated as the work of God."[1]

Sigüenza's manifesto, in spite of its moderation, evoked a response from one Martín de la Torre, who wrote a *Manifiesto cristiano en favor de los cometas* (*Christian Manifesto in Favor of Comets*). Sigüenza replied with an argumentative *Belerofonte matemático contra la quimera astrológica* (*Mathematical Bellerophon against the Astrological Chimera*). Sigüenza's text and that of his adversary have been lost. Next, a professor of surgery at the university, José de Escobar Salmerón y Castro, launched an attack against Sigüenza with his *Discurso cometológico y relacíon del nuevo cometa* (*Cometological Discourse and Report of the New Comet,* 1681). Confident in his knowledge, scrupulous and choleric, Sigüenza did not have the patience to endure the ineptitude of his contradictors. At this juncture a scholar of some repute, Father Eusebio Kino of the Society of Jesus, arrived from Europe, where he had been a professor of mathematics and had performed astronomical calculations. Expecting to have an ally, Sigüenza received him with enthusiasm, invited him to his home, shared his ideas with him, introduced him to the other intellectuals of the city, and finally took him to the locutory of San Jerónimo to meet Sor Juana.[2] Sigüenza's joy was short-lived. That same year Kino published an *Exposición astronómica del cometa* (*Astronomical Exposition on the Comet*) in which he refuted Sigüenza's arguments without even mentioning him. The pamphlet was dedicated to the Count de Paredes, Viceroy of New Spain. The omission of his name humiliated Sigüenza; the dedication to the Count de Paredes infuriated him. Kino maintained that although he could not prove that comets were a malignant source of calamities and misfortunes, they were ominous and invariably announced "sinister events." In the pamphlet's imprimatur, another Jesuit priest eloquently exalted Kino because "his comet was like a scourge or a sword that God's justice brandished from the skies."[3]

Among the few persons in Mexico to whom Father Kino sent his *Exposition* was Sor Juana. Her response was a sonnet (205) in which she places him, literally, above the comets, that is, in the incorruptible highest heavens. Sor Juana capped her praise by saying that the "heavenly lights received light" from Kino's learning. Sigüenza's surprise must have been as great as his indignation. Nonetheless, whether from generosity or by calculation, he never alluded in writing to his friend's betrayal. Two and a half centuries later, critics have asked the same question Sigüenza asked himself: why? Méndez Plancarte sees in the sonnet a simple act of courtesy—overlooking the *dis*courtesy to Sigüenza—and suggests that perhaps Sor Juana "had not read the whole of Kino's book." This criticism omits a very important fact: Kino's ties with the Duchess de Aveyro. That lady was related to María Luisa Manrique de Lara and had connections with the house of Medinaceli. Father Kino had met her in 1680 in Seville, then as now the home of the Medinacelis and their relatives. It was in that city, according to Kino's pamphlet, that he had made the observations and calculations on the comet. He also indicates that he wrote the *Exposition* at the request of the Duchess de Aveyro.

Kino was in good standing at the viceregal court. The Duchess de Aveyro was of the house of Alencastre and a descendant of John II of Portugal. She was devoted to letters and distinguished herself as a patroness of Jesuit missions and missionaries in America and Asia. This is the explanation of her long correspondence with Kino, which has been preserved. In 1683 Kino left Mexico City, first acting as a cosmographer in the exploration of the Gulf of California and later, after 1687, dedicating himself to the great enterprise for which he is remembered, the evangelization of the provinces of Sonora and Arizona. Sor Juana dedicated a laudatory *romance* to the Duchess de Aveyro (37) in which she calls her the Minerva of Lisbon, the First-Born Daughter of Apollo, the President of Parnassus, and the Spanish Sibyl. It is clear that the bonds that united Kino with the clan of the Medinacelis, the Alencastres, and the Paredes also established his ties with Sor Juana, the protégée of the Viceroy and his wife. Fidelity to the clan was and is a universal rule of survival. I need hardly emphasize again Sor Juana's prudence, her respect for authority. To these we must add intellectual conviction: unquestionably she found nothing erroneous or rash in the erudite Father Kino's pamphlet, which was studded with citations from Scholastic authorities, Latin poets, and, among other obligatory names, Kircher. Had Sigüenza not cited those same authorities?

Sigüenza's reply was a famous essay, *Astronomical and Philosophical Libra*. Although it was not published until 1690, many people saw it in manuscript. Did Sor Juana read it? If she did, she makes no mention of it. Sigüenza's essay is noteworthy not only because it ferociously crushes Kino's arguments, but also because it presages an approaching modernity in Mexico. But ambiguously so: Sigüenza mentions Descartes, Kepler, and Gassendi, but also Pico della Mirandola and Kircher. In the best-informed man of his day, Sigüenza, two eras were in conflict. I have mentioned his vacillation. Let me give one further example. Two years after his essay opposing astrology, he refers to the "malignity of stars that sterilize the earth" and deplores that there are "years under the influence of an evil star." These contradictions remained with him until the hour of his death. In his will he directed that his body be dissected so that doctors could explore the cause of the vesicular disease that killed him, but at the same time he bequeathed to a doctor, to be kept in the chapel of San Felipe Neri, the hat of Archbishop Aguiar y Seijas, said to possess extraordinary curative powers.

The friendship between Sor Juana and Sigüenza has been taken for granted, although a few skeptics have questioned it. Probably it was the sort of relationship that is usual among writers who live in a closed world; they saw one another frequently, read the same books, had similar intellectual interests, and were sometimes estranged by resentments and petty jealousies. In 1680 they were rivals: Sor Juana was placed in charge of the arch with which the Metropolitan Church welcomed the Marquis de la Laguna, and Sigüenza of the arch sponsored by the city. As I have shown, Sigüenza made clear in his *Theater of Political Virtues* that his criticism of other arches did not imply any censure of Sor Juana, whose work he respected. Sor Juana returned the compliment with a sonnet (204). It is the only time she mentions Sigüenza in her work and, significantly, the sonnet does not appear in the editions that were compiled during her lifetime. It is difficult to know whether this was from oversight or from a certain coolness. In either case it does not suggest a high esteem. Nothing distinguishes the sonnet Sor Juana addressed to Sigüenza from others of the same genre, except that in the last tercet, after protesting, with excessive modesty, that she does not dare compare her clumsy poetry to the "golden plectrum" of Don Carlos, she says:

> I would not profane integrity:
> what I comprehend, I hold most dear,
> what I do not know, my faith reveres.

In the following year, 1682, and again in 1683, there was a poetry competition sponsored by the university, held to celebrate the Immaculate Conception. Fifty poets participated, and forty-seven were awarded prizes! A society of reciprocal prizes. Sigüenza was secretary of the competition and author of the account *Triunfo parténico* (*Parthenian Triumph*; from *parthenos*, meaning "virgin" in Greek), which appeared in 1683. The jurors did not give any special distinction to Sor Juana: she received a third prize for a *glosa* (139) and a first for a *romance* (22). Sigüenza explains that in reality the first prize had been awarded to a *romance* by Francisco de Azevedo, but that he, in his "modesty and talent," had yielded to the nun. The *glosa* was signed by a Felipe de Salayzes, a complex pseudonym; Sigüenza "drew back the veil" in his epigram accompanying the trophy, a silver cup. The *romance*—in praise of the Marquis de la Laguna—was signed "Don Juan Sáenz del Cauri," an anagram of "Juana Inés de la Cruz."

Sigüenza's epigrams reveal sympathy, not resentment. Had he forgotten her sonnet praising Kino? Or would it have seemed impolitic to show signs of his chagrin on such a solemn occasion? In 1691 Sor Juana was represented in a volume compiled by Sigüenza y Góngora to celebrate the victory in the Caribbean of the Armada de Barlovento: *Trofeo de la justicia española en el castigo de la alevosía francesa* (*Trophy of Spanish Justice in the Punishment of French Perfidy*). Sor Juana's poem is preceded by the usual series of glowing epithets: Phoenix of Erudition in All Sciences, Immortal Glory of New Spain, and so on. Sigüenza was probably the author of these dithyrambs. The fact is not insignificant considering that the *Trophy* appeared at a moment when Sor Juana was battling powerful and pitiless enemies led by Archbishop Aguiar y Seijas, Sigüenza's patron and protector. And there are still other acts that show he never forgot or disclaimed her. In the prologue to Sor Juana's *Fame and Posthumous Works* it is stated that in 1700, the year of his death, among the papers of Sigüenza, a "rare treasurer of the most exquisite originals of America," was found the draft of a treatise by Sor Juana, *El equilibrio moral* (*Moral Equilibrium*). The second introductory note in the same volume adds that Sigüenza had written a "gallant and erudite funeral oration" in memory of his friend and rival. This is another of his manuscripts that have been lost.

THE MARQUIS DE LA LAGUNA governed New Spain for six years: he assumed office on November 7, 1680, and relinquished it on November 30, 1686, thus completing two terms as Viceroy. The Marquis and Marquise did not immediately return to Spain. The Duke de Medinaceli, Tomás de la Cerda's brother, was no longer first minister; since the preceding year, ill and in a kind of semi-exile, he had been living on his estates in Andalusia. Whether for this reason or because they were attached to Mexico, the Marquis and Marquise did not leave New Spain for two years. Robles notes that on April 28, 1688, the couple left the city and that "a great number of coaches accompanied them as far as Villa de Guadalupe, with many tears from the Vicereine." Sor Juana's sorrow must have been profound. It was a farewell that recalls a sonnet of Lope's: "To leave and to remain, remaining, to depart, / to leave behind a soul, but take with one, another." We know nothing of these two years, although it is probable that during this period Sor Juana wrote *The Divine Narcissus* and the *loa* that precedes it. The first separate edition of this play (Mexico, 1690) states that "the Marquise de la Laguna, Vicereine of this New Spain, most excellent patroness and admirer of Sor Juana, delivered the play to the court of Madrid for performance there." Soon after her arrival in Spain, the Marquise arranged for the publication of the first volume of the works of her friend (*Castalian Inundation*, 1689). She had taken with her many of Sor Juana's papers and manuscripts; later Sor Juana sent her others to augment the second edition of that volume (1691) and to make up the second volume of her works (1692).

Several times I have referred to María Luisa's active participation in the compilation and publication of the poems of her friend and protégée. Her devotion was admirable, and it did not cease with separation (as will be seen in the final part of this book). It is a pity we have no record of the correspondence between the two friends during those years; it would allow us to glimpse their true sentiments. After María Luisa and her husband left, Sor Juana must have felt abandoned. To live without protectors in a world that was a web of alliances, friendships, and reciprocal favors was like being in deep water without a lifebuoy to cling to. Two words defined that society: not *valor* (value) or *valer* (to be worth) but *valido* (favorite) and *valimiento* (favoritism). The lost correspondence between Juana Inés and María Luisa could also shed light on one of the most uncertain and confused periods in Sor Juana's life: those years of struggle, between 1690 and 1693, prior to her final submission. We do know from poems composed in those years that they wrote each other frequently and that their correspondence was not only personal but literary. One of the most impressive testimonies to this collaboration and to the nun's gratitude is the first sonnet in the *Castalian Inundation,* written in 1688, after María Luisa's departure. The sonnet accompanies other poems, which are the children of the "slave" (Sor Juana) and thus belong to the Countess, as the fruit of the land belongs to its owner:

> A child born of a slave shall be received,
> according to our Law, as property
> of the owner to whom fealty
> is rendered by the mother who conceived.
>
> The harvest from a grateful land retrieved,

INVNDACION CASTALIDA

DE

LA VNICA POETISA, MVSA DEZIMA,

SOROR JVANA INES

DE LA CRVZ, RELIGIOSA PROFESSA EN

el Monasterio de San Geronimo de la Imperial
Ciudad de Mexico.

QVE

EN VARIOS METROS, IDIOMAS, Y ESTILOS,
Fertiliza varios assumptos:

CON

ELEGANTES, SVTILES, CLAROS, INGENIOSOS,
VTILES VERSOS:

PARA ENSEÑANZA, RECREO, Y ADMIRACION

DEDICALOS

A LA EXCEL.ᵐᵃ SEÑORA. SEÑORA D. MARIA
Luisa Gonçaga Manrique de Lara, Condesa de Paredes,
Marquesa de la Laguna,

Y LOS SACA A LVZ
D. JVAN CAMACHO GAYNA, CAVALLERO DEL ORDEN
de Santiago, Mayordomo, y Cavallerizo que fue de su Excelencia,
Governador actual de la Ciudad del Puerto
de Santa MARIA.

CON PRIVILEGIO.

EN MADRID Por JVAN GARCIA INFANZON. Año de 1689.

Title page of the first volume of Sor Juana's works

the finest fruit, offered obediently,
is for the lord, for its fecundity
is owing to the care it has received.
    So, too, Lysis divine, these my poor lines:
as children of my soul, born of my heart,
they must in justice to you be returned;
    Let not their defects cause them to be spurned,
for of your rightful due they are a part,
as concepts of a soul to yours consigned.

The new Viceroy, Melchor Portocarrero y Lasso de la Vega, Count de Monclova, served scarcely two years in his post before being transferred in 1688 to the viceroyalty of Peru. He left the country in April 1689, five months after relinquishing the staff of command to the Count de Galve. A career officer, the Count de Monclova had distinguished himself in various military actions; in the battle of Dunkirk, fighting the French, he had lost a forearm. He wore a silver one in its place and so earned the nickname Brazo de Plata, Silver Arm.[4] The name of the Count de Monclova appears in Sor Juana's work only once, in the *loa* to *Love Is the Greater Labyrinth*. This silence in regard to Portocarrero is exceptional: the courtly poetry of Juana Inés invariably centered on the reigning Viceroy and his wife. The presence in New Spain of her protectors and friends, the Lagunas, freed her, at least temporarily, from such tedious obligations. In contrast, the arrival of the Viceroy who replaced the Count de Monclova, Don Gaspar de Sandoval Cerda Silva y Mendoza, Count de Galve,[5] immediately revived her courtly inspiration. The Count de Galve was the second son of the Duke de Pastrana, Prince of Éboli; thus he was a descendant of the councilor of state of Philip II, Ruy Gómez de Silva, and his wife, the famous, one-eyed Doña Ana de Mendoza, Princess of Éboli. Don Gaspar's older brother, the Duke de Pastrana, was the chief majordomo of Queen Mariana of Austria during the period of her regency. Like the Marquis de Mancera, he belonged to the "Austrian faction." The Count de Galve was one of the group of courtiers—including his brother, Mancera, and others—who plotted against the Duke de Medinaceli.[6] It is not far-fetched to speculate that when Medinaceli fell from power, the Count was rewarded with the viceroyalty. The Count de Galve was fifty-three when he arrived in Mexico, accompanied by his second wife, Elvira María de Toledo, by whom he had no children.

Don Gaspar de Sandoval was not as skillful as Mancera; neither did he govern with the pomp of the Marquis de la Laguna. But his administration was not inept, even though toward the end of it, during the uprising of 1692, he lost his control and his courage, and with them his authority and reputation. The end of his viceregency effaced the general approval he had earned earlier. Cruelly, today he is remembered for the disturbances of 1692 and not for the victory against the French that made him famous. Pirates had established strongholds on the island of Tortuga and from there relentlessly harassed Spanish ships and ports. The Count de Galve sent the Windward Fleet to Santo Domingo, where it was welcomed by the island's governor, Admiral Ignacio Pérez Caro. On January 21, 1691, the royal and viceregal troops defeated the French in a naval and land engagement on Tortuga and thus weakened for several years the power of Louis XIV in the region. This feat of arms, reported by Sigüenza y Góngora in his *Trophy of Spanish Justice in the Punishment of French Perfidy*,[7] was accomplished by the Windward Fleet—under the command of General Jacinto Lope Girón and Admiral Antonio de Astina—and land troops led by Francisco de Segura. In truth, the Count de Galve's role was limited to transmitting the orders he had received from Madrid, but Sigüenza and other poets in the *Trophy*, among them Sor Juana, showered him with absurd commendations. This was the last victory of the Spanish armada. It was also the last time Mexico exerted influence in the Caribbean. The poets of the *Trophy* did not suspect what impotence would follow upon their enthusiasm, their adjectives, and their hyperbole.

The Count de Galve governed from November 1688 to February 1696. In spite of the length of his tenure, longer than that of the Marquis de la Laguna, Sor Juana dedicated very few poems to him or his wife. Although the poems are decorous, to be sure, none of them is memorable. The most interesting piece is the "Encomiastic Poem to the Countess de Galve" (384), which I referred to in my chapter on music. Méndez Plancarte is enchanted with the *silva* in the *Trophy*, which he calls worthy of Pindar. It is not: it is a cold poem, constructed from the vocabulary, mythological allusions, inversions, Latinate phrases, and other legacies of a stereotyped Gongorism. It is saved by two intensely sexual strophes: one in which she compares her inspiration to a "pregnant cloud"; another, which I have quoted several times, in which she sees herself as the virgin pythoness of Delphi.

Sor Juana's courtly poetry during the viceregency of the Count de Galve fulfilled the same social and symbolic function as her writing under other viceroys: as political ritual, it was an allegory of the ideal relationship between lord and vassals. At the same time Sor Juana relied on the favor of the palace to ensure her position in the convent and to maintain her independence of the other nuns. Because of the prestige and the influence she gained with her courtly poems, she was able to defend herself from the envy, meanness, and intrigue of convent life. In our time, in order to survive and be independent, poets write for periodicals, teach in universities, give readings, and so on. The courtly poems of Sor Juana were her articles, her lectures, and her university courses, the price she had to pay in order to be left alone to write what her fantasy, her inspiration, or her whim dictated. For twenty years, in an always delicate and vulnerable equilibrium won each day, she was able to read and write in relative calm. She did not write all that she thought, or wished: the "trivial cares" of which Rubén Darío complained so bitterly devoured most of her time. Even so, the amount of her work is substantial, and it is not likely that she could have accomplished it outside the convent.

Her path was not always smooth. She never found her true niche, the place that was rightfully hers; she was always an intruder, a stranger, both in the court and in the convent. Her most personal poetry, such as *First Dream*, must be read as the coded confessions of a far-ranging soul. Its themes are flight and fall; in the heights, suddenly she grows weak and plunges to earth. That is why her hero is Phaethon: hers is a poetry of failure. In addition to this private and perhaps congenital maladjustment, she had to confront not only the intrigues and jealousies of her community but a more basic incompatibility between the free and solitary life of a writer and the collective and routine life of a convent.

FROM THE TIME SHE TOOK THE VEIL in 1669 until 1690 Sor Juana Inés de la Cruz lived a protected and secure existence. After twenty years of convent life she was fairly affluent, with funds invested in the financial ventures of the convent, a library that was admired by connoisseurs, and a collection of musical and scientific instruments, jewels, and rare objects. She protected her relatives, lent and borrowed money, and, as we have seen, defrayed the expenses of her niece Isabel María de San José, who was a nun in the convent. A nephew, Felipe Ramírez de Villena, while still an adolescent ran away from his mother and—he was nicknamed "España" for this escapade—made his way to Spain in search of adventure. Sor Juana interceded with someone close to the Count de

Galve, who set the official system in motion; the youth was picked up and returned to Mexico and to his family. The Sor Juana of 1690 was not the powerless novice of 1669.

A skillful administrator of the convent's wealth and of her own, she enjoyed a good reputation—as Dorothy Schons has established—with the city's merchants (among them Domingo de la Rea, a silver merchant, and a prebendary of the cathedral, Diego Franco Velázquez). Schons writes: "Although she had to beg for her dowry, she was toward the end of her life one of the most well-to-do nuns in the convent, perhaps in the city. Her fortune was so ample that on various occasions she supplied from her own purse what was needed to complete construction projects in San Jerónimo . . . a sharp businesswoman."[8] In addition to administering the assets of the convent, Sor Juana oversaw the work of construction and expansion of the building. Recently at San Jerónimo, during some reconstruction, a small stone box was discovered sealed in an arch; it contained two sheets of paper written and signed by Sor Juana. On one of the sheets are the first lines of the Gospel of St. John, followed by a profession of faith. The other reads: "This arch was sealed by the hand of Sister Juana Inés de la Cruz, being bookkeeper of this convent of Our Father St. Jerome, the prioress being Sister Andrea de la Encarnación, this 13 February of 1690. *Juana Inés de la Cruz.*"

She enjoyed the protection of all the viceroys. She was confidante and friend of two vicereines, Leonor Carreto and María Luisa Manrique de Lara. She provided the palace with *loas,* plays, and poems for entertainments and ceremonies, and the cathedrals of Mexico City and Puebla with *villancicos* for their liturgies; from these activities she received something more precious than economic benefits: influence and prestige. Her poems circulated from hand to hand, and no one was scandalized by the markedly erotic tone of many of them. Her plays were performed in her city, and in Madrid the appearance of the first volume of her works in 1689 was received with praise. Admirers wrote to her from Madrid, Seville, Lima, and Quito; she became as famous in Spain and South America as in Mexico. The locutory of the convent had become a kind of salon where, over cups of chocolate, biscuits, and fruit, conversations on literature and theology thrived, poems were recited and improvised, reputations were made and destroyed. In her writings she referred openly to a variety of subjects in every style possible, with one exception: until 1690 she never risked the subject of theology, in spite of her fondness for arguing subtleties. It is not difficult to guess why. She was afraid, as she herself said several times, to venture into areas that could place her in conflict with the Church. The prelates who surrounded her during these years of glory had never opposed her literary activities, at least not publicly. The austere Aguiar y Seijas must have grumbled more than once but, despite his irascibility, held his tongue.

Years later, Oviedo, Antonio Núñez de Miranda's biographer, reported that Father Antonio had often reprimanded her for her excessive dedication to secular letters, exhorting her to withdraw from such public recognition and commerce with the secular world. But Sor Juana did not change her way of life. The benevolent attitude of the Church can be explained. Not only, as I have indicated several times, had she obtained the favor and protection of the palace from the beginning, she was also loved and sheltered by several princes of the Church, from Fray Payo de Rivera, the Viceroy-Archbishop, to Fernández de Santa Cruz, the Bishop of Puebla, as well as the future Bishop of Yucatán, Juan Ignacio de Castorena y Ursúa. She was visited and sought after by high officials, ladies of the nobility, clerics, potentates, military men, homilists, and illustrious travelers such as Father Kino. She had friends and protectors in the court of Madrid, close to the throne. As she herself was pleased to note, she was a "European" as well as a local celebrity.

We can imagine her, between 1680 and 1690, in the library of her cell, as in the paintings by Miranda and Cabrera. In Miranda's portrait she is standing; in Cabrera's she is seated. Otherwise the two paintings are similar: shelves of books in the background; in the center a table; on the table a cloth; on the cloth a book and an inkwell; in the inkwell a few quill pens. There are other objects—scissors and, in the painting by Miranda, a sheet of paper with a sonnet to Hope: "Verde embeleso de la vida humana . . ." ("Human life, verdant illusion . . ."). One hand, at once slender and rounded, is white against the white sleeves of her habit and the whiteness of the paper. In Miranda's painting the hand is holding a quill pen, like a dove lifting a twig in its beak; in Cabrera's, the hand is resting on an open book, like a dove perched on a ledge. We can read the titles of the books on the shelves. There is a clock and, in Miranda's painting, a flask containing greenish liquid atop a piece of paper covered with geometric figures and calculations. How can we fail to think of the magic square in Dürer's *Melancholy 1?* In Cabrera's portrait the cloth on the table is red and sumptuous. In both paintings luxurious and theatrical draperies hang in the background.

Miranda's portrait shows us a rather tall woman about thirty years old. Her elegant habit falls to her feet without entirely disguising the slender waist. The bell-shaped skirt is banded at the hem in pale blue. In Cabrera's version the same whiteness, the same band, the same black scapular, and the same elegance; again the folds of the habit both emphasize and conceal the slightly parted legs and the bent right knee. In both portraits the left hand is caressing the beads of an enormous rosary worn as a necklace. The gesture is more courtly than devout. Like a shield, the medallion of her order on her breast: the virgin poet is also a virgin warrior. The black wimple covers the head so artfully that it resembles a mane of black hair or, even more closely, a helmet of dark reflections. The oval of the face is as perfect as the hands and, like them, full and round. The mouth is sensuous, fleshy, with just the suspicion of down on the upper lip. The nose, straight and "judicious"; the flared nostrils accentuate the vague sensuality of that remote face. Heavy eyebrows, black and well defined: "two arcs," as she herself says. In Miranda's painting the eyes are black, large, and round; in Cabrera's they are dark brown, shading to olive. But those eyes are not looking at us; they are looking at something beyond us, something that, as soon as it is seen, dissolves. They are looking at a disappearance. The brow is broad and pure. What is she thinking?

Both portraits are theatrical. We see Sor Juana among her books as we would glimpse naked goddesses through a break in mythological clouds or, through the foliage of a park, ladies in wide-brimmed, feathered hats. The figure of Juana Inés radiates elegance, not piety. The painting is not a window that allows us to view her inner nature but a curtain drawn back on an allegory. It is a monument erected in ritual space: Sor Juana appears, offers herself to the eyes of the beholder, and withdraws. The metaphor of a setting sun, illuminating the plain below before slipping behind the mountain, suits her perfectly. But the paintings spark our curiosity as much as they provoke our admiration; they allow us a glimpse of her inner self and impart an oblique lesson. In both portraits, however different the artists who painted them may have been, there is at once theatricality and reserve. Both paintings, like her poems, give an ambiguous image of seduction and disillusion. In the melancholic, not the dramatic, mode, this is the baroque contrast between being and appearance that results in disappearance. The posture and the gaze evoke the indefinable expression of Narcissus as he watches the waters change, and finally obliterate, his face—the passion for life and the immediate disenchantment that follows. Sensuality becomes melancholy, and melancholy resolves into solitude.

The portraits excite our desire to know her: what would she be like?

Through her writing and from other clues we sense that she was vivacious, ingenious, and playful, although plagued by shadows. A continuous psychic oscillation, from loquacity to silence, from good humor to hypochondria. Exposed to all winds, sometimes sunny, sometimes stormy. Reason and sensibility are intertwined in her; they quarrel, and again embrace like jealous lovers. The dialogue takes place in the theater of her inner being, and she is the only spectator. Sor Juana's poems reveal what her portraits conceal: reality is not theater—erudition, wit, fame, worldliness—but the gnawings of solitude. After seeing himself in the admiration of others, Narcissus sees himself in his own eyes and despises himself. In Sor Juana that loathing does not reach the point of self-destruction. She does not break the mirror; she contemplates her image with melancholy and ends by mocking herself. Introspection leads to irony, and irony is a way of being alone. She was contradiction itself, the epitome of her world and its negation. She represented the ideal of her era: the monstrous, the unique, the singular example. She was a species in herself. Nun, poet, musician, painter, errant theologian, embodied metaphor, living conceit, beauty in a wimple, syllogism in a gown, a creature doubly to be feared: her voice enchants, her arguments kill. But all this is the appearance, the figure on the stage. The true Sor Juana is alone, consumed by her thoughts. Consumed and consoled; if thinking disheartens, it also fortifies:

Romance 2   Let us pretend that I am gay
for a brief time, oh, doleful thought;
you may, perhaps, think to persuade me
although I know it is for naught:
they say that apprehension often
is the source of injury,
and if you think that you are happy
then less *un*happy you will be.
May it be that understanding
will briefly bring tranquillity.

Part Five

The Tenth Muse

19

Hear Me with Your Eyes

*T*HE POETRY OF SOR JUANA was published in no thematic or chronological order. There have been several attempts to establish a chronology, but, with the manuscripts lost, the results have been uncertain. Méndez Plancarte decided to organize his first volume—*Lírica personal*—by placing emphasis first on poetic form: *romances, endechas, glosas*, sonnets, *liras;* then, within each of these categories, he grouped the poems according to theme: amorous, philosophical, religious, satirical, mythological, epistolary; finally, he considered the (supposed) dates of composition or, more frequently, the dates of publication. In this review I follow a slightly different order, arranging the poems first by theme, then by form and, when possible, by chronology. I exclude the courtly poetry and the poems of loving friendship, which I have already discussed in some detail. In the present chapter I am concerned primarily with the love poems.

There are not as many love poems as courtly poems, which constitute about half her work; even so, the love poems occupy a prominent place by their number—nearly fifty—and also because among them are some of her finest creations. There are *romances, endechas, décimas, liras,* sonnets, and *glosas*. To variety of form is joined variety of subject and situation. This abundance of amatory poems published in books reprinted many times and issued under the sponsorship of important personages is truly surprising, especially when one considers that their author was a nun. Even more surprising is the fact that critics did not find it strange. In the seventeenth century the Church judged opinions more severely than behavior: the amorous literature of that period is largely the work of clerics, some of whom, like Lope de Vega, lived quite dissolute lives. However ancient and illustrious the tradition of erotic, even libertine, literature written by clerics, there is no other example of a nun who, with widespread approval, published erotic poems and even sexual satires that could have been signed by a disciple of Quevedo.[1]

My statement may seem extreme. Some, of course, will recall the letters of the Portuguese nun Mariana Alcoforado (1640–1723). Sublime as they are, we known them only in a French version (1661), and they are said to be a hoax. Nor is the example of Heloise applicable here; the theme of her letters, which were never intended for publication, was that of earthly love compared to divine love. Sor Juana's poems are very different in nature, and nowhere in them is there the slightest allusion to her religious state. The author never appears as a nun, but rather as an independent woman of the upper class, at times betrothed, at times not, almost always in interchanges with one or two suitors. Those poems must have scandalized the austere Father Núñez de Miranda and Archbishop Aguiar y Seijas, who was horrified by the female sex. Nevertheless, for years—while Sor Juana was in favor at court—the two held their silence. To mitigate the impropriety, it has been said that the poems were "commissioned." This supposition is not based on contemporary realities. It would have been most unusual for ladies and gentlemen of the viceregal court to commission a nun to write their love poems, and for those texts to be published later in books. No, Sor Juana's impunity was due to the protection of the palace and to the ambiguity of her situation: at the same time that she was writing *villancicos* for the cathedral and *loas* for the palace, she was composing love sonnets and *liras*. One activity compensated for the other. Furthermore, those poems were read not as confessions but as variations on a universal theme. At the end of her life Sor Juana paid, with interest, for this indulgence, and her persecutors were the harsher for their earlier tolerance.

There is no need to repeat what has been said about the erotic tradition of the West, from Provençal poetry to seventeenth-century Spain. Sor Juana inherited not only poetic forms, a vocabulary, a syntax, and a repertory of images, but a concept and a vision of erotic relationships. An aesthetic, an ethic, and something like a religion outside religion: the cult of love. We have inherited that tradition but our attitude toward amorous poetry is very different from that of the seventeenth century. There is a great divide between the Baroque period and our own: romanticism, with its exaltation of sincerity and spontaneity. The romantic doctrine proclaimed the unity of author and work. Baroque art differentiated and separated them to the greatest degree possible: the poem is not a testimony but a verbal form that is at the same time the reiteration of an archetype and a variation on the inherited model. The originality of the seventeenth century differs profoundly from that of romanticism. For the latter, originality lies in *genio,* creative genius; for the former, in *ingenio,* wit or cleverness. The nineteenth century conceives of creative genius as the highest of all conditions: it is an almost superhuman capacity for feeling, imagining, creating. For the seventeenth century, genius is temperament, inclination, or, as Gracián says, *vocation.* Wit, formed of intelligence and sensibility, is the faculty that discovers the secret relationships among things and ideas and hits upon the unique way to express them. Wit discovers but, especially, it combines: it is an art. It is manifest in the conceit: "What beauty is to the eyes and harmony to the ears, the conceit is to the mind." The combination of elements that compose an object or an idea reduces plurality and heterogeneity to a unity that astounds us; wit produces an object that is new or has never been seen before: an ingenuity. The highest art—a witty conceit—is an artifice that consists of a "harmonic correlation among two or three cognizables, expressed through an act of the intellect."[2]

Like all poets of her time, Sor Juana does not attempt to express herself; she constructs verbal objects that are emblems or monuments that illustrate a vision of love transmitted by poetic tradition. Those verbal objects are unique—or aspire to be—not as expressions of an experience or a personality, both unrepeatable, but as unusual combinations of the elements composing the poetic archetype of amorous sentiments. I do not mean that the poetry of Sor Juana contains nothing personal; rather, that her most intimate experiences tend to conform to and be transfigured within traditional forms, from meter to metaphor to conceit. In the most intensely personal poems of the Golden Age—those of a Garcilaso or a Lope de Vega—we find no confession or confidence, in the modern meaning of the words. Even if they are the transposition of deeply lived experiences, and even if it is easy to read the story of Lope's love affair with Micaela de Luján into the sonnets of the *Rimas,* those experiences are presented in canonical forms and take on a representative quality. Poets and their readers sought not a lived reality but the perfection of art that transfigures what has been lived and gives it an ideal reality.

A major portion of Sor Juana's amorous poetry—the same is true of her sacred writing and the rest of her poetic works—is mere exercise, ostentation, exhibition of skill. But what remains, smaller in quantity, consists of poems that satisfy the two highest requisites of art: they are beautiful works and they are authentic works. This authenticity has been questioned by allegations that many of those poems were commissioned, written at the request of male or female friends. The number and importance of these texts, however, prevents our taking this supposition seriously. It is a hypothesis that is both gratuitous and outrageous: gratuitous because it is not grounded in any proof or based on any clue; outrageous because, as I have said, it turns Sor Juana into a go-between at the service of the ladies and lords of the viceregal court, specializing in erotic missives in verse. But even if this fantastic conjecture were true, it would not diminish the authenticity of the poems. Texts stand apart from their authors and speak for themselves.

The poetry of Sor Juana, like that of all poets, is born of her life, as long as we understand that the word "life"—in all cases but especially in hers—designates imagination, ideas, and readings as well as events. As many have pointed out, her love poems must be based on lived experience, provided, I repeat, that what we call experience embraces the real and the imaginary, what is thought and what is dreamed. It is almost certain that during her years in the viceregal court she experienced love or love affairs, and she was not immune to passion once inside the cloister, as her affection for María Luisa proves. In her cell she heard, from one of her musical instruments, "a sweeping surf and a mysterious wind: / the seashell has the shape of a heart."[3] Her erotic life was almost entirely imaginary, but not for that reason any less real or intense. Calleja comments, "She writes of love without experience of love affairs." Perhaps without love affairs but not without love.

Menéndez Pelayo said that a philosophy of love can be extrapolated from Sor Juana's poems. Also a psychology, even a logic. Except that this information, codified and conceptualized through philosophical speculation and the artifices of rhetoric, is the opposite of lived information: it is not a vision but a formula set in rhyme. In *romance* 3, "with ingenious ingenuity she reflects on the passion of jealousy," as the title says, and refutes a contemporary, the Spaniard José Pérez de Montoro:

> If love is the motivating cause
> of a variety of affections,
> and if as it engenders them,
> it adds to its own perfection:

and if, among these sentiments,
to be jealous is the norm,
how, then, without jealousy
may love reach its perfect form?

The *romance* continues in this manner for three hundred thirty-six lines. Following demonstration (without jealousy there is no love) come examples—Aeneas, Theseus, Jason, Bathsheba—and, finally, an apology to Pérez de Montoro for disagreeing with him. The poem is constructed like a legal brief, and love is an examination that the student passes or fails:

A jealous person's stubbornness,
his rashness, irrationality,
are proofs of love deserving of
a grant from his academy.

Poem 99 "demonstrates the decorous efforts of reason against the vile tyranny of a violent love"; the next poem is an allegory of a soul, like Troy, besieged by love. Poem 104, in which "she defends the position that only love freely chosen is deserving of rational reciprocity," is also argued in legalistic fashion. I see the beautiful nun standing beside a blackboard, with a ruler, compasses, and chalk and, on the desk, dunce caps for the slow-witted:

In love, he who is curious
will perceive a clear distinction:
one love is chosen by election,
one chooses us, imperious.
The latter is more amorous,
because it is more natural,
more deeply felt, and thus, withal,
this is the state we call affective;
the other, which is, then, elective,
shall be labeled rational.

One series of sonnets expounds, in rhymed syllogisms, a geometry of the emotions. The triangle: she loves Fabio, who does not love her, and abhors Silvio, who does love her—a dual torment, "for I suffer both loving and being loved." The polygon: other women want to be loved by many, a single love is not enough for them, while she wants only to have her love returned by one; moral: "being loved is like the condiment of salt, we suffer from too little—or we suffer from too much." The intersection: she loves Silvio, who does not deserve her love; she would like to disavow this "base love" but notes that "it is sufficient pain to confess it." But in the following sonnet she has a change of mind: "rejected, I despise not only you, / but, for the time I loved you, myself as well." She pauses and, more rational, reflects in a different sonnet: "Who, in love, has been more fortunate?" Not all is sophistry, and in sonnet 177 the conceit becomes a surprising fantasy. The lover's vision mists over at the sight of the beloved, but then the lover sees the beloved's disdain:

> as the glances beaming from my eyes
> find resistance in your candid snows,
> what emerged as mist is turned to tears.

The majority of these sonnets are instructional and are filled with antecedents, precedents, qualifications, deductions, and corollaries. In one sonnet she proves something she refutes in the following, using the same rhyme scheme. In another she repeats the game, but this time using the end words of another sonnet. She must, writing in Spanish, define the gender of the speaker: most frequently the voice is that of a woman, but at times it is a man; it may even be a neuter voice—that of reason itself. A curious and at times touching pedantry: love is disjunctive logic, desire is rational election, and jealousy—essence or accident? As if to reward us, following so many subtleties and sophistries, the series ends with an abstruse but admirably constructed sonnet. The Scholastic terminology makes it difficult; fortunately Méndez Plancarte clarifies it: the "material form" in the upper heavens persists in its being, since—according to philosophical "probable opinion"—"it is fulfilled in its heavenly form," which is immutable and incorruptible, while here below, in the sublunar world, that same persistence leads to corruption and death. In the light of this explication the poem becomes slightly blasphemous, since it converts the Celia of the sonnet, a flesh-and-blood woman, into a "heavenly form" who instills in her beloved an incorruptible and immutable love:

> Among philosophers there is the view
> that heavenly forms maintain stability
> not through the matter's greater constancy,
> but through the form the matter changed into.
> Because a longing for vicissitude
> is sated by the form's nobility—

> and with the appetite's satiety,
> the need for change is ended, too.
>   And thus your love, with bonds invincible,
> the soul that loves you, Celia, informs:
> hence its corruption is impossible
>   and to another it need not conform,
> not through being incorruptible,
> but through the permanency of the form.

Sor Juana's love poems in the Scholastic or doctrinal mode are only a curiosity. Among the others, some are truly memorable. These are the poems that respond to real experiences, in the sense I earlier described: that imagined realities are no less real than lived ones. The imaginary nature of those compositions is patent: in all of them the lover is either absent or dead. They are love poems that are also poems of solitude, poems of nostalgia, desire, desolation, bitterness, contrition. Dialogues with shadows and reflections. But my limited list cannot describe the extreme emotions that caused her to say, in poem 79:

> I want no further pain
> from such uncertain fortunes,
> but, rather, that my soul
> exist as if forgotten.

The language is not always translucent; at times it becomes tempestuous, dark, even purple. A frequently felicitous union of disparate elements: subtle, rich rhetoric, slightly orotund but capable of true resplendence—the setting sun of our baroque; profound and flowing sentiment composed of anxiety, desire, melancholy; a lucid, alert, ironic mind. Two contradictory words, perhaps, best define these poems: wit and passion. In *romance* 6, anticipating the sorrow of an imminent separation, her eyes already moist, she says wittily: "Because water will be quenching / what fire is now igniting."

Metaphors abound on the theme of writing: paper, pen, ink, handwriting—solitude. In a funeral sonnet (189) dedicated to Laura (Leonor Carreto), in writing the verses she writes: "Misshapen are the letters that here fall, / black teardrops from my melancholy pen." In one of her *liras* (211) she speaks alone with an absent friend, and the image reappears, now more intense:

> Hear me with your eyes,
> now that distant ears cannot attend,

> and, in absent sighs,
> hear reproaches sobbing from this pen.
> And as you cannot hear a voice so faint,
> then hear me deaf, for mute is my complaint.

A frequent theme of these poems is absence, at times allied to or complicated by that of jealousy. Her love is not a happy one, as it is in the poems of loving friendship with María Luisa. She is lifted up by her fantasy, but when she opens her eyes she is once again in unhappy reality. In a poem in *endechas* (81) notable for its versification—the combination of seven- and ten-syllable lines is unusual in Spanish—she describes her fall:

> No sooner toward the Sun
> am I lifted by your eyes
> than my plummeting fall [*precipicio*]
> confers in burning signs
> revenge unto the fire, and a name upon the seas.

A scholarly note by Méndez Plancarte informs the reader that *precipicio*, precipice, is used in the archaic sense of "fall," and that the strophe alludes to Icarus, who in his fall gave his name to the Icarian Sea. But the five lines can be read with equal delight without that mythological reference: the miracle of poetry.

Poem 70, also written to someone who is absent, successfully utilizes everyday language without falling into commonness or sentimentality. This *romancillo* is a marvel of fluidity, like the murmur of running water that grows more beautiful as it flows:

> Insidious memory,
> grant some surcease;
> an instant only
> let me suffer in peace.
> Loosen the rope,
> don't twist so tight;
> with one turn more
> and life will take flight.[4]

To call memory "insidious" is something more than a lucky hit; Proust himself would have been delighted to find that adjective.

Absence is the territory where desire and imagination display their creations; Sor Juana uses other fictions to lend freedom to her erotic fantasy. In poem 75 the lover is not aware that he is loved; this gives her the opportunity to change him, literally, into a beam of sunlight that annihilates her, reducing her to "contrite ashes." The image of the lover, like the sun,

> wounds with arms of gold
> the bright moon of a mirror;
> reflecting from the glass,
> that brilliant golden ray
> reverberantly wounds
> the object nearest by.

Another fiction is the figure of death. Although usually it is the lover who is dead, in poem 76 it is she. Not dead, but dying. If we really think about the situation described in these lines, the scene is of questionable taste; if we note, however, that it is a fantasy of revenge and also that it frees her to express something intimate that she does not know how to say, then the device is quite moving. The death that separates lovers also unites them. They join hands and word play helps her say what is left unsaid:

> Hands tightly intertwined,
> palm against palm laid,
> with movements they can say
> what lips must leave unsaid.

Jealousy, absence, death: different names of solitude. Alone—and because she is always alone—she invents these situations; in turn, the inventions help her to unburden herself and come to know herself: the life of her imagination is also a means of introspection. The literary conventions of absence and death are effective because they express the personal and most intimate reality of the nun without a calling. In poem 78 the situation is equally fictitious, its theme, "the anguish suffered by a woman who mourns the death of her beloved husband." At last alone in her bedchamber, far from relatives and friends, "stolen away . . . from so many impertinent eyes," the widow surrenders to her grief. Hers is a furious and vengeful pain she wants to turn toward the destruction of creation:

> Burst forth, engendering grief,
> let all bridges be crushed
> by the torrent of my tears
> borne on the waters' crest.

The *endechas* continue in this tone of angry and slightly rhetorical grief; then follows an introspective calm that presages lines of great intensity. As always, passion heightens her inventive faculty and leads her to surprising images and figures:

> And as a blazing log
> consumed by ardent flame
> seems to us to glow
> the while it suffers pain,
> and as the vegetal
> humor perishes,
> even as it dies
> it seems to us to live:
> so I, when in my soul
> beset by mortal grief,
> am also vitalized
> in the anguish born of death.

The poet's comparison of her state to that of the blazing log is impressive: to suffer and to blaze are one and the same. Grief, like pleasure, is a kind of vital excess which as it drains life from us exalts us; that is why she is "vitalized" in her "anguish." The "vegetal humor" refers to the humor of the vegetal soul and recalls the "vegetable love" of Andrew Marvell's poem "To His Coy Mistress," except that in contrast to the English poet's love, which would grow "Vaster than empires, and more slow," Sor Juana's grief spreads as swiftly as fire.

The theme of widowhood is repeated in *liras* (poem 213) that are less intense than the *endechas* but nevertheless contain memorable lines, such as the ones in which she says she cannot tell her sorrows because "they are, tangled in their haste, / a noose around my throat, a sword plunged in my breast."

The two currents of her erotic poetry come together in poem 84: the reasoned and the sentimental. It is a fortunate fusion. The title of this composition accurately reflects its content: "In which she describes rationally the irrational effects of love." Méndez Plancarte finds in it echoes of Ruiz de Alarcón, Calderón, Rojas, and Góngora. It is curious—and revealing—that the only passages he cites are scenes from plays, even in the case of Góngora. The supreme psychological and sentimental model of the seventeenth century, like the novel in the nineteenth and film in the twentieth, was the theater. Sor Juana was the author of plays, *sainetes,* and *autos sacramentales;* general influences apart, her preference for the theatrical form of the monologue is psychological in origin. In this poem, as in others I have cited, although she is addressing herself, she is also addressing an invisible audience. She is speaking not with her departed or dead lover but with the reader, with us. As regards the echoes Méndez Plancarte hears, I checked each instance and found that the similarities are based on the use of the word "melancholy" and on the gamut of emotions and sensations it evoked in the seventeenth century. In fact, this is a question of affinities more than of influences. The first forty lines of these *redondillas* have a clarity, delicacy, and grace that is truly exceptional. The ambiguities of amorous sentiment and of language are projected in deceptive reflections: reason that is madness and grief that is happiness. Simplicity and refinement, lucidity and coquetry, internal reflection and intimate music. All this spoken before a mental mirror, a spectacle that both saddens us and makes us smile. Even though this poem is well known, I cannot resist the temptation to quote at least the first twelve lines, and four others:

> The pain and torment of this love
> that my heart cannot conceal,
> I know I feel, but cannot know
> the reasons why it's this I feel.
>
>   I suffer gravest agonies
> to reach the heights of ecstasy,
> but what commences as desire
> is doomed to end as misery.
>
>   And when with greatest tenderness
> I weep for my unhappiness,
> I only know that I am sad
> but reasons I cannot express.
>
>   First forbearing, then aroused,
> conflicting griefs I am combatting:
> that I shall suffer much *for* him,
> but *with* him I shall suffer nothing.

The language, in its reverberations and chiaroscuro, merges with the fluctuating movement of her psyche. It is a pity that the poem is prolonged in repetitious conceits and cleverness; enticed by her initial achievements, Sor Juana did not know when to stop. This is a defect found in the greatest poets of the century: Lope, Quevedo, Góngora himself. Perhaps the *romance* and *redondilla* forms, with no fixed number of lines, contributed to this verbal incontinence. A form that can be prolonged at will is an indefinite form; that is its attraction and its danger. The sonnet, by contrast, demands maximum concentration; so it is not surprising that some of the best poems of Lope and Quevedo are in sonnet form. The same is true of Sor Juana. I am thinking especially of two love sonnets: 164, "My love, this evening when I spoke with you . . . ," and 165, "Stay, shadow of contentment too short-lived . . ."

The theme of the first sonnet is jealousy, a motif that appears in a number of *romances, décimas,* and *glosas,* as well as in other sonnets. I mentioned sonnet 177, a version in the logical, discursive mode of the same theme, in which, developing the Platonic idea of sight as an organ of love, even tears become a conceit: "what emerged as mist is turned to tears." Sonnet 164, on the other hand, moves toward the specific, not the abstract. The first line declares the hour and the occasion: "My love, this evening when I spoke with you . . ." The first quatrain describes a minor emotional conflict which in the following lines becomes knotted until, in the tercets, in rapid and almost imperceptible variations, the knot is untied: the knot-heart is dissolved in tears. The denouement is a metamorphosis, like that of the other sonnet, but not an abstraction; the incredulous lover can see and touch these tears:

> My love, this evening when I spoke with you,
> and in your face and actions I could read
> that arguments of words you would not heed,
> my heart I longed to open to your view.
> In this intention, Love my wishes knew
> and, though they seemed impossible, achieved:
> pouring in tears that sorrow had conceived,
> with every beat my heart dissolved anew.
> Enough of suffering, my love, enough:
> let jealousy's vile tyranny be banned,
> let no suspicious thought your calm corrupt
> with foolish gloom by futile doubt enhanced,
> for now, this afternoon, you saw and touched
> my heart, dissolved and liquid in your hands.

Sonnet 165 is the epitome of—and more, the key to—her love poetry. Also to her erotic life. The title prepares us: it "recounts how fantasy contents itself with honorable love." Honorable because it is a fantasy, or because it is resigned to being so? A question impossible to answer.

> Stay, shadow of contentment too short-lived,
> illusion of enchantment I most prize,
> fair image for whom happily I die,

sweet fiction for whom painfully I live.
   If to your charms attracted I submit,
obedient, like steel to magnet fly,
by what logic do you flatter and entice,
only to flee, a taunting fugitive?
   'Tis no triumph that you so smugly boast
that I fell victim to your tyranny;
though from encircling bonds that held you fast
   your elusive form too readily slipped free,
and though to my arms you are forever lost,
you are a prisoner in my fantasy.

Abreu Gómez notes that the first line is very similar to one by an obscure poet, Luis Martín de la Plaza: "Amante sombra de mi bien esquivo" (Fond shadow of contentment too short-lived). Yes, but what a difference! Martín de la Plaza's line is flat and sentimental; Sor Juana's, through the simple change of *amante* (fond) to *detente* (stay), is quick and lively, dictated by anguish and desire. Méndez Plancarte cites other affinities—Calderón, Quevedo—that are predictable but not significant: the theme of the erotic phantom appears throughout Western poetry and it is natural that Sor Juana should pick up this motif. But the sonnet, like the most intense passages of her other love poems, is more than a mere variation on the theme of the phantom: it responds and corresponds to a personal need and to her very situation as a cloistered woman. What and who could have peopled her hours if not fictions? Following the anxious "Stay"—more a plea than a command—each of the lines of the first quatrain poses in a symmetrical chiaroscuro the opposition between the two worlds that make up her world: "shadow," "illusion," "image," "fiction" / "short-lived contentment," "prized enchantment," "happily I die," "painfully I live." In the second quatrain this opposition—that of her life itself—assumes the form of a perhaps insoluble conflict and is, for that reason, expressed as a question: why, "by what logic?" The image of the magnet, common in the European poetry of that century, is effective because it represents the mediation between the two worlds, the phantasmal and the real. Like the planets and the humors, magnetic attraction unites not only bodies and souls, but phantoms. The tercets resolve the conflict in a terrible way: by enshrining it. The phantom escapes the embrace of the body but is imprisoned by the mind. How can we forget the image of the lady that the cruel *spiritelli* of Dante and Cavalcanti engraved on the lover's heart?

Since the Middle Ages, the erotic tradition of the West has been one of a search, in the body, for the phantom and, in the phantom, for the body. Nothing less carnal than carnal copulation: the embracing bodies merge into a river of sensations that disperse and vanish. All that remains, the only reality, is images: the phantom. But erotic relations with the phantom, as we see in Sor Juana, are no less equivocal. Erotic fantasies that provoke the apparition of the phantom are almost always accompanied by physical experiences which—in the West but not in Oriental civilizations—have been viewed with a mixture of horror and fascination: nocturnal ejaculation, masturbation, and mental copulation accompanied by solitary orgasm. At times the appearance of the phantom was attributed to the action of infernal spirits: incubi and succubi that were sexual partners during dream and the cause of forbidden pleasures. It is impossible to believe that Juana Inés did not know some of these solitary experiences. Sonnet 165 can be read as an allegory of the transformation of incubus into phantom—that is, into an ideal fantasy, a perceivable idea. Phantoms also people the poems of Quevedo and frequently return to their original state as succubi, as in the sonnet that begins, "Ah, Floralba, I dreamed that I . . . shall I say it? / Yes, since it was a dream: that I possessed you," and ends:

> But I awakened from that sweet confusion
> and saw that living, I was there with death,
> and saw, although with life, that I was dead.

The theme of the phantom runs through the history of Western eroticism: courtly love, the *dolce still nuovo,* Petrarchism, the Neoplatonism of the Renaissance and the Baroque, eighteenth-century occultism, romanticism, and the modern period. Mexican readers of this book will be reminded of the poem by Ramón López Velarde:

> Did your flesh still cling to every bone?
> Love's enigma was completely veiled
> beneath the prudence of your long black gloves.

The phantom—whether the spirit of the dead returning to us or the image invented by our desire—is almost an obsession in the poetry of Baudelaire. In *Mon coeur mis à nu* (*My Heart Laid Bare*), he quotes an anonymous seventeenth-century sonnet that he himself could have written. I include those French alexandrines as a kind of funereal and libertine counterpoint to Sor Juana's sonnet. They are two moments of the same tradition:

Je songeais cette nuit que Philis revenue,
Belle comme elle était à la clarté du jour,
Voulait que son fantôme encore fît l'amour,
Et que, comme Ixion, j'embrassasse une nue,
 Son ombre dans mon lit se glisse toute nue,
Et me dit: "Cher Damon, me voici de retour;
Je n'ai fait qu'embellir en ce triste séjour
Où depuis mon départ le sort m'a retenue.

 "Je viens pour rebaiser le plus beau des amants;
Je viens pour remourir dans tes embrassements."
Alors, quand cette idole eut abusé ma flamme,
 Elle me dit: "Adieu! Je m'en vais chez les morts.
Comme tu t'es vanté d'avoir foutu mon corps,
Tu pourras te vanter d'avoir foutu mon âme." [5]

20

Ink on Wings of Paper

ᴏʀ Jᴜᴀɴᴀ'ꜱ ʀᴇʟɪɢɪᴏᴜꜱ ᴘᴏᴇᴍꜱ are few in number, barely sixteen: seven *romances,* four *glosas,* and five sonnets. (I do not count a
brief poem in Latin and its translation into Spanish, two Latin versions
of a *décima* written by a different author, and a translation into Spanish
of a Latin prayer: these are mere exercises.) The total is less than half
the number of her love poems and less than a tenth of the entire body of
her poetry. A closer examination reveals that almost all of the religious
poems are occasional compositions: a tribute to an artist who painted
an image of the Virgin; another to a poet who glorified the Virgin's
apparition on a hill in Tepeyac; sonnets and *glosas* sent to competitions
and contests with devout themes; a "sacred" sonnet that is actually
moral in theme; and poems written to be recited during ecclesiastical
ceremonies (feast days celebrating the Incarnation, Christmas, St. Joseph, St. Peter). That leaves three poems unaccounted for. They are love
poems to God, in *romance* form. They were not published during her
lifetime; Castorena y Ursúa included them among the posthumous
poems in *Fame,* 1700. Some critics suggest that these three *romances*
were written after 1690 and presage her conversion—her renewed professions of faith—in 1693. A questionable judgment: whatever the date
of these poems, we cannot overlook the fact that until 1692 Sor Juana
stood firm before the pressures of Núñez y Miranda and the other prelates who admonished her to abandon letters; in 1693 she yielded, and
from that time until her death, shortly thereafter, she never wrote again.
But there is no doubt that the *romances* are hers: they are closely related
to her secular love poems and also to her theological ideas.

It has often been said, at times with dismay and at times with approval, that the language of mystic poetry, especially Spanish mystic poetry, is indistinguishable from that of secular erotic poetry. Menéndez Pelayo lamented that St. Teresa used expressions appearing in the love songs of fifteenth-century palace troubadours. W. H. Auden, who surely had not read Menéndez Pelayo (and probably not St. Teresa), was similarly scandalized by the excessively sensual expressions of St. John of the Cross, and criticized the sacrilegious lack of distinction between divine ecstasy and the sexual act. Menéndez Pelayo's and Auden's qualms are not properly Christian, but Platonic. The first mystic texts of the West are later than those of the East and were the work not of Christian but of Neoplatonic authors such as Numenius and Plotinus; in them, of course, there was a clear separation of body and soul.[1] But Christianity, when it accepted Platonic philosophy, did not accept its condemnation of the body, as is demonstrated, for example, in the doctrine of the resurrection of the flesh and of the "blessed body." Christian mysticism, although derived from the Platonic, encountered in secular erotic poetry a mine of images and associations. Reading the Song of Songs as a mystic text would have been impossible if Christianity, unlike Platonism, had not been a religion of *incarnation*. The erotic coloration of mystic poetry is not, furthermore, exclusive to the West: it is the same in Sufi mysticism and in the Bhakti of India.

Sor Juana's poems of divine love continue this tradition. As its title says, *romance* 58 "qualifies as loving acts all the acts of Christ," especially in the supreme sacrament of communion. It is not surprising that she calls Christ "Sweet Lover" and says that "he in person entered into" her; what is striking is that most of these images also appear in her best known erotic sonnets. Sor Juana calls Christ "Divine Magnet"; in sonnet 165 her imaginary lover is also a magnet who attracts her with his grace. The lover in sonnet 174 is jealous and, to his misfortune, cannot see into the heart of the woman who adores him. Christ, in contrast, enters her:

> I ask: is it jealousy or love
> that causes this examination?
> For he who inspects everything
> seems to be harboring suspicion.

A "barbaric" question, because the keen-eyed "Divine Lynx," unlike the human lover, enters the heart; for him "are patent the depths of the

Abyss." Christ sees and touches the heart of his beloved but does not require that it rise to her eyes, dissolved into tears. He neither doubts nor experiences jealousy: he loves. *Romance* 57 combines, without much originality but effectively, the traditional motifs of internal struggle. Both witness and actor: "Of myself I am the jailer, I, executioner of me." Divided between the high and the low, she contemplates how

> Virtue and custom are at odds,
> and deep within my heart contend,
> my anguished heart will agonize
> until the two this combat end.

Romance 56 has been widely quoted and studied because it contains a passage—I referred to it in Part Two—in which she alludes to a different love, a mad, profane love, "a bastard love, and of antitheses composed," that died because of its own imperfections. But the poem is worthy of interest for a different reason. As in poem 57, expressions of self-castigation abound, as well as paradoxes that function as rhetorical scourges: "I am executioner of my own desires"; "I die at the hands of the thing I most love"; "the love I hold for him is cause enough for death," and so on. And what is the source of all these self-inflicted torments? The culpable desire to be loved:

> So strong is the appetite
> for being loved, so definite,
> that though we know it profitless,
> we never learn to forfeit it.

Both in the secular love poems and those of loving friendship Sor Juana maintains that the supreme love is love that does not ask to be returned. This idea distinguishes her from those who, like Ficino, believe that perfect love is requited love. The Florentine philosopher says that love of God is the finest love because when we love him we merely return, imperfectly, of course, the boundless love he has for us. But Sor Juana, who has stated the opposite view in her love poems, in this *romance a lo divino* reiterates with even greater emphasis that requited love is "profitless" and, in a different passage, that it "adds nothing." Such statements, when referring to God, were extremely serious. How were they read? Not literally but as paradoxes, hyperboles, and conceits: her century abused the art of cleverness. The concept of unrequited love reappears in the argumentation of her only theological treatise, her critique of Father Vieyra's sermon: the greatest favor God can grant us, his greatest "benefice," is not to grant us any favor. The doctrine of "negative favors" is the equivalent, on the theological level, of that of the perfect love that does not ask to be returned. There is a clear parallelism between her idea of love—divine and profane—and her concept of the relation between God and his creations.

These paradoxes, if we may call them that, verge on heresy. There is an echo of the Aristotelian God who, being the fullness of being, neither needs love nor is capable of loving. According to E. R. Dodds, one of the distinctive characteristics of the mysticism of Plotinus is the unilateral and nonreciprocal nature of ecstasy: "The soul experiences longing (eros) toward the One . . . But the One cannot experience desire, for desire is a mark of incompleteness." Although Plotinus was read in the sixteenth and seventeenth centuries, it is not easy to know whether Sor Juana read him directly; but even if she did not, she knew authors profoundly influenced by Neoplatonism. The difference—an enormous difference—is that Sor Juana transfers self-sufficiency from God to his creation. This idea, contrary to the central concept of Christianity, imposes a heroic and properly superhuman demand on the creation; to love without asking to be loved in return is a heroism that is divine, not human. Carried to its logical conclusion, the equating of unrequited with perfect love is self-deification. No hint of this can be found in Sor Juana's writings; perhaps she herself did not realize the reach of her idea.

In the *romance* I have just referred to, Sor Juana makes a confession that tempers the rigor of her doctrine. Even though love does not need love in return, we seek that reciprocity:

> To have my love return my love
> adds nothing; though I must admit,
> however much that I may strive,
> I cannot help but yearn for it.
> If transgression, I tell of it,
> and if my blame, I shall avow it.

Our yearning to be loved is an imperfection in our nature, a *fault*, in the original sense of a deficiency. We desire because our being is defective; desire is the sign of our insufficiency. The secular love poems do not allude to this imperfection, but the *romance* of divine love does admit that the natural yearning to be loved turns into guilt, punishment, and sorrow. It is not enough for the imperfect creature to give love; this is why he suffers and always will suffer. He will cease to suffer only when he loves without expecting love to be returned. Then, with a pleasure that is beyond description, he has only to close his eyes to see, with the eyes of his soul, the image of the beloved. The image: the idea. Sor Juana implies that, in spite of the creature's imperfection, some few transcend the limitation of wanting to be loved. Those few are the saints and, in the case of human love, the heroic and pure lovers. Although she does not spell it out, she hints that there is a point where human and divine love intersect: the perfect state of the one who loves without hope of having that love returned.

Sor Juana radically alters the condition of God's creature: she posits the heroic possibility of self-sufficiency. In addition, if perfect love does not need to be returned, it attenuates the other end of the love relationship: the person who is loved, whether human or divine. The other—or the Other—withdraws to an inaccessible heaven; he does not cease to exist but his presence fades into radiance, a motionless, unreachable transparency we worship without knowing whether we are heard. The traditional notion of the *other* undergoes a change as radical as that of the creation. In each case Sor Juana expands the limits of human freedom and thus, perhaps unintentionally, reduces the ambit of divine grace. God has made us free, she seems to tell us through these paradoxes and ingenious inventions, and the greatest favor he can grant us is to allow us our freedom. That is: he favors us with his indifference. She does not state it in this way, of course, but this is what she would say if her thought were translated into modern terms. Naturally we must not fall into the temptation to invest her with a modern spirit; Sor Juana is not our contemporary. But neither is she a simple person cut from whole cloth: she is a complex and dramatic being, in conflict with her world and with herself. She is not blind to our innate imperfection, our original defective being. She knows that we are fallen creations, but she also knows—an ancient knowledge more Stoic than Christian—that only the slave can speak of freedom with authority.

The doctrine of the unrequited as the perfect love is the philosophical complement to the poems in which amorous passion is presented as the pursuit of a phantasmal form. According to those poems, love is a mad race that does not end until the one who loves internalizes the desired image. Love is a solitary, imaginative, and self-sufficing activity; it is also a process of purification; the image rarefies until it is impalpable and radiant, like spirits and angelic intelligences. This is the experience defined in the doctrines of nonreciprocal love and negative favors. The shadow, the fiction, the pursued but always elusive image, acquire their full meaning as soon as they are integrated into the theory of unrequited love. All are pieces of the same puzzle. The figure formed by all those pieces is called solitude. It is also called self-sufficiency, and its third name is freedom. The first is existential, the second ontological, and the third moral. These are the three stages on the road to self-realization.

Critics have frequently referred to Sor Juana's "doctrine of love." But that doctrine, if we can call it that, is not, as the critics assume, to be found in the *romances* and sonnets where she expounds a boring erotic casuistry; it is found, scattered and not entirely formulated, in the secular and sacred poems I have mentioned. Dispersion is not incoherence, or lack of unity. On the contrary: the admirable coherence and unity of those poems show that they were a response to her psychological and intellectual circumstances—her cloistered life and her character—and her need to transcend those circumstances and to justify her life and her vocation. I have called attention to her deference to authority, her respect for established opinions, her fear of the Church and the Inquisition, her social conformity. All this was but her persona, her outer half. The other half was her profound determination to be what she wanted to be, her patient and buried quest for a psychic and moral self-sufficiency that would serve as the foundation for her life as a poet and an intellectual. The obstinacy with which she insisted on being herself, her skill and her tact in surmounting obstacles, her fidelity to her inner voices, the secret and proud pertinacity that allowed her to bend without breaking, none of this was rebellion—impossible in her time and her situation—but it was (and is) an example of intelligence and will in the service of internal freedom.

IN THE EARLY EDITIONS of Quevedo, his poems are divided according to theme, each group under the auspices of a muse. Polyhymnia is the patroness of the second group, and "sings moral poetry, that is, poems that reveal and manifest the passions and customs of man, attempting to redress them." A succinct definition that shows clearly the dual nature of these compositions: to reveal basic human nature and to instruct. These moral poems oscillate between introspection and criticism of the world and its crimes, between description of the emotions and inclinations and warning of the inevitable punishment for shortcomings. It is a genre that at one of its extremes borders on the ethical exemplum and at the other on satire. Moral poetry was popular in the seventeenth century, and all the great poets of the Spanish language distinguished themselves in it. They wrote moral poems in every form: *romances, glosas, décimas, silvas,* octaves, tercets, sonnets. It was a genre attuned to baroque genius with its love of wit, aphorism, emblem, *memento mori.* Sor Juana's work, which included almost all the poetic forms of her day, could not have excluded such poems. They form a kind of thoughtful counterpoint to her love poems and the songs to be sung and danced. Moral and moralizing reflection suited her temperament: melancholy led her to question herself; intelligence to present her ideas and experiences in conceits and aphorisms; humor to reflect in her poems the at once grotesque and absurd aspect of the passions.

Romance 2 is a good example of the virtues and defects of the form and, also, of Sor Juana. The caption is picturesque but precise: "She denounces the hydropsically immoderate thirst for learning, which she fears is useless for wisdom and harmful in life." The opening, which I quoted at the close of Part Four, is excellent: "Let us pretend that I am gay, / oh, doleful thought, for a brief time . . ." The tone recalls a *romance* by Lope de Vega, "To my solitudes I go, / from my solitudes I come . . ." The same convention rules both poems: a knowledge that is immemorial, born of experience and not of books, expressed in fluid and sententious quatrains characterized by a certain artlessness. The *romance* by Sor Juana glides along in variations on the unfortunate differences of attitude until, predictably, she comes to the pair that was the prototype of that duality: the smiling Democritus and the weeping Heraclitus. After some twenty repetitious lines, the *romance* recovers its brio. From deploring variety in opinions, the poem moves to vituperation against excessive learning and praise for blessed ignorance:

> How happy is the ignorance
> of one who's wise, naively so;
> he finds, in what would seem a flaw,
> he's blessed for what he does not know!

The ignorance that Sor Juana admires (in her *romance;* not in the reality of her life) is not the *docta ignorantia* of Nicholas of Cusa which results from extensive learning and thinking but that of the uneducated who compensate for lack of knowledge with wise resignation. This is praise of ignorance that could be made only by a learned person, and it ends with a paradox: "Let us learn to be ignorant." The *romance* is a little long, the philosophy a little short.

Some of Sor Juana's moral sonnets are among her finest work. The best is sonnet 145, which appears, and rightfully so, in every anthology. It is a perfect verbal construct; the brilliant and pithy first quatrain is a complete sentence that unfolds into a no less rounded phrase in the second quatrain. The six verses of the tercets are six phrases, an enumeration that increases in intensity until it is dissipated in the final phrase which repeats, and slightly improves upon, a celebrated line by Góngora. The subject of the sonnet is a portrait of Sor Juana:

> This that you gaze on, colorful deceit,
> that so immodestly displays art's favors,
> with its fallacious arguments of colors
> is to the senses cunning counterfeit,
>
>   this on which kindness practiced to delete
> from cruel years accumulated horrors,
> constraining time to mitigate its rigors,
> and thus oblivion and age defeat,
>
>   is but an artifice, a sop to vanity,
> is but a flower by the breezes bowed,
> is but a ploy to counter destiny,
>
>   is but a foolish labor, ill-employed,
> is but a fancy, and, as all may see,
> is but cadaver, ashes, shadow, void.

A monument of fourteen lines, a ladder of conceits that the reader ascends until he reaches the last step, the awaited final surprise. In spite of its rigorous and deliberate impersonality, this sonnet grows out of a deeply personal theme that is often a motif in her poetry: the portrait. In other poems about portraits, the theme is a dialogue between the original and the copy; in this sonnet the portrait becomes a verbal emblem that has pictorial equivalents in contemporary paintings such as Valdés Leal's *Allegory of Vanity* and *Hieroglyph of Death*. No one, to my knowledge, has addressed the question of the title; a pity, because it forces us to read the sonnet as an oblique confession: "She attempts to minimize the praise occasioned by a portrait of herself inscribed by truth, which she calls passion." The truth—in other words, the fidelity—with which her beautiful face has been portrayed on the canvas is a passion, something that passes.

Sonnet 146 is also personal: it is a defense of the love for letters that was the source of the persecutions she suffered. Méndez Plancarte praises the perfect symmetry of the three series of antitheses: "ensuring elegance affect my mind, / not that my mind affect an elegance"; to "expend finances to enrich my mind / and not my mind expend upon finance"; and "consuming all the vanity in life, / and not consuming life in vanity." Sonnet 150 returns to this theme and "demonstrates that for being praised she has been reviled," as the title claims. These two sonnets are additional proof that the story of the difficulties she experienced is not a fantasy of liberals and radicals and that finally difficulties developed into merciless persecution. She complains to fate (to whom else could she complain?): "you gave me reason / only that it be my greatest harm, / applause, only that it give offense." Sonnet 149 expresses the shattering experience I commented on in Part Two, how "spiritedly"— that is, with heroic spirit—she chose a state that was to last throughout her life; more than once she must have repented of having taken the veil. There are two sonnets to the rose on the *carpe diem* theme, intelligent exercises. I am moved by the two final lines of the second (148), direct and strong: "to die while beautiful is finer far / than to suffer the affront of growing old." There are also two sonnets (151 and 152) to Hope, not the theological virtue but the deceiver who, in preserving life, gives us protracted death. The second sonnet (152) has two final lines of a realism that is almost brutal, although not unusual in her poetry, lines that Rubén Darío would have been happy to write: "my two eyes I hold in these two hands, / and only that I touch is what I see."

Sor Juana is the author of four sonnets based on episodes from Roman history (153, 154, 155, 156). The genre had been cultivated by most of the poets of her century; the work of Juan de Arguijo, for example, consists almost exclusively of sonnets with themes taken from the history and mythology of pagan antiquity. The uniqueness of the four sonnets by Sor Juana is that they are dedicated to Roman heroines: two to Lucretia, who was raped by Sextus Tarquinius; one to Julia, the wife of Pompey; and another to Portia, the courageous daughter of Cato and wife of Marcus Brutus. The three women are proverbial examples of virtue and courage; the sonnets Sor Juana devotes to them are still further evidence of her resolute feminism, a feminism *avant la lettre* and morally no less courageous than the acts of her three heroines. The sonnets are four funeral steles, noble but cold. Another sonnet (157) inspired by ancient fable carries a curious title, "She appropriately relates, and inappropriately envies, the tragedy of Pyramus and Thisbe"; it is a rhetorical exercise. Biblical history also inspired sententious and exemplary sonnets. Lope de Vega wrote some that are unforgettable, like the one in which upon the city wall, with the encampment of Holofernes still in shadows, a "radiant" Judith appears "bearing aloft the head." Sor Juana finds inspiration in the New Testament and in Pilate's sentencing of Christ. The first verses of sonnet 207 are a warning to all magistrates: "Pilate seals what he judges another's fate; / instead it is his own."

Her funereal sonnets share much with her moral poetry. Among them is her earliest known poem, a sonnet (185) on the death of Philip IV. The news arrived in May 1666, so she was probably seventeen when she wrote it. Precocious mastery; it is no less skillful than her later sonnets. I have commented on the three sonorous sonnets (190, 191, 192) on the death in 1673 of the Duke de Veragua, and on three others (187, 188, 189), less sculptural, more emotional and translucent, to the memory of her friend Leonor Carreto, Marquise de Mancera (Laura), who died in 1674 on the road to Veracruz, as she was returning to Spain:

> and now will Love lament his bitter fate,
> for if before, in eagerness to see,
> he wished for eyes your charms to contemplate,
> now those eyes will only serve to weep.

THE SOLEMN and the sententious are ceremonial garb. There is another Sor Juana, simple and fluid, plain and ironic. Almost all of her epistolary *romances*—nearly fifty of them—contain ingenious and at times sparkling passages. The catalogue of plays on words, puns, and witty sayings is long, for almost every *romance* contains ironic or playful passages. Even those on more serious themes, such as the poems expressing her affection for María Luisa or her reply to the Peruvian poet who thought she should become a man, are larded with jests and wit. To a visiting poet from Spain who had called her a Phoenix, she replies with a veritable tirade of witticisms. One curious detail reveals her everyday life, its trivial but tedious mundane duties: thanks to her conversion into a Phoenix, "I will not have to grind chocolate / nor be ground down by / any who come to visit me."

Cleverness opens new vistas to the spirit but also confines it in symmetrical cages: it seeks novelty but debases itself in mechanical repetitions. The seventeenth century, so eager to surprise, often bores us. Its marvels are predictable while the spontaneous is really the unexpected. Sor Juana is no exception: we often see her wit as a shallow spectacle without risks, mere gymnastics. The surprise evoked by clever inventions and jests invariably results in a lowering of poetic tension: these are verbal mechanisms cloaking deception and commonplace. They are very different from irony, which is more philosophical than poetic, and from humor in the modern sense, which is the explosion of reason when faced by the unimagined and unimaginable. The anecdote of the Japanese poet Matsuo Basho and his disciple Enamoto Kikaku—they were Sor Juana's contemporaries—is a perfect illustration of the difference between poetry and wit. Kikaku presents his master with this haiku: "Dragonfly / I remove the wings / A pea pod!" Basho shakes his head, and writes: "A pea pod / I place wings on it / A dragonfly!" This is what André Breton called the ascendant metaphor. The conceit and clever invention surprise us; true grace *transports* us, it has wings. But there is more than cleverness in these *romances;* in some—those of love and loving friendship—there is passion, and in almost all there are passages of authentic poetry, that is, grace. In *romance* 50 Sor Juana praises the *romance* itself, and the words she uses have the naturalness and fluidity that she attributes to the poetic form:

> But the *romance* is a demon,
> revealing, in its occult guile,
> in every stanza, strength and force,
> in every line, a binding spell.
> Such is its suppleness of style,
> our pleasure in its tyranny,
> that what seems only to invite,
> compels, instead, with mastery.
> It has a proud humility
> that in the clamor of retreat,
> surrenders, that it may prevail
> clad in the trappings of defeat.

Sor Juana's last poem was a *romance* (51), found in her cell, says Castorena y Ursúa, "in draft and lacking the finishing touches." It was written "in recognition of the inimitable pens of Europe, who enhanced her work with their praise." The title alludes to the twelve poets and seven theologians who praised her, at times effusively, in the second volume of her *Works* (Seville, 1692). The book must have arrived in Mexico at the end of that year, so that the poem dates from the last months of 1692 or the first months of 1693. It therefore immediately precedes her alleged conversion. In addition to its biographical interest, this poem contains four lines that suggest the seductive attraction we feel in her poetry and her person:

> What are those magical infusions
> of the herbalist Indians
> of my land, that spread their spell
> through all the letters of my pen?

This seems the appropriate moment to mention the poem that saved Sor Juana from total oblivion during the two centuries—the eighteenth and nineteenth—in which her work was forgotten: the *redondillas* in which she censures men and defends women. This satirical poem has never lacked for readers and is considered one of the central pieces of her feminism. As I shall discuss that subject later in reference to the *Response,* now I will only say in passing that the satire criticizing men must be viewed within the context of the literature of her century: it was a reply to numberless satires of women circulating in her time, many of them written by famous poets. From this point of view, her satire is, once again, a literary exercise: Sor Juana wants to excel in this genre too. This does not mean she was indifferent to the theme itself. On the contrary, she was supremely aware of the problems her sex created for her, and suffered greatly because of them. Neither can it be doubted that more than once she rebelled and protested: the *redondillas* criticizing men are but further proof of her feminism. But could one be a *feminist* in the seventeenth century? At any rate, her feminism—to call it that— is not in the modern mold, even though its root cause was the same, the inferior status of women in society. Sor Juana's satire was a spontaneous and isolated response to a historical situation. In this, as in so many other things, her attitude was unique.

The poetic merits of this piece are doubtful. Not surprisingly, a critic of a previous generation, caught between two extremes—the radicalism of "pure poetry," and surrealism—found that the verses on "Misguided men, who will chastise / a woman when no blame is due," are prosaic, "her poorest work."[2] Today we have turned away from such unforgiving condemnations, although I continue to believe that any confusion between poetry and prose is fatal. Prose is the written word, and poetry is rhythmic speech. Prose is inherently discursive and that is why the militant and ideological poetry of our time has been and is discursive.

Poetry is nurtured not in written prose but in the rhythms of everyday speech or, as Eliot said, in the "music of conversation." And fortunately Sor Juana's poem, though discursive, is spoken, not written, literature— spoken in octosyllabic lines in a lively form that has survived since the fifteenth century, the *redondilla*. The theme is as ancient as the form in which it is expressed: who is to blame, "she who sins and takes the pay, / or he who pays her for the sin"? Sor Juana's defense of her sex is not ideological; it is based in the morality of the era and in common sense. It grows out of a popular topic: erotic relationships outside matrimony are sinful, but why do men insist on blaming women? Who seduces them, who compels them? Does not the act almost inevitably result from masculine initiative? It is hypocrisy to accuse an accomplice of the crime that both commit.

Sor Juana's arguments—far removed from contemporary feminism— are not new; scholars have cited many precedents in earlier Spanish poetry. Nonetheless, the great and true novelty is that a woman and not a man was the author of those satirical *redondillas*. In this sense, the poem was a historical watershed, a beginning: for the first time in the history of our literature a woman is speaking in her own name, defending her sex and, with grace and intelligence, using the same weapons as the detractors of her sex, accusing them of the very vices they impute to women. In this Sor Juana was well ahead of her time; there is nothing similar in literature by women in seventeenth-century France, Italy, or England. It is even more noteworthy that this satire should have been written in New Spain, a closed, peripheral society under two zealot powers, the Catholic Church and the Spanish monarchy.

Spanish culture in that century was markedly masculine. In Spain not even aristocratic women could enjoy the privileges of the *grandes dames* of France. Poets made a cult of the ideal lady but were insensitive to woman's true situation. Seventeenth-century Spanish literature is not rich in female characters; of course, there are women in Cervantes and in Lope de Vega—sometimes adorable, at other times horrible creatures. But these are isolated cases. Quevedo was an extreme, not an exception: the fervent Platonist who wrote the sonnet "Eternal Love That Endures Beyond Death" was also the raving misogynist who said, "After a month, any woman is a plague." It is surprising that in such a society, with its combined Arabic and Roman-Christian heritage, Sor Juana could have published her satire. More surprising still is that it could have been read with sympathy. But it was an isolated outburst that had no sequels until the twentieth century.

Sor Juana composed a number of epigrams. They are cruel and, unlike "Misguided men . . . ," attack not customs or opinions but individuals. I have mentioned the epigram that is her response to someone who had alluded to her illegitimacy: she may not have had an honorable father, "but far more generous was your mother, / offering many a likely father." This epigram is proof that her origins were common knowledge in Mexico: the version that portrays her father as a penniless Basque hidalgo was a compassionate lie that had broader acceptance in the Old Spain than the New. Another epigram has as its target an ugly woman who boasts of her beauty, to whom Sor Juana says, insolently, that with such a face she will never win a prize for beauty, but will be guaranteed a prize for chastity. A strange insult from the lips of a nun. The remaining epigrams, directed at a drunken aristocrat and two military men, are similarly acerbic. These poems, revealing a very sharp-tongued Sor Juana, were published in the second volume of her *Works* (1692), compiled from the manuscripts that she herself sent to Seville from Mexico. Thus we are not talking about poems that circulated *sub rosa*. The same is true of the series of burlesque sonnets published in the first volume of her poems (1690). The poems appeared with her approval and through her initiative. Probably, in the light of her vital need to write in all literary forms, she considered them a demonstration of her ability to undertake all the genres then in vogue, even the most audacious.

The sonnets, according to the title, were written during a "domestic respite," a social gathering. Sor Juana used a pattern of end rhymes undoubtedly proposed by the guests at such intimate occasions. Méndez Plancarte theorizes that these poems, "because of their saltiness, grossness, and impropriety," must date from the time when she was lady-in-waiting to the Marquise de Mancera, between 1665 and 1667. The theory is groundless and also unlikely: it would have been even more inappropriate had the sonnets been composed by a young girl of seventeen or eighteen who had been placed in the care of the Vicereine. It is more credible that they were written when she was a mature woman, during one of those social gatherings in the locutory of San Jerónimo for which she ground chocolate and during which, as Castorena y Ursúa records, riddles were solved and poems improvised. The sonnets are *burlescos,* not only in the Spanish sense of being humorous and witty, but also in the English sense of "burlesque," which along with the grotesque includes the licentious. It is interesting that they were written in a convent and published as the work of a nun. This is yet another example of the conjunction of opposites so prized in her time. The sonnets have a certain low humor, less caustic and somber than Quevedo's, but with a sauciness not at all nunlike and in lines suitable for reciting in a tavern:

> Though, Teresilla, you weave quite a spell,
> you treat your poor Camacho like a fool,
> and you'll give a man, through guile, a "little jewel"
> who had thought his reputation nonpareil.
>   Your love sets so many tasks he must fulfill,
> the fellow's loaded down like a pack mule
> (though with horns like those he'd make a better bull—
> they've grown so long he stoops to cross the sill).
>   As at sleight of hand you now have such great skill,
> and at getting out of tangles are the best,
> when finally that bundle you expel,
>   you will convince him, though he may suspect,
> that only to help multiply his yield,
> with neighbor's seed, his harvest you twice blessed.

Among the "portraits" I alluded to elsewhere, the one of Lisarda (214) stands out. Written in rhymed couplets like the English heroic couplet, the poem, according to its title, "paints with playful inspiration, in the manner of the famous poem of Jacinto Polo, a beauty." This kind of composition, with its random alternation of seven- and eleven-syllable lines, was used especially in the theater, another indication that Sor Juana was an avid play reader. The similarity of this poem to one by Polo de Medina ("A Gentleman Portrays a Mulatto Woman, His Lady") is undeniable, but it should also be noted that the genre was popular at the time; Sor Juana was following a convention, then, more than an isolated model.[3] The Lisarda of the portrait, like Belilla, was a young girl; according to the final lines, "For twenty birthdays she was fêted in May; / by Juana Inés de la Cruz she was portrayed." The poem pokes fun at the terms the Gongorists and euphuists used to describe their ladies. This type of satire used the euphuistic style to caricature the style itself: like mythological parody, it was a self-parodying variation frequently employed by euphuistic poets themselves. It was a literary game, not an aesthetic opinion. Sor Juana's poem is rich in vivid and witty images; it is also tiresome. It is not possible—at least, not to modern taste—to be entertaining for four hundred verses, even at the expense of the affectations of mannerist writers. Because affectation—even of simplicity—is always tedious, I fear I am being unjust: there is charm in some passages, and imagination (Lisarda's waist is "so fine / that it is pictured in just one line"); there are tender Mexican diminutives; and there are moments when good sense makes good poetry, as in this fragment on Lisarda's right hand:

> It is supremely white and fair in tone,
> being made of flesh and bone . . .
> It is esteemed, this valiant hand,
> because it clasps, and not because it's grand.

There is, finally, supreme praise from one woman to another, praise of Lisarda's clothing and bearing:

> An elegant attire, but not affected,
> that seems careless, but is care perfected;
> the special way in which this girl denotes
> her starchy scorn, her swishing petticoats
> sweeping up swains
> collected from the dust of the terrain.

Several times I have mentioned the "portrait" of Belilla (71), a song as light as a fluffy cloud and as slim as only a fifteen-year-old girl can be. Each strophe has a graceful turn of phrase; the last is a surprising pirouette:

> This is not a portrait
> of our Little Bel—
> not even a sketch:
> it's just a draft.[4]

In Mexican poetry and on this theme—the sketch of an adolescent girl in the sunlight, like a budding young tree—I find only a few lines that can compare to Sor Juana's. They are by Amado Nervo: "So blonde is this young girl that / she is invisible in sunlight."

The poem about Belilla and its counterpart, the satire of Gila (72) I mentioned earlier, bring me to the six songs (64–69) to accompany regional dances and tunes that were written for a festival in San Jerónimo honoring the Count and Countess de Paredes. (It is a curious fact that worldly dances were performed in convent patios.) They are courtly verses, stiff and formal. Better than these songs are "Three Lyrics to Be Sung" (8, 9, 10)—three delicate, translucent verbal outpourings. In the first a young girl sings, and the sound of her voice sets the stars in motion and resolves into harmony the discord of the elements.

> The great sea admires the Siren,
> ocean nymphs their voices raise,
> offering on tongues of water
> crystalline songs of praise.

These songs are the point of contact between Sor Juana's personal lyrics and those for a public audience, the liturgical *villancicos* that were sung on holy days in the cathedral of Mexico City and the other great churches of New Spain.

21

Music Box

POETIC FORMS ARE LIKE PLANTS: some are native to the soil they grow in and others are the result of grafting and transplanting. The sonnet and terza rima are Spanish by naturalization, the *romance* and *villancico* by birth. The last of these, according to a noted specialist in metrics, Tomás Navarro Tomás, comes from Galician-Portuguese *cantigas de estribillo*, which derived from the Mozarabic *zéjel*. From the medieval period to the twentieth century, the poetic fortune of the *villancico* has been extraordinary.

In the fifteenth century the *villancico* split away from the *cantigas de estribillo* to acquire its own form. Despite changes over the centuries, the form has survived to our day. The basic model is the following: a poem in short lines, almost always eight or six syllables, composed of a two- or four-line *estribillo* (refrain) that sets the theme; a variation or *mudanza* (change), ordinarily a quatrain; and a *vuelta* (envoi) that repeats the *estribillo* in whole or in part. In its beginnings the word *villancico* did not designate a specific poetic form but, rather, referred in broader terms to compositions in the manner of the songs sung by peasants and villagers. They were both amatory and devout in theme. In the sixteenth century, and now under that name, "the *villancico* became the most prevalent form of the lyric song."[1] The themes continued to be those of secular love or, as in the case of St. Teresa, divine love. *Villancicos* also appear as insertions in plays and pastoral novels. The seventeenth century is the high noon of the form, and some of the *villancicos* of Lope, Góngora, and Valdivielso are among the purest lyric poems in the Spanish tongue.

Complexity and simplicity, refinement and spontaneity: the charm of the *villancico* resides perhaps in this mixture of conflicting tonalities. There is an incessant swinging back and forth, especially during the Baroque period, between the secular amatory and the religious, the popular and the erudite: a bullfight is transformed into theological allegory; with the panache of a lady of Madrid, the Virgin treads on the head of the serpent; and St. Peter wanders the alleyways of Rome cutting a swath like a swordsman. During the second half of the seventeenth century in Spain, there are no figures comparable to Góngora, Lope, or even Valdivielso. In contrast, during those same years in New Spain the *villancico* was reaching a second but no less resplendent high noon in the works of Sor Juana. Hers was not merely a continuation, it was a rebirth.

The *villancico* came early to these shores, along with other poetic forms. The Franciscans presented in Spanish and in Indian tongues *autos, coloquios,* and other theatrical works on religious themes. The first recorded *villancico* is one sung during an *auto* illustrating the fall of Adam and Eve, performed in Tlaxcala in 1538:

> Why did she eat,
> the first wedded woman,
> why did she eat
> fruit that was forbidden?[2]

In the second half of the sixteenth century a poet of real merit appeared, Hernán González de Eslava; *villancicos* and religious songs make up the best of his work. Following him, the *villancico* became enormously popular in New Spain.

Almost all the poets who wrote in Sor Juana's time composed *villancicos,* but the truth is that none of the others could compare with her; they were not peers or rivals, only a chorus. But it was a chorus of melodic voices and well-trained throats: those poets were heirs to a century and a half of great poetry, from Garcilaso to Calderón. As skillful versifiers, masters of a repertory of images, figures, metaphors, and mythological allusions and a vocabulary of great richness, it was not difficult for them, even with moderate ability, to achieve a poetic level that Spanish neoclassical and romantic writers never reached. In fact, Mexico and the entire Hispanic world was not again to see writing of such purity and elegance until the Spanish-American *modernista* poets at the turn of this century. In this sense, even if not in philosophy or science, the literary atmosphere surrounding Sor Juana was beneficial and stimulating.

For the Spanish American poets of that generation Góngora's aesthetic revolution was still taking place, a revolution also indebted to his rivals and enemies, Lope de Vega and Quevedo. This is another of the notable differences between Spain and America. Espinosa Medrano, known as El Lunarejo, had written in Lima, "We criollos arrive late." But that tardiness was at the same time a sign of vitality: the criollos were younger. For that reason this was in Mexico a period of great experimentation, especially in the field of metrics. Sor Juana surpassed her contemporaries in this area, as she surpassed almost all the poets of the seventeenth century. In preparing a summary of the metrics and changes in Spanish verse during the Golden Age, Navarro Tomás lists the great innovators. Significantly, he omits Quevedo and Calderón, reducing the names to four: Cervantes (primarily as a humorist in verse), Góngora, Lope de Vega, and Sor Juana Inés de la Cruz.

UNTIL EARLY IN THE SEVENTEENTH CENTURY, as now, the word *villancico* referred to the Christmas carols of the shepherds of Bethlehem. This was the mode in which Góngora and Lope de Vega excelled. But around 1630, says Méndez Plancarte, the term was restricted to the compositions sung at matins on religious holidays, "leaving the simple generic name 'lyrics' for all other forms."[3] Matins are divided into three nocturnes, each consisting of three psalms. *Villancicos* adopted the same division: three nocturnes of three lyrics each, although often the last lyric was replaced by the Te Deum. Thus, each of these *villancicos* was a set or series of eight or nine lyrics. In Mexico the custom of singing *villancicos* of three nocturnes to celebrate matins on liturgical holidays goes back to the second half of the seventeenth century. The cathedrals of Mexico City, Puebla, Oaxaca, and Valladolid (Morelia), among others, celebrated all important annual holy days with these songs. The frequency of the celebrations, the accompanying pomp, and the number of faithful who attended meant there had to be a permanent organization in charge of them. The *villancicos* were a spectacle—and spectacles, besides authors, actors, and audience, require stage directors, administrators, and managers: a bureaucracy.

The institutional aspect of the *villancicos* has not been studied by historians of New Spain, regrettably. Such ceremonies fulfilled a religious function but also had social and, in the strict sense of the word, political uses. Religious, patriotic, or revolutionary holidays are ceremonies in which a society, by means of symbol or image, is made one with itself. They are a joining together of the elements that compose the society into a whole that is also a *unit:* I mean, a united whole. But they are also the society's reunion with its past—with its dead, its heroes, its saints, its founders—and with its future: its tomorrow in history and in the immeasurable time of the beyond. In New Spain, essentially a heterogeneous society, as much for its class differences as for its diversity of pasts, beliefs, and races—Spanish, criollo, Indian, mestizo, black—religious holidays were ceremonies of celebration and participation. Celebration of the principles that supposedly gave the society its being, and of the figures in whom those principles were embodied; participation of each group and of each element in a totality that encompassed all differences and annulled all hierarchies. And also a celebration of the Other, the divine, and participation in the *other* reality, the supraterrestrial. In the darkness of the church, a darkness dimly lit by flickering candles and the dawn breaking in the east, a multitude communed with a reality both marvelous and familiar: warrior angels, dancing virgins, sainted theologians, Indians and blacks, Basques and Moors, devils and lawyers. Pedantry, chanting, and soaring flight.

The existence of a permanent administration responsible for organizing such ceremonies required sufficient funds to maintain it and to pay all those who carried out their assigned tasks: poets, musicians, singers, printers of texts (booklets were illustrated with vignettes and other engravings), those responsible for decorating the altars with flowers and for the lighting, those who hung the tapestries and raised the standards, doorkeepers and ushers. None of this has been researched. We do not know how much poets were paid, or musicians, or whether some of them were permanently attached to any of the churches or cathedrals. But some basic information is available. The September 1730 issue of the *Gazeta de México* contains some interesting facts about the matins foundations of the Mexico City cathedral. The *Gazeta* lists the wealthy donors, mentions the sums they contributed to their foundations, and names the holiday to which each sum was designated: matins for the Nativity of Our Lady, six thousand pesos and three hundred in revenues donated by Don García de Legaspi y Velasco; matins for the Conception, five thousand pesos and two hundred fifty in revenues donated by someone already familiar to us, Don Juan de Chavarría, the man who provided Sor Juana with a sum of gold on the day of her profession as a nun; matins for Our Lady of Guadalupe, eight thousand pesos and four hundred in revenues donated by Don Bartolomé de Quesada; the list continues, to include all the liturgical holidays celebrated in the cathedral. The *Gazeta* mentions eleven foundations—two sponsored by Chavarría—each receiving from four to eight thousand pesos, plus revenues, except for one endowed with twenty thousand pesos and another with twelve thousand. Property and houses that produced rental income were given as well as cash.

Seventeenth-century foundations were not very different from our modern ones. Without them, the continuity of the *villancicos* would have been impossible: they were sung in the churches of New Spain from 1650 through the first third of the eighteenth century. These poems and tunes were, yes, the expression of poets' and musicians' fervor, but they were equally the result of generous financial patronage. Between 1676 and 1691 Sor Juana wrote twelve complete sets of *villancicos,* each composed of eight, nine, or more lyrics. She also composed thirty-two lyrics for the dedication of the church of the nuns of San Bernardo, three for the holy day of Our Lady, four for the Incarnation, two for the Nativity, and four for a nun's profession. In addition to all these there are another ten sets of *villancicos* that can be attributed to her and in all likelihood are hers. She wrote two hundred thirty-two of these poems. To this truly impressive quantity must be added frequency: there was scarcely a year, following 1676, when she did not write at least one set of *villancicos* and sometimes two or even three. Finally, there is geographical range: she did not limit herself to writing for the Mexico City cathedral and other churches of that city; she wrote nine series for the cathedral in Puebla and one for the Oaxaca cathedral. When we add the courtly poems—*romances, décimas,* sonnets, *bailes, loas*—we see that more than two-thirds of all that she wrote was commissioned. It is paradoxical that this literature addressed to the general public was an often enigmatic literature filled with recondite mythological allusions and embellished with displays of erudition.

Sor Juana's poetic activity was not unrewarded: the court paid her for her *loas, bailes,* and spectacles, and the Church compensated her for the *villancicos* and sacred lyrics. The income she collected from this writing helps to explain how over the years her financial condition passed from poverty and insecurity to comfort. But financial advantages, great as they were, were not the only or the most important rewards: writing for the Church provided prestige and power. What I have said about her influence at court and her use of this influence to benefit her convent and her own situation can be applied, with some reservations, to her relationship with the Church. Less centralized than that of the state, the power of the Church was distributed among the major prelates and the religious orders. This division of power and influence protected Sor Juana from the hostility of Aguiar y Seijas, at least until 1692. A nun devoted to secular literature and enmeshed in an active literary and worldly life had constantly to confront her superiors, those outside as well as within the convent. This is why she sought always to win the protection of Princes of the Church—a subject to which we will return. For now, I want to emphasize simply the material and political aspects of her collaboration with the cathedral of Mexico City and other churches, especially the cathedral in Puebla, whose Bishop, Manuel Fernández de Santa Cruz, was her friend and protector. The ambition of so many ideologues and revolutionary leaders—social poetry, art at the service of the people, and so on—was actually realized by the poets of New Spain, except that social poetry did not represent criticism and opposition but rather poetry celebrating the social order and its ideology. Official poetry was the result, then as now, of a system of rewards and punishments: on the one hand, the protection of the palace and the Church; on the other, censure and the Inquisition. The idea of the "organic intellectual" propounded by modern revolutionaries was a reality in the seventeenth century. In reaction to that reality there arose, in the eighteenth century, the idea of the critical intellectual, without a Church and without a lord.

WHEN SOR JUANA BEGAN TO COMPOSE *villancicos,* the genre was already established and it was not possible to change either the structure imposed by Church ritual or its literary and musical conventions. But even though she was not free to modify the form, with her imagination she gave it new life and with her grace gave it flight. Creative joy animates many of these poems—the almost physical pleasure born of doing things well. We sense that she enjoyed composing those singing, dancing verses. It is remarkable that using well-worn materials she was able to build such light and airy constructs. Frequently the first *villancico* of the first nocturne announces the theme and summons the audience, like a street vendor attracting the attention of people in the plazas and fairs. The tone is imperative and promises marvels, as we can see in these examples from several poets of New Spain: "Gather round, see this burning bush / that blazes, that glows, but is not consumed"; "Hurry, hurry, hurry"; "Make way, make way!"; "Pause a while, lend an ear, don't miss this, hey, there!" Sor Juana manages, while respecting the formula, to instill new freshness in the lines, as in this unusual combination of meters (poem lxvii)[4] with an echo of Góngora's *Polifemo:*

> To sing the glory of divine Pedro,
> come one, come all,
> those that come to a whistle
> or live in a sheepfold!

Or in these *seguidillas* (279) in which a blessed event, more glimpsed than seen, rises like an exhalation from the depths of time:

> Listen, hear me a moment,
> for I want to sing,
> about the blessed Moment that
> was outside of time!

The basic characteristic of the *villancico* is the blending of disparate elements. This blending at times produces the marvelous and at others the grotesque. Valdivielso's shepherdesses flirt with the Holy Spirit as they would with a lover:

> My beloved Husband,
> how beautiful your body.
> I adore its elegance.

But fifty years later a mischievous girl, Marizápalos, appears in a León Marchante *villancico* and meets the recently incarnated Jesus. She can think of no words to utter except, as she is dressed in green, this culinary joke: "if this is the night in which the Flesh triumphs, / it is not out of line that I bring the parsley." A *de*scending metaphor, Basho and Breton would say in unison. Sor Juana almost always avoids such risks: when she is on the verge of falling into the puddle, she spins away and continues along the edge of a reflection. The Virgin Mary, to whom she dedicated several sets of *villancicos*, appears in one of them as a superior student of theology: she studied all subjects, even, Sor Juana adds with wit, some she studied in herself, such as *de Incarnatione*. Mary appears later in varying guises: as the mistress of the Supreme Choir of the universe, directing the choirs "through the signs of the stars"; as a "female knight-errant"—"Bradamante in bravery, / Angelica in beauty"—torn from a page of *Orlando furioso*, "golden locks" floating on the air, surrounded by as many abject Rolands as hairs on her head; as a "great astronomer," and herself a star that "sheds beneficent influences over the Earth," outwitting even the sun and the moon; finally, in an unforgettable fantasy (228), as the "holy herb": the *Sánalo-todo* (Heal-all Herb), *Celidonia* (Greater Celadine) that "clears the sight"; *Mejor-Ana* (marjoram, and Ana, for the mother of Mary), and *Siempre-Viva* (Eternal Flower):

> No one need, from this day on, fear deadly poison,
> for with this antidote, none can be fatal.

If the Virgin is a specialist in theology, St. Peter is a student of Latin prosody and metrics, expert in syllabic quantities, in verse feet and caesuras, although, remembering that he thrice denied Christ, Sor Juana comments with irony (poem 246):

> he started in *heroic verse,*
> thrice did falter,
> then, limpingly, did imitate
> pentameter.

An obligatory reference is the malicious allusion to poor Simon Magus, customary since the Acts of the Apostles—"With an ungainly air he flies through the air"—as well as the rejoicing in his fall, which is compared to a "line of *pie quebrado*" (broken [poetic] foot). What is most surprising is to see St. Peter as a fencing master who outfences the famous Spanish masters, Carranza and Pacheco. Naturally, Sor Juana takes advantage of the occasion to recall the "act" of the apostle who struck off the ear of Malchus, servant to the high priest.

But there are serious moments, as when she refers in poem 302 to the passage in Matthew in which an angel appears to Joseph in a dream, bidding him not to abandon a pregnant Mary, "for that which is conceived in Her is of the Holy Ghost":

> Jealousy with dream,
> dream with jealousy,
> in Joseph alone
> are not contradictory.

Sometimes the lyrics have genre subtitles: *jácara, ensalada, canario, cardador,* and others. The *jácara* is a *romance* written in the language of the *jaques,* that is, braggarts and rogues; the *canario* and *cardador* were dances, and the *ensalada* (salad) was a mixture of meters and, especially, of modes of speech of blacks, Moors, Basques, Galicians, and Portuguese. In New Spain the Indians, and Indian language, took the place occupied by the Moors in Spain. A *tocotín* contained lyrics written in Nahuatl, or was colored with Aztec phrases. The tradition of the *tocotín*—probably an Indian dance—originated in the earliest evangelizing theatrical works of the missionaries. There is a *tocotín* (224) in the first set of *villancicos* written by Sor Juana on the theme of the Assumption, in 1676. The poem is written entirely in Nahuatl, but in the Castilian style of six-syllable lines of assonant rhyme.

> *Tla ya timohuica,*
> *totlazo Zuapilli,*
> *maca ammo, Tonantzín,*
> *titechmoilcahuíliz.*

Ángel M. Garibay made a literal translation: "If you go now / our beloved Lady, / do not, our Mother / forget us." The poem, says Garibay, is written "with notable grace and fluidity." Probably Sor Juana called on the help of someone who knew Nahuatl well. Here is still further indication that the composition of *villancicos* was not a solitary task but the work of a group; occasional collaborators were involved in addition to poets, musicians, and singers. The same was true of the courtly *bailes*, *sainetes*, and *loas*. Sor Juana's life was not strictly that of an anchorite.

Góngora had wrought marvels with the speech of Moors and blacks; the wonderful onomatopoeia of his *villancicos* foreshadows, and at times surpasses, the "black poetry" of modern writers such as Palés Matos, Ballagas, and Nicolás Guillén. Sor Juana's ear, and her oral gifts, rival those of Góngora, as is seen in these lively, inventive, and curiously modern resonances (258):

> *Ha, ha, ha!*
> *Monan vuchilá!*
> *He, he, he,*
> *cambulé!*
> *Gila coro,*
> *Gulungú, gulungú,*
> *hu, hu, hu!*
> *Menguiquilá,*
> *ha, ha, ha!*

How must these syllables have sounded sung beneath the vaulted ceiling of the criollo cathedral? In another *estribillo* (241) onomatopoeia is joined to black speech with comic and tender effects:

> Tumba, la-lá-la; tumba, la-lé-le;
> wheh dey be Pete, dey won' be no slave-girl!
> Tumba, tumba, la-lé-le; tumba, la-lá-la,
> wheh dey be Pete, no slave-girl dey'll be!

The Latin of the *ensaladas* is an ecclesiastical Latin with Spanish prosody and metrics; it is also a hybrid Latin studded with Spanish words, the macaronic Latin of students and sacristans. Similarly, Sor Juana's Portuguese verses are actually written in Spanish with a Portuguese accent: "Timoneyro, que governas / la nave do el Evangelio . . ." (Helmsman, you who steer / the ship of the Gospel . . . , 249). She always prided herself on her Basque heritage, so that when in an *ensalada* a Basque sings in a harsh voice we are warned that no one is to whisper, "for that is the [tangled] tongue / of my grandfathers."

Sor Juana had the ear of a dramatic poet, and may have been the first to reproduce the speech of Mexican *rancheros,* as we see in this *copla* (lviii) in which two country men enter with "jingling footsteps," singing "without the *estribillo*" (the refrain) because "up to now their feet / have disdained *estribillos*" (a pun on *estribos,* stirrups):

> God bless you, my little beauty,
> off on your way to see God!
> I think you're just as pretty
> as a picture from Michoacán.
> You rise up tall like the palm tree,
> just like the plane tree you tower,
> Those Uruápans could never catch you
> if they chased you for an hour.

The real *ensalada* is tossed not from meters or dialects but with fresh lettuce from Toluca, oil, vinegar, salt, and lime. Yet we should not take too much pride in the products of our land, as Sor Juana says in poem 311:

> Because I am so spicy,
> I like to bring salt,
> five hundred varieties
> my voice will exalt.
> You may have a fine voice, but
> don't be conceited,
> for the salt of Mexico
> is *tequesquite* [saltpeter].

Villancico 312, from a series about St. Catherine, the martyr of Alexandria, is as melodic and meandering as the river itself:

> Be calm, O sinuous Nile,
> soothe your musical waters,
> slowly, slowly,
> pause, and rejoice in seeing
> the beauty you make fertile:
> of the earth and the heavens, the Rose and Star.
>   For her, the Rose, sacred Nile,
> bid your sounding waters go
> singing, singing,
> in concerted harmony
> your swift-moving waves will be
> syllables, language, numbers, and voices.

Villancico xxxiv contains lines in *ecos*, a form also found in the *loas:*

> The waxing Moon, how beautiful,
> with grace that none can disavow,
> goes, to the rhythm of the day,
> gliding,
>   gilding,
>   golden hours.[5]

There is a little of everything in the *villancicos.* The eleven-syllable *romance* typical of the time appears alongside traditional *romances* of eight- and six-syllable lines. One of these deserves separate commentary. It is the *villancico* (315) that begins the second nocturne of the set of eleven lyrics dedicated to St. Catherine, sung in the cathedral of Oaxaca in 1691. Those lyrics, because of their fervent and militant feminism and because of the date and the place where they were sung, will be given separate analysis when we come to Sor Juana's final crisis (1690–1695). *Villancico* 315 is, however, noteworthy for a different reason. It begins by alluding to the translation of the Bible made at the order of Ptolemy Philadelphus by seventy wise men in Alexandria in the third century before Christ. Sor Juana comments that if a pagan king had instructed that the Holy Book be translated, he did it through divine inspiration, thus unknowingly preparing for Catherine's defense of Scripture centuries later. In this passage, faithful to her "Egyptian" hermeticism, Sor Juana underlies the special place ancient Egypt held in the divine plan:

> And who could doubt the plan, it was the cross
> Judea and the Roman Empire scorned,
> that Egypt, among all its hieroglyphs,
> upon the breast of Serapis adored.

Sor Juana is alluding, elliptically, to the cross (or crosses; the number varies according to the author) found among the hieroglyphs of the Serapeum, the sanctuary of Serapis in Alexandria, which was a wonder of the ancient world. The cult of Serapis, a Hellenized form of Osiris and Apis, was founded by Ptolemy Soter in the fourth century B.C. The Serapeum was destroyed in 391, a barbaric act of the monk and Archbishop Theophilus during the cruel reign of the Christian Emperor Theodosius.[6] Actually, that cross is nothing more than the ancient hieroglyph *ankh*, a cross shaped like a T with a small loop or circle at the top: the *crux ansata* or ansate cross. It was later used by Coptic Christians, and also by St. Anthony, the anchorite of the *Thebaid*. Sor Juana writes that the Egyptian cross was engraved on the chest of Serapis. She thus accepts a very ancient tradition, but one whose ramifications should have disturbed a Christian conscience. In fact, among the ancient Egyptians the *crux ansata* was a phallic sign signifying eternal life and was an attribute of certain divinities, as seen in representations of Isis, Osiris, and other deities. Although Sor Juana could not have been unaware of those associations of the *crux ansata,* motivated by her desire to exhibit her knowledge and, at the same time, obeying a deeper impulse in a poem of fervent feminism and during a time of bitter dispute, she evokes the ancient Egyptian symbol. Was she, to use current jargon, obeying an unconscious urge? Or was it conscious defiance?

According to Marsilio Ficino, the influence of the heavens is greater when its light descends in rays perpendicular to the cardinal points, thus forming a cross. That is why, he adds, the Egyptians used the sign of the cross that was for them the bearer of long life, and that was also why they engraved it on the breast of the god Serapis. For Ficino the *crux ansata* was a powerful astral talisman. But, he adds immediately, the Egyptians unknowingly adored the sign because it was a prophecy of the coming of Christ.[7] Giordano Bruno took this idea but radically, and perilously, transformed it. Some of the documents of Bruno's trial reveal that he believed that the Christians had surreptitiously appropriated an ancient and powerful Egyptian talisman. A fellow prisoner informed the inquisitors that he had heard Bruno say that "the sign [of the cross] was sculptured on the breast of the goddess Isis, and . . . was stolen by the

Christians from the Egyptians." During his interrogation, Bruno said: "I think I have read in Marsilio Ficino that the virtue and holiness of this character [the cross] is much more ancient than the time of the Incarnation of Our Lord, and that it was known in the time in which the religion of the Egyptians flourished, about the time of Moses, and that this sign was affixed to the breast of Serapis, and that the planets and their influences have more efficacy . . . when they are at the beginning of the cardinal signs."[8] Bruno believed that the *crux ansata* was the "true cross" and that it had magical powers, a belief that sealed his doom.

Kircher records in his *Oedipus Aegyptiacus* (1652) the story of the Egyptian cross graven on the breast of Serapis. He states that Hermes Trismegistus himself invented this form of the cross, which he calls the *crux hermetica*. He also cites the passage from *De vita coelitus comparanda* in which Ficino speaks of its astral and talismanic powers: the *crux hermetica* is a sign that, as it reproduces the form in which the solar rays intersect the cardinal points, creates a powerful talisman.[9] In the second volume of *Oedipus Aegyptiacus* there is an engraving (p. 206) representing a *crux ansata:* each bar terminates in one of the signs of the four elements, the cross rests on a serpent, and the Ptolemaic universe is suspended within the ring, which is transfixed by a horn, the emblem of Isis. Of course, Kircher does not allude in any way to the episode of Bruno; he, too, and with greater reason than Sor Juana, "wished no quarrel with the Holy Office." He consistently strove to stay within the bounds of orthodoxy, which is why he never accepted the new astronomy and why from time to time he denounced in his writings the "impious doctrines of Hermes Trismegistus."[10] In his attempt to present Egypt as the origin of all civilizations, Kircher finds the *crux ansata* even in the *lingam,* the phallic symbol of the Hindu god Shiva, whom he calls Insuren (Osiris). In this "infamous and monstrous disguise," the divine sign is adored in India. Sor Juana alludes to all this in the following quatrain from her *villancico* to St. Catherine (315):

> And Catherine inherited with her blood
> (though in a perverted cult) a burning zeal
> for Law and Cross, and God in her
> transformed what was perverse to the ideal.

Later, in another quatrain, and by means of an extraordinary figure, she transforms the martyrdom of Catherine into a demonstration of geometry that in turn outlines a virtuous paradigm:

> Her martyrdom was like a Cross; the wheel,
> with its opposed diameters, creates
> the holy and supreme shape of the Cross,
> which into four right angles separates.

This is the image that impressed Ficino, Bruno, and Kircher: the mysterious relationship between the cross and the circle. As the arms of the cross rotate, they engender the circle; for its part, the circle contains a cross. More than two centuries later, Alfred Jarry—in one of his most complex and still little explicated works, *César-Antéchrist*—uses the same demonstration to present a blasphemous allegory. In this enigmatic text a heraldic band appears as a character: it is also a horizontal staff, and thus symbolizes, dually, the phallus and the minus sign. As the staff-phallus rotates, exactly as in Sor Juana's quatrain, it turns upward and forms a cross that is also the plus sign, represented by a Templar who is prepared for combat against the adverse sign. There is no battle; the Templar lays aside his weapon, and the figure drawn by the two hostile signs is the sign that can only be defined negatively: zero. In its circle the two adversary principles are reconciled and annulled: phallus and cross, minus and plus, yes and no, life and death. Identity of opposites: zero is the belly of Ubu, and without contradiction, the circle that ceaselessly begins again at the exact point where it ends. The circle is Christ and it is Caesar. It is also the torture wheel to whose revolutions Catherine is bound and on which, transfigured, she escapes death:

> Catherine was bound upon the ring,
> symbol of God, the infinite hieroglyph,
> but did not die on it, and there, instead
> of circling to her death, encountered life.

Like Iphigenia, snatched by Artemis from the sacrificial altar, Catherine ascends to Heaven on the revolutions of the wheel, the emblem of the infinite God. The image of God as a circle of which the center is everywhere—a proposition both irrefutable and undemonstrable—comes from Nicholas of Cusa, although Sor Juana, as she herself says in the *Response*, took it from Kircher. In his *De docta ignorantia* Nicholas of Cusa had written that "the world has no circumference; for if it had a center and a circumference there would be some space and some thing beyond the world . . . [For this reason] it is not in our power to understand the world whose center and circumference are God." The paradox posed by Nicholas of Cusa follows in the tradition of the negative theology of Dionysius Areopagiticus. As Arthur O. Lovejoy has said, Cusanus was concerned not so much with questions of astronomy as with a species of mystical theology.[11] But Giordano Bruno uses these speculations to defend his concept of an infinite universe, and again and again repeats the metaphor of God as a circle whose center is everywhere. This image, with different shadings, reappears in two of Sor Juana's essential texts, in the central passage of *First Dream* and in the *Response:* "All things issue from God, who is at once the center and circumference from which and in which all lines begin and end." It is revealing that even in a *villancico,* a popular and devout genre, Sor Juana did not abandon her philosophical and hermetic preoccupations.

THE MERIT OF SOR JUANA'S *villancicos* is not only, or predominantly, historical, social, philosophical, metrical, or literary, but, in the strictest sense of the word, poetic. These works seduce us at times with their fluid grace, at times with their iridescent transparency, and, always, with the inexplicable attraction poetry holds for us:

> See how Love stands shivering
> in the icy blast,
> how the frost and snow
> are holding him fast.
> Who comes to his aid?
> Earth?
> Water?
> Air?
> No, none comes but Fire!

More deeply felt than *villancico* 283, just quoted, is 287, especially the *estribillo,* sung in two voices. Here is simple beauty, piercing beauty:

> "Since my Lord was born for pain,
> let him stay awake."
> "Since he is awake for me,
> let him lie asleep."
> "Let him stay awake;
> for one who loves, there is no pain
> as great as lack of pain."
> "Let him lie asleep,
> for he who sleeps is, in his dream,
> practicing for death."

Not limpid, but sumptuous and crisscrossed with cruel sensuality, are the verses of *villancico* 314 in which the poet sings to two heroic "gypsies" (Egyptians)—Cleopatra, who committed suicide for human love, and Catherine, a martyr for divine love:

> Lovingly to snowy breast
> Cleopatra pressed the asp,
> But how redundant is the asp
> when one has lain within love's grasp!
> Ay, what tragedy, dear God!
> Ay, what hapless fate!
>
> And thus heroic Catherine
> yields up a throat of ivory
> to the cruel blade, that hell shall never
> triumph over constancy;
> and, in dying, she defeats
> those who her death decreed.

We marvel at the perfect harmony and the contrasting movements and oscillations of *villancico* xxxvii. It is the dawn of the Assumption, and

> Stars fall to the earth,
> dawns rise in the skies.
> Bright sunrays shine,
> sweet perfumes rise,
> quadrilles of jasmine,
> carnations and broom,
> that run,
>   that fly,
> that strew,
>   that festoon,
> with blossoms,
>   with gleams,
> with roses,
>   with flames.

The *estribillo* of *villancico* 242 is memorable for its combination of different meters and for the play of adjectives, which make us hear writing and see voices:

> O winged seraphim and celestial finches,
> muffle your feathers and ruffle your voices,
> ruffled voice, and feather,

muffled feather and voice,
warble and write of Peter's exploits.

One of the most enjoyable *villancicos* is a diaphanous paraphrase of
the Song of Songs (221). It was one of the first Sor Juana wrote and was
sung in 1676 in the cathedral of Mexico City, at the feast of the Assumption. The *coplas,* in verses of six syllables, are simplicity itself; in contrast, the *estribillo* mixes lines of various lengths. In the *estribillo* we see
Mary as a miraculous skyrocket that ascends until it is lost in the clouds.
No commentary can substitute for the slender poem, the whirlwind of
airy words rising from the page.

> That Shepherdess
> with the serene gaze,
> enchantment in the grove
> envy of the skies,
> captured with one hair,
> wounded with one eye,
> the Sublime Shepherd
> who dwells on high;
> to her, her Beloved
> was a bundle of myrrh,
> her lily-white breasts
> gave him shelter;
> she wears rich garments
> and, for cleanliness,
> has a bowery bed
> and a cedar-filled house . . .
> to enjoy the arms
> of her Master and love,
> she exchanged humble valley
> for the Mountain above . . .
>
> To the Mountain, to the Mountain on High,
> Shepherdesses, run, run, fly,
> María is leaving, rising through the skies!
> Hurry, hurry, run, quickly, quickly fly,
> for she is stealing away our souls and lives,
> bearing off in her Person all that we prize,
> leaving our Earth barren, of all treasures deprived!

22

The Stage and the Court

OR JUANA'S WRITINGS FOR THE STAGE amount to a little more than one-third of her total work. She wrote *comedias*[1] and *autos sacramentales, loas* and *sainetes*. The religious works—I am thinking particularly of *The Divine Narcissus*—are superior to the secular, but the comedies are not to be disdained. Not everyone shares this opinion. Vossler says: "Her cloak-and-dagger comedy, *Los empeños de una casa* [*The Trials of a Noble House*], could have been composed by any of Calderón's imitators. The mythological, love-intrigue comedy *Amor es más laberinto* [*Love Is the Greater Labyrinth*], set in conventional baroque antiquity, is totally lacking in style; it was a commissioned work, written against her will, as she herself confesses." Quite apart from the fact that Sor Juana neither comments on nor confesses anything about this play, Vossler overstates his case. Among Calderón's disciples—some of great talent, such as Francisco de Rojas Zorrilla and Agustín Moreto y Cabaña—Sor Juana does not make a bad showing; *The Trials of a Noble House* is a comedy that compares favorably to Moreto's *El lindo don Diego* (*Don Diego the Dandy*), Rojas Zorrilla's *Entre bobos anda el juego* (*In the Hands of Fools*), and others by these authors. The drama of the period is not highly esteemed; most of its authors are considered to have been little more than skillful imitators. Nothing could be further from the truth. The English critic Duncan Moir states: "There was variety, considerable originality and, often, great subtlety . . . One of the more important tasks of future research will be a re-evaluation of the theater of the Calderonian school."[2]

Moir lists some of the characteristics that distinguish this type of theater from that of Lope de Vega and his followers: the conscious use of *culterano* language in the manner of Góngora's poetry, a stylistic tendency begun by Calderón himself; the most elaborate and complex intrigues, which translated into the predominance of a theater of situation over that of passion and character; conventions and norms of behavior better adapted to performance at court than in the public courtyard. Moir emphasizes the preoccupation with "the classical norm of decorum." It was obligatory that characters conform in language and conduct to the style and mores of the social class to which they belonged. Prototype triumphed over atypical reality. Earlier theater had abounded in exceptional characters who broke the norms of their world and their class; in the theater of Calderón's successors, characters by necessity adapted to the code imposed by their social status. It was an ethic and an aesthetic that glorified conformity to, not transgression of, the collective pattern.

Such are the characteristics of Sor Juana's drama: it was written not for the public stage but for the viceregal court and the palaces of the aristocracy. Her language, at times elevated and emphatic, is almost always witty, full of puns and word play. The plots are skillfully constructed. In words and deeds her characters observe the decorum dictated by their rank, age, and sex, so that even their defects and exaggerations do not challenge but instead confirm social values. Finally, dramatic conflict, without which there is neither comedy nor drama, relies not on character but on situation. The result is a comedy of errors and mistaken identities. A world of shadows and masks: *A* falls in love with the beautiful *B,* but at the masked ball, or in the shadows of the garden by night, he confuses her with *C;* meanwhile, in the darkness, *B,* who actually loves *A,* takes him for *D,* who loves her but is abhorred by her. Fate shuffles the cards again and again, until truth triumphs. The plot, the humor, the dialogues of the comic characters and the lovers, the beautiful verses, are perfection. Empty perfection. Sor Juana is a typical author of the period but, unlike Rojas or Moreto, she is locked into its conventions, and it would be futile to seek in her comedies the slightest transgression of the aesthetic of decorum.

A drama of this nature, intimately linked to the court and to the palace *galanteos,* tended, on stage, to take the form of a ceremony. In fact, plays were performed according to a kind of ritual: first the *loa,* then the *sainetes*—one between the first and second acts, another between the second and third—and, as a finale, a *fin de fiesta,* a play following the play. Everything sprinkled with dances and songs—a veritable festival. The author of the comedy was not always the author of the *loa* and the *sainetes,* although in Sor Juana's case she wrote them all. In the second volume of the *Works* (1692) we find, complete, the festival of *The Trials of a Noble House.* Thanks to the research of Alberto G. Salceda, we know when, where, and on what occasion the play was first performed: on October 4, 1683, during an entertainment for the Marquis and Marquise de la Laguna given by an important viceregal official, Don Fernando Deza, city tax collector and magistrate. The festival coincided with the entry into Mexico City of the new Archbishop, Francisco de Aguiar y Seijas, an event alluded to at the end of the *loa* with these unprophetic verses: "The happiness of his entrance / was the entrance of our happiness!" It is difficult to imagine that this praise would have impressed the dour prelate, and more difficult still to believe that he even attended the performance: he despised theater.

The function opened with a *loa* in which Fate, Diligence, Merit, and Chance are debating the source of Happiness. Happiness enters and says that she owes her existence not to any of the four but rather to the nobility of those who make us happy—in this instance, the Viceroy and Vicereine and their son. Immediately after the *loa* there is a pretty song to Lysis (María Luisa), and between the first and second acts, another song, also dedicated to Lysis, and the first *sainete.* I have previously referred to this skit, in which real courtiers become metaphysical entities. Love, Respect, Flattery, Finesse, and Hope contend for a curious prize, the ladies' scorn. Is this a comic version of the doctrine that unrequited love is the perfect love? If so, it is rather insipid. The second *sainete,* performed between the second and third acts, follows the song dedicated to José, María Luisa's son: "Tender, adored Adonis . . ." In the *sainete,* the spectacle being performed is criticized, and fun is poked at a certain Azevedo, who is reputed to be the comedy's author. According to Francisco Monterde, this Azevedo is none other than the Azevedo who yielded first prize to Sor Juana in the competition described in Sigüenza's *Parthenian Triumph* and who was also a playwright. Monterde believes that Sor Juana is making fun of one of Azevedo's comedies, which was being performed at precisely that moment in a theater in the city.[3] Likely so. But there is an additional, and less veiled, joke. Referring to comedies performed in Mexico, one of the characters says with scorn that those that come from Spain are more easily swallowed because "delicacies with the savor of brine [i.e., imported delicacies] / are much more palatable."[4]

Monterde observes that the second *sainete* foreshadows a technique of modern theater: within her fiction Sor Juana introduces a criticism of that fiction. This is a procedure that Pirandello was to employ in our century. Sor Juana was "the first to breach the invisible wall separating the actors from the spectators." It is absolutely true. Renaissance theater and the Baroque had introduced the play-within-a-play, as Velázquez in one of his paintings had included himself in the act of painting, but the dramatic poets of the sixteenth and seventeenth centuries, to my knowledge, had never broken the conventions separating stage from spectator. This *sainete* also shares a private confidence with the audience, a reference to another play recently performed in a Mexico City theater, a patched and "mestiza" *Celestina,* that is, a play written by a Spaniard and a native Mexican with joined-together fragments. Critics believe that this "mestiza" comedy is the "dramatic poem" referred to by Castorena y Ursúa in the prologue to *Fame,* left unfinished by the Spaniard Salazar y Torres and completed by the criolla Juana Inés. This play, known as *La segunda Celestina (The Second Celestina),* appeared in print in 1694, although with an ending written by Juan de Vera Tassis, a friend and publisher of Salazar y Torres, not by Sor Juana. We can infer, from the *sainete,* that the "mestiza" version was performed in Mexico City prior to the first performance of *The Trials of a Noble House.* The date is not specified but is understood to be of that same period, that is, between 1680 and 1683. The play was performed without mention of the name of the poet who completed it. With good reason: the poet was a nun. But many people were in on the secret, and this explains the sly wink from Sor Juana to the audience of her *sainete.* It is astonishing that a nun should have written cloak-and-dagger comedies—love affairs, duels, abductions, and deaths—for performance in the palace, to say nothing of the pieces she wrote for popular audiences. Equally amazing is that the theme of one of the plays was the scabrous Celestina.

As for *The Trials of a Noble House,* it is a well-structured and well-written play. Even today, three centuries after its first performance, we find it entertaining. The long monologue in the first act is famous, the heroine Doña Leonor's account of her life, a transparent transposition of Juana Inés' own, as I stated in Part Two. It is the only moment, among the whirlwind of entertaining incidents and snarled action, in which we glimpse a realistic character liberated from the conventional prototype of the young girl. The impression, however, does not last long: following this speech, Leonor becomes the lovestruck girl of every comedy, who flees her house because of love and returns to it to marry. The only character with a certain individuality is the comic Castaño, who speaks in a Mexican vernacular, thus introducing some local color into the action (which takes place in an abstract setting, the interior of a house in Toledo). Enrique Anderson Imbert observes that in the third act it is Castaño who breaks the barrier between fiction and reality "when he disguises himself as a woman and speaks directly to the audience, consulting with the ladies in the audience about articles of clothing."[5] The comedy captures the spectator's interest with its swift, almost cinematographic pace and its endless encounters and narrow escapes under cover of darkness in a hall or garden, all in a swirl of cloaked ladies and suitors blinded by desire and jealousy. The shadows are punctuated by the gleam of clashing blades and the glitter of conceits, wit, and humor. There is also a moment of magic calm as musicians sing a song whose *estribillo* asks, "Which is the gravest pain / among all the pains of love?" and each of the protagonists responds for him- or herself: jealousy, absence, suspicion, and so on.

Sor Juana's other comedy, *Love Is the Greater Labyrinth,* was performed in the viceregal palace on January 11, 1689, in celebration of the birthday of the recently arrived Viceroy, Gaspar de Silva, Count de Galve. It was preceded by a *loa* in which Sor Juana achieves one of those sleights of hand at which she was so skillful; as she transformed the Marquis de la Laguna into a new Neptune, she finds a second Janus in Gaspar de Silva. Diversity in versification is enriched by hyperbole and metaphor. The play ends in praise of both the retiring and the incumbent Viceroy and their wives (the Galves and the Monclovas). When we read the final adulatory lines, we do not know whether to smile or blush:

> Illustrious Silva, Janus sublime:
> under your ministry, may an Age
> aspire unto Eternity . . .

Love Is the Greater Labyrinth is also a comedy with lovers' intrigues, mistaken identities, and duels; this time, however, the action takes place in the Crete of Minos and the Minotaur. The suitors are the princes Theseus and Bacchus, and the ladies are the *infantas* Phaedra and Ariadne. Critics have vilified this comedy; the truth is—for me, and for a few others who have read it with sympathy—that it is a work filled with entertaining surprises and a picturesque poetry created by the superimposition of Cretan archaisms upon the baroque language and intrigue of the palace. Everything takes place amid a nebulous, chimerical architecture. *Love Is the Greater Labyrinth* is far more exaggeratedly erudite than *The Trials of a Noble House,* especially the second act, which was written not by Sor Juana but by another poet, Juan de Guevara.[6] This act has been widely—and unjustly—criticized. Like Méndez Plancarte, I find it equal to the two acts written by Sor Juana; aside from the overall dignity of the language, it has moments of drama that Moreto would have applauded, such as the scene of the masked ball in which Ariadne believes she is dancing with Theseus, although he has Phaedra for a partner. The best passage, perhaps, is the scene in which Phaedra and Ariadne recite to themselves two labyrinthine and lyrical sonnets.

The real interest of this comedy is to be found not in its ingenious and refined verse, or in the complications of the plot, but rather in Theseus' speech in the first act. When he presents himself to Minos, the Athenian prince relates his feats but first, in the manner of a prologue, expounds his ideas on the origins of the state, that is, the origins of man's domination over man. He begins by saying that although he is of royal blood, he speaks as a warrior, not a king: a good soldier can become a "supreme king," but a king, merely by being a king, can never be a good soldier. Then he declares:

> the first example of dominion
> over man evolved from deeds;
> for being that all men were equal,
> it holds that there were no means
> by which could be introduced
> the inequality we see,
> like that between a king and a vassal,
> or that between noble and plebe.
> Because were we to speculate
> that on their own men would submit
> to wear the yoke of other men,
> or answer to another's bit,
> e'en were there cause to ponder it
> there still is none for such belief . . .
> From which I only can infer
> it was the strength of force alone
> that caused divisions among men
> who all as equals had been born—
> and differences of such degree
> that although all be born the same,
> some men as master shall command
> and others live to serve as slave.

With the exception of José María Vigil,[7] no critic has even mentioned this speech. It is remarkable for several reasons: first, because it is the only example of this theme in Sor Juana's writing; second, because Theseus delivers the speech at an entertainment specifically intended to honor a Prince; third, because it is difficult to imagine how such principles could have been expounded in a viceregal palace without creating a scandal. In short, Theseus' words are remarkable simply for their content. A century earlier in *Mexican Majesty* (1604), Bernardo de Balbuena had praised *in*equality—the source of political society, of the arts and sciences—but attributed it to factors other than naked force. Theseus' point of departure is found in Spanish Neothomist philosophers. These writers, almost all of them Jesuits, and all immersed in the great controversy of the Reformation and Counter-Reformation, are the founders of the modern constitutionalism that situates the legitimate source of the power of the state in the will of the people. According to Vitoria, Suárez, Molina, and their followers, in the beginning men were free and equal. That *status naturae,* says Molina, does not admit the right to dominate others. In that state—a major difference between the Jesuits and Hobbes—natural law, not caprice or violence, reigned. According to Suárez, primitive communities lacked political organization but were not composed of nomads, as the Stoics had maintained; the first men lived in family groups. Man, says Suárez, is social by nature, and the idea of the "family community" is inherent in him.

Why did men exchange the freedom and equality of the beginning for domination and rank? This question—the same that Hobbes and Rousseau were later to ask—was answered in a very original manner. The *status naturae* is not synonymous with innocence: man is a fallen creature. If men had continued to live in those prepolitical communities, they would have been exposed to terrible and perhaps mortal dangers: injustice, violence, dispersion. Thus, as counterpoint to the optimism of natural law, Spanish theologians introduced into their theory the somber vision of fallen man inherited from St. Augustine. In order to confront evils and dangers, men decided to establish political communities and to choose "a public authority that would promote the common good." Although political power is born of the natural law that can be said to predetermine it, in each society it is the expression of human will. Men voluntarily choose domination and inequality, but along with these evils they also establish laws, peace, institutions, arts, and sciences: civilization. These ideas had led Juan de Mariana (1536–1624) to proclaim the "right to resist" the unjust Prince, even to the point of regicide.[8]

Sor Juana follows the Neoscholastics only in the first part of Theseus' discourse, the equality and freedom of the beginning; then, instead of espousing the tacit consensus that delegates authority to a lord who either through inheritance or election transmits it to his descendants, she postulates force as the cause of the leap from a natural to a political society. Of course, it is not she who is speaking, but Theseus, a character in a play. No one refutes him, however—not Minos, not the other princes and nobles who hear him. Where did Sor Juana get these depressingly realistic ideas that are in open contradiction to the prevailing doctrines of her day? How was it that no doctrinaire cleric "sought a quarrel" with her? Did she calculate the extent of her words, or did she place those ideas in Theseus' mouth with the desire to amaze and bedazzle? It is not easy to answer these questions.

Sor Juana's plays were almost surely performed in Spain, and probably also in Lima and other cities of Spanish America. Her work was widely known: it not only was published and read in Spain but had fervent admirers in Peru and other colonial centers. Recently the Mexican theater historian Armando de María y Campos published an article containing some interesting information. In 1709, Manila, like all the dominions of the Spanish crown, celebrated the birth of the first son of Philip V. The lavish and prolonged celebrations lasted nine days; there were *loas*, plays, bullfights, fireworks, masquerades, and native dances. On the first day, following solemn religious ceremonies, one of Agustín Moreto's comedies was performed; then, after a week of festivities, *Love Is the Greater Labyrinth*. On the last day, the ninth, the celebrations were climaxed by *The Trials of a Noble House*.[9] The *loas*, written by local authors, praised Sor Juana highly. In her century only Lope de Vega, Góngora, and Calderón achieved such widespread fame; later, in modern times, only Darío, Neruda, and Borges.

THE *LOAS* OCCUPY a special place in Sor Juana's work, one analogous in her secular poetry to the *villancicos* in her religious writing. Originally a *loa* was a monologue which an actor recited as a prelude to a comedy and in which, as the Spanish word suggests, the audience or the city where the performance was taking place was praised. Soon the monologue became a dialogue, and the *loa* developed into a brief theatrical piece with allegorical themes such as friendship, love, monarchy, colors, letters, and days of the week. In the seventeenth century *loas* fell into disuse, except as preludes to *autos sacramentales* and to royal performances. Sor Juana wrote five such *loas,* two for comedies and three for sacramental plays. In addition, she wrote a *loa* to celebrate the Conception, five *loas* celebrating various birthdays of Charles II, and another six to honor and celebrate birthdays of important personages: the Queen Mother, Mariana of Austria; Marie Louise d'Orléans, the first wife of Charles II; the Marquis de la Laguna; José de la Cerda, son of the Viceroy and Vicereine; Elvira de Toledo, Countess de Galve; and Fray Diego Velázquez de la Cadena, brother of her patron. Finally, a *loa* was written for a party the Countess de Paredes held in her orchard. The first *loa* Sor Juana wrote (1675?) is religious in subject but worldly in regard to the occasion: the *loa* for the Conception was performed in the house of a wealthy citizen, celebrating the birthday of his firstborn son, José Guerrero, "a handsome, pious Adonis," who sacrifices in the temple of the Virgin "the first fruits" of his youth.

In some fifteen years, between 1675 and 1690, Sor Juana composed thirteen of these brief plays. All of them center on an idea or an allegorical event: music and notes; stars and human destiny; the seasons and the elements; and the rivalry between Bellona and Venus or between Flora and Pomona, among others. Each episode and each incident was preceded or climaxed by dances and songs. A spectacle for the eyes, as much as for ears and mind; the costumes and settings must have been lavish. Composing these plays demanded constant dealings with musicians, stage designers, and actors: a bustling activity, parallel, in a certain way, to that involving the *villancicos* sung in the cathedrals, but more complex. Again, it was commissioned poetry for which she obtained both economic remuneration and court protection. The convent, as a social and economic institution, could only further and stimulate Sor Juana's activity as an official poet. The utilitarian demands of this writing did not dim her imagination or diminish her skills: the Sor Juana of the courtly and mythological *loas* was no less prolific and no less inspired than the Sor Juana of the *villancicos*. The themes of the former were less attractive than the marvelous stories of the Virgin, saints, and martyrs, but the little that could be said about the princes and the great of this world was enhanced with mythology, emblems, and erudition. It is surprising that with material as banal as the birthdays of the powerful, Sor Juana succeeded in writing these small works that, within their limitations, are perfect.

The richness and metric variety of these dramas is amazing. The *loas* not only are a complete repertory of the prevailing meters of the late seventeenth century, but include many that were infrequently used. To a versifier's mastery she added a poet's grace and imagination. In inventiveness the courtly *loas* are more complex and elaborate than the *villancicos*. Of course, none of the *loas* has lyric passages that can compare to the great poetry of the best *villancicos*. But they yield nothing in grace and freshness. A well-chosen collection of the *loas* would offer more than one surprise to a reader who is also a poetry lover. When I discussed belief in the influence of the stars, in Part Four, I referred to the fifth *loa* for the birthday of the King (378), in which the seven planets of ancient astronomy—Saturn, Jupiter, Mars, Mercury, Venus, the Moon, and, in the center, the Sun, who is Apollo—descend to Earth as a Council of Stars to reiterate the "benign influences" they had bestowed on Charles II at birth. The disproportion between astral "benignity" and the unfortunate reign of Charles II is enormous, as is the distance between the *loa's* theme and its verbal splendor. Grouped around Apollo, the planets discourse:

> Seated upon alabaster thrones,
> in seven crystal canopies, the Orbs;
> sentences of fire are their conceits,
> and constellated clauses are their words.

In the *loa* for the birthday of Marie Louise d' Orléans (379), three faculties—Intellect, Will, Memory—and three times—Past, Present, and Future—speak about music. The three faculties invoke three times:

> *Memory:* I call upon Time Past,
> World's protocol, the roll where Fate
> through corps of magistrates,
> all the ancient writings has amassed.
>
> *Will:* And I invoke Time Present,
> so swiftly passing, pliant instant,
> that he who praises you
> starts in the present, but in the past concludes!
>
> *Intellect:* I sing of Time Future,
> impregnable wall, lofty structure,
> to the Angel yet unknown,
> whose secrets are reserved for God alone![10]

When I spoke of Sor Juana's love of music I referred at some length to the "Encomiastic Poem" composed for the birthday of the Countess de Galve (384). At the beginning of that work, Sor Juana speaks in beautiful terms of the opposition between seeing and hearing, the eyes and the ears, as well as their association in every work of art or in confronting human beauty:

> If beauty may alone be found
> in the proportions of its parts,
> it may not be perceived by ear
> but is beauty that the eyes can hear.

The *loa* dedicated to María Luisa (382), written to brighten a celebration in an orchard, centers on a competition between Flora and Pomona that is resolved by a nymph in favor of María Luisa. This *loa* has wonderful lines, among them some I find especially absorbing in that they anticipate many images of modern poets. When Sor Juana writes of "the lily's white throat," for example, she foreshadows Jorge Guillén's figure of the swan as the "tenor of whiteness."

The fourth *loa* to the birthday of the King (377) is perhaps the finest of all, for the variety of its meters, the vivacity of its images, and graceful wit. In Part Four I quoted some beautiful lines when I spoke of the courtly poems: the echoing *ovillejos* with a swinglike rhythm, a rhythm formed of exquisite combinations of meters that spring like sudden freshets in a garden composed not of flowers but of vowels and consonants. This is a different fragment from the same poem:

> The fountains my voice enhance,
> let them dance!
> My echo the flowers have strewn,
> let them bloom!
> My love the green plants bestow,
> let them grow!
> And that they may deserve the praise
> of Charles, so may their glory blaze:
> fountains,
>   birds,
>   flowers,
>   plants,
> grow,
>   bloom,
>   trill,
>   dance!

This passage is an example of a technique to which Sor Juana turns repeatedly, especially in the *loas*. Here she is closely following Calderón, who was masterly in his use of the same procedure. Dámaso Alonso has studied this device.[11] The phrase bifurcates like a road or a tree into two, three, four branches or limbs that Alonso calls "members." The relation among the "members" of the phrase is a true *correlation* and centered on generic coincidence and specific differences. In the verses I have quoted, a brief sample of many dizzying combinations, the birds, fountains, flowers, and plants coincide generically in that all are a part of nature and of its movement and vitality: they trill, dance, bloom, and grow. The differences result from the fact that each has its own being, and each is sung by a different character: the birds by Aeolus; the fountains by Syrinx; the flowers by Flora; and the plants by Pan. Aeolus' monologue is the simplest and purest, a crystal fragment fashioned from weightless air:

> I who am presiding God
> of this thin and rarified air,
> am entrusted with the charge
> of governing the birds' empire,
> to see that such transparent space,
> its nebulous variety,
> is filled with flashing, winged rainbows,
> with veils of flitting vagaries.
> I am Aeolus, of the wind
> the diaphanous, drifting deity.

The entrance of Reflection is similarly memorable. The lines are crystalline in their clarity but also in the liquid sound of syllables that recall running water. Reflection, on the

> [transparent] surface of the waters,
> from glinting rays of radiant
> Sun is formed.
> And on fulgent
> crystal makes his throne.

This fragment about Reflection is only one example of the many verbal and visual felicities of the *loa* and a model, or emblem, of the perfections and limitations of these theatrical trifles. Insubstantial and fragile architectures, they are like the reflection born of light striking a smooth surface; they gleam for an instant and disappear.

23

The Float and the Sacrament

$\mathcal{A}$ ONE-ACT PLAY PERFORMED during the feast of Corpus Christi, the *auto sacramental* is one of the most singular creations of Hispanic civilization. One would expect *autos* to have had the sacrament of the Eucharist as their theme, but in the majority of cases their relation to this mystery was tangential and artificial. Critics and historians of Spanish literature have studied the evolution of the genre, from the end of the fifteenth to the middle of the eighteenth century, as an aesthetic phenomenon and as a manifestation of the religious fervor of the Spanish people. But there is another aspect to the *autos:* the economic system which made possible their continuity for more than two centuries and which was itself the manifestation of the policies of Church and monarchy. Marcel Bataillon, some decades ago, revealed the reverse of that tapestry: without the Counter-Reformation, which was also, as this French critic emphasizes, the reform of Spanish Catholicism, the phenomenon of the *autos* would be unintelligible.[1]

The *autos* derived from medieval religious theater, which was still pervaded with ancient ceremonies and pagan festivals. These sacred mysteries, accompanied by games and pantomimes, were performed in the atriums of churches. Frequently the processions and mummery invaded the church, even while mass was being celebrated. The tradition in Spain is an ancient one. The processions for the festival of Corpus Christi were begun in the thirteenth century. In the fifteenth century these parades were at the height of their popularity; the great attraction was the *carros*, which were not very different from the floats of a modern carnival or those of the great religious festivals of India. You could find anything on them, says Bataillon, "from St. George's dragon to Noah's Ark." Along with painted images and sculptures, there were actors and clowns, reciting, singing, and dancing. During the festival there was eating and drinking, and masked figures, followed by the crowds, snaked through the churches amid a great din and tumult. The Spanish processions and festivals were not very different from those in the rest of Europe. But the Reformation abolished this reputedly pagan popular diversion in the countries under its influence. Perhaps impressed by the example of Lutheran severity, the Church decided at least to refine if not abolish these popular celebrations. The procession was shortened; the spectacles took place outside the church; and the centerpiece of the festivities became the performance of a religious work that had previously been approved by the authorities. The *auto,* says Bataillon, "was a compromise between the custom of celebrating the Corpus with theatrical performances and the demands for Catholic reform" publicly endorsed by the Council of Trent.

Each major municipality was responsible for providing—almost always generously—for the needs of the authors, players, and designers. The city of Madrid commissioned Lope de Vega, Tirso de Molina, Mira de Amescua, and other famous poets to write the *autos* that were performed every spring. When the genre was at its peak, Calderón reigned supreme over it. The best actors performed in the *autos;* the decorations and costuming were sumptuous. Cities paid considerable sums to the directors of the companies, usually two for the two *autos* performed. The companies enjoyed additional privileges. The choicest was a monopoly: no other group was allowed to perform plays; another was a prize of one hundred ducats awarded to the best performance. As a vestige of the original procession, an open-air stage was erected between two floats in a plaza. The performances began early, were repeated several times, and lasted two days, Thursday and Friday. Sacred and secular theater had much in common; the poets, actors, directors, and designers were the same for both. The *auto sacramental* was an activity—artistic and commercial—of professionals. It was not unusual to see a famous actress represent Faith or Chastity while displaying the jewels given her by one of her wealthy lovers. The secular drama not only lent its poets and actors to sacramental worship but served as an aesthetic model; in turn, the *auto* subsidized the drama and lent it respectability. This system—at once economic, religious, and artistic—was essentially no different from that of the *villancicos* sung in the cathedrals of New Spain.

As a literary genre, the *auto sacramental* was born at the end of the fifteenth century, although with characteristics quite different from those it would later have. This primitive period—represented by a great name, Gil Vicente, and by lesser writers such as Juan de Timoneda—flowed into the mainstream of the Spanish theater during the time of Lope de Vega. Lope's *autos* are actually devout legends, ruled by magic and marvel; Valdivielso's are lyric poems in dialogue, stories based on a slim plot. Mira de Amescua continued in the devout and edifying vein, which is closer to miracle than theology. Calderón radically changed the nature of the *auto sacramental,* which ceased to be a story of miracles and became an intellectual allegory. In its final and finished form, the *auto* is a construct not of conceits but of image-conceits, not of ideas but of character-ideas. Symbolic theater, and itself a symbol, the *auto* is an emblem of the world and what lies beyond the world. A dance of allegories: each conceit is embodied in an image that is tied to another, until a garland is formed that suddenly vanishes in a flash of bright light: the allegory has been nothing more than a triumphant demonstration. The God of Calderón is a Maker but, above all, he is a Thinker. His perfection is the perfection of geometry: the universe that issues from his hands is as coherent as a system.

Ratiocinations dance; arguments twine through a *décima* or are sculpted in a sonnet; syllogisms turn in a tight circle, heels tapping out a *seguidilla*. Scenic artifices of the speculative mind: footlights, painted drop curtains, stage machinery, and above all the fantasy that projects onto the scene a second, mental scene, as on a movie screen. A theater of strict conventions and curious artifices, as stylized as a ballet and as rigorous as a chain of deductions. Conjunction of a place and a time, *autos* could have been born only in Spain and only in the atmosphere of the seventeenth century. The Europeans of the Baroque Age contemplated the universe in the mirror of analogy that converts things and beings into images that irradiate contradictory and complementary meanings; even so, I do not find in the dramatic tradition of other countries anything similar to the Spanish *auto*. In the *auto*, love for philosophical argument and its stringencies was allied with dancing frenzy, and both with a fascination for emblems and hieroglyphs. Across the hanging bridge of allegory and symbol, an extraordinary traffic took place between the most abstract thought and the most sensual art, between logic and dance, theology and buffoonery.

Many years ago in Tokyo, watching a performance of Noh theater, I thought of Calderón. It occurred to me then that Noh, contrary to Arthur Waley's thesis, has a greater affinity with the *auto sacramental* than with Greek tragedy. Both *auto* and Noh are very close to liturgy, and in both poetry is mixed with theology. Most important, both are theaters ruled by symbol. At that time I wrote:

> It is not arbitrary to compare the plays of Kanami and Seami to the *autos sacramentales* of Calderón, Tirso de Molina, or Mira de Amescua. The brevity of the works and their symbolic nature, the importance of poetry and song—in one, the chorus, in the other, singing—their strict dramatic architecture, religious tone, and, especially, the importance they place on theological speculation—from within, not in confrontation with, dogma—are features common to both artistic forms. The Spanish *auto sacramental* and the Japanese Noh are intellectual and poetic. Theater in which life is a dream and dream is the only possible life. The world, men, have no existence of their own: they are symbols. A theater suspended between heaven and earth by rational threads, constructed with the precision of a philosophical argument and with the phantasmal violence of desire embodied only to be obliterated.[2]

Today I would modify that final sentence; the theme of desire is precisely what distinguishes Buddhism from Christianity. Buddhism aims at the obliteration of desire, the source of error and misfortune; the characters of the Noh, souls in pain, resurrect desire in order to dissipate it: they seek *dis*incarnation. Inspired by a theology that is the opposite of Buddhism, the *auto sacramental* celebrates the mystery of the Eucharist: God himself, moved by loving desire, is made flesh, dies, and is resurrected.

THE CUSTOM OF CELEBRATING the festival of Corpus Christi with theatrical performances reached New Spain almost immediately after the Conquest; in 1539 that festival was celebrated in Tlaxcala with four plays. Shortly thereafter, in 1565, the municipal council of Mexico City agreed to award "a prize of gold or silver in the value of three hundred gold crowns to the best performance." From that time on, throughout the sixteenth century, the minutes of the Council record the sums given to the directors of the companies of players for performances during the celebration.[3] Among Mexican colonial authors of that period the name of Hernán González de Eslava again stands out. In the first half of the seventeenth century, according to José Mariana Beristáin y Souza, numbers of *autos* were written in native Indian languages, and Calderón's *El gran teatro del mundo* (*The Great Theater of the World*) was translated into Nahuatl. We have very few facts, as Méndez Plancarte points out, about *autos* written in Mexico during the seventeenth century, even though we know that every spring, in front of the cathedral, an *auto sacramental* and an accompanying *loa* were performed.

Sor Juana wrote three *autos,* each preceded by a *loa: El divino Narciso* (*The Divine Narcissus*), *El mártir del Sacramento: San Hermenegildo* (*The Martyr of the Sacrament: St. Hermenegild*), and *El cetro de José* (*Joseph's Staff*). The first was written in 1688, or slightly earlier; the Countess de Paredes took it with her to Madrid, and it was probably performed there in the celebration of Corpus Christi in 1689 or 1690. *The Martyr of the Sacrament* was also written to be performed before the court in Madrid, because it ends with greetings to the King and both Queens, Marie Louise d'Orléans and Mariana of Austria. The date of composition of this *auto* is unknown, but because of the dedication to the royal family and because of the intervention of the Countess de Paredes, who was surely the intermediary between Sor Juana and the Madrid court, it would not be rash to suggest that it was written between 1680 and 1688. We have less information about *Joseph's Staff;* probably it belongs to the same period. *The Divine Narcissus* was published in 1690; in 1691 it was included in the enlarged edition of the first volume of her works. The other two, with *loas,* were published the following year in the second volume of her works. There is no record, strange as it may seem, that they were performed in Mexico. During those years, between 1690 and 1693, Sor Juana's star was in decline and it is possible that no one wanted to offend Aguiar y Seijas by performing one of her works in the atrium of the cathedral. The year in which she wrote the militant and feminist *villancicos* to St. Catherine was 1691 (it is significant, however, that they were sung in Oaxaca, not Mexico City).[4] A careful examination of the records of the municipal council could perhaps resolve these minor enigmas.

The *loa* accompanying *The Martyr of the Sacrament* is of interest not for its dramatic construction, or for its poetic worth, but for the light it sheds on Sor Juana's theological preoccupations. The *loa* is a dramatic treatment of a subject typical of the Baroque and of a clerical society: two theology students debate which is Christ's greater demonstration of his love—his having given his life for us, or his having left us the sacrament of the Eucharist, in which he gives of Himself as the food of immortality, and in which we partake of His being. This—the beneficence of Christ—is the theme of Father Vieyra's Sermon of the Mandate and of Sor Juana's critique of that famous text, the *Carta atenagórica.* In other poems, although more briefly, she again touches on the same matter. In one of the *villancicos* to St. Bernard (345), she maintains that Christ's greatest beneficence was to die for us, although immediately following that, she postulates a paradox: Christ, in the sacrament of the Eucharist, "being in glory / is as if dead." She means, in a state that encompasses the two extremes, life and death, the impassiveness of God and the suffering of his creation. In another *villancico* from the same series (351), she openly inclines toward the gift of the Eucharist, while in two verses from *The Divine Narcissus,* through the mouth of Satan, she elects the other: his having died for the sake of "his image" (humankind).

This vacillation indicates either that she was uncertain when confronted with several possible answers or, more probably, that she slanted her judgment to the circumstances of the moment. It is not easy to take her theological opinions very seriously; rather than deep convictions, they were brilliant speculations to be uttered in a lecture hall, in the locutory of a convent, or on the stage of a theater. What interested her was to present herself in the best possible light or, as in her critique of Vieyra, to refute arguments. In the *loa* to *The Martyr of the Sacrament,* a third student appears who resolves the debate in favor of the Eucharist. The student argues exactly the opposite of what Sor Juana was to write only a brief while later in her critique of Father Vieyra. A revealing detail: the third student is a personification of Sor Juana. He says that he has been charged with writing an *auto,* that he chose the story of the martyr Hermenegild, and that he is going to use the debate between the students as "the framework for a *loa.*" Thus at the end of her life Sor Juana succeeded in realizing her adolescent dream: to dress as a man and to study at the university. Theater within theater, and a hint from the author to the public concerning the identity of the third student— none other than the author of the *loa,* and of the *auto* about to be performed.

The action of *The Martyr of the Sacrament* takes place in the last third of the sixth century, in the Spain of the Visigoths, during the reign of Leovigild. The theme is the misadventures of that Arian King, and of his son, Hermenegild, a convert to Catholicism. Sor Juana closely follows Juan de Mariana's *Historia de España.*[5] There is a devout play by Lope de Vega—*La mayor corona (The Finest Crown)*—that Méndez Plancarte considers very poor because it is filled with far-fetched incidents and grotesque inventions and digressions. Sor Juana's *auto* suffers from the opposite sin: being overly schematic. It seems that in her haste to send it to Madrid she did not take time to polish it. The scaffolding is still visible in the work, and it lacks several windows and a stairway. Sor Juana's version of the story of Leovigild and Hermenegild is not only cursory but unjust. She paints a picture of a vacillating Leovigild, cruel, like all tyrants, subject to the perverse influence of an Arian Bishop she names Apostasy, while Hermenegild and his wife, the Frankish Catholic Ingunda, are the images of faith, charity, and filial devotion. According to Modesto Lafuente, Leovigild was "a great monarch, a valiant warrior, and an astute statesman." He was, in fact, the founder of the institution of the Spanish monarchy. The historical Hermenegild, perhaps out of hatred for his stepmother, who was also an Arian, or because of ambition, rebelled against his father, who had made him King of what today is Andalusia; he formed an alliance with the enemies of his country, the Byzantines and the Swabians; he surrendered his wife and son, as pawns, to the former, fought, was defeated, was pardoned by Leovigild, again rebelled, was taken prisoner, rejected the communion offered him by an Arian Bishop, and was executed by his father's order.

Sor Juana was insensitive to this terrible story, a drama of a struggle between blood relations and, at the same time, a political and religious conflict. It is futile, of course, to search for realistic characters and psychological analyses in doctrinaire works; still, the modern reader is offended by the prejudiced view of events and by the rudimentary and simplistic characters and ideas. There are unpleasant moments, such as the scene in which, as he rejects the Arian Bishop, the intolerant Hermenegild calls him a "*comunero* traitor." It is not the anachronism that irritates me but the fact that Sor Juana calls the *comuneros* traitors. This was not, naturally, Sor Juana alone; it was her time.[6] But bias is ideological, an illness of the spirit that is found in all times. In great works we are presented with a vision of man as a being with more than one facet; the true poet always shows us the *other* side of reality. Spanish religious theater at times escapes the chains of dogmatism precisely by means of one of its dogmas, free will, which conceives of man as a contradictory being who has the capacity for choice. Why did Sor Juana not show us the *other* Hermenegild, the ambitious, tyrannical rebel before martyrdom transfigured him?

The Martyr of the Sacrament is a hastily written play, marred by aesthetic carelessness and imperfections in its moral arguments. Méndez Plancarte acknowledges the carelessness, and even that the play contains a "theological lacuna": Hermenegild rejects the communion offered him by the Arian Bishop Apostasy "because it is not a true sacrament"; according to Church doctrine, however, even when administered by a schismatic Bishop or a heretic, the holy sacrament of the Eucharist is valid. Hermenegild should have rejected communion not for the reason given but because to accept it "would have been to participate in the sacrilege of schism and to take communion with non-Catholics." Fortunately, not all is theology. There is a pause in the action: Leovigild is following through the corridors and chambers of his palace a shadow that he can neither overtake nor relinquish. Finally, he asks, "Who are you?" and the shadow answers, "Do not be surprised / that, contained within your melancholy, / your Fantasy should speak with you." The shadow, a projection of Leovigild, offers him a panoramic view of the triumphal history of the Visigoths, protected by the Arian faith, and images of Visigoth kings, their battles, and their victories parade before his eyes, as if across a movie screen. This is another technique Sor Juana borrowed from Calderón. She uses it in three *autos* and in the *loas;* each *loa* contains an *auto* that, like a Russian doll, in turn contains scenes that are "views" of other realities and histories. This is allegory in motion, pictorial perspective transported to the stage and endowed with movement: film before the time of film.

In *Joseph's Staff* (372) the art of literary trompe-l'oeil is continuous and felicitous. The action unfolds on two planes. One follows the biblical history of Joseph, who is sold by his brothers but who, after the adventure with the wife of Potiphar and various misadventures, because of his prudence and his gifts of prophecy becomes counselor and minister to the Pharaoh. The second plane, superimposed on the first, is a commentary on the action, communicated by Lucero and his inseparable companions and confidantes: his wife, Intelligence; Conjecture; and Envy. Lucero (Bright Star) is the devil; Intelligence, Conjecture, and Envy are his multiple projections. The commentaries of Lucero and his retinue, at times refuted by Prophecy and Science, are verbal and visual: the spectator sees all that the shrewd and eloquent devils relate. The commentary uncovers an allegory in the acts of Joseph and, little by little, the demonic spirits realize the true meaning of the story of the young Hebrew: it is a prefiguration of the story of Christ. The first hint is found in the meaning of Joseph's name. Intelligence says that "Joseph" means "expansion of God." "Is that not strange? In those syllables may lie a mystery." With philosophical aplomb, Lucero rejects the insinuation: "God is infinite, and infinity neither expands nor contracts." Intelligence replies, "Very well, though I fear—" but before she can finish, Conjecture steps in:

> I mean, in short, I fear that, although infinite,
> divine essence could into itself admit
> a different nature,
> thus (although nothing can increase its stature)
> what essence had not previously contained
> would be "expansion." Is this not plain?

The devil, to his misfortune, exhibits extraordinary shrewdness: by reading the name of Christ in Joseph's name, he foretells his eventual defeat. Adam and Eve appear in another passage, one that similarly manifests omens of the future in episodes from the past. Although Eve is deceived by the serpent, she will later triumph over the devil through one of her descendants, Mary. Lucero is frightened by this omen for, he says, the Egyptians made the serpent "the most feared hieroglyph" of freedom: a reappearance of "Egyptian" hermeticism. And thus, step by step, the devils discover in the story of Joseph the allegorical prefiguration of Christ's incarnation in human form. It was a stroke of genius to have made the devils the interpreters of the holy story. In the final scene, these malign spirits see Jacob on his deathbed, surrounded by his children. The patriarch speaks his last words to them and, before he dies, kisses Joseph's staff, which is topped by a round loaf, a sign foreshadowing the sacrament of the Eucharist, instituted by Christ for our redemption. A miraculous nourishment:

> The manna's flavors
> were many—different;
> this has but one,
> but it is infinite.

The *loas* to *Joseph's Staff* and *The Divine Narcissus* are identical in subject and in intent. In each, Sor Juana addresses the theme of the affinities between pre-Columbian religion and Christianity. The *loas* show that early pagan rites contained signs that, although encoded and allegorical, foreshadowed the Gospel. This is a theme that since the second century had absorbed the Church Fathers and later would be the subject of discussion and speculation among Renaissance philosophers and theologians. The Baroque Age inherited the theme and made it the subject of theological polemics. In Spain it inspired *autos* and devout dramas. The discovery and conquest of America gave it extraordinary currency, especially when the Spanish began to note strange and inexplicable similarities between certain native rites and the mysteries of baptism, communion, confession, and sacrifice. Some, like Sahagún and the first missionaries, held that those resemblances were tricks and lures of the devil; others, especially the Jesuits, inclined toward the opinion of some of the first Church Fathers, that ancient religions contained glimpses and foreshadowings of the true religion. The Society of Jesus adopted this interpretation in China, in the south of India, and in Mexico and Peru. In the second half of the seventeenth century, Manuel Duarte and Sigüenza y Góngora turned this type of allegorical explanation into orgies of speculation—that Quetzalcoatl was St. Thomas, and Neptune an Indian chieftain. In this, as in so many other areas of her thought, Sor Juana followed the Jesuits, although with moderation and intellectual sobriety. In *Joseph's Staff* she repeats the process, although with one major difference: seeing a foreshadowing of the Eucharist in the rites of cannibalistic idolaters is quite different from seeing it in an episode from the Bible.

The characters in the *loa* (371) for *Joseph's Staff* are Faith, the Law of Grace, Natural Law, Nature, and Idolatry. There is a symmetrical relationship among the first four: Faith is to Nature as the Law of Grace is to Natural Law. The action takes place in America, recently converted to Christianity. Faith wants to commemorate "such an illustrious and glorious event"; immediately, Nature and Natural Law propose that the natural order of the beginnings, perverted by Idolatry, be reinstated. It is Nature's opinion that above all they must demolish the altars "where their blood had so often been spilled." Natural Law wants to abolish the Indians' polygamy, a transgression against the natural contract. The Law of Grace interjects: it is "of greatest importance to rid the altars of the statues of false gods" and replace them with the cross. Faith goes further: upon the altars where human blood had been shed, they must enshrine the symbols of the mystery of the Eucharist, the chalice and the host. Then comes an outburst from Idolatry, "plenipotentiary of all the Indies," in which she defends the ancient rites. In the end she capitulates, agreeing that only one God should be adored but insisting on preserving human sacrifice, for two reasons:

> the first, from the belief
> that the gods are more subdued
> when given noble human flesh,
> the second, that of all our food
> the one held as most savory
> is flesh given in sacrifice,
> a dish, our peoples all believe,
> not only the most highly prized
> but one invested with the gift,
> the virtue, of prolonging life.

Idolatry's arguments are the traditional ones, except the argument that the Indians considered human flesh the "most savory" dish. No text confirms this; they ate, unsalted, a minimal portion of the sacrificial body, in true religious communion. Faith and the Law of Grace, confronted with Idolatry's arguments, turn to their theological arsenal to explain to Idolatry the secret meaning "of the allegory of human sacrifice" and its supernatural ties with the mystery of the Eucharist. Partially convinced, Idolatry replies "that Christ as victual is a perplexing tenet." Faith then invites her to watch the *auto sacramental* about Joseph, "in whose life are found only mysteries of bread and wheat."

The subject of the *loa* (367) to *The Divine Narcissus* is substantially the same. Sor Juana follows the historian Juan de Torquemada who, in *Monarquía indiana,* describes a rite the Aztecs celebrated every year on December 3: with grains and seeds (among them the innocent sesame, with which Mexicans today make sweetmeats), mixed and kneaded with the blood of sacrificed children, the priests formed a man-sized figure of the god Huitzilopochtli, which they then riddled with arrows until it tumbled to the ground. They broke the figure into bits and each of the participants ate a small piece. The ceremony was called *Teocualo,* "God is eaten." The similarities of this terrible ritual to the Catholic communion and mystery of the Eucharist are evident. As in the other *loa,* Religion, dressed as a Spanish gentlewoman, promises America, costumed as a "noble Indian," a food better than that of the god of the seeds. America, convinced, sings:

> My agony is exquisite,
> come, show me how in bread and wine
> this God gives of himself to me.

To place these two brief works in their true perspective—and also as an introduction to *The Divine Narcissus*—I must return to the origin of this kind of interpretation. From their earliest days the Church Fathers had confronted pagan religions and Greek philosophy. They experienced mixed feelings of attraction and repulsion, an impulse to assimilate and, simultaneously, combat those ideas and beliefs. The second century was a time of peace and prosperity, but also of philosophical sterility and great religious unrest. It was marked by the final crumbling of Greek rationalism, which, bereft of its gods, found itself incapable of reconstructing civilized life on a purely rational basis. Pagan rationalism, Festugière states in his famous study of those centuries, ended "by devouring itself" and led to skepticism or to eclecticism and erudition.[7] Pythagoreanism was reborn, and with it were resurrected the beliefs of the ancient peoples of Judea and Chaldea, of the Druids, of the Indian gymnosophists and the Persian magi—and, especially, Egyptian wisdom. For the Greco-Roman world, Egypt *was* antiquity. Astrology, magic, mysticism. Syncretist writings appeared, gnostic movements arose, and amid all this rumble of sects and doctrines spread the revelations of Hermes Trismegistus, the Egyptian god Thoth. His were the original teachings from which Platonism, Judaism, and all other doctrines derived.

The existence of hermetic texts and their supposed antiquity posed a problem, however: if only the chosen people, the Hebrews, had been graced with pre-Christian revelation, then all the writings attributed to Hermes and other pagan theologians were Gentile interpretations of Judaism—something in manifest contradiction to the professed antiquity of those doctrines. This opened the way to the possible existence of partial, pre-Christian revelations independent of biblical revelation. Some of the Church Fathers, like Lactantius and Clement of Alexandria, were inclined toward this opinion, which centuries later was adopted by the Jesuits. In essence, this is the doctrine Sor Juana expounds in the two *loas* (367 and 371). With the doctrine came the ancient lists of the "first theologians," later accepted by the Neoplatonists of the Renaissance, that indiscriminately included Adam, Enoch, Zoroaster, Moses, Hermes Trismegistus, Orpheus, the Sibyls, and Plato. The Middle Ages knew this tradition, although it had been shaken by the attacks of St. Augustine, who saw in it remnants of astrolatry. I have related how hermeticism was revived toward the end of the fifteenth century and how, through Ficino, Pico della Mirandola, and others, it became the intellectual belief of the humanists, poets, and artists of the Renaissance.

A document that confirms the persistence of Neoplatonic hermeticism in the sixteenth century is the dedication to Pope Gregory XIV of Francesco Patrizi's *Nova de universis philosophia* (1591), counseling the Church to reject Scholastic philosophy and adopt hermeticism in its place:

> I would have you then, Holy Father, and all future Popes, give orders that some of the books which I have named [prominent among these was the *Hermetica*] shall be continually taught everywhere, as I have taught them for the last fourteen years at Ferrara. You will thus make all able men in Italy, Spain, and France, friendly to the Church; and perhaps even the German Protestants will follow their example, and return to the Catholic faith. It is much easier to win them back in this way than to compel them by ecclesiastical censures or by secular arms. You should cause this doctrine to be taught in the schools of the Jesuits, who are doing such good work.[8]

The Jesuits did not adopt Neoplatonic hermeticism, but they did make use of the syncretistic method of interpretation employed by Lactantius and Clement of Alexandria. Furthermore, many Jesuits—foremost among them Father Kircher—introduced certain hermetic notions into Scholastic doctrine. The syncretism of the hermetic tradition, as I explained in Part One, was admirably suited to their project of spiritual conversion "from the top down." This syncretism allowed for the reappraisal or, rather, the "redemption" of ancient national religions, whether that of the Druids in the case of the Gauls, that of Confucius in the case of the Chinese, or that of Quetzalcoatl in the case of the Mexicans. Sigüenza y Góngora's historical works on Quetzalcoatl, and the two *loas* by Sor Juana on the theme of the supernatural relation between human sacrifice and the mystery of the Eucharist, belong to this tradition.

THE THEME OF *The Divine Narcissus* is taken from Ovid's *Metamorphoses,* the source of inspiration for so many poets. Narcissus, son of the nymph Liriope and the river-god Cephissus, was a youth with extraordinary beauty who loved the hunt and scorned nymphs. Of the many nymphs who adored him, the most ardent was Echo. Punished by Juno for her talkativeness and her assistance to Jupiter in his dalliances, she was condemned to repeat only the final words of everything she heard. Echo fell so deeply in love with Narcissus that she wasted away until there was nothing left of her but her voice. Narcissus, in his wanderings, came to a pure fountain; he saw himself in it and fell in love with his own image. Unable to touch or kiss his reflection, he languished until he died. Then he was transformed into the flower we call the narcissus. Echo, the Fountain, Narcissus: the myth recurs throughout antiquity, the Renaissance, the Baroque, neoclassicism, and the modern age. In addition to Ovid and countless poems on the theme, Sor Juana was directly inspired by a mythological play of Calderón's, *Eco y Narciso*. Sor Juana's *auto*, however, is more complex and of greater intellectual and lyrical richness than the work of the Spanish poet. She also adapted from the Vulgate several fragments from the Song of Songs and others from Jeremiah, as well as the passage from the gospel of Matthew relating Jesus' temptation on the mountain (4:8–11). The final verses are a translation of a hymn written by Thomas Aquinas. There are also echoes of Garcilaso, St. John of the Cross, and Lope. The play is an example of the exquisite art of the mosaic or, as we say now, the literary collage, in which Eliot and Pound excelled. Although *The Divine Narcissus* combines several styles and modes, this diversity in no way damages its unity or originality.

The *auto* converts Ovid's fable into an allegory of the passion of Christ and the institution of the Eucharist. The interpenetration of the two traditions, the mythological and the biblical, was constant; even the novels of chivalry were transmuted: Jesus appears in one of Lope's *autos* as Amadis, and his twelve apostles as the twelve peers. Calderón used and abused this technique, in *El divino Orfeo* (*The Divine Orpheus*), *El verdadero dios Pan* (*The True God Pan*), *El divino Jason, Psiquis y Cupido* (*Psyche and Cupid*). These precedents situate Sor Juana's *auto* within a tradition, but they do not indicate a direct influence, as in the case of his *Echo and Narcissus*. Another possible source I have found is Francisco de Aldana's *Epístola* to Arias Montano. Although he was later forgotten, Aldana enjoyed great and deserved prestige during the Golden Age—Cervantes, Gil Polo, Quevedo, and Lope de Vega praised him—and Sor Juana undoubtedly read him. Aldana writes that God is a "Narcissus of the upper heavens" and compares the soul to the nymph Echo, who distantly repeats the divine "sweet sound." Sor Juana's allegory is more complex: God is Narcissus, but Echo is not the human soul, she is the devil. A remarkably apt and suggestive invention: the devil is the imitator, the ape, of God, who repeats the deity's words but converts them into meaningless sounds.

Sor Juana preserves the three central elements of the fable: Narcissus, Echo, and the Fountain. She adds Human Nature and Grace. God created man in his own image, but the Fountain, clouded by original sin and other sins of man, cannot cleanse the face of Human Nature, which had, originally, been made in the image of God. Grace shows Human Nature a pure pool in which she will be able to see herself clean and innocent. The pool is an allusion to Mary, who, although human, would be conceived free of original sin. Echo appears, an "impetuous shepherdess." She is a fallen angel, Satan. She is accompanied by Pride and Self-Love. Sor Juana's originality lies in her transformation of the pagan myth: Christ does not, like Narcissus, fall in love with his own image, but with Human Nature, who is and is not himself. In Ovid, the soothsayer Tiresias prophesies that Narcissus will die "when he knows himself": knowledge is equivalent to death. In Sor Juana's *auto* knowledge does not kill; it resurrects.

Sor Juana's central allegory offers a truly extraordinary similarity to a passage from the *Pimander,* the first book of the *Corpus Hermeticum.* There is no way to know whether she had read that text—very popular and widely discussed in her time—in Ficino's translation or whether she was inspired by Valeriano's, Moya's, Kircher's, or some other version. It can be summarized as follows:

> Mind, the Father of all beings, created a Man similar to himself. Man, handsome to look upon, was made in the image of his Father. This Man of eternal substance, this demiurge, had absolute power over the world of mortal creatures and unreasoning animals. It happened that God looked down through the spheres and showed the beauty of his form to Nature below. And Nature, seeing such beauty, smiled, enamored of Man, having seen the beautiful form reflected in the water. And upon seeing in Nature a form so like his own, he loved it and wished to dwell in it. No sooner did he desire it, than it was done, and he entered into matter-devoid-of-reason. Then Nature, welcoming her beloved into herself, bound herself to him. So they became one, and were inflamed with love. And that is why man, unlike all other living creatures upon earth, is twofold. He is mortal by reason of his body; he is immortal by reason of the Man of eternal substance.[9]

This fragment is not without touches of the sublime, and we can understand how Ficino would have read it with wonder and why it would later have impressed Sor Juana. The similarities are disquieting: unlike the ignorant Narcissus, who does not recognize himself, Sor Juana's Christ and the *Pimander*'s Man of eternal substance do not fall in love with their shadows; on the contrary, being Wisdom, as they fall in love with their own image they also fall in love with something that is not that image, something mortal: Nature. But there is a fundamental difference, the great dividing line between Neoplatonic hermeticism and Christianity: while dwelling within Nature, the Man of eternal substance of the *Pimander* falls; Christ, in contrast, redeems Nature. Gnostic pessimism becomes Christian optimism.

The Divine Narcissus (368) is a marvelous mosaic of poetic and metric form. Profundity and complexity of thought are matched by beauty of language and perfection of dramatic concept. In spite of the intricacy of theme and thought, the language is limpid. The scene of Jesus' temptation, transposed into a *romance* in the amatory-pastoral style, is graced with a fluidity that recalls, as Méndez Plancarte so accurately notes, the Lope de Vega of the barks afloat on the seas of love and jealousy. This *romance* is an adaptation of one by Calderón on the same theme; Sor Juana achieves the miracle of lightening and making liquid the weighty verses of the eloquent Spaniard. Echo is displaying her riches to Narcissus:

> See milk, whiter than the snow,
> that as it thickens into whey
> is white that shames the jasmine flower
> in the light of dawning day.
> See, from the reddish ears of wheat,
> forming in the fields afar,
> a cloth of wheaten tapestry
> woven by the waves of air.

The scene in which Human Nature, led by Grace, discovers the fountain where Mary will be conceived without sin is another passage of translucent poetry. Again we see the six-line *lira* that Sor Juana used in other compositions, with its final hendecasyllabic line dividing into four "members":

> Oh, forever crystalline,
> beauteous, transparent fountain:
> stay your flowing,
> that my ruin be reversed
> in your rushing watercouse,
> transparent, cleansing, luminous, life-giving.

Human Nature, who despite her long history of infidelities and betrayals has not entirely lost the memory of her origins and her first love, wanders through the mountains in search of her beloved. The para-phrase by St. John of the Cross of the Song of Songs is purer and more intense, but Sor Juana's is memorable in its opulent description of the "traits of the beloved," a daring combination of Ovid and the Bible:

> like the dove's, his eyes engender love,
> he dwells in the transparent, living waters,
> his breath is sweet, like the perfume of myrrh,
> his hands are turned, perfectly formed, and filled
> with hyacinths, for splendor
> or as signs of all that he must suffer;
> for if the hyacinth is "ay!" it brings
> purpled sighs as well as jeweled rings.[10]

The song of Narcissus as he searches for the lost sheep is another biblical paraphrase. It is a fragment that again is more reminiscent of Lope de Vega than of St. John of the Cross. The mention of the "broken wells" introduces a concrete element into an abstract passage. Sor Juana achieves the near-impossible: effortless fusion of the real and the alle-gorical.

> Oh, where is the lost lamb
> who has strayed from her pastor?
> Where have you gone,
> where do you wander?
> Straying from me, from life you are sundered.
> You drink troubled water
> from the broken wells . . .

Echo surprises Narcissus kneeling over the pure Fountain in which he is contemplating—in the image of Human Nature, hidden among the grasses and reeds of the shore—his own image. Echo's fury is so great that, as in the pagan myth, she loses the power of speech and can repeat only the final words of the speeches of her companions, Pride and Self-Love. Symbolism within symbolism, a technique favored by Calderón and also Sor Juana; joined together, Echo's words give a fragmented summary of the situation: "I have—pain—rage / to see—that—Narcis-sus / a fragile—human being—loves." The disruption of speech may take two opposing forms: first, the freeing of the tongue of the faithful that occurs when the Spirit descends and bestows the miraculous gift that St. Paul calls the "gift of tongues"; second, the stammering that results when jealousy, anger, and envy—experiences known to all—cloud our intellect and tie and tangle our tongues. The "echoes" that in several *loas* seemed an affirmation of life are in *The Divine Narcissus* a net of air and sound that traps "fallen" Intellect within its reverberations.

In another scene, Narcissus, searching for the lost sheep and speaking to himself, hears a voice repeating his words. It is Echo, hidden in the thicket. A hallucinatory duet, as the Divine Spirit's words are repeated in the devil's echo:

> Who from that leafy portico,
> *Echo*
> in tones so gloomy and downcast,
> *downcast*
> to every cry of mine responds?
> *responds*
> Who are you, then, O voice, and where
> do you lie hidden in those fronds?
> Who is it calls in such despair?
> (Together) *Echo, downcast, responds.*

Following this scene, the divine Narcissus lies down beside the Fountain to die. As he dies he recites a sonnet that is, once again, a paraphrase of Scripture. The sonnet is unusual for its repeated enjambment, a technique not highly favored by the poets of the seventeenth century. No doubt Sor Juana intended in this way to emphasize the utterance of a dying man:

> I bid death come; the ghost I now
> yield up, that from my body it be rent,
> although in both resides, forever immanent,
> my godliness . . .

Later, Human Nature, weeping over the death of her beloved—before Grace announces his resurrection in the "white disguise" of the flower we call the narcissus—sings a diaphanous song:

> O nymphs and naiads of this place,
> who dwell within this sylvan glade,
> some in the verdure of the trees
> and others in the crystal waves . . .
> come grieve with me, come share my pain,
> come weep as I do at his death!

Sor Juana's drama, secular and sacred, moves within the orbit of Calderón. Her comedies, *loas,* and *autos sacramentales* are planets and satellites to the Spanish poet's sun, but *The Divine Narcissus* beams its own scintillating light. A hybrid genre, the *auto sacramental* is foreign to modern sensibility, despite the symbolic nature of much of modern drama. Nevertheless, some few works, four or five, redeem the form and give it that timeless contemporaneity that is the mark of all true poetry. Among those works—along with *Life Is a Dream, The Great Theater of the World,* and *Belshazzar's Feast*—stands *The Divine Narcissus.*

24

First Dream

N SPITE OF ITS EXTREMELY intellectual nature, *Primero sueño*[1] is Sor Juana's most personal poem; she herself says so in the *Response:* "the only piece I remember having written for my own pleasure was a little trifle they called *El sueño.*" The belittling tone should not deceive us; it is her longest and most ambitious poem. The date of composition is unknown. It was published for the first time in the second volume of her *Complete Works* in 1692, but one can assume it was known and discussed before that date. It must have been written around 1685, when she was approaching her fortieth birthday: it is a poem of full maturity, a genuine confession, in which she relates, and analyzes, her intellectual adventure. In the *Response* (1691) the poem is called, simply, *El sueño;* in the 1692 edition the title was lengthened to *Primero sueño, que así intituló y compuso la madre Juana, imitando a Góngora (First Dream, for Thus It Was Entitled and Composed by Sister Juana, in Imitation of Góngora).* It is doubtful that the publisher would have presumed to add the adjective "first" without the author's instruction. Perhaps she intended to write a *Second Dream,* and thus the allusion to Góngora, author of the "First" and "Second" *Soledades (Solitudes).* Nevertheless, some critics argue that the poem is self-contained, that it does not need a second part, that Sor Juana never intended to write one, and that the adjective was impertinent meddling on the part of her editors. I do not believe this, and later I shall explain why.

Is *First Dream* an imitation of the *Solitudes?* Only in the sense I have mentioned. Or of Góngora's poetic style? Many critics, beginning with Father Calleja, have cited the influence of Góngora.[2] In its Latinisms, mythological allusions, and vocabulary, *First Dream* is a Gongorist poem. It is Gongorist also in the repeated use of inversion, which reverses the normal order of phrases in an attempt to accommodate them to the pattern of Latin. And there are traces of Góngora in certain passages. This said, we must add that the differences are greater and more profound than the similarities. By nature Sor Juana always tended more toward the clever conceit than toward the brilliant metaphor. Góngora, a poet of the senses, excels in the description—the visual re-creation— of things, figures, beings, and landscapes, while Sor Juana's images are intended more to be grasped intellectually than to be seen. The language of Góngora is aesthetic; that of Sor Juana, intellectual. The world of Góngora is a space crowded with colors, forms, people, and specific objects; the two long *silvas* of his *Solitudes* are descriptive: the sea and the fields, their labors and festivals. *First Dream* is also in *silva* form. It is not a description, however; it is a rational discourse on an abstract theme. Its phrases are prolonged in grammatical complexities and parenthetical comments, a technique learned from Góngora but used by Sor Juana to a different purpose: not to describe but to tell a single story, in which each episode is a spiritual experience. In Góngora, light triumphs; everything, even shadow, is resplendent; in Sor Juana black and white prevail. Replacing the profusion of objects and forms of the *Solitudes* is the uninhabited world of celestial spaces. Nature—sea, mountain, river, trees, beasts—disappears, transformed into geometric figures: pyramids, towers, obelisks. In Góngora's poetic scheme an ideal reality replaces seen reality; the Andalusian poet does not question reality, he transfigures it. The Mexican poet proposes to describe a reality that is by definition invisible. Her theme is the experience of a world that lies beyond the senses. Góngora: a verbal transfiguration of the reality perceived by the senses. Sor Juana: a discourse on a reality seen not by the senses but by the soul.

Intellectual poetry? More exactly, a poetry of the intellect confronting the cosmos. In this sense, it could be said that *First Dream* is strangely prophetic of Mallarmé's poem *Un coup de dés* (*A Throw of the Dice*), which also recounts the solitary adventure of the spirit during a voyage through outer and inner infinities. The resemblance is even more striking if one notes that both voyages end in a fall: vision resolves into nonvision. The world of Mallarmé is that of his time, an infinite or transfinite cosmos; Sor Juana's is the finite universe of Ptolemaic astronomy, but the intellectual emotion she describes is the vertigo of being on the edge of the infinite. Hovering on the heights of her mental pyramid of conceits, the soul finds that what opens before it is a bottomless abyss. In *First Dream* a new and different space appears, unknown either to Fray Luis de León and the sixteenth-century Neoplatonists or to the seventeenth-century poets Góngora, Quevedo, and Calderón. For the former, space was the harmony of the spheres, a visible, although in-audible, model of the divine presence. For the latter, space was the accident-beset reality perceived by our senses, a *here,* or a theological concept, a *beyond.* The space revealed by Sor Juana is an object not of contemplation but of knowledge; it is not a surface over which human bodies move but an abstraction we apprehend, not the celestial or infer-nal beyond but a reality that cannot be conceptualized. The soul is alone, not before God but before a nameless and limitless space.

The "dream" of the title has caused its share of confusion. Alfonso Reyes is astonished by the "layers of subconscious" in the poem and asks, "Have the surrealists peered into Sor Juana's dreams?" Ezequiel Chávez speaks of a "chaotic poetry," and Méndez Plancarte sees in the poem a world that is "unclear, like the world of dreams." Nearly all critics believe that this is a "dreamed" poem, and they recall the passage in the *Response* in which Sor Juana relates that she sometimes solved problems in her dreams. But her poem is too architectural and too com-plex to be confused with a dream in the ordinary sense of the word. We need go no further than Father Calleja's excellent, brief synopsis to dis-miss any similarity of the poem to the kinds of dreams that Reyes and the others were referring to. "As it was night, I slept; I dreamed that I wanted to understand totally and instantly all things of which the uni-verse is composed; I could not, not even divided into categories; not even an individual one. Disappointed, at dawn I awoke." In Spanish we use the word *sueño* to describe different experiences: the act of sleeping, the fantastic and irrational images we "see" while we sleep, the psychic or physiologic faculty that produces those images, desires, ambitions, and dreams, and, finally, the strange experience to which Sor Juana re-fers. The confusion is increased because, unlike French, to cite the lan-guage most closely related to it, Spanish does not distinguish between *rêve* (an ordinary dream) and *songe* (a visionary or prophetic dream). Sor Juana's contemporaries had a clearer notion of these things. In a book she must have known well, Macrobius' commentary on the dream of Scipio, five classes of dream are defined; two of them—nightmare and apparition—are of the type we describe to our friends and our psychoanalysts. In ancient times such dreams were considered deceptive and without value.

Sor Juana's poem recounts the pilgrimage of her soul among the superlunary spheres while her body slept. The tradition of the voyage of the soul during bodily sleep is as ancient as shamanism. Despite its antiquity it is a belief that presupposes a radical distinction between *body* and *soul*. In the history of ideas and the poetry of the West, this concept of the body and the soul as two independent and separable entities was first formulated, with extraordinary clarity, by Plato and his disciples. For the Homeric Greeks, the body and the soul, *soma* and *psyche,* were consubstantial. In the *Iliad* and the *Odyssey,* the souls of the dead are not actual spirits, in the later meaning of the word, but shades, that is, entities composed of a matter less substantial than that of the body. Similarly, spirit (*pneuma*) was a breath. The idea of the soul as a reality separate and distinct from the body was, according to Erwin Rohde, "a drop of foreign blood in the body of Greek culture." That drop of blood, E. R. Dodds ventures, was most likely Scythian or Thracian.[3] Through Pythagoras and Empedocles it reached Plato, and from Plato, in a long and sinuous trajectory that blends with the spiritual history of the West, it came down to us.

This belief is based on a strict dualism (moderated by Aristotle and later by Scholasticism): the soul, being by nature different from the body, is able to leave its carnal sheath in exceptional moments, as in ecstasy or in certain dreams. Visions are those superlunary realities that the soul *sees* in its spiritual voyage. Soul and body act in opposition: the former is more active when the body is least active, and vice versa. Xenophon says, "When the body sleeps, the soul reveals with greater clarity its divine nature . . . ; the soul is liberated from the body in sleep." The soul awakens when the body sleeps. Hence the belief that intensely corporeal states—physical exercise, manual labor, sexuality—are not spiritual and that on the other hand the life of the spirit is passive and quiescent. Action is the body and its senses; contemplation is the soul and its superior faculties. Thus the soul is a prisoner of the body, an idea the Church never approved of and always looked on with suspicion. Nevertheless, the influence of Platonism was so strong that this belief never completely vanished but reappeared in more or less diluted form in many Christian mystics and philosophers. Another consequence of this dualism is that, though fragmentary and transitory, sleep and the ecstatic trance replicate death; during those states the soul is freed to soar from the body. This is the tradition to which *First Dream* belongs.

In ancient times the dreams in which the soul voyages while the body sleeps were held in special reverence. Festugière informs us that the second and third centuries produced an abundance of texts relating this type of experience, expeditions into the world of the spirit. Every age has modified the genre—we are, after all, talking about a literary and philosophical genre—adapting it to its specific needs, to its ideology and its sensibility. In the Middle Ages the voyage of the *spirito peregrino* reached its fullest, most complex, and perfect form in the *Divine Comedy*. The Renaissance and the Baroque modified the genre. In some cases it became the vehicle for political and religious satire (Donne's voyage to the moon, *Ignatius His Conclave,* was a ferocious attack against the Jesuits); in others, the spiritual voyage was transformed into an astronomical expedition (Kepler's *Somnium* and later Kircher's *Iter exstaticum*). Sor Juana inherited this tradition, but instead of a prose account of her voyage she wrote a philosophical poem. Because her treatment of the theme differs substantially from that of her predecessors, it can be said that her *First Dream* both prolongs and alters the tradition. It is the last manifestation of a genre and the beginning of a new one. The universal significance of her poem—a significance that, strangely, no one has yet understood—rests on this fact. But before proceeding we should stop to consider the authors who probably influenced the making of *First Dream*.

First, we must underscore Sor Juana's absolute originality; nowhere in all of Spanish literature of the sixteenth and seventeenth centuries is there anything like *First Dream*. Neither do I find precedents in earlier centuries. It is obvious that the poem has not the slightest relation to satirical works like Quevedo's *Sueños* or to moral and philosophical allegories like Calderón's *Life Is a Dream*. Herrera wrote a song entitled "Al sueño," as did Quevedo. Herrera's *sueño,* "crowned in poppies," simply means sleep. Similarly Quevedo; tormented by love affairs and by remorse, the poet suffers from insomnia and so promises that "if sleep [*sueño*] banishes wakefulness," he will stay awake "only to celebrate sleep." Lupercio Leonardo de Argensola wrote a sonnet against, not in praise of, sleep, "Imagen espantosa de la muerte" ("Awesome Image of Death"). Nothing could be further from Sor Juana's poem. In a valuable study Georgina Sabat de Rivers has made a thorough analysis of the poem's literary, mythological, religious, historico-legendary, and scientific themes.[4] This American scholar believes that Sor Juana was above all inspired by a poem by Francisco de Trillo y Figueroa, "Pintura de la noche desde un crepúsculo a otro" ("Portrait of a Night from Dusk to Dawn"). Although the similarities that Sabat de Rivers has discovered are indisputable, it must be noted that they are commonplaces of the period, mythological allusions and descriptions of night and dawn which both poets appropriated from the allegorical and emblematic repertories in vogue during the seventeenth century. The themes of the poems, however, could not be more dissimilar. Trillo y Figueroa's night is one of sleeplessness caused by love; Sor Juana's poem relates a dream of a spiritual voyage.

In Garcilaso's second eclogue—the most enigmatic poem of the Spanish Renaissance—there is a strange passage about dream and sleep. Unlike the other poets I have cited, Garcilaso in this poem makes ambiguous use of the word *sueño*. It is restorative sleep and grants oblivion to the sad or dejected spirit, but it is also the mysterious power that engenders deceitful fantasies: the fickle dream that vanishes "on swift wings through the ivory door." Here Garcilaso is repeating the traditional distinction made by the ancients between dreams that enter through doors of horn (truthful dreams) and those that enter through doors of ivory (deceptive dreams). Herrera's commentary on this passage is of great interest but is, first of all, a description of dream as a physiological phenomenon. He pauses briefly, nevertheless, to consider a certain kind of dream that, inspired by the stars and other causes, "stirs and awakens the imagination and fantasy of the sleeper . . . causing him to see things in accordance with the arrangement of the heavenly bodies."[5] Sor Juana's poem could be included in this category except that she makes no allusion to the influence of the stars. At any rate, Herrera's note is too brief to be considered an antecedent of a poem as long and complex as *First Dream*.

In a brilliant, if brief, essay accompanying his translation into German of *First Dream*, Karl Vossler signals a precedent that undoubtedly did directly influence the composition of the poem: Kircher's astronomical voyage, *Iter exstaticum*. Other authors have cited Scipio's dream, narrated in Cicero's *De Republica* and preserved in the commentary of the Neoplatonist Macrobius. But Vossler and others mention these precedents only in passing, without stopping to consider or analyze them. In his lucid essay on *First Dream*, Robert Ricard made a major contribution by demonstrating the poem's debt to the tradition of spiritual dream voyages such as the *Somnium Scipionis* and to the doctrines and revelations collected in the *Corpus Hermeticum*. Ricard stated that Sor Juana knew the hermetic literature of ancient times only at second hand, and

suggested that the poem's Neoplatonism came probably from Leo Hebraeus and his *Dialogues of Love*. But there is no trace of erotic Platonism in *First Dream*. Ricard also singled out Garcilaso's first elegy, in
which some of the final tercets are a reflection of Cicero's description of
the heroes in the pagan pantheon; this is too vague and, especially, too
remote from Sor Juana's theme.[6]

This brief review shows that Vossler and Ricard, each and independently, made essential contributions to a better understanding of *First
Dream*—Vossler with his reference to Kircher and his astronomical voyage, and Ricard by identifying the poem with the tradition of the "ana-
basis dreams" of the first centuries of the Christian era. For years these
were isolated insights; it fell to me to tie up the loose ends and to prove
that the hermetic tradition, of which an essential part is the vision of the
soul freed through dream from its bodily chains, came to Sor Juana
primarily through Kircher, and also as filtered through the treatises of
Cartari, Pierio Valeriano, and others.[7] It would have been impossible to
reach this conclusion, however, without the work of the English historian Frances A. Yates, who traced the development of the modern hermetic tradition from its reappearance in the fifteenth century in Cosimo
de' Medici's Florence to seventeenth-century Germany, where it influenced the Rosicrucians, on the one hand, and, on the other, various
members of the Society of Jesus. Yates demonstrated that Father Athanasius Kircher was one of the last representatives of hermeticism in the
seventeenth century. Categorical though it is, her assertion is substantially true: more than once Kircher and his disciple, Father Gaspar
Schott, had to defend themselves against the accusation of following too
closely the "impious doctrines" of Hermes and his disciples.

A curious event is related in the second chapter ("Road to the Moon")
of *Iter exstaticum*,[8] which marks the beginning of the voyage through
the celestial spheres: Theodidactus, who is the transparent mask for Father Kircher, is invited to a private concert offered by three Roman musicians. He is overwhelmed by the mastery of the three artists and feels
as if "all things were conspiring to intensify the harmony of the universe." Shortly after, one day when the "images of the said symphony
were stirring his spirit with their ghostly apparitions . . . suddenly, as if
overcome by intense drowsiness, . . . he found himself lying prostrate in
the middle of a vast plain." Then "appeared a male figure of uncommon
aspect," winged, awe-inspiring, and beautiful, who immediately soothed
him, saying, "I am Cosmiel, minister of the God of Heaven and earth.

Arise; do not fear, Theodidactus; your desires were heard and I have been sent to show to you, insofar as may be permitted to mortal eye, the supreme majesty of the God Optimus Maximus, who shines in splendor in all his works." Thus begins the voyage of Theodidactus through starry spaces, during an ecstatic dream provoked by the music. Schott, Kircher's disciple and editor of the book, adds in an explanatory note that the ecstasy was not "fiction but a true story"; that he personally knew the three musicians (he gives their names); and that "the dream occurred the night after the concert." Theodidactus-Kircher, guided by Cosmiel, visits the planets, the upper heavens, and the firmament of the fixed stars. "Each star is governed by an Intelligence . . . that moves it in its predestined orbit." Cosmiel, leading Theodidactus, faithfully follows the astronomy of Tycho Brahe, a system in which the planets and the stars orbit the sun while the sun and the moon orbit the earth.

Kircher's is a hybrid book. The form derives from the hermetic and Neoplatonic literature of the voyage of the soul; its astronomy, taken from Brahe, is a compromise between the old and new astronomies; and its information about planets and stars is a mixture of known facts, fantasies, wild hypotheses, and authentic religious sentiment. The account conforms to a literary model that reached its highest point around the second century after Christ. This is the period of the decline of ancient rationalism and of the rise of obscure cults inspired by the revelations of numerous prophets, demiurges, and divinities. "It is natural," says Festugière, "that certain widespread beliefs should have given rise to a number of literary fictions as a manner of expressing different aspects of the divine gift." It is useless to ask "in every instance of this *logos* of revelation whether the author is sincere or whether he is merely creating a literary fiction that will be avidly received by the public." Festugière underscores the ambiguous attitude of the authors of these accounts of revelations experienced during an ecstatic dream: "although they speak of ecstasy and of ascending to the heavens, they have a clear awareness that they are recounting a psychological phenomenon, not a real event."[9] The Jewish Neoplatonist Philo says that those magi and prophets "voyage in spirit to the sun, the moon, and the choir of the moving planets, for although they are bound to the earth by their bodies, their souls have wings." Kircher's book repeats this ambivalence: the title page speaks of a "feigned rapture," but in the text itself Theodidactus reports his ecstasy as real, and Schott adds his verification, even to the date: the night following the concert by the three Italian musicians.

This is not, however, the only or the most important similarity between Kircher's ecstasy and the accounts of the voyages of the soul. The revelations of a god, angel, or demiurge always take place after the subject falls into a deep sleep (the "intense drowsiness" of Theodidactus); then he sees a divine figure, hears a voice, and, sometimes, ascends to the upper heavens guided by a deity or a heavenly messenger. The vision of Hermes, in the first book of the *Corpus Hermeticum,* follows this pattern in detail:

> Once on a time, when I had begun to think about the things that are, and my thoughts had soared high aloft, while my bodily senses had been put under restraint by sleep—yet not such sleep as that of men weighed down by fullness of food or by bodily weariness—methought there came to me a Being of vast and boundless magnitude, who called me by my name, and said to me . . ."I am Poimandres, the Mind of the Sovereignty . . . I know what you wish, for indeed I am with you everywhere . . ."[10]

I need not point out all the features that distinguish this religious text from Kircher's merely literary account. But they are both in the same lofty pattern. And so is the account Cicero places in the mouth of Scipio the Younger, although Scipio, a Roman, holds forth in terms less majestic than Hermes and more sober than Theodidactus. Cicero's general relates how in his youth, in Africa, after a magnificent banquet and a conversation that lasted far into the early hours with King Masinissa, who had been a friend of his grandfather, Scipio Africanus,

> I fell into a deeper than ordinary sleep. Then there appeared unto my spirit, still preoccupied with the matter of our dialogues, an apparition . . . It was Africanus, perfect in every feature, whom I knew more through contemplation of his portrait than from having seen him. I recognized him at once, and felt a sudden shudder; but he said to me: "Be calm, Scipio, and engrave upon your memory what I am about to tell you . . ."

These were, probably, the texts that inspired Sor Juana. She was an avid reader of Kircher, and several times in her writings she cites Cicero and Macrobius: she undoubtedly knew and studied them. In her theorizing about music there is more than one echo of Macrobius' commentary on Scipio's dream. As for Hermes' vision and his dialogue with Pimander: the authors of her much-favored books on mythology frequently alluded to this theme: in *Oedipus Aegyptiacus* Kircher not only cites the treatises of the *Corpus Hermeticum* but transcribes several fragments. Yet Sor Juana's dream does not fit the traditional mold. The first difference is formal: the dreams relating the ascent of the soul to the heavenly spheres are written in prose, while Sor Juana's account is a poem. Prose is the language of history. That is why the authors of the gospels wrote in prose: they were writing history. Verse, on the other hand, is the favored medium for poetic fiction. Thus *First Dream* must not be read as an account of true ecstasy; it is the allegory of an experience that cannot be encompassed in the space of a single night but spans the many nights Sor Juana spent studying and thinking. The night of the poem is an exemplary night, a night of nights. The complement to *First Dream* is the *Response:* a prose version of the same theme, the search for knowledge—but over a lifetime, not in the course of a single night.

The second difference is the impersonality of *First Dream*. The protagonist has no name, age, or gender: it is the human soul. Not until the last words of the last line ("the world was filled with light, and I awakened") do we learn that the soul is Sor Juana's. This information in no way alters the impersonality of the poem; Sor Juana had said again and again, "Souls have no gender." The impersonality accentuates the allegorical and exemplary nature of the poem: it does not tell us a story, in the strict sense of the word "story," but unfolds before us as a model, a synthetic archetype. Personality and individuality have been carefully excluded. Naturally, the pretense of impersonality breaks down at the end: the poem is simultaneously allegory and confession.

The third difference is more than a difference: it is a break with tradition. According to Macrobius, dreams that truly reveal—unlike nightmares and chimeras—are of three classes: enigmatic, prophetic or visionary, and oracular. In all three types a supernatural agent—god, demiurge, dead ancestor—always intervenes to lead and instruct the soul during its voyage. Festugière, in his study of "the *logos* of revelation in literary fictions," follows Macrobius: the apparition of the demiurge or messenger at the beginning of the ecstatic dream is the point of departure for the revelation. In Sor Juana's dream we witness the same sequence of events: the body falls into a deep sleep, the soul awakens, ascends, and contemplates the universe. But there is a fundamental difference, one already noted by Ricard: in Sor Juana's dream there is no dead grandfather, no Pimander, no Virgil or Beatrice, no Cosmiel. Thus Sor Juana's poem continues the ancient tradition of the soul's voyage during a dream but at the same time, on an essential point, breaks with it.

First Dream's break with tradition is something more than a simple literary anomaly. And it is something different: it is a sign of her times. Something ends in that poem and something begins. This spiritual departure implies a radical change in the relationship between the human being and the beyond. The supernatural intermediaries and celestial messengers who were our link with the beyond have disappeared, dispelled by analytical powers; the soul is left in isolation. The break is truly momentous, and we still suffer its historical and psychic consequences. There is yet another difference between Sor Juana's dream and traditional ecstasy. In *First Dream* she relates that, while her body slept, her soul ascended to the upper sphere; there her soul had a vision so intense, so vast, so luminous and dazzling, that she was blinded; once recovered, she longed to ascend again, now, step by step, but she could not; as she was wondering what other path she might take, the sun rose and her body awakened. The poem is the account of a spiritual vision that ends in nonvision. This second break with tradition is even more important and more radical.

The theme of the voyage of the soul is a religious theme and is inseparable from revelation. In Sor Juana's poem not only is there no demiurge, there is no revelation. *First Dream* is the first example of an attitude—the solitary soul confronting the universe—that later, beginning with romanticism, would be the spiritual axis of Western poetry. The solitary confrontation is a religious theme, like that of the voyage of the soul, but religious in a negative way: it denies revelation. More precisely, it is the revelation of the fact that we are alone and that the world of the supernatural has dissipated. In one way or another, all modern poets have lived, relived, and re-created the double negation of *First Dream:* the silence of space, and the vision of nonvision. The great and until now unrecognized originality of Sor Juana's poem resides in this fact. And this is the basis for its unique place in the history of modern poetry.

FIRST DREAM IS A *SILVA* OF nine hundred seventy-five verses. The poetic form of the *silva*—a combination of seven- and eleven-syllable lines with no fixed rhyme pattern—is both demanding and flexible. The poem flows without interruption, without set divisions: a true discourse. The rhythm is slow, although in some passages, in accordance with the demands of the text, it picks up speed or slows down. Every time there is a shift in direction or subject, Sor Juana constructs verbal bridges to make the transition less abrupt. This allows for various groupings of themes in different modes and tonalities. The poem's voyage occurs in the space of a single night, and its shifts reflect the imperceptible variations in shadow, light, and temperature which take place between the setting of the sun and its reappearance in the east. This is one of Sor Juana's great artistic achievements: just as we cannot perceive the precise advent of dusk, midnight, or dawn, so the poem flows in long intervals until suddenly the wan light of dawn filters through the window. It is artificial, therefore, to divide the poem into parts and sections; at the same time it is indispensable—and legitimate, as long as we remember that divisions in the text are never clear-cut and that there is a continuous interpenetration of themes and motifs. Throughout the poem—tacitly, not explicitly—two series of oppositions are in conflict: day and night, body and soul. Their fluctuating interplay constitutes what could be called the substance of the poem.

Critics cannot agree on the number of parts that compose the poem: Méndez Plancarte says twelve, Chávez six; José Gaos reduces it to five, Ricard to three. Vossler sees the poem as a continuous flow, which was also Calleja's view. Like Ricard, I tend toward the tripartite division, although my parts are different from his: "Sleep," "The Voyage" (the dream proper), and "The Awakening." The three parts of the poem subdivide into seven sections, its basic components. The first part splits into two sections, "The Sleep of the World" and "The Sleep of the Body"; the third part replicates that division in "The Awakening of the Body" and "The Awakening of the World"; the second part, the voyage or dream itself, is divided into three sections: "The Vision," "The Categories," and "Phaethon." There is a perfect correspondence between the first and seventh sections, and between the second and the sixth: the sleep and the awakening, respectively, of the world and the human body. Within the symmetrical frame formed by those four sections appears the triptych of the voyage of the soul: the ascent of the soul and its vision; its fall and its attempt to climb the pyramid of knowledge step by step; its doubts and the example of the hero Phaethon.[11]

A word of warning before I turn to a description of the poem. The word *sueño*, in the text, has four principal connotations: *sueño* as sleep; *sueño* as dream that is vision, not deception; *sueño* as the name of that vision; and *sueño* as ambition, desire, or an unrealized dream. These distinct meanings are enclosed in another: *sueño* is the almost total cessation of bodily functions, the passivity that stimulates the activity of the soul. It is a state close to death—the provisional death of the body that means the liberation, also provisional, of the soul. Sor Juana's *sueño* is not the disorderly and chaotic product of the libido, the subconscious, or instinct; it is rational and spiritual vision. Her *sueño* is the soaring of the soul freed from its bodily chains, not the delirium of the body liberated from the censorship of reason. Thus it differs radically from Freud's—and our—view of sleep. For Freud, *sueño* liberates desire, instinct, the body; for Sor Juana, *sueño* liberates the soul.

"The Sleep of the World" could also be called "The Triumph of Night." The first twenty-four lines describe a strange scene: the earth projects a "pyramidal shadow" with which it hopes to assault the highest heavens, "to ascend and touch the stars." Normally we say that night falls from above and that its shadow descends over the earth; Sor Juana describes the opposite phenomenon: shadow issues from the earth and is a projection of it. Her description is symbolic, not realistic: shadow emanates from the "black vapors" of terrestrial corruption, and with it the earth hopes to obscure the superlunary sphere, the region of celestial intelligences and angels. In a different passage (lines 340–412) she again speaks of a pyramid, but one of light, not shadow. Vossler has suggested the "symbolic significance" of these geometric forms: the pyramid of light represents the soul's ascent and stands in opposition to the pyramid of shadow in the opening lines. He recalls that Kircher writes in one of his books that "the Egyptians were wont to distinguish between a pyramid of light that descends from the heavens to the earth and another of shadow that aspires to rise toward the sky."[12] Vossler's comment is appropriate, with the simple addition that in Sor Juana's poem this opposition between the pyramids, the luminous and the shadowy, is one of conflict: the hosts of night assaulting the skies. That Sor Juana assigns a negative symbolism to the pyramid of shadow there can be no doubt; she calls it "baneful." It is the image of the sublunary world, where accident, sin, and corruption reign.

Night does not reach to the stars and merely brushes the sphere of the moon. But below, it extends its dominion over all beings, admitting only the "muted voices" of nocturnal birds, so solemn and subdued that their muffled sound does not disturb the silence. The dualism of the first lines disappears, and in a passage strongly reminiscent of Góngora—except that it is in tones of black and white—Nyctimene the owl, the three daughters of Minyas transformed into bats, and Pluto's minister Ascalaphus pass before our eyes. The god Harpocrates—another reminder of Egypt—imposes silence upon the lugubrious choir. The wind dies down; dogs sleep; the fish are doubly mute (because they are fish and because they are asleep); sleep has come to Alcyone, to Acteon the hunter whose hounds turned on him, to the lion that keeps watchful eyes open even in slumber, to the birds, to Jupiter's eagle—to everything and everyone, not excepting thief and lover. Sleep reigns.

Bodies sleep. Sleep is a law no one can escape, King or fisherman, Pope or laborer. Sleep is as universal as death: *Somnium imago mortis.* Temporal death: "the body is a corpse without a soul." False death: the body, "dead in life, alive in death," lives in motionless, secret life. The soul, inversely, is immortal, and the sleep of the body relieves it of its material burden. Then begins the description of the bodily organs during sleep: the heart, "the kingly organ"; the lungs, "magnet of the wind"; the stomach, "temperate hearth of human warmth." Sor Juana's medical knowledge, like her cosmography and astronomy, is that of her time (in Spain and its possessions). Méndez Plancarte says that she follows Fray Luis de Granada. Perhaps. In any case, she did read books on medicine, although not Harvey, as Vossler supposed. More realistically, Emilio Carilla cites Galen and his successors. Most of her knowledge must have come from the manuals of the time, although bookshelves in the portraits by Miranda and Cabrera show volumes by Hippocrates and Galen and other tomes on anatomy, surgery, and pharmacy. Her medical science, in fact, derived from philosophy and theology. The Spanish scholar José Gaos observes that the images in this section allude to the mechanical arts: the heart is the balance wheel of the human clock; the lungs are bellows; the trachea is an aqueduct. He asks, "Descartes's animal machines?"[13] A literary echo seems more likely to me: the poetry of the seventeenth century used and abused scientific metaphors almost as much as mythological ones. But Sor Juana's fondness for those images is greater than that of other Hispanic poets; in this she is closer to Marvell and Donne than to Quevedo and Góngora. Another characteristic that distinguishes her from her tradition.

How does the body, which even while sleeping continues to labor, communicate with the soul? Sor Juana calls upon two separate theories without clearly distinguishing between them in the poem: the theory of humors and the theory of the vital spirits. The four humors combine like the four elements: cold, warm, moist, and dry form the blood, phlegm, bile, and black bile or melancholy. These humors pass through a process of purification until they reach the brain and, from there, the "internal senses." The spirits, for their part, are born of the blood; the warmth of the liver converts them into vapor and they are transformed into natural spirits. They then undergo a further refinement and become vital spirits, and in the brain are converted into animal spirits. The order, and the names, change from author to author, but the process is the same.[14] Body and soul communicate through these spirits; in Donne's words:

> As our blood labours to beget
> Spirits, as like soules as it can,
> Because such fingers need to knit
> That subtile knot, which makes us man.

So, during that night of the *sueño,* the body dispatches, already refined, the spirits and humors to the "internal senses," which are responsible for collecting sensations and perceptions from the external senses (sight, hearing, smell, touch, and taste), purifying them, and, once they are images, transmitting them to the rational soul for consideration, thought, and contemplation. The internal senses are the estimative, the imaginative, memory, and fantasy.[15] The external and internal senses constitute the sensible soul (*anima secunda*), and through them the rational soul (*anima prima*) communicates with the world and the body. In turn, the rational soul is composed of two faculties—*Ratio* and *Mens,* Reason, which communicates with the sensible soul, and Intellect, which is the organ of spiritual vision. The sensible soul, said Bruno, is a Jacob's ladder that leads us to Reason, where we receive, "like a shadow," the image of God himself, "reflected in the intellect." So in Sor Juana's night, the estimative sense—the one most directly in touch with the external senses—receives "simulacra" from the external world, transmits them to the imaginative sense, which then, "for better custody," delivers them, purified, to memory, whence they ascend to the highest sense, fantasy, which forms "diverse images" with them. So begins the motionless voyage of the soul and its vision. In these passages, and even more in those that follow, the mixture of Scholasticism and Neoplatonism is constant.

In lines 280–284, fantasy serenely copies "the images of all things" and with its "invisible brush" paints "mental figures," "without light" and with "bright colors." Vossler points out that the idea that colors exist in themselves, *in potentia,* and are manifest, *in actu,* without being generated by light, in a medieval concept derived from Aristotle and found in Kircher's *Ars magna lucis et umbrae* (1646). The distinction between potential and actual is Aristotelian, but the speculations about different types of light and about colors that shine of themselves without need of external light are more Neoplatonic than Aristotelian. Kircher was probably following Neoplatonic Renaissance hermeticism: Ficino, Patrizi, Bruno. The brush of fantasy is invisible precisely because it is formed from the internal light that illumines dream visions. This invisible and incorporeal light was a spiritual substance well known to the Neoplatonists and hermeticists. Its purest manifestation, says Bruno, was *Lux*, God's first creation in Genesis. Ficino enumerates a variety of lights: the light of God, followed by the intellectual light of the angels; then the rational light of man; below that, the light of the sensible soul; then the light of the astral body, in which the material body is enveloped; and, finally, everyday sunlight.[16] The light with which fantasy paints mental figures is the light of the rational soul: like the Neoplatonists, Sor Juana blurs the distinction between fantasy and understanding. (The twentieth century has its own curious version of these ideas: Marcel Duchamp, in several notes on his *White Box*, states that "there are colors that are luminous in themselves, source colors independent of external light." Bruno had said the same thing, although less categorically, attributing this property to colors and metals that are opaque in the sublunary world but shine of their own light in the stars.)[17]

Fantasy's bright copies and reflections are compared to those of Pharos, the lighthouse of Alexandria, in whose mirror one could see ships plying the seas beyond the line of the horizon. The lighthouse built by Sostratus on the isle of Pharos, by order of Ptolemy Philadelphus, was one of the seven wonders of the ancient world. The legend—of Arabic origin—concerning the mirror in which ships sailing at incalculable distances were reflected was current throughout the sixteenth and seventeenth centuries. Among the mathematicians and physicists interested in this fiction were Descartes, Mersenne, and Newton himself. Kircher was surely among those who, without denying the mirror's miraculous properties, attributed them "to a diabolic illusion condemned by the Church."[18] Fantasy, however, copies not only sublunary objects and beings but the "light of intellects in the stars"—that is, the intelligences that move the stars (Cosmiel was one of them). Neoplatonism, insinuated in the preceding lines of the poem, is now manifest, palpable. The soul contemplates those celestial intelligences, revealed to it in the "only possible way / that the invisible may be conceived." That "way" was through fantasy, which at the time meant not unreality but the intermediary between the spiritual and the sensible. Aristotle had said that man needs images "to think, in time, of what lies outside time."

Intellect, on the wings of the soul's "immaterial being," sees in itself a spark of the Supreme Being. This is the poem's first mention of divinity. Sor Juana does not use the word God, but Supreme Being. A rationalist deism, even Robert Ricard concurs. There is not a single allusion to Christ anywhere in the poem; Sor Juana speaks of a Supreme Being, a Prime Cause, and an Author of the World, but never of God the Father, the Savior, or Jesus. Nor does she say that the soul was created by God; rather, it is a "spark of divine fire." This expression echoes the hermetic tradition, not Christianity. There are additional traces of Neoplatonism. For Plato, knowledge obeys the law of similitude; to contemplate is to participate: the spiritual eye, the intellect, or *Nous,* sees the divine light and rejoices in seeing it because the intellect itself is illuminated by it and participates in all that it sees. Sor Juana says this in terms that could not be more purely Platonic: the soul, seeing itself as part of the Supreme Being, rejoices in the similitude. And she adds that, enraptured in its joyful contemplation, it judges itself "nearly released" from the "corporeal chain" that bound it and prevented it from soaring. Méndez Plancarte deplores such overt dualism: "This, and the 'liberation' of the soul during dream, seems to us more the simple poetic fantasy of Sor Juana than philosophical conviction." In contrast, Vossler sees in these expressions, and in those that follow, evidence not only of her Neoplatonism but of her interest in the ideas of Bruno and Galileo, "about whose trials she probably was informed, not without a certain apprehension." An apprehension that was well founded, as she later found out.

Hovering at its highest point, the soul contemplates the movement of the stars and the celestial sphere. A lengthy digression follows: the famous passage on the pyramids. Sor Juana compares the pyramid of light, the soul, with the two pyramids of Memphis. A new echo of hermeticism: Egypt is the site of Hermes' revelation, and Platonism was a doctrine considered by many, among them Kircher himself, to have originated in Egypt. Vossler suggests that Sor Juana was also referring to the pyramids of Teotihuacán, but the truth is that she never mentions them. Furthermore, both Kircher and Sor Juana believed that the Mexican pyramids were derived from those of Egypt, origin of all the arts and philosophies of the ancient world. Most important, we must not forget that the landscape of the poem is *mental.* The Egyptian pyramids appear as allegories of the soul and of its rise toward the light. Sor Juana describes a symbolic landscape that can be read as if it were a written text. The significance of that stone text is its Platonic theology: the soul's longing to ascend toward its origin. Sor Juana cites the authority of

Homer and says that the pyramids are "barbaric hieroglyphs . . . , material embodiments" of the human mind, for in the same way that pyramids rise toward their apex, so the mind "aspires always toward the Prime Cause." Some critics are surprised by the mention of Homer in connection with the symbolism of the pyramid. There is no reason for surprise: from the second century on, Homer and Virgil were reinterpreted by hermeticism. The allusion to the Prime Cause immediately evokes another of Sor Juana's favorite images: the circle whose center is everywhere. In the *Response* she says she borrowed this idea from Kircher, but, as I have already shown, the source is Nicholas of Cusa. This image is one of the axes of Sor Juana's thought, as it was for Bruno and others.

The soul has reached a point higher than the pyramids and the Tower of Babel. It has created a "peak of its own soaring" and, there on the apex of its "mental pyramid," believes it has "left its self behind and entered a new region." Is that region the Supreme Being, the light which illumines Intellect and in which Intellect rejoices in contemplating itself, or is it the complex mechanism of the universe? Is it union with God or knowledge of the heavens and their worlds? Perhaps both; for Sor Juana they are one and the same. A new and still more radical departure from Christian mysticism: the soul in *First Dream* does not aspire to join with God as a *person* but, as in Plato, wants to know and contemplate him as the First Being and Prime Cause. This knowledge and this contemplation include contemplation of his works, especially the highest, the celestial universe. Faithful to Platonic tradition, Sor Juana seeks contemplation of the Supreme Being through knowledge of the universe. To see the stars in their movement—to see them with spiritual eyes, the light of similitude—is to see the Supreme Being in his very essence, indistinguishable from his thought and his acts. "Rejoicing, hovering," the Queen of all sublunary things—the rational soul and, in particular, the intellect—casts her gaze into the distance and her "eyes of beauty and intellect" embrace "all creation." Intellect sees, but Reason cannot understand, that immensity and that richness. Just as we close our dazzled eyes against the too-bright light of the sun, so the soul hesitates and shrinks back into itself, unable to bear the heavenly light. Vertigo and dizziness: the end of the vision.

Reason has been defeated, overwhelmed by "the immensity and vastness of the workings of the universe" and simultaneously by the diversity of its components. Intellect itself has clouded over. The soul, incapable of finding a path, founders "in the impartiality of a sea of amazement." Then, prudently, it emerges from the sea and clings to the "mental shore." Nevertheless, it is not dispirited and stubbornly continues to search for an alternate course: either to dwell on a single matter or "to ponder one by one" each entity and each object, until they are arranged in the ten "artificial categories." This "discourse on method" has suggested to some a possible influence of Descartes. No such thing: Sor Juana relies on Aristotle and Scholasticism. She proposes, by their example, to attain the "science of universals" through the reduction of all existing things to the ten Aristotelian categories. She calls them "mental fantasies," an expression which Méndez Plancarte disparages as "lacking in rigor" but which actually is a residue of Neoplatonism: I have already shown that in Ficino and Bruno the operations of fantasy are confused at times with those of intellect. "Mental fantasies" is the same as "rational concepts." Literally *reanimated,* with new spirit, the soul sets out to climb, step by step, from the mineral realm to the vegetal, and from it to the animal. The idea of the categories blends here with another, related but distinct: that of the "great chain of being," to use the phrase of Macrobius, which stretches from God to the inanimate, passing through angelic intelligences, man, animals, and plants.

The concept, and the expression "chain of being," are Neoplatonic in origin. If the world exists, it is because God, in his fullness of being, overflows, in a manner of speaking, and produces the world and its entities. Plato, says Lovejoy, converts the Self-Sufficing Perfection that is divinity into Self-Transcending Fecundity.[19] Plotinus perfected this concept with that of the Emanations: "The One is perfect . . . and being perfect, it overflows, and thus its superabundance produces an Other . . . Whenever anything reaches its own perfection, we can see that it cannot endure to remain in itself, but generates and produces some other thing." The One is plethora that manifests itself as plurality.[20] The "chain of being" assumes in the thought of Aristotle the eminently logical form of serial continuity: "Nature passes gradually from the inanimate to the animate . . . and between them there is a middle kind that belongs to both orders." The same occurs in the transition between plants and animals. Aristotle emphasizes the idea of transition among the species, orders, and families, and thus conceives of the natural world as a vast system of links or, to use Sor Juana's word, hinges. St. Thomas is heir to the dual legacy of ancient philosophy: the Neoplatonic belief in the ascent of things and beings toward God, and the Aristotelian connected series (*connexio rerum*). Both ideas are present in *First Dream*, as they would be throughout the eighteenth and nineteenth centuries. Forty years after the publication of Sor Juana's poem, Pope addresses the same theme:

> Vast chain of being! which from God began;
> Natures ethereal, human, angel, man,
> Beast, bird, fish, insect, what no eye can see,
> No glass can reach; from infinite to thee,
> From thee to nothing . . .

Pope's series is descendant and Sor Juana's ascendant, but at either end both poets stumble over two incommensurables: infinite being and nothingness. Two forms of the circle that defy reason. Nevertheless, in the midst of the series, Reason finds the prodigious "hinge," the "marvelous threefold composite," Man. He is threefold because he is the compendium of the three natural realms; threefold also because the soul is composed not only of the "five sensible faculties" (the senses) but of the three internal ones that rule the rest. Almost certainly this refers to the three functions of the soul according to Plato: desiring, which pertains to the senses; reasoning, corresponding to the rational; and, mediating between the two, the spirited, or passionate, faculty that subjects irrational desire to reason as the warrior is subject to the magistrate.[21] The fragment devoted to Man is, along with the description of the soul hovering above its "mental pyramid," one of the most beautiful in *First Dream*. If God is the circle whose center is everywhere, man is the point of convergence of creation, the link between mortal creatures and immortal spirits, the absolute compendium "of angel, plant, and beast." He is a "lofty baseness" whose brow brushes the heavens but whose mouth is "sealed by dust." A dual and contradictory creature who resembles the eagle of Patmos "that measured the stars and the earth," or the statue of Nebuchadnezzar, with golden brow and feet of clay. These are the only biblical allusions in the poem.

Why is man the convergence and point of intersection? Because "he would be exalted through the mercy of Union." Thus the section that I have called, rather arbitrarily, "The Categories" ends by evoking union with God as the goal of knowledge. Sor Juana knew perfectly well, however, that knowledge of the divine is essentially different from knowledge of worldly sciences. Unlike the philosophical schools of antiquity, whose ultimate goal was wisdom and an upright life, no manual of

Christian mysticism prescribes the study of geology, botany, physics, and mathematics in order to reach God. The distinction between the two kinds of knowledge is not made clear in either *First Dream* or the *Response*. Sor Juana defends her love of the secular sciences as being a path toward the divine: this attitude was more philosophical than Christian, as her critics and censors did not fail to point out to her. Intellect, in the poem, does not succeed in passing through all the gradations of knowledge. It cannot comprehend even the simplest fact, such as the capricious course of an underground spring—a pretext for a mythological digression—or the reason for the shape, fragrance, and color of a flower—another pretext, this time for some more or less felicitous variations on the baroque *topos* of flowers—or, finally, the transition from individual to species and genus. The endeavor "to investigate Nature" is revealed as a task whose weight would crush a Hercules, or Atlas himself.

As it contemplates "the awesome machinery" of the universe, Reason hesitates and steps back. But to hesitate is not to give up. Then it recalls Phaethon, the young mortal who refused to yield in his arrogant determination to drive the chariot of the Sun, even after his father, Apollo, had warned him of the certain dangers that lay ahead. Phaethon is an archetype, because he was determined "to immortalize his name in his ruin," a memorable line and a perfect example of what Breton called the "ascendant metaphor." Like the pyramids in an earlier passage, Phaethon is "the embodiment, the model," that gives wing to the spirit, the third and most generous of the faculties of the soul. Newly emboldened, the soul defies immensity and "spells out glory / among letters of devastation." This passage, one of the most beautiful in the poem, is abruptly interrupted: the body, deprived of nourishment for several hours, awakes. The "phantoms" flee from the unoccupied brain like the fleeting figures projected on the wall by Kircher's magic lantern. The body's awakening is followed by the awakening of the world. Announced by Venus and Aurora, "Amazons clothed in light," the sun rises between the mountains. Cosmic symmetry: the combat of the beginning is repeated, but now day triumphs, routing the black squadrons of the night. The combat is cyclic, and night establishes its empire in the other hemisphere, where perhaps another Juana Inés is dreaming the same dream. Light filters through the windows, and she awakes.

ALTHOUGH CONSTRUCTED WITH DELIBERATE and rigorous objectivity, *First Dream* is threaded with personal emotion. The daring of the soul, its ecstasy, its doubts, its vacillations, and the praise of the tragic figure of Phaethon are a true intellectual confession. To confirm this we need only compare the poem with what Sor Juana says in the *Response* about her desire for learning, her psychic wavering, her method of study, meditations, and reasonings. In the space of an ideal night, in a consciously abstract manner, Juana Inés recounts her intellectual life. The poem ends inconclusively: the soul does not know what path to choose—all are "quicksand and reefs"—the body awakens and the dream dissipates. The abrupt awakening puts an end to the dream, not to the intellectual adventure of the soul. This explains and justifies the adjective *primero*, first. But *First Dream* also portrays the history of a defeat, although some Catholic critics, contrary to what is explicit in the text, insist in seeing in the poem the "beautiful embrace of faith and piety." What, then, is the meaning of that "defeat"?

The idea that learning is impossible divides into two other ideas: either man cannot know because he is man, or he is precluded from knowing by some particular circumstance—for example, in Sor Juana's case, because she was Sor Juana. This is the distinction perceptively set forth by José Gaos in his essay "El sueño de un sueño" ("Dream of a Dream"). According to Gaos, "Sor Juana did not philosophize in verse on the limits of human knowledge . . . but on the primary experience of her life: the failure of her quest to learn." And he adds, "Is this failure of a woman's desire to learn the result of being a woman or of being the woman she is? A feminist or a personal skepticism?" As a person, Sor Juana was "inclined toward learning," but soon she realized that "being female was a basic barrier to the realization of that desire. She attempts to neutralize being female by means of religion . . . but even this neutralizing fails." Gaos does not clarify whether this barrier was natural for Sor Juana—that is, her condition as a woman—or imposed by society. Sor Juana's texts make clear that she did not believe that being a woman was a natural barrier: her obstacles originated in customs, not in her femaleness. That is why she turns to religion: to neutralize the social barrier. Furthermore, the protagonist of *First Dream* is not the female soul but the human soul that for Sor Juana—it cannot be repeated too often—has no gender. The barrier is not her womanhood but the fact that the soul is prisoner of the body. Failure derives not from her sex but from the limitations of human comprehension. The defect of "not knowing in one instant the whole of creation," as we read in the middle section of the poem, is a defect of fallen man. Sor Juana did reflect on the limitations of reason: this is the theme of her poem and is at the center of her inner life.

Most critics believe that the poem is about "the dream of knowledge." They immediately invest the word "dream" of the title with the sense of illusion and vanity. The soul "dreams" of knowing, fails, and, now awakened, realizes that knowledge is a delusion. Sor Juana's skepticism, like that of so many others, leads to surrender to God. At the end of her life, faced with the failure of her dream of learning, Sor Juana renounces human studies, renounces the word itself, to enter the silent world of contemplation and charity. This is the opinion of Ricard, Ramón Xirau, and Gaos as well: "from vital and intellectual disillusion, to mystic release, refuge in God."²² *First Dream* is the poem of Sor Juana's intellectual crisis and the initial act of her conversion. This proposition has a corollary: the poem is yet another example, the most radical, of the baroque poetry of disillusion. It must be said, first of all, that this idea has no basis in chronology: many years passed between the writing of *First Dream* and the crisis of 1693. The causal relation between the poem and the so-called conversion, therefore, is tenuous. An even more pertinent question: are the dream and vanity of knowledge actually the theme of the poem?

I believe that the interpretations to which I have just referred are a reading we have imposed on the poem in order to make it coincide with the baroque poetry of disillusion and the view of skepticism as a road toward faith. Sor Juana tells us a dream about the voyage of the soul through the celestial spheres, her bedazzlement, and her efforts to convert her *vision* into *idea*: Intellect sees but Reason does not comprehend what it sees. The dream the poem relates is an allegory of the *act of knowing*. It describes the vision, the difficulties encountered by Reason, its wavering and its daring, its heroic spirit; it yearns to know, although it is aware in advance that surely it will fail. The model of the soul—the prototype, Sor Juana emphasizes—is Phaethon, the youth Jupiter strikes down, but who is immortalized in his fall. Earlier, she had compared the aspiration of the soul toward the First Cause to the Egyptian pyramids. The symbolic model of spiritual yearning is the pyramid: the mythic model is Phaethon, with whom—for reasons I shall explain in a moment—Sor Juana secretly identifies. The poem is all upward impulse: there are falls, yes, but again and again the soul is determined to soar.

The parallel between *First Dream* and the *Response* is complete. In the latter, written years after the poem, Sor Juana, in closing, says that *she will continue to write:* there is not the slightest sign of any intention to stop writing, nor is there any notice of a renunciation or a surrender to silence. In *First Dream,* more profound and intimate in its abstraction and objectivity (she is talking with herself, not with a prelate), she makes the same affirmation, but in a tragic vein: she is determined to persist in her endeavor, and she spells out her glory in her fall. No: *First Dream* is not a poem about knowledge as a vain dream, but a poem about the act of knowing. This act adopts the form of a dream, not in the sense of an ordinary dream or of an unrealizable illusion, but in the sense of a spiritual voyage. During the dream the soul is awake, something most critics forget. The voyage—a lucid dream—does not end in a revelation, as in the dreams of hermetic and Neoplatonic tradition; actually, the poem does not *end* at all: the soul hesitates, recognizing itself in Phaethon, whereupon the body awakens. An epic of the act of knowing, the poem is also the confession of the doubts and struggles of Reason. A confession that ends in an act of faith: not in learning but in the desire to learn.

Góngora's *Solitudes* is the great poem of Spanish disillusion. Góngora's disenchantment—his skepticism—ends not in an act of faith but in aesthetic affirmation. In the *Solitudes* there is no desire for learning, but neither is there faith. For Góngora there is neither a *here* (world and history) nor a *there* (Heaven or Platonic idea) but only the word: light and air. Góngora responds to the horror of the world and to the nothingness of the beyond with a language beyond language, that is, with words that have ceased to be communication to become spectacle. The sign becomes an enigmatic object that, once deciphered and seen, we admire. *First Dream* recounts the confrontation between the human spirit and the cosmos: Sor Juana does not want to clothe nothingness in a language of equivocal splendor, she wants to penetrate being. Sor Juana's vertigo has a different name: poetic rapture. Like all unique and singular works, *First Dream* cannot be reduced to the aesthetic of its time—that is, to the poetry of disillusion. This is true of all great poets: they express their age but simultaneously transcend it; they are its exception, everything that in some way escapes the tyranny of styles, tastes, and canons. Without denying Sor Juana's debt to her time, Vossler has said that *First Dream* prefigured the philosophical poetry that was to follow: "The cosmic poem of the Mexican nun was, historically, both late and premature: a late fruit of the baroque and the jubilant precursor of the Enlightenment." The great German critic is right in pointing out that the poem is doubly displaced in time, but wrong as to the nature of that displacement. Although it takes the form of Gongorist poetry, *First Dream*'s ties are to the tradition of the voyage of the soul belonging to the ancient hermeticism rediscovered by the Renaissance. It is a prophecy not of the poetry of the Enlightenment, but of the modern poetry that centers on the paradox at the heart of her poem: the revelation of nonrevelation. In this sense *First Dream* resembles Valéry's *Le cimetière marin* (*Graveyard by the Sea*) and, in the Hispanic world, José Gorostiza's *Muerte sin fin* (*Death without End*) and Vicente Huidobro's *Altazor*. And, above all, the poem in which all that poetry is subsumed: Mallarmé's *Un coup de dés*. Sor Juana's poem inaugurates a poetic mode that is central to the modern age; more precisely, a mode that *defines* modern poetry in its most radical and extreme form: the very antithesis of the *Divine Comedy*.

A baroque poem that negates the baroque, a belated work that prefigures the most modern modernity, *First Dream* is a verbal obelisk rising out of a nebulous zone of mist, precipices, and dizzying geometry. Like its author, it is of the dusk and the dawn. If we are to understand its unique situation better, we must again turn to Sor Juana's cosmography. Was it really Ptolemy's cosmography? Yes and no. That traditional image of the universe instilled a security we have lost. The earth was in the center, surrounded by seven planets, from the moon to Saturn; beyond, the firmament of fixed stars and the empyrean, with the Prime Mover. A finite universe, with well-defined limits and a center. A harmonious universe. The distances between the earth and the stars were enormous but, as C. S. Lewis says, man experienced no fear: the cosmos, like one of the walled cities of the Middle Ages, protected and defended him. Everything changed with the Renaissance: the walls crumbled and the center vanished. It is clear that Sor Juana had information, even though imperfect and vague, of the changes in the status of the earth, the sun, and the planets. Kircher alludes in his works to the new astronomy, although with prudence; he lived in Rome, where they had burned Bruno and tried Galileo. Sor Juana's reserve on these themes should not surprise us; it was typical of her class and her world. We must not forget, in addition, that she was familiar with Neoplatonism, which exercised a decisive influence in changing the image of the universe.

It is customary to attribute the triumph of the new image to the diffusion of the ideas and discoveries of Copernicus, Galileo, Kepler, and others. This is only partly true. According to modern historians, Neoplatonism was the true source of that change. This philosophical and spiritual current had been repressed throughout the Middle Ages but toward the end of the fifteenth century resurfaced with renewed vigor to win the best minds of the sixteenth century. In refuting Scholasticism, it outlined a different idea of the world, one linked with the new physical and cosmographic sciences. We know that the great scientific innovators were greatly indebted to Neoplatonism. What determined the image of the world that displaced the Ptolemaic finite universe, therefore, was not so much the heliocentrism of Copernicus, which was rather slow to be accepted, as certain propositions that were not, strictly speaking, derived or deduced from the new science: the infinity of the universe, the lack of a cosmic center, the plurality of inhabited worlds.[23] More than in Copernicus and Galileo, the new ideas originated in Neoplatonism and in the speculations of philosophers like Nicholas of Cusa, who had postulated the coincidence of opposites. Cusanus, several centuries before Kant, confronted the antinomy of the infinite and attempted to negate it with the paradox of the circle whose center is everywhere. The circle does not enclose the infinite, does not *define* it, but it is an image that allows us, if not to think it, to *intuit* it.

The new universe was a challenge to man's reason as well as his sensibility and fantasy. The extreme attitudes it produced are exemplified in two minds, Bruno and Pascal. They are divided not by a century but by something more profound: temperament. They are like hot and cold, wet and dry. Giordano Bruno was a passionate defender of the astronomy of Copernicus, but he also, and with still greater passion, believed in an infinite and decentralized universe with a plurality of inhabited worlds. His spiritual relationship to Nicholas of Cusa was more profound than the merely intellectual ties that joined him to Copernicus. His reasons for postulating an infinite universe were not what today we would call scientific, but rather ontological, moral, and temperamental: "it is incomparably better that Infinite Excellence should express itself in innumerable individuals than in some finite number of them . . ." Bruno rejoiced in the idea of an infinite universe, and in that idea there is an echo of Plato: all that exists, even the bad, is good. Again and again he repeats that there are no differences, everything is center, and all is circumference. Lovejoy comments that there is "an essentially cosmical piety" in Bruno, but "to Pascal's imagination the vision of the *infini créé* is not exhilarating but oppressive." The infinite does not elate Pascal; it humbles him. The image of the circle reappears in the French philosopher but with a negative coloration: "It [the universe] is an infinite

sphere, of which the center is everywhere and the circumference nowhere ... What is a man, in the midst of infinity?"[24] Confronting this
infinite and incomprehensible universe, Pascal, in order to become a
chrétien soumis, chooses first to be a *pyrrhonien accompli.* Was Pascal's
experience shared by Sor Juana?

It is impossible to confuse the world of *First Dream* with that of traditional cosmography. In her descriptions of celestial space Sor Juana
never alludes to the discoveries of the new astronomy, and we do not
know what she really thought about controversial and dangerous subjects such as heliocentrism, the infinity of the universe, and the plurality
of inhabited worlds. No matter; her emotions and sentiments about the
cosmos tell us as much as her ideas. First of all, her world has no clear
outlines or precise limits. This distinguishes it radically from the traditional cosmos, which was a harmonious world. Another difference: distances are not only immense but immeasurable. Last—and this is a
modern characteristic—her world lacks a center and man feels lost in
its uninhabited spaces. It is a world that, if not infinite, produces sentiments and images that are a response to infinity. This is why Sor Juana,
in order to think about the infinite, turns quite naturally to Nicholas of
Cusa's paradox of the divine circle: she does exactly the same as Bruno
and Pascal, who did believe in an infinite universe. Sor Juana feels that
the "machinery of the world" is both "immense and terrifying." Her
emotions are not those of a Dante, or even a Fray Luis de León: neither
metaphysical certainty nor supernatural rapture. The cosmos no longer
has shape or measure; it has become unfathomable, and the Intellect
itself—not even Neoplatonism can rescue her at this point—has experienced vertigo confronting its abysses and myriads of stars. Sor Juana
is awe-struck. But this emotion soon becomes a different sentiment that
is neither the jubilant elation of Bruno nor the melancholy depression of
Pascal. The sentiment appears in the last part of *First Dream,* when
everything seems about to end on a Pascalian note. It is rebellion. Its
emblem is Phaethon.

In the myth of Phaethon, Sor Juana is appropriating a motif from the
poetry of her time, a very popular theme during the Golden Age. In
Alciati's *Emblemata* he appears as an example of temerity; the Spanish
translator, Bernardino Daza, turns the myth into a model for "the vain
princes" who "destroy their kingdoms" and then "plummet to the earth
and die." In the poetry of the sixteenth and seventeenth centuries there
are innumerable sonnets, *décimas,* and *romances* on the theme of Phae-

thon and his fall. Francisco de Aldana wrote a long and ponderous *Fábula de Faetonte*, a free translation from the Italian, which is one of the least felicitous compositions by this great poet. In contrast, *Fábula de Faetón* by Juan de Tassis Peralta, Count de Villamediana, is, in the words of Juan Manuel Rozas, "one of the most ambitious endeavors of our baroque lyric."[25] Rozas points out that the myth "serves some as a moral; for others it is an exemplum for lovers; and finally it is a model of glory and honor, of the desire to climb to the heights and undertake great enterprises." Villamediana's Phaethon fits the latter category. Epaphus having questioned whether Phaethon is the son of Apollo, the youth goes to his father's palace to seek recognition; the god grants it willingly, but for Phaethon this satisfaction is not sufficient. He yearns to show the world—and himself—that he is worthy of being Apollo's son and capable of driving his chariot through the sky. The theme of questionable birth is allied with that of honor, and both are allied to the theme of forfeiting life for a glorious death: "You have fallen, Phaethon, you have yielded to your fate . . ." Sor Juana's hero is more complex; Phaethon is herself. Although she is moved by the desire for glory, she is attracted by a passion unknown to Villamediana: love of knowledge.

A new passion in the history of our poetry appears with *First Dream*: love of learning. Let me clarify. The passion, of course, was not new; what was new was that Sor Juana used it as a poetic theme and invested it with the fateful intensity of erotic love. For her, intellectual passion is as strong as the love of glory. In the best Platonic tradition, intellectual passion—reason—enlists the spirit to accompany it in its adventure. But the next step is an even greater break with tradition: if knowledge seems unachievable, one must somehow outwit fate and dare to try.

Daring becomes defiance, rebellion: the act of knowing is a transgression. The infinity of the universe elates Bruno and depresses Pascal. In *First Dream* Sor Juana moves from inspiration to fall, and from fall to defiance. Hers is an intellectual and lucid hero who wants to learn even at the risk of falling. The figure of Phaethon influenced Sor Juana in two ways. First, as the intellectual example that joins love of learning to daring: reason and spirit. Second, because he represents freedom in its most extreme form: transgression.

The theme of Phaethon appears several times in her work, always as an image of the freedom that dares to cross boundaries. I have commented on sonnet 149, which portrays her envy of the person bold enough to seize the reins of the chariot of the Sun, "heedless of the danger," and who does not, like her, resign himself to a "state to last his span." A terrible confession for a nun. Phaethon attracted her in still another way: for her, too, the question of birth, bastardy, was a sensitive one. But, as we have seen, she transcended the theme of honor; her theme was learning. This may be why she does not share Pascal's dilemma; Sor Juana is not torn between "total Pyrrhonism" and "submissive Christianity." She separates the two orders, the religious and the strictly philosophical; she is a Christian but, in a different sphere, she is *un*submissive. This sentiment was the secret core of her psychic life. Very early, as I attempted to demonstrate in Part Two, Juana Inés proposed to transcend her allotted role, and identified with her grandfather and with the masculine world of learning and books. Her choice of Phaethon, in her mature years, realizes her childhood desire in the world of symbols. Juana Inés saw herself in three figures: in the pythoness of Delphi, in the goddess Isis, and in the youth Phaethon. The three images are interwoven with literature and knowledge: the maiden of Delphi is inspiration; Isis is wisdom; and Phaethon is the unfettered desire for learning.

The act of knowing, even if it ends in failure, is learning: the nonrevelation is a revelation. I compared *First Dream* with *Un coup de dés:* the two poems have as their protagonists the starry sky and the human spirit; in both the *act of knowing,* since it is not knowledge, is a *learning.* Mallarmé says something that is entirely applicable to the experience of Juana Inés: "In an act where chance is in play . . . , negation and affirmation cancel each other out." (Note that this phrase is another version of the paradox of the circle.) But there is another work that has a no less profound and disquieting similarity to *First Dream.* It is not a poem but an engraving, Dürer's *Melancholy 1.* The theme is the same: the contemplation of nature and the distress of the spirit—anguish, doubt, discouragement, rebellion—at not being able to transform that contemplation into form or idea. The female angel in the engraving— actually, a figure composed of two types: Geometry and Melancholy— could be a personification of the soul in *First Dream,* captive to doubt and sorrow, at the end of its spiritual adventure. The resemblance is not fortuitous but is born of similar experiences: *Melancholy 1* and *First Dream* are intellectual confessions, and Dürer's work is no less enigmatic than Sor Juana's poem.

Dürer's engraving has been admirably analyzed by Erwin Panofsky, Raymond Klibansky, and Fritz Saxe in their famous study *Saturn and*

Melancholy,[26] which explains the connection between Dürer and Neo-platonic hermeticism. Dürer borrowed from Ficino the new vision of the melancholic temperament as the spiritual disposition of poets, philosophers, and contemplatives. Dürer's direct source was Cornelius Agrippa's *De occulta philosophia.* According to Agrippa, the melancholic humor attracts certain spirits (daemons) that produce visions and ecstasy. These spirits act on the imagination of visual artists and those who use number and proportion: architects, painters, draftsmen; on reason when it pertains to poets, philosophers, or orators; and, finally, on the intellect in the case of prophets and founders of religions. The figure in *Melancholy 1* personifies the first type and is in a sense an intellectual self-portrait. It is the portrait of his soul, Sor Juana would say, drawn "in the only possible way": an image fixed in fantasy.

In addition to their being symbolic self-portraits, there is another striking resemblance between the engraving and the poem. Agrippa's text explains why the numeral "1" appears after the word "melancholy": the engraving represents the first type of melancholy, that is, the melancholy of the artist. Did Dürer plan to complete the series someday? This is the very question we ask about the adjective "first" preceding the word "dream." Whatever our answer, both the engraving and the poem present but an initial image, the first phase of a process. In this sense they are works that, although formally complete and finished, open toward the unfinished and still unnamed. They are works that, spiritually, verge on infinity. What is unsaid is an essential part of their mysterious seduction. The image in *Melancholy 1* seems to be a prophetic illustration for the passage in *First Dream* in which the soul, lost in the geometric night and its prospects of obelisks and pyramids, "looks on everything, and sees nothing." The character the two works draw is identical: the question mark.

Part Six

The Traps of Faith

25

An Ill-Fated Letter

At the end of November 1690 a pamphlet was published in Puebla with the abstruse title *Carta atenagórica de la madre Juana Inés de la Cruz, religiosa profesa de velo y coro en el muy religioso convento de San Jerónimo . . . Que imprime y dedica a la misma sor Philotea de la Cruz, su estudiosa aficionada en el convento de la Santísima Trinidad de la Puebla de los Angeles* (*Athenagoric Letter of Sister Juana Inés de la Cruz, a Professed Nun in the Most Spiritual Convent of San Jerónimo . . . Printed and Dedicated to That Same Sister by Sister Filotea de la Cruz, Her Studious Follower in the Convent of the Most Holy Trinity in Puebla de los Angeles*).[1] *Atenagórica* means "worthy of the wisdom of Athena"—supreme praise from Sor Filotea. Sor Juana's text, in the form of a letter, is a critique of a Sermon of the Mandate given by the Portuguese Jesuit Antonio de Vieyra. The Sermon of the Mandate is delivered on Maundy Thursday at the ceremony of the washing of the feet, and takes as its theme a verse from St. John: "A new commandment I give unto you: that you love one another as I have loved you." Vieyra belongs as much to the history of Brazil as of Portugal. Considered one of the great prose writers of his century, he was widely read and discussed in Spain and its domains. His sermons and letters were published in Spanish, in Mexico City and elsewhere. Vieyra preached more than one Sermon of the Mandate, but the one analyzed by Sor Juana was delivered in the royal chapel in Lisbon in 1650—that is, forty years earlier. It is curious that its author, an expatriate in Brazil, never knew of Sor Juana's critique.[2]

The theme of the sermon is also curious. At the end of his life, Christ did not love man *more*—his love was, from the beginning, perfect and infinite, without possibility of increase or diminution—but his love, effectively, if not affectively, was greater and more extreme: "It combined purpose [*fin*] with fineness [*lo fino*]." Of all of Christ's expressions of love [*finezas*] at the end of his life, which was the greatest? This, according to Vieyra, "is the matter of the sermon." Ricard observes that the words *fino* and *fineza* are common to Spanish and Portuguese. *Fino* seems to combine "ideas of purity, tenderness, and subtlety." Vieyra defines the word this way: "love that is *fino* is love that does not seek cause or effect; it loves because it loves, and it loves for loving's sake." In fact Vieyra is quoting the words of St. Bernard, except that in translating it from Latin to Portuguese he adds his own invention, the adjective *fino*. That is, he bestows—unknowingly?—a *fineza* on St. Bernard. The *Diccionario de autoridades* says that "*fineza* is the perfection, purity, and goodness of a thing of its kind." It is also the "action or declaration by which one communicates one's love for another. Also used for tactfulness and delicacy." The latter two meanings are those favored by Vieyra and Sor Juana. In defining "what *fineza* is," she says: "Is it, perhaps, a *fineza* to love? Of course not; rather, it is the demonstrations of love that are *finezas*. Those external demonstrative signs, the lover's actions if their motivating cause is love, are what constitute *fineza*." This is a theme, it will be remembered, that had always fascinated her, and appears in her love poems as well as in a *sainete*.

The *Carta* is written in clear and direct language; the sentences are not overly long; the reasoning is sometimes dry and labored—as a polemical and theological composition it is doubly serious—but in the pauses there is a hint of alleviation and a knowing smile to the reader. Sor Juana is writing for a small group and knows that none of her barbs will pass unnoticed. As happens with all doctrinaire documents once their moment has passed, it is difficult to become excited by Sor Juana's arguments; at the same time, it is impossible not to admire their solidity, their coherence and energy. As we read this text we note another unsuspected facet of her genius: Sor Juana is a true intellectual pugilist. Fortunately, she never abandons either good manners or irony. The *Carta* is addressed to an unidentified recipient, although, to judge by her respectful and deferential tone, it is someone of high rank. She writes this critique not of her own will but to obey him. She recounts that on some occasion he had listened to her "prattle," which he generously found "clever," on "the sermons of an excellent orator," and was so pleased by what he heard that he asked her to write down her argument. Sor Juana bows to the wish of her superior, although with one condition: the document is to be read only by him. At the end of the *Carta* she repeats the restriction: "Finally, this paper is so private that I write it down only because Your Mercy so commands me and in order that Your Mercy may see it." She refuses to sanction any public dissemination of her composition.

No less strange are two notices that appear at the beginning of the *Carta*. The first states that she writes "purified of all passion," since she has three reasons for loving the orator in question (she never names him; she is writing for the initiated): because he is a member of the Society of Jesus, of which she feels she is a "daughter"; because of his highly esteemed intellect; and because of her "hidden sympathy" for his nation. (Very well hidden.) The second is even more remarkable. She is writing solely for her correspondent: "To other eyes it would seem disproportionate arrogance, especially coming from a sex universally discredited in literary matters." Sor Juana does not hesitate to dwell on the unworthiness of her sex, and at the end of the *Carta* she harps on that theme: her daring is extreme, since "compared to the author's intellectual eminence even giants seem like dwarfs. What, then, can be expected of a mere woman? But it was a woman who lifted the club from the hands of Heracles, which was one of the three impossible feats venerated in ancient times."[3] And she adds that she is the "frail instrument" God chose to punish the orator's pride: "It is no faint chastisement, for one who believed there was no man who dared reply to him, to see that an ignorant woman dares, one for whom study of this nature is so foreign, and so remote from her gender; but equally foreign to Judith was the mastery of arms, and to Deborah, that of judicature." These ardent feminist declarations seem even more ardent when we note that they are written by one nun and published by another.

It is difficult to share—although not to understand—the admiration provoked by the sermons of a Paravicino, Donne, Bossuet, or Vieyra. With great ingenuity and in a language of studied deliberation and swift inferences (the aesthetic of surprise applied to divine subjects), Father Vieyra refutes the opinions of three saints—Augustine, Thomas Aquinas, and John Chrysostom—on Christ's expressions of love just before his death. To each of their choices he opposes a different *fineza*, and then expounds his ideas on which is the greatest among them. Rather boastfully, he forewarns his listeners that "for my choice of Christ's greatest *fineza,* none can pose an equal." St. Augustine proposed that the greatest expression of Christ's love was to have given his life for man; according to Vieyra, however, the greater sacrifice was to have absented himself from us: "Christ our Lord loved man more than life . . . and while to die is to leave life, to absent himself was to leave man." In *The Divine Narcissus,* as has been seen, Sor Juana says that the greatest *fineza* of Christ was to have died for man, the creature made in his likeness. In the *Carta* she reiterates that argument: "For man, Christ gave the most that one could give, which is life." Furthermore, did Christ truly absent himself? No: "He is still present in the transubstantiation of the Eucharist." And that presence, as she herself had written in a *villancico* (345), is a state that embraces both life and death, since the Lord, "being in glory, is as if dead."

For St. Thomas, says Vieyra, "the greatest *fineza* of Christ's love was to remain with us as he absented himself from us." He clarifies: Christ remained in many ways, but especially in the sacrament of the Eucharist. This was also Sor Juana's opinion in the *loa* to *The Martyr of the Sacrament;* the student who is her personification refutes St. Augustine's opinion and declares himself in favor of that of St. Thomas. Vieyra's departure is most original: "It was a greater *fineza* for Christ, rather than to remain, to conceal himself in the sacrament of the altar; although he is there in body, he has no use or mastery of his senses." Sor Juana comments: "What manner of argumentation is this? St. Thomas proposes in genus and the orator responds in species." This breach in the rules of logic leads her to say, "The argument is invalid . . . it is sophistic." St. John Chrysostom's opinion was that "the greatest *fineza* was Christ's having washed the feet of his disciples," among them Judas himself, his betrayer. Vieyra ingeniously maintains that Christ washed Judas' feet, like those of the others, because "*amor fino* does not seek cause or effect: it loves for loving's sake." Sor Juana, as I have mentioned, refutes the orator, defining *fineza:* the cause of the act is love and the foot-washing is its *fineza,* that is, its expression or external sign. Thus, the fact that Jesus washed the feet of Judas *did* have a cause: his love for his creatures.

I do not know whether my brief and cursory summary allows a glimpse of the subtlety and ingenuity of Vieyra and Sor Juana—a vain subtlety and an empty ingenuity, since they were applied not to any real object but to sophistries unrelated to true philosophy. This is rhetorical passion, enamored of itself and devoid of authentic religious sentiment:

shadowboxing. The section that follows has more substance. After defending the three saints, Sor Juana confronts Vieyra's opinion and broaches a theme she had often treated in her secular works: requited and unrequited love. Vieyra maintains that "Christ did not wish his love to be returned for his own sake but for man's sake, and this was his greatest *fineza:* to love without being loved in turn." Sor Juana had said something similar in her love poems and her poems of loving friendship dedicated to Lysis; also, in a sacred *romance* (56) she repeats that supreme love does not need to be reciprocated; if we insist that love be returned it is because of a flaw in human nature. How to get around this problem? First, by calling on the authority of Scripture. There are numerous texts in the Old and New Testaments that state that we must love God above all things. From love of God is born the love we have, or should have, for our fellow man and for ourselves. Does Christ, therefore, need our love? No: "In being returned, human love finds something that would be missing were it not returned; but in Christ's love nothing is lacking, even when it is not returned." When she reaches this point, the most vexing, Sor Juana sets forth the second part of her argument:

> Christ's love is very different from that of man. Man wishes love to be reciprocated for his own good. Christ desires that same reciprocation for the good of others, of man himself. In my opinion, the author [Vieyra] wandered some distance from this point, for he misunderstood and stated the opposite; seeing a selfless Christ, he persuaded himself that Christ did not desire his love to be requited. The fact is that the author did not distinguish between reciprocation and the utility of that reciprocation . . . Hence the author's proposition that Christ desired requited love not for himself but for man. My own view is that Christ did wish that his love be returned, but he desired the utility resulting from that reciprocation for the sake of man.

The reasoning is more subtle than solid, and an example of the casuistry she criticized in the Jesuits. Viewed from a modern perspective, the root of Sor Juana's difficulty (and Vieyra's as well) is to be found in the dual nature of Christ: man and God. Christ as man feels a need for requited love; Christ as God does not require it. It is an impenetrable mystery, and one that had amazed Porphyry: it seemed to him incongruous and blasphemous that Christians should adore a God who sought their love. Sor Juana replies with brilliance but does not resolve the dilemma:

The lover makes requited love a means to his end; Christ makes reciprocation a means to man's well-being . . . The requited lover desires the good for his beloved that results from his love, but he wants the good for himself from his beloved's love. Christ desires the good from the love he holds for man, and the good from man's love for him, all of the good, for man alone.

Sor Juana distinguishes between requited love and utility but does not answer the terrible question: why does Christ desire to be loved by man? Earlier, in *romance 56*, which is closer in spirit to Plotinus than to the Scriptures, she had said that we must love God without desiring that the love be returned, and that such love is the supreme love. She had said the same thing in her poems of secular love and in the poems of loving friendship dedicated to María Luisa. But in the *Carta* she affirms that Christ, who is both God and man, seeks our love in return for his. Finally, she adds a not entirely convincing argument: the need for requited love is born of free will, "the charter of authentic liberty" that God gave to man. Since love for God "is the supreme well-being of man, but cannot exist unless man desires it," it follows that "God desires, solicits, and commands man to love him." It seems to me that this conclusion is not unlike Vieyra's, except that Sor Juana transfers the contradiction from the divine to the human sphere. The love of God does not deny but intensifies human liberty: because of his love for man, God has made man free. The two extremes that God suffers as Christ—loving / being loved—men also suffer as free beings. This idea, as we have seen, is at the heart of her inner life. In a certain way, the *Carta* confirms what she had written earlier: "reciprocal lovers" achieve a kind of happiness, but there are others who love for the sake of loving. The love of heroic lovers who do not seek to be loved in return is the fullest love.

At the end of the *Carta* she expounds her own opinion on divine *finezas*. Her conclusion is puzzling: having affirmed that Christ seeks our love, she says that "the greatest *finezas* of divine love are the gifts he does not grant us." She calls them "negative benefactions." To mitigate slightly the reader's dismay, she clarifies that she is speaking not "of the *finezas* of Christ at the end of his life," Vieyra's theme, but of "the *finezas* of God as God." Thus the human element that represents the specific originality of Christianity disappears from the divine nature. "God as God": a strange formula that recalls *First Dream*, from which Christ is similarly absent. Sor Juana's development of the argument is somewhat abrupt. Knowing our ingratitude and our wickedness, God does not grant us benefactions: "We appreciate and we ponder the exquisiteness of divine love, in which to reward is a benefaction and to chastise is a benefaction, and the absence of benefaction is the greatest benefaction, and the absence of *finezas* the greatest *fineza*." A divine version of her idea of supreme love as the love that does not seek to be reciprocated: we must love God not for the benefactions he bestows upon us but because his greatest *fineza* is not to grant us his favor. God's *fineza* consists of releasing us from his hand, for in this way he increases our liberty. This is without question the most notable consequence of the "negative favors" and must have alarmed more than one of her readers. The notion of human liberty as God's grace does not disappear but, in a manner of speaking, changes coloration: it becomes a "negative favor" through divine *abstention*. In this Sor Juana is closer to Pelagius than to St. Augustine.

Sor Juana's reasoning on the subject of "negative favors" is an echo of the great polemics of her time on the subject of grace and free will. Domingo Báñez and the Dominicans had posed free will as a reflection of divine grace; the Jesuit Luis de Molina had attempted to reconcile freedom and predestination while increasing the sphere of liberty. *Sufficient* grace was the primary grace; *efficacious* grace worked not over or above, but *through,* free will. Sor Juana, especially in her conclusions, appears to subscribe to Molinism. Dorothy Schons, in an intelligent open letter to the archconservative writer Alfonso Junco, maintains that "in the much-debated argument between the Augustinians' sufficient grace and the Jesuits' efficacious grace, Sor Juana opts for sufficient grace. She declares that both the lack of grace and excessive (efficacious) grace are damaging; that is, that sufficient grace is enough. From this point of view, Sor Juana is the Port-Royal of New Spain—or could have come to be so."[4] I do not agree. St. Augustine's vision of fallen man—radicalized by Jansenism—is founded in predestination, and the idea of "negative favors" represents the precise opposite: divine abstention. "Negative favors" do not negate free will; they augment it. They work like Molina's efficacious grace. Using Jesuitical ideas and procedures, Sor Juana attacked a Jesuit, one of the most illustrious among them. Her attack was not directed, like Pascal's, against a doctrine, but rather against a person and a group.

In its published form, the *Carta* was preceded by another letter—a sort of prologue—addressed to Sor Juana and signed by a Sor Filotea de la Cruz, a nun in a convent of Puebla who declared herself a "student" of the poet. The prologue by Sor Filotea is brief. It begins with words of high praise: in spite of the fact that in his sermon Vieyra had soared "above himself like a second Eagle of the Apocalypse," Sor Juana had "sharpened her quill to a finer point," and the Portuguese scholar could "glory in seeing himself refuted by a woman who is the honor of her sex." Subsequently, Sor Filotea praises the "energetic clarity" of Sor Juana's prose and reminds her—the first reproach—that if it is true that "the one who has received most from God is the one most obliged to return that gift, I fear that Your Mercy finds herself deeply obliged, for few creatures are more indebted to His Majesty for greater natural talents." She is not to be censured for writing verses as "highly praised as those of St. Teresa," but it is regrettable that she does not imitate the saint "in her choice of subjects." Sor Filotea's reprimand is tempered: it would be "ignoble" to deny women the exercise of letters. It is true that St. Paul says that women should not teach, "but he does not command that they not study . . . He wished only to avoid the risk of pride in our sex, always inclined toward vanity . . . Literary learning that engenders pride God does not wish in a woman, but the Apostle does not criticize letters as long as they do not lead a woman from a state of obedience." Sor Filotea exhibits no particular tenderness for the female sex, but concedes that study and learning have held Sor Juana in a state of submission. Had they really? Sor Filotea's letter reveals precisely the contrary; one of its aims is to return her to obedience.

Sor Filotea does not intend, like others, that Sor Juana alter her "natural inclinations by renouncing books," but that she "better them by reading occasionally in the book of Jesus Christ . . . You have spent much time in the study of philosophers and poets; now it would be well for you to better your occupation and improve the quality of the books . . . Any science that does not light the way to salvation God regards as foolishness." Condemnation of secular learning is joined to exhortation: "What a pity that such a great intellect should so lower itself by unworthy notice of the Earth as to have no desire to penetrate what comes to pass in Heaven; and, having already stooped to the Earth, may it not descend farther to consider what comes to pass in Hell." Following this ominous warning, Sor Filotea, again mixing the sweet with the bitter, alludes to the "negative favors," and hopes that "the Lord God, who has so profusely rained positive benefactions upon you in the natural sphere, will not find Himself obliged to bestow solely negative benefactions upon you in the supernatural sphere, for however

much you may view them as *finezas,* I must hold them as punishments."
Sor Filotea not only censures the idea of the "negative favors" but quite
openly threatens Sor Juana with them in her afterlife. The conclusion is
more gentle. Sor Filotea hopes that Sor Juana will be blessed by divine
favor and, recalling other times, adds, "This wish is sent you by one
who, from the time your hand was kissed many years ago, lives enamored of your soul, one who has experienced no cooling of that love with
distance or time, for spiritual love does not suffer the assaults of
change."

Sor Filotea so much admires Sor Juana's critique of Vieyra's sermon
as to have it published at her own expense. At the same time she criticizes Sor Juana's dedication to secular letters and reprimands her for not
devoting herself to "holy matters"—that is, theology. A strange attitude
that blends love with severity, and in which praise veils a stern admonition. Sor Juana's reaction was equally curious: although in the *Carta
atenagórica* she had said she wrote under instructions and with the condition that what she wrote not be made public, when the *Carta* was
published she accepted the fact and later in the *Response to Sor Filotea
de la Cruz* even said, "I do not know how to express my gratitude for
your immeasurable kindness in publishing my scribblings."

In order to throw some light on these mysteries, we must first ask and
attempt to answer certain questions. Who was this Sor Filotea de la
Cruz? Why did Sor Filotea publish Sor Juana's critique of Vieyra's sermon? To whom was Sor Juana's *Carta* addressed? A contemporary of
these events would reply, "No need to belabor the obvious." In fact, it
was an open secret: Sor Filotea de la Cruz and the person addressed in
the *Carta* were one and the same person, the Bishop of Puebla, Manuel
Fernández de Santa Cruz. He also wrote the document's imprimatur.
Only the recipient could have disseminated the letter, and only a recipient who had the Bishop's high rank could have dared publish it. The
reason for hiding behind a female pseudonym will be made clear in a
moment.

The friendship between Sor Juana and the Bishop was of long standing, as can be seen in the tone of both the *Carta* and the affectionate but
stern prologue. The relationship between the nun and the prelate must
have begun during the viceregency of Fray Payo Enríquez de Rivera,
when Fernández had just arrived in New Spain and Juana had but recently taken her vows in San Jerónimo. One of the Bishop's intimates
and his future biographer, Fray Miguel de Torres of the order of Our

Lady of Mercy, was the nephew of Sor Juana—the son of her half sister Inés and of José Miguel de Torres, a poet and secretary of the university. It seems reasonable to conjecture that Fernández de Santa Cruz, Sor Juana, and others—among them, perhaps, Castorena y Ursúa—formed a group bound by friendship and common interests. Many of them had become prominent in public life during the era of Fray Payo. Some were criollos and others Spaniards with long years of residence in New Spain. It is likely that the head of this circle was the Bishop of Puebla. The appointment of Aguiar y Seijas as Archbishop of Mexico, with his Spanish loyalties and his excesses, must have irritated the Bishop of Puebla and the Bishop's friends.

Manuel Fernández de Santa Cruz y Sahagún was born in Palencia in 1637. Miguel de Torres relates that he nearly drowned as a boy when he went to play with friends at the river, and that on another occasion he was close to death when candles he had left lit set fire to the bed where he was sleeping.[5] This may explain his caution. He studied with the Jesuits and later, in Salamanca, was a disciple of Pedro de Godoy, a famous Dominican theologian. Once he was ordained, his spiritual adviser for a time was Tirso González, who was to become general of the Society of Jesus. At the age of thirty-five he was appointed Bishop of Chiapas. Before he set sail he was named to a more important diocese, in Guadalajara. He arrived in Mexico in 1673 and in 1675 was consecrated by Fray Payo Enríquez de Rivera. According to Torres' account, the young Bishop enjoyed Fray Payo's friendship and protection. In 1676, at the age of thirty-nine, he was named Bishop of Puebla, a post he held until his death in 1699. In Puebla he founded schools for virgin girls (a strange adjective for children), schools for nuns, and a house for indigent women. He also added to the library founded by his predecessor, the great Palafox, and was a driving force in the school for theologians. From this brief summary of his activities his two main concerns are easily deduced: theology and women in religious life. He was also an ascetic. He frequently retired, Torres recounts, to the sanctuary of San Miguel del Milagro, "for much prayer, poor food, and no few scourgings." Perhaps Torres exaggerates: his biography is a hagiography, as was also the case with the lives of Núñez de Miranda and Aguiar y Seijas written by Juan de Oviedo and José de Lezamis.

His dedication to theology resulted in three books, his life's work, devoted to reconciling the "apparent" divergences and contradictions among various sections of the Bible. His solicitude for women in reli-

Manuel Fernández de Santa Cruz, Bishop of Puebla

gious life led to his reform of lax practices in the convents. According to Torres, "many of those virgins, among the number of the foolish, not only failed to polish their lamps but in fact allowed them to tarnish through certain communications inappropriate to their professed purity, and whose lack of propriety was cause for wicked effrontery on the part of some who, from the lay world, disturbed them with the frequency of their visits to the grilles and blind windows, scandalizing the unwary." The Bishop of Puebla visited the nuns, conversed with them, instructed them, and, most important, wrote them inflamed letters that Torres classified as "spiritual." In one of them the Bishop says, "To suffer for Christ, to seek out scorn, to crush your will, that is your path, as beloved of the crucified Christ." In another letter, the fire of the violently sensual metaphors becomes cruelty: "However much I strive to strip you, I do not achieve it; you will condemn yourself, be forsaken by God, forgotten and abandoned by your confessor." Torres published thirty-six of these letters, among them the comparatively moderate one addressed to Sor Juana. He—her nephew—comments with a certain hypocritical compunction: "This letter had its desired effect . . . because, as His Excellency intended, she lived as an example to the nuns and died showing clear evidence of salvation."

In spite of Torres' unvarying and boringly encomiastic tone, he provides occasional glimpses of the real Fernández de Santa Cruz. The Bishop was not a saint but a true Prince of the Church: a cautious but not cowardly politician, energetic but realistic. He knew how to confront the Viceroy of Mexico in 1692, and he also knew how to yield to Archbishop Aguiar y Seijas in the matter of the "oblations." When they administered the sacraments, priests received certain gifts, inappropriately called "oblations." Aguiar y Seijas, with the Pope's backing, denounced this "sacrilegious custom." The two prelates met in Chilapa in 1686 (it was their only encounter). Fernández de Santa Cruz commented on the interview as follows:

> I distribute among the poor any proceeds from those oblations and it saves my carrying money for alms . . . but my only wish is to do what is most proper, for although the Pontiff spoke as a private person, still his authority carries great weight. I know, too, that this will harm my successors, but I do not take that into consideration . . . although I do not understand how the reverend Archbishop can call this practice sacrilegious and even diabolic.

These expressions of ecclesiastical humility do not entirely conceal Fernández' bad humor over the Archbishop's words and actions. But why did the Bishop publish Sor Juana's *Carta,* and why did he hide behind the name Sor Filotea de la Cruz? To answer these questions we must first answer another: against whom was Sor Juana's critique *truly* directed?

The Jesuit Antonio de Vieyra was born in Lisbon in 1608 and died in Salvador, Brazil, in 1697. A celebrated homilist, the author of memorable letters, master of baroque prose, a missionary in Brazil, and an ardent defender of Indians and blacks, Vieyra enjoyed great influence and good standing with John IV of Portugal. He was a skillful diplomat and a defender of converted Jews. He lost favor at court, returned to the delta of the Amazon to live among the Indians, learned Tupi-Guaraní and other native languages, returned to Portugal, was again expelled, was persecuted by the Inquisition, took refuge in Rome, became the confessor of Christina of Sweden, returned to Brazil, again fought in behalf of the Indians, and died at the age of eighty-nine. I have already pointed out that he was completely removed from the imbroglio of the *Carta.* Why, and for what purpose, did Sor Juana write a critique of a sermon preached forty years before? Why, and for what purpose, was the Bishop of Puebla so determined to publish that text? How can its publication have left the Bishop completely unscathed while evoking such criticism of Sor Juana? In 1950, in a brief essay, I stated that Sor Juana's intellectual and psychological crisis could be understood only from the perspective of the social and historical crisis of New Spain at the end of the seventeenth century. No one took account of my observation until in 1967 the Italian critic Dario Puccini adopted it and proposed a hypothesis that is at once solid, reasonable, and intellectually satisfying. I shall follow it in this section, although from time to time, as is only natural, I shall deviate slightly from his interpretation.

Vieyra was admired in Spain and in Mexico. That glory was in great part a reflection of the supremacy of the Society of Jesus. In Mexico the Jesuits not only dominated higher education but, through Archbishop Francisco Aguiar y Seijas, exercised a very profound influence over Church and state. The appointment of Aguiar y Seijas was largely the work of the Society, and among the friends and admirers of Vieyra, Aguiar y Seijas was at the forefront. His friendship was so valued that when in 1675 and 1678 two volumes of Vieyra's translated sermons were published in Madrid, both were dedicated to Aguiar y Seijas, then

Bishop of Michoacán.[6] In 1683, *Conclusiones a toda la teología* (*Some Conclusions on Theology*) was published, dedicated to Vieyra by the Real y Pontificia Universidad de México—surely, says Dario Puccini, "at the suggestion of Aguiar y Seijas, who had recently risen to power." The dedication by the university coincided with Vieyra's fall from favor in Lisbon and can be interpreted as a kind of compensation.[7] Finally, in 1685, Vieyra's sermon "Heráclito defendido" ("In Defense of Heraclitus") was published in Mexico. It is impossible not to see the intervention of Aguiar y Seijas in this new publication. And it is not difficult to deduce from all this that the person who might feel affected by Sor Juana's critique was not Vieyra, absent and far removed from it all, but Archbishop Francisco de Aguiar y Seijas. An attack on Vieyra was an oblique attack on Aguiar. It was also a confrontation with influential Jesuit friends of the Archbishop.

The cause of the rivalry between Fernández de Santa Cruz and Aguiar y Seijas remains to be examined. Fernández had been the first of the two to arrive in Mexico. The bishopric of Puebla was the most important in New Spain with the exception of Mexico City, and it was natural that, at the departure of Fray Payo, Bishop Fernández de Santa Cruz should aspire to his post as well as to the post of Viceroy. In an effort to prove Fernández de Santa Cruz's lack of interest in the position, some critics have alleged that later "he not only refused the archbishopric of Mexico City and viceregency of New Spain, but resigned his bishopric in Puebla, though the latter resignation was disallowed."[8] This information, coming from an author with as little credibility as Torres and repeated without further proof by Beristáin and others, is today viewed with justifiable skepticism by the great majority of historians.[9] The other aspirant for the archbishopric of Mexico City was Aguiar y Seijas, then Bishop of Michoacán. Texts from the period, in spite of their reserve, reveal that the struggle between the prelates was long and bitter. Santa Cruz, says Puccini, "was more popular in New Spain; he was more experienced, more moderate in temperament, and he had greater gifts for dealing with civil authority." Aguiar enjoyed the support of the Jesuits and other ecclesiastical authorities in the mother country; he was known to be a man of severe principles, moral intransigence, and intellectual prestige, as demonstrated by Vieyra's dedication. In order to compensate for his disadvantages, Santa Cruz attempted, without great success, to capture the good will of the Society of Jesus. In a letter to Charles II, he praises the Jesuits and their work in the Colegio de San Ildefonso. The election of the Archbishop was carried out in a mysterious manner that has never been clarified. In Antonio de Robles' *Record of Notable Events* there are four references to the election: the first says that the Bishop of Santo Domingo had been named Archbishop of Mexico City; the second, dated May 1680, states that the person named was Manuel Fernández de Santa Cruz; the third confirmed that the appointee was Santa Cruz, Bishop of Puebla; the name of Aguiar y Seijas appears for the first time in the fourth, dated March 1681.

What happened between May 1680 and March 1681? It seems that Santa Cruz had been named Archbishop, but then some power in Madrid intervened and the decision was changed in favor of Aguiar. There are indications, Puccini affirms, of a festering but not overt rivalry between Aguiar and Santa Cruz. Only within the context of such a rivalry can we answer with any glimmer of truth the questions we have posed. The *Carta atenagórica* is a polemical text in which criticism of Vieyra veils criticism of Aguiar. That criticism came from a woman, a new humiliation for Aguiar, who despised and scorned women. The *Carta* is published by the Bishop of Puebla, who thus cloaks Sor Juana in his authority. The Bishop writes a prologue hidden behind a female pseudonym: ridicule and insult for Aguiar y Seijas. Why has it taken until now to shed a little light—although many shadows remain—on the enigma of the *Carta atenagórica*? Perhaps because in the twentieth century we have learned to remove from such tragedies and comedies the masks that covered them in societies ruled by orthodoxy and bureaucracy. Nadezhda Mandelstam tells in her memoirs (*Hope against Hope*) that the terrible criticism Zhdanov directed against Anna Akhmatova shortly after World War II was in fact an attack against his rival Malenkov, then Akhmatova's protector. Less prudent than Akhmatova, Sor Juana intervened in the quarrel between two powerful Princes of the Roman Church and was destroyed in the process.

In order to understand Sor Juana's attitude, we must bear in mind the personality of the Archbishop of Mexico City, Francisco de Aguiar y Seijas. He was Galician, from Betanzos. His family, ancient and distinguished, was said to have descended from a Roman knight in the household of Julius Caesar. When the apostle St. James reached the coast of Spain, he was reputedly met on the shore by one of the ancestors of Aguiar y Seijas. This was why the family coat of arms displayed five seashells and a cross. Two determinant circumstances: he was a premature baby and fatherless. As a child he was cared for by strangers and at a tender age was made a familiar to a prelate. He had a good record in theology at the Universidad de Santiago de Compostela. From that time on he was known for his wildly eccentric temperament, his extreme devoutness, and his irascibility. Rigorous with others but with himself as well, he earned the reputation of being an exemplary priest in spite of his eccentricities. He moved in an atmosphere of devout exaltation and blind faith. Father José de Lezamis, who accompanied him in his travels and was his confessor, has left us a biography of Aguiar y Seijas filled with very curious stories.[10] For example, Lezamis recounts that when Aguiar set sail for New Spain, devils "attempted to sink the fleet," fearing that the new Bishop would seize many sinners from their claws. They failed: "a handmaiden of God" had a vision in which she saw St. Ursula and the eleven thousand virgins calm the sea and set the devils to flight.

Aguiar y Seijas' good relations with the Jesuits must have begun during his student years. Perhaps he met Vieyra in person or at least corresponded with him; otherwise Vieyra would not have dedicated the two volumes of translated sermons to him. Being Galician, Aguiar y Seijas probably had friends and acquaintances in Portugal. During the time he was Bishop in Michoacán, one member of his entourage was a Portuguese Jesuit, Antonio Soares. A letter the Bishop received from Father Oliva, general of the Society of Jesus, thanking him for "the extraordinary kindnesses and favors that Your Excellency has been good enough to grant our Society" dates from that same period in Michoacán. Almost as soon as he was named Archbishop of Mexico City, Aguiar y Seijas instituted a policy of austerities that few applauded. One of his first measures was to forbid the nuns of the Immaculate Conception and of San Jerónimo to receive in their locutories their "devotees" (a euphemism for the nuns' admirers), a widely accepted custom throughout Spain and Spanish America. With the same severity, he denounced public spectacles, especially theater, bullfights, and cockfights. Lezamis says: "A primary cause of many sins is wont to be plays and bullfights; for which reason His Excellency despised greatly these and other similar festivities . . . He preached with great bitterness against these bullfights and plays, and always prevented them whenever he was able."

The arrival in Mexico City of this enemy of the theater coincided with the performance of one of Sor Juana's plays (*The Trials of a Noble House*) during an entertainment honoring the Marquis and Marquise de la Laguna. In the *loa*, without naming him, Sor Juana praised the new

RETRATO DEL ILLVS.^{mo} IV.^{mo} S. DOCTOR DON FRANCISCO D. AGVIAR
SEIXAS, IULLOA; NATVRAL DE REINO DE GALICIA COLLEGIAL MAYOR
DEL COLLEGIO DE CVENCA EN SALAMANCA; MAESTRO D PHILg SOPHIAEN

Francisco de Aguiar y Seijas, Archbishop of Mexico

Archbishop. But the prelate, who did not attend the ceremony, never acknowledged the praise. What did he think of a nun who wrote plays, and lyrics for dances and other spectacles? Would he have known that Sor Juana had written a sonnet in praise of a bullfighter? Did he learn of the nun's burlesque sonnets and love poems? In 1682 the Inquisition banned, for trifling reasons, a comedy written by the famous playwright Juan Pérez de Montalbán, *El valor perseguido y la traición vengada* (*Bravery Persecuted and Betrayal Revenged*), which was being performed at the city theater, the Coliseo. Among the inquisitors who denounced the work was Núñez de Miranda, Sor Juana's confessor. The tribunal often banned plays; Irving Leonard attributes the action taken against Montalbán's comedy to the animosity of Aguiar y Seijas.

In a curious way, the Archbishop combined hatred of the theater with love for the poor. His biographer writes:

> He attempted to put an end to books of plays and to distribute devout books. When we came here from Spain, he brought with him fifteen hundred books entitled *Consuelo de pobres* (*Consolation of the Poor*) . . . and he persuaded the booksellers to take no more books of plays; and he traded with some among them all they had of the above books of plays for the aforementioned *Consuelo de pobres;* and then he burned the books of plays.

Lezamis does not tell us what measures the Archbishop employed to persuade the booksellers. But we know through other sources that he never hesitated to use threats, moral coercion, and even confiscation, leaving a simple receipt as the only record. Possessed of a kind of rage for charitable works, he was not content with giving what was his, but, using and abusing his ecclesiastical authority, forced others to exorbitant acts of charity. Toward the end of his life he was unable to contain this passion and surrendered to a frenzied distribution of alms, always preceded by a more or less forced collection of funds. Lezamis records that "he could not control himself . . . and in that time he not only accepted what was given him, but solicited further, and drew up lists of the wealthy of the city . . . and amassed a great deal of money and performed extraordinary acts of charity." In truth, those who yielded to his mania for generosity were not the truly wealthy, who had the means and the power to refuse him, but people of ordinary means who for various reasons owed him obedience. One of the victims of these pious exactions was Sor Juana. Dorothy Schons notes: "The Archbishop died in 1698, and he was scarcely buried before several convents and private persons presented claims for what the Archbishop had plundered. And so a suit was filed against the estate of the defunct prelate."

His fever for charity was inseparable from his miracles. Lezamis writes that once during a time of floods in Mexico City, the Archbishop, accompanied by one of his almoners—he had several—and another priest, passed through the outlying districts in a canoe, equipped with five or six sacks of bread. After blessing the bread, they began to distribute it, but there was such a crowd—more than fifteen hundred people—that they feared they would not have enough. Imagine their surprise when they saw that it provided for everyone! Then "they passed it out a second time; they gave each of the poor two or three portions of bread and, even so, they did not exhaust the source, and there was bread remaining to be apportioned the following day." Charity, miracles, and humility: Aguiar went around in old clothes; he wore tattered stockings; he erased his family coat of arms from his Archbishop's seal; he ate in hospitals; and his horror of pomp and ostentation was so great that "he evoked the murmuring of worldly men." He wore a hair shirt and scourged himself twice weekly. He slept in a borrowed bed and, at his death, was discovered to be swarming with bedbugs, in "a horrible state." But, Lezamis adds, a marvelous fragrance emanated from his corpse.

The harshness the Archbishop inflicted on his body did not calm his spirit. He went from devotion to rage, from fervor to acrimony; his charity was more hatred than love, his humility more self-loathing than fraternity. He knew neither friendship nor trust; he addressed everyone he knew in formal terms. He was distant, choleric, imperious, and rude. Once when entering the church to preach he saw in the atrium a woman with her head uncovered; he immediately jerked her shawl from her shoulders and threw it over her head and face. Aguiar y Seijas professed esteem for Sigüenza y Góngora; he appointed him chaplain of the Hospital del Amor de Dios and, a much-prized favor, named him one of his almoners. Nevertheless, shortly after the uprising of 1692, during a conversation in which a difference of opinion arose, the Archbishop lost control, berated him, and, to Sigüenza's amazement, physically attacked him. Robles reported the incident in his *Record:* "Altercation. Saturday 11. As Don Carlos de Sigüenza y Góngora, a priest, was calling upon the Archbishop for some purpose, the aforesaid Don Carlos asked that His Excellency observe that he was speaking with him, upon which His

Excellency fell upon him with a crutch, breaking his eyeglasses and bathing him in blood."

If humility is often a mask for pride, what is to be said of chastity? Aguiar y Seijas was famous not only for his charity but for his horror of women. In his history of the Mexican Church, Francisco Sosa reports that "the Archbishop's aversion toward women was so extreme that it could be classified as true mania. It is evident that from his earliest years he avoided any encounter with them; it is no surprise that once he became a priest, he tried to avoid even a glimpse of a woman's face."[11] Sosa overlooks several facts I have already mentioned: Aguiar y Seijas was born prematurely; he lost his father at a very early age; and his mother, when he was still a boy, placed him in the service of a prelate friend of the family. His premature birth, his mother's abandonment of him, and his having lived all his childhood and youth among clerics separated him forever from the world of women. It is not difficult, however, to perceive in that hatred the two contradictory components of fascination: fear and attraction. "In his service," Sosa continues, "he never allowed any woman; in his frequent doctrinal addresses he vehemently attacked any defects he thought present in women; he went so far as to reprimand one of them from the pulpit, personalizing his attacks." Lezamis recalls having heard the Archbishop say "that if he knew that a woman had so much as entered his house, he would have to order the bricks she had stepped on removed . . . He did not want a woman to touch anything in his house or to cook his meals; he did not want to hear them sing, or even to hear them mentioned." Nor did he allow anyone who visited him to bring a woman with him, a prohibition that irritated many people. He was so strict in this rule that when the Count de Galve assumed his post as Viceroy, the Archbishop did not, as demanded by protocol, go to call on him, so he would not have to greet the Vicereine. Aguiar y Seijas gave thanks to God that he was nearsighted, since that prevented his having to see women.

Lezamis' testimony reveals the true nature of Aguiar y Seijas' misogyny: "I remember during the time I heard his confessions, which was when he was Bishop and Archbishop, he detailed with great clarity the battles and temptations he suffered in this matter." Lezamis is referring to the temptation of lust, and he adds: "Before he was Bishop he did not suffer as much as when he was Bishop and Archbishop. And His Excellency attributed the cause of this to the fact that before holding those posts he did not visit women." His dealing with women, even though from a distance, was a threat to his spiritual health. The chastity of the prelate was "heroic," but the more he mortified his body, the more his lust increased. Not only did the painful humbling of his flesh cruelly stimulate his imagination, it is also revealing that the temptation increased with his new rank of Archbishop, as if there were a secret connection between desire and pride. Lezamis comments, "A prolonged martyrdom was the chastity of the reverend Archbishop." In spite of the admiration and love he professed for him, the portrait Lezamis draws is one of a violent and capricious man, apprehensive and choleric, suspicious, cruel with himself and with others, constantly visited by the ghosts of wrath and lust. His charity was despotism, his humility pride, and his chastity a mental debauch.

Aguiar y Seijas' impatience and anger in regard to Sor Juana's worldly and literary activities must have been extreme. Nevertheless, for years that antagonism was not openly expressed. Indirectly, through clerics and nuns, the poet received continual rebukes and reprimands. Núñez de Miranda, her confessor, undoubtedly transmitted many of these complaints, in addition to his own. But Sor Juana enjoyed the friendship and protection of the Viceroy and his wife, the Countess de Paredes. After their departure, though her friendship with the Galves was not as intimate, she retained the favor of the palace. Sor Juana, for her part, must have felt a mixture of fear and repugnance for the bizarre and formidable Archbishop. She must have viewed his condemnation of theater and secular poetry as a condemnation of her work and her life; his hatred of women must have seemed to her both comic and horrible. She was never ashamed of being a woman, and her work is a glorification of the female spirit. Aguiar y Seijas inspired fear, but she did not bow before him. On the contrary. Writing a critique of a sermon by Vieyra, the theologian venerated by Aguiar y Seijas, was a way of teaching the arrogant prelate a lesson. In the *Carta* she states it very clearly: a "mere woman"—she herself—is God's instrument in punishing an arrogant man.

Puccini believes that Sor Juana's participation in this matter was merely that of an involuntary instrument of Fernández de Santa Cruz's machinations. I find it impossible to overlook her emotions and her motives for attacking the Archbishop. Those motives, in addition to being legitimate, were deeply personal: defense of herself and of those of her sex. In its complexity, the incident reflects one of the characteristics of Hispanic society in that period: rivalries between prelates were expressed only in veiled ways. Theology was the mask of politics. But there is a new factor in this incident, unknown until then in the history of Hispanic culture: the appearance of a female consciousness. This factor is what gives the event its real significance. I repeat: Sor Juana was not the instrument of the Bishop of Puebla. She was his ally. We do not know whether the idea of humiliating Aguiar y Seijas through a woman's criticism of a sermon by his much-admired Vieyra—a perverse and brilliant example of "Aesopian language"—originated with Sor Juana or with Fernández de Santa Cruz. What can be stated is that she would never have written that text without the support of the Bishop of Puebla: the *Carta* was addressed to him; he wrote the ecclesiastical imprimatur that allowed it to be published; he wrote the prologue; and he bore the costs of publication. Sor Juana could not have foreseen the consequences of her act. She felt secure in the protection of powerful patrons in Madrid and Mexico. But another power, faceless and nameless—chance? destiny? history?—was waiting just around the corner.

26

The *Response*

Sor Juana and Fernández de Santa Cruz must have fore-
seen that the publication of the *Carta atenagórica* would provoke replies
and commentaries. Their number, however, and the violence of some,
must have amazed them both and slightly frightened Sor Juana. Only
echoes from this polemic and a few actual documents have survived to
our day; nevertheless, from what the *Response* tells us, we know that a
number of clerics were involved and that some attacked Sor Juana fu-
riously, despite the fact that she was a woman and a nun. The polemic
reached across the sea, although there it lacked the acrimony and heat
of the debate in Mexico.[1] From the beginning, through a kind of tacit
agreement—there is nothing the Church detests more than scandal—
there was an attempt to avoid publicity. This policy continued even after
the death of the principal protagonists. In *Fame*, Castorena y Ursúa refers only in passing to the incident, although we know that he was one
of Sor Juana's defenders; Calleja praises the critique of Vieyra's sermon
in effusive terms but does not go to the heart of the matter; Oviedo is
preoccupied with defending Núñez de Miranda and tries to show that
Sor Juana did not return his affection; Torres, similarly, exalts and defends the memory of Santa Cruz; as for José de Lezamis, he does not
even mention the affair. This silence is an attempt to conceal what actually happened.

Almost none of the commentaries were printed. Some were delivered
from the pulpits of churches and in the lecture halls of schools and seminaries. Others circulated in manuscript. Sor Juana relates that her most
rabid critic made and distributed copies of his comments. Dorothy

Schons speaks of a "storm of criticism" and cites, among the works that circulated in manuscript, one written by a priest, Manuel Serrano de Pereda, and one by a friar, Francisco Ildefonso de Segura. But we need not dwell on this: Sor Juana always refers to her critics in the plural, calling them "impugners," "slanderers," and "persecutors." Among the documents discovered by Ermilo Abreu Gómez was a pamphlet entitled "La fineza mayor" ("The Greatest Act of Love"), a sermon delivered on March 20, 1691, by the Valencian priest Francisco Xavier Palavicino Villarrasa in the convent of San Jerónimo itself. Sor Juana had sent off her *Response to Sor Filotea de la Cruz* barely ten days before. Palavicino's sermon holds special interest for us: it is an indication of the proportions the affair assumed in the months following the appearance of the *Carta atenagórica*. Palavicino disagrees both with Vieyra's and Sor Juana's opinions: in his eyes, Christ's greatest *fineza* is to conceal Himself during the sacrament of the Eucharist. He begins his sermon with disproportionate praise of Vieyra: a Portuguese Demosthenes, a Jesuit Cicero, and "the Tertullian of our blessed age." He continues by praising Sor Juana, although he concludes with the familiar reservation: "The choicest intellect of this blessed century, Minerva of America, great talent limited by the handicap of her being a woman . . ." Probably the nuns of San Jerónimo, with the hope of calming high feelings, had invited the diplomatic Palavicino to intervene. What the Valencian priest wrote was vastly inferior both to Vieyra's sermon and to Sor Juana's critique, but at that moment the weight of the reasoning was less important than the personalities of the antagonists. It is revealing that the nuns of San Jerónimo thought it prudent to invite a homilist whose opinion on the *finezas* of Christ differed from those of Vieyra and Sor Juana, in this way demonstrating their detachment from the controversy. Sor Juana must have considered this a defection on the part of her sisters.

The reactions caused by the *Carta* were not exclusively negative. In spite of the "handicap of her being a woman" there were those who defended her, and in the *Response* she refers to their comments, although without naming the authors. She is particularly effusive in praising one of them, probably Castorena y Ursúa, to whom she also dedicated a poem of gratitude, in which she says gracefully: "you must let the light of your intellect / shine brightly in my defense." Castorena y Ursúa's defense, like most of the others, does not appear anywhere— still another indication that there was a concerted attempt to erase all traces of the scandal. This reticence, this silence and ambiguity, along with a fondness for pseudonyms and veiled allusions, is characteristic of all bureaucracies identified with an orthodoxy. This also explains the strangely ambiguous prologue by Sor Filotea de la Cruz. First, the pseudonym. The famed Juan de Palafox y Mendoza, Fernández de Santa Cruz's predecessor as the Bishop of Puebla, had in 1659 published "Peregrinación de Filotea al Santo templo y monte de la Cruz" ("Pilgrimage of Filotea to the Holy Temple and Hill of the Cross"), written in imitation of Francisco de Sales' "Filotea francesa" ("French Filotea"). As Filotea means "one who loves God," even the pseudonym chosen by the Bishop of Puebla was an invitation to leave secular letters and take up sacred subjects. The contrast between the first paragraph of the prologue and what follows is also remarkable. The text begins with extravagant praise of Sor Juana: in addition to Vieyra, she had surpassed another Portuguese preacher, Meneses, who had been Vieyra's teacher. Not without malice, Sor Filotea expresses amazement that a woman should have vanquished a great theologian. Following that statement, Sor Filotea agrees with the notion that women may study provided that study not make them arrogant. All this can be considered as a series of oblique thrusts against Aguiar. Then the author voices a reservation, one that is essential: what a pity that Sor Juana had devoted herself to secular and not sacred writing.

The Bishop of Puebla has been accused of intolerance. Rightly so, although it seems to me that this cautiously worded text has not been read with care. The paragraphs condemning Sor Juana's predisposition toward secular writing probably were intended to deflect any criticism that might arise from friends of the Archbishop of Mexico. I also believe that Fernández de Santa Cruz's reprimand, in addition to its tactical utility as a weapon of self-defense, accurately represented his point of view. Sor Juana's style of thinking and writing collided violently with his views. He believed that "any science that does not serve Christ is but ignorance and vanity." Sor Juana paid lip service to those ideas, but the attitude that ruled her life was radically different: her true passion was knowledge. Another source of conflict was the limits imposed on a woman's learning. Sor Juana wants them broadened, and in this she does not yield. Although her rebellion is undeclared, she does not give in: she advances with prudence, retreats, again advances. I emphasize the Bishop's ambivalence: he asks Sor Juana to write a critique of Vieyra; he publishes it, and does not hesitate to give it his imprimatur; he hides behind a pseudonym with ambiguous connotations and writes a no less ambiguous prologue in which he praises Sor Juana on the one hand and criticizes her on the other. If Sor Juana's enemies attack the Bishop, if they are startled that he published such a text, he can reply that he had already reprimanded the nun; at the same time, that reprimand offers her an opportunity to defend herself. José María de Cossío assumes that there was a prior agreement between Sor Juana and the Bishop: the prelate's letter was an invitation for her to present her case and defend herself. Possibly. But the Bishop could not have known what Sor Juana's response would be, nor could she have foreseen the prelate's cruel desertion. At the heart of their relationship there was something equivocal, something unstated; almost as soon as it came to light, the relationship dissolved. The Bishop's comments brought Sor Juana face to face with the problem of her vocation; that is, with the very meaning of her life. Christ's *finezas* and other theological points faded into the background.

Sor Juana was not long in replying; the *Carta atenagórica* appeared at the end of November of 1690, and the *Response to Sor Filotea de la Cruz* was dated March 1, 1691. It is a text written in different modes, ranging from that of a legal brief to autobiography to intellectual discourse. Certain passages—a mark of her time and her religious training—are pedantic and interlarded with Latin; others are simple, written in an admirable and fluid familiar prose. In spite of blemishes and lacunae, the *Response* is a unique document in the history of Hispanic literature, in which there are few confessions relating to the life of the mind, its illusions and disillusions. Reflection on the solitary adventures of the mind is a theme seldom explored by the great Spanish and Spanish American writers. In this, the *Response* departs from the prevailing tendencies of our culture and forms the complement to *First Dream:* if the latter is the isolated monument of the mind in its hunger for learning, the *Response* is the account of the everyday labors of that same mind, told in a direct and familiar language.

The *Response* is more than a kind of prose version of *First Dream;* it is also, and first of all, a reply to the Bishop of Puebla. That reply, naturally, had to be a defense of secular letters. Sor Juana could not say that they were equal or superior to sacred writing—to say that would have led, ipso facto, to the Inquisition—but she used all her ingenuity to praise secular literature and to demonstrate its value and necessity. She was answering not just the Bishop but all her adversaries and critics. She realized that she was being attacked above all for being a woman, and thus her defense was immediately transformed into a defense of the female sex. To us, this is the part of her brief that is most vital and closest to present-day concerns. Finally, there is an invisible interlocutor with whom Sor Juana is in continual dialogue: herself. All her life she has lived in ambivalence: is she a nun or a writer? As she replies to the Bishop and others, she is writing to herself; she recounts the beginnings of her love of letters, and attempts to explain and justify that love to herself. The contradiction that pervades her life—she says it again and again—is born not of her nature but of circumstances imposed upon her: she was a nun because she had no other choice. But she always fulfilled her religious obligations, and more than twenty years after taking her vows she continued to believe in the compatibility of her two vocations. Any careful reader can perceive on reading those pages that if the *Response* was an examination of conscience, Sor Juana emerged from that examination unrepentant. Further, writing that text was a liberating experience that reconciled her with herself. Although its language is cautious and abounding in reservations and parentheses, the final impression is clear: she is not ashamed of what she is or has been. And this is what must have disturbed, pained, and offended men like Fernández de Santa Cruz and Núñez de Miranda.

Sor Juana begins her response with a long and ingenious preamble. She confesses that she was moved when she saw her "scribblings" published, and adds that "when the letter which you saw fit to call *atenagórica* reached my hands, in print, I burst into tears of confusion (although tears do not come easily to me)." The words are less than sincere: surely the Bishop would not have published her critique of Vieyra without her assent. Sor Juana prolongs the fiction by not disclosing the identity of the person to whom the *Carta* was addressed; she insists that she wrote it on the order of someone she cannot disobey, and reiterates that she had no hand in its publication. Neither is she sincere when she calls the Bishop's action a favor from God, who is thus chastising her for her ingratitude. She says she has not written much on theological matters, but the entire *Response* is specifically intended to explicate and justify that omission! The passage ends with a formal promise: she accepts Sor Filotea's admonition. Although "it comes in the guise of counsel," it will have for her "the force of a precept," and she will dedicate herself to the study of the Sacred Books (a promise not fulfilled, as we shall see). After this humble and conciliatory prelude, she takes up her defense.[2]

Why has she not written more on sacred subjects? The answer is disconcerting: she is not capable of penetrating the subtleties of theology. She invokes the authority of St. Jerome, who recalls that, among the Jews, those dedicated to the priesthood were forbidden to read the Song of Songs "until they have passed thirty years of age . . . in order that the sweetness of those epithalamia not prompt imprudent youth to translate their sentiment into desires of the flesh." Fear of misinterpreting the Holy Scripture often "has plucked my pen from my hand . . . , a scruple I did not find when it came to secular matters, for a heresy against art is punished not by the Holy Office but by the judicious with derision, and by critics with censure." The paragraph is ambiguous; it is clear that she did indeed have sufficient talent to deal with theological abstractions but, just as clearly, she preferred writing plays and sonnets. She affirms that she never wrote "except when compelled and constrained, and then only to give pleasure to others"—a surprising declaration if one recalls the effort she put into having her works published. Immediately, however, she modifies that statement: she says that this "repugnance" for writing refers specifically to sacred matters, and repeats, "I wish no quarrel with the Holy Office." Her true passion has been learning, not literature. The statement must be understood in its true sense: by *learning,* she means not only the sciences and philosophy but what in her time was called humane letters, with classical literature in the forefront.[3]

In the paragraphs that follow she defends not only her passionate dedication to literature but her womanhood:

> From the moment I was first illuminated by the light of reason, my inclination toward letters has been so vehement that not even the admonitions of others . . . nor my own meditations . . . have been sufficient to cause me to forswear this natural impulse that God placed in me; the Lord God knows why, and for what purpose. And he knows that I have prayed that he dim the light of my reason, leaving only that which is needed to keep his Law, for there are those who say that all else is unwanted in a woman.

The "those" referred to are the ones who according to the Bishop were guilty of ignobly "denying women the exercise of letters." Then she makes a remarkable confession, although again she blends the true with the false:

> I have sought to veil the light of my reason, along with my name, and to offer it up only to Him who bestowed it on me, and He knows that none other was the cause of my entering into religion, notwithstanding that the

spiritual exercises and company of a community were repugnant to the
freedom and quiet I desired for my studious endeavors.

A glaring contradiction: in the first part of the essay she says that in the
convent she had wanted to veil not only her name but the light of her
reason, which would have meant, specifically, renouncing her bent toward study; in the second part she says that she took the veil even
though she knew that life in the convent would hinder her intention to
study and read. Here, for the first time, we see a theme that will appear
and reappear throughout the course of the *Response:* the conflict between the vocation of a solitary scholar and the obligations of communal life in a convent.

Sor Juana's confessions do not entirely correspond to reality: she
seems to forget how few roads were open to her in 1669. If not the road
of the convent, what would her choice have been? A disastrous marriage, like those of her two sisters? Nonetheless, it is true that she entered San Jerónimo knowing that a convent was not the most propitious
place for an intellectual like herself. That is why she had hesitated, and
confessed her doubts to "only the one who should know," that is, her
confessor, Núñez de Miranda. But he did not accept her uncertainty,
"saying it was temptation: and so it would have been." A terrible admission that is also a veiled accusation: Núñez de Miranda had told her
that it was temptation to want to bury her name and renown, along
with her person, in the convent. He had urged her to take the veil, telling
her that she could continue her studies without harm to her religious
obligations. Surely Sor Juana is speaking the truth. For Núñez de Miranda, the first order of business was to get her into the convent. Later,
gradually, he would persuade her to abandon poetry and secular letters
and to consecrate herself to the religious life. It is clear that Núñez de
Miranda changed during the course of his relationship with Sor Juana:
at first he was kind; later, increasingly severe. He was a "fisher of souls,"
and in order to catch Sor Juana he minimized the conflict between religious life and dedication to study and letters. That is why, faced with
her hesitation, he called it temptation. The Jesuit's transformation was
the slow product of circumstances. During the long period in which Sor
Juana was totally involved in literary affairs, Father Antonio did not
overtly express his strong opposition; Sor Juana had become something
akin to an official poet, linked to the palace by the double ties of com-
missions from the court and personal friendship. At the end of the paragraph, Sor Juana writes with true passion: "If it were in my power, my

lady, to repay you in some part what I owe you, it might be done by telling you this thing which has never before passed my lips, except to be spoken to the one who should hear it [Núñez de Miranda]." These pained words reveal a private disagreement, until then kept secret, between her and her confessor.[4]

In the paragraphs that follow, she tells of her efforts: of having attended at the age of three "a school for girls we call the Amigas" in Nepantla (she lived in Panoayán, several kilometers away); of her voluntary abstention from eating cheese—her favorite treat—because she had heard that it made one "slow of wits"; of her scheme to attend the university dressed as a man; of her readings in her grandfather's library; of having learned grammar, and the punishment she voluntarily inflicted on herself: cutting her hair four or six fingers' breadth and not letting it grow back until she had learned some lesson or other. I referred to these passages in Part Two, interpreting them there. A pity that they are so few, and that Sor Juana skimmed so rapidly over her childhood and youth. The account of her love of study leads again to her reason for having chosen the religious life. This is one of the themes that haunted her thoughts. She confesses that she had felt "a total antipathy to marriage," and that she had deemed life in a convent "the least unsuitable and most honorable I could elect." Hers is a case not of a call from God but of a rational choice: Sor Juana weighs her situation and with a clear head chooses San Jerónimo, in spite of "all the trivial aspects of my nature, such as wishing to live alone, and wishing to have no obligatory occupation that would inhibit the freedom of my studies, or the sounds of a community that would intrude upon the peaceful silence of my books." That is why, she repeats, she hesitated in taking her vows until "certain learned persons enlightened me, explaining that [my wishes] were temptation." Again the theme that she returns to throughout the *Response:* for her, although she was aware of the conflict between intellectual and convent life, entering the convent did not entail renouncing humane letters. This conflict was not one of substance but of regimen: the many obligations of the convent made studious concentration next to impossible. The result, naturally, was that her thirst for knowledge was not sated but, rather, intensified: "I brought with me my worst enemy, my inclination, which I do not know whether to consider a gift or a punishment from Heaven, for once dimmed and encumbered by the many activities common to religion, that inclination exploded in me like gunpowder, proving that *privatio est causa appetitus.*"[5]

In the convent she continued the pursuit "of reading and more read-ing, of study and more study." There is bitterness in her account: it is difficult to study without a master. Although her studies were secular, her ultimate goal was to arrive at theology. This, again, sounds to me less than sincere. She herself confesses that if she dwelled so long on the preliminaries, it was "to flatter and applaud my own inclination, pre-senting its indulgence as an obligation." She explains then that one can-not understand "the style of the Queen of Sciences [theology] if one has not first come to know her servants." Without logic, rhetoric, music, arithmetic, geometry, history, law, languages, astrology, and even the me-chanical arts, it is impossible to comprehend passages from Holy Scrip-ture. Sor Juana's plan, aside from its intrinsic difficulty, was superfluous: the highly speculative nature of theology made unnecessary much of the knowledge she speaks of. With the exception of Albertus Magnus, his disciple St. Thomas, and one or two others, no theologian mastered all the sciences of his time. Besides, Sor Juana was too intelligent to believe what she was saying.

Her confidences continue; she tells us that she foundered in the va-riety of her studies, "having an inclination not toward any one thing in particular but toward all in general." Nevertheless, even in these appar-ently unstructured readings she held to a certain rhythm, moving from study to enjoyment. Sor Juana is severe with herself: "though I have studied many things I know nothing." This judgment on her method of acquiring knowledge, and its results, could perhaps justify José María de Cossío's opinion that she was a dilettante. Not so; her ideal was many-faceted knowledge. By that I mean that she wanted to be profi-cient in the themes and sciences central to the culture of her day, in the hope of discerning the links and connections that joined that disparate knowledge into a whole. This was an unattainable ideal in the New Spain of the end of the seventeenth century, although she probably did not know that. She was almost entirely ignorant of the great intellectual revolution that was transforming Europe. In view of that ignorance, her desire becomes even more poignant. Nevertheless, if her information was out-of-date and incomplete—especially in physics and astron-omy—her concept of culture was singularly modern. It was the view not of the specialist but of the mind that attempts to discover the hidden links among disciplines. She would undoubtedly have been fascinated by the reasoning of a Lévi-Strauss, who finds hidden analogies between primitive thought and music; she would also have been excited by the

ideas of modern linguistics, in which the phonemes and their components fulfill the same functions as elementary particles in physics and
blocks of color in cubist painting. In spite of the fact that many of her
notions were outdated, the view that modern science—from microbiol-
ogy to astronomy—has given us of the universe as a vast system of communications would not have surprised her unduly.

After describing her experience with many and diverse disciplines in
rather negative terms, in a sudden about-face—a common procedure in
her writing—she says the opposite: familiarity with many matters is
very advantageous, for "what I have not understood in an author in one
branch of knowledge, I may understand in a second in a branch that
seems remote from the first . . . And thus it is no apology, nor do I offer
it as such, to say that I have studied many subjects, seeing that each
augments the other." She invokes as a primary example "the chain the
ancients believed issued from the mouth of Jupiter, from which were
suspended all things linked one with another." Sor Juana attributes the
image to Father Kircher. It comes, as we have noted, from Macrobius,
who used it to illustrate the idea of the descending progression from the
One to the Multiple: "From the Supreme God even to the fish in the
depths of the sea there is one tie, binding at every link and never broken.
This is the golden chain of Homer which God ordered to hang down
from the sky to the Earth."⁶ In the same paragraph, also as if it were
taken from Kircher—"in his learned book *De magnete*"—she repeats
her favorite maxim: God is at once center and circumference.⁷

When she reaches this point, she ponders her labors: not only has she
lacked a teacher, she has had no fellow students. This comment reveals
that during twenty years in the convent she has found no one interested
in the sciences, letters, or arts. Instead, the nuns have hindered her with
their incessant interruptions. The busy and empty life of the convent:
unexpected visitors in her cell, constant gossip, songs and laughter from
adjacent cells, the servants and their quarrels. A small world possessed
by a fever for the trivial. But the difficulties of communal life—she calls
them "inevitable and accidental obstacles"—were but a small part of
the problems she experienced. In addition to her obligations as a nun,
and the chatter and busyness of her sisters, she suffered the persecution
of men and women who wanted to prevent her from studying and writing. Among them, the worst were

> not those who persecuted me with open hate and malice, but those who in
> loving me and desiring my well-being . . . have mortified and tormented

me more than those others: "Such studies are not in conformity with sacred innocence; surely you will be lost; surely you will, by reason of your very perspicacity and acuity, grow heady at such exalted heights."

Among these pious persecutors was Núñez de Miranda. Sor Juana was also maligned for her "unfortunate facility in making verses, even if they are sacred verses." This entire passage is written with admirable subtlety. Imperceptibly, she moves from the defense of her hunger for learning to the defense of the art of writing poetry, whether sacred or secular. Thus she asserts, without stating it, her right to read and write on themes that were not religious.[8]

To read is a passive occupation; to write is the opposite of burying one's name in the obscurity of a nunnery: it is to emerge into public view. Eminence, however, always entails penalties: the rule of this vulgar world "is to abhor one who excels, because he deprives others of regard. And thus it happens, and thus it has always happened." The Pharisees' hatred of Christ was born of envy. They killed him "because that is the reward for one who excels." That is why, too, the ancients adorned the figure of Fame, placed on the highest point of their temples, with iron barbs: "the figure thus elevated cannot avoid being the target of barbs." Any superiority, "whether in dignity, nobility, riches, beauty, or knowledge, must suffer this punishment, but the eminence that undergoes the most severe attack is that of intelligence . . . for, as Gracián stated so eruditely, 'a man favored by intelligence is favored by nature.'" Sor Juana then launches into a disquisition on Christ as the victim of envy, although she notes that in her case she has been persecuted not "for my knowledge but merely for my love of learning." That love brought her "closer to the fire of persecution, to the crucible of torment, and to such straits that they have asked that study be forbidden to me." Who would "they" have been—Aguiar y Seijas? Núñez de Miranda? On one occasion they succeeded, and an abbess, "very saintly and ingenuous, who believed that study was a matter for the Inquisition . . . , commanded me not to study." The prohibition lasted three months. This incident illustrates another aspect of Sor Juana's character, one that separates her from her contemporaries and from Hispanic tradition: love of experimentation. Everyday objects, parallel shadows cast by a headboard, the tracings left on the floor by a spinning top—everything she saw and touched served as an excuse for posing questions and attempting to answer them. The kitchen was also her laboratory: "And what shall I tell you, lady, of the secrets of nature I have discovered while cooking . . . ?"

And she asks, "What can we, as women, know if not the philosophies of the kitchen?" On the other hand, "had Aristotle prepared victuals, he would have written more." All these struggles, sleepless nights, hardships suffered for love of learning, were they merits? In the case of a man they would be, but not in a woman. No matter; she has been true to her inclination, she "cannot but study." She does not offer a judgment of herself; she leaves that to Sor Filotea.[9]

Although her love of letters was so great that she would not have needed examples to imitate, she always had in mind the names of women who had excelled in human and divine studies. Here begins a long and erudite enumeration embracing famous women of history—poets, philosophers, jurists, and others—from classical antiquity and the Bible to contemporaries such as the Duchess de Aveyro and Queen Christina of Sweden. Among the "learned women" she lists, many belong to pagan times, and to hear the name of some—such as Hypatia, "who taught astrology, and studied many years in Alexandria"—on the lips of a nun is somewhat startling. Hypatia of Alexandria, beautiful and intelligent, virtuous and wise, a Neoplatonic philosopher, was murdered in March of 415 by a band of Christian monks. Sor Juana must have known the circumstances of Hypatia's death, a martyr not to her professed faith but to philosophy. As when she mentions the wife of Simon Magus, the gnostic Ennoia, her admiration for these illustrious women was stronger than fear of going beyond the limits of orthodoxy. Two rival beliefs were at war within her: Christianity and feminism, her religious faith and her love of philosophy. Frequently, and not without risk, feminism and philosophy triumphed. Remarkable courage.[10]

The list of learned women offers her the opportunity to introduce a theme that obsesses her: can women teach and interpret Holy Scripture? It was St. Paul's opinion that they could not: "Let women keep silence in the churches; for it is not permitted them to speak." Basing her argument on the ideas of a Mexican theologian, Dr. Arce, on other authorities, and on her own wit, through a long, circuitous dialectic she reaches the conclusion that women *may* study, interpret, and teach Holy Scripture, with one limitation: they must do so not from the pulpit but in their homes and other private places. She proposes something akin to universal education for women, to be the responsibility of elderly educated women. She argues that women should also be taught the sciences and secular letters. She bases her idea in the reasoning she had expounded at the beginning: direct knowledge of the Scriptures is impossible without the study of history, law, arithmetic, logic, rhetoric, and music. The study of holy books "demands more learning than some believe, who, knowing only grammar . . . cling to that 'Let women keep silence in the churches.'" She scoffs at the idea, current in her day, that women are intellectually inferior. As stupidity is not confined to women, neither is intelligence an attribute only of men.[11]

The long passage on women brings her back to her own case. Why do they attack her? She does not teach or write theology. The *Carta atenagórica?* It was not a crime to write it. If the Church did not forbid it, why should others do so? Vieyra's opinions are not articles of faith. Furthermore, she writes with passion, "I maintained respect at all times . . . , and I did not touch a thread of the robes of the Society of Jesus." She complains that one of her critics has been lacking in decorum, and has labeled her letter rash and heretical—"why then does he not denounce it?" But the defense of the *Carta* is only one aspect of her brief; she is even more hurt by attacks on her "oft-chastised gift for making verses." She has searched for the harm that could result, and has not found it. She quotes the great poets and poetesses of the Bible and Catholic tradition to demonstrate that writing poetry is not at variance with the religious life. If so many holy women have cultivated poetry, why is what she has written evil? She states with assurance that "no verse of mine has been deemed indecent." (What about the burlesque sonnets and epigrams?) Immediately she falls back on the questionable argument she has repeated throughout the *Response:* "Furthermore, I have never written of my own will, but under the pleas and injunctions of others." This gives her the excuse to slip in the information that "the only piece I remember having written for my own pleasure was a little trifle they called *El sueño.*" Although we have no reason to believe her literally—she surely must have been pleased with much of what she wrote—we can see why she would single out her spiritual autobiography.[12]

The end of the *Response* is more rambling: she repeats herself and skips about, as if she could not find a way to end. She persists in her statement that she wrote her critique at the request of someone she could not disobey, and that she had never thought it would be published. The blemishes and lacunae in the *Carta* are primarily due to the haste with which it had been composed: several arguments and proofs had been left in her inkwell. She does not venture to remit those "reasonings" directly to Sor Filotea, but "if they should wing your way (and they are of such little weight that they surely will), then you will command what I am to do." So it seems that Sor Juana sent the Bishop other "reasonings" that amplified and rounded out her critique of Vieyra's sermon. Fernández de Santa Cruz did not publish them, however, or even so much as mention them. How are we to judge this devious behavior? As for those who impugn her: others have responded for her; she has seen some of these replies and is sending one that is especially learned. Neither Fernández de Santa Cruz nor anyone else left any information concerning the content or the fate of those writings. Sor Juana continues: the attacks do not discourage her, as they are the price she has to pay for public notice: "calumny has often mortified me, but never harmed me." Having vented her feelings, without much logic, she repeats that she has never published anything of her own will, with the exception of two devotional compositions: "Ejercicios de la Encarnación" ("Exercises for the Incarnation") and "Ofrecimientos de los Dolores" ("Offerings for the Dolors"), two folios that circulated unsigned among the nuns of the city.[13]

Before closing with the customary formulas of respect and gratitude, she makes the Bishop an offer: "If ever I write again, my scribbling will always find its way to the haven of your holy feet and the certainty of your correction." She is undoubtedly referring to theological writings or compositions; clearly she did not propose to send him poems on secular subjects.[14] Thus she ends this remarkable document. The form of her argument is that of a spiral; every advance is a withdrawal. The apparent complexity of her argument can be reduced to a few points: the conflict between religious life and secular study is not one of substance but of regimen; secular studies have always been, and are, steps toward higher and more difficult sacred subjects; the honest practice of poetry is not reprehensible; she claims for herself, and asks for women in general, the chance to be educated in secular as well as sacred literature and science; finally, none of this seems to her to be contrary to the laws of the Church. The *Response to Sor Filotea de la Cruz* is not only a confession but a defense of her intellectual bent; Manuel Fernández de Santa Cruz was seeking a retraction, but Sor Juana's answer was a refutation.

27

And the Responses

$\mathcal{T}$HE RESPONSE TO SOR FILOTEA DE LA CRUZ was not published until after Sor Juana's death, in *Fame and Posthumous Works* (1700), although it must have circulated in manuscript among her friends and admirers. The attitude of Fernández de Santa Cruz revealed a caution that bordered on duplicity and hypocrisy. He did not answer the letter of his protégée, nor do we know what his reaction was when he received it. His silence is all the more striking in view of the fact that the *Response* was an exceptional piece of writing, not only because of its authorship, but for the subjects it treated, among them the education of women and women's right to comment on and interpret Scripture. How could a man who had shown his concern for the welfare of the nuns in so many edifying letters have confronted Sor Juana's reasoning with such indifference and silence? The disdainful silence that followed the *Response* contrasts strangely with the affectionate though exacting attentiveness that had preceded it. The prelate's attitude was shared by his biographer, Fray Miguel de Torres, Sor Juana's nephew. That mediocre apologist recounts a thousand trivial details in the life of Fernández de Santa Cruz but never once mentions the *Response*.

It is difficult, nearly three centuries after the events, to offer an explanation of Fernández de Santa Cruz's behavior. A logical supposition is that he did not wish to irritate the choleric Aguiar y Seijas further. It was better to abandon the nun than to prolong and embitter a dispute with the Archbishop of Mexico and his friends and with many Jesuits as well. The latter consideration must have been decisive. Moreover, Fernández himself was persuaded of the justice of the criticism Sor Juana was receiving. The *Response to Sor Filotea de la Cruz* confirmed his opinion: her writing and the renown she had won had fed her natural vanity and rebelliousness. In spite of her protestations of obedience and the obsequiously humble tone she affected, the Bishop of Puebla could not have been happy with her response; he had wanted a frank and unequivocal renunciation of secular letters, not a reasoned defense, even if the defense viewed secular learning as a path toward divine learning. In the eyes of the prelate, Sor Juana had fallen into the very sin he had denounced in his letter as the most serious risk for educated women: the pride, the presumption, that "leads a woman from her state of obedience."

The reaction of Sor Juana's confessor, the Jesuit Antonio Núñez de Miranda, was even more harsh; he withdrew his spiritual aid from her and refused to see her. Núñez de Miranda was a figure of great prestige and influence—a professor of theology, rector of the Colegio de San Pedro y San Pablo, a renowned homilist, a man in good standing with the powerful, an untiring counselor to nuns, and censor for the Holy Office. The last responsibility consisted of examining, censoring, and, in his case, condemning the books and proposals submitted to the authority of the Inquisition. The censors were the guardians of orthodoxy. Sor Juana often alluded to her fear of the tribunal of the Holy Office. The desertion of Núñez de Miranda must have been a blow to her. How could she forget that he was the one who had persuaded her to choose the path of religion, and that on the day she took the veil he himself had lighted the altar candles? Such an intimate and long-standing relationship as that between Núñez de Miranda and Sor Juana—two conflicting temperaments, he domineering and she independent—always engenders misunderstandings and ill will. The confessor was the father and the tyrant, the venerated image and the hated ghost. It must have been distressing to have as father confessor a man who specialized in detecting heresy and sins against dogma.

With some uncertainty I have given the date of Núñez de Miranda's withdrawal from her as that of the *Response,* that is, the early months of 1691. This is the opinion of the majority of critics. It is possible, however, that he had withdrawn earlier. Our information on all this is vague and incomplete. Calleja, faithful to his role as apologist, does not even mention the incident; if it were not for Oviedo, we would know nothing about it at all. Determined to clear Núñez de Miranda of any blame for his lack of understanding or excessive severity toward Sor Juana, Oviedo committed the indiscretion of revealing some of the details of what occurred: "When Father Anonio saw that he could not achieve what he desired [Sor Juana's renunciation of secular letters], he withdrew totally from assisting Sister Juana, lamenting that if those remarkable gifts were not entirely wasted neither were they as well directed as he would have wished." Oviedo does not say when he withdrew, only when he returned: in 1693, two years before her death. The withdrawal may have been caused by the *Response*, since in it Sor Juana expresses no intention of renouncing secular writing; it is also reasonable to think it may have been earlier, considerably earlier. Even in 1680 it was clear that, far from dedicating herself to theology or the ascetic life, Sor Juana was determined to participate increasingly in the flurry of literary affairs. Between 1680 and 1690 her literary and worldly life reached its greatest intensity, with the salon of San Jerónimo, the friendship with María Luisa, the plays and *loas,* the courtly and amatory poems, the uninterrupted correspondence with colleagues and admirers in Madrid, Seville, Lima, and Quito. Perhaps Núñez de Miranda withdrew his ministrations during this period.*

How did Sor Juana feel about Núñez de Miranda's defection? We know nothing at all. This is one of the many lacunae in her biography. Nevertheless, contrary to what we might have expected, her literary and intellectual activity during those years—whether ten years or two—suggests that Father Antonio's abandonment did not seriously affect her and her work. This indirectly confirms my supposition regarding the ambiguity of her feelings toward her former confessor. Another lacuna: we do not know who the priest was who replaced Núñez de Miranda. It would have to have been a person of authority and prestige, someone who would support her both publicly and in private. Francisco de la Maza discovered a strange bit of information in a biography of Father Pedro Arellano written by Juan José de Eguiara y Eguren.[1] Eguiara says that after the death of Núñez de Miranda, Sor Juana's confessor was Father Arellano, a man the nun termed "holy." Arellano enjoyed great prestige "among the important personages of Mexico City," so that he could take Núñez de Miranda's place without any disadvantage to Sor Juana. Probably he was less severe than the Jesuit: he was an *extático,* a contemplative, not an intellectual. Eguiara, however, says that Arellano was Sor Juana's confessor *after* the death of Núñez de Miranda. That is not possible. Núñez de Miranda died on February 17, 1695, and Sor

---

* For a new light on this matter, see the Appendix.

Juana on April 17, exactly two months later. This is either an error on Eguiara's part or, more likely, another example of the clerical mania for hiding the truth and replacing it with edifying fiction: the episode of the confessor's withdrawal did not flatter either Sor Juana or Núñez de Miranda. So we may reasonably assume that Arellano replaced Father Antonio from the time of his withdrawal until his return in 1693.

In her final years, Sor Juana had to face up to a conflict that had been present since the day she became a nun but which twenty years later came to a head. That conflict can be defined, briefly, as the opposition between the religious and the intellectual life—but stated in those terms it sounds like a thesis topic, not a vital and compelling question. What was in balance was the true meaning of her life and the direction her life would take in the future. The conflict placed her identity, her innermost being, into question. From the beginning she had been aware of the contradiction she was living and had avoided confronting it. The road she had chosen was not an unusual one: the Church had always served as refuge for impoverished talents. Poets, dramatists, and even writers of fiction were common in the secular clergy and the religious orders. None of them had been persecuted for writing secular works; they were allowed remarkable freedom as long as they wrote nothing that conflicted with dogma. Sor Juana's decision to take the veil, in spite of the inconveniences of communal life, was sane, proper, and in line with tradition. Since she had no taste for marriage and no means to marry suitably, the convent was a reasonable compromise between the free but solitary existence of the intellectual and the servitude of domesticity. For twenty years her tact and skill had won her protectors in many places, especially the highest, the palace. As a result, she had been able to balance her profession as a nun and her true vocation as a writer. Suddenly, the scales are tipped and a few intransigent prelates corner her, attack her, and forbid her to write except on religious subjects. Why?

The difference between Sor Juana and other clerical writers—Lope de Vega, Góngora, Calderón, among many—was very simple: she was a woman. Lope and Góngora were not good priests, but no Fernández de Santa Cruz scolded them publicly for not writing theological treatises, nor did a Núñez de Miranda withdraw his spiritual aid because they were writing love sonnets and décimas. A nun could be forbidden what a bad priest could not. Sor Juana was fully aware of the fact that her sex was the cause, declared or tacit, of the censure and admonitions. This is why the *Response* argues for the education of women, listing notable female writers of ancient and modern times. Her admiration for certain women from the past was so great that she devoted a series of moral sonnets, verbal cameos, to Lucretia, Julia, and Portia. The irritation provoked by a literate nun who was not ashamed of being a woman and who counted on protectors in high places was exacerbated by an additional factor: the narrowness of the world in which she moved. Life in her city revolved around a court that imitated the court in Madrid, in which quarrels over rank and position acquired ridiculous proportions. Disputes over questions of precedence were constant, and the Princes of the Church participated in these squabbles with the same passion as the peninsular and criollo nobility. Sor Juana's preeminence offended many prelates; they were her superiors, and almost all considered themselves theologians, literati, or poets. The nun's sex and her intellectual superiority were a double affront.

In Aguiar y Seijas all these sentiments were crystallized. He was her evil genius. Consumed by a sick hatred of women, he saw in Sor Juana an example of perdition and dissoluteness. An enemy of theater and poetry, he regarded as an abomination the conduct of a nun who instead of scourging herself wrote plays and poems. Aguiar y Seijas' animosity was at first expressed as indifference; as he could not attack her, he ignored her. His restraint was calculated: it was not prudent, even for an Archbishop, to alienate the powers that protected Sor Juana. The Marquis de la Laguna was not only the Viceroy of New Spain, he was the brother of the Duke de Medinaceli, a favorite of the King and also his prime minister. The return to Spain of the Marquis and Marquise de la Laguna in 1688 weakened Sor Juana's position, but not unduly; she soon won the support of the new Viceroy, the Count de Galve. Furthermore, in Spain she could still count on the friendship of the Marquise, Countess de Paredes, her publisher and sponsor in Madrid and Seville. María Luisa's husband, the former Viceroy, had been named chief majordomo to the new Queen, Maria Anna, and after the fall of the Duke de Medinaceli the couple had regained their position at court. The first volume of Sor Juana's works (*Castalian Inundation*) appeared in 1689 and a second, corrected and enlarged edition in 1690. It was very well received in Spain and enhanced her reputation and consolidated her position.

The incident of the *Carta atenagórica* finally gave the advantage to Aguiar y Seijas and other of Sor Juana's enemies. The widespread but until then unspoken hostility aroused by this nun who presumed to be an author, and whose fame had spread across the seas, gradually gathered support until it became an issue that touched on the very principles of ecclesiastical discipline. Hostility and jealousy were cloaked in appeals to high principle: respect for authority, obedience, devotion to religious duty. The flood of opinion unleashed by the animosity of Aguiar y Seijas was, in fact, a wave of shameful passions: envy, fear, misogyny, mistrust. Some wanted to convert her into a student of theology, others into a plaster saint; everyone wanted to humble her, silence her.

It would be a mistake to think that Sor Juana was the object of a deliberate conspiracy: it was a general climate of opinion that grew stronger with time. Gradually, she was caught up in the tide of opposition. She felt the tide and resisted it. Until the very last, she never lost her self-control. Even during those two years she was not lacking for friends and protectors, in the palace, in the Church, and among other persons of high standing. Her greatest strength lay in her patrons in Spain. Among them, in addition to the Countess de Paredes and her husband, she counted on her long-time protector, the Marquis de Mancera, who had regained royal favor following the Queen Mother's return to the court of Madrid. For all these reasons—and also because her past triumphs had made her dangerously self-confident—she stood firm in the face of censure. Praise still outweighed criticism. Her writing and other activities in that period, 1691 and 1692, reveal a tranquil Sor Juana fully in control of herself. The *Response* had been not an abdication but an affirmation, and the most impressive testimony of her will to preserve her independence was her continued and imperturbable dedication to literary endeavors.

Early in 1691 Sigüenza y Góngora published his anthology celebrating the victory in the Antilles of the Spanish American armada over the French, *Trophy of Spanish Justice*. Among the poems in that collection is the *silva* "Epinicion to the Count de Galve," a long poem in which Sor Juana attempts the heroic genre. The Viceroy was surely flattered by her homage. In 1691 the third edition of the first volume of her works was published in Barcelona, an edition "corrected and enlarged by the author." Three *villancicos* were added and, even more noteworthy, the *loa* and *auto sacramental* of *The Divine Narcissus*. These changes could not have been made without Sor Juana's participation and consent. A task requiring even greater effort was the preparation of the second volume of her works: it involved collecting, selecting, revising, and arranging the originals, as well as supervising and correcting the work of the copyists. She was probably engaged in this task at the time she was writing the critique of Vieyra's sermon. The publication of this volume in Seville has a significance that has not been appreciated until now: it was a projectile fired from Seville against her enemies in Mexico.

The second volume of Sor Juana's *Works* (Seville, 1692) is dedicated to a Knight of the Order of Santiago, Juan de Orve y Arbieto. Sor Juana's curious dedication begins with an odd declaration: she asks that Orve y Arbieto not defend her works against "the detractions of the vulgar," nor "curtail the freedom of readers' opinions"—odd, since one-third of the book is composed of prefatory vindications, panegyrics, apologies, and laudatory poems that amount to an impassioned defense of Sor Juana's writings, especially on those points for which she had been criticized in Mexico. Next, her rationale for the dedication is that she has Basque blood, like the "noble families of Orve and Arbieto," and thus the "brooklets of her meditations are flowing back to the sea in which they recognize their origins." After this explanation that explains nothing, she apologizes for the imperfections of her writings: they are the work of a woman, "in whom any defect is pardonable," and a woman who had no masters but "the mute teachings of books." She ends with a quotation from St. Jerome that also appears in the *Response*: "of what effort I have expended, what difficulties I have suffered, the times I have despaired, how often I have ceased my labors and turned to them again, driven by the hunger for knowledge, my conscience is witness." The thirty-six lines of the dedication can be read as a continuation of the themes of the *Response*: the "defect" of being a woman; the absence of masters; her love of learning; and the hardships she has suffered for that love. More than a dedication, it is a summation of her defense.

Juan de Orve y Arbieto was never in Mexico and never met Sor Juana. Their shared Basque heritage does not explain either the dedication or the fact that Orve y Arbieto published the book. As we know, the publication of the first volume of Sor Juana's poems in 1689 was due to the efforts of the Countess de Paredes. The man responsible for that and subsequent editions was Juan Camacho Gayna, also a Knight of the Order of Santiago and a former majordomo to the Marquis de la Laguna. Probably Juan de Orve y Arbieto, like Camacho Gayna, was a relative, friend, or protégé of the Duke de Medinaceli or the Marquis de la Laguna, or of some other member of that powerful family, such as the Duchess de Aveyro. My point is that the Basque knight was a figurehead for the Countess de Paredes. The book is illustrated with a mediocre engraving by Lucas de Valdés: a cameo of Sor Juana, her quill in its holder, Minerva and Mercury on either side, and overhead a winged Fame with her trumpets. The resemblance to Miranda's portrait is striking; there is no doubt that we are looking at a true image. Valdés obviously was inspired by a portrait of Juana Inés shown him by the Countess de Paredes, perhaps the miniature that was the subject of several *décimas*.

An additional sign of María Luisa's not-too-well-hidden intervention in this affair is the fact that the book was printed in Seville, the ancestral home of the Medinacelis and to this day the site of their principal residence. Also, the majority of the theologians, scholars, clergy, and poets who signed the opinions and panegyrics were from, or lived in, Seville. Many of them find occasion to praise the Countess de Paredes and to say that it was through her that they first learned of the genius of the Mexican nun. One of them has composed three "panegyric anagrams" in honor of Sor Juana, "Unique Queen of Poetry," dedicating them to Doña María Luisa Manrique de Lara, Countess de Paredes and Marquise de la Laguna. In the third of those anagrams he ingeniously incorporates lines from the *romance* Juana Inés dedicated to the "great wisdom of the Señora Duchess de Aveyro." Each of the four lines of this *copla* is an arrow aimed at Sor Juana's enemies:

> To women you bring great esteem,
> to learned men, acute offense,
> by proving gender plays no part
> in matters of intelligence.

The enthusiasm of the two censors and the author of the *aprobación* (imprimatur) was unusual; as the third says, "it would be impertinent to say 'approved'; better, I shall say 'praised.'" The first censor, Fray Juan de Navarro Vélez, begins his *censura* by declaring that "the second volume is worthy of the same acclamation and applause as the first." He continues, advancing an already familiar argument: "Sister Juana did not write these pages with the ambition or hope that they would be printed . . . but rather for her own licit pleasure or because they had been requested by persons whom she could not refuse." To be sure "certain scrupulous persons are surprised at a religious quill that writes verses." There is no need for such concern; "the verses of Sister Juana are as pure" as she is. Praise of the poems ends with admiration for *First*

Dream, which Navarro Vélez deems the best of all. Quickly (it was more difficult), he approves the plays and, as is to be expected, praises the *autos sacramentales* to the skies. But the "jewel of this volume and of all the works of Sister Juana" is her critique of "a sermon by an illustrious homilist." The *censura* by Cristobal de Báñez is even more enthusiastic: his judgments are briefer and more vague than those of his fellow censor, but he agrees with him in his praise of a woman who, not content with her sublime ability to write poetry, is also a matchless theologian. The *aprobación,* by Pedro Ignacio de Arce, still another Knight of the Order of Santiago and a councilman of Madrid, ends with a glowing exclamation: "Celebrated woman and of all illustrious women the exemplar!" All of this praise was written to be read and appreciated in Mexico.

The volume has a unique feature that distinguishes it from ordinary editions. Orve y Arbieto, as he explains in a note, sought the opinion of "various illustrious men in religion and letters" regarding the contents of this second volume. Their replies were a collection of "brilliant tributes" published in lieu of the usual introduction. In defense of her friend, the Countess de Paredes had recruited a team of theologians and literati. Among them are a dozen poets, all unknown today except for José Pérez de Montoro, whom Sor Juana had occasionally quoted. The theologians—seven of them—were all esteemed in their time, although today, understandably, they are forgotten. Two were Jesuits, proof that in Spain Sor Juana's critique was not considered an attack on the Society of Jesus. It would be tedious to repeat the theologians' arguments. They agree on three points. First, their admiration for Sor Juana is heightened by the fact that she is a woman (one of them says, gracelessly, "This woman is a man in every respect"), which leads several to compose long lists of the illustrious women of ancient times, the Christian tradition, and their own day (including poets from convents in Lisbon and Seville). Second, they are particularly enraptured by the theologian, the woman who has vanquished the great Vieyra. And, third, it occurs to none of them to admonish Sor Juana or reproach her for her devotion to letters: in this their position is diametrically opposed to that of Fernández de Santa Cruz and Núñez de Miranda. The seven texts of the seven theologians are seven vindications.

This is the most important volume of Sor Juana's writings: it is the most varied and the richest and contains her best work. The book opens with the critique of Vieyra's sermon, now less grandiosely entitled *Crisis* [*crítica*] *sobre un sermón de un orador grande entre los mayores . . .* (*Crisis* [*Critique*] *of a Sermon by an Orator Great among the Finest . . .*). Publication of this text confirms that Sor Juana *did indeed intend it to be made public*. The section of lyric poetry opens, correspondingly, with *First Dream*. The comments of nearly all the theologians and both censors reveal that they must have been deeply impressed by this poem. One says that with the *Crisis* and *First Dream* Sor Juana had outdone both the greatest poet and the greatest orator of the century, Góngora and Vieyra. The sections of "comedic" poetry contain the three *autos sacramentales*, two plays, and brief works; the sections of lyric poetry, secular and sacred, contain sonnets, *romances*, *décimas*, *glosas*, and *villancicos*. The inclusion of *The Martyr of the Sacrament* is further testimony to Sor Juana's feverish literary activity during those years. As I have pointed out, the flaws in this *auto* can be attributed to the haste with which it was written, undoubtedly to enable it to arrive in Seville before the book went on press. The volume was a long time in production: the *censuras* are dated July 1691, and the *aprobación,* permission, and tax, May 1692. Possibly the attacks in Mexico modified the original plan, forcing Orve y Arbieto (that is, the Countess de Paredes) to counterattack by soliciting the opinions of the theologians. The dates of their comments range from September 1691 to April 1692. Thus the volume became a powerful defense of Sor Juana, countering the criticism of her enemies in Mexico with the praise of respected religious authorities in Spain. Unfortunately, it came too late: 1692 was a year of radical changes in New Spain that affected Sor Juana's personal fate.

On November 25, 1691, the *villancicos* written in honor of St. Catherine of Alexandria were sung in the cathedral in Oaxaca. I have already written of this group of eleven poems, which include some of Sor Juana's most beautiful verses, many resonant with autobiographical references and several proclaiming a defiant feminism. Perhaps they were sung in distant Oaxaca because she did not dare offer them to the cathedrals of Mexico City and Puebla, for which she wrote regularly. Neither the Archbishop of Mexico nor the Bishop of Puebla would have listened in good humor to such aggressive and strident praise of a "learned maiden." Sor Juana saw herself in Catherine of Alexandria: like Isis and "the maiden of Delphi," Catherine was one of her symbolic doubles. The Roman Catholic breviary explains that Catherine, noble virgin of Alexandria, combined the liberal arts with the ardor of her faith, and at the age of eighteen surpassed the most learned males. Maximinus, who persecuted all things Christian, convoked the greatest philosophers from far and wide to confound her, but she, "with the strength and subtlety of her argument," conquered and converted them. Calleja recounts an analogous episode: the Viceroy Mancera was so astonished by the precociousness and learning of Juana Inés, then sixteen or seventeen, that he summoned forty learned men to question and examine her, and she answered all of them with consummate skill. Another similarity between Catherine and Juana Inés was their beauty. They were persecuted for the same reasons:

> For beauty, all do envy her,
> her learning, all do emulate,
> how endlessly in this poor world
> has blame sought worth to regulate![2]

In a different *villancico* (317), singing of the triumph of Catherine over the philosophers, she repeats what she has previously said about women, but now in a tone that is both ironic and passionate. When she wrote these stanzas she was thinking of herself:

> There in Egypt, all the sages
> by a woman were convinced
> that gender is not of the essence
> in matters of intelligence.
> *Victor! Victor!*
>
> A victory, a miracle;
> though more prodigious than the feat
> of conquering, was surely that
> the men themselves declared defeat.
> *Victor! Victor!*

God does not wish women—especially women in religious life—to be ignorant; that is why he honors Catherine, patroness of "learned women":

> It is of service to the Church
> that women argue, tutor, learn,
> for he who granted women reason
> would not have them uninformed.
> *Victor! Victor!*
>
> No man, whatever his renown,
> accomplished such a victory,

and we know that God, through her,
honored femininity.
Victor! Victor!

Tutelar and holy Patron,
Catherine, the Shrine of Arts;
long may she illumine Wise Men,
she who Wise to Saints converts.
Victor! Victor!

The final *villancico* (322), written in everyday language, is mischievous, swift-moving, stinging:

Once there was a girl,
as I here relate,
whose years when added up
numbered ten plus eight.
Wait, listen well,
to what I have to tell.
    They say (I've no idea
how it could be true)
that though a girl, men wondered
at all the things she knew.
Wait, listen well,
to what I have to tell.
    Because, as it is told,
by whom I do not know,
girls can only learn
to spin and cook and sew . . .
Wait, listen well,
to what I have to tell.
    Well, it seems this girl
convinced great men, with poise,
though any girl at all
can swaddle baby boys.
Wait, listen well,
to what I have to tell.
    They even say this girl
was a blessed saint,
and learning, in her case,
left not the slightest taint . . .

The year 1691 ended with the *villancicos* to St. Catherine: self-portrait, defense, mockery, and defiance. Also a prophecy of what awaited her:

Now all her learned arguments
are lost to us (how great the grief).
But with her blood, if not with ink,
she wrote the lesson of her life.

28

The Siege

$\mathcal{D}$URING THE SUMMER OF 1691 it rained incessantly in the Valley of Mexico. The crops were ruined and the capital was flooded. Sigüenza y Góngora recounts, "No one could enter the city and there was a shortage of coal, firewood, fruit, vegetables, fowl, and all that comes from outside the city." [1] Bread and maize especially were in short supply. Many adobe houses collapsed and for several weeks the city was again a lake. On August 23 there was a solar eclipse, and the people believed that its malign influence was the cause of a new calamity: a plague of *chahuixtle* weevils, which eat maize and wheat. Hoarding and speculation increased the shortages. Bread became smaller in size and higher in price; tortillas were scarce. The Viceroy did what all indecisive governors do: held meetings. Summer passed, and autumn; winter arrived and the decisionmakers were still deliberating. Extreme measures were tried: there were solemn prayers, processions, and public flagellations; miraculous images were paraded through the streets and plazas; the Virgen de los Remedios, a patron saint of the Spanish, was removed from her sanctuary and carried to the cathedral. Messengers were sent to obtain needed supplies from the granaries of Chalco, Puebla, Atlixco, Celaya, and elsewhere. Growers, however, were reluctant to sell at the price set by the authorities, and many hid their grain; in addition, there were not enough mules to transport it. People whispered that, if not the Viceroy, at least his protégés and intimates were involved in the shortages and speculation.

This situation lasted into 1692; the government seemed powerless to remedy it. On April 7 a solemn Easter mass was held in the cathedral. A

Franciscan, Antonio de Escaray, delivered a sermon described as "inflammatory and indiscreet." In the congregation were the Viceroy and members of the Audiencia and the court: the entire government. An eyewitness describes Escaray's sermon in these terms: "He spoke so imprudently of the scarcity of provisions that his words had the effect of stirring up the people, and if before they had spoken of this matter with reserve, thereafter they began to do so openly, declaring the efforts the Viceroy was making to solicit provisions for the city to be for his own use and benefit, and they applauded the speaker mightily."[2] This sermon and the favorable reception accorded it demonstrate that, contrary to what was later reported, discontent was widespread and embraced all social classes. Those most affected by the shortages were the poor, but the most vocal complainers were groups of criollos and clergymen like Escaray, the same social classes that a century later would fight for independence. During April and May the authorities attempted to store maize and wheat in the public granary of the city. Demand was overwhelming because the people, alarmed, rushed to buy all the available grain. To their disappointment there was very little to buy.[3]

On June 6 there was a panic: a rumor spread that supplies had run out; people rushed to the granary, crowding the doors. The guards were unable to keep order, and one of them clubbed a pregnant Indian woman, who miscarried on the spot. She was gathered up by indignant Indian women, placed on a litter, and carried in a procession to the palace of the Archbishop by fifty women and about twenty men. They wanted to complain to the Archbishop "that not only were they not given maize for their sustenance in return for their money, but the guards had beaten a poor woman and made her miscarry." Aguiar y Seijas' attendants did not allow them to enter. They then went to the viceregal palace; there guards barred the way, refusing them permission to see the Count de Galve. They returned to the Archbishop's quarters but were not allowed through the doors, "where"—says Sigüenza y Góngora—"no woman had entered since that venerable prelate had taken up residence." From the street talk in front of the Archbishop's palace, Sigüenza alleges maliciously, some students ascertained that the Indian woman had feigned the miscarriage. Now several hundred strong, the protesters returned to the Viceroy's palace, with no better luck than before. In the course of their comings and goings, night had fallen, and they dispersed. Saturday, June 7, passed peacefully, although everyone realized that the calm was merely a respite. Crowds continued to gather at the public granary, and the Viceroy ordered the soldiers to be ready for any emergency. (They were not.) Persisting in his distortion of the events, Sigüenza y Góngora says that the Indians spent Saturday night drinking pulque and plotting the assassination of the Viceroy, the burning of the palace, and the sacking of the city, a sign of the "culpable lack of protection for those of us living among such rabble."

The morning of Sunday, June 8, was also peaceful. The Count de Galve attended mass at Santo Domingo and had to put up with the insults of several women. Perhaps this incident made him fear for his safety, for that afternoon he paid a visit to the monastery of San Francisco and stayed there all day. The Vicereine, after visiting the Virgen de los Remedios in the cathedral, went to the gardens for a bit of relaxation and from there to San Francisco to join her husband. Unquestionably the couple had chosen the monastery as a refuge. At the granary, Friday's events were repeated, and word flew that the guards had beaten another Indian woman. She was exhibited, nearly lifeless, and borne in a new procession to the Plaza Mayor and the residences of the Viceroy and Archbishop. Once again the attendants of Aguiar y Seijas refused entry. The crowd waited until six in the evening, then marched to the palace of the Viceroy. More people began to gather. They shouted "insults and obscenities" at the Count de Galve and his wife. Someone threw a stone at one of the balconies; others followed. The Viceroy's majordomo alerted the guard corps, a few poorly armed soldiers. With the servants, they managed to form a small contingent of men armed with pikes. This detachment charged the rioters, who at first retreated but soon counterattacked, forcing the militia to take refuge in the palace. A few soldiers fired at the crowd from the flat roofs; to prevent casualties, they were ordered to load their muskets with powder only. The rioters grew bolder. Now they numbered ten thousand, from "every class of society." This passing remark by Sigüenza proves that it was not only Indians who protested. The plaza was full of stalls and vendors' stands made of wood or reeds; the crowd tore off boards and reeds, ignited them, and used them to set fire to the doors of the palace. The fire quickly spread throughout the building. The municipal building, which stood opposite, met a similar fate.

Some clerics tried to intervene. They soon desisted, however, threatened with becoming the victims of the infuriated mob, which had begun to pillage the stalls in the plaza. Then a peculiar thing happened: a priest surrounded by altar boys and other priests emerged from the cathedral, bearing on high the Holy Sacrament. The rioters knelt as the holy symbol passed by: the tabernacle was illuminated by flames from the blazing buildings. The procession circled the plaza twice and returned to the cathedral. A priest came to the doorway and preached to the crowd in Nahuatl. They listened respectfully. They did not attack Sigüenza y Góngora, who, with a group of students, rushed into the municipal building to save the archives—a courageous action, and one that allows us to overlook to some degree his slandering of the rioters. Sigüenza succeeded in rescuing many of the papers. At nine o'clock the crowd began to disperse. Another indication that this was a spontaneous riot and not a planned uprising is that there were no visible leaders, and the rioters made no attempt later to regroup and organize a second assault.

Sunday night the Viceroy, along with his counselors and several priests, outlined the most suitable measures for dealing with the situation. In fact, like a summer storm, the riot had, all by itself, concentrated and at the same time dissipated the people's anger. As there were no leaders to spearhead or organize feelings of discontent, no ideas to change those feelings into programs of reform, popular sentiment, having been purged, returned to its habitual apathy. If the riot proved anything, besides the vulnerability of the institution of the viceregency, it was the solidity and vitality of the Church and the power that religious belief held over individual consciences. On Monday morning the Viceroy was able to gather his troops, along with a considerable number of citizens, all well armed. At their head, on horseback, the Viceroy traveled the few streets separating the convent of San Francisco from the palace and the cathedral. The Vicereine followed in a carriage. Before the church of La Profesa, Archbishop Aguiar y Seijas awaited, also in a coach. The two highest authorities of the land entered the deserted plaza together and circled it twice, followed by troops and spectators. The dead bodies had been cleared away. Robles reports in his *Record of Notable Events* that there were many. The palace was still burning; a sign tacked to a wall said, "For rent: this chicken yard for local cocks and Spanish hens." The pasquinade was clearly the work of criollos. Other lampoons appeared during the days that followed, almost all of them bearing defamatory captions aimed at the Count de Galve. These posters, like the secret letters sent to the King of Spain complaining of the blunders of the Viceroy and his government, reveal the extent of the differences between criollos and the Spanish bureaucracy. The malcontents signed all the broadsides with the phrase "His Majesty's most loyal vassals," prefiguring the attitude of Hidalgo and the first insurgents in the struggle for independence: loyalty to the King but not to his viceroys or Spanish emissaries.

The Count de Galve began to conduct business from the house of the Marquis del Valle's family, descendants of Cortés, near the palace and adjacent to the cathedral. Officials were dismissed and the military contingents in the capital increased (an unnecessary measure according to "His Majesty's most loyal vassals"; if justice were done, all that would be needed for the safety of the city was "a company of one hundred soldiers, even if headed by a lady in a toque—but not the Countess de Galve"). The sale of pulque was prohibited and instructions were given that no Indian could enter the city. One ominous sign: the rioters had burned the gallows in the Plaza Mayor and the Viceroy ordered it rebuilt. On June 10 the arrests began and on June 11 the executions: four Indians were condemned to death. Only three were executed; the fourth committed suicide. Their hands were cut off and exhibited in the plaza. The punishments continued through the following days. According to Rubio Mañé, a total of ten Indians, one mestizo, and one Spaniard were executed. We have to agree that the Count de Galve was relatively moderate. On the other hand, he had revealed himself to be indecisive and less than courageous. He defended himself against this charge by saying that if he had abandoned his refuge in the monastery to confront the rioters, he might have lost his life and thus caused irreparable harm to the country. Besides, although "the citizens of means and their families and domestic servants wanted only leaders [to oppose the rioters] with the authority to mete out justice . . . , I found myself without resolute ministers to come to my aid . . . since the first ministers of the Audiencia, civil and criminal, have little spirit for such undertakings . . . because of their personal weakness and faintheartedness."[4] The Viceroy's complaints revealed that there had been, and still was, friction between him and the Audiencia; the two highest organs of political power in New Spain were at odds, and each paralyzed the other. Their quarrel produced a vacuum of power, into which, inexorably, moved the Church, and the visible head of that Church, Aguiar y Seijas.

The Viceroy explains that "the people's animosity" toward him was due to the "error of believing that I had held back grain for my own profit," and that "their rage, the assault on the palace, and the death threats against myself and all my family . . . resulted from the drunkenness of a large part of the crowd." Sigüenza y Góngora made the same charge: the cause of the tumult "was the general drunkenness of the common people," although he also admits that in part the blame fell on "the excesses of the militia and their carelessness in dealing with the drunken Indians." A cleric, writing to a friend in Puebla, offers a different view:

> Many Indians were asked whether this tumult was motivated by the shortage of maize and they said that it was not, that they had quantities hidden in their houses. And being asked why they had hidden it, they responded, "You see, señor, as we wanted to rise up against the realm . . . and as the harvest of maize had been lost . . . the chiefs ordered us to buy much more than we needed . . . so there would not be enough for the poor and they would take our part when we rebelled."[5]

A fantasy; it makes the hapless Indians guilty for the abuse committed by wealthy criollos and Spaniards: hoarding wheat and maize. Further, it converts a spontaneous uprising into a conspiracy plotted by mysterious Indian chiefs. But it is true that both racial and social resentments were responsible for the riot: differences in New Spain were determined by origins and wealth. "His Majesty's most loyal vassals" offered reasons of greater substance: "the tyranny of the Viceroy, judges, and other persons . . . selling justice," banishment to Texas without cause and without prior trial, "for which reason hearts were filled with ill will, as were the spirits of the Indians who had been made to labor on the roads, aqueducts, and ditches from sunrise till sunset for half a *real*."

All the motives alleged by the participants are worthy of consideration, from natural catastrophes to racial strife. Some were incidental, however, such as drunkenness (if in fact that was not slander), while others were decisive, such as bad government, exploitation, and corruption. The uprising of 1692—the most serious of all those that occurred in Mexico City during the era of the viceroyalty—was the expression of a deep historical crisis that involved the social structure and institutions as well as the cultural establishment; in the final chapter I shall try to decipher the meaning of that crisis. As for its repercussions, there were also disturbances in Tlaxcala, Guadalajara, and elsewhere: all were harshly repressed. In Puebla, Bishop Fernández de Santa Cruz averted an insurrection by buying grain from growers at a high price and selling it to the people for less than he paid. The immediate consequence of all this was that the authority of the Viceroy was so diminished that in normal times he would have been dismissed. But the Count de Galve had relatives and influential friends at court, and the war with France was absorbing the full attention of the government in Madrid. The Audiencia was also weakened. The only institution that not only preserved but actually increased its influence was the Church.

Several events reveal the strengthening of the institution of the Church. In order to ease the situation in Mexico City—the shortages lasted until 1693—the Viceroy attempted to commandeer the grain the Bishop of Puebla had deposited in warehouses. The Bishop defied the command, saying that before the Count de Galve's messengers achieved their aim they would see "his holy vestments stained with his own blood."[6] The Viceroy yielded and answered with a conciliatory letter. The true winner was the Archbishop of Mexico, Aguiar y Seijas, the highest ecclesiastical authority in the land and the only leader, following the discredit of the Viceroy and his administration, respected by the people. The Count de Galve issued an ineffective proclamation condemning hoarders who were stockpiling maize and wheat. Then Aguiar y Seijas issued an edict against speculators and ordered anathemas to be read against them in the cathedral and in all the temples. In this way the Church became the bulwark of the other institutions. The efficacy of its spiritual measures should not be underestimated; in a society that viewed epidemics and droughts as punishments from God, anathemas, excommunications, prayers, and processions were proven remedies.

Thus a totally unforeseen series of public events radically and irrevocably changed the private life of Juana Inés, demolishing the edifice she had skillfully and patiently constructed over a period of twenty years. Her design had been to create for herself a small space that, without dereliction of her religious duties, would offer her freedom to dedicate herself to letters and defend herself against the envy of the other nuns and the jealousy of intolerant prelates. One after another her defenses fell. The imprudence of writing the critique of Vieyra's sermon, and the even greater imprudence of answering the Bishop of Puebla with a defense of her vocation as a writer, had been grave but not irreparable errors. She had lost the support of Fernández de Santa Cruz and Núñez de Miranda, but not that of the palace or, especially, Spain. History, however, whether public or private, cannot be reduced to cause and effect: chance and the unforeseen alter all calculations and change the destinies of peoples and individuals. The riot, an unexpected happening, strengthened Aguiar y Seijas. In his new circumstances, the Viceroy did not dare support Sor Juana against the imperious prelate. Thus Sor Juana was suddenly without friends or protectors in New Spain.

The cruelest, most crushing—and equally unexpected—blow came from Spain: on April 22, Tomás de la Cerda, Marquis de la Laguna, majordomo to the Queen, died suddenly. His widow, the Countess de Paredes, in mourning and faced with the problems of her new situation, must not have had time or opportunity to concern herself with the tribulations of her friend in distant Mexico. Neither could Sor Juana count on her other protector, the Marquis de Mancera: he was more Núñez de Miranda's friend than hers. Father Antonio had been his confessor in Mexico, and from Spain the Marquis wrote him letters of fervent admiration signed "Son and friend of your paternal care . . ." Most serious of all was the wave of religious superstition sweeping across New Spain: the rains, the plague, the hunger and riots, were deserved punishment for crimes and sins committed by all. It is entirely possible that Sor Juana, a true believer, shared these sentiments and saw in her past life—lukewarm in matters of religion—one of the causes of the calamities raining down on New Spain. Her case suggests once again that inevitably we are our enemies' accomplices.

Loneliness is a test but also a trap for the afflicted: we have no choice but to leap over it or give up. Sor Juana's isolation was more and more menacing: outside, she was encircled by prelates whose power was as great as their severity; within the convent, by fanatic nuns of weak and limited talents. Her saintly confessor had abandoned her to an uneasy conscience that questioned itself incessantly and turned upon itself. She had lost her patrons and was in the hands of her critics; someday, if she persisted in her ways, she would have to confront them, no longer as critics but as accusers and judges. The idea terrified her. Then it became her ally, and she saw in her present suffering the natural result of her past life: she had used religion as a screen in order to devote herself to worldly, frequently sinful, passions and desires. What had poetry been to her? A ghost that insatiably fed her sensual dreams and her intellectual fantasies, a chimera carved from her vanity and lust, her love of the world and of herself. Lost in endless brooding over their imaginary guilt, temperaments such as hers end by condemning themselves. Where to turn for aid and support? Whom to go to? At bottom, the self-accusations of melancholics are merely a ruse to seek what they most desire: a lover, a father, a protector. The stage was set for the return of her confessor, Núñez de Miranda.

She had met him when she was sixteen and living alone in the viceregal palace as lady-in-waiting to the Marquise de Mancera. For many years he had been her guide and counselor, also her critic and her judge.

At first he was gentle and comforted her; later, severe, he became her tormentor. Probably she venerated him, but more than anything she feared him. According to Oviedo, she called him her "true father"; nevertheless, the only father, the only masculine direction, Sor Juana had known was her grandfather's tenderness. She knew that with Núñez de Miranda neither intellectual conversation nor gentle spiritual release awaited, only unyielding soul-searching, harsh meditation, hair shirts for the body and humiliations for the mind. Why did she ask him to return? She had no choice: Núñez de Miranda was the bridge between her, a misguided nun, and the Church. No one but he could defend her from Aguiar y Seijas and neutralize his malign influence. The Jesuit confessor, as the image of authority, was the key to the security she yearned for. In her decision, as in almost all human actions, there was calculation—the desire to end her loneliness, and repentance for errors magnified by misgivings. First and foremost, there was fear. In her last years she was never free of it. Núñez de Miranda was the embodiment of everything she desired and feared: if he instilled fear in her, she also hoped to find in him sympathy and, perhaps, protection. It seems likely that her other confessor (Arellano?) and the Mother Superior of San Jerónimo may have urged her to take this fateful step.

Reconciliation with the austere priest meant reconciliation with the world around her, perhaps even with herself. This last was the crux of the matter. She had lost her self-assurance, and it would have been difficult to recognize in her the author of the *Response to Sor Filotea de la Cruz* and the *villancicos* to St. Catherine. She had suffered the worst of personal ills: loss of faith in herself. That is why she placed her faith in her former confessor. All her contemporaries speak of the great change she went through in her last years, and the suddenness of that change. In spite of our distance from the events, and the lack of documentation, we can detect the reasons for that change in the combination of external circumstances I have described in this and the preceding chapters. When she lost her protectors she had no choice but to find a new source of support. Her only salvation, however, was the very thing she had fought against for the last two years: submission. The destruction of the fragile space of calm and independence she had managed to create and preserve through so many years of patient effort meant the destruction of her life plan. That plan, as we have seen in the pages of the *Response* and other texts, postulated the coexistence of her religious life and her literary vocation. The plan, and the space that housed it, had collapsed. During her fatherless childhood and adolescence she had lived in the ambiguous position of the outsider who sleeps in a house that is not hers and eats bread that belongs to others. The convent had given her, if not a home, a place of her own; her cell quickly became a worldly and intellectual center. Suddenly the lights go out, the illustrious visitors disappear, and once again, as in the early years, she is abandoned. Everything turns to smoke. Nothing could be more natural than to look to her first guide and protector, even though she knew that to turn to him was to give in. She was beaten.

The change was precipitated by three circumstances. The first, external in nature, was the riot; in a few days the balance of power was radically altered, the Viceroy weakened, and the influence of Aguiar y Seijas expanded. Thus, when the second volume of her *Works* arrived in New Spain with the laudatory opinions of the seven Spanish theologians, the effect must have been just the opposite of what was desired: the book was seen not as a refutation but as a challenge. The second circumstance was the wave of religious superstition that swept over New Spain following the natural and political disasters that were seen as punishment from God. Third, although by temperament Sor Juana was reasonable, even a rationalist, it is difficult to imagine that she would not have attributed to her past attitudes a part, however minimal, of the calamities suffered by New Spain. Guilt always finds an outlet, especially during times of upheaval and catastrophe. In Sor Juana, as is seen in many of her poems, this feeling was powerful and sank its roots in both her intellectual and her emotional life. The poems of loving friendship for María Luisa, the disquieting presence of the erotic ghost in others, and her sacred poems, with their insistence on the theme of unrequited love, reveal the pervasiveness of her guilt feelings. In isolation, none of the three circumstances would have sufficed to cause the change; the combination of the three was irresistible. Some have insisted that Sor Juana was neurotic in the extreme. I cannot agree. Naturally, she was not what we would call a "normal" person. Who is? But neither was she unstable, plagued and tormented by immoderate anguish, manias, and aberrations. Considering the adversities of her childhood and the obstacles she had to overcome in her adulthood, I perceive not psychic instability but self-confidence, ability, and good sense. I do not see a neurotic; I see a woman lucid and whole.

Closely related to her feelings of guilt—indistinguishable from them—was the awareness, heightened during those days, of her inner conflict. Throughout her life, as we can glimpse in her poems, she went through periods of inexplicable sadness and ill-defined anxieties. Something gnawed at her thoughts and consumed her hours, an invisible visitor that appeared at night to prevent her from sleeping or thinking. These attacks of melancholy were channeled into poems. This is the difference, still unexplained, between the creative artist and the simple neurotic. But during the last period of her life, when the very writing of poetry became a sinful activity, the feeling of disgust was transformed into self-hatred. Her soul-searching worked against her. Always, in her innermost self, there was an empty space that neither the image of God nor the ideas that helped her pass her sleepless nights could fill; perhaps the ghost that appears in some of her amorous poems had occupied it but, inevitably, had disappeared. Sor Juana had always mourned for someone who never existed. One of the recurrent themes of her best poems is her quest of that chimera, always resolved into solitude and hatred of her own image. Those poems reveal that, if it is true that she loved herself, it is also true that frequently that love turned to disgust. Furthermore, in the effort to speak with ghosts and to clasp phantoms in her arms, she herself became a ghost. Then she looked on her image with horror. More than once she wrote in the margins of her books, "I, the least worthy of all." It is true that this phrase was often used by both monks and nuns, but her fondness for it is revealing. To understand it, we must contrast that formula with her portraits; she moved continually between those two extremes. The events of 1692, in leaving her on her own, confronted her with her own image.

According to Oviedo, Sor Juana's decision was made two years before her death, that is, at the beginning of 1693:

> Moved by Heaven, and ashamed of not having responded as she should have to the divine mercies she had received, she sent for her former father confessor . . . He refused repeatedly, either because he did not grasp the purpose for which she called him, or because he feared some fickleness in so sudden a change, or, which is most probable, to fan the fire of her wishes by his delay. Finally, with the counsel and approval of his superior, he did go.

Oviedo's account confirms what we already know: the change was sudden. In a few months' time Sor Juana passed from defiance to acceptance of the criticisms made by Fernández de Santa Cruz and Núñez de Miranda. Father Oviedo—and with him the majority of Catholic critics—

attribute the change to divine intercession. More likely it was due to the unwonted solitude in which she was living and to the anxiety caused by increasingly overt hostility on the part of her ill-wishers. The cautious reaction of Núñez de Miranda—the agent God had chosen to convert her—helps us place the conflict in its true setting; this was a public matter, not merely a case of personal conscience. This is why intervention by the prominent Jesuit immediately assumed the form of psychological and moral intimidation. The verb appropriate to this situation is not so much "convert" as "subject." Sor Juana's dominant emotion was fear; Núñez de Miranda acted with calculation. He proceeded like a politician: at first he refused to go to her—to "fan the fire of her wishes," Oviedo comments—and he did not yield until after many pleas, and then only after consulting with his superior.

All this corroborates that Sor Juana's attitude and the debates that followed the publication of her critique of Vieyra's sermon had created a scandal in certain circles and had been the object of commentaries and deliberations among Church authorities. Núñez de Miranda's reluctance, whether real or feigned, and the intervention of the Superior of the Society of Jesus in his final decision, reveal that the matter had public dimensions. There is nothing more private and personal than the choice of a confessor and spiritual director, but in Sor Juana's case the choice immediately extended beyond the sphere of her personal life: to call Núñez de Miranda was equivalent to a tacit retraction. So it was understood by her contemporaries, not excluding Núñez de Miranda and Sor Juana herself. She knew that the step she was about to take was irreversible, and the thought simultaneously terrified and fascinated her. Her predicament was similar to her dilemma in the months preceding her taking the vows. A fateful symmetry: the point at which all her soul-searching converged was the same as in 1669—Núñez de Miranda. Master of the keys to her existence, he had opened the doors of the convent to her to enable her to escape an inhospitable world, and now he was preparing to close the doors to her essential vocation, letters, irrevocably.

29

The Abjuration

$\mathcal{F}$ATHER ANTONIO NÚÑEZ DE MIRANDA was a criollo, like Sor Juana. Her elder by thirty years, he was born in 1618 in Fresnillo, near Zacatecas, of a family of military men and clerics; his father was a captain. Throughout his life he had a passion for discipline, fostered by the military tradition as well as the rules of the Society of Jesus. At the age of fourteen he took his preliminary vows and was sent to Mexico City. He studied in the Colegio de San Pedro y San Pablo, a school run by the Jesuits, and after a brilliant record there he entered the Society. He had no further involvement with his family; his life was totally absorbed in that of his community. He completed his studies in the famous school of Tepotzotlán and became a professor of Latin and later of philosophy and theology, in Valladolid (Morelia), then Puebla, Guatemala, and Mexico City. He became rector of the Colegio de San Pedro y San Pablo and for two years was Provincial of the Society of Jesus. But the posts he held longest—thirty years each—were those of censor for the Holy Office and prefect of the Congregación de la Purísima Concepción de la Virgen María (Brotherhood of Mary). Both positions entailed heavy obligations but, at the same time, great authority and influence.

By their nature these were public posts, and Father Núñez de Miranda was above all a public figure, respected and feared. As censor for the Inquisition, he was the guardian of doctrine; as prefect of the Brotherhood of Mary, he ministered principally to the aristocracy or, more precisely, the ruling class. The activities of the Church in seventeenth-century Hispanic society, though guided always by the same principles and goals, were distributed among various orders and adapted to the needs of different social groups. Furthermore, although the Church was intimately linked with the throne, its function was not strictly governmental, and this allowed for a certain diversity of opinion, as shown by the sermon the Franciscan Escaray delivered in the presence of the Viceroy. In many cases criticism of governmental abuses came from the Church, or, more accurately, from certain orders and from individuals within those orders. The Brotherhood of Mary directed by Father Núñez de Miranda, however, had exactly the opposite mission: not criticism but defense and justification of the institutions and their representatives.

The Brotherhood of Mary embraced the most influential personages of New Spain. It was directed by nine Jesuit priests, one for each of the nine months Mary had carried Jesus in her womb. The supreme authority was the prefect. The members met every Tuesday. They began with prayers, followed by a session of self-examination, at the end of which the prefect imparted a lesson. His talk lasted a little more than an hour and was followed by questions from the listeners based on the subjects he had addressed. Among those attending were judges, inquisitors, prebendaries, and gentlemen of the highest rank. It was frequently the custom of the viceroys to participate in these gatherings; the Marquis de Mancera was assiduous in attendance, as was the Count de Galve. Father Núñez de Miranda's weekly talks were directed toward the spiritual edification of his listeners; the subjects included good behavior, charity, the power of prayer, and the need for daily soul-searching. He reproached members for attending plays and other spectacles. Almost all those who participated confessed, in the privacy of Father Antonio's quarters, their moral conflicts and sought his counsel. As the talks often touched on death and the need to prepare oneself for it, many consulted him on this subject and on the best way to set their affairs in order and to dispose of their worldly goods before dying. Clearly, therefore, his talks dealt with both this life and the next. It is true, as Oviedo never fails to emphasize, that he warned all those who sought his counsel not to come to him with temporal problems. Yet when we consider that the members of the Brotherhood were from the highest levels of government and public life, his influence over his hearers and, through them, over the entire society must have been extraordinary.

The activities of the Brotherhood were varied and many. In each neighborhood it supported a kind of agency charged with aiding the poor, an activity that extended into hospitals and prisons. Father Antonio paid weekly visits to hospitals, where he fed the sick; he also helped penniless prisoners and the "innocent," that is, the mad. As a friend of the rich and powerful, he obtained money to construct churches and chapels. His energy in construction was remarkable, and the same can be said of his untiring zeal on behalf of the nuns. With funds from Juan de Chavarría he built the nunnery of San Lorenzo. The same philanthropist provided the money that allowed many impoverished maidens to enter the convent. In all these pious transactions, Núñez de Miranda conducted himself with uncommon political and business acumen. He could squeeze blood from a turnip, and today would have been the director of one of the cultural foundations that subsist on donations from millionaires. Oviedo reports one of his maxims on the best way to approach a donor: "Confine myself entirely to the character and prudent benevolence of the patron, without mentioning or proposing any arrangement, but following his own at his pace." The guile of a Machiavelli in the service of Christ.

Father Antonio visited all the nunneries of the city, preached in them, and heard the nuns' confession. Sor Juana was not his only confessional daughter. If Fernández de Santa Cruz wrote "spiritual letters" to the nuns of Puebla, Núñez de Miranda was the author of a primer of religious doctrine "in which, by means of a dialogue of questions and answers, he smoothed out all the stumbling blocks and difficulties that might present themselves to the nuns." Remarkable the affection these clerics had for the nuns. In this matter, Aguiar y Seijas was the most circumspect: he chose not to expose himself to temptation. But Núñez de Miranda's solicitude for the "brides of Christ" was rigorous, not indulgent. He continually exhorted them to honor their four vows: poverty, chastity, obedience, and enclosure. It was said that, among his triumphs, he once moved a nun so greatly that she disposed of her jewels, an act that foreshadows the sale of Sor Juana's library and collections. The strictness and zeal of Father Antonio contrasts with information we have from other sources on conduct in the nunneries. According to accounts by Gemelli Carreri and other travelers, as well as glimpses afforded by the laconic accounts in Robles' *Record,* in most convents the rules were liberally, even laxly, observed. I am inclined to believe these testimonies; they show no proselytizing bias. The laxity of convent life was proverbial, as is illustrated by the very attempts of Aguiar y Seijas and Fernández de Santa Cruz to correct it.

The activities to which Núñez de Miranda devoted his time and ener-

V.P. Anttonio Nvñes de Miranda dela Compañia de Jhs. Prefecto de la mui illustre Congregacion dela Purissima por espacio de 32 años. Varon insigne en sabiduria, observancia religiosa, i zelode la saluacion de las almas. Murio en Mexico de edad de 77 años a 17 de Febrero de 1695. Bernardin. Aleman. Sculp. Mexico Año 1705.

Antonio Núñez de Miranda, S.J.

gies were comparable to those of a public figure in our own day: meetings in the Holy Office; the weekly talks to the Brotherhood of Mary; private conversations with members who sought his counsel; frequent visits to the viceregal palace and other high places; work in the hospitals and prisons; sermons in the nunneries. Did he have a spiritual life? Oviedo refers repeatedly to daily self-examinations and the constant recitation of prayers. But formal self-examination pertains really to moral hygiene and has an eminently practical significance; it is not meditation on the mysteries and spiritual verities but a rigorous moral accounting. Self-examination is an exercise for keeping the soul agile, ready for the battles of everyday life. The good priest is an athlete for God. Prayer, in turn, is ritual, not an expression of one's innermost being. It is inseparable from religious life, but linked especially to that group of practices that joins the individual on the one hand to the community and, on the other, to the supernatural.

Father Antonio excelled in the energy, skill, and zeal with which he performed the public activities that devolved upon him. He also distinguished himself—although secretly, Oviedo says—in virtues such as humility, chastity, and obedience. He was clothed and shod like a pauper; he mended his own garments; every Saturday he swept the church and on Tuesday he scrubbed the kitchen plates. Humility is often the mask for pride. Núñez de Miranda knew that: "Make me, O Lord, humble of heart, of heart. Not this pretentious humility of mine." Was he sincere? Yes and no. He wanted to be humble but, surreptitiously, pride interfered with his desire. Pride is a sin that lies in wait for ascetics. The only remedy is simplicity of heart. Father Antonio was not simple.

Oviedo, Torres, and Lezamis allude frequently to the demonic influence of bodily passions; but they never describe the temptations their subjects had to overcome. More fortunate than St. Augustine, St. Francis, and other saints, they apparently did not have to combat desires of the flesh, pride, or the ambition for power. Aguiar y Seijas was the only one of the three besieged by the demons of lust. Oviedo recounts that Father Antonio was very cautious in his dealings with women; when he spoke with them he lowered his eyes, and he never visited them or received their visits. Like Aguiar y Seijas, he congratulated himself on being nearsighted, thus prevented from seeing women. He was also scrupulous in observing the vow of obedience, and in one of his notes wrote: "The subject is the instrument of his superior, and the instrument has no value other than its submissiveness . . . The subject must live for the wishes and needs of the superior." So rigorous a concept of discipline worked in both directions: his harshness with Sor Juana was merely the obverse of his harshness with himself.

"Prayer and mortification," says Oviedo, "are the wings on which the spirit soars toward the peak of perfection and union with God." Núñez de Miranda mortified himself unceasingly; he scourged himself "seventy-three times, in reverence for the seventy-three years of the Blessed Virgin's life . . . and the blows were so cruel and delivered so pitilessly that they could be heard outside the chamber, inspiring sorrow and compassion in all who listened. Those waiting outside the door feared they might find him dead." [1] He scourged himself three times a week and on official feast days. The doors and walls of his room were spattered with blood. He wore a hair shirt three or four times a week and when preaching. He had a "more painful hair shirt," however: "the one caused by the vermin that bred on him and which the mortified father suffered with patience and joy."

Núñez de Miranda had always suffered from poor vision, and in the last year of his life he was almost completely blind; even so, although his superiors insisted he stop, he continued his activities. If in writing of mortifications and penances Oviedo varies little from Torres and Lezamis—each of the three adapting to the prototype of innumerable lives of saints and pious men—in his chapter on miracles and prodigies Oviedo is more restrained than the other two biographers: he offers no multiplying of loaves, no fragrance from a deathbed swarming with bedbugs, no battle on the high seas between devils and the eleven thousand virgins. On the other hand, he does report that Father Antonio was capable of mental telepathy, and the departed faithful visited him more than once. On one occasion the soul of the recently deceased philanthropist Captain Chavarría visited him and confided that he had spent only a week in purgatory.

Núñez de Miranda repressed his passions as severely as he castigated his body. He was by nature excitable, pugnacious, and choleric, but constantly attempted moderation. At times the effort was so great that "he turned as white as paper and his body seemed to come unjointed in his heroic efforts to contain himself." Once he confessed that he was afraid he would die during one of these attacks. Impatience usually accompanies a strong sense of self. Father Antonio, in spite of his exercises in humility, does not seem ever to have questioned the truth and justice of his opinions. He not only was sure of what he believed, his words and deeds reveal that invariably he *knew* he was right. Like all those who do not know doubt, he did not hesitate to condemn to hell those who opposed his opinions:

> An honorable Viceroy [Oviedo conceals the name] consulted with him in a quite difficult case; the good father replied to him what according to God it seemed he should do and, recognizing in the Prince some repugnance in carrying it out, . . . said to him with all resolve, "Your Excellency may do what he pleases but I am sure that this is what must be done and if you do not do it you will go to Hell unquestionably and without passing through purgatory." The Viceroy revised his opinion, following to the last detail everything Father Antonio had counseled him, saying that his fear of him was great.

If a Viceroy feared him, how must Sor Juana have felt?

Oviedo says that in his dealings with the world, Núñez de Miranda "was in continual battle with himself, struggling for self-control." But those victories reaffirmed his assurance; they did not humble his natural arrogance but put it to strategic use. Pride became a tactic, and thus his human relationships were converted into a political game. In his notes he says, "I need to amend the haste, moderate the vehemence, and temper the harshness of my words." Calculation, not virtue, inspired this maxim: it was designed not for self-improvement but for more ready triumph. His humility was a sham. The same duplicity appears in his relation with his family. He refused his brother—because it was his brother, not because the request was unreasonable—a sum of money he needed. The day his mother died, she had scarcely given up the ghost when he left her to deliver a sermon; as he was slightly late in arriving, he explained that he had been delayed in assisting a dying woman; he did not say who she was. Admirable or abominable? When Núñez de Miranda died at seventy-seven years of age, one of his panegyrists wrote that his "exemplary life allowed us to see revived in our own time the examples of the prelates of the early Church." The praise is only partially deserved; it is one thing to be an apostle of a persecuted Church, quite another to represent a Church triumphant.

There were two seemingly contradictory but in fact complementary sides to Father Antonio: the man of action and the ascetic. He was not a contemplative, and that is why I question whether he had a spiritual life. All his being was directed outward, toward the duties and struggles of this world. As both prefect of the powerful Brotherhood of Mary and censor for the Inquisition and as the spiritual guide of nuns, he was a man devoted to the affairs and battles of everyday life. Devout and self-less but also astute and shrewd, he was, in the strictest sense of the term, a militant politician in the service of the Church, of its princes and its interests. Politics is power, and power is impure. His ascetic mortifications did not open to him the doors of ecstatic vision, beatitude, or mystical union. His asceticism served an exacting morality, a kind of spiritual athleticism; it was not a path to supernatural realities but a test for tempering his spirit. These mortifications strengthened his soul but did not purify it, nor did they endow it with the sixth sense that is said to be the sign of true spirituality. According to what his biographer tells us, and his own notes, he had no visions of Heaven or, which is equally strange, of Hell. The appearance of Chavarría's ghost was trivial, as was the ghost's message. Bloody penances and sugar-coated visions: this contrast is a further sign of the decline of official Hispanic Catholicism.

Although he was a professor of philosophy and theology, Núñez de Miranda was not a true intellectual; he did not love ideas or show any passion for knowledge. Everything he said and everything he wrote pertains to practical questions: what to do and how to proceed in this or that case. Everyday behavior, not great philosophical and theological themes, was his daily preoccupation. Was he a moralist? Only in a very limited sense. Interested in righteousness, his own and others', he had a certain knowledge of the human soul and its hidden turnings; but, once again, that knowledge was pragmatic. He was not interested in knowing what the soul entrusted to him was truly like: he wanted to know the most efficient means of winning it. He was never attracted by human complexity and ambiguity, and in this sense, the most basic, he did not truly love. His knowledge of souls was a combination of recipes, formulas, and techniques for moving and manipulating them. I have said it before: he was a fisher of souls. But can one save someone without knowing and loving him? The quality that distinguished Núñez de Miranda, even as a spiritual guide, was not comprehension but will, the obligation to win new converts. A curious perversion that makes preaching a battle and a dialogue between two souls a stratagem.

Nor was Núñez de Miranda a defender of the principles of his religion, although it appears he was a good theologian; total unanimity in religious matters was the rule in New Spain, and there was no one with whom to argue and nothing to defend. Theological controversy, as we have seen, was restricted to inoffensive and subtle arguments on themes such as the *finezas* of Christ. A controversy such as the one that divided Jansenists from Jesuits was unthinkable in end-of-the-seventeenth-century New Spain. As he lived in a society in which there was officially no religion but Catholicism, neither was Núñez de Miranda's work that of a missionary who converts idolaters. What a difference between him and Vieyra! Not a man of ideas and doctrines, nor a preacher in pagan lands, nor a defender of Indians and blacks, Núñez de Miranda was a righteous judge of customs and beliefs. His task as a censor for the Holy Office was to detect and denounce heresy and heretics; as prefect of the Brotherhood of Mary, to guide the elite that governed the country and watch over the rectitude of their opinions and behavior. In both functions, he was one of the pillars of constituted power. It is impossible to imagine him preaching a sermon criticizing inept government, as the Franciscan Escaray had done on June 6, 1692, in the presence of the Viceroy and judges. His every action was inspired by unconditional adherence to the status quo. Núñez de Miranda was a conformist and could only have been scandalized by Sor Juana's attitudes, her poems, her intellectual curiosity, and her belligerent feminism.

Upright but underhanded, capable of striking a deal and of temporarily accepting compromise and delay, inflexible yet devious, intransigent in regard to principles but tolerant in regard to means, Father Antonio was a sectarian and a militant. The picture Pascal draws of Jesuit casuistry applies to him: blindness to the complexity of souls but a strategic relativism in the means used to win them. In relation to Sor Juana, he at first understated the incompatibility between convent life and intellectual life; later he overstated it, to the point of demanding that she renounce letters altogether. Like the militant revolutionaries of the twentieth century who seek to win converts by any means, Father Antonio saw in every human being a convert or a reprobate. Ideological militance of whatever kind inherently disdains liberty and free will. Its vision of the *otherness* of each human being, of his unlike likeness to us, is simplistic. When the *other* is a unique being, irreducible to any category, the possibilities of winning or netting him vanish; the most we can do is enlighten him, awaken him; he, then, not we, will decide. But the *other* of the militant is a cipher, an abstraction, always reducible to an *us* or a *they*. Thus the proselytizer's concept of his fellow man is totally lacking in imagination. Imagination is the faculty of discovering the uniqueness of our fellow man. The great limitation—the sin, I was going to write—of minds like Núñez de Miranda's is precisely their lack of imagination. It is also their great strength.

Calleja says that "in the year 1693 the divine grace of God found in the heart of Sister Juana its dwelling place and abode." Oviedo gives the same date; two years before her death, Father Antonio again became her spiritual director. Thus she must have passed the second half of 1692 amid doubts and fears, watching as one after another her defenses crumbled, realizing that she was more and more alone and at the mercy of her critics and persecutors. The second volume of her *Works*, with the defenses and the tributes from the Spanish theologians and poets, probably arrived in Mexico at the end of 1692. She must have written at that time her poem (51) "in gratitude to the inimitable pens of Europe, who made her works greater with their praise: which was found unfinished." Castorena y Ursúa included it in *Fame* (1700) and says that it was found "after her death, in draft form and without her finishing touches." Apparently, her renunciation had not been so final as to cause her to destroy that last poem. The poem does not reveal the least wish to abandon literature or to change her way of life; on the contrary, it continues the themes of the *Response:* her only merit had been her studying, though a woman and without teachers. A person who writes so effusively and so enthusiastically about her work is not on the verge of abandoning it. Nevertheless, shortly afterward she sent messengers to Núñez de Miranda, asking him to return and stating that she was prepared to change her life and confess her errors—an additional indication that during the second half of 1692 she was subject to a great deal of censure, criticism, and pressure. We cannot doubt that she felt threatened, or that her fear unleashed the reactions I alluded to above. She feared others, and as fear undermined her personal defenses, breaches were opened through which old phantoms escaped. In those moments of anguish and insecurity, many of her friends must have counseled her, and even urged her, to seek reconciliation with the highest Church authorities.

From everything we know about Núñez de Miranda and his methods, he must have been kind and paternal in his first interviews with Sor Juana. Gradually, once he regained her confidence and secured his position, his demands increased and his stipulations became more severe. An uneven battle: Sor Juana, in exchange for concessions, was seeking protection and defense; Núñez de Miranda was proposing total surrender. There can be no doubt that Sor Juana's latest writings—the *Response,* the *villancicos* to St. Catherine, and the second volume of the *Works,* containing the defenses and encomiums of the seven Spanish theologians—had been seen as rebellion by members of the ruling ecclesiastical hierarchy of Mexico. Calleja and Oviedo relate that one of Sor Juana's first acts was a general confession that included all of her past life. Calleja adds, without irony, that fortunately "her most felicitous memory" aided her in this arduous undertaking. The confession probably lasted several weeks. This act was decisive, the hub on which everything that followed turned and the first step in the series of retractions and abjurations. To submit to an examination of her entire life, in spite of the fact that periodically, during her many years in the convent, she had confessed and been absolved, was to submit for judgment the matter that had been the center of her discussions and disagreements with Núñez de Miranda, Fernández de Santa Cruz, and other clerics: her dedication to secular letters to the neglect of the sacred.

In the course of the confession, the amatory poems, the moral ones, the witty ones, the plays, and in a word, her entire work must have been closely scrutinized. None of it could have found favor in the eyes of Núñez de Miranda, although perhaps he judged as minor peccadilloes the secular works, such as the plays, written for official festivities, and he could not have disapproved entirely of the *loas* honoring the monarch and the viceroys. All the rest, except the *autos* and *villancicos,* was condemned. Among her other major faults were her constant communication with the external world, by word and writing, the salon in the locutory, the portraits, and the other worldly distractions in which she had passed the best of her time. The worldly friendships had been serious offenses against her commitment as a nun devoted to God. The review of her friendship with María Luisa Manrique de Lara must have taken several days. Núñez de Miranda's views on the subject were very different from the modern ones; in the intensity of that friendship he did not see sexual or erotic deviation but a sin against the love a nun must have for God, infidelity to the Divine Husband. The use of Platonism as justification for that attachment must have seemed to him proof that all Sor Juana's failings had a common origin: her immoderate love of secular learning. The assessment of her faults led inevitably each time to the theme of her devotion to letters, which had led her to live her religion imperfectly and, in the end, to rebel. There was a close and causal connection between her dedication to letters, her worldly occupations and affections, the sin of pride, and—the most serious failing of all—rebelliousness. The general confession was Núñez de Miranda's first great triumph. It was also the decisive one; everything that followed was its natural consequence.

Calleja says that, following the general confession, Sor Juana presented to the "Divine Tribunal a petition that, in forensic form, begs forgiveness for her sins."[2] Such must have been the sequence of events, for this disturbing document is the direct effect of the abjuration of her past life with which she must have ended her confession. The "Tribunal" is God, and the prosecutor, her own conscience. Although she recognizes that her sins are "great and without equal" and that she deserves "to be condemned to eternal death" in "infinite hells," she implores forgiveness and mercy. All of these expressions, however excessive and terrible they may seem to us, were traditional. There is nothing personal in them; they are devout formulas. In the second part, although the language does not change, we find more personal confessions: as God knows "that for many years *I have lived in religion without religion, if not worse than a pagan might live* . . . it is my will to renew my vows and pass a year seeking your approval." Two themes are interwoven in this statement. The first is the admission that during her twenty-five years of convent life she has lived outside religion, that is, devoted to secular, even pagan, occupations and affairs. The second theme is that of her jubilee: Sor Juana had taken her vows in 1669, and in 1694 she was completing her twenty-fifth year as a nun; now, as a symbolic act, she was to take her vows a second time, under the patronage of St. Jerome and—for a year, as prescribed—subject to the approval of the heavenly court. Thus, allegorically, she reenacted her profession of faith of 1669. The culture of the seventeenth century was a symbolic culture, by which I mean that their symbols had a reality ours do not have. The sense of the petition is clear: I entreat that my previous life be considered as never having existed and I promise a new and truly religious life.

On February 17, 1694, Sor Juana signed another sad document (with her blood, Calleja says, but the text makes no mention of it): "Docta explicación del misterio, y voto que hizo de defender la Purísima Concepción de Nuestra Señora, la madre Juana Inés de la Cruz" ("Learned Explication of the Mystery, and Vow Made by Sister Juana Inés de la Cruz to Defend the Immaculate Conception of Our Lady"). Neither the explication nor the vow contains anything noteworthy from a literary or theological point of view; they are standard reiterations of the dogma of the Immaculate Conception. The paper does have an item of informational interest: for thirty-two years Núñez de Miranda had been the prefect of the Brotherhood of the Immaculate Conception of Mary, so that Sor Juana's vow to defend that mystery with her blood was an additional sign of the ties that joined her to her spiritual director. Another interesting detail: Sor Juana names as intercessors and witnesses St. Joseph, St. Peter, her guardian angel, St. Augustine, St. Ignatius, St. Rosa, and others, but she does not mention St. Catherine. Nor had she named any learned women saints in the petition. Last, the impersonal style of the document, which seems copied from a book of devout formulas, reveals either that Sor Juana did not write it or that, totally renouncing literature, she stayed within standard formulas.

According to Calleja and Oviedo, she began to mortify her flesh, following her confessor's example. She had never previously shown any ascetic inclinations; when she speaks of anguish in her sonnets and *décimas,* she is referring either to the suffering of love and jealousy or, in the sacred poems, to moral torment. Oviedo says (repeating what Núñez de Miranda had confided to him):

> Sister Juana was alone with her Husband, and as she saw how he was nailed to the cross by the sins of man, love gave her strength to imitate him, endeavoring in her undertaking to crucify her appetites and passions, with such fervent severity in her penance that she had need of the prudent care and attention of Father Antonio, that he take her by the hand, so that her life not end at the hands of her fervor.

Except for the exaggeration of the final phrase, what Oviedo relates must be true, for Calleja repeats that

> her counselor endeavored to persuade her to lessen the pitiless severity to which she subjected herself . . . "It is necessary," said Núñez de Miranda, "to mortify her that she mortify herself less, taking her by the hand in her penitence that she not lose her health and incapacitate herself."

It is difficult to believe that the self-confident and defiant person of 1691 and 1692 had turned into the raving penitent of 1694. But we have no reason to believe that Oviedo and Calleja were lying. In the twentieth century we have seen even more astounding changes, such as Bukharin's confession to the fantastic crimes Vyshinsky had accused him of.

On March 5, Sor Juana signed a distressing document: "Protesta que, rubricada con su sangre, hizo de su fe y amor a Dios la madre Juana Inés de la Cruz, al tiempo de abandonar los estudios humanos para proseguir, desembarazada de este afecto, en el camino de la perfección" ("Profession That, Signed with Her Blood, Sister Juana Inés de la Cruz Made of Her Faith and Her Love to God, at the Time of Abandoning Humane Studies in Order, Released from That Attachment, to Follow the Road of Perfection"). Despite the title, nowhere in the rather brief declaration is there any reference to giving up the study of humane letters. The first paragraph reiterates her firm belief in the dogmas of the Roman Catholic Church; in the second, after saying that it pains her "exceedingly to have offended God"—although without detailing or naming her offenses—she asks forgiveness for having sinned and calls upon the intercession of the Virgin; the third paragraph reiterates the vow she had made to believe in and defend the mystery of Mary's Immaculate Conception. She ends by saying, "And as a sign of how greatly I wish to spill my blood in defense of these truths, I sign with it." There is not a word about humane studies. Moreover, no one has seen the original document. The text appeared for the first time in *Fame,* and the title, like the other titles, was the work of Castorena y Ursúa. There is, therefore, *not a single declaration in which Sor Juana formally and expressly renounces letters.* I have no doubt that she defended herself to the last and refused to sign an abdication and nullification of her entire life. The purpose of the title superimposed by Castorena is to prove that the long process that had begun with the admonitions of Núñez de Miranda, the recommendations of Fernández de Santa Cruz, the withdrawal of the former, and the other incidents that she recounts in the *Response,* had ended with a spectacular abjuration.

During that time, she surrendered all her books and musical and scientific instruments to Archbishop Aguiar y Seijas to sell in order to use the proceeds to aid the poor. Calleja adds that "her cell was left bare except for three small books of devotions and a number of hair shirts and scourges." Sor Juana's contemporaries and many later critics considered this a sublime act. It seems to me the gesture of a terrified woman attempting to ward off calamity with the sacrifice of what she most loves. Relinquishing her library and her collections of instruments and other objects was a propitiation intended to appease the enemy, Aguiar y Seijas. Calleja himself, in spite of his efforts to paint all these sad events as wondrous acts illuminated by divine mercy, could not but write, "The bitter pill that Sor Juana had to swallow, although she did so without flinching, was to give up her beloved books." It seems likely, considering the Archbishop's ever-present need for money to fund his charities, that the books and other objects were sold for far less than their worth. Thus was the library of one of America's great poets dispersed.

Not content with disposing of the books, instruments, and other objects, Aguiar y Seijas confiscated funds, some belonging to Sor Juana, some to the convent. As bookkeeper of her community, she managed substantial sums while carrying out the financial transactions her post demanded. The convent had considerable wealth and she administered it. In fulfilling her duties, she dealt with agents and merchants. Dorothy Schons has shed light on these aspects of the last period of Sor Juana's life, following the sale of her books:

> It seems certain that there was some agreement between Sor Juana and the Archbishop that caused him to believe he was entitled to the nun's property. Don Francisco Aguiar y Seijas had asked for money in her name. Diego Velázquez [one of the agents] declared that as Sor Juana had contracted to buy some materials with money that she had given him [for building repairs], "the Señor Archbishop learned that I owed her some return and, although I pointed out the truth, he asked me for one hundred pesos for his charities. On a different occasion, according to the same witness, His Excellency having made a certain person press me to sell him a slave, I did so, following his command, and His Excellency received three hundred pesos for his just worth and when I appeared to claim them he said that he was applying them to the accounts of Sister Juana."[3]

Nevertheless, although Sor Juana had fallen completely under the domination of Núñez de Miranda and Aguiar y Seijas, her native skill did not abandon her and she was able, as we shall see, to hide away certain sums. Was she hoping for better days?

Antonio Núñez de Miranda suffered from cataracts. The surgeon who attended him saw that they had matured and decided to operate, in spite of the priest's age—he was seventy-seven. The operation was performed successfully, but several days later Father Antonio caught a cold; there were complications, and he died suddenly on February 17, 1695. Two months later an epidemic broke out in the convent of San Jerónimo—because of the vagueness of the information we still do not know the nature of the disease—and the death rate was very high. Calleja says that nine nuns died out of every ten who fell ill. Sor Juana demonstrated her charity in caring for her sisters; she contracted the illness, and at four o'clock on the morning of April 17 she died. She had lived forty-six years and five months. In the convent's Book of Professions, several months previously, she had written:

> In this place is to be noted the day, month, and year of my death. For the love of God and his Most Holy Mother, I entreat my beloved sisters the

nuns, who are here now and who shall be in the future, to commend me to God, for I have been and am the worst among them. Of them I ask forgiveness, for the love of God and his Mother. I, worst of all the world, Juana Inés de la Cruz.

The frequency with which self-deprecatory formulas were used in that century—Núñez de Miranda's notes abound in similar expressions—partly explains Sor Juana's extremely harsh judgment of herself; she cannot, no matter how severe her opinion of her own life and behavior, have believed she was the "worst of all the world." She was simply using a common formula of vilification. But there was an ounce of real self-contempt in her judgment: her narcissism was the other face of her self-loathing, and that feeling stayed with her until the hour of her death.

Calleja describes the final days: "The illness was extremely contagious and Sister Juana, by nature compassionate and charitable, attended all without rest and without fear of their proximity." It was useless for them to counsel her at least "not to go near the very ill . . . Finally she fell ill . . . but the severity of the sickness, so extreme as to claim her life, had not the least effect on her mind." I distrust the exemplary quality of this picture; nevertheless I recognize in this pious account two of Sor Juana's distinguishing characteristics: her generous nature and her lucidity. What Calleja does not tell us is the medical treatment to which the sick women were subjected: purges and bloodletting. The strongest defense against the plague was religious in nature: prayers, masses, rogations, and processions. The priest Cayetano de Cabrera y Quintero wrote a book, *Escudo de armas de México* (*Mexican Coat of Arms*), in which he describes the measures taken to battle the epidemic that devastated New Spain between 1736 and 1738.[4] He reviews all the epidemics suffered in Mexico City, pausing briefly at the one that took Sor Juana's life. He does not mention the heroism with which she nursed her sisters, but describes the processions, rogations, and flagellations practiced by nuns in times of plague. His descriptions paint a vivid picture of the ways in which religion attempted to combat natural calamities.

The vow of seclusion prevented the nuns from going out into the streets and plazas as the monks did to perform propitiatory ceremonies and to dispense pardons and indulgences. The nuns held their processions inside the cloisters, almost always "veiled, even from one another, by the common mantle of night." As they wound their way through the corridors and patios of their convents, singing and praying, they

Page of the Book of Professions of the Convent of San Jerónimo on which the death of Sor Juana is recorded scourged and lashed themselves. To sharpen the punishment, they removed some of their clothing. In the light of candles and torches, these processions inevitably recalled ancient pagan ceremonies. Cabrera y Quintero says that the nuns resembled "souls in pain from the other world . . . their cries rising to the heavens . . . their blows drawing blood . . . and their harsh hair shirts, until then kept out of sight, wondering at finding themselves uncovered and in the open air." A Christian version of the bacchantes and maenads: the nuns in the night shadows, half naked, bodies bleeding, singing and wailing. There were other, briefer processions, says Cabrera y Quintero, in which the nuns, shoulders bleeding, dragged enormous, heavy crosses. But in the most distressing ceremony of all, the nuns licked the ground—which was usually tiled or paved—"until they drew a cross, their tongues sweeping it as clean as a brush, but with a painful difference: the ground being harder than the brush, they wore away their tongues as they drew the cross." The cross was covered with saliva, and their tongues with blood.

There are those who have said that Sor Juana was buried with a solemn mass in the cathedral. Nonsense; she was buried in San Jerónimo, like the other sisters. Sigüenza y Góngora, according to Castorena y Ursúa, composed a funeral oration. No one has seen it, however, and it must be considered lost. It is revealing that Castorena y Ursúa did not publish Sor Juana's posthumous works until five years after her death, in 1700, in Madrid, when all the protagonists of the events that darkened the last years of her life were gone: Núñez de Miranda, Fernández de Santa Cruz, and Aguiar y Seijas. The survivors—Castorena y Ursúa, Calleja, Oviedo, and Torres—attempted in their accounts of the events to smooth over the rough edges; even Aguiar y Seijas emerges as a kind and paternal figure for whom Sor Juana professed veneration and gratitude. It is also revealing that we have no biography of Sor Juana written by a contemporary, except for the summary by Calleja, who never met her and who wrote from hearsay. Perhaps it is all for the best: it spares us a hagiography like those written by Torres and Lezamis, in which we would have been presented with a miraculous Sor Juana practicing levitation and curing the blind.

Thanks to Dorothy Schons's research, we have a more reliable idea of what actually happened. On the day after her death, representatives of Aguiar y Seijas appeared in her cell to claim everything there: jewels, money, promissory notes, and other documents. Later the nuns of San Jerónimo estimated (and proved) that the Archbishop's agents had removed, in addition to the jewels, a sum equivalent to five thousand two hundred pesos.[5] This shows that Calleja was not entirely accurate when he wrote that after Sor Juana surrendered her library and collections to the Archbishop she kept only two or three small books of devotions and a few hair shirts. How can we interpret the evidence to the contrary except as a sign that some part of her remained unvanquished? At the Archbishop's death in 1698 a suit was filed against his heirs, with the aim of recovering some portion of the loans and requisitions he had coerced from different persons and institutions. Among the institutions petitioning for the return of monies owed them were several convents: Jesús María, San Lorenzo, the Hospital del Espíritu Santo, and San Jerónimo. In the document from the nuns of San Jerónimo it says that the Archbishop, "in his zeal for bestowing charity, ordered that all the jewels, writings, and monies [of Sor Juana] be carried away, both those that were in the convent and those that were deposited outside it."

The nuns make no mention of books or musical and scientific instruments because these had been ceded by Sor Juana to the Archbishop. They add that there were other jewels and money on deposit that they do not claim because they have no trace of them. Among the sums Sor Juana was able to save from the zealous greed of the Archbishop were, in addition to the five thousand two hundred pesos claimed by the nuns (they considered themselves the legitimate heirs of her wealth), another two thousand pesos given to Domingo Rea to be invested, "declaring that the principal and interest were to be enjoyed by Sister Juana during the days of her life and afterward by her niece, Sor Isabel María de San José."[6] Is it not strange that, fully penitent and on the path toward sainthood—as Calleja, Oviedo, and others claim—Sor Juana kept poetry, jewels, and money in her cell? In her so-called conversion, we see none of the signs that accompany this kind of psychic turnaround: no poems, declarations, letters, or other expressions of the soul. Only stereotyped formulas. The one act that might corroborate her change—the surrender of her library—was more likely intended to conciliate Aguiar y Seijas and is partially invalidated by the sums she managed to hide from the prelate's charitable mania. There was a little of everything in Sor Juana's actions: eagerness for a reconciliation with the Church authorities, and also eagerness, no less intense, to break the siege of those terrible prelates. Especially, and above all, fear, a great deal of fear.

My generation saw the revolutionaries of 1917, the comrades of Lenin and Trotsky, confess false crimes before their judges in a language that was an abject parody of Marxism, just as the sanctimonious language of the affirmations of faith Sor Juana signed with her blood is a caricature of religious language. The two cases—the Bolsheviks of the twentieth century and the poet-nun of the seventeenth—are very different, but they share an essential and disturbing similarity: such events can occur only in closed societies ruled by an all-powerful bureaucracy governing in the name of orthodoxy. Unlike other regimes, whether democratic or tyrannical, orthodoxies are not satisfied with punishing dissent: they demand confessions, repentance, and retraction from the guilty. In those ceremonies of expiation, the faith of the accused is the surest ally of the prosecutors and inquisitors.

Faith and ideology made Sor Juana an accomplice of her executioners; and they continue to blind her interpreters. How else can we explain that three centuries after her humiliation, most Catholic critics continue to speak of her *conversion?* The three texts of 1694 are examples of devout formulas of the time, not mystical literature—and lamentable both as literature and as religious language. Yet Alberto G. Salceda has called the "Petition," an impersonal document not worthy of her either morally or as literature, "Sor Juana's ultimate literary composition." A judgment worthy of a scribe of the Holy Office. March 5, 1694, the day she renounced humane letters, inspires in Alfonso Méndez Plancarte a kind of macabre unction: it is her "most beautiful hour." According to Alfonso Junco, on that day Sor Juana, who was "always enchantingly good, became arrestingly saintly." Is not this desire to sanctify her an attempt—perhaps not entirely conscious—to hide the true meaning of her life and work? If her last years are misrepresented, the true meaning of what she wrote will also be misrepresented. A great deal of her writing was an imitation of models then in vogue and an intelligent variation on the rhetoric of her century, but some of it distinguishes her from, even contradicts, her time. The same is true of her life and her person: a solitary figure, Sor Juana is the image of contradiction, and she knew it. She said it in many poems. Nun and skilled politician, poet and intellectual, erotic enigma and businesswoman, a Mexican and a Spaniard, a lover of Egyptian esoterica and of witty poetry, Sor Juana perpetually contradicts herself and, in so doing, contradicts her age. She also contradicts those panegyrists who prefer a plaster saint to a living writer.

I believe that the circumstances I have spelled out earlier explain—to the degree that a human life *can* be explained—Sor Juana's conversion. I have tried to place personal circumstances in their historical context.

History includes chance, the unforeseen: those events that we humans, with our limited understanding, cannot measure or predict. History was the misogyny of Aguiar y Seijas and his rivalry with Fernández de Santa Cruz; the obsessions of Núñez de Miranda, intent on making a saint of a woman who had no religious vocation; the politics of the Society of Jesus in China and Mexico; the loving friendship with the Countess de Paredes; Father Kircher as transmitter of the hermetic tradition; Juana Inés' illegitimate birth, and her lack of fortune; her years in the viceregal court; and her labors as a semiofficial poet for the palace and the cathedral. In short, everything that was her life and at the same time the history of the society in which she lived. Without the riots of 1692 or the death of the Marquis de la Laguna, she might have found protection against the wrath of Aguiar y Seijas and the severity of Núñez de Miranda; without her imprudent decision to follow Fernández de Santa Cruz's command to write the critique of Vieyra's sermon, she might never have been disturbed. Her personal history was made of the same perpetually fluctuating substance as the history of her world.

Among all these factors, two, as I have emphasized, are basic, although insufficient in themselves to explain her final fall. The first is the opposition between the intellectual life and the duties and obligations of convent life. The second is the fact that she was a woman. The latter was the more decisive; if she had been a man, the zealous Princes of the Church would not have persecuted her. Deeper than the incompatibility between secular and religious pursuits was the perceived contradiction between writing and being a woman. That is why, finally, Sor Juana the poet does not become a theologian but a penitent who "buries, along with her name, her intellect." She yields, but not without a struggle; for more than two years, in growing isolation, she must contend with a siege that at times assumes the sweetness of paternal advice, at others the severity of persecution. As the net closes around her, the foundations of her world are shaken: power is exposed as both vacillating and cruel, great men quarrel, the people rise up and burn the symbols of authority. Sor Juana's faith was an accessory in her defeat. She relinquished her books to her persecutor, scourged her body, humbled her intelligence, and renounced the gift that was most her own: the word. Her sacrifice on the altar of Christ was an act of submission to proud prelates. Her religious convictions provided the justification for her intellectual abdication: the powers that destroyed her were the very ones she had served and praised.

Epilogue

Toward a Restitution

*T*HE TEMPTATION TO SEE CULTURE—the arts, sciences, beliefs, ideas—as a reflection of society and of the forces at war within society is probably as old as history itself. In the last century and a half, under the combined influence of Marxism and positivism, many historians have adopted this view. I confess that I have always felt it was an aberration to see Provençal poetry as a consequence of the social system of the twelfth century, or Sappho's poems as a product of slavery. What has always struck me is the opposite phenomenon: art's relative independence from social determinism. What ties do Courbet's splendid nudes have with the society in which he was fated to live, or even with the artist's ideology? How is it that art from other eras, expressing ideas different from our own, based on themes that no longer excite us, and invoking strange mythologies, continues to stir our passion and our admiration?

I am not the only one who has asked this question. Marx also asked it, and he too was unable to answer it: "The difficulty, however, does not lie in understanding that Greek art and the Epic are associated with certain social developments. The difficulty is that they still give us esthetic pleasure and are in a certain respect regarded as unattainable models."[1] I also distrust the opposite view. Plato saw reality as an imperfect copy of ideas. In turn, art was a copy of a copy. But I ask: how, in the presence of certain paintings, symphonies, and poems, can we fail to feel that we are before a heightening of reality, not a diminished idea? We shall never live in a world as perfect and joyous—one in which every chord is in accord—as the world we journey through when we hear

Mozart's Jupiter Symphony. For the Greeks, nature was the paradigm and art the copy, but to us the natural world is no longer sacred; science and technology have reduced it to a complex of forces and reactions. Nature, for us, is not wise or intelligent: it is a blind *process*. The same has happened to all other ideas and mythologies. Heaven has been stripped of its symbols and divinities; theology is an uninhabited mansion. The *idea* is not the model of art.

In sum, I distrust both views equally: I cannot see culture—that is, the sum of the inventions and creations by which man has become man—either as the reflection of changing social forces *or* as the imperfect imitation of immutable ideas. It seems to me that what both views fail to take into account is the creature without whom none of these marvels would exist. In a given situation, and within certain limitations, man conceives, imagines, invents: he fashions an ax, designs a symbol, conceives the image of a divinity. Man is subject to the laws of social development and to those of thought (he cannot think a circular triangle), but within those limits he invents, transforms, and creates. Culture is freedom and imagination.

Once this has been said, how can we deny that there is a kind of harmony, or correspondence, among a society's tools, institutions, philosophies, and works of art? I do not know whether Nahuatl poetry, with its obsessive reiteration of the words "flower," "blade," and "jade," is actually a metaphor for one of the principal institutions of Aztec society, the Flower War, in which the heart of the victim was identified with the flower, and jade with the restorative power of nature. Nonetheless, there is a clear correspondence between the metaphorical system of Aztec poetry and the ritual of the Flower War. Neither do I know whether the Flower War was an enactment of the solar myth of the daily creation of the world, or whether the myth was an ideological projection of the social relationships that formed the Aztec world. Argument on this theme can be (is, has been, will be) unending. What cannot be denied, however—regardless of Plato and Marx—is that there is a visible correspondence between the metaphors of Nahuatl poetry, the Flower War, and the Aztec solar myth. The same sorts of correspondences could be established in the Roman and Gothic worlds, fourteenth- and fifteenth-century Florence, and eighteenth-century France. The inherent style or manner we detect in each period corroborates what I have just said; however profound the differences between one artist and another, something unites them: the style of their age. Style is what makes abstract time concrete and historical. Yes, time passes, but it passes always through a "here," through a community. And style records that passing.

The autonomy of works of art and their inevitable correlation with history and society seem to be contradictory or even incompatible ideas. Perhaps they are, but reality is also contradictory. The culture of a society at any given moment is a fluid system of interconnections. It is impossible to explain those interconnections by appealing to strict determinism; it is also impossible to deny their existence. Many modern historians seem to have given up the idea of causality; causes are too numerous, so numerous that it is practically impossible to detect and to measure them. And events are the product not only of so-called causes but also of chance. Perhaps what we call "chance" is a cause that our reason and the methods of investigation at our disposal are powerless to foresee or recognize. In any case, we can discount causes while retaining the principle of correspondence. At first a philosophical concept, then an aesthetic, the notion of correspondence can enlighten history. Events, works, and even persons "correspond." More, they "rhyme." Vermeer's painting rhymes with the merchant middle class of the Low Countries in the seventeenth century. If in Monet's landscapes nature has ceased to be clear outline or architecture and has become vibration, how can we fail to realize it is a projection of sensations and ideas, of the ideas in Monet's time about the innermost structure of nature?

This brief digression has had a double purpose: first, to justify my attempt to establish certain correspondences or rhymes—it would be too much to call them explanations—between the history of New Spain, the person of Sor Juana, and the character of her work; second, to show that her "conversion" and the social and political events of 1692 were joined not by an impossible causality but by a real correspondence.

The disturbance of 1692 was not a revolution, not even a revolt, but a riot. Governmental indecision, excessive rain, an agricultural disaster, difficulties in transporting grain, hoarding to drive up prices, and an unfair system of distribution spurred popular discontent. Two circumstances precipitated the events: the sermon by the Franciscan Escaray criticizing the government, and social friction. In New Spain social and racial differences were interrelated; the resentment that had built up among the indigenous population, the *castas* and the criollos, aggravated their righteous anger over the scarcity of maize and wheat. The widespread belief that the Viceroy and his supporters were guilty of hoarding and speculation threw oil on the fire. A slightly more detailed examination of the events will shed further light.

Without Escaray's sermon, that is, without religious sanction, the riot might not have exploded. The clergy were the people's conscience, and the words of the Franciscan were incendiary—up to a point. We do not know the text of the sermon, but however violent it may have been, we can assume that it criticized the errors of those who governed, not the principles of social order. Ortega y Gasset has made a perceptive distinction between the revolutionary and the reformist set of mind: the former criticizes uses; the latter, abuses. Escaray's sermon belonged in the second category. From the accounts of the time we know that the sermon was heard with approval and applause. It was delivered in the cathedral, in a solemn ceremony at which government officials and high clergy were present. The Indians and groups of people who later burned the viceregal palace and the municipal building were not in the audience. Who, then, were those who received the Franciscan's critical remarks with such approval? Perhaps a few Spaniards, but especially criollos, a group represented by a broad social and economic spectrum: property owners, miners, and wealthy businessmen, but also clerics, doctors, lawyers, students, and shopkeepers, all of whom considered New Spain their true homeland. In spite of their economic and social differences, the criollos were united in their resentment toward the Spanish. They did not contribute significantly to the riot itself, but they were the ones who justified it with their complaints and fanned the flames with their invective. Criollos were the "loyal vassals" who wrote long accusatory letters to the King and his first minister attacking the viceregal administration, and criollos were the anonymous authors of the pasquinades that slandered the Count de Galve and his family.

The social classes and groups that participated in the uprising were the same that a hundred years later fought for the independence of Mexico. But the riot was not a foreshadowing of independence; the forces of rejection had no project for reform. It was a spontaneous outburst that faded as rapidly as it had spread. What lack kept it from developing into a full-scale, modern-style revolution? First of all, an intellectual class allied with the lower and middle classes. The intellectual class was composed predominantly of the clergy, but even the most cultured clerics, like Sigüenza and Sor Juana, had very unformed notions of modern ideas, especially in the area of politics. New Spain lacked the intellectual equipment to start, if not a revolution—unthinkable at the end of the seventeenth century—even a timid reform. In Spain itself, such a movement would not have been viable. The Spanish empire was a formidable political and intellectual edifice ruled by two powers, the throne and the Church, both armed with powerful bureaucracies. The monarchic-Catholic orthodoxy, the foundation and the steeple of the edifice, extended via its two bureaucracies into every corner of public and private life. Thus there were no guiding principles on which to base a reform in New Spain. When, shortly afterward, with the advent of a Bourbon dynasty, reform was attempted during the reign of Charles III, it originated at the top and remained incomplete; although it limited the power of the Church, the power of the monarchy increased. The end result was the reinforcement of one of the vices of Hispanic societies: centralism.

Criticism of orthodoxy had begun in Europe with the Reformation. It was a criticism of Roman Christianity within Christianity, a religious criticism of established religion. This critical tradition was transported to the American continent by the English colonists; the religious democracy of the New England Puritans eventually became the political democracy of the United States. This means that within the tradition of New England there existed in embryo the principles that were so sorely lacking in New Spain. In other countries, notably France, the criticism originated from outside Christianity, not within; it was philosophical, not religious, criticism. The target of the *philosophes'* attacks was Catholic dogma and, especially, the Church and the clergy. Another French revolt, Jansenism, while remaining within the limits of orthodoxy, was related to both the Reformation and philosophical criticism. Spain, however, did not know the Reformation or Jansenism or the Enlightenment. The American Revolution and the French Revolution were each a consequence of their respective intellectual, religious, and moral traditions. They were breaks, but breaks that in a certain way were continuations of tradition: the religious democracy of Puritanism and the philosophical criticism of Church and monarchy. In both instances the societies were renewed from within. The same can be said of earlier political reforms in Holland and England.

The riot of 1692 is not in itself of great importance, except as a sign of the historical situation of New Spain and the mother country at that time. The lack of a philosophical and religious critical tradition in Spain, and in her possessions, was the reason why a century after the riots of 1692 Mexicans looked outward rather than to their own past. They did so, in the beginning, with extraordinary timidity: Hidalgo's cry initiating the struggle for independence—"Long live Ferdinand VII! Down with Bad Government!"—is very similar to the formula the criollos used to sign the letters criticizing the Count de Galve to their King: "His Majesty's most loyal vassals." True, the Jesuits and criollos had conceived a vague idea, a transformation of the Spanish and Aztec empires into a Mexican empire, but this concept was more an emotion than a plan and it died out at the beginning of the nineteenth century. By then, as events demonstrated, it was unworkable. It was necessary to adopt a different plan, brought from outside—the models were the United States and France—and forced upon the country like a straitjacket. New Spain, which had outlived itself for a century, died of strangulation. In its place was born a different society, the Republic of Mexico. This accounts in part for the fragility of our democratic institutions and the difficulties we have encountered in becoming a modern nation.

It is scarcely necessary to point out the similarities between Sor Juana's personal situation and the obstacles we Mexicans have experienced during the process of modernization. There was an insoluble contradiction between Sor Juana and her world. This contradiction was not merely intellectual; it was fundamental, and can be located in three main areas. The first was the opposition between her literary vocation and the fact that she was a nun. At other moments, although not in New Spain, the Church had been tolerant and had harbored writers and poets who, often in blatant disregard of their religious responsibilities, had devoted themselves exclusively to letters. Their cases, however—the most notable being those of Góngora, Lope de Vega, Tirso de Molina, and Mira de Amescua—differ from that of Sor Juana in an essential point: they were poets and dramatists but not intellectuals. Both vocations, poet and intellectual, converged in Sor Juana. In late seventeenth-century Spain and its domains, a priest or nun with an intellectual vocation was restricted to theology and sacred studies. This incompatibility was aggravated by the fact that Sor Juana's extraordinary intellectual restlessness and her encyclopedic curiosity—Sigüenza's also—coincided with a moment of paralysis in the Church and exhaustion in Hispanic culture.

The second area of discord was Sor Juana's gender. The fact that a woman—what is more, a nun—should devote herself so single-mindedly to letters must have both astounded and scandalized her contemporaries. She was called the "Tenth Muse" and the "Phoenix of America": sincere expressions of admiration that must have set her head spinning at times. She tells us in the *Response* that no lack of criticism and censure accompanied this praise. The censure came from influential prelates and was founded on a point of doctrine. It was not by chance that in his appeal to Sor Juana asking her to forsake secular letters the Bishop of Puebla quoted St. Paul. It was one thing to be tolerant with Lope de Vega and Góngora, both bad priests, and another to be lenient with Sor Juana Inés de la Cruz. Although her conduct was beyond reproach, her attitudes were not. She was guilty of the sin of pride, a sin to which the vain feminine sex is particularly susceptible. Pride was the ruin of Lucifer, because hubris leads to rebelliousness. Sor Juana's critics saw a causal relationship between letters, which lead a woman from her natural state of obedience, and rebelliousness. Sor Juana had disproved the inferiority of women in intellectual and literary matters and made her attainments a source of admiration and public applause; to the prelates this was sin, and her obstinacy was rebellion. That is why they demanded a total abdication.

Finally, the knowledge to which Sor Juana aspired—as we have seen in *First Dream* and the *Response*—was not the learning religion can offer. Her intellectual and moral concerns were different from those of a St. Teresa or a St. John of the Cross. She did not seek, like St. John, to obliterate reason, but to sharpen it. Unlike St. Teresa, she did not long to be penetrated by divine light; she wanted, with the light of reason, to penetrate the opaque mysteries of all things. It is difficult to define exactly the kind of knowledge she sought. It certainly was not union with God. Although not clearly defined, two types of learning can be identified in *First Dream,* as I have shown in my analysis of the poem. One, derived from Platonism, was the fruit of contemplation, not so much of ideas or essences as of the marvelous machinery of the universe, to use Sor Juana's own expression. To see what *is,* not in its abstract or ideal form but in its real motion and harmony. Another, more modern type of learning she yearned for corresponds to what we call encyclopedic knowledge: knowledge of the secrets of each individual science, as well as the links that join one with another. Neither of these forms of knowledge was appropriate in a nunnery. In the *Response* we can see even more clearly what she was after: an understanding of the things of this world. Of course, she says that all such learning is preparation for theology, the highest of the sciences. But she says this to ward off her critics; she was well aware of the fact that one need not study chemistry in order to speculate on efficient grace or to achieve union with God.

If Sor Juana had allowed herself to carry these contradictions to their ultimate conclusions, she would have ended up shaking her spiritual universe to its foundations and negating the precepts and intellectual convictions that had shaped her. To go forward would have been to deny her world and to adopt other principles. Which principles? Those of emerging modernity. But we have already seen in the examination of her library and *First Dream* that she had only vague notions of the two sciences that in her day had transformed the image of the universe: astronomy and physics. Neither was she informed in the current philosophy that had shattered the foundations of the Neothomism in which she had been educated. Like the criollos and the Indian rioters of 1692, she lacked the means or principles by which to complete the critical demolition her situation demanded. Like them, too, she lacked a public arena in which to expound her point of view. The immediate response would have been the Inquisition. Was there a solution other than surrender and abdication? New Spain was teetering between rebellion and submission, between Sor Juana's *Response* and her renunciation of secular writing. There is a striking parallel between cultural crisis and social unrest in New Spain: the same historical situation is inherent in both of them.

My reflections on the state of New Spain are not inexact, but they are one-sided. In the three centuries of its existence, New Spain was a peaceful, stable, and reasonably prosperous society. Mexico City became larger, richer, and more beautiful than Madrid. The remarkable growth of agriculture and mining gave rise to a class of wealthy criollo proprietors, and a second group that distinguished itself in the Church, the university, and the military. The wealthy criollos were generous; they built churches and hospitals we admire today. Culture itself, within the stringent limitations I have defined, showed vitality. Despite the kind of gilded paralysis in which it lived, New Spain reached levels of achievement that we, its descendants, have not surpassed. In the social domain: three centuries of almost uninterrupted peace; in the forging of a common faith: the Virgin of Guadalupe, an image that has done more to shape our sense of nationhood than all the official and pseudo-official myths propagated by successive nineteenth- and twentieth-century republican governments; in the legal sphere: a series of prudent and intelligent measures—not always carried out, it is true—intended specifically to protect the weakest among us, the Indians; in matters of urban development: amazing monuments and buildings and, especially, a number of cities almost without parallel on our continent: Morelia, Oaxaca, Guanajuato (not to mention those we have ruined in the last thirty years); in the field of letters: a group of notable poets in the sixteenth century and, in the seventeenth, one of the great writers of our language, Juana Inés de la Cruz. For all these reasons, the look we throw back over New Spain always ends in *recognition*, in every sense of that word.

Of course we must not look upon that society as a model or a lost paradise. Social inequities abounded, and the narrowly hierarchical and authoritarian nature of the regime precluded, as we have seen, either denunciation or correction of injustices. We cannot close our eyes to the abuses of power or ignore the inherent injustice of that society that consecrated privilege. It must also be said, however, that New Spain was not an exception either in its time or in the history of the human race. Gibbon said that if one were asked to pick "the period in the history of the world, during which the condition of the human race was most happy and prosperous, he would, without hesitation, name that which elapsed from the death of Domitian to the accession of Commodus" (A.D. 96–180).[2] Who today would subscribe to that opinion? The empire of the Antonines was an enlightened despotism that engaged in perpetual war and ruled over countless subject nations and a population of slaves. The age in which Gibbon wrote, the eighteenth century, was similarly one of enlightened despotism; monarchs warred ceaselessly among themselves, or undertook wars of conquest on other continents: the slaves were now the peoples of colonized America, Asia, and Africa. In the areas where European powers had not yet established empires, barbarous and cruel governments ruled or, as in China and Japan, cultured despots like those of Europe.

From the sixteenth century on, many European writers, followed in the nineteenth century by writers in Spanish America, branded Spanish and Portuguese domination with the iron of opprobrium. In order to right the scales slightly, we have only to recall that the Indians of Latin America, however terrible their plight, escaped the fate suffered by their brothers to the north: extermination. How then do we explain the decline of New Spain and the historical stumbling blocks their descendants have confronted? I have already indicated the answer in Part One: New Spain was a society that could not move forward. Once they won independence, Mexicans felt lost; nothing and no one had prepared them to confront the dominant force in the modern world: change, progress. But time works its revenge. Today many Europeans and Americans, disillusioned, even terrified, by the disasters of progress, are looking for ways to slow it. Progress has become synonymous with death.

WHAT DISTINGUISHES A GREAT POET? According to Eliot, three qualities: excellence, abundance, and diversity. Sor Juana is a prolific poet, even though with her, as with most poets, only a few poems can meet the ultimate test, perfection. She is also diverse, not only in the variety of her forms and meters but also in themes and tonalities. Finally, some of her poems, as we have seen, can be compared with the finest works of the Spanish language. Her work—I am thinking of *First Dream, The Divine Narcissus,* and a handful of amatory poems—belongs not only to the literature of our tongue but to the great tradition of Western civilization.

Sor Juana demonstrates her abundance, variety, and excellence first of all as a versifier. Navarro Tomás places her alongside Góngora and Lope de Vega in the seventeenth century. We can go further and say that throughout the eighteenth and nineteenth centuries there is no poet who used with such exquisite mastery so much variety in meter and form. We find her equal only at the beginnings of our own century, in the modernist poets, principally Rubén Darío and Leopoldo Lugones. Sor Juana skillfully employed a wide variety of verse forms and excelled in little-used metric and strophic combinations. Oddly enough, there were forms she did not employ, the most notable example being terza rima, inherited from Dante and used by all sixteenth- and seventeenth-century Spanish poets. It is also worth noting that in spite of the perfection and formal variety of her poems she did not influence poets who came after her. Tastes changed, and for two centuries her work was forgotten. Rather than a beginning, like Darío, she was an ending: she inherited almost all the forms of her age and in many cases carried them to their ultimate perfection. If, as is natural and predictable, curiosity about and love for metrics should be rekindled among our new poets—poetry is above all a rhythmic verbal art—perhaps one of them will discover a model and stimulus among the combinations of her *villancicos* and *loas.*

Her contemporaries praised her for having followed Góngora's example. Eighteenth-century theorists, the romantics, and early twentieth-century critics condemned her for the same reason. They excepted only that part of her work not tainted by the plague of Gongorism. Then came Góngora's revival and Sor Juana was once again praised for Gongorism. The influence of the Cordoban poet on her was both deep and broad. On the one hand, she appropriated many of Góngora's processes: syntactic inversion, arcane terminology, periphrasis, antithesis, metaphor; on the other, she displayed this influence in many poems, among them two of her most notable compositions: the decasyllabic *romance* to the Countess de Paredes and *First Dream*. Most of these techniques, however, were used by the majority of the poets of the time, including those who, like Lope de Vega and Quevedo, professed enmity for Góngora's literary doctrines. Góngora is not the only presence: there are echoes of other poets in Sor Juana's poems, as I have already demonstrated. At times she writes poems of great purity and translucence, closer to the sixteenth century than to some of the poetic trends in vogue in the seventeenth. I am referring to parts of *The Divine Narcissus* and especially to the *liras* on love. Those poems reveal another facet of her genius: not the slightly chilly sensuality of the convoluted *romance* to the Countess nor the self-reflecting melancholy of the *décimas* on her portrait, but a limpid fluidity.

The influence of Calderón was as decisive as that of Góngora. This great dramatist and mediocre lyric poet, Gerardo Diego has astutely observed, "substitutes wit for sensitivity . . . , prefers symmetry where in Góngora there is balance . . . , reduces surprise to commonplace . . . Calderón is Góngora's academy." A severe but exact judgment. What did Sor Juana learn from Calderón? Method, manner, that is, the mechanics of poetry. Fortunately, although she uses Calderonian models and formulas, she is frequently saved by her sensibility. In Sor Juana, Calderón's "artificial flowers" suddenly bloom, release perfume, shed their petals. In sum, when we reread her works we note that her best poems are not those that flaunt the influence of Góngora—with the exceptions I have noted—nor those that follow Calderón. The poems that reveal either influence are in the minority. Some of her most deeply felt *romances* on love and on her inner life, certain *endechas* and *décimas* (especially those on the theme of the portrait she sent to the Countess de Paredes), are poems only she could have written. In them, all influences have evaporated. I shall go further and say that only in a very few instances, despite echoes and influences, is she other than herself. Sor Juana writes at the end of a great poetic era, although one tainted by rhetorical affectation; she inherits the tendencies of her time and shares in its style or styles. Like all great poets, she was saved by her sensibility, her creativity, and her instinct. Almost always she said what had to be said. What only she could say.

It is not easy to express in words and concepts what we feel and think as we read a poem. Sentiments and thoughts, fleeting as time itself, that leave us more an impression than a clear idea. It is the impression that causes us to say we prefer one poem to another. Judgments based on such impressions have provoked the distrust of professional critics, who prefer less uncertain methods and who approach the poem with procedures that range from philosophical reflection to scientific analysis. Acuity of critical description, however, and precision of judgment invariably depend more on the sensitivity and intelligence of the critic than on the excellence of the method. An obtuse critic, whatever system he employs, will end his study of a poem with an obtuse judgment. A critic who is intelligent but devoid of sensitivity will write an essay in which he treats each and every aspect of a poem except the most crucial: the poetry itself. Methods for understanding, enjoying, and judging a poem are legitimate when they take two factors into account. The first is the impression we have as we read the poem (the word "impression" is not very exact and not in fashion, but others are similarly unsatisfactory). The second is what we think as we feel what we feel. An understanding of poetry, in other words, is rooted in feeling and insight, impression and reflection. We could add another requisite, a sense of proportion and number, although I believe that is included in the first two. I have reiterated the obvious because without bringing all these factors to bear we can neither understand Sor Juana's poetry nor respond to the question of what distinguishes it from that of her contemporaries.

It is impossible to define the distinctive element of Sor Juana's poetry in a word or a phrase. It is an elusive though clearly perceivable quality. Lucidity? Irony? Knowing how far to go and where to stop? Love of clarity of thought and clarity of design? Passion that ends in melancholy? A taste for introspection? Although this handful of words and phrases I have flung on the page could serve as a point of departure, I would rather pause briefly to consider some of her love poems and to compare them to poems by her contemporaries. These poems in a certain way define her. When I say love poems I include those of loving friendship, a few sacred *romances,* and those in which she reflects upon herself. Love is a passion, a longing that forces us outside ourselves in search of the desired one and then back to search within ourselves for the trace of the beloved, or to contemplate the beloved's ghost in silence. Sor Juana's poetry reproduces this dialectic movement with extraordinary authenticity. But the dialectic is fulfilled in all the good amatory poetry of the time, including, of course, the two poets who have left us the most intense love poems of seventeenth-century Spain: Lope de Vega and Quevedo.

The two have opposite visions and experiences of love: Lope de Vega, a succession of women and love affairs; Quevedo, misogyny and Platonism. In the former, diversity of experience does not deny the oneness of passion. Into each of his loves he put the wholeness of love. In the case of Quevedo we would have to speak of single-mindedness, even obsession, rather than wholeness. His love is phantasmal, whether in the Platonism of his sonnets or in their complement, those satiric compositions in which the female body becomes corpse and corruption. Quevedo's love is, in truth, a meditation on mortality. Amorous passion, disembodied, is transformed through antithesis and paradox into an *ars moriendi*. To know love is to know death, or to know life in death. Nothing could be further from Lope de Vega. For him love is neither contemplation of death nor meditation on life; it is fate. What does he seek in a woman? Perhaps he seeks nothing; he is attracted to her as to a star. Desire and its recurrent images, at once motionless and in frenzied motion, the interminable hours of solitude, with their ghostly presences, sudden thirsts, torrents of tears, jealousy and despair, meetings and leave-takings, hopes, the river of tenderness in an empty room—all passions nourish Lope's passion, which is at once cynical and innocent.

It would be pointless to look in Sor Juana's poems for Quevedo's fury, which resolves finally into smoke, or for the vastness, variety, and richness of Lope de Vega. Her experience was more limited. She could not know what Lope's senses knew from touching and being touched, discovering the warmth of another's flesh, and feeling the waterfall of a lover's laughter on one's breast in the middle of the night—a knowing that knows what no philosophy knows. Neither did she, like Quevedo, have intimate congress with the skeleton that will one day be our partner. (What is terrible in Quevedo is that the partner becomes a specter *before* the act of love.) Sor Juana's poetry is unique because passion, in her, means neither fulfillment, as it does in Lope, nor condemnation, as in Quevedo, but awareness. Sor Juana experiences intensely but never touches the desired person; in this she might seem to resemble Quevedo. The difference is that her passion is not transformed into a philosophy in which bodies blaze in order that souls may emerge from their ashes. Her love is here and now: despite her Neoplatonism, it is not, as in Quevedo, a transference to a beyond peopled with disembodied spirits. At the same time, her love is *not* here and now: bodies fade at her touch. Although she probably never, not even during her years in the viceregal palace, had a real—except, perhaps, a solitary—erotic experience, Sor Juana perceived with astounding insight the paradoxical nature of pleasure: we merely touch a body and it disappears; it has only to disappear to recover its reality. The mirror play of the *décimas* on the portraits expresses this intuition. Between the portrait and the original there is a transition from the real to the unreal, and vice versa, without our being able to perceive where the true reality lies: "of this body you are the soul, / and of this shadow, the body."

What shall we call the gaze that sees the invisible transition between what is and what ceases to be, between what is not and then again is? "Lucid" is the only word that comes to mind. If anything distinguishes Sor Juana's poetry from that of other poets, it is a clear-sightedness that is immediately transformed into awareness. Lope is vast but he is not lucid; Quevedo lives the opposition between passion and reason; Sor Juana unites them: as she feels, she thinks. Lucidity is, at the same time, a sense of where one's outer limits lie. Lope and Quevedo are excessive; Sor Juana has a keen awareness of the "thus far and no farther." That awareness is both existential and aesthetic. Existentially, love borders on melancholy, that is, on absence, solitude, and self-reflection. Sor Juana constantly questions herself and the images of her solitary musings: love is knowledge. And the art made with that knowledge is neither excess nor verbal extravagance but rigor, restraint. The poet's imagination constructs a limited space wherein spirit and passion—now converted into words, images, and conceits—unfold.

Sor Juana lived toward the end of the Baroque Age and inherited all its manias and extravagances but never lost her basic sense of proportion. Even in *First Dream,* her most complex poem, the design is clear. Among all the Spanish poets of the seventeenth century, Sor Juana is the best at design. The others are luxuriant; what they draw disappears beneath the foliage or breaks under the weight of branches and fruit. In Sor Juana, forms are strict and the brilliance of color restrained: a Juan Gris compared with a Picasso.

Two of her distinguishing qualities, born of her ironic self-consciousness and of the limits of words, were ingenuity and gracefulness. The first, although outstanding, is not the stronger of her gifts; she did not have the ingenuity of a Góngora. The second is wingèd, and soars through water, fire, and air, as in her *villancicos*. Design, proportion, clarity, gracefulness, self-awareness, irony, lucidity. Need I add that her lucidity is melancholy, not tragic?

Sor Juana was predisposed toward the theater, yet, whether because it was a declining art form in her day or for some other reason, she left no single outstanding play. *The Trials of a Noble House* is a pleasant comedy, one that can still be enjoyed—but nothing more. Some of the *loas,* although they were official art, deserve to be remembered for their versification and language. I know that few modern readers will care to wander through those artificial verbal labyrinths; it is a pity, for the stroll is its own reward. Her sacred drama is more substantial. These plays were written at the urging of the Countess de Paredes, for performance at the royal court in Madrid. But who today wants to see or read an *auto sacramental?* Unlike the Noh, which has been preserved with admirable fidelity by the Japanese through six centuries, the tradition of the *auto sacramental* was lost following its prohibition by Charles III in 1765. The loss is unfortunate; the genre has very modern scenic effects. *The Divine Narcissus* is outstanding not only in Sor Juana's work: along with three or four *autos* by Calderón, it represents the most felicitous moment in this theatrical form. What in *The Divine Narcissus* can attract us today? First, the originality of the conception, with its hermetic resonances: the story of a creator enamored of himself through his creation, Human Nature. It is an idea that would have delighted Schelling, perhaps Hegel himself. A less than Christian idea, incidentally. Second, some of the *endechas* and songs are of remarkable purity. Is all this a little or a lot? It is for the reader to judge.

Sor Juana was not mistaken in awarding *First Dream* a special place in her work. I am not sure that in this case the influence of Góngora is fortunate: this is a taxing poem and the syntactic complications that increase the intellectual difficulties add nothing. I have shown that Góngora's influence is superficial. We see the poetry of Góngora; we think the poem of Sor Juana. Góngora surprises us with his metaphors, his colors, his verbal associations; Sor Juana recounts her spiritual biography. *First Dream* is unique in Hispanic poetry, not because it is an exposition—already an anachronism in her time—of the vital functions or of the system of the universe, but because it is a poem of the adventure of knowledge. There were poems in Spanish literature whose theme was the contemplation of the music of the spheres and the harmony of the universe, such as those by Fray Luis de León and Francisco de Aldana. Or poems of union with God, like those of St. John of the Cross. Sor Juana's poem is totally different in subject: the desire to know; the soul's ascent; its vertiginous fall; and its painful, step by step, climb up the staircase of learning. As a poem of knowledge, there is nothing like *First Dream* until Mallarmé's *A Throw of the Dice,* a poem that also ends in an ellipsis, the "perhaps" traced by the stars of the constellation as they revolve through the heavens. Another striking resemblance: the protagonists of the two poems are the same—the human spirit, nameless, without history or country, confronting the starry sky. I have noted that Sor Juana appropriated the voices of the great Spanish poets of her century in order to say something only she could say. The originality of *First Dream* is of a different and more essential nature; the poem says something that no one had said before in Spanish, something that would not be said in other languages until two centuries later. In this sense, *First Dream* belongs to the history of world poetry.

THERE IS A THIRD ASPECT of the personality of Juana Inés: she was, in the words of Dorothy Schons, "the first feminist of America." I have already indicated my reservations about the use of this term; neither the word nor the concept existed in the seventeenth century. It is undeniable, however, that awareness of her womanhood is inseparable from her life and her work. As a girl she conceived the idea of disguising herself as a man in order to attend the university; as a young woman she made the decision to enter the convent because otherwise she would not have been able to devote herself to study or to letters. As a mature woman she proclaims again and again in her poems that reason has no gender; defending her inclination toward letters, she composes long lists of famous women writers from antiquity on; she invokes Isis, the mother of wisdom, and the Oracle of Delphi, the prototype of inspiration; she chooses St. Catherine of Alexandria, a learned virgin and martyr, as her favorite saint; she defends her right to secular learning as a preliminary to sacred learning; she writes that intelligence is not the privilege of men nor is stupidity restricted to women; and, a true historical and political novelty, she advocates the universal education of women, to be imparted by older learned women in their homes or in institutions created for that purpose.

Juana Inés quickly discovered that her gender was an obstacle, not natural but social, to her learning. As a young girl, she was also aware of the fate of women who remained in the world: matrimony, concubinage, or prostitution. The example of her mother must have impressed and marked her forever: a mother of six children, all illegitimate; illiterate, but nonetheless capable of directing the affairs of the hacienda she had inherited. The troubled lives of her sisters, who lived, unmarried, with different men, confirmed her ideas about the lot of women, especially the abandonment this often meant for their children, as in the case of Sor Isabel María de San José, Sor Juana's niece. All this, along with her difficulties with various prelates and with a mother superior, led Sor Juana to communicate to the Bishop of Puebla her ideas on the education of women. Neither the Bishop nor any other prelate ever commented on this idea; it was considered presumptuous. The result of all this was the surrender of her library and the nights spent not in the study of books but in penitence with scourges.

Several factors make Sor Juana's last years seem sadly "modern." The first is the theological—today we say ideological—nature of her personal difficulties and quarrels. At the end of his admirable autobiography, Trotsky affirms with innocent pride that there is nothing personal in his drama: history has been and is the true protagonist. Sor Juana's reiterated affirmations, in her critique of Vieyra's sermon, that God had chosen an ignorant woman (herself) to humble a proud man foreshadows to some extent the Russian revolutionary's rationale. Personal quarrels disguise themselves as clashes between ideas, and the true protagonists of our acts are not we but God or history. Reality is transformed into an enigmatic book we read with fear: as we turn the page we may find our condemnation. We are an argument with which a masked person challenges another, also masked; the subject of a polemic whose origins we are ignorant of and whose denouement we shall never know. Neither do we know the identity of the masked powers who debate and toy with our acts and our lives: where is God and where the Devil? Which is the good side of history and which the bad? Like the quarrels of the gods, humble terrestrial quarrels are a masquerade: Sor Juana, in criticizing Vieyra, is actually attacking Aguiar y Seijas; Mao's campaign against Confucius is intended to destroy Lin-Piao and his followers. Men are converted into names, and names into ideological signs.

Another resemblance between our age and Sor Juana's is the complicity, through ideology, of the victim with his executioner. I have cited the case of Bukharin and others accused in the Moscow trials. Sor Juana's attitude—on a smaller scale—is similar; we have only to read the declarations she signed following her general confession in 1694. This is not surprising; her confessor and spiritual director was also a censor for the Inquisition. Political-religious orthodoxies strive not only to convince the victim of his guilt but to convince posterity as well. Falsification of history has been one of their specialties. In the case of Sor Juana the travesty nearly succeeded; several generations saw in her last years not a defeat but a conversion. Through the mouths of a Bishop and of a high official of the Holy Office, aided by a crazed Archbishop, God called her, and she obeyed his call. A strange call, and an even stranger conversion, that transformed a great writer into a mute penitent. The "conversion" of Sor Juana leaves us nothing, absolutely nothing, except three pious declarations written in prose unworthy of her and, on one of their pages, a thread of blood, quickly dried.

The unfortunate last years of Sor Juana do not, as some of her commentators would have had us believe, give a new meaning to her work. On the contrary; in the light of her work, it is her defeat that takes on a new meaning. Her writings, especially the *Response* and *First Dream*, are the best antidote for the moral righteousness that would make an edifying example of her fall. The moment we begin to weaken, seduced by guilt and punishment, we remember those texts and, as if questioning a mirror, we ask them: what was the real meaning of her defeat? On the smooth surface of the mirror appears the ambiguous image of Phaethon. Ambiguous like most mythic figures, Phaethon is the aspiration toward the heights and the attraction of the abyss. He is the paradoxical image of freedom: flight and fall, transgression and punishment. These two impulses were joined in the character of Sor Juana, and thus it is that we can see her as the emblem of both. Contradictory impulses that perhaps, in some moment of rare divination, she saw as one. Rising and falling intersect at some magnetic point in space, and in that instant, "amid the letters of devastation,"[3] join in the same hieroglyph.

Appendix
Notes on Sources
Spanish Literary Terms
Notes
Index

Appendix

Sor Juana: Witness for the Prosecution

AMONG THE MANY enigmas of Sor Juana's life and work, none has sparked more controversy over the years than that of her relations with the Church hierarchy. A recent discovery, however, has put an end to the debate. I am referring to a small book by Father Aureliano Tapia Méndez: *Audodefensa espiritual de Sor Juana (Sor Juana, A Self-Defense;* Monterrey: Universidad de Nuevo Leon, 1981). This booklet, published by the Universidad de Nuevo León, contains a letter from Sor Juana to her confessor, Father Antonio Núñez de Miranda. The transcript of the letter is followed by a detailed and convincing study by Tapia Méndez. In the first pages Tapia Méndez relates the circumstances of his discovery. In the library of the Seminario Arquidiocesano of Monterrey he found a large quarto volume entitled *Varios Ynformes (Miscellany)*, containing eighteenth-century manuscripts and printed documents, most of them from Mexico City. In looking through the volume he came across a five-and-a-half-page manuscript bearing the title "Carta de la Madre Juana Inés de la Cruz escrita al R.P.M. Antonio Núñez de la Compañía de Jesus" ("Letter from Sister Juana Inés de la Cruz Written to the R[everend] F[ather] M[aster] Antonio Núñez of the Society of Jesus"). The calligraphy is that of the early eighteenth century. Although the letter is undated—and the omission of the date on the part of the copyist is unusual—this circumstance does not suffice to call into question the document's authenticity.

I want to comment on the style and language of the letter. Sor Juana weaves long, sinuous sentences, studded with quotations and allusions, abounding in digressions and subordinate clauses. A love of undulations and convolutions, as well as of figures of logic and ratiocination, is typical not only of baroque prose but also of legal and theological literature. Sor Juana was an irrepressible reasoner, arguer, and debater. The style of the letter to Núñez de Miranda exemplifies these intellectual and stylistic tendencies. If the sentences are long, longer at times than those in the *Response to Sor Filotea de la Cruz,* they never offend syntax or logic. Similarly, although the letter is not as carefully phrased as the *Response,* I find nothing in the vocabulary that suggests a forgery. Throughout I recognize not only most of the themes that appear in the *Response* but many of the characteristic expressions of Sor Juana's prose as well, such as the use of "more" for "moreover." Is my judgment definitive? In these matters no judgment is definitive. I am speaking of my impressions and my opinions. All I can say is that the language and peculiarities of style are those of Sor Juana, or of someone who adopted her manner of writing and thinking. If the latter, why—for what reason?

At times the letter resembles a draft of the *Response to Sor Filotea de la Cruz.* At first I found these similarities suspicious: how could two texts separated by an interval of more than ten years be so much alike? My doubts were ill-founded. The continuity between the themes of the letter to Núñez de Miranda and those of the *Response* to the Bishop of Puebla is that of Sor Juana's very life. There is correspondence between the documents because, even though separated by ten years, they mark two stages of the same conflict. The document discovered by Tapia Méndez confirms that Sor Juana's difficulties with various dignitaries of the Church predated the affair of the *Carta atenagórica* (1690), and must have begun around 1680.

I have granted the presence of some careless phrasing. In one passage she writes, "The basis, then, for the anger of Y.R. . . . has been none other than those miserable verses granted me by Heaven so expressly against the will of Y.R." Obviously Heaven had endowed her not with the verses but with the faculty for composing them. The following phrase also amazes me: "I have extremely resisted in the writing of these . . ." There are two or three other solecisms. We can only suppose that we are reading a private, almost intimate, letter (or perhaps a draft of one), written with undisguised impatience and anger in reaction to the defamatory gossip of Father Núñez de Miranda.

The letter is a major find, not only because it is a previously unknown writing of Sor Juana's but because it has a biographical value comparable to that of the *Response to Sor Filotea de la Cruz.* First of all, it informs us about one of the decisive events of her life: the break with Núñez de Miranda. This is a subject about which the majority of her contemporaries kept silent, and about which we would have no information at all were it not for an indiscretion on the part of Oviedo, Father Núñez' biographer. Through the letter we learn that this truly major decision was made not by Núñez, as Oviedo reports, but by Sor Juana herself: "I beg of Y.R. that if you do not wish or find it in your heart to favor me (for that is voluntary) you think of me no more, for although I shall regret so great a loss, I shall utter no complaint, because God, Who created and redeemed me and Who has bestowed so many mercies upon me, will supply a remedy in order that my soul, awaiting His kindness, shall not be lost even though it lack the direction of Y.R., for He has made many keys to Heaven and has not confined Himself to a single criterion; rather, there are many mansions for people of as many different natures, and in the world there are many theologians, but were they lacking, salvation lies more in the desiring than in the knowing, and that will be more in me than in my confessor." These forthright words also shed light on the reasons for her having chosen, after the *theologian* Núñez de Miranda, the *contemplative* Arellano as her confessor: the "desiring" weighs more than the "knowing." Sor Juana continues: "What obligation is there that my salvation be effected through Y.R.? Can it not be through another? Is God's mercy restricted and limited to one man, even though he be as wise, as learned, and as saintly as Y.R.?" With a few phrases, unearthed three centuries after her death, Juana Inés de la Cruz demolishes an edifice of pious lies.

The letter, furthermore, gives explicit information about matters that previously had been the subject of mere conjecture. For example, speaking of the triumphal arch of 1680 (*Allegorical Neptune*), she corroborates what I had supposed: the commission from the Cabildo (the cathedral chapter) was arranged by the Viceroy-Archbishop Fray Payo de Ribera. Núñez de Miranda's involvement in Sor Juana's decision to enter the convent is known; in his biography of the Jesuit, Oviedo gives the impression that Núñez obtained the dowry (three thousand pesos). Sor Juana contradicts this: "In the matter of my dowry, long before I met Y.R., my godfather, Captain D. Pedro Velázquez de la Cadena, had arranged it." On the other hand, she adds, "I do not deny that I owe to Y.R. other affectionate acts and many kindnesses for which I shall be eternally grateful, such as that of paying for my instruction." Instruction in what? Probably theology. She rejects—spiritedly—the enforced saintliness Núñez has prescribed for her: "Am I perchance a heretic? And if I were, could I become saintly solely through coercion? Would it were so, and that saintliness were a thing that could be commanded, for if that were so, I should surely be saintly; but I judge that one is persuaded, not commanded." These expressions are more audacious than similar ones in the *Response*. The intimate nature of the letter excuses her frankness. Above all, one must remember that the letter to Núñez de Miranda was written at the time when she was in favor with the Countess de Paredes. She felt safe and secure.

Tapia Méndez' discovery, I repeat, is a major one. There are three points that I find essential. First, the letter confirms that the conflict that clouded the last years of Sor Juana's life was not the invention of liberal critics. Second, the cause of the conflict (at least the apparent cause: what do we know of the cabals that formed and dissolved inside the viceregal palace, the cloisters, and the sacristies?) was the contradiction the high prelates found between her situation as a nun and her literary aspirations. Added to this was their animosity toward women: the prelates shared the ideas of their time and could only view female excellence with hostility. The third point is perhaps the central one. All modern students of Sor Juana have believed that her break with Núñez de Miranda coincided with the crisis of 1690, that is, with the scandal provoked by the publication of her critique of Father Vieyra's sermon. In Chapter 27 of this book I ventured a different hypothesis: that Núñez de Miranda might have withdrawn his support years earlier. Sor Juana's letter has corroborated my supposition.

In his erudite and perceptive analysis of the letter, Father Tapia Méndez states its probable date of composition as 1681. My opinion is that it could be either 1681 or 1682. Sor Juana mentions some of her public writings, referring expressly to the arch, that is, the *Allegorical Neptune* (November 1680), and to two *loas* written for the birthday of the King, one commissioned by Fray Payo (before 1680) and another by the Countess de Paredes (which according to Méndez Plancarte should be dated November 6 of either 1681 or 1682). On the other hand, the letter does not mention the poetry competition sponsored by the university, in which Sor Juana received two prizes. Thus the letter was written before the competition. Actually there were two competitions: one in 1682 and the other in 1683. Sor Juana was awarded a prize in the second competition. It is reasonable to assume that the letter was written after November 6, 1681, and before 1683. The break with Núñez de Miranda lasted a little more than ten years. How was Sor Juana able for more than ten years to defy the powerful Núñez de Miranda? First of all, with the support of the viceregal palace. In addition, she took advantage of the rivalry among high dignitaries, and very probably was protected by the Bishop of Puebla until 1690.

The struggles and the last years of Juana Inés de la Cruz compose a dramatic chapter in the history of the conflict between intellectual freedom and authority, between the individual and ideological bureaucracies. The significance of this conflict has been obscured by the doctrinaire passion of various Catholic critics, some of them truly eminent, like Father Méndez Plancarte. Only now, at the end of a century that has known ideological persecutions on a scale greater than that suffered by Sor Juana, can we comprehend her life and her sacrifice. To comprehend is something more than to understand: it means to *embrace* in both the physical and the spiritual sense.

March 31, 1983   O.P.

～ THE LETTER

Letter from Sister Juana Inés de la Cruz
Written to the R[everend] F[ather] M[aster]
Antonio Núñez of the Society of Jesus

Pax Xpti [Peace in Christ]
For some time now various persons have informed me that I am singled out for censure in the conversations of Y[our] R[everence], in which you denounce my actions with such bitter exaggeration as to suggest a *public scandal,* and other no less shocking epithets. Although my conscience might move me to my own defense, for my good name is not mine alone but is linked with my lineage and with the community in which I live, nevertheless I have chosen to bear my suffering in view of the supreme veneration and filial affection that I have always felt toward Y.R., preferring that all your objections fall upon me rather than have it seem that I had crossed the line of what was proper or that I was lacking in respect in replying to Y.R.—in which I confess openly that I deserved no credit from God, for it was more human respect for your person than Christian patience. Not being unaware of the veneration and high esteem in which Y.R. (and justly so) is held by all, and that they listen to

you as if to a divine oracle and appreciate your words as if they were dictated by the Holy Ghost, and that the greater your authority, the more is my good name injured; with all this, I have never wished to yield to the entreaties made to me, I know not whether by my reason or my self-esteem (which at times beneath the mantle of reason sways us all), that I reply, judging that my silence might be the most delicate way in which the anger of Y.R. would be cooled; until with time I have come to realize that on the contrary it seems that my patience irritates you, and thus I determined to reply to Y.R., without impugning my love, my obligation, and my respect.

The basis, then, for the anger of Y.R. (most beloved Father and dear sir) has been none other than those miserable verses granted me by Heaven so expressly against the will of Y.R. I have extremely resisted in the writing of these and have excused myself in every possible way, not because in them I found a source of good or evil, for always I have held them (as they are) to be inconsequential, and although I might note how many holy and learned people have employed them, I do not wish to enter into their defense, for they are neither father nor mother to me; I say only that to please Y.R. I would cease to write them without seeking, or ascertaining, the reason for your abhorrence, for it is befitting love to obey blindly; in addition there was the natural repugnance I have always felt in writing them, as all those who know me can attest; but this was not possible to observe so rigorously that there were not some few exceptions, such as the two *villancicos* to the Most Blessed Virgin, which after repeated petitions and a lapse of eight years' time I wrote with the permission and license of Y.R., which I then held more necessary than that of His Excellency the Archbishop Viceroy, my Prelate, and in them I proceeded with such modesty that I did not allow my name to be put to the first and it was put to the second without my consent or my knowledge, and both were corrected beforehand by Y.R.

This was followed by the Arch for the Church. This is my unpardonable offense, which was preceded by my having been asked three or four times and my having as many refused, until two lay magistrates came who before calling upon me called first upon the Mother Prioress and then upon me, and commanded in the name of His Excellency the Archbishop that I do it because the full chapter had so voted and His Excellency approved.

Now it would be my wish that Y.R., with all the clarity of your judgment, put yourself in my place and consider what you would have replied in this situation. Would you answer that you could not? That would have been a lie. That you did not wish to? That would have been disobedience. That you did not know how? They did not ask more than I knew. That the vote was badly taken? That would have been impudent audacity, vile and gross ingratitude to those who honored me by believing that an ignorant woman knew how to do what such brilliant minds solicited. So I had no choice but to obey.

These are my published writings that have so scandalized the world, and so edified the good, and so we pass to the unpublished: there are scattered here and there a *copla* or two written for a birthday, in honor of some person I esteemed, and to whom I was indebted for assistance in my personal wants (which have not been few, being as I am so impoverished and without income). A *loa* for the birthday of Our Sovereign King written at the command of His Excellency Don Fray Payo himself, another by order of Her Excellency the Señora Countess de Paredes.

Well, now, my Father and dear sir, I beg of Y.R. to put aside for a moment your affectionate counsel (which sways even the most saintly) and tell me, Y.R. (since in your opinion it is a sin to write verses), on which of these occasions was the transgression of having written them so grave? For if it were an offense (for myself I do not know by what reason it could be called so), it was excused by the very circumstances and the requests in which I acted so against my will, and this is clearly proved, for as all know the facility I have, if to that were joined the motive of vanity (perhaps it is a motive of mortification), what greater punishment would Y.R. wish for me than that resulting from the very applause that confers such pain? Of what envy am I not the target? Of what malice am I not the object? What actions do I take without fear? What word do I speak without misgiving?

Women feel that men surpass them, and that I seem to place myself on a level with men; some wish that I did not know so much; others say that I ought to know more to merit such applause; elderly women do not wish that other women know more than they; young women, that others present a good appearance; and one and all wish me to conform to the rules of their judgment; so that from all sides comes such a singular martyrdom as I deem none other has ever experienced.

What else can I say or instance?—for even having a reasonably good handwriting has caused me worrisome and lengthy persecution, for no reason other than they said it looked like a man's writing, and that it was not proper, whereupon they forced me to deform it purposely, and of this the entire community is witness; all of which should not be the subject for a letter but for many copious volumes. Then again, what things have I said that are so blameworthy? Did I solicit the applause and public celebration? And the private favors and honors bestowed upon me by the Most Excellent Marquis and Marquise, only out of their deigning and their matchless humanity—did I seek them?

On the contrary, and Sister Juana de San Antonio, Prioress of this Convent and a person who would never lie, is witness to the fact that the first time Their Excellencies honored this house, I asked her permission to retire to my cell and not see them or be seen (as if Their Excellencies had harmed me in some way), with no other reason than to flee the applause that now is converted into such stinging thorns of persecution, and I would have done so had not the Mother Prioress forbidden it.

What fault was it of mine that Their Excellencies were pleased with me? And though there was no reason for their pleasure, could I deny such sovereign figures? Could I regret their honoring me with their visits?

Y.R. knows very well I could not, as you could not during the time of Their Excellencies the Marquis and Marquise de Mancera, for on many occasions I have heard Y.R. complain of the duties which attendance on Their Excellencies caused you to miss and yet you could not do otherwise; and if His Excellency the Sr. Marquis de Mancera at will entered convents as holy as those of the Capuchins and Teresians, and without anyone's considering it wicked, how should I deny that His Excellency the Sr. Marquis de la Laguna enter this one? More, I am not in charge and running the convent is not up to me.

Their Excellencies honor me because they please to, not because I am deserving, or because I first solicited it.

I cannot, nor would I wish to even if I could, be so boorishly ungrateful for the favors and affection (as undeserved as poorly returned) of Their Excellencies.

My studies have not been to the harm or detriment of any person, having been so extremely private that I have not even enjoyed the direction of a teacher, but have learned only from myself and my work, for I am not unaware that to study publicly in schools is not seemly for a woman's honor, because this gives occasion for familiarity with men, and is sufficient reason for barring them from public studies, and that if women may not challenge men in such studies as pertain to them alone, it is because the body politic, having no need of women for government by magistrates (from which service, for the same reason of honor, women are excluded) has not provided for them; but private and individual study, who has forbidden that to women? Like men, do they not have a rational soul? Why then shall they not enjoy the privilege of the enlightenment of letters? Is a woman's soul not as receptive to God's grace and glory as a man's? Then why is she not as able to receive learning and knowledge, which are the lesser gifts? What divine revelation, what regulation of the Church, what rule of reason framed for us such a severe law?

Are letters an obstacle or do they, rather, lead to salvation? Was not St. Augustine saved, St. Ambrose, and all the other Holy Doctors? And Y.R., with such learning, do you not plan to be saved?

And if you reply to me that a different order obtains for men, I say: did not St. Catherine study, St. Gertrude, my Mother St. Paula, without harm to her exalted contemplation, and was her pious founding of convents impeded by her knowing even Greek? Or learning Hebrew? Analyzing and comprehending the Holy Scriptures under the tutelage of my Father St. Jerome, as the Saint himself reports? Who also, in one of his epistles, praised the broad learning of her daughter, Blesilla, and at a very tender age, for she died at twenty?

Then why do you find wicked in me what in other women was good? Am I the only one whose salvation would be impeded by books?

If I have read the secular prophets and orators (an imprudence of which St. Jerome himself was guilty), I also read the Holy Doctors and Holy Scripture, besides which I cannot deny that I owe to the former innumerable riches and rules of sound living.

Because what Christian is not ashamed of being wrathful in view of the patience of a pagan Socrates? Who can be ambitious in view of the modesty of the Cynic Diogenes? Who does not praise God in the intelligence of Aristotle? And finally, what Catholic is not confounded when he contemplates the sum of moral virtues in all the heathen philosophers?

Why must it be wicked that the time I would otherwise pass in idle chatter before the grille, or in a cell gossiping about everything that happens outside and inside the house, or quarreling with a sister, or scolding a hapless servant, or wandering through all the world in my thoughts, be spent in study?

And all the more as God so inclined me, and I have not seen that it was against His most holy law nor contrary to the obligation of my state; I have this nature; if it is evil, I am the product of it; I was born with it and with it I shall die.

Y.R. wishes that I be coerced into salvation while ignorant, but, beloved Father, may I not be saved if I am learned? Ultimately that is for me the smoothest path. Why for one's salvation must one follow the path of ignorance if it is repugnant to one's nature?

Is not God, who is supreme goodness, also supreme wisdom? Then why would He find ignorance more acceptable than knowledge?

That St. Anthony was saved in his holy ignorance is well and good. St. Augustine chose the other path, and neither of them went astray.

What, then, is the source of your displeasure and of your saying "that had you known I was to write verses you would not have placed me in the convent but arranged my marriage"?

But, most beloved Father (only compelled and with diffidence do I utter what I would prefer not pass my lips), whence your direct authority (excepting what my love gave you and will give you always) to dispose of my person and the free will God granted me?

For when that happened I had only for a brief time had the good fortune to know Y.R., and although I owed to you the realization of many desires concerning my state, which I shall value always, as is only fitting, in the matter of my dowry, long before I met Y.R., my godfather, Captain D. Pedro Velázquez de la Cadena, had arranged it, and it was in his negotiating this endowment for me and in no other thing that God provided me the solution; so that such an assertion is baseless; although I do not deny that I owe to Y.R. other affectionate acts and many kindnesses for which I shall be eternally grateful, such as that of paying for my instruction, and other favors; but why, then, instead of continuing, have these favors turned into vituperation, and why is there no conversation in which my offenses are not mentioned and my conversation does not serve as the subject of your spiritual zeal?

Am I perchance a heretic? And if I were, could I become saintly solely through coercion? Would it were so, and that saintliness were a thing that could be commanded, for if that were so, I should surely be saintly; but I judge that one is persuaded, not commanded, and if by command, I have had Prelates to so command; but precepts and external coercion that make one circumspect and modest when they are moderate and prudent cause despair when they are too strong; only God's grace and assistance can make a saint.

What then is the cause of such anger? And of the injury to my reputation? Or holding me up as scandalous before everyone? Do I offend Y.R. in some manner? Have I asked you to assist me in my needs? Or have I disturbed you in any other spiritual or worldly matter?

Did my correction fall to Y.R. by reason of obligation, of relationship, upbringing, prelature, or other such thing?

If it is mere charity, let it be seen as mere charity and proceed as such, gently, for vexing me is not a good way to assure my submission, nor do I have so servile a nature that I do under threat what reason does not persuade me, nor out of respect for man what I do not do for God; and to deprive myself of all that can give me pleasure, though it be entirely licit, it is best that I do as self-mortification, when I wish to do penance, and not because Y.R. hopes to achieve it by means of censure, and then not given in secret with fatherly discretion (since Y.R. has set yourself to be my father, a thing in which I hold myself to be greatly blessed) but publicly before everyone, where each can think as he chooses and speak as he thinks.

Must I not regret this, Father, from one whom I love with such veneration and with such love revere and esteem?

If these reprimands were to fall upon some scandalous communication of mine, I am so docile (notwithstanding that neither in my worldly nor in my spiritual writings have I been directed by Y.R.) that I would set it aside and attempt to better my ways to satisfy you, even though it were not to my liking.

But if you are censuring only my gainsaying an opinion by stating, in substance, that it amounts to the same whether I write verses or not, and if I abhor them so that there would be no penance greater than always to be writing them, whence your displeasure?

Because if in gainsaying an opinion I were to speak passionately against Y.R. as Y.R. speaks against me, innumerable times your words have been exceedingly repugnant to me (because after all, views on minor matters are *alius sic, et alius sic* [a matter of opinion]); yet I do not for that reason condemn them but, rather, venerate them as yours and defend them as my own, even perhaps those directed against myself, calling them kind solicitude, extreme affection, and other terms that are prompted by my love and reverence when I speak with others.

But to Y.R. I cannot fail to say that by now my breast is overflowing with the complaints that over the course of the years I could have spoken, and that as I take up my pen to state them, rebutting one I venerate so highly, it is because I can stand no more and, as I am not as humbled as other daughters in whom your instruction would be better employed, I am too sorely tried.

And thus I beg of Y.R. that if you do not wish or find it in your heart to favor me (for that is voluntary) you think of me no more, for although I shall regret so great a loss, I shall utter no complaint, because God, Who created and redeemed me and Who has bestowed so many mercies upon me, will supply a remedy in order that my soul, awaiting His kindness, shall not be lost even though it lack the direction of Y.R., for He has made many keys to Heaven and has not confined Himself to a single criterion; rather, there are many mansions for people of as many different natures, and in the world there are many theologians, but were they lacking, salvation lies more in the desiring than in the knowing, and that will be more in me than in my confessor.

What obligation is there that my salvation be effected through Y.R.? Can it not be through another? Is God's mercy restricted and limited to one man, even though he be as wise, as learned, and as saintly as Y.R.?

Surely not, nor up to now have I received special light or inspiration from God that He so orders; I shall therefore be able to govern myself by the general rules of the Holy Mother Church, until God enlightens me to do otherwise, and choose freely the spiritual Father that I wish; for if, as Our Father inclined my wishes to Y.R. with so great a love, He had also allowed me my choice, it would have been no other than Y.R., whom I beg not to regard this candor as boldness, nor as lessening of respect, but as simplicity of heart that does not allow me to say things except as I feel them; rather, I have attempted to speak in a manner that cannot leave Y.R. any trace of resentment or complaint; nevertheless, if in this exposition of my faults there were any word written through culpable inattention that might seem to show a wish to offend or even be disrespectful of the person of Y.R., I of course retract it, and I hold it badly said and worse written, and would of course erase it, if I knew which it was.

I reiterate that my intention is only to beg of Y.R. that if you do not wish to favor me, you not think of me, unless it be to commend me to God, which I believe in your great charity you will do with all fervor.

I ask that His Majesty keep Y.R., as is my wish.

From the convent of my Father St. Jerome, Mexico City.

Your

Juana Inés de la Cruz

Notes on Sources

Biographical Studies

The first biography of Sor Juana was the narrative of Father Diego Calleja, published in 1700 as a preface to her posthumous works. In Calleja's pious and edifying account, the career of Juana Inés is the saga of a gradual ascent toward saintliness. A majority of the Catholic scholars who have written on Sor Juana's life have followed Calleja's example. Among them are Father Alfonso Méndez Plancarte, to whom we are indebted for what is still the standard edition of her works, and Albert G. Salceda, who ably completed the edition; also Robert Ricard, who wrote perceptively on her poem *First Dream*. The passion for edification blinded them. The same can be said of Ezequiel A. Chávez. Another critic, Genaro Fernández McGregor, maintained that Núñez de Miranda, Sor Juana's confessor, was wiser, more generous, more upright than she: a saint. Fortunately, he says, Núñez de Miranda's superior qualities finally prevailed; Sor Juana renounced writing and she, too, undertook the path toward saintliness. If these points of view had triumphed, the real Sor Juana would have been forever hidden.

A perceptive and intelligent woman named Dorothy Schons opened the way to critical biography. Her research was sound and honest. In 1926 she published an essay which was the first reasoned inquiry into the three principal mysteries in Sor Juana's life: Why did she take the veil? What was her real name, Juana Ramírez or Juana de Asbaje? Why, at the height of her fame and intellectual maturity, did she renounce literature?[1] In a later essay[2] she showed, beyond a shadow of a doubt, that Sor Juana's difficulties with the Archbishop Aguiar y Seijas and various Jesuits were not imaginary but very real. Although Pedro Henríquez Ureña compiled the first bibliography of Sor Juana (1917), it was Dorothy Schons who took the definitive step with her article "Some Bibliographical Notes on Sor Juana Inés de la Cruz."[3] Ermilo Abreu Gómez followed her lead; we owe to him not only the first critical editions but also two works of basic research: *Iconografía de Sor Juana Inés de la Cruz*[4] and *Sor Juana Inés de la Cruz, Biografía y biblioteca.*[5]

Schons broke new ground in attempting to place the life and work of Sor Juana within the context of the seventeenth-century society of New Spain. This American scholar tried to understand Sor Juana's feminism as a reaction to Hispanic society, its extreme misogyny, and its closed masculine universe. She was the first to show that the final conflict of Sor Juana's life, which ended in her defeat, was an episode in the history of ideas—the history of freedom, I would say—not without analogies to the confrontation between Pascal and the Jesuit Order. Unfortunately, Dorothy Schons did not gather her observations, scattered in several articles, into a book. Ermilo Abreu Gómez attempted to continue the line of her research, but his interpretations were schematic and biased.

A far cry from Dorothy Schons's work was a ponderous volume by Ludwig Pfandl,[6] ponderous both literally and figuratively. Despite his exaggerations and one-sided conclusions, the German professor makes a plausible observation: I am referring to Sor Juana's narcissism, which he relates to masculine tendencies. Pfandl was not the first to broach this subject. Sor Juana herself hints at it in several poems and in the *Response*, and other scholars had taken it up before Pfandl.[7] It is only fair to say that no one previously had written a study as detailed as his, although one might add that it is this very excess in arguing his case that leaves him open to criticism. Pfandl's point of departure was the idea—current in his time, especially in Germany—of fixed, immutable biological types. The ideal female type was full-bodied, Aryan, blonde, with strong maternal instincts and no pretension to intelligence or inclination to study. Pfandl identified intellectual pursuits with masculinity and saw Sor Juana's devotion to books and writing as a sign of sexual aberration. Unlike other writers who had referred to her narcissism and her masculine tendencies, Pfandl was blind to the fact that there are no pure types and that most humans are bisexual to a greater or lesser degree. He so overstated his argument—bolstering it with voluminous pseudomedical erudition (he was not a psychiatrist)—as to turn psychological analysis into caricature. I do not believe that Sor Juana's personality fits Pfandl's textbook description; it seems to me that her so-called masculinity was more psychological than biological and more social than psychological.

Obsessed by the neurotic aspects of Sor Juana's personality, Pfandl ignored nearly all the social and historical circumstances surrounding her. Through several hundred pages he turns again and again to Sor Juana's psychic and physiological conflicts, from infantile penis envy to the disorders of menopause, but he overlooks one circumstance that was no less determining than psychology and physiology: the masculine character of the culture and world in which Sor Juana lived. How, in a civilization of men and for men, could a woman gain access to learning without becoming masculinized? Pfandl failed to see that in individual destinies the influence of social and cultural conditions is no less powerful than psychic and physiological predisposition. Pfandl's book is inadequate on another level: he did not write a concrete study of Juana Inés; he limited himself to applying the etiology of others to her case. His method was deductive and based almost entirely on analogy. If a biographer is hampered by an absence of documents, he must content himself with hypotheses. That is what Pfandl did not do: he produced a handful of affirmations and set them forth with an air of triumph. Strange as it may seem, he was not really interested either in the flesh-and-blood Juana Inés or in the historical and social figure. He simply applied the schemata of psychoanalysis—of the Jungian more than the Freudian variety—to the nun's biography and to her works. Occasionally the theoretical model coincides with the facts and illuminates them; more frequently it obscures them.

At certain moments Pfandl's method verges on the inadvertently comic. In the *Response* Sor Juana speaks of the kitchen and of cooking eggs; the German professor gravely reminds us of the symbolic function of the egg in the *Rig Veda* and the Sioux epic, in Orphic philosophy and among the Gnostics. ("In the universe the sky occupies the place of the white in the original egg.") One of the *topoi* of the poetry of her time, the owl Nyctimene, thief of oil (mentioned in *First Dream*), is transformed into evidence of the nun's incestuous feelings. Bent on deciphering the latent content of Sor Juana's writings, Pfandl did not notice that almost always the manifest meaning is the richer and more vivid. Thus he converted extraordinary texts like *The Divine Narcissus* and *First*

Dream into tedious repertories of the commonplaces of psychoanalysis. It may be that the speculations of Descartes or the tragedies of Racine are masks for the pleasure or nirvana principle. No matter; these works exalt and beguile us in themselves.

On the subject of Sor Juana's capitulation in her final years, Pfandl writes with astounding assurance that "the enigma is resolved": she was the victim of psychosomatic disturbance. A neurotic constitution, menopause, and, as a determining external cause, the extreme emotions prompted by the Jubilee of 1694 explain her great change. In contrast to Pfandl's conception of the ideal woman, poor Sor Juana was brunette and bisexual; her case was aggravated by asthenia and thinness of physique (the portraits indicate the opposite). The clinical portrait is completed with her immoderate tendency to brood, her masculinity, her narcissism, and the fact that she "must have suffered the most severe and excruciating climacteric known." Her "manic-depressive disposition," a consequence of all these factors, overwhelmed her during the Jubilee of 1694; this external event released her masochistic tendencies.

One cannot read Pfandl's lengthy description without being struck by the rashness of the claims and the brashness of the conclusions. Of course Sor Juana was bisexual, but what does that say? All but a handful of humanity is bisexual. Furthermore, any somatic masculinity in her case is pure fantasy: look at her portraits. Neither is it psychological: read what she wrote. Her masculinity—if we can even use that word to describe her—was neither physical nor psychic but, rather, a response to a societal prohibition that made it impossible for her to study, attend the University, or lead the retired and solitary life of a scholar. This was, without doubt, the basis of her lifelong conflict, as we have seen. I further argue that what is surprising in her poetry is precisely the keen awareness of her femininity, which can range from coquetry to melancholy or take the form of a defiant challenge to men. Thus it would be more exact to speak of erotic ambiguity, which is not the same as bisexuality. This is a subject I have discussed at length in various chapters of this book, especially those dedicated to the poems of loving friendship for María Luisa Manrique de Lara. But even those inflamed poems cannot be described as Sapphic, except in the sublimated sense of the Renaissance Platonic tradition.

As for brooding: it is not a cause of melancholy, as Pfandl seems to believe, but an effect. Certain traces of the melancholic temperament are clearly visible in Sor Juana; so are certain narcissistic traits. The close connection between melancholy and narcissism has been pointed out any number of times. The differences, nevertheless, are so profound as to suggest they may be opposing tendencies. The melancholic is not in love with himself but with someone who is absent; this is why Freud associated melancholy with mourning. The melancholic believes, furthermore, that he is responsible for the absence of the beloved, hence the unrelenting accusations he directs against himself. The narcissist, in love with himself and his unattainable (but not absent) image, suffers from an incapacity to love another being. He cannot objectify his desire. Clearly, in Sor Juana melancholy dominates over narcissism. Finally, neither melancholic nor narcissistic traits—separately or in combination—made Sor Juana a manic-depressive, as the German professor proposes. A neurotic? In the clinical sense of the word, no. Repressed and conflicting tendencies waged war within her, as in all of us, but in spite of her inhibitions she was able to live a relatively full life: not only was she actively involved in practical affairs—administering the convent's finances, overseeing the work of building and reconstruction, and shrewdly managing her own small fortune—she also wrote constantly, leaving an admirable body of work. She transformed her tendencies and impulses into actions and poems.

It scarcely seems necessary to mention the factor that Pfandl believed triggered her crisis: her menopause. First, because we have no idea at what age Sor Juana experienced the climacteric: in 1693 she was forty-five, and the age of menopause varies from woman to woman. Second, because the effects of the climacteric are not as severe as Pfandl describes them and, what is more important, they are stronger in married women and women with an active sexual life, which was not the case with Juana Inés. To believe that the Jubilee was the external factor that brought on the double crisis—manic depression and menopause—is arbitrary at best. The date must have been a significant one for Sor Juana, and—in accordance with the spirit of the times—a symbolic one for her spiritual director. We must not, however, overlook the surrounding circumstances: the admonitions of Fernández de Santa Cruz; the *Response;* Núñez de Miranda's withdrawal; the publication of the belligerent second volume of the *Obras* and the composition of the even more belligerent *villancicos* to Saint Catherine; the riots of June 1692; the Viceroy's loss of influence and the resulting elevation of Aguiar y Seijas; the sudden death of the Marquis de la Laguna; and the return of Núñez de Miranda.

What is truly eccentric in Pfandl's interpretation (others have followed his lead) is the energy it expends on Sor Juana's supposed instability while failing to devote a single line to the mental problems of the three prelates who censured her. Fernández de Santa Cruz's now-sugary, now-sadistic letters to the nuns of Puebla are filled with disquieting expressions that combine the fragrance of incense with the stench of the sewer. In Núñez de Miranda's notes his self-contempt over his eternal defeat in his battle with pride knows no bounds: "I am a sack of corruption, stinking and abominable, and what is worse is that, knowing this, I am not humble." On one occasion, when removing lice from another priest's cassock, he said, "See this, my brother, our harvest: lice, corruption, and stench—yet we are filled with vanity." As for Aguiar y Seijas, I need not recall his obsessions and manias, his hatred of women and his pathological charity. The lives of these prelates are not examples of "normality"; not one of them can be termed a well-balanced man. But no one dwells on their lunacies—only on Sor Juana's neuroses. A curious blindness. To my mind, the fact that Juana Inés was able to resist so long, that only at the end of the siege did she abdicate and follow her critics in their inhuman mortifications, is glorious proof of her spiritual fortitude.

In an essay first published in 1951 (translated, with other essays, in *The Siren and the Seashell,* 1976), I suggested that Sor Juana's personal crisis at the end of her life could be explained only within the context of the broader crisis of New Spain in the late seventeenth century. No one took my reflections seriously until 1967, when the Italian Hispanist Dario Puccini published a study of Sor Juana.[8] In the opening pages of his small and valuable book he referred to my observation and developed it with insight and learning, offering a new hypothesis. I have benefited from his interpretation and in Chapter 25 have discussed it in some detail. Other works relating to Sor Juana's life are referred to in the notes.

Editions

In her *Response* to the Bishop of Puebla, Sor Juana alleges that she has never given permission for the publication of her writings; through no fault of hers, others have taken the liberty of printing her poems and attaching her name to them, without her consent. It is a disclaimer that no one close to her could take very seriously, and is belied by what we know of her life—the endless exchange of letters with acquaintances of a literary bent, the gatherings in the locutory of the convent, the poems in homage to writers and intellectuals. She lived immersed in the business and busyness of literature. It was not for nothing that her last book was entitled *Fame:* she sought it and she achieved it. Nevertheless, taken out of context, this statement in the *Response* has served to portray her as an exemplar of modesty, indifferent to worldly acclaim. The Argentine critic Juan Carlos Merlo, in his otherwise judicious introduction to his anthology of her works, maintained, "The circumstances surrounding the publication of the first volume of her works are a clear testimony that she never wrote with a desire to have her writing in print." The circumstances, it seems to me, point in the opposite direction. She gathered her poems together, had them copied, sent them to Spain, and composed a prologue in verse for the volume. The texts that make up the second volume of her works were similarly gathered, copied, and sent to Spain. On that occasion, by way of a prologue she wrote several pages in prose dedicating the book to her sponsor, Juan de Orve y Arbieto. Unlike Góngora and others, she was fortunate enough to see most of her writing, including much of the best of it, published in her lifetime, thanks to her own efforts and those of the Countess de Paredes.

Editions of her poems appeared very early, starting with the first *villancicos* in 1676 and continuing at intervals until 1691. The first volume of her works, *Inundación castálida de la única poetisa, musa décima* . . . , is dated 1689. Even in that hyperbolic century it must have seemed excessive to describe the inspiration of a nun from across the seas as an inundation from the Castalian spring; this is undoubtedly why the phrase did not appear in subsequent editions. On the other hand, in the second edition (1690) a word was added that was retained: . . . *única poetisa* AMERICANA, *musa décima.* Sor Juana's editors in Madrid were probably unaware that forty years earlier, in 1650, other publishers, Protestants and Londoners, had used the appellation "Tenth Muse" for a different poet who was also American and also unique, Anne Bradstreet (1612–1672). The book by this poet—a Puritan, a transatlantic disciple of the Huguenot Du Bartas, wife of the governor of Massachusetts and mother of eight children—was published with a title that rivals Sor Juana's: *The Tenth Muse, Lately Sprung Up in America, or Several Poems, compiled with Great Variety of Wit and Learning* . . . "Tenth Muse" is an expression that appears in an epigram by Plato, referring to Sappho, in the *Palatine Anthology.* Editions of Sor Juana's first volume came out in rapid succession; according to Ermilo Abreu

Gómez there were nine in all. In 1692 the second volume was published in Seville; this one, and also the third (*Fama y obras póstumas*, Madrid, 1700), appeared in five successive editions. Few modern poets have had so many editions of their work published in so short a time. In 1725 the three volumes were reissued for the last time. Then there was nothing—until late in the nineteenth century.

The first modern edition is not Mexican but Ecuadorian: *Obras selectas de la célebre monja de México, Sor Juana Inés de la Cruz (Selected Works of the Celebrated Nun of Mexico . . .* , Quito, 1873), with a prologue by Juan León Mera. This was the beginning of what could be called, without exaggeration, the revival of Sor Juana. It is significant that this first recognition came from someone other than a Mexican writer. And the first essay of significance was written not by a Mexican but by the well-known Spanish literary historian and critic Marcelino Menéndez Pelayo. This is a pattern that is repeated again and again in the literary history of Mexico. A South American, the poet and critic Juan María Gutiérrez, published an extensive study of Sor Juana in three issues of *Correo del Domingo* (Buenos Aires, March and April 1865), followed by an anthology. Finally in Mexico, just before the turn of the century and during the next few decades, some studies and anthologies began to appear. The first worthy of mention is Manuel Toussaint's *Obras escogidas (Selected Works*, 1929). Two years earlier Toussaint had made a major contribution by publishing *Poemas inéditos, desconocidos y muy raros de Sor Juana Inés de la Cruz (Unpublished, Unknown, and Very Rare Poems . . .*). It was in those years that Ermilo Abreu Gómez began his labors. It has been said that his work was undisciplined and careless; it must also be said that he was the founder of modern studies of Sor Juana. In addition to his *Bibliografía y biblioteca* and *Iconografía* (both 1934), we owe to him the first modern editions of *First Dream* (1928), the *Response to Sor Filotea de la Cruz* (1930), and the *Carta atenagórica* (1936). During this same time, Sor Juana was being read by the poets of the Mexican "Contemporáneos" group, a reading that was reflected especially in the *conceptista* sonnets of Jorge Cuesta. The poet Xavier Villaurrutia published her *Sonetos* in 1931 and, in 1940, her *Endechas*. In 1941 Karl Vossler, who had already published a seminal essay on Sor Juana's work, translated *First Dream* into German, with an introduction, notes, and a prose redaction.

All these efforts prepared the way for the excellent edition of Alfonso Méndez Plancarte. In 1951 he published his edition of *El Sueño (First*

Dream), with an introduction, notes, and a new prose version; then, from 1951 to 1957, came the four volumes of the *Obras completas*. The first three (*Lírica personal*, 1951; *Villancicos y letras sacras*, 1952; *Autos y loas*, 1955) are the work of Méndez Plancarte; the fourth (*Comedias, sainetes y prosa*, 1957) is that of his friend and disciple Albert G. Salceda. Without exaggeration, Antonio Alatorre writes, "The edition by Méndez Plancarte is truly exemplary. No Spanish poet of the Golden Age has received a similar tribute." Little can be added to his judgment. For myself, I can say that without the versions of the texts established by Méndez Plancarte, without his erudite and intelligent notes, without his learning and his sensitivity, I would not have been able to write this book. I am obliged to add, nevertheless, that anyone consulting the *Obras completas* must read the historical and biographical discussions with caution. Méndez Plancarte, an incomparable guide in literary matters, was at the same time a doctrinaire who, *ad maiorem Dei gloriam*, did not hesitate to conceal a fact or weave a pious lie.

Two other editions in Spanish deserve to be mentioned. In 1953 Juan Carlos Merlo published in Buenos Aires a critical edition of *First Dream* with a prose summary inspired by those of Vossler and Méndez Plancarte. In 1976 there appeared, in Barcelona, an excellent *Antología de Sor Juana Inés de la Cruz*, edited by Georgina Sabat de Rivers and Elias L. Rivers. The introduction is one of the best modern studies of Sor Juana's work, and the book contains a new prose version of *First Dream*.

Spanish Literary Terms

Advertencia : a foreword, prologue, or explanatory note.

Aprobación : ecclesiastical license to print or perform; imprimatur.

Arte mayor : the principal meter of fifteenth-century Spanish courtly poetry; characteristically a twelve-syllable line divided into two hemistichs.

Auto sacramental : an allegorical or religious play.

Baile : a poetic form based on a dance rhythm; also a very brief dramatic work combining words, pantomime, and music, generally staged between the first and second acts of a play.

Cantiga de estribillo : an ancient Castilian / Galician-Portuguese song; a forerunner of the *villancico*.

Censura : ecclesiastical approval during the time of the Inquisition.

Conceptista : a practitioner or adherent of *conceptismo*.

Conceptismo : a literary style prevalent in seventeenth-century Spain, characterized by its reliance on the conceit, on wit, on cleverness and word play.

Copla : a term with various meanings including couplet, line, and stanza, and, in the plural, ballad and popular song.

Cosante : a Castilian / Galician-Portuguese verse form based on a series of couplets in which each new couplet picks up part of the sense of the previous one and adds some new thought.

Culteranismo : a seventeenth-century Spanish literary style reliant on learned allusion, euphemism, preciosity.

Décima : a stanza form of ten octosyllabic lines, with a pause after the fourth.

Eco : a stanza or series of lines in which the end-rhyme of certain lines is repeated, as if by an echo.

Endecha : quatrain of five-, six-, or seven-syllable lines with assonant rhyme in the even-numbered lines.

Endecha real : quatrain of three seven-syllable lines and one eleven-syllable line, with assonant rhyme in the even-numbered lines.

Ensalada [literally, salad]: poem with a mixture of meters and rhyme schemes.

Entremés : a short one-act play performed between the acts of a full-length play.

Epinicio : a triumphal ode honoring a victory.

Estribillo : a refrain; usually an introductory stanza repeated, totally or partially, following each subsequent stanza.

Gaita gallega : a sprightly Galician rhythm used in Spanish popular verse.

Glosa : poem formed with an initial statement of a theme and a series of stanzas that expand on the theme and usually repeat one or more lines of the text being glossed.

Jácara : an irreverent and ribald ballad.

Laberinto : a poetic palindrome.

Letrilla : a usually light poem generally written in short lines, often with a refrain.

Lira : a rhymed stanza of four to six lines, combining lines of seven and eleven syllables.

Loa : a brief theatrical piece played as prologue to a principal play, often in praise of visiting or newly arrived dignitaries or for royal anniversaries.

Modernismo : Spanish American literary movement beginning in the 1880s, influenced by French symbolists and Parnassians but American in essence. Its most famous figure was Rubén Darío of Nicaragua (1867–1916).

Octava real : stanza of eight eleven-syllable lines, rhyming *a b a b a b c c*, used in Spanish epic poetry.

Ovillejo : a complicated stanza form consisting mainly of rhymed couplets, with shorter lines interspersed among longer ones.

Pie quebrado : octosyllabic verses with one or more lines of each stanza "broken" or shortened, generally to four syllables.

Redondillas : stanzas of four lines rhyming *a b b a*.

Romance : the Spanish ballad, in octosyllabic meter with alternate assonant rhyme; generally narrative in content.

Sainete : a lighthearted one-act play.

Seguidilla : a popular four-line stanza with a mixture of seven- and five-syllable lines in assonant rhyme.

Silva : a poem mixing seven- and eleven-syllable lines with no set rhyme scheme or stanza length.

Tocotín : an Indian-style dance form.

Ultraísmo : an avant-garde Hispanic literary movement that flourished briefly after World War I.

Villancico [from *villano,* peasant] : originally a poem in short lines in the manner of the songs sung by peasants; in Sor Juana's time, one of a sequence of lyrics composed to be sung at matins on a religious holiday.

Zarzuela : a light musical dramatic performance.

Notes

1. A Unique Society

1. *La supervivencia política novohispana: Reflexiones sobre el monarquismo mexicano* (Mexico City: Fundación Cultural de Condumex, Centro de Estudios de Historia de México, 1969).

2. *Historia de la revolución de Nueva España, antiguamente Anáhuac* (London: G. Glindon, 1813). Fray Servando (1763–1822) claimed that Quetzalcoatl was in fact St. Thomas; America, consequently, owed nothing to Spain, not even Christianity. The Dominican was exiled to Spain for this revolutionary position.

3. "The Heritage of Latin America," in *The Founding of New Societies,* ed. Louis Hartz (New York: Harcourt, Brace and World, 1964).

4. Max Weber, *Economy and Society: An Outline of Interpretive Sociology* (Berkeley: University of California Press, 1978). Originally published as *Wirtschaft und Gesellschaft* (Tübingen: J. C. B. Mohr, 1922).

5. All poem numbers are those assigned by Alfonso Méndez Plancarte (for volume 4, by Alberto G. Salceda) in his edition of Sor Juana's *Obras completas* (*Complete Works*).

6. Ignacio Rubio Mañé, *Introducción al estudio de los virreyes de Nueva España, 1535–1746,* vol. 1, *Orígenes, jurisdicciones y dinámica social* (Mexico City: Ediciones Selectas, 1955; reprinted by Fondo de Cultura Económica, 1982).

7. Ibid. See especially chap. 6, "El virrey como presidente de la Audiencia."

2. The Dais and the Pulpit

1. *Baroque Times in Old Mexico* (Ann Arbor: University of Michigan Press, 1959), p. 160. (The Marquis de la Laguna governed for six, not three, years.—O.P.)

2. *The Court Society,* trans. Edmund Jephcott (Oxford: Blackwell, 1983). Originally published as *Die höfische Gesellschaft* (Neuwied: Luchterhand, 1969).

3. In *The Founding of New Societies,* ed. Louis Hartz, p. 151.

4. *Über den Prozess der Zivilisation* (Bern: Francke, 1969).

5. J. Corominas, *Diccionario crítico etimológico de la lengua castellana* (Bern: Francke, 1954).

6. Suárez (1548–1617) was a Spanish Jesuit philosopher-theologian of the Scholastic school.

7. *Quetzalcoatl and Guadalupe,* trans. Benjamin Keen, foreword by Octavio Paz (Chicago: University of Chicago Press, 1976). Originally published as *Quetzalcóatl et Guadalupe* (Paris: Gallimard, 1974).

3. Syncretism and Empire

1. Fray Bernardino de Sahagún (1500?–90) was a Franciscan friar who recorded much of our extant information on Aztec culture.

2. Lafaye, *Quetzalcoatl and Guadalupe.*

3. Sigüenza y Góngora (1645–1700) was a Mexican mathematician, astrologer, humanist, and writer.

4. Lafaye, *Quetzalcoatl and Guadalupe.*

5. D. P. Walker, *The Ancient Theology* (Ithaca, N.Y.: Cornell University Press, 1972), p. 197. In Jonathan D. Spence's selection of the texts of K'ang Hsi (*Emperor of China: Self-Portrait of K'ang Hsi* [New York: Knopf, 1974]), one may glimpse the cat-and-mouse game the Chinese monarch played with the Jesuits and their enemy, the papal ambassador. Finally, I call attention to Etiemble's book *Les Jésuites en Chine* (Paris: R. Julliard, 1976).

6. See the studies on hermeticism by Frances A. Yates, especially *Giordano Bruno and the Hermetic Tradition* (London: Routledge and Kegan Paul, 1964) and *The Rosicrucian Enlightenment* (London: Routledge and Kegan Paul, 1972).

7. See my *Children of the Mire,* trans. Rachel Phillips (Cambridge, Mass.: Harvard University Press, 1974). Also published as *Los hijos del limo* (Barcelona: Seix Barral, 1974).

8. Lafaye, *Quetzalcoatl and Guadalupe.*

9. See Irving A. Leonard, *Don Carlos de Sigüenza y Góngora, a Mexican*

Savant of the Seventeenth Century (Berkeley: University of California Press, 1929).

4. A Transplanted Literature

1. Leonard, *Baroque Times.*
2. Juan de Torquemada (1557–1664), historiographer, author of *Monar-quía indiana.*
3. Alva Ixtlilxóchitl (1568–1648), the great-grandson of the Emperor of the Chichimecs, was called the "Livy of Anáhuac" by the historian Prescott.
4. Mexico City: Ediciones de la Universidad Autónoma, 1942–1945, 3 vols.: *Primer siglo, 1521–1621* (1942); *Segundo siglo, 1621–1721, I* (1944); *Segundo siglo, 1621–1721, II* (1945).
5. *European Literature and the Latin Middle Ages,* trans. Willard Trask (New York: Harper and Row, 1963). Originally published as *Europäische Literatur und lateinisches Mittelalter* (Bern: Francke, 1948).
6. Frank Warnke, *Versions of Baroque: European Literature in the Seventeenth Century* (New Haven: Yale University Press, 1968).
7. *Idea: A Concept in Art Theory,* trans. Joseph J. S. Peake (Columbia: University of South Carolina Press, 1968), p. 71. Panofsky is referring to theories about art during the second half of the sixteenth century in Italy, but his observation is perfectly applicable to poetry.
8. *Der gegenwärtige Stand der romanistischen Barockforschung* (Munich: Verlag der Bayerischen Akademie der Wissenschaften, 1961).
9. *The Baroque Poem* (New York: Dutton, 1974).
10. John Shearman, *Mannerism* (London: Penguin, 1967).
11. See Alfonso Méndez Plancarte's *Poetas novohispanos, 1621–1721,* vols. 2 and 3.
12. *Obras,* ed. José Pascual Buxó (Mexico City: Fondo de Cultura Económica, 1986).
13. An example of *ecos* given by Leonard, "si el alto Apolo la s*agrada agrada* . . . mid*a* / de veloz tiempo en la jorn*ada nada,*" can be translated roughly as follows: "if lofty Apollo is *plea*sed by holy *pleas* . . . / in day's swift time no mea*sure* may be *sure.*" An example of the word play called *paranomasías* is, in Spanish, "el inglés con fr*ascos frescos* / ebrio con su b*aba, beba* / y haga de la g*ula, gala* / que con él se tr*ata, treta*"; in English, "the Englishman does b*attle* with b*ottle,* / does d*rip* and d*rool,* and d*runk,* does d*rink,* / of rage and r*amp* he would make r*omp:* / for fools will r*ise* to any r*use.*"—*Translator's note.*
14. A reply by a Portuguese nun, Sor Margarita Ignacia, the *Apologia a favor do R. P. Vieyra,* came too late; it was published in Lisbon in 1727. This

rebuttal was actually the work of Margarita Ignacia's brother, the priest Luis Gonçalves Pinheiro. (See Robert Ricard, "Antonio Vieyra y Sor Juana Inés de la Cruz," *Revista de Indias,* 10 [April 1951].)

5. The Ramírez Family

1. *Poesías completas,* compilation and prologue by Ermilo Abreu Gómez (Mexico City: Ediciones Botas, 1940).

2. A series of laws prohibiting communal ownership of property. The Indian tradition of the *ejido* was affected, as well as the Church and religious orders; the effect of the laws was to diminish the wealth of the Church and disband communities of monks and nuns.

3. Guillermo Ramírez España, *La familia de Sor Juana* (Mexico City: Imprenta Universitaria, 1947); Enrique A. Cervantes, *El testamento de Sor Juana Inés de la Cruz y otros documentos* (Mexico City: n.p., 1949). The research of these two scholars—Ramírez España is a distant kinsman of Sor Juana's—has been very fruitful in this area. Thanks to their findings, we now have a clearer idea of her origin and of the position of her family.

4. This is probably the same person Dorothy Schons mentions in her study *Algunos parientes de Sor Juana* (Mexico City: Imprenta Mundial, 1934). Also see Alberto G. Salceda, "El acta de bautismo de sor Juana," *Abside,* January–March 1952.

5. English translations of many of Sor Juana's poems are (with minor changes) from *Sor Juana Inés de la Cruz: Poems,* ed. and trans. Margaret Sayers Peden (Binghamton: Bilingual Press, 1985).

6. Schons, *Algunos parientes.*

7. Cervantes, *El testamento de sor Juana Inés.*

8. Ramírez España, *La familia de Sor Juana.*

9. Cervantes, *El testamento de sor Juana Inés.*

10. Their two daughters, Antonia and Inés, were born in 1658 and 1659, if we accept document IV in Enrique A. Cervantes' *Petición de Antonia e Inés Ruiz, primas hermanas* [sic] *de Sor Juana Inés de la Cruz, para ingresar en el convento de San Jerónimo, 15 de diciembre de 1672.* It is significant that her father placed them in the care of Sor Juana Inés de la Cruz in order to "remove them from the perils of the lay world." Were Ruiz Lozano and Isabel Ramírez already separated by this date? We know that Don Diego later married Doña Catalina Maldonado Zapata.

11. Leonard, *Baroque Times,* quoting Agustín de Vetancourt. A liquid *arroba* is 2.6 to 3.6 gallons.

12. Paz, *Conjunctions and Disjunctions,* trans. Helen R. Lane (New York:

Viking, 1974). Originally published as *Conjunciones y disyunciones* (Mexico City: Joaquín Mortiz, 1969).

13. Dorothy Schons, "Some Obscure Points in the Life of Sor Juana Inés de la Cruz," *Modern Philology*, 24 (Nov. 1926).

6. *May Syllables Be Composed by the Stars*

1. Translations of quotations from the *Response to Sor Filotea* are (with minor changes) from *A Woman of Genius: The Intellectual Autobiography of Sor Juana Inés de la Cruz,* trans. Margaret Sayers Peden (Salisbury, Conn.: Lime Rock Press, 1982).

2. A simple calculation justifies my hypothesis: Diego, the oldest child of Ruiz Lozano, must have been about eight years younger than Sor Juana, since the sister who followed him, Antonia, was ten years younger than she. So he was probably born in 1656, that is, the year Juana Inés' grandfather died and she was sent to Mexico City to live with the Matas. Antonia was fourteen when, on December 15, 1672, her father asked that she be allowed to enter the convent of San Jerónimo to be under the care of Sor Juana, who was just twenty-four. See Enrique A. Cervantes, *El testamento de sor Juana Inés.*

3. As may be deduced from Sor Juana's will (February 24, 1669). But was it true that Asbaje had died? There is no documentary proof.

4. *Sor Juana Inés de la Cruz: Bibliografía y biblioteca* (Mexico City: Secretaría de Relaciones Exteriores, 1934).

5. My copy of *Teatro de los dioses de la gentilidad* is the 1673 Madrid edition, although there are earlier editions. The first is dated 1620 (vol. 1) and 1623 (vol. 2). Sources for Vitoria's account are the same used by Sor Juana in her *Allegorical Neptune* and other writings: Vincenzo Cartari, Pierio Valeriano, Ravisius Textor, Natalis Comes, and others.

7. *The Trials of Juana Inés*

1. See Gabriel Gamazo, Duke de Maura, *Vida y reinado de Carlos II,* 2d ed. (Madrid: Espasa Calpe, 1954).

2. Duke de Maura, *Vida y reinado.*

3. Antonio de Robles, *Diario de sucesos notables* (Mexico City: n.p., 1853).

4. There is a revealing relationship between this idea and that of "the negative favors of Our Lord" expounded in the final part of her critique of Father Vieyra's sermon on the Mandate (the washing of feet on Maundy Thursday). Both are examples of the baroque love of paradox and the conceit.

5. Duke de Maura, *Vida y reinado.*

8. Taking the Vows

1. Miguel de Torres, *Dechado de príncipes eclesiásticos* (Puebla de Los Angeles: La Viuda de M. de Ortega y Bonilla, 1716; revised edition, Madrid: M. Román, 1722).

2. Quoted by Schons in "Some Obscure Points," from Julián Gutiérrez Dávila, *Vida y virtudes de Domingo Pérez de Barcia* (Madrid, 1720).

3. Ignacio Rubio Mañé, *Introducción al estudio de los virreyes de Nueva España*, vol. 4, *Obras públicas y educación universitaria* (Mexico City: Fondo de Cultura Económica, 1983).

4. Juan de Oviedo, *Vida ejemplar, heroicas virtudes y apostólico ministerio del venerable padre Antonio Núñez de Miranda, de la Compañía de Jesús* (Mexico City, 1702).

5. Oviedo, *Vida ejemplar*.

9. Life in the Convent

1. Giovanni Francesco Gemelli Carreri, *Giro del Mondo* (Venice: Presso G. Malachin, 1719). There is a translation into Spanish of the part relating to Mexico: *Viaje a la Nueve España* (Mexico City: Sociedad de Bibliófilos Mexicanos, 1927).

2. *The English American: A New Survey of the West Indies, 1648* (modern edition, London: G. Routledge & Sons, 1928). Quotations are from *Travels in the New World* (Norman: University of Oklahoma Press, 1958).

3. Josefina Muriel [de la Torre], *Conventos de monjas de la Nueva España* (Mexico City: Editorial Santiago, 1946).

4. Muriel, *Conventos*.

5. Artemio de Valle-Arizpe, *El Palacio Nacional de México* (Mexico City: Impr. de la Secretaría de Relaciones Exteriores, 1936), and Leonard, *Baroque Times*.

6. The Spanish playwright Antonio Mira de Amescua (1574–1644) wrote *El esclavo del demonio* in 1605.

7. *Juana Inés de la Cruz, die zehnte Muse von Mexico: Ihr Leben, ihre Dichtung, ihre Psyche* (Munich: H. Rinn, 1946).

8. Josefina Muriel, in *Conventos*, says: "When the convent was opened, it was not given the name San Jerónimo, but Santa Paula, in honor of that saintly matron who gave her home to St. Jerome as a site for a temple." Nevertheless, it has commonly been called by the name of the male saint.

9. Francisco de la Maza, "El convento de sor Juana," *Divulgación Histórica* (Mexico), 2, no. 5 (1941).

10. "La vida conventual de sor Juana," *Divulgación Histórica*, 4, no. 12 (1943).

11. Today Isabel la Católica and Izazaga streets, respectively. See de la Maza's "El convento de sor Juana."

12. Juan Carlos Merlo in the prologue to his anthology, *Sor Juana Inés de la Cruz: Obras escogidas* (Barcelona: Editorial Brughera, 1968).

13. Pope, "Rape of the Lock," III, 11, 16.

14. The pillar of Tepeaca (in Puebla) is not a simple stone column but an octagonal tower, partly Moorish, partly Gothic, constructed in the sixteenth century. It served as a pillory as well as a watchtower. (Manuel Toussaint, *Arte colonial* [Mexico City: Impr. Universitaria, 1962].)

10. Political Rites

1. *Introducción al estudio de los virreyes de Nueva España, 1535–1746*, vol 1: *Viaje de los virreyes a su destino, llegada y recepción* (Mexico City: Ediciones Selectas, 1955; reprinted by Fondo de Cultura Económica, 1982).

2. Lucas Alamán, *Disertaciones sobre la historia de la República Mexicana* (Mexico City: Impr. de J. M. Lara, 1849), vol. 3, appendices.

3. Alamán, *Disertaciones.*

4. Rubio Mañé, *Introducción.*

5. Richard Alewyn and Karl Salzle, *Das grosse Welttheater: Die Epoche der höfischen Feste in Dokument und Deutung* (Hamburg: Rowohlt, 1959).

6. *L'Espagne de Charles Quint* (Paris: Société d'Enseignement Supérieur, 1973).

7. Chaunu, *L'Espagne de Charles Quint.*

8. Rubio Mañé, *Introducción.*

9. Rubio Mañé, *Introducción.*

10. *Explicación sucinta del arco triunfal que erigió la Santa Iglesia Metropolitana de México, en la feliz entrada del excelentísimo señor conde de Paredes, marqués de la Laguna, virrey, gobernador y capitán general de esta Nueva España, que hizo la madre Juana Inés de la Cruz, religiosa del convento de San Jerónimo de esta ciudad, México, 1680.* Modern commemorative edition published by the Universidad Nacional Autónoma de México, with an introductory study by Manuel Toussaint (Mexico City: Universidad Nacional Autónoma de México, 1952).

11. Introduction to *Obras*, vol. 4.

12. Lafaye, *Quetzalcoatl and Guadalupe.*

11. The World as Hieroglyph

1. This is one of the rare times when Sor Juana diverges from Vitoria, for whom the centaurs were not learned but abominable and lascivious monsters.

2. On the *diua Angerona,* goddess of the winter solstice, divinity of the *angustos dies,* that disquieting period when the light of the sun grows more faint, see Georges Dumézil, *La religion romaine archaïque* (Paris: Payot, 1966). Of particular interest is his observation on the magic value of silence as concentrated spiritual energy.

3. Jurgis Baltrušaitis, *La quête d'Isis* (Paris: O. Perrin, 1967).

4. A. J. Festugière, *La révélation d'Hermès Trismégiste,* 4 vols. (Paris: Le Coffre, 1933–1954). The hermetic texts have been edited by A. D. Nock and translated by A. J. Festugière, *Corpus Hermeticum,* 4 vols. (Paris: Société d'Edition Les Belles Lettres, 1945–1954).

5. M. W. Bloomfield, *The Seven Deadly Sins* (East Lansing: Michigan State College Press, 1952). Quoted by Frances A. Yates in *Giordano Bruno and the Hermetic Tradition.*

6. Yates, *Giordano Bruno,* pp. 223, 263.

7. In 1974 the Jesuit priest Conor P. Reilly published *Athanasius Kircher: Master of a Hundred Arts* (Rome: Edizioni del Mondo, 1974), an excellent source of information for Kircher's innumerable scientific works and for his intellectual evolution. Reilly does not deal with Kircher's hermeticism except in passing; nor, perhaps for religious reasons, does he discuss his syncretism.

8. Yates, *Giordano Bruno,* pp. 417–418, quoting Kircher's *Oedipus Aegyptiacus.*

9. "Architecture and Magic: Consideration on the Idea of the Escorial," in *Essays in the History of Architecture, Presented to Rudolf Wittkower,* ed. Douglas Fraser (London: Phaidon, 1967).

10. See Frances A. Yates, *Theatre of the World* (Chicago: University of Chicago Press, 1969). This English scholar quotes an article by Hugh Tait, "The Devil's Looking Glass: The Magical Speculum of Dr. John Dee," collected in *Horace Walpole: Writer, Politician and Connoisseur,* ed. Warren Harding Smith (New Haven: Yale University Press, 1967).

12. *Sister Juana and the Goddess Isis*

1. Franz Cumont, *Les religions orientales dans le paganisme romain* (Paris: P. Buenther, 1929; previously published by E. Leroux).

2. See Hans Jonas, *The Gnostic Religion,* 2d ed. (Boston: Beacon Press, 1963), and H. D. Leisegang, *La gnose* (Paris: Payot, 1951).

3. Baltrušaitis, *La quête d'Isis.*

4. Ibid.

5. Auguste Viate, *Les sources occultes du romantisme (1770–1820),* 2d ed. (Paris: Champion, 1969).

6. Amsterdam, 1699.

13. Flattery and Favors

1. Duke de Maura, *Vida y reinado.*

2. See Manuel Rivera Cambas, *Los gobernantes de México* (Mexico City: Imprenta J. M. Aguilar Ortiz, 1872); Vicente Riva Palacio, *México a través de los siglos: El virreinato* (Mexico City: G. S. López, 1940); Rubio Mañé, *Introducción,* vol. 2: *Expansión y defensa* (1959).

3. J. H. Elliott, *Imperial Spain, 1469–1716* (New York: St. Martin, 1963).

4. Ibid.

5. Ibid.

6. "*Loa* a los años del rey, IV." The Reflection represented José, son of the Viceroy and Vicereine, who had not yet had his first birthday.

7. *La pensée chinoise* (Paris: A. Michel, 1950).

14. Council of Stars

1. That was the Duke de Medinaceli's position in the royal palace before he was named first minister.

2. Number 16.

3. René Nelli, *L'érotique des troubadours* (Toulouse: E. Privat, 1963).

4. Robert S. Briffault, *The Troubadours* (Bloomington: Indiana University Press, 1965).

5. Nelli, *L'érotique des troubadours.*

6. Méndez Plancarte says of these verses: "This is one of the passages for which the Inquisition—had it chosen, as some have fantasized—could have, and not without justification, looked for a quarrel with her." Sor Juana had said in her *Response to Sor Filotea* that she "wished no quarrel with the Holy Office."

7. In a commentary on the sonnet honoring Father Kino, and in commenting on verses 303–308 of *First Dream.*

8. C. S. Lewis, *The Discarded Image: An Introduction to Medieval and Renaissance Literature* (Cambridge: Cambridge University Press, 1964).

9. Diogenes Laërtius, *Vies et opinions des philosophes* (Book 7, *La doctrine stoïcienne*), in *Les Stoïciens,* Bibliothèque de la Pléiade (Paris: Gallimard, 1962).

10. *The Anatomy of Melancholy.*

11. Lewis observes that Coleridge, like all moderns, inverted the positions of fantasy and imagination. When I examine *First Dream,* I shall return to this question.

12. *Stanze: La parola e il fantasma nella cultura occidentale* (Turin: G. Einaudi, 1977).

13. Robert Klein, *Form and Meaning,* trans. Madeline Jay and Leon Wie-

seltier (New York: Viking Press, 1979). A number of these essays are contained in *La forme et l'intelligible* (Paris: Gallimard, 1970). I have referred especially to the section entitled "Spirito Peregrino." Another author who has dealt knowledgeably with these themes is D. P. Walker, *Spiritual and Demonic Magic* (London: Warburg Institute, 1958).

14. See the song "Donna mi prega."

15. Klein, *Form and Meaning.*

16. "Quand'elli è giunto là dove disira, / vede una donna che riceve onore / e luce sí, che per lo suo splendore / lo peregrino spirito la mira." Translation into English by Mark Musa (Bloomington: Indiana University Press, 1962).

17. See Paul Oskar Kristeller, *The Philosophy of Marsilio Ficino,* trans. Virginia Conant (New York: Columbia University Press, 1943).

18. Ibid., p. 277f.

19. See my *Conjunctions and Disjunctions.*

15. Religious Fires

1. The caption of poem 18 reads: "The Lady Vicereine was wont, so jealously infatuated was she with the Poet, to reproach her for any interruption in her expressions of regard.

2. *Poètes du XVI siècle,* texts established and with an introduction by Albert-Marie Schmidt (Paris: Gallimard, 1953).

3. "Throughout the ages our love will stand / As proof that woman's love for woman / Surpasses any love offered by man."

4. Antonio Alatorre, "Avatares barrocos del romance (De Góngora a Sor Juana Inés de la Cruz)," *Nueva Revista de Filología Hispánica,* 36, no. 2 (1977). Alatorre calls this decasyllabic *romance* "an erotic poem," and briefly underscores the interest of the "Advertencia" in poem 16. He is the only person, as far as I am aware, who has noted this aspect of the poem. Or the only one who has been open enough to say so.

5. See Chapter 21, "Music Box."

6. The cumulative effect of the Spanish *dura/dureza/duración* cannot be recreated in English.—*Translator's note.*

7. In Spanish there is a pun on *retratada,* appearing in a portrait, and *retractada,* repenting of affection.—*Translator's note.*

8. José F. Montesinos in his introduction to *Poesías líricas de Lope de Vega,* vol. 1 (Madrid: Ediciones de "La Lectura," 1925).

16. The Reflection, the Echo

1. The poem is preceded by this note: "This paper was found without the name of its author; it seems to have been composed immediately following the

arrival in Spain of the news of the poet's death." Castorena y Ursúa, in his introduction, intimates that the poem is by Calleja. It is my opinion that Calleja also wrote the anonymous sonnet that follows his imprimatur: "On Sister Juana Ines' Disillusion at the Time of Her Death." In addition to the fact that Father Calleja uses the same naive stratagem to conceal his name, the sentiments, ideas, and language recall those of the tercets. These are two truly *felt* poems, and this distinguishes them from the other compositions in *Fame and Posthumous Works.*

2. "Primer retrato de sor Juana," in *Historia Mexicana,* 2, no. 1 (July–Sept. 1952).

3. Pietro Cerone (1565–1625?), a Neapolitan musician, lived in Spain for many years and was Kapellmeister for Philip II and Philip III. He wrote a treatise on music in Italian in addition to *El melopeo y maestro,* which was famous in Cerone's time but written in a Spanish plagued with Italianisms. (In Spanish we have *melopea* and *melopeya,* but *melopeo* is not listed in any of the standard sources—the *Diccionario de autoridades,* the dictionary of the Academia, or Corominas' etymological dictionary.)

4. José Subirá, "La musique en Espagne (siècle XVII)," in *Histoire de la musique,* Encyclopédie de La Pléiade (Paris: Gallimard, 1955).

5. See Alice M. Pollin's essay "Toward an Understanding of Cerone's *El melopeo y maestro,*" *Romanic Review,* 53, no. 2 (April 1962), for an examination of Cerone's Platonism.

6. Macrobius, Book II, first chapter of his *Commentary on the Dream of Scipio,* trans. William Harris Stahl (New York: Columbia University Press, 1952).

7. Joscelyn Godwin, *Athanasius Kircher: Renaissance Man and the Quest for Lost Knowledge* (London: Thames and Hudson, 1979).

8. Kircher claimed as his own the invention of the megaphone, or "speaking trumpet" (*tuba stentorophonica*), and devoted to the subject another treatise on acoustics, *Phonurgia nova* (1673). On the question of the polemic between Kircher and Samuel Morley, see the book by Conor P. Reilly, *Athanasius Kircher: Master of a Hundred Arts* (Rome: Edizioni del Mondo, 1974).

9. According to Godwin, *Athanasius Kircher.*

10. "Sor Juana y el regateo de Abraham" (1979).

11. Reilly, *Athanasius Kircher.*

12. Godwin, *Athanasius Kircher.*

17. Realm of Signs

1. Leonard, *Baroque Times.* See the chapters "Scenes, Writers, and Reading, 1620"; "The Strange Case of the Curious Book Collector"; and "On the Book Trade, 1683."

2. A number of collections of *romances*—narrative poems—published beginning in the sixteenth century.

3. Tomás Navarro Tomás, *Métrica española* (New York: Syracuse University Press, 1956); Alatorre, "Avatares barrocos del romance."

4. A curious misconception: Spain did not yet exist. We do the same with Nezahualcóyotl and Nahuatl poetry. A literature is defined not by nation—an imprecise and rather late, modern concept—but by language.

5. *Visión y símbolos en la pintura española del siglo de oro* (Madrid: Aguilar, 1972).

18. Different from Herself

1. Leonard, *Don Carlos de Sigüenza y Góngora: A Mexican Savant of the Seventeenth Century.*

2. Leonard reports that it was Sigüenza who most frequently brought visitors to the locutory of San Jerónimo, where they were received by Sor Juana. Other authors mention this practice. In his biography of Sor Juana (Mexico City: José Porrúa, 1936), Juan José Eguiara y Eguren states that Juan de Aréchiga took the Spanish theologian Antonio Gutiérrez to San Jerónimo, as was his custom whenever persons of intellectual standing arrived in Mexico. Castorena y Ursúa also refers to these visitations.

3. See Elías Trabulse, *Ciencia y religión en el siglo XVII* (Mexico City: El Colegio de México, 1974).

4. The Count de Monclova died in Lima, as Viceroy of Peru. One of his daughters, Josefa, fervently inclined toward the religious life, had vowed to become a nun but was prevented by her father from doing so. At the death of the Count, while his widow and daughters were still living in Lima, the girl renewed her entreaties but met with the no less categorical refusal of her mother. One night, as if in a romantic play, she climbed over a balcony in the palace and, sliding down a rope, fell into the arms of an awaiting priest, who immediately led her to a convent. She was the founder of the convent of Santa Rosa in Lima. Never suspecting what was to be her fate, Sor Juana mentions this daughter of the Count de Monclova in a line of her *loa* to the play *Love Is the Greater Labyrinth.*

5. Rubio Mañé calls attention to the Count de Galve's indiscriminate use of his names and titles.

6. See Duke de Maura, *Vida y reinado.*

7. See Rubio Mañé, *Introducción,* vol. 3: *Expansión y defensa.*

8. "Nuevos datos para la biografía de sor Juana," *Contemporáneos* 9 (February 1929).

19. Hear Me with Your Eyes

1. See sonnets 159–163.

2. *Agudeza y arte de ingenio,* Discurso II.

3. The lines quoted are the last two lines of Rubén Darío's sonnet "Caracol" (Seashell): "un profundo oleaje y un misterioso viento: / el caracol la forma tiene de un corazón."—*Editor's note.*

4. Translation by Alan S. Trueblood from *A Sor Juana Anthology* (Cambridge, Mass.: Harvard University Press, 1988).

5.   Phyllis, I dreamed this night, within my chamber showed
As lovely as erstwhile beneath the light of day,
Seeking to give her ghost again to amorous play,
That, like Ixion, I should couple with a cloud.
   Her ghost crept in my bed, naked, without a shroud,
And said: "Dear Damon, back to thee I find my way. ˙
I am but grown more fair whilst I did darkling stay
In that grim region whence at last I am allowed.
   "I come to kiss again the handsomest of blades,
I come to die again within thy body's mesh."
Then, when the image had exacted its full toll,
   It said, "Farewell! And now I go back to the shades.
Since thou hast boasted oft of lying with my flesh,
Now canst thou boast anew, of lying with my soul."

Translated by Norman Cameron.

20. Ink on Wings of Paper

1. See E. R. Dodds, *Pagan and Christian in an Age of Anxiety* (Cambridge: Cambridge University Press, 1965). According to Dodds, the first Christian mystic was St. Gregory of Nyssa, who was familiar with the work of Plotinus and appropriated his vocabulary. To that extent and in that sense Christian mysticism springs from a pagan source.

2. Angel Valbuena Prat, *Historia de la literatura española,* vol. 2, 8th ed. (Barcelona: Gustavo Gili, 1968).

3. There are many examples in seventeenth-century poetry of humorous poems in rhymed couplets—for instance, these ballads by Quevedo: "A una dama hermosa, rota y remendada"; "A una mujer flaca"; "A una mujer pequeña"; "A Marica." Méndez Plancarte criticizes Henríquez Ureña for calling Sor Juana's poem in couplets a *silva;* Lope de Vega, nevertheless, titled the first canto of *La gatomaquia,* composed almost exclusively of couplets, "Silva primera."

4. Translation by Alan S. Trueblood, *A Sor Juana Anthology.*

21. *Music Box*

1. Navarro Tomás, *Métrica española.*

2. See Othón Arróniz, *Teatro de evangelización en Nueva España* (Mexico City: Universidad Nacional Autónoma de México, 1979), and José Rojas Garcidueñas, *El teatro de Nueva España en el siglo XVI* (Mexico City: Secretaría de Educación Pública, 1973).

3. In his "Estudio liminar," vol. 2, *Obras completas.*

4. Small roman numerals indicate poems attributed to Sor Juana by Méndez Plancarte.

5. In the Spanish word play, *voladoras,* "flying," is echoed in *doras,* "you gild," and rhymed with *horas,* "hours."—*Translator's note.*

6. It is curious that Méndez Plancarte says, in regard to this *villancico,* "We find no evidence of a cross on the breast of Serapis." Jurgis Baltrušaitis states that "the history of the figure of the cross found among the hieroglyphs of the temple of Serapis has been told by Rufinus (311–420), Sozomen (384–425), Socrates Scholasticus (379–440), Cassiodorus (480–575). It was collected by Suidas (tenth and eleventh centuries), Nicephorus Callistus (fourteenth century), and Marsilio Ficino" (*La quête d'Isis*). I would add the mythologists, especially Cartari; in his book many engravings of Egyptian and Christian gods are presented on facing pages. In the *Allegorical Neptune* Sor Juana quotes Cartari; in the *Response,* Cassiodorus.

7. Marsilio Ficino, *De vita coelitus comparanda,* quoted by Yates in *Giordano Bruno.*

8. Ibid.

9. Frances A. Yates must be credited with pointing out the ties that link Kircher to the hermetic tradition of the preceding century, in contrast to his biographer Father Reilly, who overlooks this basic aspect of his personality and work.

10. An example of Kircher's attitude on this subject is the elaborate defense his disciple Gaspar Schott made of the orthodoxy of his points of view in the second edition of *Iter exstaticum* (1671). A Dominican priest, Melchior Carnam, had denounced some of the statements of that book as heretical, saying that Kircher was falling into the same fatal error as Bruno: postulating an infinite universe and a plurality of inhabited worlds. This belief had led Bruno to the stake. In his biography of Kircher, Father Reilly confuses Melchior Carnam with Melchor Cano, who lived a century earlier.

11. *The Great Chain of Being* (Cambridge, Mass.: Harvard University Press, 1936), p. 113.

22. The Stage and the Court

1. The Spanish word *comedia* is the general term for dramatic work; it does not mean comedy in the modern sense.—*Translator's note.*

2. E. M. Wilson and D. Moir, *The Golden Age: Drama 1492–1700* (New York: Barnes and Noble, 1972), vol. 3 of *A Literary History of Spain.*

3. *Sainetes de sor Juana* (Mexico City: Editora Intercontinental, 1945).

4. The Spanish pun is on *cosas . . . pasadas por agua,* literally, "passed through water" (as foodstuffs imported from Spain would be); idiomatically the phrase means "soft-boiled."—*Translator's note.*

5. *Spanish-American Literature: A History,* trans. John V. Falconieri (Detroit, Mich.: Wayne State University Press, 1963). Originally published as *Historia de la literatura hispanoamericana,* I (Mexico City: Fondo de Cultura Económica, 1954).

6. The learned Francisco Fernández del Castillo believed that Guevara was a cousin of Sor Juana's, a supposition that has since been rejected. The priest Juan de Guevara was born in Mexico—date unknown—and died around 1692. In his time he was a well-known and appreciated poet. A fervent Gongorist, he was awarded prizes in several poetry competitions. Few of his works have survived. The few examples Méndez Plancarte was able to include in vol. 3 of *Poetas novohispanos* reveal a clever, competent, and impersonal imitator of the ruling poetic styles of his day.

7. In an address delivered at a literary celebration honoring Sor Juana, on November 12, 1874, in Mexico City. Vigil finds a vague prefiguration of the ideas of Hobbes in the words of Theseus. The Mexican critic did not know the writings of Suárez and his disciples on the origin of the state.

8. See Quentin Skinner, *The Foundation of Modern Political Thought,* vol. 2: *The Revival of Thomism* (Cambridge: Cambridge University Press, 1978).

9. Armando de María y Campos, "El teatro de sor Juana Inés de la Cruz en Manila, en 1709," Sunday supplement, *México en la Cultura,* of *Novedades,* 145 (November 11, 1951).

10. Angelic intelligences cannot know the future, the realm of freedom, says Méndez Plancarte, finding his authority in St. Thomas. Nevertheless, there is a minor theological problem here: Dante tells us that the souls of the wicked condemned to hell have the gift of dual vision and *can* know the future.

11. "La correlación en la estructura del teatro calderoniano," in Dámaso Alonso and Carlos Bousoño, *Seis calas en la expresión literaria española* (Madrid: Editorial Gredos, 1970).

23. *The Float and the Sacrament*

1. "Explicación del auto sacramental" (1940). This essay was included by Manuel Durán and Roberto González Echevarría in their excellent collection with a perceptive introduction, *Calderón y la crítica: historia y antología* (Madrid: Editorial Gredos, 1976).

2. *Las peras del olmo* (Mexico City: Fondo de Cultura Económica, 1957).

3. Rojas Garcidueñas, *El teatro de Nueva España*. See also his *Autos y coloquios del siglo XVI* (Mexico City: Universidad Nacional Autónoma de México, 1939).

4. The *villancicos* to St. Peter sung in the cathedral of Mexico City in 1692 and included by Méndez Plancarte among the attributed compositions: are they really hers?

5. A slightly less prejudiced version of the events is found in Modesto Lafuente's *Historia general de España*, vol. 1 (Barcelona: Montaner y Simon, 1877). Lafuente follows the version of the chronicler Juan de Vidara, "a contemporary writer, the person closest to the theater of events," although he also accepts "Gregory of Tours, also a contemporary, but writing farther from the scene."

6. Two centuries after the rebellion of the Comuneros of Castile the *Diccionario de autoridades* (1726 edition) still offered the definition: "*Comunero:* He who in the name of the commoner or people joins with others to rise up and conspire against his sovereign."

7. Festugière, *La Révélation d'Hermès Trismégiste*.

8. Quoted by Yates in *Giordano Bruno*.

9. *Corpus Hermeticum,* Book I. The summary given here is a paraphrase based on the Nock and Festugière edition.

10. Méndez Plancarte footnotes the long and complex symbolism of the hyacinth, including Pliny's report that the Greek letters *AI* can be read in its veins: "Thence, those *hyacinths,* on the hands of Christ, are both rich jewels and purple flowers (his wounds) and, in his *AIes,* allude to the suffering of his Passion."

24. *First Dream*

1. I render the Spanish title as it appears in the first editions, although modern usage demands *Primer sueño*.

2. Eunice Joiner Gates, "Reminiscences of Góngora in the works of Sor Juana Inés de la Cruz," *PMLA,* 54 (September–October 1939); Emilio Carilla, "Sor Juana, ciencia y poesía: el *Primero sueño,*" *Revista de Filología Española,* 36 (July–December 1952); Alfonso Méndez Plancarte, *El sueño* (Mexico City:

Imprenta Universitaria, 1951); José Pascual Buxó, *Góngora en la poesía novo-hispana* (Mexico City: Universidad Nacional Autónoma de México, 1960).

3. *The Greeks and the Irrational* (Berkeley: University of California Press, 1963).

4. *El "Sueño" de Sor Juana Inés de la Cruz* (London: Tamesis, 1977).

5. See Antonio Gallego Morell, *Garcilaso y sus comentaristas* (Madrid: Editorial Gredos, 1972).

6. Vossler published two essays on Sor Juana, "Die Zehnte Muse von Mexico" (Munich, 1934) and "Die Welt im Traum," which appears with his translation of *First Dream* (Berlin, 1941). The former, as "La décima musa de México," translated by Carlos Clavería, was collected in Vossler's *Escritores y poetas de España* (Buenos Aires: Espasa Calpe, 1947). The second, as "El mundo en el sueño," translated by Gerardo Mondenhauer, appeared in Juan Carlos Merlo's edition of *Primero sueño* (Buenos Aires: Universidad de Buenos Aires, 1953). The dream of Scipio, the only surviving fragment of the sixth book of *De Republica,* comes to us through the commentary of Macrobius. For commentary on Scipio's dream—in addition to Macrobius, and William Harris Stahl's introduction to his translation of Macrobius' *Commentary*—see Pierre Boyancé, *Études sur le songe de Scipion* (Paris: Boccard, 1936). The essay by Robert Ricard ("La poésie savante: 'El sueño,' deuxième leçon") is one of a series of lectures on Sor Juana given by the French historian in Paris in 1957. They were collected in a mimeographed pamphlet entitled "Une poétesse mexicaine du XVIIème siècle."

7. The ideas I present in this chapter were first formulated in 1971 during a course I offered on Sor Juana at Harvard University, and repeated in 1973 and 1975. They took on something close to their present form in the fifth lecture in a series, "Sor Juana Inés de la Cruz, Her Life and Her Work," delivered in 1974 at the Colegio Nacional de México.

8. There are three editions. The first is *Itinerarium exstaticum* (Rome, 1656). The title varies slightly in the subsequent editions: *Iter exstaticum* (Würzburg, 1660, and Nuremberg, 1671), both annotated and with scholia by Schott. I have used a microfilm copy of the 1671 edition. I want to take this opportunity to thank my friend the poet Rubén Bonifaz Nuño for his translation of the second chapter. The wording of the title page is worth quoting, at least partially: "The ecstatic heavenly voyage of the Reverend Father Athanasius Kircher, Society of Jesus, in which, with new hypotheses, is expounded, in strictest truth, the workings of the world . . . through the veil of a feigned rapture, the Interlocutors being Cosmiel and Theodidactus . . . with the consent of the author, the work was elucidated with headnotes and scholia . . . and expurgated, by Father Gaspar Schott, Society of Jesus, of the errors that had been introduced in the first edition in Rome . . ." I wonder whether the first edition

termed the "ecstatic rapture" as "feigned." As for the "errors": this refers to the accusations that Kircher held theories similar to those of Bruno and others on the infinity of the universe and plurality of inhabited worlds.

9. Festugière, *Révélation*, vol. 1, chap. 10: "Les fictions littéraires du *logos* de révélation."

10. *Hermetica*, ed. and trans. Walter Scott (repr., Boulder, Colo.: Hermes House, 1982).

11. After this book was written, José Pascual Buxó published a thought-provoking essay, "*El sueño* de Sor Juana: Alegoría y modelo del mundo," in *Sábado* (August 15, 1981). Buxó also favors the tripartite division. He indicates that it corresponds to a medieval "model of the world" prolonged in the Renaissance tradition: "The three parts of *El sueño* conform to a tripartite model of man and the world, in which the world is conceived of as divided into three orbs, or spheres (the earth, the sun and the planets, and the empyrean), which in turn are homologous to the parts of the human body"—the inferior, the location of the reproductive organs; the intermediate, the heart and lungs, seat of the vital spirits; and the superior, the head, "simulacrum of the spiritual world." Buxó analyzes only the first part of the poem and finds that Sor Juana, to describe night in the sublunary world, uses the emblems current in her time— for example, in Saavedra Fajardo—following the pattern of Alciati's famous *Emblemata*. He argues that the other parts of *First Dream* pertain to the same emblematic system. The poem, he concludes, "displays not only a considerable number of symbols sanctioned by humanist tradition . . . but also a Neoplatonic model of the world." Buxó is correct in underscoring the importance of emblems in *First Dream,* and he makes a perceptive analysis of the symbols and allegorical figures of the first part of the poem. More questionable, in my opinion, is his view of the poem as merely a representation of a "Neoplatonic model of the universe." The tripartite division of the world is not exclusive to Neoplatonism. Furthermore, the second part of the poem does not correspond to the zone of the vital spirits (the heart and lungs) or to that of the sun and the stars; neither is the third part homologous to the empyrean and, in man, to comprehension and the intellect. Finally, in conceiving of the poem as an allegorical "model" of the cosmos, its most essential theme is omitted: the adventure of the soul liberated from the body during sleep. Sor Juana is telling us of an action, a feat: the saga of the soul in stellar spaces and personal abysses. This is why *First Dream* can justly be called an epic of the spirit.

12. The book is *Obeliscus Aegyptiacus* (Rome, 1666). In the *Oedipus Aegyptiacus* (pages 115 and 418 of the second volume) and in the *Musurgia universalis* (page 393 of the second volume) appear engravings representing pyramids of light and shadow that, according to Kircher, emblematically sum up Egyptian philosophy. Joscelyn Godwin says that Kircher took the theme of the intersection of the pyramids of light and shadow from Robert Fludd.

13. José Gaos, "El sueño de un sueño," *Historia Mexicana,* 10, no. 1 (July–September 1960).

14. See Chapter 14, "Council of Stars."

15. Authors generally mention common sense (*sensus communis*) in addition, but Sor Juana omits it.

16. Klein, "L'imagination comme vêtement de l'âme chez Marsile Ficino et Giordano Bruno," in *La forme et l'intelligible.*

17. See my *Apariencia desnuda,* 2d ed. (Mexico City: Ediciones Era, 1978). In English, *Marcel Duchamp: Appearance Stripped Bare,* trans. Rachel Phillips and Donald Gardner (New York: Viking Press, 1978).

18. Jurgis Baltrušaitis, *Le miroir: Essai sur une légende scientifique* (Paris: Elmayan, 1978).

19. Lovejoy, *Great Chain of Being,* p. 49.

20. Proclus carried this idea to its extreme: negation is part of the process. Hegel's admiration for Proclus is well known.

21. *The Republic,* Book IV. Jesús Tomás García, Spanish translator of *The Republic,* points out that the Greek corresponds to the Latin *animus.* Léon Robin translates it as *ardeur de sentiment,* and calls this faculty *la fonction médiatrice.* In the *Timaeus,* the soul is also composed of three parts: an indivisible, immutable substance identical to itself, which is the One and corresponds to the intelligible; another, divisible, subject to change, which is the Other and corresponds to the sensible; and a third, which is a combination of the other two and which relates them one to another, since it belongs to both the sensible and the intelligible. In Renaissance Neoplatonism the mediating function is effected by comprehension or reason in the rational soul, and fantasy in the sensory.

22. Ramón Xirau, *Genio y figura de sor Juana Inés de la Cruz* (Buenos Aires: Editorial Universitaria de Buenos Aires, 1967).

23. Lovejoy, *Great Chain of Being.*

24. Ibid., p. 126.

25. *Obras* of Juan de Tarsis y Peralta, Conde de Villamediana, edited with an introduction and notes by Juan Manuel Rozas (Madrid: Editorial Castalia, 1969).

26. London: Nelson, 1964. I call attention to two essays that rectify certain points and open new perspectives: Robert Klein, "Saturne: croyances et symboles," in *La forme et l'intelligible,* and Giorgio Agamben, "I fantasmi di Eros," in *Stanze.*

25. An Ill-Fated Letter

1. A translation is available in pp. 86–120 of Fanchón Royer's *The Tenth Muse* (Paterson, N.J.: St. Anthony Guild Press, 1952).

2. See Robert Ricard, "Antonio de Vieyra y sor Juana Inés de la Cruz," and Dario Puccini, *Sor Juana Inés de la Cruz: Studio d'una personalità del Barocco messicano* (Rome: Edizioni dell'Ateneo, 1967). Ricard believes that Vieyra delivered the sermon between 1642 and 1652. Puccini states that Sor Juana must have read it in a translation that appeared in editions published in 1678 and 1680.

3. Omphale, who dressed Hercules in women's clothes and forced him to spin and weave while she, clad in a lion's skin, wielded his war club (Macrobius, *Saturnalia*, 3). Sor Juana refers to the same passage in *First Dream*.

4. *Carta abierta al señor Alfonso Junco* (Mexico City: Imprenta Mundial, 1934).

5. Torres, *Dechado de príncipes eclesiásticos*.

6. *Las cinco piedras de la honda de David en cinco discursos predicados a la serenísima reina de Suecia, Cristina Alejandra, en lengua italiana. Por el reverendísimo padre Antonio de Vieyra . . . Dedicados al ilustrísimo señor don Francisco de Aguiar y Seijas, obispo de Michoacán . . .* (Madrid: I. Fernández de Buendía, 1675). And the second volume: *Sermones varios del padre Antonio de Vieyra de la Compañía de Jesus, dedicados al ilustrísimo señor don Francisco de Aguiar y Seijas* (Madrid: I. Fernández de Buendía, 1678).

7. In a letter to the Marquis de Gouvela (June 24, 1683), Vieyra refers to the honor with satisfaction. Relations between the university and the Archbishop, Puccini indicates, were excellent.

8. José Mariano Beristáin y Souza, *Biblioteca hispanoamericana septentrional* (Mexico City: A. Valdés, 1816–1821); second edition, in facsimile, 1980.

9. According to Torres, when Fray Payo departed, the "cédula de arzobispo de México" was sent to Fernández de Santa Cruz, but he, "poised on the bright speculum of disillusion," did not accept the post. Torres neither copies nor mentions any document to prove his claim. He adds that the Viceroy Count de Galve informed him that he had named Fernández "interim Viceroy," but that the Bishop again refused. In this instance he does reproduce the *cédula* in which Charles II accepts the rejection (Madrid, April 8, 1698). I emphasize that Fernández de Santa Cruz refused the Viceroy's temporary position, not a permanent appointment. Torres' account is unclear, and purports to show that the 1698 appointment is a consequence of the Archbishop's supposed refusal sixteen years earlier! (See chapter 41, pp. 266–70, of *Dechado de príncipes eclesiásticos*.)

10. José de Lezamis, *Breve relación de la vida y muerte del Ilmo. y Revmo. Señor Doctor Don Francisco Aguiar y Seijas* (Mexico, 1699).

11. Francisco Sosa, *El episcopado mexicano* (Mexico City: H. Iriarte y S. Hernández, 1877–1879).

26. The Response

1. I stated earlier that an *Apologia a favor do R.P. Antonio Vieyra* was published in 1727, in Lisbon, signed by an Augustinian nun, Sister Margarita Ignacia. The author of this booklet was actually her brother Luis Gonçalves Pinheiro. Again, pseudonyms and sex changes—unusual symbolic "transvestism."

2. Lines 1–128. (I refer to the line numbers in volume 4 of the *Complete Works*.)

3. Lines 129–183.

4. Lines 184–215.

5. Lines 216–289.

6. Macrobius, chapter 14 of his *Commentary on the Dream of Scipio*, ed. William Harris Stahl. The image comes from the *Iliad* (VIII, 9). It also appears in Proclus.

7. Lines 290–440. Kircher did not write a book entitled *De magnete*. Sor Juana may be referring to *Magnes, sive de arte magnetica* (Rome, 1641), which is Kircher's most extensive study on magnetism. I previously pointed out the origin of the image of God as a circumference: Nicholas of Cusa. The frontispiece of *Magnes* contains, among other images, that of the chain descending from the heavens. This symbol appears in two additional books by Kircher: as a frontispiece in *Magneticum naturae regnum* (Rome, 1667) and in *Mundus subterraneus* (Amsterdam, 1678).

8. Lines 441–532.

9. Lines 533–844.

10. Between Hypatia and Sor Juana there are clear similarities of which she was undoubtedly aware. Beautiful, young, chaste, and learned, both were persecuted by intolerant prelates, although those who victimized the Alexandrian were incomparably more cruel and barbaric. Hypatia was the daughter and disciple of the Neoplatonic mathematician and philosopher Theon. She was perhaps the first woman to excel in the physical sciences: mathematics and astronomy. She lectured in the Platonic school of Alexandria, which rivaled that of Athens, and wrote several scientific treatises, now lost, commentaries on Diophantus, Apollonius of Perga, and Ptolemy. It is probable that, like all Neoplatonists of her day, she combined astronomy with astrology. She was the teacher and friend of Synesius of Cyrene, Bishop *malgré lui* and author of a famous book on dream, *De insomniis,* which Sor Juana might have read, or known indirectly through quotations and commentaries. Hypatia, friend of another pagan, the prefect Orestes, a rival of the awesome patriarch of Alexandria, St. Cyril, a contentious and bloodthirsty theologian, was the target of the animosity of the groups of fanatic, patriarch-led monks who terrorized the city. One

day in 415, during the Lenten season, these monks stopped her carriage, killed the coachman, stripped her of her clothes, and raped her. They then took her to the church, where they tore her body to pieces. Gibbon adds a horrible detail: "Her flesh was scraped from her bones with sharp oyster-shells." Her murder was the beginning of the end of Alexandria's position as the world center of learning. Her fate inspired the ancients. In one of his letters, Synesius speaks of her as "mother and sister, teacher and benefactress in everything and of everyone." A century later the poet Palladas dedicated a poem to her memory (*Palatine Anthology*, IX, 400). In modern times Hypatia has been memorialized by historians, philosophers, and scholars. Gibbon devoted a moving page to her, and the now-forgotten Charles Kingsley made her the heroine of his historical novel *Hypatia; or, New foes with an old face* (1853). Leconte de Lisle wrote two poems in her honor and, more recently, Charles Péguy delivered an exalted elegy of that soul "si parfaitement accordée à l'âme platonicienne." On the subject of her relationship with Synesius, I cite the essay of H. I. Marrou in *The Conflict Between Paganism and Christianity in the Fourth Century*, ed. Arnoldo Momigliano (Oxford: Clarendon Press, 1963). As in the case of Sor Juana, all these writers speak of Hypatia's beauty and love of learning. Gibbon writes with his customary eloquence, "In the bloom of beauty and in the maturity of wisdom, the modest maid refused her lovers and instructed her disciples." She probably died a virgin, for in the poem Palladas dedicated to her, he sees her as one of the stars in the constellation of Virgo.

11. Lines 841–1150.

12. Lines 1150–1267.

13. They are interesting neither as literature nor as examples of ascetic or spiritual writing.

14. Lines 1267–1432.

27. And the Responses

1. *Vida del venerable padre Pedro de Arellano y Sosa* (Mexico City: En la Imprenta Real del Superior Gobierno, 1753). See Francisco de la Maza, *Sor Juana ante la historia* (Mexico City: Universidad Nacional Autónoma de México, 1981).

2. *Villancicos* to St. Catherine (316).

28. The Siege

1. *Alboroto y motín de México el 8 de junio de 1692. Relación de don Carlos de Sigüenza y Góngora en una carta dirigida al almirante don Andrés de Pez*, ed. Irving A. Leonard (Mexico City: Talleres Gráficos del Museo Nacional, 1932).

2. "Relación del tumulto acaecido en México el año de 1692 por un testigo

presencial," in vol. 10 of *Documentos inéditos o muy raros para la historia de México,* ed. Genaro García (Mexico City, 1907).

3. Ignacio Rubio Mañé, *Introducción,* vol. 2, *Expansión y defensa* (1959).

4. Letter from the Count de Galve to his older brother, Gregorio María de Silva y Mendoza, Duke del Infantado, August 23, 1692. Quoted by Rubio Mañé.

5. "Letter written by a monk in Mexico City to an intimate gentleman friend in Puebla de los Ángeles, recounting the uprising in that city, June 8, 1692," in *Documentos para la historia de México,* series 2, vol. 3 (Mexico City: Impr. de J. R. Navarro, 1853–1857). Quoted by Rubio Mañé.

6. Torres, *Dechado.* Manuel Fernández de Santa Cruz was noted for his belligerence, and Francisco de la Maza, in *Sor Juana ante la historia,* refers to a watercolor in which Fernández appears dressed as a musketeer, sword in his belt, probably painted during the expedition of the Armada de Barlovento against the French in the Antilles. Santa Cruz tried to form a small army composed of clerics and laymen, to join the Hispano-Mexican troops.

29. The Abjuration

1. Such pious accounts were standard, and Lezamis writes a similar report of Aguiar y Seijas' penances. In a different passage Oviedo attributes the same zeal to Sor Juana.

2. The "Petition" appears at the end of volume four of the *Complete Works.* But it is undated, and Salceda does not indicate why he placed it where he did. I prefer Calleja's version: the "Petition" derives from the confession.

3. Schons, "Nuevos datos."

4. Mexico City: Impresso por la Viuda de J. B. de Hogal, 1746. Written to commemorate the end of the tragic epidemic. Facsimile edition with a historical study and a chronology by Victor M. Ruiz Naufal (Mexico City: Inst. Mexicano del Seguro Social, 1981).

5. Schons, "Nuevos datos."

6. Ibid.

Epilogue

1. *On History and People,* trans. Saul K. Padover (New York: McGraw Hill, 1977). Originally published as *Kunst und Epos.*

2. *Decline and Fall of the Roman Empire,* chap. 6.

3. *First Dream,* line 810.

Notes on Sources

1. "Some Obscure Points in the Life of Sor Juana Inés de la Cruz," *Modern Philology,* 24 (November 1926), 141.

2. *Carta abierta al señor Alfonso Junco* (Austin, 1934).

3. *University of Texas Bulletin,* 2526 (July 8, 1925).

4. *Anales del Museo Nacional de Arqueología. Historia y Etnología,* 1 (Publicaciones del Museo Nacional de México, 1935).

5. Mexico City: Secretaría de Relaciones Exteriores, 1934).

6. *Juana Inés de la Cruz, die zehnte Muse von Mexico: Ihr Leben, ihre Dichtung, ihre Psyche* (Munich: H. Rinn, 1946). Spanish-language edition, *Sor Juana Inés de la Cruz, la Décima Musa de México; Su vida, su poesía, su psique,* translated by Juan Antonio Ortega Medina (Mexico City: Universidad Nacional Autónoma de Mexico, 1963).

7. For example, Ermilo Abreu Gómez in his *Semblanza de sor Juana* (Mexico City: Ediciones Letras de México, 1938). E. Urzaiz Rodríguez published his essay "El espíritu varonil de sor Juana" in *El hijo pródigo,* 25 (April 1945), a year before Pfandl's book; and in an essay written in 1950, published in *Sur* in 1951 and later collected in *Las peras del olmo* (Mexico City: Imp. Universitaria, 1957), independently of Pfandl and without dwelling on psychosomatic "masculinity," I alluded to questions relating to Sor Juana's psychology, especially in regard to the ambiguity of her emotional relationships with several female friends.

8. *Sor Juana Inés de la Cruz: Studio d'una personalità del Barocco messicano* (Rome: Edizioni dell'Ateneo, 1967).

Index